Also by William E. Burrows

Deep Black
On Reporting the News (a textbook)
Vigilante
Richthofen

EXPLORING SPACE

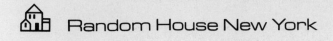 Random House New York

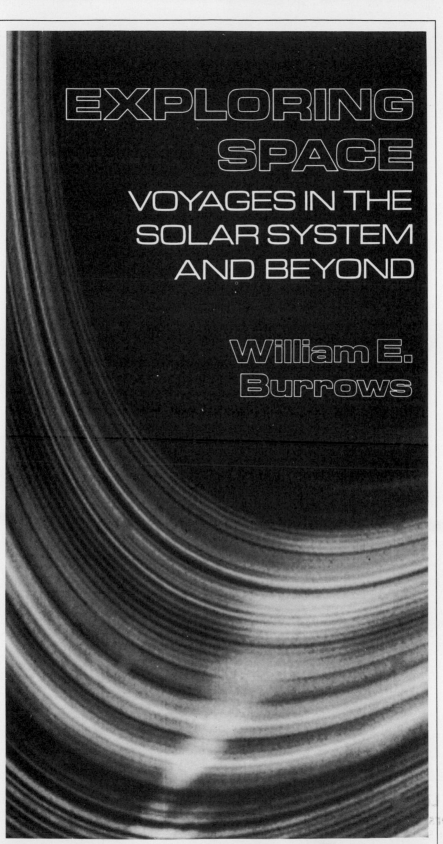

EXPLORING SPACE

VOYAGES IN THE SOLAR SYSTEM AND BEYOND

William E. Burrows

Copyright © 1990 by William E. Burrows
All rights reserved under International and Pan-American Copyright
Conventions. Published in the United States by Random House, Inc., New York,
and simultaneously in Canada by Random House of Canada Limited, Toronto.
Photos courtesy of JPL (Jet Propulsion Laboratory).

Library of Congress Cataloging-in-Publication Data
Burrows, William E., 1937-
Exploring space : voyages in the solar system and beyond / by
William E. Burrows.
p. cm.
Includes bibliographical references and index.
ISBN 0-394-56983-0 : $22.95
1. Outer space—Exploration.   I. Title.
TL793.B847   1990
919.9'04—dc20   90-53133

Manufactured in the United States of America
23456789
First Edition

To Joelle

Provide ship or sails adapted to the heavenly breezes, and there will be some who will not fear even that void. . . . So, for those who will come shortly to attempt this journey, let us establish the astronomy: Galileo, you of Jupiter, I of the Moon.

—Johannes Kepler

When you get an answer you couldn't formulate the question for, that's exploration.

—Merton E. Davies

For a successful technology, reality must take precedence over public relations, for nature cannot be fooled.

—Richard P. Feynman

FOREWORD

My first visit to the American Museum–Hayden Planetarium in New York, on a ninth-grade class trip was profoundly intimidating.

Whatever the intention of our guide, I came away from my initial encounter with a representation of the solar system struck by the alien nature of the other planets and stupefied by the distances separating them. The distances were so enormous I could not grasp them: they made everything beyond where I stood hopelessly untouchable and therefore forever abstract. Or so I thought.

The planetarium people seemed to take some satisfaction in the fact that everything was so far away it was inaccessible except through telescopes. Somebody said that the Sun was ninety-three million miles away, which caused in me a kind of seizure of the imagination. Ninety-three million miles was so far away that it didn't make sense: it was literally inconceivable and it therefore lacked all meaning. Trying to imagine such a distance was like trying to imagine what God looked like. It couldn't be done. That was in 1951.

One morning early in August thirty-eight years later while driving eastward toward Pasadena on the 210 Freeway, I looked up, over the tops of the San Gabriel Mountains, and saw the disk of the same Sun clearly etched behind swirling milky gray clouds. "Look," I said to my wife, "there's the Sun. It's only ninety-three million miles away." We were going to the Jet Propulsion Laboratory for the Voyager 2 encounter with Neptune: to look at vivid close-up pictures of the planet eighth in order from the Sun and its extraordinary major moon, both nearly three billion miles away. Neptune had been nothing more than an insignificant blob in the biggest telescope in the world when I was in the ninth grade, and no power on Earth (excuse the pun) could change that. It was simply out of reach, a situation to which I had long been reconciled.

In 1951 I would have been hard pressed to find more than one paragraph on Neptune in any college-level astronomy text, more than a page on the rings of Saturn (no one knew that there were also rings around the other gas giants and that Neptune's were very strange indeed), or an unambiguous description of Venus and Mars. Thirty-eight years later the shelves of universities and research institutions practically groan under the weight of knowledge acquired in the space age. There are hefty tomes published by the University of Arizona Press, for example, each of which is dedicated specifically to planetary satellites, comets, rings, or the planets themselves (*Saturn* is printed in small type and is a hefty 968 pages long). There is a splendid color photograph of Mars on my wall—actually a montage of shots—taken in 1976 by a spacecraft named Viking that is so clear I can spend hours just studying Valles Marineris, a truly grand canyon the length of the United States that runs east and west across its face. I have richly detailed photographs of the moon Io, which bears an unmistakable resemblance to an anchovy pizza and is definitely the strangest place in this solar system, and another of Triton, Neptune's bizarre cantaloupe, shot by Voyager 2 on the last leg of its Grand Tour. It took that picture four hours and six minutes just to get here traveling 2.7 billion miles at the speed of light. Given that kind of distance, what's ninety-three million miles? It's almost trivial; a relatively short hop, to be taken for granted. So by 1989, I felt at home in my part of the galaxy. Neptune was no longer a mere blob. It was a neighbor. What had changed?

For one thing, radio telescopes had come into widespread use for scrutinizing parts of the electromagnetic spectrum not covered by optical telescopes. And optical telescopes themselves had grown increasingly capable in any number of ways.

But the big change was that spacecraft had actually been sent out to the planets and their several moons, not only to inspect them up close, but in the case of the Moon and Mars, to land. What had happened, in essence, is that we had extended our capability from merely looking helplessly from afar to conducting audacious inspections at very close range with extraordinary exploring machines and even to touching these other worlds: alighting on their surfaces to collect information about them for use on the home planet. These exploring machines and the instruments they carried—their eyes and ears—were always pitifully small for what was expected of them. Yet they were so brilliantly conceived and operated, the knowledge they provided so prodigious compared with their cost, that they did great credit to a race whose technology has in many other ways gone seriously awry. Many of the missions, and certainly Voyager 2's epic Grand Tour of Jupiter, Saturn, Uranus, and Neptune—our four large gas giants—exemplified the highest ideal of man and machine working in harmony for the real benefit of Earth itself. It was the interplanetary exploring machines that finally bridged the void of my youth, simultaneously drawing in the edges of the world and expanding them.

This is the story of these machines and their role in space science and planetary exploration: the spacecraft that Oran Nicks, the former head of NASA's lunar and planetary programs, called the "far travelers." But it is necessarily only one aspect of a much bigger story.

Lunar and planetary exploration and space science are not the same thing. The former is the physical process of going to the planets and their moons with manned spacecraft or with smart robots. The latter is the wider process of collecting scientific data—biological, chemical, or physical—about the solar system, the galaxy, and the universe beyond.

The planetary explorers collect scientific information from wherever they go. That's the reason they're sent out in the first place. But they are far from alone. A variety of satellites that circle Earth—the Infrared Astronomical Satellite, the Cosmic Background Explorer, and the troubled Hubble Space Telescope, to take only three—also engage or have engaged in space science, as do both optical and radio telescopes, sounding rockets, and even balloons and airplanes. But as used here, space science is meant in the more restrictive sense of having to do with experiments carried out by the lunar and planetary explorers themselves.

So this book is about the machines we send across the solar system and into the galaxy beyond. It is therefore about extraordinary journeys through time and space: about very high technology. But while the exploring machines fly into a vacuum, they don't come from one. In a more fundamental sense, this is also about their creators: about the scientists, engineers, managers, and politicians, often in intense competition or outright conflict with one another, whose intellects and passions have shaped planetary exploration. All voyages of discovery are inevitably done by and for people. This one is no exception. And this enterprise, no less than the others, is replete with its own heroes and with those who are somewhat less than heroic. It is, in the journalistic argot, a true "people" story.

My ultimate reconciliation with the solar system and with the rest of the galaxy would have been eased considerably, in fact, if someone at the American Museum–Hayden Planetarium had told me in 1951 what Bruce Murray told me at Caltech nearly four decades later: Space is a reflection of Earth.

William E. Burrows
Stamford, Connecticut
March 27, 1990

ACKNOWLEDGMENTS

An undertaking as necessarily complex and emotionally charged as the writing of a book like this is dependent on generous amounts of time, and in many cases enthusiastic encouragement, given by a variety of individuals who hold deep and often passionate beliefs. It is a never-ending source of wonder to me, as I'm sure it is to even the most seasoned of my colleagues, that there are so many good and dedicated people out there who are willing to give freely of themselves in return for the simple reward of having a story they consider to be important told honestly and accurately.

I am deeply grateful to all of the individuals listed in the section on sources who generously made themselves available for taped interviews that helped reveal the story's human dimension, often in telling quotation. I would like to particularly thank Chas Beichman, Mous Chahine, Lonne Lane, Bill McLaughlin, Bruce Murray, Bill Pickering, "Turque" Standish, Homer Joe Stewart, and Joe Tatarewicz for participating not only in initial interviews, but in important follow-ups as well.

Archivists and librarians went out of their way to be helpful. Paula Hurewitz at Caltech, Vladimir Petrov at JPL, Sandra Kitt at the American Museum–Hayden Planetarium, and David R. Smith at Walt Disney Productions were very generous with their time and effort. Special thanks must go to Lee D. Saegesser at the NASA History Office in Washington who put a great deal of effort not only into meeting my needs but in anticipating them, and maintaining an ebullient disposition to boot.

Then there were the public information people. I appreciate the help I received from Pete Waller at the Ames Research Center; Don Bane, formerly of JPL; and Charles Redmond and Paula Cleggett at NASA Headquarters. In lending me all three volumes of the *NASA*

Historical Data Books, Ms. Cleggett saved me untold hours in which I would otherwise have had to track scores of pieces of information, including budgets, separately. At JPL, Jim Doyle and Jurrie van der Woude put in endless hours ferreting out material, arranging interviews, and also anticipating my needs. Jurrie repeatedly provided material well beyond what his job called for—in some cases, material I didn't know I needed. I came to understand during several research trips to Pasadena why the Flying Dutchman has a special place at JPL. Alan Wood also was most helpful in finding much of the line art that appears in the text. I am also grateful to Ann Collins of the New York Academy of Sciences for providing the tape of an important meeting and a great deal more through the years. The academy is lucky to have her, as hundreds of science writers know.

Thanks, too, are due Penny Crafton of the Galileo Project Office at JPL, Craig B. Waff of the Galileo History Project, Alan Ladwig of NASA's then Office of Exploration, Jeffrey T. Richelson of the National Security Archive, Robert Windrem of NBC News, and Dick Meserve for making my task easier in a lot of ways. Alton Blakeslee was kind enough to open his and his father's prodigious files and allow me to borrow what I needed.

There are also some very old interviews to acknowledge: specifically, those done at the time of Apollo with Phil Morrison, Owen Gingerich, Isaac Asimov, Bernard Lovell, and the late Margaret Mead, Arnold Toynbee, and Mark Van Doren.

David Morrison, an extremely knowledgeable astronomer and longtime participant in many of the events described on these pages, not only gave me a long and incisive interview, but then went through the arduous process of reading the manuscript in its initial form. He provided many helpful comments while saving me from making some egregious errors. Similarly, John M. Logsdon of the George Washington University's Space Policy Institute brought his vast knowledge of the space program to bear, first by providing a moment of acute insight during an afternoon at JPL, and then by also going over the entire rough draft in considerable detail. John Casani made many helpful suggestions and corrections in the chapter on Galileo, while Bob Shapiro, my friend and NYU colleague, did the same for Viking and the search for life on Mars. Bill Pickering was kind enough to read and critique the Ranger material. Mert Davies of RAND, a universally respected founding father and guiding light of remote sensing (for the collection of information both on Earth and on the other planets), not only heaped a wealth of insight and information on me, but relinquished his only copy of the long-out-of-print *Space Handbook*. It occupies a place of honor on my desk.

I am also most grateful to Bob Bunim, a sharp-eyed old friend, who assiduously looked after my interests in California in a number of ways, one of which was by making me the only client of "Bunim's Clipping Service." Sarah Whitworth, my secretary and administrative assistant at NYU, once again ministered to my graduate students and kept the science writing program functioning smoothly during my thirty months of distraction in Pasadena, Mountain View, Washington, Cape Canaveral, and Stamford. Bob Loomis, my editor, is to publishing what JPL is to planetary exploration: the best in the world. I was very fortunate to have the benefit of his intelligence, insight, and imagination, all brought to bear through the telling prism of his self-described "ignorance."

Adequately expressing appreciation to my family for helping with this book is in some respects harder than it was to write it. How proud I am that having tried to help Lara with her writing throughout her childhood, she was able to repay the favor by helping me with my own at my relatively advanced age. She also learned to be philosophical about her father's stress and to handle it better than he did. Lara was therefore doubly his teacher. Joelle repeatedly scrutinized the manuscript with typical fastidiousness, making important points with her intelligence, dedication, and steadfast belief in the project. She also endured the whole seemingly interminable process of doing yet another long book. I can only repeat what I said in similar circumstances two decades ago: Now she knows why authors acknowledge their spouses' forbearance and why acknowledgments do not suffice.

CONTENTS

EXPLORING SPACE

AT THE JET PROPULSION LABORATORY

The first near encounter with Uranus by a machine from Earth happened in January 1986. The machine was named Voyager 2, and it had come a very long way to take the measure of the giant turquoise planet from up close. At eight o'clock on the morning of the last day of the near encounter, Edward C. Stone met with some fifty scientists to sort out the discoveries that had been made by Voyager 2 during the previous twenty-four hours. The meeting was called a science operations review, or SCORE, and its purpose was to refine and consolidate the new data. Stone led the SCORE meeting that morning, as he had each morning since the near encounter began eight days earlier, because he was the project scientist, the one to whom the other scientists reported.

The meeting took place in a large conference room at the Jet Propulsion Laboratory in Pasadena, California. JPL, as the sprawling 176-acre facility just below the San Gabriel Mountains is generally called, was where the spacecraft was designed and made and where it was now sending its stream of data for analysis by the scientists.

Stone and all of the men and women who represented the mission's science and engineering teams were particularly excited that morning. For months Voyager 2 had been obediently sending back an enormous amount of data about the large, mysterious planet— the planet that, unaccountably, had long ago gotten knocked on its side by some colossal force. Four days earlier the spacecraft had come closest to Uranus, skimming over its pale blue methane cloud tops at an altitude of only fifty thousand miles, its sensors collecting information continuously. Now, with Voyager 2 safely past the sul-

try planet, the hundreds of scientists and engineers who participated
in the mission were looking forward to one of the most memorable
days of their lives: the finale of a great planetary encounter. They
could have no way of anticipating, however, just how memorable a
day it would turn out to be.

As had become customary during visits to other planets, each
daily SCORE meeting was followed two hours later by a news conference at which the "instant science" that had come in and been
clarified during the night—the preliminary findings—was announced to the news media that gathered at JPL especially for the
occasion. As project scientist, it was Stone's job to summarize the
new scientific findings for the press and then introduce those of his
colleagues who would make specific reports on developments in their
particular specialties. He therefore went to his own office when the
SCORE meeting ended in order to think about the most important
of Voyager 2's discoveries at Uranus and ready himself for the questions that would be directed at him by the reporters at the news
conference. Certainly, the project's science teams had sent their own
questions to Uranus: thousands of them. Yet as Merton Davies, a
stalwart of the imaging team had said, the joy of exploration was
finding answers—discovering things—that are so surprising no questions have been formulated for them.

For starters, there was a singularly strange magnetic field. While
the other planets' fields are more or less at a right angle to the
orbital plane and therefore parallel to the poles (the difference between true and magnetic north on Earth, for example, is only 11.7
degrees), Uranus's field is not only a whopping 60 degrees off its
rotational axis, but the hypothetical dipole magnet inside Uranus
that causes the field in the first place is offset from the center: it
doesn't run roughly up the middle, the way it does inside Earth and
the other planets, but stays off to the side. It was presumed that
whatever delivered the colossal blow that turned Uranus on its side
also caused its magnetic field to be so strange. The fact that Uranus
had a magnetic field was no surprise, but its angle was positively
astonishing.

The picture on Stone's television monitor was coming over NASA
Select, a closed-circuit channel that was carrying a picture from
Kennedy Space Center. As the lanky scientist, holder of a doctorate
in physics from the University of Chicago, thought about other ques-
tions that were likely to require answers at the news conference—
What was Uranus's rotation period? Did it emit radio signals? What

was the composition of its atmosphere?—he saw a space shuttle on the screen. It had recently been released from the steel embrace of Launch Complex 39B's gigantic fixed service structure at the Kennedy Space Center at Cape Canaveral and it looked as if it were about to fly. In fact, the shuttle had less than seven minutes left on Earth, according to the large digital countdown clock at KSC, which ticked off the seconds to liftoff with remorseless precision.

Stone concentrated on the work at hand, however, not on what he took to be yet another routine shuttle launch on the other side of the continent. So did the other scientists, some of whom were also half watching NASA Select as they prepared to make their own presentations to the world press. The news conference that was scheduled to begin at 10:00 A.M.—in an hour and a half—would be especially important because it was to summarize all of the discoveries at Uranus, in effect bringing down the curtain on a brilliant encounter. Less obviously, it would also celebrate a triumph of the will, since this particular spacecraft had traveled a daunting distance politically as well as physically. It was 8:30 A.M., Tuesday, January 28, 1986, in Pasadena. But it was three hours later at Cape Canaveral.

AT THE KENNEDY SPACE CENTER

The object that appeared on Edward Stone's monitor, as well as on scores of others around JPL, was a flying machine of enormous complexity and formidable (no one would say beautiful) appearance: a winged behemoth designed under the supervision of the great Maxime Faget to carry people and cargo to the edge of space and then return to Earth for refitting and relaunching. It and its three sisters were therefore the first true spaceships.

By that morning this particular spaceship, named Challenger after a converted Royal Navy corvette that had done pioneering ocean exploration a century earlier, had made the audacious journey out of the atmosphere and back again nine times without loss of life. Now, held securely to its massive gray launch platform by eight explosive bolts, it stood poised for another try. There were seven in its crew. Its manifest consisted of two satellites and some equipment for scientific experiments, all of which was secured in its hold, or payload bay.

The mission had been scheduled to begin six days earlier, but bad luck had caused the launch to be postponed three times and scrubbed once. There had also been a series of last-minute glitches, including a stuck outer hatch handle, as well as very poor weather.

The weather was the worst of the problems. Dangerously high winds were moving down Florida's east coast at the head of a cold front. Only the day before, on Monday the twenty-seventh, cross-winds gusting across the Kennedy Space Center's runway had been so strong that had the spaceship been forced to come around for an emergency landing immediately after launch because of an abort, as the plan required, it might have been swept sideways into a crash as it tried to touch down. Accordingly, it had been decided with great reluctance at 12:36 that afternoon to scrub the launch and reschedule it for the next day, Tuesday.

From a purely technical standpoint the decision to stay on the ground had been judicious and certainly not unique. Only the previous July, even as this same spaceship's three main engines (the most powerful in the world) were pouring a torrent of fire into the flame pit underneath the launch platform as they worked up to thirty-seven million horsepower, they were automatically shut down because a coolant valve in the number two engine had failed to close. That had been a relatively small problem. In fact, there was even a redundant mechanism for closing the valve within the labyrinthine tangle of pipes and tubes that constituted the engine's intestine. But the computer that monitored the engine's vital signs had decided that the margin for failure had suddenly become unacceptable, and it had therefore acted decisively, as it was programmed to do. It hadn't cared that the difficulty was technically minor. The shuttle's computers were untroubled by political considerations, so they carried out their assignments unambiguously. For them, every choice, like the colors of the spaceship itself, was reducible to black and white.

Not only had the wind remained stiff after sunset that Monday, but the cold had intensified. As Challenger, the massive external fuel tank to which it was attached, and its two solid rocket boosters stood bathed in floodlight, the temperature had dropped to below freezing: to 27 degrees Fahrenheit. Although the glare all but blotted out the sky above Challenger, it was in fact an exceptionally clear night, with stars sprinkled everywhere. The four constellations that form Argo, the ship assigned by Greek myth to Jason and his fifty Argonauts for the pursuit of the Golden Fleece, were making their nocturnal voyage westward, just above the horizon to the south. Argo was sailing backward, however, as if it were correcting for a navigational error.

As Monday night wore on, thousands of foot-long icicles had begun growing on the fixed service structure, the giant gantry that stood beside Challenger and even towered above its external tank, whose brown bullet-shaped nose stretched 184 feet above the surface of the launch platform. The ice had formed because a fire hose near the top of the fixed service structure had been left running all night in order to keep the water in it moving so it wouldn't freeze. But the subfreezing temperature had partly clogged the drains into which the hose spilled, causing them to overflow onto the service structure itself. Then the spreading water, trickling down the fixed service structure a level at a time, had slowly turned to ice.

At first light on Tuesday long slivers of ice, some grown to a foot and a half, hung from nearly every pipe and girder on the fixed service structure's upper reaches the way stalactites hang from the roofs of caves. A communication box down below was almost completely entombed in clear ice, while two large water troughs were thickly frozen over despite the fact that more than 20 percent of the liquid they held was antifreeze. By 11:00 A.M. Eastern standard time, even as Ed Stone was listening to his science teams make their reports on the other side of the continent, a specially designated "ice/frost team" had inspected the fixed service structure's several levels, the launch platform, and the shuttle itself three times. It reported to the space center's director of engineering and to the spacecraft's launch director that thick ice covered the part of the structure from which the five astronauts and their two payload specialists were to enter Challenger, that it coated part of the launch platform, the area around the launch pad, and even the lower section of the spaceship's left solid rocket booster.

"You feel comfortable with what you see out there, Charlie, now?" asked Horace L. Lamberth, the director of shuttle engineering, as he sat in the space center's firing room.

"We have a lot of ice, if that's what you mean," answered Charles G. Stevenson, who headed the ice/frost team. "I don't feel comfortable with what's on the FSS."

"Then what choices have we got?" Lamberth wanted to know.

"Well, I'd say the only choice you got today is not to go," Stevenson answered matter-of-factly. "We're just taking a chance of hitting the vehicle," he added. As it was to turn out, though, Stevenson need not have been concerned. Flying ice was not going to figure in what was about to happen.

Stevenson, relatively low on the administrative ladder, was not the only one who was worried about the possibility of serious harm coming to Challenger. Several of his superiors who had a wider perspective of where matters stood that Tuesday morning were also concerned, and with far better reason. Beginning at 5:45 the previous afternoon and continuing well into the morning of the twenty-eighth, a series of meetings and teleconferences had taken place between NASA officials and representatives of the Rockwell International Corporation, the spaceship's prime contractor, and the Thiokol Chemical Corporation's Wastach Division at Brigham City, Utah, which manufactured its two solid rocket boosters.

The bitter cold was the subject of several worried discussions that night. There was so much concern, in fact, that it was decided at one point to delay the launch from 9:38 A.M. to 11:38 A.M. in the hope that two additional hours of sunshine would generate enough warmth to substantially reduce what was seen by some space agency officials and manufacturers' representatives as a potentially dangerous problem.

The temperature of the air around the spaceship at 11:18 that Tuesday morning stood at 36 degrees, or 15 degrees lower than at any previous launch. The middle-level technocrats from the space agency and the corporations, whose responsibility it was to decide whether to launch or to hold, considered the weather very carefully. They were particularly troubled by the way the cold might affect the solid rocket boosters, which were especially vulnerable to low temperatures because they were made in eight sections that had to hold together securely under extreme heat and pressure.

The managers considered possible ice damage and also the likely effect of the cold on the two boosters and the system's other parts. They considered all of the problems, sometimes debating them heatedly, and finally announced their decision at 11:18. They would go for it. The spaceship's crew members, all of whom had been strapped into their seats by 8:36, were not told that the weather was considered by the launch team to be potentially hazardous.

The decision to launch, however, rested on a great deal more than balancing engineering factors. Its apparent substance may have been technical, but it was shaped by political considerations, however unarticulated. On the morning of January 28, 1986, at least three considerations having nothing to do with physics or engineering, though unspoken and perhaps even sublimated, weighed on the managers' minds.

For one thing, the launch rate of the so-called space shuttles had slipped so badly from the fifty-five or so a year that had been advertised to sell the program to Congress in the first place that it amounted to an abiding embarrassment for the space agency. Since the shuttles were supposed to be only the first link in an extended program to include a space station, there was considerable pressure on NASA and its contractors to keep the winged rockets in space as much as possible—to make them appear to be efficient and dependable.

Of more immediate concern was the fact that one of the seven people who were supposed to go into orbit on this mission, a thirty-seven-year-old New Hampshire high school social studies teacher named Christa McAuliffe, had long been scheduled to give two lessons to the nation's schoolchildren live from space on the fourth day of the flight. That would put the lessons on Friday, the last day of the school week, if the shuttle went up on Tuesday. Just one more delay would have effectively killed the feat's public relations impact, which had been the whole point of trying to send the ebullient woman into space in the first place. (McAuliffe had been preceded by two congressmen and was to be followed by a journalist mandated to describe the exhilaration of spaceflight for those who remained behind to pay the shuttle's massive bills.) Public relations were one of the linchpins of the shuttle program. And that program itself constituted the heart of the space agency. It was therefore judged extremely important that McAuliffe deliver her inspiring lesson before the end of the week.

Finally, the president was supposed to deliver the State of the Union address that very night. Whether or not Ronald Reagan made specific reference to the mission, having seven Americans orbiting overhead even as he spoke would add a patina of prestige to him, to the United States, and therefore to the agency responsible for the mission.* That's the way points are made in Washington and no one in NASA had any illusions about it.

AT URANUS

Meanwhile, in the much colder reaches of deep space, just beyond Uranus, Voyager 2 sped on even as Ed Stone sat contemplating its

---

*NASA told the author that material relating to Challenger's flight was sent to the White House for inclusion in the address. The Reagan White House steadfastly refused to say whether reference to the mission was actually included in the speech prior to the accident, however.

accomplishments as Challenger stood poised for flight. Like the shuttle, its distant relation, it flew under the aegis of the National Aeronautics and Space Administration. But that was substantially where the similarity ended.

Indeed, there were at least two fundamental differences between Challenger and Voyager 2. Unlike the manned shuttle, which was a captive of gravity and was therefore restricted to making relatively low orbits around Earth, Voyager 2 was a robotic deep-space probe whose sole mission was planetary exploration and scientific investigation: reconnaissance of the solar system. Also, Voyager 2 was very far from home. At the moment the decision was made to launch Challenger, in fact, it was slightly more than 1.84 billion miles from Earth and streaking toward Neptune at 44,227 miles an hour, or slightly more than 12 miles a second.

There were actually two Voyagers—twins—heading toward the edge of the solar system that Tuesday morning. Both had been conceived and designed at JPL as a single project to advance planetary exploration by a giant leap. Both had been launched in the late summer of 1977 on roughly the same initial route. Both had followed approximately the same trajectory past Jupiter and then Saturn, and had sent back an unparalleled amount of new scientific data from the two giant liquid-gas planets.

But the twins had separated at Saturn, each going its own way. Voyager 1, its planetary exploration over, was directed to climb up and out of the plane on which the planets orbit around the Sun—the plane of the ecliptic—and send back information on the particles and other things it found there. Voyager 2, however, continued on in a far more ambitious undertaking. It too had ostensibly been launched to reconnoiter only Jupiter and Saturn. But Stone and his colleagues in science and engineering had quietly dreamed of going beyond them, to where no other man-made object had ever been: to Uranus, to Neptune, and then beyond.

Lunar and planetary exploration was a far different proposition from orbiting Earth. Those who worked Voyager 2 from Pasadena were overcoming the immensity of time and space, of a distance so great that it took two hours and forty-five minutes for instructions to reach the solitary explorer and just as long for the data it collected to come back. In addition, there were dangers from radiation, the possibility of running into a meteorite, and a darkness so pervasive that taking pictures of a passing planet and its moons was like trying to photograph people in a football stadium at night by the light of a single candle.

The twin spacecraft were to spend their working lives and after-lives in the vacuum of deep space, and they had therefore been designed to function most efficiently in that environment. Stream-lining was unnecessary; aerodynamics didn't matter because there was no air. Consequently, Voyager 2 and its twin looked like large insects, and not very pretty ones at that.

The heart of the spacecraft was a container, shaped like a ten-sided doughnut and called a bus, which was arranged as a series of bays that held computers, tape recorders, the navigation system, radio transmitters, and other equipment. From the bus sprouted a large dish antenna that always faced Earth, a scan platform that held cameras and other remote sensing devices, a long spindly boom on which was mounted a meter that measured magnetic fields, two other antennas (each as long and thin as a wand), sixteen tiny thrust-ers that were occasionally fired to keep the probe on course and pointed precisely where it was supposed to be pointed, and three small nuclear generators that had to supply power to the spacecraft because they were flying so far from the Sun. Solar panels would be of no use as energy collectors, after all, where the Sun was the size of a receding dot.

Voyager 2's coordinates—where it was—at a little after 11:00 A.M. on Tuesday, the twenty-eighth were precisely known to those who operated it. Although it was far from home, it wasn't very far from Uranus, at least in astronomical terms. Its closest approach four days earlier had amounted to an extraordinary navigational bull's-eye. It had sped into the heart of the Uranian system with its scien-tific instruments recording thousands upon thousands of bits of data about the planet's elusive rings and their tiny shepherd moons, windblown clouds, atmospheric composition, magnetic field, and a great deal more. That same day it also streaked past Uranus's five known moons, its cameras and other instruments going full bore in what amounted to a robotic frenzy. In the process, Voyager 2 not only had returned plentiful data on the moons that were expected to be there, but had discovered ten new ones as well.

Time was so short during the actual encounter, the amount of information to be collected so vast, and the instrumentation so nec-essarily limited, that some of the scientists who wanted the data had argued, often passionately, for their own experiments over those of their colleagues. They had understood that Voyager 2's arrival at Uranus would be profoundly important, perhaps the most important event of their professional lives.

The planetary scientists had anticipated a bonanza as one revela-

tion after another materialized in the bursts of data streaming back
from Voyager 2 as it swept past Uranus. So competition for a place
on board (in a manner of speaking) had turned some ordinarily
taciturn individuals into highly vocal advocates of their particular
specialty. And once on board, the privileged few still had to compete
with one another over which experiment was to be done when. A
camera, for instance, could point in only one direction at a time.
Which way it was going to point when Voyager 2 passed between a
planet and one of its moons therefore became a matter of intense
concern to those who wanted pictures of the planet (the atmosphere
people, for example) and those who wanted them of the moon (usually geologists).

The climax of the Uranus encounter—closest approach—had actually begun to unfold seven days earlier, on the morning of Friday,
the twenty-fourth, while Challenger remained on hold. At 4:01 A.M.
Pacific standard time a message had come from the craft saying that
it had rolled slightly and locked its celestial navigation system onto
Canopus, whose brightness and relative lack of close neighbors make
it a favorite star to steer by. Twelve minutes later Voyager 2 had
begun making ultraviolet observations of Uranus, which was only
265,000 miles in front of it and getting nearer very quickly. Anticipation had turned to exhilaration inside the Jet Propulsion Laboratory's Space Flight Operations Facility, which sent commands to
Voyager 2 and continuously monitored where it was and what it was
doing.

At that moment and in the hours that followed, Voyager 2 had
done just fine. It had sent back seven pictures of Uranus showing the
planet's atmosphere in unprecedented detail, although given the
fact that it looked as bland as a turquoise egg, that wasn't necessarily saying much. These had been followed by two extremely clear
pictures of Umbriel, one of the five known moons. There had been
other imagery showing Oberon, another of the Uranian moons, in
such stunning detail that it would be used to make exceptional maps
of the satellite's surface. There were data based on ultraviolet and
infrared observations of the moons and of the planet itself, pictures
of Titania, the third moon, and of Ariel, the fourth. Voyager 2 had
come closest to Oberon at 8:12 that morning, and eight minutes later
it had come closest to Ariel, sweeping past the small moon at a
distance of 81,000 miles. The closest approach to Miranda, the fifth
moon, had come at 9:03, when Voyager 2 had passed within a mere
20,000 miles of its icy surface. And only thirteen minutes after that,

the probe had shot through Uranus's ring plane as it continued to close in on the planet itself. The data had kept pouring in as the minutes passed, and as they had poured in, the mission scientists had grown progressively more excited.

The closest approach to Uranus had come just before 10:00 A.M. that Friday, the twenty-fourth. A few minutes later Stone had announced the closest approach to reporters from around the world who had been straggling into JPL since the previous Monday and who at that moment filled the von Karman Auditorium.

"Just a few minutes ago, at approximately 9:59 A.M., Voyager 2 made its closest approach to the planet Uranus," Stone had reported solemnly. The science and space writers, whose nonchalance was legendary even by journalistic standards, had broken into loud applause at the news. In an appropriate prelude to the mission's scientific findings, which were shortly to be recounted by several specialists sitting at a dais at the front of the auditorium, Stone had related how William Herschel, at first believing that he had spotted a new comet, discovered Uranus in 1781. Then Stone, who was also a professor of physics at the California Institute of Technology, had gone on to read a letter of congratulations sent by the mayor of Bath, England. Bath was where Herschel lived when he saw the new ball of light for the first time.

There had been more press conferences and science meetings over the weekend as fresh data continued to stream in from Uranus and its environs. Although there had been no way of knowing it months earlier when the finale—the last news conference of the encounter—had been planned, it would coincide almost exactly with the launching of Challenger.

AT THE KENNEDY SPACE CENTER

Challenger's sixty-foot-long payload bay held two satellites: not interplanetary travelers like Voyager 2, but Earth-huggers that were supposed to do their jobs while circling the home planet itself.

The larger of the satellites was an advanced communication type called a tracking data and relay satellite, or TDRS, which was to be used by the space agency and the Department of Defense to relay both open and secret messages from the shuttles and as many as twenty-three satellites to a ground facility at White Sands, New Mexico. Two of the tracking and relay satellites existed in operational condition on the morning of January 28, 1986. One, TDRS-A, had previously been delivered to orbit by Challenger and was working. The second, TDRS-B, was now bolted in the spaceship's payload bay, ready to go. The two spacecraft shared more than their name. Both were fated to ride this same orbiter. And both had been afflicted with a spate of very bad luck.

TDRS-A, launched on Challenger's maiden flight in early April 1983, had been sent spinning out of control by the errant booster that was supposed to push it away from the shuttle and into a permanent orbit 22,300 miles over the equator. But even after that problem had been corrected through frantic repositioning from the ground, one of the communication links on the $100 million spacecraft had failed and command problems developed, significantly reducing its capability.

TDRS-B had originally been scheduled to ride Challenger to orbit on March 3, 1985. But when NASA officials became suspicious that the second satellite could have the same command problem as its predecessor, and also discovered that one of its batteries had failed and Department of Defense encryption equipment had malfunctioned, they had abruptly scrubbed Challenger's seventh flight and removed its problem-plagued cargo. Challenger did go on to fly again, but not with TDRS-B, which had to undergo extensive testing and some modification by TRW, its manufacturer. Now there was going to be another attempt to park the satellite in a permanent geosynchronous orbit, 22,300 miles above northern Brazil.

The second, smaller satellite in the payload bay was also a problem, though for political, not technical, reasons. It was called Spartan-Halley and it was supposed to be released from Challenger on the third day of the mission. It would observe and photograph Halley's Comet while the exotic visitor was near the Sun and then be retrieved two days later and brought back to Earth so the data it had collected could be analyzed. That was fine as far as it went. The problem, however, was that where the space science community was concerned, it didn't go nearly far enough. There were many at the Jet Propulsion Laboratory and elsewhere who were chagrined because a small armada of more sophisticated spacecraft from the Soviet Union, Japan, and the European Space Agency had gone out to examine Comet Halley closeup. The United States, on the other hand, had to be content with releasing and then retrieving a simple instrument package from the shuttle rather than sending a proper spacecraft. It was sending no spacecraft to Halley because of lack of funds.

While most scientists gave higher priority to spacecraft other than one that could intercept the comet—to the long-grounded Hubble Space Telescope, for example—many were irked because it had been the horrendously expensive development of the shuttle itself that in effect killed the Halley mission by gobbling up so much of NASA's resources. And what the shuttle had done to the Halley mission it had done to many others as well. Four and a half years earlier, in fact, both of the Voyagers themselves had very nearly been turned off because of the shuttle. The threat of ending their mission, and particularly Voyager 2's record-breaking race to Uranus and Neptune, had ended only after an intense lobbying effort by the planetary science community.

Voyager's near demise, the devastation in other interplanetary programs, and the failure to send a spacecraft to Halley had engendered a suppressed but abiding bitterness in many of the same people who now watched Challenger poised to fly on JPL's ubiquitous television monitors, several of which were even located in the cafeteria.

AT THE JET PROPULSION LABORATORY

The monitors were on over in von Karman as well, though it was far less populated than either the cafeteria or Building 264, next to it, where Stone and the others continued to labor over the data from Uranus.

The building at JPL that is commonly known as von Karman is ordinarily divided into two large rooms: an auditorium complete with an audiovisual booth on one side and, to its left, a museum-display area containing replicas or actual backups of several JPL spacecraft. But during the Uranus encounter, as was customary during all JPL-run lunar and planetary encounters, both rooms had been turned over to the press.

The auditorium was in turn divided into three sections: a raised wooden platform at the rear on which the television cameras were positioned; more than one hundred chairs set in neat rows in the center of the room; and, in front, the stage on which the scientists stood each morning to tell the reporters what they had learned the previous day before they sat with them to take questions. A third Voyager, built mostly from scrap and carefully configured to look exactly like the two in space, dominated the left side of the auditorium. "Voyager 3" was complete down to a replica of the gold-plated,

twelve-inch records containing hundreds of Earth sights and sounds
that Voyagers 1 and 2 were carrying ever deeper into the reaches of
space. The probe's infrared spectrometer and radiometer, jutting out
on the end of its scan platform like a copper-colored eye from *The
War of the Worlds,* was turned toward the center of the room, where
the reporters sat. Behind Voyager 3, on the other side of the wall,
the artifacts of space exploration had been evacuated and replaced
by desks for perhaps forty reporters. There were also television
monitors so that the news conferences in the auditorium, as well as
frequent special broadcasts on the progress of the mission carried on
NASA Select, could be followed by those who were writing on dead-
line.

It was now 11:37:52 A.M. back at the Kennedy Space Center, where
Challenger's three main engines were about to ignite. But it was still
only 8:37:52 at JPL and the last news conference was not due to start
until 10:00. Since many of the reporters saw no reason to be on hand
an hour and twenty-two minutes early, they were scattered in hotel
rooms in nearby Pasadena and elsewhere, leaving the press room to
perhaps a score of stalwarts who were going over feature material,
boning up on the end of the encounter, poring over newspapers, or
just gossiping with JPL public information representatives on the
building's portico over the lab's notoriously potent coffee.

AT THE KENNEDY SPACE CENTER

The mood at KSC at that moment was festive. The families of Challenger's crew were among about ten thousand spectators, all invited
by NASA, who filled grandstands about four miles from the launch
site. Among them were 112 of the teachers who had lost out to McAuliffe in the competition to ride Challenger to orbit. They were nonetheless fully committed to spreading the gospel according to NASA
throughout the land. "There's nothing more thrilling than the space
program," chirped Lynne Haeffele, a "space ambassador" from Illinois, who added that she and the others were going to give presentations to civic groups like the Kiwanis "to get people excited about
space and education in general." Not to leave anything to chance,
the space agency had even hosted a three-day conference in Orlando,
the home of Disneyworld, to instruct the finalists on such topics as
"Mapping Your Way to a Successful Space-Age Presentation." The
irrepressibly effervescent winner had said earlier that "space is for

everybody, that it's a new world out there, a new frontier." Some four hundred reporters and photographers were also present. Their number would swell to fifteen hundred within twenty-four hours. Most of the VIPs and reporters were bundled against the cold. The temperature was 36 degrees.

Seeing that nothing appeared to be amiss, Challenger's general-purpose computer instructed the first of the three main engines to fire at 11:37:53, followed almost instantly by identical orders to the others. The spaceship began to rumble and strain at the eight hold-down posts to which its solid rocket boosters were held by explosive bolts. As the engines quickly came up to power, columns of blue-white flame and seared gases poured out of each exhaust nozzle. The shuttle began lurching forward, then backward, in what crews call "twanging." There was a loud roar in the flight cabin, expected by the crew, as the three main engines worked to pull free.

Six seconds later, at T minus 0, there was another roar as the orbiter's four master computers ordered the solid rocket boosters to ignite. Solid propellant began turning into 6.4 million pounds of thrust inside the two blast furnaces. Gregory Jarvis (a civilian engineer), Christa McAuliffe, and the five astronauts, all of them strapped to their seats on two levels in Challenger's cabin, were jolted again, this time even harder.

Below, most of the way down the length of the right solid rocket booster and therefore obscured from the seven people inside Challenger, a puff of black smoke blew out of the crack that separated two of the booster's lower sections. Then there was another, and another after that, each pointed inward toward the bottom of the external tank—right at the section that held 225,000 gallons of liquid hydrogen. With white flame now blasting out of all five engines to a roar that shook the earth beneath it—a thunder so deep and pervasive that it seemed to pound the heads of those who heard it—the eight hold-down posts popped open. At that instant, two external "umbilicals" that were plugged into Challenger to supply external power and a communication link separated from it. The spaceship's master timing unit, event timer, and mission event timers were started, and the three main engines neared 104 percent of their rated thrust. Challenger began to rise.

BEYOND URANUS

Although Voyager 2 was now almost ninety-five hours, or 3,175,000 miles, past its closest encounter with Uranus and heading toward its next objective, Neptune, it was looking back at the planet that was spinning on its side and continuing to soak up data and relay them back home. Soon the probe would enter the void between the two planets and the opportunity to gather useful information would temporarily end. A series of ultraviolet and infrared observations had already been made that morning to help determine the composition of the Uranian atmosphere and to search for activity in the auroras of its polar regions. One series of such observations had been completed at 10:22 A.M., Eastern standard time, and another series was scheduled for 12:32 that afternoon. Voyager 2 was also programmed to take parting pictures of Miranda and Titania. This was not only scientifically justifiable but important for purposes of navigation. The two Uranian satellites would be used to help set Voyager 2's route to its next and final port of call, Neptune, which it was supposed to reach in late August 1989. With Uranus encountered, and Neptune still to come, the mood at JPL was also festive as Challenger lifted off Launch Complex 39B and began to climb on top of its five cylinders of fire.

OVER THE ATLANTIC

Less than a second after the solid rocket boosters ignited and the explosive bolts fired open, a series of eight black puffs of smoke abruptly shot out of the right booster's aft field joint. The joint connected the booster's lower section with the lowest of its three middle sections and was sealed with a rubber ring and putty. The puffs meant that there was a leak in the joint's seal. No one was close enough to the launch platform to see the small puff balls. But it wouldn't have mattered even if there had been an observer. So many things happen at once during a shuttle launch—so many objects fly around, fall off, smoke, steam, and spit as the thundering machine struggles to break away from Earth—that he or she would scarcely have noticed the tiny puffs of acrid smoke coming out of the side of the SRB. And even if the telltale danger sign had been noticed, it would have been too late.

The spaceship rose very slowly at first, seeming to inch past the

massive 347-foot-tall fixed service structure, which turned from bat-
tleship-gray to glowing orange as it reflected the fire coming out of
the engines. The crew felt intense vibration now, like being on a
mechanical paint mixer, as Challenger slid slightly sideways while
its main engines redirected their thrust. At seven seconds it was just
clearing the service structure and picking up momentum quickly.

"Houston, Challenger roll program," Mission Commander Francis
R. Scobee radioed to the Johnson Space Center, which directed shuttle flights. Scobee was simultaneously verifying that Challenger had
a communication link with Johnson and telling those who were
monitoring the flight from Houston that the spaceship's computers,
which were flying it, had started the shuttle on a 90-degree roll to
the right while simultaneously easing over on its back 20 degrees.
Smoke billowed out over the manicured grass surrounding Launch
Pad 39B, over the nearby water tank, and out as far as the large
white dome-shaped container that could hold up to 850,000 gallons
of supercooled liquid hydrogen. Challenger kept climbing away from
the smoke and debris, over the clean beach that separates the grass-
land from the sea, gradually arcing toward the east, out over the
Atlantic.

"Go, you mother," Commander Michael J. Smith, the pilot, urged
Challenger in a fit of unbridled exuberance.

"Shit-hot," said an awed Judith Resnik, using a term that was
common among the flying fraternity to express exhilaration. Resnik,
who was thirty-six years old and held a doctorate in electrical engineering, was strapped into the seat behind and between Scobee and
Smith. She had been the second American woman to go to space,
after Sally Ride, and had run up almost 145 hours on Discovery's
maiden flight. Although she was technically a mission specialist,
Resnik was also handling the flight engineering job during launch
and was assigned the task of taking pictures of Halley's Comet after
orbit had been established.

"Looks like we've got a lotta wind here today," Smith observed
nineteen seconds after liftoff, as Challenger's computers turned its
main engines down to 94 percent of their rated thrust. Then they
rolled the spaceship again and further reduced thrust to 65 percent.
Challenger was now approaching the speed of sound in the part of
its flight envelope the engineers called the maximum dynamic pressure region, so it was slowed to keep stress to a minimum. It made
it safely past the danger zone thirty-three seconds later. The main
engines were once again throttled up to 104 percent.

"Feel that mother go," Smith said as the extra push from the three main engines pressed him and his six companions even more tightly into their seats. The sensation of being thrust upward with such force has been likened to being fired out of a giant slingshot. It made astronauts and the crews of other high performance flying machines almost giddy.

At that moment, exactly sixty seconds after liftoff, the puffs of black smoke that had come out of the right solid rocket booster's aft field joint turned to fire. Then the fire began attacking the external tank's thin skin and therefore the liquid hydrogen behind it.

Four and a half seconds later the exhaust plume coming out of the three main engines abruptly changed shape and color, and although no one in the grandstand was aware of it as they watched Challenger climbing steeply away from them, this meant that the flame from the SRB had ruptured the external tank and was lapping at the liquid hydrogen. During its final two seconds, Challenger struggled against the forces that were destroying it (in the words of those who were shortly to investigate the accident). But it was futile. The lower strut linking the right solid rocket booster to the main tank gave way, allowing the booster to break free at that point and rotate as it hung from only the upper strut. Then the hydrogen container inside the external tank broke open with such force that it caused the entire bottom of the tank to fall away, releasing thousands of gallons of the fuel. Almost simultaneously, the dangling solid rocket booster smashed into the section of the external tank that held the liquid oxygen, causing it to rupture and pour its contents downward, where it mixed with the liquid hydrogen.

As Challenger neared twice the speed of sound, eight and a half miles over the Atlantic, the mixture of liquid hydrogen, liquid oxygen, and flame that was still pouring out of the main engines did what the laws of chemistry said it was supposed to do: it turned into a gigantic fireball. The explosion happened within full view of the very important people, the reporters, hundreds of NASA employees both at the site and watching elsewhere on the Select channel, and thousands of ordinary Americans, including youngsters at McAuliffe's school, who were watching the launch on the Cable News Network. (Having decided that shuttle launches had become too routine to warrant live coverage, the other three major networks did not interrupt their regular schedules for the event.)

The end of Challenger, its colossal fuel tank, and its two boosters was spectacular: an orange and white flower that suddenly bloomed at the end of a long smoky stem. But this flower quickly sent ugly pointed sprouts all across a dazzling blue sky. Each sprout was a piece of the Space Transportation System trailing fire and smoke. Out of the fireball came the spaceship itself, broken into several large pieces, along with the two solid rocket boosters. The SRBs' burning propellant pushed them away from each other at high speed. The main engines, firing as they were supposed to and still attached to the tail, emerged from the far side of the cloud of putrid smoke and arced gracefully away. One of the orbiter's wings—the left one—came out at another place and floated down slowly, like a dead leaf. Somewhere else the forward fuselage, including the crew compartment with its seven occupants inside, appeared trailing a slew of wires, cables, and other lines from its rear bulkhead—electronic veins and arteries—that had connected it to the payload bay. The crew cabin's velocity propelled it almost twenty thousand feet higher after it emerged from the fireball. The emergency oxygen system in Challenger had not been designed to kick in automatically, as it does in an airliner, so Resnik and Ellison Onizuka, another mission specialist, threw switches releasing their own oxygen masks and then one of them apparently threw a third to Michael Smith. It took the cabin about two and a half minutes to complete its long plunge to the sea, which it hit at 207 miles an hour.

The two solid rocket boosters, empty of their propellant, burned out and harmless, were to have separated from the external tank less than sixty seconds after the explosion occurred. It was that close. Yet it was an eternity. Challenger had defied gravity, defied the atmosphere, and even defied the motion of Earth itself. But then it defied those who created it, and the result was terrible.

AT THE JET PROPULSION LABORATORY

In his office on the third floor of Building 264, Ed Stone was thinking about what he would say in concluding one of the most brilliant encounters in history while his television monitor droned on. Then he noticed the flower growing in the sky over the Atlantic off Cape Canaveral. The flower broke into his musing. He found himself staring at the screen for several moments in stunned silence, trying to grasp the enormity of what he was seeing as a NASA commentator narrated the event. But it took a long time for his mind to catch up with his senses. "I couldn't believe it," he was to recall later, "I simply couldn't believe it."

Arthur L. "Lonne" Lane, a veteran JPL scientist and a specialist in the analysis of ultraviolet light, was scheduled to talk about Uranus's rings at the news conference. "We had our graphics ready so we'd have pretty things to show," Lane remembered of that morning. After the SCORE meeting, he had walked downstairs to the graphics room to look at the pictures he wanted to show the press. There was a small black-and-white monitor in the room, and it was showing the launch. Lane, intent on his graphics, did not bother to watch Challenger leave its pad, although he half listened to the usual launch chatter in the background. Then, he remembered, "the two girls behind me got very quiet." So he turned, looked at the screen, and realized right away that there was trouble. "I saw the solid boosters going off like that," he added, moving his hands away from each other, "and I knew something was really wrong. We were just staring at the screen from then on."

Lane's first reaction was horror. But his second, which, like that of many of his colleagues, came quickly, was frustration and a tinge of anger. "Here was a major presentation I and some other scientists were about to give of the culmination of the Uranus encounter. And then I realized, Hey, the thing had blown up, and I personally knew they weren't going to survive. I was very low, very morose. People weren't going to be interested in our story. I felt very badly because of what happened to Challenger and its people," Lane explained, "but I also felt sort of sorry for all of the people who had worked on Voyager for so many years, and who do not get direct limelight, but who shine in the reflected glory of a good science mission with good press. It was not a good time; not a good time at all."

William I. McLaughlin, the manager of JPL's Mission Profile and Sequencing Section, followed events with two monitors he kept on his desk. One showed Voyager 2's parting shot of Uranus, taken with the Sun on the planet's far side, so that only a graceful blue crescent curved along one edge of the Uranian disk. The other monitor was switched to the NASA channel. An hour or so after the accident, McLaughlin remembered, "They focused their cameras at Cape Kennedy on the ocean as the water was rolling in. It was the memorial thing. The ocean is so final. If you want to talk about the irony . . . the juxtaposition . . . I've never seen a greater. . . . I had that crescent of Uranus, three billion kilometers away, and I had this ocean rolling in on the other one. That's the greatest contrast I think I'll ever see in my life: one a dirge, a mournful thing, and the other, one of the greatest accomplishments we've ever done. . . . the farthest contact we've had in outer space."

None of the reporters in von Karman really grasped what they were looking at during the first full minute after the explosion. But when the realization struck, many, and especially those who worked for daily newspapers, raced to make plane reservations for Florida or Texas. In most cases, the same science writers who covered planetary exploration also covered the shuttle. The story had moved elsewhere, and they understood that they had to move with it. Most of those who had lingered over their coffee somewhere else that morning, waiting for that last news conference, never even got to JPL.

After some initial discussion, it was decided that holding a wrapup news briefing that day would be not only disrespectful of the dead, but unproductive. It would be sparsely attended and whatever stories did emerge would only end up buried by the blizzard of news about Challenger. The last meeting with the reporters was therefore postponed until the following day.

There were some tears at JPL that morning. But mostly there was bewilderment and vexation as the scientists and engineers reflected on how Challenger's demise was likely to affect the Lab, the planetary exploration program, and their own fortunes. Never in the history of the space program had victory and defeat come so close together and in such equal measure. It was one of the enduring ironies of the space age that Challenger's destruction occurred barely ninety minutes before the start of Voyager 2's celebratory finale at Uranus.

The irony did not escape McLaughlin; neither did it escape Stone and many of their colleagues. "And so, if you like, Voyager just kind of disappeared from the scene, overwhelmed by the Challenger accident," Stone would reflect ruefully.

Bobby Brooks, who worked on Voyager's sequencing—the order in which it performed its science-collecting tasks—was more explicit. "We knew that there were a bunch of dead people now, and that the space program was in deep trouble. And we knew we had been cheated, intentionally or not, out of our encounter," he said, his voice rising with emotion. While Brooks was upset at the loss of life, and at the setback suffered by the space program as a whole, his overriding feeling on the morning of January 28, 1986, was one of bitterness. The shuttle had been the nemesis of planetary exploration in its formative years. And now, from its grave at the bottom of the Atlantic, it was stealing the explorers' thunder. "Here we were, flying high, and they took it away from us," Bobby Brooks said, his eyes burning with anger and resentment.

1.

Dreams of Ships to Sail the Heavenly Breezes

The urge to leave Earth to explore other worlds is so old that it has no discernible beginning. But the will to explore, and the means of doing so, were unreconciled until relatively recently. And the first machine to bridge the gap was not one that defied gravity but one that defied distance: the telescope.

In the first decade of the seventeenth century, Galileo turned his homemade telescope to the night sky and beheld the new worlds there from a vantage point closer than any who had come before. In the words of the physicist Philip Morrison, he thereby finally "healed the ancient split between the heavens and the Earth."

Then Galileo was driven to get closer, and closer still. Having raised the magnification of the three-power telescope that had shortly before been invented in Holland to nine-power by August 1609, the professor of mathematics and his craftsman-assistant pushed the cutting edge of the technology still further: to twenty-power by November and then to thirty-power by January 1610. That year he discovered the four largest of Jupiter's moons, and, in doing so, showed that not everything in the solar system orbited Earth. He also discovered that the Sun had spots—"blemishes"—which contradicted the religious and philosophical view, popularized by Aristotle, that it was perfect. These observations, in addition to others showing that Venus went through phases, like Earth's own moon, were another strong indication that Earth was not the center of the universe, as religious dogma had it, but that it circled the Sun just as the Polish astronomer Copernicus had insisted as far back as 1543.

While the origin of astronomy is lost in time, the use of optics to explore the heavens dates from Galileo. Metaphorically speaking, he and his telescope were the forerunners of today's rocket-propelled space probes. His observations of planetary motion, meticulously recorded on grids, were the equivalent of the mechanical sensors—

the eyes and ears—on a deep space probe. The telescope amounted to being his booster. It was the means by which Galileo's intellect was able to reach the target: it got his "sensors" to where they needed to be. From his time to ours, astronomers have depended upon a succession of improved telescopes to get them ever closer to ever more distant destinations.

Within thirty-five years of Galileo's observations of the Moon, richly detailed maps had been made of the lunar surface showing some three hundred features, including prominent craters. During that time, William Gascoigne mounted a micrometer on his telescope so he could measure the diameters of planets and stars in a way that he called "strangely precise." The English astronomer reported that he got the idea for the measuring device after God—the "All Disposer"—had caused a spider to spin a thread in an open case while he was experimenting with a view of the Sun.

There was an explosion of science from England to Italy in the waning years of the seventeenth century, much of it focused on the heavens. In 1676 Edmund Halley cataloged 341 stars in the Southern Hemisphere. The following year he made the first complete observation of the transit of Mercury. He also calculated the orbit of the comet that bears his name. This was the time of Isaac Newton, the brightest star in the European scientific firmament, and an individual who was to lay the groundwork for the eventual physical move off the planet and into space.

But touching—going there—was the thing. The great voyages of exploration in which Columbus, Vespucci, Balboa, Magellan, Cabot, Drake, and the others prowled their puzzling world, in effect fitting its disparate pieces into a comprehensible whole that could be studied at first hand rather than merely envisioned as abstract geometry, would before long trace a route that came to point upward.

If the New World was similar to the Old in fundamental respects, might not some of the spheres of the night also share characteristics with the place from which they were observed? It was an invigorating idea and one upon which Galileo himself mused. His discovery that the Moon's surface was "uneven, rough, and full of cavities and prominences, being not unlike the face of the Earth" was published in a historic pamphlet, *The Starry Messenger,* in 1610. The implication of Galileo's observations was clear. If the Moon was similar to Earth, then sending people to it was possible, at least theoretically. It would only be a matter of getting there, of finding a way to break free of Earth and embark on an extended voyage.

The difference between the watchers and the wanderers was that the former had to content themselves with observation—with being able to look but not touch—since they had to stay home. But the wanderers had the means to go where they pleased and touch where they went because they had an infinite source of propulsion. They had sailing ships for boosters and they had the power of the wind.

Exploration would be spiritually uplifting, to be sure. But where science was concerned, the difference between merely seeing and being able to touch would also be of fundamental importance. Going to space, instead of merely looking at it, would open the way to a higher order of science because it would allow actual experimentation, rather than only observation.

Problem-solving through observation requires the sifting of vast quantities of data over years or centuries, a complex, protracted, and arduous process, Lloyd V. Berkner and Hugh Odishaw would explain in a pioneering work about space science soon after the space age began. Berkner, an eminent geophysicist, was chairman of the National Academy of Sciences' Space Science Board when he and Odishaw edited the book *Science in Space,* which would appear in 1961. But experimentation "permits the gifted experimenter to devise his measurements in such a fashion as to separate the variable of interest from the many unwanted ones." It is the difference between observing a hundred criminal suspects over a long period of time to discover which exhibits suspicious behavior, a laborious sorting-out process, versus being able to associate with them and devise a specific trap to ensnare the guilty party.

The longing to touch space, but not be able to do so for lack of a means to get there, caused a frustration that led to flights of fantasy. As early as the second century A.D. the Greek satirist Loukianos, generally known as Lucian of Samosata, wrote an apparent parody of Homer's *Odyssey* called *True History.* The hero, lifted by a giant whirlwind, goes to the Moon and encounters fantastical humans and animals. In 1638 Bishop Francis Godwin's *The Man in the Moone, or a Discourse of a Voyager thither by Domingo Gonzales, the Speedy Messenger* had its hero breaking the bonds of Earth by using trained swans. The story was imitated in the mid-seventeenth century by Savinien Cyrano de Bergerac in two stories that usually appear together as *Voyages to the Moon and the Sun.* Jonathan Swift in turn borrowed from either Godwin or de Bergerac when he penned Gulliver's voyage to Laputa. A spate of science fiction having to do with space travel came out of France in 1865, including Alexander Dumas's *Journey to the Moon* and Achille Eyraud's *Voyage to Venus.* The latter described a propulsion system consisting of a reaction motor that used water under pressure. It wouldn't have moved a real spacecraft an inch, but the essential principle was on the mark. *The First Men on the Moon,* which was written by H. G. Wells and published two years before the Wright Brothers' airplane flew at Kitty Hawk, used an antigravity device to escape the pull of the Earth. And undoubtedly the work that did most to popularize the concept of spaceflight was Jules Verne's *From the Earth to the Moon,* in which a nine-hundred-foot-long cannon sunk in the ground in Tampa, Florida, shot a 19,250-pound manned aluminum shell all the way to the Moon.

In many ways, one of the most remarkable of the fictional odysseys in space was written by an astronomer himself, the eminent Johannes Kepler, and was published posthumously by his son in 1634. *Somnium* (Dream), an allegory, was loaded with footnotes that went into specifics about the scientific aspects of a voyage to the Moon. Kepler, himself a pioneering student of optics, was imperial mathematician to Rudolph II in Prague when he discovered the law of elliptical orbits and made important contributions to the understanding of gravity and the tides, which he theorized were created by lunar attraction. His work on gravity, in fact, foretold Newton's law of universal gravitation. Kepler was among the first scientists whose abundant imagination and creative urge spilled over into fiction because physical science alone could not provide an adequate milieu for them.

Galileo sent a copy of his *The Starry Messenger* over the Alps to Kepler soon after it was published. On April 19, 1610, Kepler replied in an open letter titled *Conversation with the Starry Messenger.* "Who would have believed that a huge ocean could be crossed more peacefully and safely than the narrow expanse of the Adriatic, the Baltic Sea or the English Channel?" Kepler asked Galileo in evident reference to the voyages of Columbus and the others that were being made across the Atlantic with increasing frequency. Then Johannes Kepler, grasping the fact that the exploration of the Moon was only an extension of the exploration of Earth, went on to make a prediction that was as prescient as it was hauntingly beautiful. "Provide ship or sails adapted to the heavenly breezes, and there will be some who will not fear even that void [of space]. . . . So, for those who will come shortly to attempt this journey, let us establish the astronomy: Galileo, you of Jupiter, I of the Moon." As Kepler correctly pointed out, the problem with going to the Moon was not the destination itself, but the means of getting to it.

. . .

The pendulum finally swung back from fantasy to reality in Russia in the last two decades of the nineteenth century when a poor and unknown schoolteacher named Konstantin Eduardovich Tsiolkovsky developed theoretical models for rocket propulsion. He based his work on Newton's calculations, first published in his *Philosophiae Naturalis Principia Mathematica* in 1687. The treatise included a thorough account of the principles of sending objects into orbits around Earth and even included a still-famous diagram illustrating the technique. Tsiolkovsky was trained in physical science and mathematics and had a special interest in astronomy. These interests combined to produce a unique synergy: relatively early on he became an apostle of space travel and spent his life working on the means to achieve it. When he died in 1935, at age seventy-eight, the world outside the Soviet Union was largely ignorant of his many innovations. But he has subsequently been recognized throughout the world as the master theoretician of the space age: the "father of space travel."

Early in January 1920, barely two months after the end of the first war to be fought in the air, the Smithsonian Institution in Washington published a paper that was to have a profound effect on man's reach even beyond the air itself. The paper was titled *A Method of Reaching Extreme Altitudes,* and Robert Goddard was its author. In the course of only sixty-nine pages, the Clark College professor precisely described a machine that could be used to finally escape from Earth and travel through the infinite vastness of space itself. The machine was the rocket motor.

In the paper, Goddard never mentioned getting people to space. Instead, as he explained in the report's opening lines, "A search for methods of raising [a] recording apparatus beyond the range for sounding balloons (about 20 miles) led the writer to develop a theory of rocket action. . . ." He pointed out that "the most interesting, and in some ways the most important, part of the atmosphere lies in this unexplored region," where balloons could not go. Scientific investigation in a number of areas, including the density, chemical composition, and temperature of the atmosphere, the nature of the aurora, the alpha, beta, and gamma particles that radiate from the Sun, and the ultraviolet spectrum, would be accessible by rocket propulsion, Goddard asserted. He also dismissed any discussion of the instruments that would be carried on his rocket in order to make such measurements, claiming that "their construction is a problem of small difficulty compared with the attainment of the desired altitudes."

Accordingly, Goddard went on to describe in painstaking detail a solid-fuel rocket consisting of two stages and carrying a parachute that was supposed to open when the vehicle reached its maximum altitude, thereby allowing the scientific instruments to float down for recovery. Ever practical, Professor Goddard explained that sending recording instruments to moderate altitudes—five or six miles—would permit weather forecasters to conduct "simultaneous daily observations of the vertical gradients of pressure, temperature, and wind velocity, at a large number of stations." And since the instruments would not be carried very high and would return to the ground by parachute about where they had been launched, he was careful to note, the expense would be relatively slight: it would only entail putting fresh fuel in each rocket.

But then came the exception to all of the hardheaded engineering calculations. He concluded the paper by noting that hitting the Moon with a rocket would be a feasible demonstration of its ability to reach extreme altitudes. And the way to prove that it scored a direct hit over so long a distance, Goddard explained, would be to load its nose with flash powder that would go off when it struck the Moon's dark surface.

News accounts of Goddard's paper were for the most part straightforward, though in the case of *The New York Times,* the Moon angle figured more prominently than he liked. The *Times* referred to the Moon shot in the first paragraph and even played it in the story's headline: BELIEVES ROCKET CAN REACH MOON. The next day, January 13, 1920, a *Times* editorial writer who probably had seen only the article, not the paper, attacked it in Topics of The Times. He took strong exception to the possibility that Goddard's device could be propelled as far as the Moon. In other publications Goddard was simply dismissed as the "Moon Man." He steadfastly rebutted by insisting that the Moon aspect of his paper had been overblown, while its practical elements were unnecessarily played down. But the attack would drive the inventor to a near-reclusive state, which, in turn, would have serious effects on the development of the rocket in the United States.

On March 16, 1926, Goddard, his wife, and a couple of assistants took a small rocket and its six-foot-high A-frame launch tower to a farm at Auburn, Massachusetts, not far from his physics laboratory at Clark. While his wife took notes and prepared to make motion pictures of the test, the rocket's gasoline and liquid oxygen were lit with a blowtorch. Up it went, arcing some 184 feet in two and a half

seconds, as timed by a stopwatch. The world's first liquid-fueled
rocket came down in a cabbage patch.

Grants from Daniel Guggenheim and the Carnegie Foundation
allowed Goddard to take his wife and a small entourage to a place
that was far more conducive to rocket testing than New England,
with its long and often harsh winters. They went to Roswell, New
Mexico, in July 1930. On December 30, using a pressure tank to force
gasoline and liquid oxygen into the combustion chamber where they
were ignited, Goddard sent an eleven-foot-long rocket that weighed
thirty-three and a half pounds to an altitude of two thousand feet.
This development, as well as the adaptation of gyroscopes to stabilize
the launch vehicles, were described by Goddard in a second Smithsonian paper, *Liquid-Propellant Rocket Development,* published in
March 1936. The use of gyroscopes, spinning like children's tops,
would prove to be important for stabilizing not only rocket vehicles
but artificial satellites as well. By that year—1936—a great deal of
serious rocket work was also taking place in Nazi Germany. And
nobody there was snickering.

By the time Hitler came to power in 1933, the German Army was
already in the rocket business, in large measure because several
amateur rocket societies already existed in Germany. The largest
and best known of these was the Verein für Raumschiffahrt, or VfR:
the Society for Space Travel. The VfR, founded in Breslau in 1927,
had the dual purpose of popularizing space travel while advancing
rocket propulsion to the point where such journeys were actually
feasible. The first liquid-fueled rocket to fly in Europe was built by
Johannes Winkler, a VfR member, and launched on February 21,
1931.

Meanwhile the Army, which was technically prohibited by the
Treaty of Versailles from securing any but specified defensive weapons, began to take a particular interest in rockets for use as long-
range artillery rounds. The treaty made no mention of rockets, after
all, since there had been none in 1919. So in the spring of 1932
Captain Walter Dornberger, who was mandated by the Army to
develop in absolute secrecy a liquid-fueled missile with a range exceeding that of any artillery piece in existence, paid a visit to the VfR
with three of his superiors.

Whatever the VfR's members wanted out of rockets, the Army
ordnance officers had their own wish list, and it did not include
interplanetary travel. Dornberger was explicit on that score: "The
value of the sixth decimal place in a calculation of a trajectory to

Venus interested us as little as the problem of heating and air regen-
eration in the pressurized cabin of a Mars ship," Dornberger was to
explain. "We wanted to advance the practice of rocket building with
scientific thoroughness. We wanted thrust-time curves of the performance of rocket motors (how much thrust a rocket develops during the stages of its burn).

Wernher von Braun, who was one of the early members of the
VfR, recalled in an interview shortly before his death in 1976 that
the visiting officers did not like "what they called our 'circus-type'
approach. We would invite people for an entrance fee to witness our
launches," he said. But Dornberger and the others soon set the VfR
straight. "What we really want is data," von Braun quoted them as
saying, "meaningful scientific material."

Von Braun and the rest of Dornberger's rocket team would receive
increasing encouragement from the Wehrmacht to design and build
ever larger and more powerful rockets during the years that remained before another war broke out. By the autumn of 1936, in fact,
the Germans were already conceptualizing the huge rocket, at first
designated the A-4, that would evolve into the vengeance weapon
they would finally call Vergeltungswaffe Zwei, or the V-2.

The principles of liquid rocket propulsion were well understood by
the eve of World War II. It was widely known that a liquid fuel—
ethyl or methyl alcohol, kerosene, methane, turpentine, ammonia,
or hydrogen, for example—mixed with an oxidizer, such as liquid
oxygen or hydrogen peroxide, would produce a sustained explosion
when ignited. If that explosion occurs in a metal chamber having
only one opening, the burning gases produced by the explosion would
rush out of that opening and, in doing so, "thrust" the closed end in
the opposite direction. Newton's third law says precisely that: for
every action there is an equal and opposite reaction. The amount of
thrust that is produced—how much power the motor develops—
depends on several factors: the type of fuel that is used, the pressure
under which it is forced into the firing chamber, the size and shape
of the nozzle through which the hot gas escapes, and a great deal
more. The quality of the fuel is measured by how hot it gets for how
long. The hotter the exploding fuel, the more efficient it becomes: the
more thrust it produces. And the more thrust it produces, the more
weight it can lift into space.

It would be difficult to overestimate the importance of the V-2. The
world's premier long-range ballistic missile was the first such
weapon to be designed for mass production on an assembly line, the

first to be truly large, and the first to incorporate engineering advances that would set the basis for the large rockets that were to follow after the war. Although it was conceived and built strictly as a weapon, it was nonetheless the prototype of every rocket that came after it, military or civilian. Not coincidentally, it was also the device that made Wernher von Braun valuable war booty in 1945 and a key player in shaping the American space program in the years that followed.

The entire missile stood nearly forty-six feet high and weighed a bit less than four tons empty and almost thirteen tons when fully fueled. It was divided into four sections. The top, or pointed end, contained a payload compartment for its high-explosive warhead (and, after the war, for scientific instruments). Next came the missile's five-foot-long control compartment, its brains. Here was the flight control equipment, including batteries, a pair of gyroscopes mounted on a guidance platform, radio receivers, instruments that measured the weapon's velocity, fuel cutoff equipment, alternators, and three compressed air bottles, which were used to pressurize the fuel tank. The third and largest section of the V-2 contained two tanks, one holding a little more than 12,000 pounds of liquid oxygen, and the other, which was more tapered because it was closer to the nose, held 9,200 pounds of ethyl alcohol mixed with water. The fourth and final segment of the V-2 was the rocket motor itself.

After a series of failures, the first successful V-2 launch occurred on October 3, 1942. "We have invaded space with our rocket for the first time," Dornberger bragged that night at a party for the highest-ranking members of the rocket team. "Mark this well: we have used space as a bridge between two points on Earth; we have proved rocket propulsion practicable for space travel. To land, sea, and air may now be added infinite empty space as an area of future transportation, that of space travel. So long as the war lasts, our most urgent task can only be the rapid perfecting of the rocket as a weapon. The development of possibilities we cannot yet envisage will be a peacetime task. Then the first thing will be to find a safe means of landing after the journey through space."

But as Dornberger explained, the war came first. Between 5,789 and 6,915 V-2s were manufactured by the end of the war (depending on who did the calculations), of which 3,225 were fired at targets in England, Belgium, France, and elsewhere. Along with V-1 "buzz-bombs," the large rockets killed 11,965 people and seriously wounded another 26,433, while destroying some 33,700 homes and buildings in London, Antwerp, and Liège alone.

And the fertile German imagination ranged quite a bit beyond the vengeance weapons as rocketry made the transition from theory to well-established fact. Even as the engineers and technicians were working on the V-2 at Peenemünde in the early 1940s, a Stuttgart professor named Eugene Saenger laid out plans for a giant winged rocket plane, called an antipodal bomber, that would be able to skip along the top of the atmosphere like a flat stone on water and reach all the way to North America with ten tons of bombs. Plans called for the craft to be launched on a highly lubricated rail, its engine generating a fantastic 1.2 million pounds of thrust, and then carry its weapons load to New York, Washington, and Pittsburgh. Another project, this one coming out of von Braun's shop, involved a monster ballistic missile that would be capable of producing four hundred thousand pounds of thrust and whose booster would have air brakes and a parachute so that it could be reused.

While the Germans labored mightily to build more powerful rockets as a means of sending explosives over increasingly long distances, their American counterparts worked at far more modest projects, initially with neither government interest nor support. Amateur rocket societies began to proliferate throughout much of the United States during the late 1930s. And, of course, Goddard continued his own increasingly complicated and productive experiments in the splendid isolation of the New Mexico desert. But the most fertile seedbed was started on the edge of Pasadena, California, some six miles north of the City of Roses itself, just in the shadow of the San Gabriel Mountains. Compared with the huge engines of destruction being designed and built by von Braun and his rocket team, not to mention their embryonic but increasingly detailed plans for going to space itself, the Californians' efforts were so pathetic that they would not bear mentioning except for one thing. The seedbed in Pasadena would germinate and then grow into the world's preeminent facility for the exploration of deep space: an undertaking, in fact, that would one day even put it into a limited partnership with the great von Braun himself.

On October 31, 1936, in the Arroyo Seco, a dried-up riverbed four hundred yards southeast of the heart of what is now the Jet Propulsion Laboratory in Pasadena, a small group of Caltech students and their friends managed to get a rocket fueled with gaseous oxygen and methyl alcohol to work for three seconds. That was good stuff, particularly for rank amateurs. Yet many aeronautical engineering students at the Guggenheim Aeronautical Laboratory of the California Institute of Technology, or GALCIT, continued to believe that

rocketry was as dangerous as it was irrelevant. So they contemptuously called the Arroyo Seco rocketeers the Suicide Club.

The rocket builders were led by Frank J. Malina, a doctoral candidate in aeronautics who had read Verne and believed him. Besides
Malina, who studied under the venerable Hungarian expatriate
Theodore von Karman,* there were six other members of the Suicide
Club. Two, John W. Parsons and Edward S. Forman, had not gone
to college and had no formal connection to Caltech. Not only had
Parsons not gone to college, but he believed in the occult and prac-
ticed black magic. William A. Bollay, a protégé of von Karman's,
followed rocket experiments in Europe and reported them to Malina.
These four were soon joined by three others: Apollo Milton Olin
Smith, William C. Rockefeller, and Carlos C. Wood. Later, the original seven would be joined by two other Caltech students, Hsue-shen
Tsien and Weld Arnold. Smith and Hsue-shen would figure prominently in the development of rocket technology.

Having gotten nowhere with anyone else at Caltech, Malina and
his colleagues went to von Karman for support. "The gap between
experimental demonstration of rocket engine capabilities and actual
requirements for space flight was just too great to inspire serious
interest among men of science," von Karman noted in his memoir.
"Knowing this, the young men who came to me set forth modest
aims. They wished to build and test liquid and solid [fueled] rockets
which could be propelled perhaps twenty to fifty miles into space.
This was not flying to the moon, the vision of most space pioneers,
but a small rocket when properly instrumented could bring back
information about cosmic rays and weather at the edge of outer
space, an altitude which balloons had not been able to penetrate."
The unconventional aeronautical genius, who was by nature sympathetic to any innovator laboring under a hail of scorn or in the
vacuum of indifference, agreed to take them under his already prodigious wing.

In setting the goal of building a rocket that could take instruments
for making measurements beyond the range of balloons, rather than
taking aim at the distant heavens, Malina and the others carefully

*Von Karman, who was born in Budapest, emigrated to Germany for his higher
education and later did pioneering work in aerodynamics there, particularly as the
director of the Aeronautical Institute at Aachen, where he built Germany's second
wind tunnel and did important work on Zeppelins, gliders, and monoplanes. The rise
of Nazism sent him to the United States in 1930. He soon became a professor at
Caltech. His later work in both aeronautics and rocketry earned him the nation's first
National Science medal, bestowed by President John Kennedy in 1963, two months
before von Karman's death at the age of eighty-one.

eschewed the kind of grandiose scheme they knew would not play well on their staid campus. Instead, they followed Goddard's far more conservative route of using rockets to slowly accumulate information about the physical world. This was the prelude to the development of the sounding rockets that would begin extracting data from the atmosphere and beyond immediately after the coming war. It was therefore seminal for the far-ranging spacecraft that would follow the sounding rockets ever deeper into space. And it was more than that. It was also the true beginning of the Jet Propulsion Laboratory.

At one point Malina went to Roswell to confer with Goddard. The fact that he and Goddard were engaged in similar work notwithstanding (or perhaps because of it), however, the reclusive "Moon Man" was blatantly unresponsive to the notion of sharing information. When Jack Malina returned to Pasadena, he reported to a disgusted von Karman that Goddard, displaying the *New York Times* article that had ridiculed him more than a decade and a half earlier, had pointedly avoided showing him either the rocket engines he was building or the reports that documented the results of their tests.

Goddard's rebuff of his young protégé evidently so angered von Karman that he had not gotten it out of his system a quarter of a century later. Reflecting on Goddard's having all but ignored Malina, von Karman went out of his way to attack both Goddard's penchant for secrecy and the quality of his work. However interesting Goddard's first liquid-propelled rocket flight might have been from a historical standpoint, he asserted, it was in no serious sense important scientifically. The Wright Brothers had been first to fly an airplane, he added, but that feat was not more important than was the theory of lift developed by George Cayley. Goddard's rocket therefore was reduced to being a mere historical curiosity. "I believe Goddard became bitter in his later years because he had no real success with rockets, while Aerojet-General Corporation* and other organizations were making an industry out of them," von Karman wrote. "There is no direct line from Goddard to present-day rocketry. He is on a branch that died. He was an inventive man and had a good scientific foundation, but he was not a creator of science, and he took himself too seriously."

Work on rocketry at GALCIT, however, progressed in fits and

---

*Von Karman, Malina, Parsons, Forman, and others started the Aerojet Engineering Corporation, eventually to be called Aerojet-General, in 1942.

starts through the remainder of the 1930s without help from Robert Goddard. In January 1938 Malina presented a paper he and Apollo Smith had authored, "Flight Analysis of the Sounding Rocket," at the Institute of Aeronautical Sciences meeting in New York. The trip was notable in at least three regards. First, Malina was given two hundred dollars to make the cross-country trip, thereby placing Caltech's resources behind rocket development for the first time and showing that the institute was taking a real interest in rockets. Second, the paper was published two months later in the *Journal of the Aeronautical Sciences,* an unmistakable sign that the propeller-driven academics in the aeronautical establishment were beginning to take rockets seriously. Finally, the paper got extensive and positive press coverage from the Associated Press, *Time,* the *Los Angeles Times,* the *New York Herald Tribune,* and even from a Hollywood radio station that wanted to get the sound of a rocket motor on the air, indicating, perhaps, that rocketry had an element of mass appeal.

Mindful of the way Goddard had been savaged by the press because of his reference to the Moon, von Karman and Malina stressed repeatedly that their vision extended only to about twenty miles up, where their rockets would be used for the study of meteorology and cosmic rays. But now it was the journalists who became fixated on fantastic voyages to the Moon, complete with sketches of passenger-carrying rocket ships blasting off from the Civic Center in Los Angeles. The reporters "seem to have better imaginations than we do," Malina quipped, though he never allowed himself to be baited into joining boundless flights of fancy.

GALCIT's first serious enterprise, in fact, was extremely practical. Even before the war began, von Karman was asked by the War Department to develop a device that would help airplanes take off in the shortest possible space. His and Malina's answer was JATO, or jet-assisted takeoff, in which small rockets were attached to the plane to bring it up to takeoff speed more quickly, and therefore with a shorter roll down the runway. This would prove useful on short or partially finished airfields on Pacific islands, in the Aleutians, and elsewhere, and eventually on aircraft carriers as well. Faced with a scarcity of funds, von Karman decided to do what von Braun and the others in the VfR had done: take research money from the military rather than close up shop.

Meanwhile, GALCIT had leased from Pasadena a seven-acre site in the Arroyo Seco. The desolate scrub-covered riverbed was more suitable for research than was the Caltech campus, which remained the preserve of a professoriat and student body whose sensibilities were offended by the rocket's sudden earsplitting noise and its propensity to explode without warning, sending hot shrapnel, fuel, and oxidizer in all directions. The owners of the homes that overlooked the facility in the Arroyo Seco weren't enthralled by its presence either, but they were persuaded to bear it for patriotic reasons. They were assured by the city of Pasadena that the rockets, unheated corrugated metal and wood structures, protective sandbags, and other test-range paraphernalia would be removed right after the war. They would, indeed, but the Arroyo Seco would never be the same.

In the early autumn of 1943 Malina and Hsue-shen Tsien were asked by the War Department to study the possibility of using GALCIT's experience in rocketry to develop an engine that could propel a long-range ballistic missile ("long" in those days being measured in scores, not hundreds or thousands, of miles). The resulting report concluded that a ten-thousand-pound liquid-fueled rocket could be produced that would have a range of seventy-five miles. Von Karman forwarded the study, along with his own recommendation that a long-range missile program be started without delay, on November 20, 1943. The document called for a fundamental expansion of the rocket research being carried out at the Arroyo Seco, including experimental work on ramjet engines and on three rocket missiles having ranges of between ten and seventy-five miles. It was also the first to carry the fledgling organization's new name: Jet Propulsion Laboratory. Although "Jet" was a misnomer for an organization engaged in rocket research, it was considered to be broad enough to cover both jet and rocket power plants. Besides, it was hoped that it would not be subject to the kind of ridicule that was still being heaped on anything smacking of the kind of rockets that were in the funny papers.

Urged by the army's ordnance rocket branch, which had awakened to the possibilities of getting into the long-range missile business, JPL then submitted a second, more comprehensive report early in 1944. This one outlined work not only for the development of propulsion systems but for guidance, control, and the other elements that went into a complete rocket-powered missile. The Pasadenans were soon rewarded with a one-year $3 million contract, a colossal amount of money at that time. Caltech's Board of Trustees approved

the agreement in February. The Jet Propulsion Laboratory thereby
became the first institution in the United States to engage in formal
long-range missile studies and associated space research, albeit with
military funding. As the coming years would show, JPL's special
relationship with the Army, while happy and constructive, established a free-wheeling environment that was to lead to painful problems when the soldiers were forced to surrender the lab to a new
civilian space agency.

Although JPL belonged to the California Institute of Technology,
an academic institution with outstanding credentials, Caltech's
board of trustees had given it permission to temporarily engage in
war work—developing guided missiles for the Army—until the end
of hostilities. So by late 1945 more than three hundred scientists,
engineers, and support personnel were working at the Arroyo Seco
site, which now included two laboratories, rocket test facilities, an
administration and office building, and even a supersonic wind tunnel. The intention was to develop a series of ballistic missiles, each
named after a successive Army rank. As it was to turn out, there
would be only three: Private, Corporal, and Sergeant.

Corporal, the second in the trio, would have the distinction of
being the first ballistic missile to be deployed by the U.S. Army. More
important, at least where science was concerned, it was also the first
true sounding, or research, rocket and flew under the name of WAC
Corporal (named after the Women's Army Corps because its developers thought of it as being Corporal's "little sister"). The sleek missile
was a little more than sixteen feet long, only a foot in diameter, and
weighed a mere 665 pounds. It could carry only forty-four pounds of
recording instruments.

On October 11, 1945, the Suicide Club's oldest dream was finally
realized when the first WAC Corporal blasted off from the Army's
new missile proving ground at White Sands, New Mexico, and kept
going until it disappeared at the end of its white smoke plume.
Although the rocket's engine ran out of fuel and oxidizer at about
76,000 feet, its formidable velocity propelled it to slightly more than
228,000 feet, or about thirty-three miles, before it plunged back down
seven and a half minutes later. The Jet Propulsion Laboratory's
sounding rocket thereby became the highest-flying object to leave
Earth up to that time.

But WAC Corporal's importance extended beyond its ability to
streak high into the atmosphere. It was designed and crafted at JPL,
which belonged to a civilian seat of higher learning. It was funded

by the United States Army, which saw a clear military benefit to be gained by it and by the research instruments it would carry to the edge of space. Its engine was made by Aerojet Engineering, a private firm started by von Karman and some associates from Caltech. And it was used by scientists whose research would be so applicable to war as well as to peace that it was effectively inseparable (a detailed knowledge of the upper atmosphere, for example, is useful for designing ballistic missile warheads as well as for predicting the weather).

At the very outset of the U.S. space program, then, a highly complex infrastructure was already forming in which lines of cooperation extended in all directions among scientists, engineers, technicians, military officers, managers, and industrialists until they formed a vast web that held together a tight, mutually supportive technology.

In a matter of weeks after the armistice, von Braun and a few others from the rocket team were sequestered at White Sands. They had surrendered to the U.S. Army, been rushed to the United States, and were now spoils of war. Their vengeance weapons, dropping out of the sky with impunity, had pummeled Allied cities from impressively long range. Now the victors insisted on having no less capability to obliterate targets than their vanquished foe. The advance party was shortly joined by other rocket-team alumni, as well as by the components of more than sixty-five captured V-2s that arrived in three hundred Santa Fe freight cars.

U.S. Army interrogators who questioned von Braun and his colleagues were astounded as the German engineers told them matter-of-factly of almost unbelievable plans to send manned machines to the fringes of space and beyond. The German engineering prodigy himself eagerly described multistage piloted rockets that would reach speeds approaching twenty-eight thousand miles an hour, and that would not return to Earth, but would stay in orbit as gravity and centrifugal force balanced each other out. "In such a case," Werner von Braun explained as if describing the movement of a sailboat across a lake, "the rocket would fly along a gravitational trajectory, without any power, around the earth, in the same way as the moon." And instead of using rockets as observation platforms, "it would be possible later on to build a station especially for this purpose and send components up into the interstellar space by means of rockets to be erected there. The erection should be easy," von Braun assured his transfixed captors, "as the components would

have no weight in the state of free gravitation." It was 1945 and von
Braun was inventing a permanent space station to orbit Earth.

Von Braun's new home, the White Sands Proving Ground, was
where missiles of all kinds were soon to be proven to work (or not)
under the auspices of the U.S. Army. The terrain upon which it
sprawled was flat and desolate, with weather that was predictably
hot and dry. It was no coincidence that the site was 120 miles southwest of Roswell, where Goddard performed his experiments in isolation, and about eighty miles south of Alamogordo, where the world's
first atomic bomb had been tested only a few months before.

The V-2s were brought to New Mexico for testing for a variety of
reasons, foremost among them being that they provided the Army
and civilian defense contractors. such as the General Electric Company, with working models on which to base their own designs. The
V-2s and their creators would provide invaluable experience in operating ballistic missiles, integrating components, and collecting atmospheric and other data necessary for America's own embryonic
missile program. The Americans would thereby benefit from the
Germans' achievements at relatively little cost while at the same
time avoiding many of the pitfalls that had plagued the V-2 program
in its formative years.

The first V-2 to be launched from White Sands went up on April
16, 1946, but it didn't make it past three and a half miles. One of its
four fins fell off. But the next try, on May 10, was a success. With a
group of generals, admirals, reporters, and assorted scientists and
businessmen looking on, the black-and-white bullet-shaped missile
roared off its pad and soared to an altitude of seventy-one miles
before falling back to Earth again.

Most of the sixty-four V-2 launches that followed between April
1946 and September 1952 went comparatively smoothly. But as was
the case with postwar rocketry everywhere, there were occasional
exceptions, and one of them was hair-raising. This was the launch
on the morning of May 29, 1947, when the gyroscope in one of the
V-2s developed a problem, causing the large missile to streak south
toward El Paso. It flew over the city, crossed the Rio Grande, and
finally plowed into a hillside a mile and a half beyond Juarez, where
a fiesta was taking place. Although no one was reported hurt, the
wayward missile caused sufficient alarm in Washington to prompt
telephone calls to the base commander at White Sands from Dwight
Eisenhower, the Army chief of staff, and from Secretary of State
George C. Marshall.

"We had already been called the only German task force that managed to invade United States territory and penetrate as far westward as El Paso," Krafft Ehricke, one of the expatriate rocketmen, was to recall with amusement many years later. "Now, we were known as the only German team that also managed to attack Mexico from their base in the United States!"

The Navy, too, was determined to carve its own niche in the nation's soon-to-be-started space program. In October 1945 its Bureau of Aeronautics set up a Committee for Evaluating the Feasibility of Space Rocketry. Within a few weeks the group concluded that a single-stage liquid-hydrogen-oxygen-propelled "earth satellite vehicle" was feasible and recommended that such a project be funded so the resulting satellite could carry electronic equipment for scientific test purposes. Because of the committee's favorable recommendation, the Bureau of Aeronautics contracted with the Guggenheim Aeronautical Laboratory at Caltech that December to do research on the relationship between orbital altitude, rocket engine and fuel performance, structural characteristics, and the payload of such a spacecraft. It soon became clear, however, that the sort of satellite the committee had in mind would cost between $5 million and $8 million and that funding from the Navy for the project would not be made available. Given the fact that their own service would not finance the project, the committee members decided to approach the Army Air Force in the hope of establishing a joint earth satellite project. But they were rebuffed. The Army's airmen had their own study under way.

Simultaneously, the Naval Research Laboratory in Washington established a Rocket Sonde Research Section so it could use its experience in missiles and communication (including television) to study the upper atmosphere. Although the NRL at first considered developing its own satellite, it quickly concluded that such a vehicle would be prohibitively expensive (possibly because word of the fate of the Bureau of Aeronautics' project had spread) and instead decided to put its measuring equipment on the rockets themselves. The NRL envisioned relatively small and inexpensive rockets that would be fired straight up with instruments in their noses and then come straight down, like arrows. They would either transmit the data they collected by radio telemetry or have instrument packages that would float down under parachutes. The little missiles would come to be called "sounding" rockets, after the nautical term used to gauge the depth of water beneath a vessel, and they would figure importantly in collecting valuable preliminary data during the early stages of the space science program. The progression from sounding rockets to Earth orbiters to deep space probes was essentially only a matter of increasing thrust to extend range.

Whatever the military aspects of the V-2 program, civilian scientists were included from the beginning. On January 16, 1946, even before the first V-2 rose off the New Mexico desert, Ernest H. Krause, who headed the NRL's Communications Security Section, invited a number of military officers and astronomers and physicists who were interested in cosmic ray, solar, and atmospheric research to meet on a preliminary basis at the Naval Research Laboratory. Krause told the group that the Army had offered to allow qualified scientists to place experiments in the empty nose sections of the big missiles. For people whose life's work was the study of the upper atmosphere, but whose research had been severely restricted by the altitude limitations of airplanes and balloons, the availability of a vehicle that could rise to a height of more than a hundred miles— beyond the distorting blanket of the atmosphere—was profoundly exciting.

"The drive for myself and my colleagues to go into space was not particularly inspired by science fiction, or the idea of manned space flight," James A. Van Allen, a preeminent space scientist and one of the group's founding members, was to recall more than four decades later. "Our motivation was an improvement in technique for performing scientific experiments in a new way and to investigate matters which had previously been only areas of, let's say, educated conjecture." Van Allen was interested in such projects as studying cosmic rays, measuring the ozone content of the atmosphere, and doing high-altitude photography of Earth. "I'd just been dying for an opportunity to go to higher altitude to do some of these things." Van Allen, a cosmic ray physicist then with the Applied Physics Laboratory at the Johns Hopkins University, was so impatient to get his instruments above the atmosphere that he also took to launching small sounding rockets from balloons that had already risen to high altitude. These were called "rockoons" and were occasionally launched from ships.

Given the level of interest expressed at the first meeting, a second, organizing meeting, was held at Princeton University on February 27. Besides Krause, there were three representatives of the General Electric Company, one from the Army Signal Corps, and four scientists (W. G. Dow of the University of Michigan, M. H. Nichols of

Princeton, Fred Whipple, the Harvard astronomer, and Van Allen).
General Electric was heavily represented because it was the contractor that Army Ordnance was using to assemble and fire the captured
rockets. One of the G.E. representatives, a scientist named Charles
F. Green, would explain the significance of the V-2 research this way:
"Right now, we know as much about upstairs as a fish does about
land." The fish knows what a fisherman looks like, Green added, but
it cannot explain him. Similarly, the V-2 would allow man to explain
things about the upper atmosphere that he had only been able to
guess at previously.

The group, which at first was called the V-2 Panel, had no formal
charter and no objective specified by a parent organization. It was
therefore free, in the words of one scientist who was at White Sands
at the time and who went on to become a high-level administrator
in NASA, to "pursue its destiny in keeping with its own judgment."
Colonel James G. Bain and Colonel Holger N. Toftoy, who were the
V-2 Panel's representatives at Army Ordnance, gave the scientists
free rein to schedule whatever experiments they pleased with the
understanding, which was subsequently challenged, that all results
were to be unclassified. The panel, which eventually grew to include
more than fifty of the most celebrated scientists and engineers in the
country, was adamant in fighting military classification. Secrecy,
the members felt, was antithetical to science because it impeded or
prohibited the free exchange of ideas that constitutes the very core
of the scientific process.

"Basically, it was a very permissive policy as far as the details of
how we went about what we did," Van Allen explained, adding that
there were no formal contracts and no overt attempts to get participating scientists to conduct experiments that would benefit the military. But military applications from the research were definitely on
the minds of the officers in Army Ordnance and elsewhere who
participated in the V-2 research program, he added. "For example,
the structure of the atmosphere—the density and temperature of
the atmosphere as a function of altitude—is of obvious importance
to guided missiles. The measurement of radiation above the atmosphere, which is my special field, was of obvious interest for radiation effects on components of vehicles in flight. I would say that the
military services had a broad view of the virtues of this type of
research, not a very narrow view."

Since the noses of the V-2s were designed to carry explosives, not
scientific experiments, the Naval Research Laboratory supplied spe-

cially designed nose sections to accommodate research instrumentation. It also provided equipment in the V-2s that collected and transmitted research data to White Sands and built receiving stations there, complete with antennas, so that the radio signals carrying the scientific data could be pulled in.

The V-2s, in common with spacecraft and other rockets, would send back the data they collected in a stream of radio signals. These signals are called radio telemetry, or simply telemetry, and they inform those on the ground about either what's happening to the rocket or what research data have been collected. Flight telemetry, for example, shows how fast the rocket is flying, how its instruments are performing, what its fuel consumption is, and a great deal of other data having to do with its vital signs. Since sounding rockets, boosters, and guided missiles do not have crews, such information is the only means by which those who operate them can make improvements or diagnose problems.

Research telemetry provides the same service for the experiment packages that the rockets carry. A Geiger counter carried in the nose of a V-2, for example, would register varying levels of radiation as the rocket flew along. A device called a transducer would convert the reading from the Geiger counter into radio waves in the same way that words being spoken into a microphone are converted into radio waves. The information would then be transmitted—broadcast—to the ground as a radio signal traveling at a particular frequency. After being collected by an antenna, the data would be restored to the state they were in when they were registered in the first place, just the way the voice that comes over the radio is converted from the signals that travel through the atmosphere. In order to be able to take advantage of all of the recording instruments that could be fitted into the V-2's large nose section, the Naval Research Laboratory built master telemeters to match: first, one that offered twenty-three channels of information, and then one that offered thirty.

Whatever the quality of the scientific measurements made by the instruments in a V-2's nose, and however accurately they were telemetered to the ground, they would be virtually useless unless the rocket's whereabouts were known at every stage of its flight. Knowing that one of the rockets had passed through a field of intense radiation without knowing where it had been when it ran into the radiation would be just as pointless, for example, as an aerial reconnaissance pilot's returning from a mission with splendid photographs of a new military installation without knowing what part of the country he had been flying over when he took the pictures. Because of this, it was necessary to precisely track the rockets at every stage of their flight, an undertaking that was to evolve into a vital specialty as the sounding rockets gave way to earth satellites and then to probes that reached first to the Moon and the inner planets and then billions of miles into remote space.

In order to keep precise track of where the V-2s and other rockets were, radar signal enhancers, called transponders, were installed in them. These picked up the radar signals beamed from tracking stations such as the one at White Sands and in effect sent them right back down in a highly amplified form that could easily be picked up by the facility's own radar antennas. In this way the rocket's position could be calibrated with the time it transmitted the data it collected to show exactly where it was when it gathered whatever information it was supposed to get. In addition, theodolites (the instruments on tripods that surveyors peer into to measure horizontal and vertical angles), powerful cameras, and other optical instruments were set up at strategic locations around White Sands to help track the rockets.

And the V-2s, in common with all of the rockets that were to come after them, had to be made to go where they were supposed to go, and this—guidance—was one of the knottiest problems of all. It was well understood by the spring of 1946 that there were two basic ways to guide rockets: command guidance, in which they were told what direction to take by means of direct radio commands from the ground, and inertial guidance, in which gyroscopes were preset to follow a given course and ordered the vehicle's steering rudders and vanes to move however much was necessary to keep it there.

With the advent of computers, however, a third technique—celestial guidance—would come into use to keep spacecraft on course as they flew away from Earth. Telescopic "eyes" would be programmed to lock onto three objects in the sky—generally the Sun, Earth, and a bright star, such as Canopus—and keep its bearings relative to their positions. If a spacecraft was supposed to go to Mars, for example, that planet's location would be loaded into the computer relative to the positions of the three other objects. As long as it kept those objects in view, then, it would stay on its trajectory to the red planet. If it veered—if it lost one or more of them—tiny steering thrusters would gradually move the spacecraft until they reappeared in its field of view.

But the main challenge was, and remains, systems integration. A rocket-propelled launch vehicle or a spacecraft is made of thousands of separate components, most of which have to work together in close harmony, and many of which can cause the destruction or incapacitation of the whole machine when they fail by even a slight margin. Unlike automobiles and ships, which can be stopped and examined, or airplanes, which can usually be landed for a detailed look at a problem, a rocket that has been fired is for all practical purposes usually gone for good. Some return to Earth smashed almost beyond recognition, while others disappear in balls of fire, leaving practically no trace of their components, let alone a clue as to the nature of the malady that killed them. Still others plunge into the ocean, or disintegrate during reentry, or shake apart so violently that their subsystems scatter over a wide area. Others never reenter at all, but remain orbital derelicts for years or forever. That is why telemetry is crucial for launch vehicle and spacecraft diagnostics, as well as for the return of research data. Rocketry was a risky business in 1946. It still is.

Nor was the actual flight the only problem. In the beginning—during White Sands's first year of operation—managerial issues and procedures emerged that had to be settled in order for the rockets to be able to function at all. There were, in Homer Newell's words, "safety considerations, provision for terminating propulsion of the missile in midflight, tracking, telemetering, timing signals, range communications, radio-frequency interference problems, weather reports, recovery of instruments and records, and all that went into assembling, instrumenting, testing, fueling, and launching the rocket." (Newell certainly knew all this. He worked on missiles during World War II, was at White Sands during the late 1940s, and went on to become a leading specialist in NASA's space science program and eventually an associate administrator.)

As 1946 wore on, routine procedures were worked out at White Sands to deal with all the details that went into making the place run. Typically, in a bureaucracy as structured as the civil service, the procedures were cut into formal, written operational plans. All projects had to be submitted in advance so that the proper procedures could be issued to every participant. "In only a few years," Newell remarked ruefully, "experimenters were harking back to the 'good old days' when operations were free and easy and red tape had not yet tied everything into neat little inviolable packages."

As Army Ordnance and General Electric worked to assemble and fire the V-2s with help from the resident Germans, the members of the Rocket Sonde Research group, loosely led by Van Allen, tried to develop instrumentation for their experiments. Some of the equipment was inventive if crude, so considerable amounts of data soon started coming.

Atmospheric pressure, for example, was ordinarily measured by something called a Pirani gauge, in which an electrically heated wire under low pressure lost heat by conduction through gas as atmospheric pressure changed. Lacking a Pirani gauge, however, Ralph Havens of the Naval Research Laboratory took the bulb out of an ordinary automobile headlight, knocked off the part that plugged into the socket, and rigged it to work like a Pirani gauge. The device went up in the V-2 that was fired on June 28, 1946, and actually collected data.

By the end of the year, rockets that had been designed to destroy and kill were popping up nearly one hundred miles through Earth's atmospheric canopy at relatively frequent intervals. They carried spectrographs to measure never-before-recorded levels of ultraviolet light from the Sun, radio transmitters that sampled the electrification of the ionosphere, telescopes whose cosmic-ray counters analyzed radiation at the threshold of space, and a great deal more. Data that could be collected no other way, and for which scientists had waited for decades, began to come down in prodigious quantities. There was information on atmospheric temperatures, pressures, densities, composition, ionization, and winds, on Earth's magnetic field at very high altitude, cosmic rays, and radiation as it existed both in the atmosphere and as it came in from the Sun.

But whatever the V-2's advantages for research—chiefly the fact that it was a proven launch vehicle, could carry a great deal of instrumentation because of its size, and was available in quantity (at least at the beginning)—it also brought problems. First, and most obviously, their number was finite and decreased with every launch. And their size, which allowed for the heavy payloads, also restricted their launching to White Sands, which had been painstakingly set up in the middle of nowhere to accommodate them. Finally, their very size and complexity made them expensive to assemble and operate. It was clear by the time the first V-2 flew in the spring of 1946 that smaller and cheaper sounding rockets were needed. And they were on the way. The last war-surplus V-2's launch took place in the autumn of 1952.

During the time between WAC Corporal's first flight and the launching of Sputnik, a flurry of rockets were used to sound the atmosphere and beyond, most of them either directly supported by the military or derived from military launch vehicles. Aerobee, a Navy Bureau of Ordnance project, was conceived in 1946 and turned out to be one of the longest-lived and most versatile sounding rockets. Not to be outdone, the Naval Research Laboratory again began work on its own high-altitude research vehicle, named Viking, that same year. Viking was an expensive flop and turned out to be the precursor of still another Navy high-altitude vehicle, the notorious Vanguard.

Meanwhile, the push for altitude—always more altitude—intensified. The Army accepted an idea, first proposed by Malina and Martin Summerfield of JPL, to mount a WAC Corporal on top of a V-2 and use both stages to get a payload higher than was possible at that point with only a single stage. The combination was called Bumper-WAC. During its two-year lifetime, the hybrid booster established a bittersweet record that was all too typical of rocketry during that period. The first flight, on May 13, 1948, ended prematurely when the WAC Corporal's motor cut off. The next three launches were also failures of one sort or another and included another abrupt shutdown and the explosion of a V-2.

But Bumper-WAC number five, launched from White Sands on February 24, 1949, flew flawlessly. The Corporal separated from the V-2 at the high point of the German missile's trajectory and shot up to a height of 244 miles. It broke the altitude record for rockets and in the process became the first machine to penetrate extraterrestrial space. Science had finally stuck its head beyond the atmosphere and taken a tentative first look around. The view was magnificent.

2.

A Plan to Conquer Space

There was a competition between the so-called manned and unmanned space programs even before the dawn of the space age itself: competition between those who believed in the primacy of getting men to Earth orbit and beyond for political and spiritual reasons and others who were equally convinced that proxies—robots—could accomplish a great deal more than humans in the realms of science and applied technology at far less cost.

Those who favored a strong manned program were persuaded that a kind of manifest destiny demanded sending humans to space, just as it had sent Magellan and other explorers to distant lands. Even before Sputnik, as the cold war intensified, they called for the "conquest" of space and warned that Communism's worldwide onslaught extended to the heavens. Sputnik only seemed to make their case irrefutable.

Those who differed from them—notably scientists—maintained that the true value of going to space derived from the knowledge of Earth, the Moon, and the worlds beyond that could be gained there. Indeed, they tended to see astronauts—the frailest elements in the equation and therefore the most expensive to maintain—as impediments to the valuable work that might otherwise be done.

While generally ambiguous in setting national goals for space, the National Space Act of 1958, which brought the National Aeronautics and Space Administration into being, was explicit in stipulating that science and technology be central to U.S. endeavors in space. It reflected President Eisenhower's aversion to extending a military presence to Earth orbit and beyond. Yet Sputnik and the Soviet satellites that followed it quickly set off a national frenzy and an interservice rivalry to answer the immediate challenge. Almost simultaneously, space strategy began to focus on the old dramatic dream of sending men to the Moon and then devising an appropriate rationale for doing so. The heart of the matter had less to do with science and exploration than with beating the Soviets by any means possible and deriving favorable propaganda in the process. Lunar and planetary exploration, while inherently valuable in their own right and theoretically above politics, were therefore relegated to a supporting role as the space race wore on. Besides, scientists were not perceived to be as heroic as astronauts, and it was derring-do that seemed to capture the popular imagination. Thus the space agency itself, reflecting the priorities placed by successive administrations, came to lose sight of its own charter. This, in turn, created a space program that was obsessively man- and mission-oriented and lacked a coherent and balanced long-range plan.

The heart of the American space program was graphically foretold not in a fat government report but on the pages of a popular magazine called *Collier's*.

It was laid out in eight installments that began with the issue of March 22, 1952, and appeared periodically for the next two years, ending with the one of April 30, 1954. Taken as a whole, the series amounted to a blueprint for occupying space. Scrupulous in detail and strident in tone, the articles called for nothing less than the wresting of supremacy in space for the United States. At a newsstand price of fifteen cents an issue the entire plan, meticulously constructed and lavishly illustrated, could be had for $1.20. That was quite a bargain. And it came during the Korean War, during the first real throes of what was increasingly seen as a pervasive international Communist conspiracy.

The series grew out of three symposiums on space travel held at the American Museum–Hayden Planetarium in New York between October 1951 and May 1954. The first meeting took place on Columbus Day (with due homage paid to "that outstanding conqueror of space and earth") and mainly involved Fred Whipple, chairman of Harvard's Astronomy Department; Robert F. Haviland, a General Electric rocket engineer; Heinz Haber, an expert on space medicine; Oscar Schachter, a space law specialist at the United Nations; and Willy Ley, one of the founders of the prewar German rocket society and a prolific popularizer of space travel.

All except Haviland made presentations on man's physiological suitability for space travel and the legal and technical means by which it might be accomplished. Haviland was supposed to deliver a paper on the uses of satellites to relay television pictures, but GE canceled the presentation at the last minute saying, lamely, that his fellow engineers considered it too speculative. In fact the use of cameras in space to collect military intelligence was at that time the subject of a number of top secret studies under Air Force auspices. The first operational space reconnaissance satellite, which did not use a television camera, would be launched nine years later in a program code named Corona. It was made by General Electric.*

Wernher von Braun, by then firmly established at the top of the U.S. rocket apparat, delivered a paper, "The Early Steps in the Realization of a Space Station," at the second symposium, on October 13, 1952. "The station in space," von Braun declared, "will be the most fantastic laboratory ever devised. It will also be the springboard to man's further ventures into outer space, to the Moon and the near planets. But it will become a reality because of its tremendous potentialities as a deterrent of war," he added, noting that powerful telescopes would be able to "pull up any Iron Curtain." He predicted that the man-carrying stations, "as big as light cruisers," would be in orbit within fifteen years. Dr. Milton W. Rosen, director of the Naval Research Laboratory's embryonic Viking rocket project, took a more conservative approach in his paper, "A Down to Earth View of Space Flight." There was a vast difference, Rosen cautioned, between firing a guided missile to space as an experiment and putting passengers on board rockets on a regular basis. Both men had their pictures taken beside a cutaway of von Braun's rocket, which stood some twelve feet high.

The first part of the *Collier's* series, "Man Will Conquer Space *Soon,"* appeared the previous March under the editorial supervision of Cornelius Ryan, who would go on to write *The Longest Day* and other best-sellers. Chesley Bonestell, an acclaimed painter of astroscapes, was one of three artists hired to do the illustrations. Whipple, Haber, Ley, Schachter, von Braun, and an atmospheric physicist named Joseph Kaplan did the articles. If Rosen was invited to participate, he did not accept.

*By 1952 the United States had become obsessed with the possibility of a nuclear sneak attack by the Soviet Union. Accordingly, it conducted extensive strategic aerial reconnaissance within its limited capability. This soon gave rise to the U-2 program. At the same time, it was well understood that satellite photography would prove to be the ultimate way in which to snoop on the USSR because the spacecraft had access to the whole country and were believed to be impervious to attack: a RAND Corp. report had said as much in 1946 and subsequent studies reinforced it. The Department of Defense was therefore loath to give away potentially useful space reconnaissance techniques and classified whatever it could.

Whatever the contributors' vision of man's role in space, the tone of the series was set up front by the magazine's editors, and it was blatantly jingoistic.

"What you will read here is not science fiction. It is serious fact. Moreover, it is an urgent warning that the U.S. must immediately embark on a long-range development program to secure for the West 'space superiority,' " the introduction to the series warned. "If we do not, somebody else will. That somebody else very probably would be the Soviet Union. The scientists of the Soviet Union, like those of the U.S., have reached the conclusion that it is now possible to establish an artificial satellite or 'space station' in which man can live and work far beyond the earth's atmosphere. In the past it has been correctly said that the first nation to do this will control the earth. . . . A ruthless foe established on a space station could actually subjugate the peoples of the world," the article went on to explain. "Sweeping around the earth in a fixed orbit, like a second moon, this man-made island in the heavens could be used as a platform from which to launch guided missiles. Armed with atomic warheads, radar-controlled projectiles could be aimed at any target on the earth's surface with devastating accuracy." But in ten years and at a cost of $4 billion, the article continued, a U.S. space program on the scale of the one that was to be outlined in the pages that followed—one that would amount to another Manhattan Project—could instead produce "an instrument which would guarantee the peace of the world." Seen in that light, *Collier's* concluded, the investment would be negligible.

The articles themselves amounted to a conceptual tour de force. The core of the material—specific, detailed engineering concepts concerning the various vehicles that would have to be used to break away from Earth—was provided by von Braun, by now the ubiquitous technical director of the Army Ordnance Guided Missiles Development Group at the Redstone Arsenal at Huntsville, Alabama. The Army took its bead on space mainly at Huntsville.

What he proposed, in essence, was a Space Transportation System that would be used to construct an orbiting space station from which manned expeditions would be sent to explore and then colonize first the Moon and then Mars. Thirty-five years later Dr. Sally K. Ride, mandated by NASA to plot a long-term strategy for the nation's space program in the wake of the Challenger accident, would recommend precisely the same scenario in a report, *Leadership and America's Future in Space.* With a single notable exception, in fact, von

PARANOIA OF SOVIET UNION
MOTIVATES SPACE PROGRAM

Braun's and Ride's concepts were strikingly similar. The exception had to do with the exploration of planets in addition to Mars, as well as comets, by unmanned probes that were supposed to make significant contributions to mankind's knowledge of the solar system. Ride was for it.

Von Braun ignored unmanned spacecraft for deep space exploration as inconsequential compared with the titanic political benefits that could be gained only by getting people into the loop. For his part, Whipple wrote enthusiastically about orbiting a space observatory that would finally get a telescope out from under the distorting effects of the atmosphere. (This would eventually be realized as the Hubble Space Telescope.) But when reference was made to it in a subsequent book that expanded on the articles, there was an added reference to the fact that such a telescope could also be used "for taking pictures in minute detail of the earth." Since no astronomer, and certainly not Whipple, would advocate using a space telescope for spying on Earth, it would seem there was another hand at work during the transition from article to book.

"Within the next 10 or 15 years, the earth will have a new companion in the skies, a man-made satellite that could be either the greatest force for peace ever devised, or one of the most terrible weapons of war—depending on who makes and controls it. Inhabited by humans, and visible from the ground as a fast-moving star, it will sweep around the earth at an incredible rate of speed in that dark void beyond the atmosphere which is known as 'space.'" So began von Braun's description of the centerpiece of his manned space system, the station from which all expeditions were to be launched.

While von Braun's space station was not as big as a light cruiser, it was conceived on a grand scale. It would be shaped like a wheel with a bar running across its diameter, circling Earth in a polar orbit 1,075 miles high. The selection of an orbit that would take the station over both poles at that altitude was significant because it meant that the entire planet would rotate beneath it every two hours, making it perfect for surveillance of Earth, a capability the German master engineer clearly prized. Specially designed telescopes "will keep under constant inspection every ocean, continent, country, and city. Nothing will go unobserved," von Braun explained. As the station revolved around Earth it would itself slowly rotate, so that centrifugal force would create "synthetic" gravity. A cutaway diagram of the 250-foot-wide wheel showed forty-five "spacemen" working in jackets or shirt sleeves inside the station or in spacesuits outside it. Some observed the Earth in varying degrees of detail, while others gazed at far-off galaxies, and still others performed the routine chores that kept the station going. One, sitting in his khakis, could even be seen reading *Collier's*. Visible were communication and meteorological sections, sleeping quarters, a computer, water recovery plant, loading area, power cables, airtight doors, hook-on rings for personnel in spacesuits, an air-testing laboratory, an air lock, a solar mirror used to focus the sun's rays on a mercury boiler, a space taxi approaching the station and another already docked in its landing berth, and quite a bit more. The picture, by Fred Freeman, had been done in close consultation with von Braun and reflected an astonishing amount of engineering detail.

The shuttle that was to carry prefabricated pieces of the space station to orbit, where it was to be put together, was no less finely detailed and carefully conceived than the station itself. Shaped like a giant inverted cone with wings and huge fins, von Braun's shuttle and the two boosters on which it stood in the form of a three-stage rocket were 265 feet long, or as high as a twenty-four-story building (making it eighty-one feet longer than the Space Transportation System that was to fly twenty-nine years later). Citing his own V-2s as examples of the way ballistic rocketry worked, von Braun went on to assert that his calculations showed that the shuttle would have to be accelerated to 18,468 miles an hour in order to make it to orbit with its crew and up to thirty-six tons of cargo. At a gross takeoff weight of fourteen million pounds, it was to require a cluster of fifty-one rocket motors in the first stage, thirty-four in the second, and five in the shuttle itself to gain enough velocity to reach its 1,075-mile-high altitude. Von Braun's shuttle was to return to Earth exactly as the real ones would: by gliding down and landing like an airplane. Unlike the actual shuttle, which used its ceramic tiles to dampen the heat caused by atmospheric friction during reentry, von Braun's streamlined spaceship was shown by Chesley Bonestell to glow red-hot as its temperature rose to 1,300 degrees Fahrenheit.

And there was more, much more. Subsequent installments described the way fifty scientists and technicians would use three transport craft (each exactly nine feet higher than the Statue of Liberty) to hop from the space station to the Moon, how actual exploration would be done and a permanent lunar base established, and how the spacemen would be selected, trained, clothed, and protected while in space (including details on a cleverly designed escape cylinder that was supposed to get them out of the shuttle and floating down on parachutes in case of trouble. No detail was too small to go unaddressed. "We have no knives, spoons, or forks," von Braun noted in describing a journey to the Moon in which the occupants of the three spacecraft and their materiel were weightless. "All solid food is precut; all liquids are served in plastic bottles and forced directly into the mouth by squeezing. Our mess kits have spring-operated covers; our only eating utensils are tong-like devices; if we open the covers carefully, we can grab a mouthful of food without getting it all over the cabin."

As befitted an enterprise of such extravagance, the *Collier's* series finally came to rest on Mars with the issue of April 30, 1954—barely one week after Senate hearings began in which Joe McCarthy, alternately sighing in feigned weariness and hammering in his patented nasal drone, doggedly tried to convince a captivated national television audience that Communist subversives had even succeeded in penetrating von Braun's employer, the U.S. Army. The chief of guided missile development himself coauthored an elaborately conceived article with "Connie" Ryan titled "Can We Get to Mars?"

The Mars mission dwarfed even the space station in complexity. It required the construction of a special space station, an armada of ten spacecraft for the two-and-a-half-year round trip, ski-equipped landing planes for use on the polar ice cap and inflatable and pressurized spheres mounted on tractors in which the members of the expedition would live when they weren't out exploring. First, however, Whipple paved the way with a short introduction that asked in boldface type the tantalizing question, to be repeated through the years every time someone tried to sell a mission to the red planet: "Is there life on Mars?" Well, maybe.

The Martian polar caps melt in spring, Whipple noted, and "strange blue-green areas develop near their retreating edges." And then, he wrote, "some months later these color patches, now covering great areas of the planet's surface, turn brownish. Finally in the deep of Martian winter they're a dark chocolate color. Do these seasonal color variations indicate some sort of plant or vegetable life? That's one of the riddles we'd like to solve."

And there was another. Although most astronomers had long since come to ignore Giovanni Schiaparelli's (and later Percival Lowell's) assertion that the surface of Mars was etched with a network of canals, there remained no satisfactory explanation of what the canals were, if indeed there were canals at all. That, the astronomer asserted, needed to be resolved. Finally, Whipple posed a question

that continues to intrigue cosmologists and others who are interested in the universe to this day. "How can we say with absolute
certainty that there isn't a *different* form of life existing on Mars—a
kind of life that we know nothing about? We can't. There's only one
way to find out for sure what is on Mars," Whipple concluded, "and
that's to go there."

No astronomer or planetary scientist would quibble with the notion of going to Mars to collect the sort of data Whipple wanted. The
real question, which was soon to generate an enduring and bitter
controversy, was whether the journey had to be made by humans or
whether robots were better suited to such a task.

For his part, Wernher von Braun saw himself as having two missions. One of them, his primary task, took place at Huntsville and
consisted of working with colleagues on the hard engineering that
would produce the rockets and spacecraft that would take men to the
Moon and Mars. The other had to do with his public persona and how
it was used.

By the time of Sputnik, von Braun had already blossomed into
America's savant of space. This "von" was no debauched aristocrat,
no idle and decadent wastrel, of the sort de Tocqueville's Middle
Americans instinctively found so slimy and contemptible. To the
contrary. Here was an individual with rugged Saxon good looks and
European urbanity who was also a master technologist—a young
Wagnerian nobleman, wielding a slide rule, whose prodigious imagination, Teutonic discipline, and absolute dedication conjured up
thundering devices that rode on pillars of fire and could reduce
whole cities to radioactive rubble or carry men to other worlds. The
combination was charismatic and the wily von Braun used it unabashedly.

The *Collier's* series spawned four books on space travel done alone
or in collaboration with Willy Ley and some of the other Hayden
symposia alumni: *Across the Space Frontier, The Exploration of
Mars, The Mars Project,* and *Conquest of the Moon.* Von Braun
lectured tirelessly and testified before any number of congressional
committees (some of whose members were sure to have their pictures taken with him). He was even the subject of a melodramatic
movie, *I Aim for the Stars,* in which he was played by the suave Curt
Jurgens.

Von Braun was quick to grasp the power of the visual medium: to
understand that television was a perfect vehicle for spreading a
gospel that had inherently dramatic graphic possibilities.

So on Wednesday, March 9, 1955, the former chief rocket designer
of the Third Reich took his place with Goofy, Tinkerbelle, Jiminy
Cricket and Davy Crockett on Disneyland, the network television
series. "Tomorrowland," one of the program's four permanent segments, was billed as "science factual" (as opposed to science fiction):
"The promise of things to come."* The animation, which was drawn
from the *Collier's* illustrations, was reminiscent of *Fantasia* in its
powerful, almost ominous tonality, vivid sound effects, and dramatic
score.

Billed as "one of the foremost exponents of space travel," a shirtsleeved von Braun gamely used props and diagrams to bring key
elements of the magazine series to life. He painstakingly showed
how an expedition to Mars, consisting of six "ships" assembled at the
space station like an interplanetary wagon train, could make the
trip in thirteen months and six days.

Von Braun also predicted that a "practical passenger rocket could
be built in ten years." This was no doubt the genesis, at least in the
popular mind, of the notion of commuting to orbit that would be used
more than a decade later to sell the space shuttle. Disney, the great
animator himself, held out the possibility of life on other planets,
particularly Mars. "Some observers claim the canals are only optical
illusions," the voice-over teased while alluding to the red planet's
many similarities to Earth.

The National Aeronautics and Space Act of 1958, which established
NASA, was not the result of a fundamental need within the people
of the United States to go to space—of a widespread yearning to
follow manifest destiny into what those who wanted to popularize
space exploration liked to call the "final frontier." Certainly trying
to get off the planet carried neither an economic nor a social imperative. There were no delusions even among the loudest and most
persistent advocates of space exploration that going there would do
for the coffers of the United States what previous expeditions had
done for Portugal, Spain, and Great Britain. No one would go crazy
or become physically impaired or die if Americans did not blast off
for the heavens. There was nothing in such an enterprise that made

*The three other segments were "Fantasyland," "Frontierland," and "Adventure-
land." Together with "Tomorrowland," they also constituted the elements of the
Disney theme parks in California and Florida. "Tomorrowland" itself appeared in
three subsegments: "Man in Space" (the premiere), "Man and the Moon" (1955), and
"Mars and Beyond" (1957). Disneyland itself—the series as a whole—premiered in
October 1954.

it inherently necessary where the safety or well-being of society was concerned. And with the possible exception of a few souls on the lunatic fringe, no one seriously believed that the journey literally amounted to a matter of life or death. To the contrary, as Dwight Eisenhower kept saying, it would simply be damnably expensive. The conquest of space had no broad, heavily committed constituency before the advent of Sputnik.

Sputnik 1, launched on October 4, 1957, changed everything. Alarmists—and suddenly there were many—ran to the barricades denouncing what they took to be a somnambulant president, a miserable, failed educational system, and a society that had grown too fat and dangerously complacent in the area of "scienceandtechnology" (which most of them and their bewildered fellow citizens took to be the same thing). The uproar that followed Sputnik has been described so often, however, and so well that there is no need to discuss it again. It would turn out that in and of themselves Sputnik and its follow-ons constituted no technical or scientific threat to the United States. The nation had an embryonic space program of its own in place the night the first Sputnik flew. And that program would prove that it could more than hold its own with the opposition.

If there was a real danger, it came not from the satellites themselves but from the huge boosters that carried them to orbit: monster boosters with enough lifting capacity to carry nuclear warheads to America as well as a beeping ball or a mutt to orbit. "The capacity to lift a satellite ninety or a hundred miles above the surface of the earth, and to place it into orbit, ominously suggested a capacity to lift a nuclear bomb into the upper atmosphere and send it hurtling down upon the target of choice," the late James R. Killian, who became Eisenhower's science adviser as a result of Sputnik, observed.

Whatever the apparent threat posed by the Soviet Union's ICBMs, however, it was Sputnik that provided the Kremlin with one of the most extraordinary propaganda coups of the century and set off a chain of events that led to the destruction of Challenger. For sheer drama and the demonstration of what appeared to be unexcelled scientific and technical prowess, there could have been nothing to equal Sputnik—certainly not an announcement that some dread disease had finally been eliminated, a new strain of wheat developed to reduce starvation, or the advent of an airliner that could dash from New York to Tokyo in six hours. Diseases had been overcome before, new strains of food had been developed, and airplanes were always being made to go higher and faster.

But nothing had ever been sent up to circle the whole world. For what Sputnik accomplished in public relations—an apparent demonstration of unequivocal Soviet scientific and technical superiority (and by implication the inherent vitality of Marxism-Leninism)—it was as cheap as it was brilliantly conceived.

The United States was profoundly humiliated, not because its science and technology were unequal to the Soviet Union's, but because its image suffered by comparison. Thus the space age visited two of its own ironies on the United States. First, the nation that gave the world "Madison Avenue" advertising, press agentry, public relations, and much of the attention-getting, image-building, sparkling, smell-good razzmatazz used to promote everything from soap to starlets was beaten at its own game, and by Bolsheviks to boot. "Our policy makers seem to have had no appreciation of the international reaction that would follow the accomplishment of the scientific feat [of Sputnik]," Lloyd V. Berkner, chairman of the National Academy of Science's Space Science Board, was to observe sometime later.

It would not take America long to define and then build its own space program. But that program would not be shaped to use science and technology in a grand design, a long-term master plan for the careful, integrated, progressive movement of man and machine off Earth for the exploration and perhaps settlement of other worlds, as well as for the management of Earth itself. Instead, it would become an instrument of politics on all levels: local, national, and international. Substance would almost invariably give way to form, to how the program was perceived, both at home and abroad. A bureaucracy that owes its existence not to the threat of armed aggression from abroad, or to the necessity of upholding the law, or to ensuring that food is safe, but to a 184-pound ball has to have exceptional PR to stay in business.

And within the technotheater a dangerous myth would evolve following a series of spectacular feats, the most notable of which were nine successful manned flights to the Moon, six of which landed and then returned safely to Earth. The myth, unceasingly promoted by the space agency for purposes of the public relations upon which it thought its survival rested, was that it (and by implication its manned forays into space) were infallible. To even consider that the Apollo crews that were to make it back safely from the Moon carried with them an element of luck would have been to diminish the technological precision upon which NASA's cachet rested. Infallibility, after all, cannot depend on the vagaries of fate. So the second irony was that the space agency would come to believe the myth it had created. The resulting hubris would have tragic and far-reaching consequences.

Sputnik was the ostensible impetus for the creation of NASA. But there was another motivating factor, less obvious but no less real. That was a growing awareness that science was moving to space with its own momentum.

The agency's technical genesis was contained in a report titled *Introduction to Outer Space,* which the President's Science Advisory Committee created on Eisenhower's order in the immediate aftermath of the Sputnik launchings and the national dismay they engendered. It was written in the form of an easily understood essay offering a rationale for going to space and carried an opening statement by the president himself, dated March 26, 1958. Eisenhower, in fact, used the report in a press conference that was designed to calm the nation about the supposed Soviet advantage in space and urged the news media to give it considerable play.

"What are the principal reasons for undertaking a national space program?" the report asked rhetorically before listing four of them under the rubric of the "advancement of space technology." The first reason had to do with the urge to explore and discover, which was all the more compelling because most of the home planet had already been combed over. Defense was the second factor, the report noted, adding that the United States had to be prepared to use space for defensive purposes if that became necessary. National prestige came next. "To be strong and bold in space technology will enhance the prestige of the United States among the peoples of the world and create added confidence in our scientific, technological, industrial, and military strength." Finally, the advisory panel stated, space technology afforded new opportunities for scientific observation and experiments "which will add to our knowledge and understanding of the earth, the solar system, and the universe."

Introduction to Outer Space went on to single out two likely targets, the Moon and Mars, for space exploration, explaining how they would be approached in terms of levels of difficulty. The prospect of landing men on the Moon was raised by the report, and also the always intriguing possibility that an expedition to Mars might find life there. "We know quite enough about Mars to suspect that it may support some form of life," the document noted.

The report concluded with a rough timetable for space exploration, divided according to four progressive stages. "Early" activity would include work in physics, geophysics, meteorology, minimal Moon contact, experimental communication, and space physiology. Later, there would be astronomy, extensive communication, biology, scientific lunar investigation, minimal planetary contact, and human flight in orbit. "Still Later," there would be automated lunar exploration, automated planetary exploration, and human lunar exploration. "And Much Later Still," human planetary exploration (meaning Mars) would begin. It is probably fair to say that none of the report's drafters—and they included such science luminaries as Edward M. Purcell, Hans Bethe, George Kistiakowsky, Edwin Land, I. I. Rabi, Jerome Wiesner, and Herbert York—thought that Americans would be planting the Stars and Stripes on the Moon in eleven years. But there was no doubt in the spring of 1958 that whatever the timetable, strong and intelligent leadership would be necessary, not only to ensure technological excellence but to navigate through treacherous political waters while maintaining a high level of public confidence and support.

Given the nature of the President's Science Advisory Committee, it was understandable that the Purcell panel's report would emphasize space science and exploration rather than military applications, which it all but dismissed with one short section that mentioned the need for satellite communications and reconnaissance systems and the possible development of such exotic weapons as orbiting bombs. Indeed, the name of the new organization—the Space Exploration Agency—chosen by the PSAC underscored its view of the situation. The president, to whom the PSAC reported, after all, harbored deep misgivings about his former comrades in arms' designs on national policy. Where they could encroach, Eisenhower believed, they would encroach. Unless they were kept in check, they would end up dictating national policy. He was therefore adamant in wanting to keep the Department of Defense's ballistic missiles and related hardware out of the national space program as a whole and to keep the respective policy lines distinct as well. But this would prove to be far easier ordered than obeyed.

Ike's fears were not misplaced. There were those, particularly in the Army and in the Air Force, who thought that placing the management of the country's space program in civilian hands, especially in the face of the overwhelming Soviet threat, was stupefying, if not treasonous, in its naïveté. Major General John B. Medaris, who commanded the Army Ballistic Missile Agency and was therefore von Braun's boss, was particularly forceful in trying to wrest a central role in space for the Army.

"Medaris and von Braun campaigned with fierce religious zeal to obtain a central role in space for the army," James Killian was to recall in his memoir. "Medaris vehemently proclaimed that military satellites should have greater priority than ballistic missiles, that the space program rightfully belonged to the Department of Defense, and that it would be a terrible mistake to give the responsibility for the U.S. space program to an independent civilian space agency."

In his capacity as science adviser to Eisenhower, Killian regularly moved in Washington's power establishment, and he therefore saw his share of political maneuvering from the inside. But there seems to have been a quality about Medaris's exceptionally forceful lobbying tactics, rooted in zealotry, that Killian found particularly distasteful. The former president of MIT, ordinarily circumspect and taciturn in open discussions about those he had encountered in public life, evidently could not resist taking an uncharacteristically gratuitous parting shot at Medaris in his autobiography. "I have noted with interest the post-army career of the dedicated, outspoken, belligerent, and pious general. He retired, first to become president of the Lionel Corporation, builder of toy trains, and later to become an Episcopal priest, Father Bruce." Killian ended his riposte by quoting a comment attributed to Medaris in *People* magazine: "No human being, without the guidance of the Lord, could have been right as much as I was."

And the Air Force was also covetous of the space program. Leaving nothing—certainly not nomenclature—to chance, Air Force public affairs specialists even came up with the term "aerospace" to get the public used to the idea that air (in which the Air Force operated) and space (in which it wanted to operate) were an indivisible continuum.

Aside from Sputnik and the threat from the military, there was also a growing groundswell for a formal organization from the science community itself.

The U.S. sounding rocket program, begun tentatively with the V-2s in 1946, had achieved a string of impressive successes well into the 1950s as the "sounders" were progressively refined. During the

International Geophysical Year, which began on July 1, 1957, and ended on December 31, 1958, sounding rockets by the score were sent aloft to gather data on X rays coming from the Sun and elsewhere in space, on solar flares, the shape of the Sun's corona during an eclipse, ultraviolet radiation coming from early stars, and a great deal more. The rockets, together with aircraft and balloons, formed one of several components in an unprecedented joint international examination of Earth and its surroundings conducted by more than sixty thousand scientists from sixty-six nations. Sputnik's ostensible purpose, just as the Soviets claimed, was to participate in the IGY.

The Navy's beautifully sleek and versatile Aerobees were used for many of these experiments. In addition, the National Advisory Committee for Aeronautics, which was for the most part responsible for the development of aviation technology, sent up its own sounding rockets. Most of these depended on Nike boosters, which had been developed by the Army as an air defense missile against Soviet bombers. Nike-Ajax, the first and most widely produced of the anti-aircraft missiles, had a range of twenty-nine miles. With its explosive warhead replaced by a rocket-propelled Cajun second stage carrying instrumentation, its ceiling was extended to an impressive 145 miles.

The high-altitude rocket soundings were for the most part conducted under the auspices of the Rocket and Satellite Research Panel (renamed from the V-2 Panel in evident recognition that the German booster had become anachronistic and, in any event, that the group's mandate was not limited to any one propulsion system). There was also increasing involvement by the National Academy of Sciences, as well as by the PSAC itself. Not only did the civilian scientists depend to a great extent on military equipment—the Nikes, like the V-2s, were basically war surplus—but, as has been noted, their research results almost invariably benefited the military one way or another.

The International Geophysical Year was in large measure responsible for the coming together of a space establishment because participation required the formation of specialized panels to carry out particular sets of experiments. Furthermore, there was a growing awareness by the mid-1950s that if science and engineering depended upon government not only to deliver research apparatus to space but to fund the research in the first place, it was important to have organizations that could lobby for the necessary support from Washington. So the demands of participation in the IGY, mutual dependence within the community itself, and the need to lobby effectively coalesced into a true space establishment even before Sputnik.

"Gradually the idea emerged that the United States should go further [than participation in the IGY] and establish some kind of permanent space agency," Homer Newell has written. He and a committee of colleagues therefore roughed out a plan in the summer of 1957 for a "National Space Establishment" to be organized and funded solely to carry out "unmanned space research and applications and manned exploration of outer space."

Within seven weeks of the flight of the first Sputnik, Newell's committee hammered out a paper, eventually to be called National Space Establishment, which came out squarely for a civilian space agency. It was one of the seminal documents creating the National Aeronautics and Space Administration.

The new agency's founding fathers, not only within the Rocket and Satellite Research Panel but in the White House, the National Academy of Sciences, the universities and institutes, the military, and in industry, amounted to the cream of the nation's science and engineering crop. Besides many of the notables who produced *Introduction to Outer Space,* they included Detlev Bronk (president of the National Academy), Killian, Lee DuBridge (president of Caltech), William Pickering (the director of the Jet Propulsion Laboratory), Homer Joe Stewart (also of JPL), plus Krause, Nichols, Whipple, Van Allen, Ehricke, von Braun, and several others.

NASA was born on October 1, 1958. Its enabling legislation, the National Aeronautics and Space Act of 1958, was pounded out only after a sometimes acrimonious debate between the Department of Defense and the White House. The generals remained stubbornly convinced that civilian control of a program whose technology was derived up to 90 percent from military requirements was not only absurd but hypocritical. Eisenhower nonetheless prevailed. The basic guidelines set out by Killian's PSAC became the essence of the Space Act, which was signed into law on July 29, 1958, and which mandated "the preservation of the role of the United States as a leader in aeronautical science and technology. . . ."

The Space Act made no mention of sending Americans to the Moon or of manned spaceflight of any kind. Yet almost everyone within the fledgling national space establishment—including its handful of scientists—was beginning to understand that "winning" the space race was going to be taken to require a human, not merely a robotic, presence up there.

And so it was that on December 15, 1958—just seventy-six days after NASA came into existence—its first administrator, T. Keith Glennan, sat with some of his aides in the space agency's first headquarters, the old Dolly Madison House in Washington, and listened while a presentation was made on how to capture the imagination of the world and one-up the Russians at the same time. The plan, an audacious one, called for landing Americans on the Moon. The planners, from the Army Ballistic Missile Agency at Huntsville (soon to be NASA's George C. Marshall Space Flight Center), were Heinz H. Koelle, Ernst Stuhlinger, and Wernher von Braun.

Koelle predicted that the country would have the technological wherewithal, particularly where extremely powerful boosters were concerned, to put men on the moon by 1967. "And," he quipped teasingly, "we still hope not to have Russian Customs here." Von Braun addressed the question of what it would take to get men to the Moon and back again by mentioning five possible techniques. Four of them entailed rendezvousing in Earth orbit on the way while one, requiring an immense booster, went straight for the target in a so-called direct ascent. Von Braun was against the direct ascent approach—a single, relatively straight shot without reboosting from orbit—because, he calculated, it would require a stupendous launch vehicle weighing 13.5 million pounds. The launch vehicle that was to carry three Americans to the Moon eleven years later, a 360-foot-tall monster called Saturn V, would weigh less than half of what von Braun had calculated and would use a rendezvousing maneuver. It would nevertheless be the largest rocket ever built. And it would be designed by von Braun himself.

Ernst Stuhlinger, the next to speak, had worked with von Braun at the German rocket development facility at Peenemünde and had once been an assistant to Johannes Geiger, the eminent atomic physicist, at the prestigious Technische Hochschule in Berlin. "The main objective in outer space, of course, should be *man* in outer space," Stuhlinger remarked. "And not only man as a survivor in space, but man as an active scientist, a man who can explore out in space all those things which we cannot explore from Earth."

Whatever the scientific embellishments of the plan, it was presented by engineers, and its goals were engineering-specific. Engineers are different from scientists. Whereas scientists' goals tend to be open-ended—the more new questions that are raised, the better—

engineers' goals are carefully delineated and closed. In effect, the engineers tend to see their essential task as getting from point A to point B as cheaply, safely, and efficiently as possible without unnecessarily burdening themselves with esoteric considerations; they are builders, not explorers. And they are therefore a pragmatic bunch, far more easily conscripted to grand feats of technology than are the scientists. It was therefore only natural that von Braun and the other engineers defined themselves by setting the technical challenge of propelling people to space and then meeting that challenge. In this context, getting humans into orbit and then to the Moon and beyond were thoroughly justified ends. And there was no doubt about the propellant that would be used for the journey. It would be the Soviets themselves.

Yet others, including Killian, had serious reservations about staging space spectaculars in order to compete successfully against the Soviet Union. He felt that the enormous expenditure of funds required for such an enterprise might be used for better scientific return elsewhere. And he also fretted that trying to match the Soviets feat for feat, even if it resulted in outdistancing them, would mean that the Soviets were in effect shaping, if not dictating, U.S. space policy. That ought to have been beneath the nation's dignity.

"In the long run we can weaken our science and technology and lower our international prestige by frantically indulging in unnecessary competition and prestige-motivated projects," Killian said in an address to the MIT Club of New York in December 1960. While it could be argued that the appeal of manned space exploration is so great that nothing can deter it, he warned, an argument could also be made that the program was moving too quickly and was becoming "excessively extravagant" for the sake of the prestige that could come with beating the Soviets into space. "Many thoughtful citizens are convinced that the really exciting discoveries in space can be realized better by instruments than by man," Killian added, no doubt thinking of Van Allen and a growing number of other space scientists who were looking with growing apprehension at all of the limbering up that was taking place behind the race's starting line. He advised Eisenhower to go slowly on flinging Americans into orbit. Ike took his advice, but the matter soon became moot.

John Kennedy was inaugurated the following month. On April 12, almost before the new president was fully unpacked, Flight Major Yuri Alekseyevich Gagarin became the first human to orbit Earth in a spacecraft named Vostok. James E. Webb, whom Kennedy had appointed to succeed Glennan as head of NASA, went on television to congratulate the Russians. Then he went to the Hill to face angry and frustrated legislators who had created NASA two and a half years earlier precisely to prevent this sort of thing from happening.

But Vostok wasn't the only problem. Exactly one week later the invasion of the Bay of Pigs collapsed. The Cuban fiasco was hardly the only factor that Kennedy took into consideration when he thought about the role of the nation's space program. But the coincidence of its happening immediately after Gagarin's triumph—a one-two punch—seems to have persuaded the young president, a prideful and competitive Irishman, that he needed a rousing victory. And he needed that victory in space, in a place that was innately dramatic and in which the United States stood a better chance than ever of coming in first. Applied technology, after all, was allegedly what the country was best at. So on April 19, the day the invasion of Cuba disintegrated, as shown in the lenses of press cameras from around the world, Kennedy called Lyndon Johnson into his office and ordered the vice president to find a "space program which promises dramatic results in which we could win."

On May 5 Alan Shepard blasted off from Cape Canaveral on top of one of the Army's Redstone boosters and rode Freedom 7, a Mercury capsule, 304 miles downrange in fifteen minutes twenty-two seconds. Although the flight was suborbital, reaching a maximum altitude of a little more than 116 miles, it parted the clouds that hung over Washington. No doubt it was also decisive in persuading Kennedy to go for the Moon. An American had finally reached space. But he had not orbited the world, and even when one of the astronauts did, it would only be in Gagarin's wake. Measured by firsts, low orbit therefore belonged to the Soviets, so there was literally nowhere to go but still farther out. The signpost pointed right at the Moon.

On Saturday, May 6, 1961—the day after Shepard's flight—Webb and ranking members of the space agency met at the Pentagon with Secretary of Defense Robert McNamara and other officials to shape the final recommendation on space that Johnson had to give to Kennedy. Bringing the two organizations into a collaborative effort to send Americans to space, which Eisenhower would have abhorred, seemed to make sense given the amount of planning both had already done in this area. It was no longer possible to keep them separated for appearance sake, as Ike had wanted, particularly if doing so perpetuated the thrashing the country was taking at the hands of the Soviets. What did it matter if the space program appeared to the world as untarnished by a military influence if it was simultaneously taken to be a bumbling also-ran operation?

Three years earlier the Air Force had developed a plan to cannonball one of its own fliers into orbit before any civilian agency could do so. The project, Man-in-Space-Soonest (MISS), was to have progressed to long-duration orbital flights and finally to a manned landing on the lunar surface. It had been driven at a frantic pace, but it was finally killed by Eisenhower in August 1958 in deference to the space agency that was to come into existence less than two months later. Now time seemed to be running out; the Pentagon had to cooperate whether NASA was in charge of the space program or not.

Webb, McNamara, and the other civilian and military apostles of a strong American presence in space ended the day by producing a memorandum calling for astronauts—men, not machines—to go to the Moon. The rationale for sending humans was contained in their classified memorandum to Johnson. It was so clearly articulated and so basic to events that are still unfolding that it warrants quotation:

> It is man, not merely machines, in space that captures the imagination of the world. All large-scale projects require the mobilization of resources on a national scale. They require the development and successful application of the most advanced technologies. Dramatic achievements in space therefore symbolize the technological power and organizing capacity of a nation. It is for reasons such as these that major achievements in space contribute to national prestige.

Then the memorandum whittled the matter to a finer point.

> Major successes, such as orbiting a man as the Soviets have just done, lend national prestige *even though the scientific, commercial, or military undertaking may by ordinary standards be marginal or economically unjustified.* . . . [Italics added.] Our attainments are a major element in the international competition between the Soviet system and our own. The non-military, non-commercial, non-scientific but "civilian" projects such as lunar and planetary exploration are, in this sense, part of the battle along the fluid front of the cold war.

And so on May 25, toward the end of a speech on "Urgent National Needs" that he delivered to a joint session of Congress, Kennedy announced that he wanted to land Americans on the Moon before the end of the decade and asked the nation to approve such a commitment. "No single space project in this period will be more exciting, or more impressive to mankind, or more important for the long range exploration of space; and none will be so difficult or expensive to accomplish," Kennedy averred.

In all ways except one, JFK's statement would prove to be prophetic. Sending men to the Moon would indeed be exciting, impressive, difficult, and expensive. The program's long-range importance for the exploration of space, however, would turn out to be very different from what the young president seemed to have in mind.

In any case, there it was. The United States of America was finally pointed right at the Moon, just as von Braun, Ley, and the others had prophesied a decade earlier. The decision rested on four fundamental principles that were so important they would constitute the essential underpinnings of the space program for decades to come:

• The crusade to land Americans on the Moon would be unabashedly political, and would be dictated by a perceived competition that the Kennedy administration resolved to win at all costs. The Soviet Union, and specifically its presence in space, would thereby become a force that was used to consolidate, shape, and focus the national will in a patriotic enterprise of unparalleled scope. Competition with the USSR was therefore to become an intrinsic part of the U.S. space program. And if winning was everything, any means of doing so could be justified, even if it involved technologically dubious strategies. The science and technology would have to support the politics, not the other way around.

• Since winning would be measured in terms of prestige—how the world viewed the American space program—favorable public relations would become a fundamental part of the process. Being best would matter only as it related to popular perception. And that would apply at home no less than beyond the nation's borders because there would be no program without public support. The country would have to have its appetite whetted for the competition—the game—and kept interested enough to finish. That in turn would require a campaign to portray the conflict in epic terms, with the astronauts depicted as true heroes in the Arthurian tradition and the opposition as the embodiment of evil. In this regard, *Life* magazine's exclusive coverage of the original seven Mercury astronauts would be reminiscent of the *Collier's* series, which in part dealt with the astronaut selection and testing process, portraying successful candidates as examples of the ideal American male.

• The space program would now be firmly man-centered, since

only men could be heroes and heroes were to be the order of the day. That, too, would prove to be costly. Not only were astronauts incapable of performing even a fraction of the tasks that machines could do, but sending them to space and keeping them there would be extremely expensive because their lives had to be protected in an environment that was relentlessly dangerous and potentially lethal. Furthermore, while the race to get men on the Moon would usher in a period of robust space science and planetary exploration, the Space Transportation System that followed Apollo would force NASA to plunder the budgets of many valuable unmanned programs just to keep the shuttle going. This would have a divisive effect within the space agency itself, not only pitting manned and unmanned programs against one another, but forcing unmanned programs to compete on their own level for the crumbs dropped by the shuttle. The Hubble Space Telescope and other space-based astronomical projects, for example, had to vie with projects involving planetary exploration.

• Finally, Project Apollo would be goal- or mission-oriented, not part of a larger, more comprehensive endeavor. Because landing astronauts on the Moon was to be an end in itself, rather than the means to a greater end, it would conclude abruptly after the sixth trip without realizing its true potential: that of being a sizable step in the larger process of securing an expanding foothold in the solar system. The Apollo experience would therefore leave a confusing void. The morning after the party, so to speak, many thoughtful Americans who remained convinced that the lunar landings were good would find themselves wondering what, in fact, they were good for.

The goal of getting Americans to the Moon would be a sharply focused undertaking, but an exceedingly narrow one, and that too would have telling effects on the space program as a whole. It would haunt both the shuttle and the space station in years to come. The system—NASA, successive administrations, and Congress—would prove incapable of creating and sustaining a comprehensive ongoing space program. Instead, the program (if, indeed, it could be called that) would be constantly subjected to the vagaries of partisan politics and a mercurial budget that would leave almost everything severely malnourished. And the most scientifically and technologically productive of the space agency's programs—space science in all of its manifestations on the ground, in Earth orbit, and beyond, and the exploration of the solar system—would be the least nourished of all.

3.

JPL: "Able, Extremely Brilliant and Spoiled Brats!"

NASA's basic problem at the outset was that it did not evolve; it accumulated. The heart of the agency itself was a transmogrification of the NACA, the old National Advisory Committee for Aeronautics.* In order to accomplish the task mandated by Congress—to establish an ostensibly peaceful U.S. presence in space—an infrastructure had to be created from scratch. Components needed by the new organization had to be invented, negotiated for, or pried away from armed services that begrudged its existence. Deals had to be struck. Facilities and equipment had to be sequestered.

The result was an organizational nightmare. T. Keith Glennan, NASA's first administrator, not only had to contend with the ire of the three services and the disgruntled factions that made up the NACA's own far-flung empire, but with a legion of individuals from many otherwise disparate areas who had their own ideas as to how NASA and its space program should evolve. "The individual motivations—political objectives, commercial goals, professional aspirations—and the differing philosophical backgrounds of the industrialist, academician, legislator, administrator, soldier, scientist, and engineer set up cross currents and conflicts of varying intensity that run through the early years of NASA's history," according to Homer Newell. They run through many of the subsequent years as well. In addition, Glennan and his aides had to contend with the Jet Propulsion Laboratory's own special mixture of genius and hubris. Relations with JPL, in fact, would prove to be especially nettlesome.

*As noted, the NACA had a solid reputation for developing innovative aeronautical designs. But by 1958 it was generally considered to be a lumbering organization that would probably not be able to make a smooth (and quick) transition to the requisites of heavy-duty rocketry. It was therefore resolved to collapse the NACA and fold whatever viable parts were left into the new space organization.

The Jet Propulsion Laboratory would abandon the guided missile business and move into deep space: it would be assigned the primary role of getting NASA's robot spacecraft to the Moon and the planets, in addition to developing and operating much of the infrastructure and ground hardware that were necessary to accomplish that lofty goal. But the assignment would evolve through a period of bitter political turmoil between the lab and Headquarters, as well as within a maelstrom of exasperating, near-ruinous technical defeat.

It is therefore appropriate to return briefly to JPL's own postwar history, and specifically to its relationship with the Army, its part in helping to salvage the national honor by answering the challenge of Sputnik, and how both of those elements came to play an important if not decisive role in molding JPL's institutional character and therefore its relationship with NASA.

William Hayward Pickering was born in New Zealand in 1910 and came to the United States for his education, graduating from Caltech with a B.S. in electrical engineering in 1932. He received a master's degree in the same field the following year. In 1936, the year Frank Malina and the rest of the Suicide Club had their first sputtering success in the Arroyo Seco, he completed his Ph.D. at Caltech and was invited to join its faculty. In 1944 he moved to JPL and set to work developing telemetry techniques for transmitting cosmic ray data from sounding rockets to receiving stations on the ground. Since this peaceful endeavor, like so many others, had applications that were suited to ballistic missilery, the military adopted it in 1947.

And that was more or less how Pickering, along with the rest of JPL, got into the missile business with the Army in the first place. Pickering was appointed professor of electrical engineering at Caltech in 1946, began working on Corporal two years later, and was promoted to become JPL's director in 1954. The appointment seemed to be a good one. Bill Pickering was generally known to be a solid, levelheaded, low-key engineer who was good at conceptualizing innovative ways to solve problems. His Scottish ancestry had imbued him with the kind of grit that was needed at an institution as new and as vulnerable to petty jealousy as was JPL. But it also made him more competitive than his conservative demeanor showed. And it made him abidingly stubborn.

The year he was made the lab's director, Pickering also began work on Corporal's intended successor, Sergeant. By that time, however, he had become convinced that the new tactical missile would have no successors—at least, none spawned at JPL. Instead, like von Braun, he saw his and his organization's future on the Moon and the planets. Missiles went up here and landed there, and after you got the knack of how to make them do that, it just wasn't very challenging.

"It was quite clear to us that our future lay in the space program," Pickering explained many years later. "In other words, as a university laboratory we did not see a future in just continuing to make missiles for the Army. After all, we had all sorts of ideas of things we wanted to do and the space program offered the possibilities." He therefore resolved to trade on JPL's reputation as an innovator in missile guidance, telemetry, and other instrumentation—already a solid reputation by Army standards—to move the lab into what he and some others in Pasadena were convinced was the enormous new frontier of space.

So late in 1954 JPL, teamed with Medaris's ballistic missile agency at Huntsville, was heavily involved in preparations to launch a scientific satellite as the U.S. contribution to orbital research for the International Geophysical Year. The idea was to use one of the Army's Redstone medium-range ballistic missiles and clusters of smaller rockets as upper stages to shove the little satellite into orbit. The engineers, who were not given to extravagant flights of fancy when it came to naming projects, called the orbiter "orbiter." While JPL continued to refine its satellite, the Army Ballistic Missile Agency worked on its own, in addition to readying one of the Redstones to carry to space whichever was finally selected.

Meanwhile, the Naval Research Laboratory had seized the opportunity offered by the IGY to get back into crafting a satellite and a launch vehicle of its own. Since that satellite and its booster were designed from scratch as scientific vehicles and were therefore politically clean, Eisenhower gave the Navy the go-ahead to be the first to carry the nation's colors to space. He would come to suffer the consequences of that decision. The launch vehicle–satellite was the infamous Vanguard.

As it happened, Secretary of Defense Neil McElroy was visiting Huntsville on the night of October 4, 1957. When news of Sputnik came in, von Braun, unable to contain his frustration, pleaded to be allowed to answer the Communist challenge. "Vanguard will never make it," he told the Secretary of Defense. "We have the hardware on the shelf. For God's sake, turn us loose and let us do something. We can put up a satellite in sixty days, Mr. McElroy! Just give us a green light and sixty days," begged von Braun. "Sixty days!" Medaris, interceding, persuaded his wildly exuberant rocketeer to allow ninety days to get the country into space. But it wouldn't take that long.

Within hours of his return to Washington, the Army's biggest guns, led by no less than Secretary of the Army Wilbur M. Brucker himself, began to pelt McElroy with requests to launch their own satellite. The launch vehicle of choice was Jupiter, an improved Redstone and a well-proven intermediate-range ballistic missile (but rechristened Juno for the occasion in deference to the president's abhorrence of using weapons of war to launch satellites of peace). Throughout the rest of October, Brucker, Generals Maxwell Taylor, James Gavin, and Medaris, plus von Braun, beseeched the Department of Defense and Congress for permission to launch. Their frustration—no, anger—was all the more intense because they knew they could have beaten the Soviets to space a whole year earlier, but had been forbidden to do so.

Sending the first U.S. satellite to space would not only cover the victorious service with glory, the reasoning went, but it would in the process give it a substantial edge in dominating the new arena of space. Or at least that was what the contestants had every reason to believe.

Vanguard, the nation's immediate answer to Sputnik, was a sphere measuring six inches in diameter and weighing three and a quarter pounds. It looked like a chrome grapefruit with spikes. Following a successful test of its immediate predecessor, an attempt was made to launch one of the little satellites from Cape Canaveral on December 6, 1957, just about two months after Sputnik went up. The Navy, already conscious of the importance of image, named its spacecraft TV-3, for Test Vehicle No. 3. If the thing actually made it to space it would revert to its right name, Vanguard. If something catastrophic happened, though, all the world would know that it was merely a test vehicle and that test vehicles, after all, were bound to fail on occasion.

Something catastrophic happened. With reporters and cameramen from around the world gathered at Cape Canaveral to see the NRL-Martin launch vehicle and its diminutive payload rescue the nation's honor, disaster struck. Two seconds after ignition, at an altitude of four feet, the beautiful pencil-slim rocket lost thrust and fell back down onto its launch pad, disappearing in a ball of exploding liquid oxygen and kerosene. As if that weren't bad enough, the nose cone landed away from the flaming launch pad, giving up the little satellite. The grapefruit obediently continued to chirp its telemetry even after it had rolled to a full stop. It was promptly dubbed Puffnik, Flopnik, Kaputnik, Stayputnik, and other epithets by the press.

"As we watched the Vanguard having its troubles, and as we heard various reports coming out of Russia about how they were doing, we got more and more frustrated. The Army was just being kept on the sidelines," Pickering would recall of those intense times. "Until Sputnik flew, neither the Russians nor the Americans understood the importance of it. And then all of a sudden Sputnik was up there, and it scared the daylights out of the Americans to realize that this Russian thing was going over, happily beeping away; anybody could hear it. And there wasn't a thing they could do about it. Those peasants over there had put this thing up while we were fooling around," he added, making reference to the way most Americans thought of Soviet science and technology in the 1950s. "And so it was natural, I think, that the Americans would respond by saying, 'Okay, you wait; we'll do better.' "

And "better" was the operative word. It was a measure of the competitiveness that permeated JPL that its reflexive reaction was not merely to match the Soviets by placing its own satellite in orbit, but to leapfrog them by going right to the Moon. While continuing to work on a satellite that was competitive with Vanguard, Pickering and others at both Caltech and JPL looked farther out, well beyond Earth orbit, to the Moon and the planets. Both Pickering and his boss, Lee DuBridge, tried to persuade the Army to go beyond Earth satellites and send a series of rockets on lunar missions. The plan, named Red Socks, entailed landing some spacecraft on the surface of the Moon to measure temperature, pressure, and light intensity, while others would follow and even orbit around it. Predictably, the Army proved to be enthusiastic enough, but the administration would not countenance such an ambitious plan.

So quickly and intensely did a sense of competition with the Soviets take hold in Pasadena following Sputnik, so clearly did the people at JPL comprehend the nature of the propaganda war that had just begun, that imaginations groped for spectacular ways to get on page one even if it meant temporarily ignoring good science for good PR. No doubt chief among these was the possibility, mentioned by Pickering to DuBridge, of firing an atomic-bomb-tipped missile at the Moon and having it explode right on the lunar surface. The huge blast, unrestrained by an atmosphere, would "shower the earth with samples of surface dust in addition to producing beneficial psychological results." Nothing came of the notion—Pickering said years afterward that it amounted to "coffee table talk"—but it was nonetheless indicative of the lengths to which some at JPL, and by inference at Army Ordnance as well, would go to enhance their competitive positions at home by upstaging the audacious Soviets.

But Pickering and his subordinates did resolve to accomplish two tasks, both of which were well within the realm of possibility, during that long and arduous winter of 1957–58: get an American satellite developed by JPL into orbit as an immediate response to the Soviet challenge and, using that feat and others following it, lobby for all they were worth to become the nation's center for lunar and planetary exploration within the new national space agency.

Nor did the competition exist only between the ABMA/JPL team and the Navy. Maneuvering for position was also going on among the team members themselves, as JPL and Huntsville vied to see which would actually produce the satellite. JPL had one satellite in mind to fit on top of Jupiter, while the Army Ballistic Missile Agency had another. But just before the meeting in which roles were to be assigned for the new program, Pickering got Medaris alone and pitched hard for JPL to do the satellite work on the basis of all of the laboratory's expertise in related areas. Medaris, evidently persuaded that there was merit to what Pickering said, and also no doubt feeling that JPL was a valuable ally, agreed.

The general's decision was a fateful one. Rather than being relegated to a background role in the development of America's first Earth-circling satellite, a position from which it might never have recovered, the Jet Propulsion Laboratory was to give the United States the spacecraft that evened the score. And that considerable victory would in turn set the basis for a long series of accomplishments in deep space, none of which could have been foreseen in 1958.

Now it was the Army's turn. Huntsville, which had finally received permission to launch on November 8, five days after the orbiting of the huge dog-carrying Sputnik 2 and well before the Vanguard's ignominious demise, had spent the following eleven weeks furiously preparing to get JPL's satellite off the ground.

At 10:48 on the night of Friday, January 31, America's first operational spacecraft, bathed in floodlight as it stood fastened atop the Jupiter-Juno first stage, rose slowly at first, then ever more quickly, as it swung far out over the ocean and headed for space in front of a yellow paraboloid of fire. Medaris, wary of the kind of prelaunch publicity that had resulted in the embarrassment suffered by the Navy at Vanguard's inglorious debut, had virtually clamped down on press coverage before the launch. The reporters and photographers at Canaveral, as well as their superiors back home, readily accepted the blackout. (They also agreed not to publicize what turned out to be the Navy's heartbreaking last-minute attempt to get a second Vanguard off before Jupiter-Juno went up. Six days before the Army launch, the problem-riddled booster got to within fourteen seconds of ignition when its first-stage motor malfunctioned, effectively killing the Navy's bid to be first in space.) The Navy had suffered the humiliation of seeing the December 6 Vanguard explosion portrayed in the press as a "disaster" for the United States. Medaris had no wish to see the Army subjected to the same treatment in the event of yet another failure.

Going along with the scheme betrayed an abandonment of the kind of objectivity for which the mainstream news media prided themselves. Indeed, the Fourth Estate itself would become an eager and highly vocal cheerleader for the U.S. space program in all its manifestations. But the price of participating in the technodrama, for overidentifying with the thundering machines and the imperatives of the race in which they flew, would one day prove to be very high indeed.

At any rate, minutes after its launch, the Army's satellite was picked up by large tracking antennas in the Caribbean as it continued to accelerate toward an orbit that was inclined a little more than 33 degrees off the equator. By midnight the race for space had been joined by a small American satellite designed and built by JPL. It was named Explorer 1.

After the Jupiter-Juno and a cluster of upper stages had fallen away over the Atlantic, Explorer 1 headed toward its programmed orbit, which had an apogee of 1,580 miles and a perigee of 233 miles. Van Allen, along with Brucker, Medaris, von Braun, General Lyman Lemnitzer, Pickering, and some others were in the Pentagon's War Room when Explorer went up.

Although downrange tracking indicated that the rocket was climbing as it should, confirmation that an orbit had been achieved was agonizingly slow in coming. There was, in Van Allen's words, an "exasperating lack of information. The clock ticked away, and we all drank coffee to allay our collective anxiety. After some ninety minutes, all conversation ceased, and an air of dazed disappointment settled over the room. Then, nearly two hours after launch, a telephone report of confirmed reception of the radio signal by two professional stations in Earthquake Valley, California, was received. The roomful of people exploded with exultation, and everyone was pounding each other on the back with mutual congratulations." The United States was in space.

Within minutes, an Army car sped Van Allen, von Braun, and Pickering across the Potomac to the National Academy of Sciences, hard by the Mall, where they were "smuggled" through a back door. After making a preliminary report to IGY staff members, the three jubilant men were led into the building's Great Hall, where a throng of reporters, photographers, and others waited. The three, with Pickering and von Braun beaming on either side of Van Allen, held up a replica of Explorer 1 as flashbulbs went off. Pickering noted that his satellite's apogee of "well over 1,000 miles" put it farther out in space than either of the Sputniks that had preceded it. Medaris, who had also come to the triumphant gathering, was more to the point. He claimed that the satellite was probably better than its Soviet counterparts by virtue of the fact that it was flying higher. Explorer 1's altitude had nothing to do with its quality, of course, but it showed the lifting capability of its Army launch vehicle and the little upper stages that had given it its final push.

If Sputnik 1 amounted to an orbiting cannonball that went beep in the night, Explorer 1 was a marvel of electronic miniaturization. The satellite was basically a cylinder eighty inches long and six inches wide. It was divided into two parts. The rear, or motor case, was a solid propellant rocket—actually a scaled-down version of the Sergeant motor—that injected (in the engineer's argot) the satellite into its final orbit.

The front part, the instrumentation section, was only thirty-three inches long and weighed just under thirty pounds. Eighteen and a half of those pounds represented measuring instruments for three experiments, plus two radio transmitters that had been developed at JPL. The three experiment packages were squeezed beneath and between the two transmitters (one, a "high-power" transmitter, weighed all of two pounds and ran on a one-and-a-half-pound battery; it was to transmit data for two weeks).

The first two instruments were mundane enough. One would record the temperatures that the spacecraft passed through as it plunged successively into darkness and sunshine on its twelve daily orbits, as well as the temperature within the satellite itself. A second was designed to measure the impact of micrometeorites that struck Explorer by picking them up on a microphone, amplifying the sound they made, and then radioing that sound back to Earth.

The third instrument, however, would make history. It was technically referred to as a cosmic ray and micrometeorite package. In fact, it was essentially a Geiger counter (or a Geiger-Müller tube) nestled under the second, low-power transmitter, near Explorer 1's nose. It was put there to measure charged particle activity—cosmic rays—in the pristine reaches above the atmosphere.* The package, which had been designed for Vanguard but was put on Explorer at Pickering's suggestion, belonged to James Van Allen, who had moved from Johns Hopkins to the University of Iowa in 1950. Van Allen's experiment, using the little gas-filled Geiger counter tube and related paraphernalia during Explorer 1's historic odyssey around Earth, was shortly to bear results that would figure profoundly in the new space science and planetary exploration programs.

It was well understood by Van Allen and other physicists that the intensity of cosmic radiation increases with altitude: the farther away from Earth, beyond the protective blanket of the atmosphere, the heavier the dose of radiation from the Sun and other objects in the galaxy. The sounding rockets had shown that much. Van Allen therefore had reason to assume that the charged particles that slammed into his Geiger counter would increase in a progressive way each time Explorer 1 swung out toward its apogee during each 113-minute orbit around Earth. But that didn't seem to have happened. In fact, as the transmitters continued to relay signals to sixteen receiving stations around much of the world during the minute or two it took Explorer 1 to pass over each of them, it had seemed as though the Geiger counter wasn't registering any hits at all.

As it was to turn out, though, the apparatus hadn't escaped being struck by particles. On the contrary, it had been so saturated by them that it had become overwhelmed; mechanically speaking, it had become paralyzed. The preliminary data, substantiated by more detailed experiments on Explorer 3,† which went up on March 26,

---

*"Cosmic ray" is a catchall for several elements, including protons which hurl through space at nearly the velocity of light, high-energy electrons, the nuclei of helium atoms (called alpha particles), and others. They are thought to radiate from the Sun, as well as from supernova explosions and other objects or events outside the solar system.

†Explorer 2 never made it to orbit because of a fourth-stage ignition failure.

indicated, much to Van Allen's and his colleagues' surprise, that a massive belt of radiation circled Earth. Data from Explorer 1 during its first two weeks in orbit were so extraordinary, in fact, that, in Van Allen's words, they were "regarded with a very jaundiced eye."

He was confident enough of the results, however, to present them to a joint symposium of the American Physical Society and the National Academy of Sciences in Washington on the morning of May 1, 1958, barely three months after Explorer 1 went up. "Above an altitude of about 1,000 kilometers we have encountered a very great increase in radiation intensity which is vastly beyond what could be due to cosmic rays alone," Van Allen told the gathered scientists during the first moments of the finest hour of his professional life. "In fact, it is of the order of, or greater than, 1,000 times the intensity of cosmic rays as extrapolated to these greater altitudes. . . ."

What James Van Allen did, in essence, was to use the Explorers to map a belt of trapped radiation (later understood to be two belts, both roughly doughnut-shaped, with one extending well beyond the other) by means of repeated orbits around the planet. This was used (in his words) to provide a detailed analysis for the symmetry in Earth's magnetic field.

In other words, mapping the radiation belts was to allow geophysicists to accurately determine the size, shape, and intensity of the magnetic field that circles Earth and protects it from a potentially dangerous bombardment of cosmic rays.

Although there had been speculation about the field's existence for years, it was generally thought to trace the kind of pattern that would come if a bar magnet ran through the center of the planet, north to south, with most activity taking place at the poles. But the belt's size, location, and influence came as a surprise to the scientific community. In recognition of the importance of the discovery of James Van Allen's belts, they were named after him.* It was a singular triumph for the physicist, who would go on to become one of the nation's most outspoken advocates of unmanned space flight, as well as an implacable opponent of the manned program. And, of course, it was also a triumph of enormous magnitude for the JPL/ABMA team that produced the Explorers and their boosters.

For his part, Eisenhower not only avoided making any comparison

*He was also awarded the Crafoord Prize, comparable to the Nobel Prize, by the Royal Swedish Academy of Sciences in 1989 for his discovery.

between Explorer 1 and the two Sputniks that had preceded it, but was scrupulous in couching the event as a purely scientific, and therefore civilian, accomplishment. "Dr. J. Wallace Joyce, head of the International Geophysical Year office of the National Science Foundation has just informed me that the United States has success-fully placed a scientific earth satellite in orbit around the earth," Ike said in a statement released by his press secretary, James C. Hagerty, even before the pad from which the modified Army IRBM had blasted off had cooled to its normal temperature. "This launching is part of our country's participation in the International Geophysical Year. All information received from this satellite promptly will be made available to the scientific community of the world." Hagerty was careful to note that further information about the little satellite's condition and whereabouts would come from the National Academy of Sciences.

And by coincidence, just a few hours before the launch of Explorer 1, John P. Hagen, the Navy scientist who directed the Vanguard program, complained to a Washington audience that the U.S. satellite program was in such a sorry state because it had been given "minimum funds and low priority" despite the fact that going to space required a maximum commitment by the United States. Speaking at the Sertoma Club, which gave him an award for service to mankind, Hagen vented his frustration with the Eisenhower administration by complaining that its frugality had put the Soviet Union ahead of the United States in the move to space. Furthermore, Hagen warned, it was time for Americans to begin to "look up to the egghead" who was going to shape the nation's "progress in this new world [of space]" and "get rid of our anti-intellectual notions and begin to respect and revere learning." The article in *The New York Times* reporting Hagen's speech appeared beside another one, datelined London, which said that Radio Moscow reported that at ten o'clock that night Sputnik 2 had completed 1,263 orbits around the Earth. But who was counting?

The successes of Explorers 1 and 3 further convinced Pickering that JPL not only belonged in space science and exploration, but that the lab had now earned the right to be the nation's preeminent facility for those enterprises by virtue of having led the way to space.

He therefore wrote a letter to Killian in July—the month the National Aeronautics and Space Act of 1958 became law—to request such a role for JPL in the new space agency. Pickering urged the president's science adviser to help ensure that NASA "accept the concept of JPL as the national space laboratory." Pickering warned, "If this is not done, then NASA will flounder around for so long that there is a good chance that the entire program will be carried by the military." Not wanting to risk losing his case for being too subtle, Pickering went so far as to tell Killian that JPL's guidance would establish a realistic space program while maintaining its civilian character, just as the president wished.

At the same time, Pickering and Homer E. Newell, then of the Naval Research laboratory's upper atmospheric research division, were having their own flirtation. Vanguard's troubles—there was a successful launch on March 17, 1958, followed by four more failures, all of them caused by booster or guidance malfunctions—were unrelated to the generally impressive scientific work done by Newell's group.

So while John Hagen's Vanguard contingent transferred directly from the Naval Research Laboratory to the National Advisory Committee for Aeronautics preparatory to NACA's turning into NASA in October, Newell went to Pasadena to talk to Pickering about the possibility of bringing his group out there, rather than directly to the new space agency. After talking with Pickering, however, Newell and a few of his associates decided to go to Washington instead of California. "Our conclusion after I came back and we discussed it among ourselves," Newell later remarked, "was that we'd be nearer the center of action if we joined NASA," whereas "we felt we'd be only a part of a piece of the action out at JPL." He evidently concluded that formidable egos were at work in Pasadena and he had no intention of being devoured by them.

The Army was not happy about losing von Braun and the entire ballistic missile agency to NASA, where they were to concentrate on building the space agency's large boosters. Medaris, for one, was doubly thunderstruck by the creation of NASA in the first place and then by the loss of the entire ABMA to it. For John B. Medaris, Huntsville might as well have been overrun and captured by an enemy power. In fact, it *was* captured by an enemy power.

Here was the Army's reward for bringing the V-2s and the rocket team to the United States; for providing the expatriates with a hospitable environment at White Sands; for bankrolling so much of the early sounding rocket science work; for providing von Braun and his colleagues with a nurturing sanctum in Alabama within which they could chart the nation's future in space (while at the same time encouraging the prophet of planetary travel to lead a growing legion of captivated congressmen, taxpayers and their star-struck offspring across the pages of *Collier's* and through Tomorrowland's mocked-up missiles, moon craters, and Mars-scapes). And finally, and most ironically, here was the Army's reward for coming off the bench to get the team back in the game after the opposition was allowed to score twice while the Navy did nothing but lose yardage. The general was vehement in his insistence that the space program rightfully belonged to the Department of Defense and that handing it to civilians was a mistake tantamount to treason. This, according to Killian, he and von Braun believed with a religious fanaticism. The transfer was nonetheless made.

Conversely, JPL eagerly embraced the new space agency. "We wanted to be in the space program and, if you like, we lobbied to make sure that we'd be included in the NASA family. NASA started in October and by December," Pickering would recall, "we were signed up." And by January the Jet Propulsion Laboratory and the National Aeronautics and Space Administration, its contractual parent organization, were locked into the early stages of a long feud.

Since JPL belonged to the California Institute of Technology, a private institution, it could not simply be expropriated for the national good. A deal had to be struck—a contract signed—between Caltech and NASA in which the laboratory would become a government facility while its engineers, technicians, scientists, and administrative staff remained employees of Caltech and therefore out of the civil service. They were in fact the only employees in NASA who remained outside the civil service. And that was to become just one of the sticking points in the relationship.

Another, more important cause of friction from the beginning was the fundamental nature of the working relationship between the two organizations. Glennan, looking around his disparate, far-flung empire, knew that if NASA was going to survive to accomplish what it was supposed to, especially in the venomous environment that had been created by Medaris and his comrades in arms in the other services, its operations would have to be spread out while being tightly controlled. Having centers and contractors all over the country would broaden the agency's political and economic base, measured in jobs and contracts. But he and his successors also understood that if such an operation wasn't rigidly controlled, there would be chaos in short order.

This meant that while every facility was to have a specialty, tight coordination would have to come from Headquarters in Washington. The Goddard center in Maryland would concentrate (though not exclusively) on unmanned Earth-orbit work, for instance, while Huntsville would produce the giant boosters; the eventual Johnson center in Houston would handle the manned program, while the Ames Research Center in California, with its massive wind tunnels, would specialize in aeronautics; Wallops Island, off the Virginia coast, would fire the sounding rockets, while JPL would be responsible for deep space exploration, and so forth. But they would have to be led like a philharmonic orchestra. And the baton would remain in Washington.

But Pickering and others at JPL saw things somewhat differently. By virtue of their pioneering work in missilery, their role as designer of the first U.S. satellite to make it to orbit, and their intimate relationship with the prestigious Caltech (known at JPL, with understated reverence, as the "campus") they considered themselves to be special, an elite. This imbued the Pasadenans with a palpable disdain for the civil servants (read lackluster automatons) everywhere else in the empire. Where JPL was concerned, the operative word in civil servant was "servant." Civil servants were notorious for going by the book. Well, JPL *wrote* the book.

"JPL was always an anomaly in the NASA system. All of the other laboratories were civil service labs, and NASA didn't quite know how to handle us, particularly since, if you go back to the beginning of NASA, we felt we knew more about rockets than all of those other NASA types put together because we had been working on these rockets for the Army," Pickering asserted in an interview years later. "We designed them, built them, and knew quite a lot about them. And so our reaction was that we were the experts, and 'you guys are a bunch of aeronautical types who are now trying to learn something about rockets.' "

Pickering, like von Karman before him, said he believed that Goddard has been given too much credit for the advancement of rocketry, that Goddard's reclusiveness ultimately left him in a backwater and that Malina and the other Arroyo Seco irregulars were the ones who had made the real advances in American rocket propulsion. The distinction is more than esoteric. It was ingrained in JPL's folklore and constituted much of the basis of its self-image as the institution that really implanted rocketry in America. Pickering himself indicated as much by dismissing his new masters in 1958 as "aeronautical types." And if JPL was the nation's leader in rocket research, the reasoning went, it was because of the free-spirited academic vitality that flowed like an elixir directly from the parent body, the California Institute of Technology.

Caltech rivaled MIT as the nation's most celebrated academic incubator of innovative engineering and high technology. And no one doubted that it was the intellectual atmosphere of the class-rooms and research laboratories of the great institution, an atmo-sphere of total academic freedom as solid as its adobe walls and unencumbered by seemingly endless federal rules, that was the linchpin of its success. That tradition, carried by scientists and engi-neers who held joint appointments at both Caltech and the lab, pollinated JPL from the beginning and made its employees wary of the morass of red tape they correctly sensed would be headed their way from Washington—Back East—when they officially entered NASA's fold.

Nor had the Jet Propulsion Laboratory's relationship with the Army prepared the way. If anything, the Army's laissez-faire atti-tude toward JPL made working with the lab more difficult for NASA's new, somewhat insecure but straightlaced administrators.

"We used to think about the good old days when we were working for Army Ordnance," Pickering was to recall nostalgically. "In those days, we reported directly to an office in the Pentagon, our work was entirely classified, we did our research work there at White Sands, and if we blew up a bunch of rockets, it never made the newspapers. When it came budget time, the Army would say, 'What do you want to do this year, and how much do you think it's going to cost?' And we would say, 'Oh, about $25 million.' And they'd say, 'OK, do it.' And that was it."

W. E. "Gene" Giberson, who came to JPL in 1951 to work first on Corporal and then on Sergeant, and who went on to become assistant laboratory director for flight projects, shared Pickering's recollec-tion of the halcyon days before NASA. "We were, very frankly, quite spoiled in the sense that, living in the Army era, we had a tremen-dous amount of freedom, and there was very little even close moni-toring of what we did." But the freedom led to growing responsibility, Giberson added, as well as to a goal-oriented work ethic that was impatient with what was taken to be excessive paper-work. Getting it done was the thing.

But the obsession with circumventing what it took to be minutiae in order to get right to work on problems threatened the new NASA leadership and made it apprehensive about JPL. Giberson commented, "Most of the [NASA] people came from the old NACA back-ground, which was a different cultural background; it was a slower life, not nearly as aggressive, or as rambunctious. So I'm sure we were viewed with a certain amount of suspicion. . . ." Suspicion and then irritation. The cavalier attitude and disdain for meticulous record-keeping—the engineering equivalent of flying by the seat of the pants—would soon exact a high toll on the Pasadenans and, therefore, on Headquarters as well.

Jack N. James, a contemporary of Giberson's who also worked on the Army's ballistic missiles and who actively participated in the transition to NASA, reminisced about the pre-NASA era the way a henpecked spouse might remember life before the vows were ex-changed. In a February 1987 talk on the early history of JPL to a lunchtime audience of JPL employees he provided a flavorful glimpse of the period. It was a time, James recalled, when engineers packed their own equipment in crates and shared the all-night 850-mile drive to White Sands, then spent the day launching their Cor-porals with cronies in Army Ordnance. Ordnance controlled tactical missiles like Corporal and Sergeant, while the ballistic missile agency worked on longer-range strategic weapons like Redstone and Jupiter.

"The Army seemed to love us. They were very tolerant; tolerant of errors," he recalled, recounting how one Corporal rolled 90 de-grees backward after launch and came down uncomfortably close to the town of Las Cruces. "But we sort of went on," he said, adding that there were "no boards of inquiry, no investigations, no cost disallow-ances."

James had anecdotes of those days similar to those shared at college reunions about particularly wild fraternity parties. Some-one's office was completely boarded up—"entombed"—as a practical joke. Someone else paid for an expense account long in arrears by inventing a mechanism that sent a blizzard of nickels flying out of a container the instant it was opened in the accounting department. The arrival of an Army steering committee, whose members favored loud sport shirts, frequently caused food fights that on at least one occasion resulted in damages to the White Sands banquet hall of thousands of dollars. General James Gavin, who had led the 101st Airborne Division on D-Day, was an especially enthusiastic partici-pant, according to James.

And so it was that the two institutions, JPL and NASA, came together in Pasadena early in December 1958 to get acquainted and set the basis for their relationship. A clash was inevitable.

"I remember when [Hugh] Dryden and Glennan first took over, and came out to see what they were buying," William Pickering said. "They gave me a little lecture on the fact that things were going to be different, and that working with Ordnance, I was basically working with a group of colonels who didn't quite *understand* the technical business that I was involved in and [that's why] they were prepared to leave me alone. But now I was going to be working with a group of people who were primarily trained in the NACA, and they thoroughly understood the technical problems, and so on and so forth, and that Washington was going to look over my shoulder in a lot more detail than Ordnance ever did. I didn't quite say go to hell. . . ."

The feeling was mutual. Years later, Homer Newell asked Glennan to go over the manuscript for *Beyond the Atmosphere,* his history of the early years of space science, for errors and omissions. Of Chapter 15, titled "Jet Propulsion Laboratory: Outsider or Insider?" Glennan noted pointedly that he thought "JPL was the beneficiary of tolerance by NASA peers. . . . I suppose that the pay off of success is the final answer—but did it need to cost so much in $—in tolerance and accommodation by Newell and others? I again use the terms—able, extremely brilliant and spoiled brats." Glennan also noted in a cover letter that he preferred Newell not to use the "spoiled brat" quote for fear of needlessly hurting feelings in Pasadena. "Could you use an alternative descriptive wording such as 'administratively undisciplined'? I think these words would be unmistakable in intent, yet would avoid the description of childish avoidance of administrative responsibility."

Whatever their differences in temperament and managerial style, there was no disagreement on the broad notion that JPL was to be NASA's primary deep space exploration facility, and that unmanned space probes to the Moon and the planets were to be an integral part of the nation's space program. Given Eisenhower's penchant for using space in pursuit of peaceful endeavors, it could not have been otherwise, at least at that juncture. George Kistiakowsky and Edward M. Purcell agreed early on that space exploration by unmanned probes should be emphasized as a way of keeping NASA out of the cold war, leapfrogging the Soviets, and looking squeaky clean in the process.

Kistiakowsky, who had access to U-2 intelligence pictures depicting the handful of elephantine SS-6 ICBMs whose civilian version lifted the Sputniks, understood that the Soviets needed to build monster boosters because they could not yet miniaturize their thermonuclear warheads. The United States, on the other hand, had already become adept at miniaturizing both warheads and scientific instruments. He therefore resolved not to compete with the Soviets on their own terms, which was lifting heavy satellites to low orbit, but rather to send relatively light scientific probes much farther out. "Let's outsmart them," Kistiakowsky thought. "We have a higher technology, a more sophisticated technology, we can miniaturize things, we can design very clever automated systems. Let's use unmanned probes and, that way, we can acquire far more scientific information than they can."

By January 1959, with JPL newly in the NASA fold, Kistiakowsky's sentiments were being echoed from several directions. But there were ramifications, some of them thorny.

The National Academy of Sciences' International Geophysical Year committee had metamorphosed into its Space Science Board the previous June. While the National Space Act placed the nation's civilian space program in NASA's hands, as noted, it was ambiguous about precisely what that program was supposed to be. This led to jurisdictional problems and repeated clashes not only between NASA and the military but also between the space agency and the Space Science Board. Although NASA was not legally bound to accept recommendations made by the board, the fact that several of the leading scientists in the country sat on it made it worthwhile for NASA to pay close attention to what it said. Many of the scientists on the board were by definition strong-willed individuals who had risen to the top of their disciplines. They therefore had firmly held views about what they wanted to see accomplished in the areas of space science and lunar and planetary exploration. Consciously or otherwise, members of the Space Science Board tended to want to set the national civilian space agenda. And the fact that this shadow government must by law be consulted as an expert body (as other academy boards are consulted by other government agencies involved in science) only added to its feeling of self-importance. The attitude in the venerable bastion of intellect that anchors northwest Constitution Avenue, to paraphrase Clemenceau, is that space science is too important to be left to the space agency.

For their part, Glennan and his successors were loath to see a system develop in which space science and exploration proposals would routinely come to their agency through an appendage of the National Academy or, worse, in which the Space Science Board would have the power to decide which programs and experiments NASA would undertake.

It was not that Headquarters questioned the board's scientific competence. But encroachment would create formidable problems. First, and most obviously, NASA was responsible for the civilian space program and its authority could not be transferred. Second, there would be many more factors involved in conducting space science and exploration than pure science alone, and the board would be in no position to understand or cope with them. Besides dreaming up and shaping missions, there were, in Homer Newell's words, such other considerations as the availability of funding, facilities, launch vehicles, manpower, and the spacecraft themselves, all of which had to be coordinated among the various centers. Even the salability of the various science and exploration programs at the White House and on the Hill, it was felt, could only be properly assessed by NASA itself.

And although it is not documented, there would have been a third reason to resist encroachment by the Space Science Board or any other outside body in the space agency's decision-making process, a reason familiar to legions of federal administrators. Once the board was allowed to rip off a piece of NASA's flesh, other hungry and covetous predators would surely follow, with the likely result that the fragile new agency would have been caught in a bureaucratic feeding frenzy that might well have effectively finished it at the outset.

The root problem from the beginning was a low-keyed but persistent mutual contempt between successive NASA administrators, along with their staffs, and much of the outside science community. There were many in the space agency who scorned scientists in universities and elsewhere as being ivory tower snobs who had no idea of how difficult it was to get things done in what they saw as the real world. The belief was that the objectivity that purportedly constituted the essence of their existence evaporated in pure parochialism when the scientists had to compete for funding or a scarce place on a mission, or when their work was challenged.

"Should it not be said somewhere that no major operating agency ever gave more consideration to the very much less than objective cries of the 'scientists'?" Glennan was to complain bitterly in a margin elsewhere in Newell's book manuscript. "Within the Administration—that is, NASA, we had solid and often brilliant scientists who were able to plan a truly 'NATIONAL' science program in spite of the often controversial advice and complaints so freely given by the scientific community."

Newell did not disagree. "The complacent assumption of the supe-

riority of academic science, the presumption of a natural right to be
supported in their researches, the instant readiness to criticize, and
the disdain which many if not most of the scientists accord the
government manager, particularly the science manager, were hard
to stomach at times," he would write in his memoir. "When Lloyd
Berkner [then chairman of the Space Science Board] undertook in
person to lay before NASA's first administrator some of the criti-
cisms and demands of the Space Science Board, Glennan could not
restrain an outburst of indignation at the arrogant presumptuous-
ness of the scientists. His vexation was shared by Silverstein, who
from time to time cautioned NASA's space scientists to guard
against losing control of their destiny." Abe Silverstein was the
feisty director of NASA's Office of Space Flight Development.

Newell, who majored in mathematics at Harvard and had a doctorate from Illinois, would spend fifteen years in NASA's space science programs. He would come to readily admit that most of the
space agency's science managers were better managers than scientists. "But repeated efforts throughout the years to lure working
scientists into NASA management only occasionally bore fruit," he
complained. "In spite of the enticement of top positions in the [space
science] program, none of the senior 'establishment' came."

The establishmentarians, in other words, feared for their independence and the attendant quality of their science (not to mention
their standing within their own communities) if they ventured out
of the pristine majesty of their university or corporate laboratories
to join a Washington bureaucracy that could only be expected to
swallow and corrupt them, making them part of the problem rather
than the solution. The scientists tended to think of themselves,
somewhat sanctimoniously, as being an impoverished but proud
elite that fate had conspired to force into a Faustian dilemma. They
believed that as scientists it was primarily they, not NASA managers, who were in the best position to decide which fields to pursue and
what methodology to use. And they wanted to be allowed to do that
for the national good with as little meddling as possible. Ideally, in
their view, the federal government—NASA—would simply provide
funding and the means to get to space and otherwise leave them
alone.

The Space Science Board's own participation in planetary exploration dated from July 1958, when Dryden, then NACA's director, had
sought advice on separate missions to Venus that were proposed by
both JPL and the Air Force. Knowing that the Eisenhower adminis-

tration was obsessed with curtailing the budget, and that it therefore did not relish a large-scale expansion of the space program, Dryden had asked for the board's advice on the merits of going directly to the Moon and the planets in the apparent hope that it would be negative. (This lack of a real appetite for space exploration by NACA had exasperated the space crowd and been taken as proof that its mossbacks were too rooted in aeronautics to ever be of real help in space science and exploration. And that, in turn, had helped to precipitate NACA's end.)

Lloyd Berkner had taken the occasion of Dryden's request to set up an ad hoc Committee on Interplanetary Probes and Space Stations. It had come out in favor of not only dispatching a probe to Venus but also sending one to Mars, stating that both missions were technically feasible and extremely important. And it had gone on to unanimously recommend that it was "urgently necessary to begin the exploration of space within the solar system with any means at our disposal if a continuing USA program of space science and exploration is to proceed at an optimum rate."

The report had specified that such areas as the radiation environment of the various bodies in the solar system, their electronic and magnetic fields, and their density, composition, and physical properties be measured. In addition, it had called for accurately calculating the length of an astronomical unit (the mean distance between Earth and the Sun, and the standard unit of measurement within and beyond the solar system), as well as for studying radio signals and their sources in outer space, plus a detailed study of meteorites. The recommendations, which were contained in a special report by the Space Science Board to Glennan in December 1958, two months after NASA was born, had urged that planning for a mission to Mars in 1961 be undertaken without delay.

In addition, scientists around the country, intrigued with the notion of being able to send exploring machines to the Moon and planets rather than merely look at them, were now agitating for solar system exploration. Many astronomers, on the other hand, were not interested in studying the planets. The solar system had for the most part long since been abandoned as an academic backwater, with telescopes trained instead on less known and more interesting targets elsewhere in the Milky Way and beyond. Carl Sagan of Cornell would become one of the notable exceptions. Some of the others would be wooed back by federal grants in the years immediately ahead.

Harold C. Urey, who won the Nobel Prize in chemistry in 1934, began pondering the origin of the solar system in the early 1950s and by 1958 was a highly vocal proponent of lunar and planetary exploration. His *The Planets: Their Origin and Development* was a seminal work on the origin of the solar system. Urey's impatience with what he took to be NASA's misordering of priorities would make him one of its most impassioned and persistent gadflies. It was his belief that the Moon held the clues to the origin of the solar system which in part led to the Ranger and Surveyor probes there and, to a significant extent, to the scientific aspect of the manned landings that followed them.

And the new space agency itself also began to look to the Moon as a likely destination for its rockets. But its motive for wanting to go there would in most respects not coincide with the aspirations of the scientific community. The mission to the Moon, and the manned spaceflight program leading to it, would reflect an agenda that went well beyond satisfying the scientists' thirst for knowledge of Earth and the cosmos in which it existed. Pragmatism would be the thing. Pragmatism—the imperatives of the real world—would decide where the new space agency's priorities would lie.

So as JPL officially joined NASA on New Year's Day, 1959, the two organizations saw planetary science and exploration from distinctly different perspectives. The Pasadenans were busily drawing grandiose long-range missions for what they took to be a mandate to explore the solar system. They even decided that it would be splendidly appropriate—most efficient—if they accomplished a sizable amount of that exploration with their own upper stage, a rocket booster called Vega that would be designed to work optimally with their own spacecraft. But their dreams were taking shape in a political vacuum that in some respects was as pervasive as the physical one they wanted to send their spacecraft to explore.

At the same time, Glennan and his aides at Headquarters were trying to weld several scattered and technically divergent space centers into a cohesive organization. Meanwhile, they were also trying to forge ties with industry, finesse relations with generals and admirals who were undergoing political hyperventilation because of NASA, and break bread with a suspicious, egoistic scientific establishment, which thought of them as a well-off but ignorant and unsavory suitor. More fundamentally, they had to reconcile their own need for sending and probably keeping people in space—soon to be a presidential directive to land them on the Moon—with the requirements of their own charter. A complex dynamic therefore began to take shape in the waning months of the fifth decade of the fourth century after Galileo's and Kepler's observations. Plans to go to the Moon and the planets, some of them contradictory and all of them fragmented, were incubating within both the manned and the unmanned camps. And the able, extremely brilliant and spoiled brats from Pasadena would be in the thick of it.

4.

Ranger: Racing with the Moon (and Losing)

Having decided that JPL was going to forsake designing guided missiles in order to spearhead exploration of the planets, William Pickering made one more resolution. He determined that, to the greatest extent possible, the lab would maintain its traditional independence. It was "essential for some competent group to be given a clear cut responsibility and told to draw up a realistic long term [space science and exploration] program which they can successfully complete on schedule," he wrote to Killian in July 1958, adding that JPL was the obvious choice to become *"the* [italics added] national space laboratory" because of its knowledge "in all phases of the problem."

As a consequence, a memorandum by Abe Silverstein to Pickering on October 28, less than a month after NASA officially came into existence and two months before JPL itself joined the space agency, suggested that Pasadena begin thinking about possible space projects. The memo was taken as a mandate to come up with a detailed long-range plan for lunar and planetary exploration. This was entirely as it should have been where Pickering and his colleagues were concerned, since JPL's getting the "deep space mission" had been a condition of Caltech's allowing it to contract with NASA in the first place.

So a week later, Pickering sent a proposal to Silverstein calling for the preparation of a five-year plan, or "Space Flight Program Study." The proposal led, in turn, to the creation of a seven-member NASA Program Study Committee that met on November 18 to begin trying to lay the groundwork for getting science into space and for starting exploration. JPL was of course represented. But the Pasadenans showed up fresh from their own meeting at which the lab's own position had been resolved after a vigorous debate. JPL wanted to head right for the planets and relegate the Moon to a subsidiary role. It therefore quickly became apparent to everyone else on the Program Study Committee that JPL was for all intents and purposes locked on the planets.* Headquarters, on the other hand, was becoming increasingly resolved to begin the exploration process with the Moon. They were therefore at cross purposes.

Since the Moon was close—extremely close, astronomically speaking—there would always be ample opportunity to send spacecraft to circle it or land on it, Pickering and his colleagues believed. As with all shots at other bodies in the solar system, a spacecraft would in effect have to be aimed ahead of the orbiting body so as to meet it at a predetermined point. It was like shooting a bullet ahead of a moving target. There were optimal times to do this, depending on the relative positions of Earth and the object in space, and they came to be known as launch "windows." For JPL, launch windows for the Moon were boringly frequent, and the whole business was therefore not all that interesting, even in 1958.

The planets, on the other hand, were farther out, more difficult to reach because of fewer windows and other obstacles (the lack of adequate boosting, communication, navigation, and tracking being but four), and were in any case far less understood than the Moon. Where Pickering and his colleagues were concerned, then, the planets held the key to the lab's future. The engineering challenges that would have to be overcome in order to get to them would be formidable. At the same time, the cornucopia of scientific information yielded once they were reached would benefit mankind, bring renewed pride to American science and technology, and, not uncoincidentally, steep JPL in deserved glory. In that regard, Pickering in California was in total accord with von Braun in Alabama (though, of course, it was Huntsville, not Pasadena, that von Braun had in mind when he thought about glory). Pickering and his top managers became convinced that since the Soviets were cleaning up on Earth

---

*JPL's plan called for twenty-three missions through October 1963. These were to include a circumlunar flight and two Mars flybys in 1960; two Venus flybys and three more lunar missions, including a rough landing on the Moon itself in 1961; another rough landing on the Moon and four missions to Venus in 1962; and three soft landings on the Moon, a circumlunar flight with an animal on board, and two flybys each of Jupiter and Mercury in 1963. Mission objectives called for studies of interplanetary conditions; photographs of lunar and planetary terrain; gamma ray, atmospheric, and magnetic experiments; seismography experiments and surface analysis of the Moon; and weather sampling of Venus. The plan called for JPL to actively conduct the planetary missions and supervise those that were going to the Moon.

orbit anyway, and would undoubtedly get a probe to the Moon before the United States no matter what NASA did, the next prudent step was to beat them to the planets.

But Headquarters saw the situation differently. For one thing, exploring the Moon before the planets seemed logical to Glennan, who reasoned that Earth sciences had come before the Moon and planets in the development of the space sciences, so the Moon ought to be next in the logical order of progression.* But that was arcane stuff.

The real point, made during the sometimes acrimonious preliminary meetings between Headquarters and JPL on January 12 and 13, 1959, was that NASA was engaged in a race to space with the Soviet Union. And the race was taking place on several levels. It was presumed that JPL would not lose sight of that fact.

Abe Silverstein, renowned for his toughness, explained that while he accepted the need for long-range planning, NASA first had to overcome serious short-range problems. Foremost among these was building a broad base of support in Congress and across the country so that the longer, more ambitious missions would get funded later on. It was hoped, Silverstein emphasized, that the people from Pasadena would see themselves as part of the greater space agency rather than as outsiders intent on going their own way—that they would see the bigger picture.

As Washington saw that picture, a multifaceted race was brewing between the superpowers. The contest was going to involve sending people first into Earth orbit and then, undoubtedly, on to the Moon. Silverstein was a shrewd individual. But he didn't have to be prescient to know that American citizens, not just robots, were headed for space. On January 5, just one week before the first day of the two-day meeting between JPL and Headquarters, guidelines had been set for selecting the nation's first astronauts. And only three days before, on the ninth, the winner of a design competition for the one-man capsules that were to carry those astronauts had been picked. The McDonnell Aircraft Corp. of St. Louis, Missouri, would get the contract. The project even had a name: Mercury, for the

---

*The space sciences are in fact extensions of the earth sciences and of science in general, rather than being separate entities. Geological techniques that are applicable on earth are also applicable on Mars, for example, and the laws of physics are the same in both places. A chemist who investigates the chemical composition of the Martian polar cap is conducting space science; if he investigates the chemical composition of Earth's poles, he is doing plain old chemistry.

fleet-footed son of Zeus and the grandson of Atlas. Abe Silverstein knew that, too. He had named it.

So however badly Pickering and the others at JPL wanted to go right to the planets, NASA in 1959 was becoming preoccupied with going to the Moon, mostly for political reasons that were becoming increasingly clear. Yet politics was not the only reason for wanting to go there.

The previous November, Newell, who was assistant director of Space Sciences in the Office of Space Flight Development, had created two small divisions within the office. One of them was to concentrate on practical science, while the other would handle theoretical problems having to do with basic research in astronomy, cosmology, and planetary science. He had picked Robert Jastrow, a physicist who had been a colleague at the Naval Research Laboratory, to head the Theoretical Division.

Jastrow hadn't claimed to know a great deal about the specialties for which he was suddenly responsible, but he had enough sense to know where to go to get a good briefing on them. He had promptly headed for La Jolla, California, to confer with Harold C. Urey. Urey was convinced that the Moon held important clues to the formation of Earth and the other planets. (In that connection, he would also become the quintessential gadfly of the planetary sciences program, Glennan's and Newell's stereotypical arrogant and presumptuous scientist.)*

At any rate, the irascible chemist had sat Jastrow down, handed him a copy of *The Planets* opened to the chapter on the Moon, and began briefing the young physicist on the unique importance of that body as a kind of Rosetta stone for understanding Earth and the other planets. Urey had an almost messianic effect on Jastrow.

"I was fascinated by his story, which had never been told to me before in fourteen years of study and research in physics," Jastrow would remember. He was told for the first time how stars are born, how the solar system was formed, what the primitive Earth may have been like, and how life may have developed. This was a revela-

---

*In 1963, for example, Urey publicly criticized NASA for lacking first-rate scientists and therefore with not being able to make the best use of scientists outside the agency because, in effect, it was unable to understand them. He indicated at a press conference at the National Academy that the United States might do well to emulate the Soviet Union, where space activities were headed by outstanding members of the Soviet Academy of Sciences. The following year he challenged the space agency for not selecting astronauts with science backgrounds and for severely limiting the amount of scientific experiments they were allowed to perform in orbit.

tion for Jastrow, whose work had focused on the atom and the nucleus, and who, in common with many of those in his discipline, had considered biology to be an alien subject and a lower form of science. "Yet the fact is that a single thread of evidence runs from the atom and the nucleus through the formation of stars and planets to the complexities of the living organism," Jastrow would later recount in awe.

A week later, Jastrow showed up at Newell's office in Washington with Urey in tow. The two of them then convinced the assistant director of Space Sciences that sending reconnaissance spacecraft to the Moon was a scientific imperative. Newell would say years later that Project Ranger "was in effect born on [that] day. . . ."

That same January, at about the time Silverstein, Newell, Pickering, and the others were grappling with who was going to be responsible for what (and who would be answerable to whom), Newell also started an ad hoc Working Group on Lunar Exploration. It was chaired by Jastrow and included Urey and three other eminent scientists, James Arnold, Harrison Brown, and Frank Press. The group's purpose was to devise ways in which NASA could interact with outside scientists in order to determine what experiments should be sent around the Moon and landed on it. The group came up with four different possible kinds of missions during its first meeting the following month: a circumlunar orbit in which a spacecraft circled the Moon and collected data, including pictures; uncontrolled impact, in which a spacecraft would simply plow into the lunar surface; a rough landing, in which a package of experiments would survive what amounted to a controlled crash by using retrorockets to brake its descent; and a soft landing, in which a spacecraft alighted gently.

Meanwhile, the Soviets were continuing to stage space extravaganzas. Sputnik 3, the last of their initial battery of Earth satellites, was successfully orbited on May 15, 1958, less than two months after the ascent of Explorer 3. This one, at nearly three thousand pounds the heaviest of the trio, was crammed with more than a ton of scientific apparatus, including equipment to measure solar and cosmic radiation, electrical fields, the geomagnetic field, micrometeorites, and ion density and composition. It also carried an advanced telemetry system that allowed collected data to be stored on tape and then "dumped" as the satellite passed over the Soviet Union. Sputnik 1 may have been little more than a beeping ball, but the two spacecraft that followed it, both technically flying under the aegis of the International Geophysical Year, were impressive except for the relatively cumbersome nature of their instruments. Sputnik 3 continued to transmit scientific data until it decayed nearly two years later.

And there was more. After remaining grounded for the rest of 1958, the Soviets sent Luna 1 (also known as Mechta, or "Dream") to the Moon on January 2, 1959 (a bare ten days before the JPL-Headquarters meeting). The heavily instrumented sphere, which outwardly resembled Sputnik 1, sailed thirty-six hundred miles above the lunar surface after releasing a cloud of sodium and then continued on toward the Sun, becoming the first man-made object to orbit it. On September 12—three days before Nikita Khrushchev was to begin a trip to the United States that would start in New York and end at Disneyland—Luna 2 was dispatched on a direct trajectory to the Moon. The spacecraft, which was virtually identical with Luna 1, performed several experiments, including measurement of Earth's radiation belt. Like its immediate predecessor, Luna 2 released sodium (which was duly photographed by an observatory on Earth, lest anyone doubt that it was where it was claimed to be), and then slammed into the lunar surface, becoming the first man-made object to accomplish that as well. The spacecraft carried two small spheres bearing the hammer-and-sickle insignia of the USSR.

Next came Luna 3, launched on October 4, 1959, to mark the second anniversary of the launching of Sputnik 1. The Luna 3 mission, which Soviet space expert Nicholas L. Johnson has called "one of the most astounding technological achievements of any nation, considering the state of the art at the time," involved photographing the far side of the Moon. The Automatic Interplanetary Station, as its creators called it, was able to develop its pictures on board and then transmit them to ground stations when its orbit swung closest to Earth. President Eisenhower, the Congress of the United States, and the people who elected them were soon treated to never-before-seen views of the Sea of Moscow, the Gulf of Cosmonauts, the Tsiolkovsky and Lomonosov craters, and the Sovietsky Mountain Range. Senator Lyndon B. Johnson, who was still tormented by the memory of Sputnik 1, took each successive Soviet triumph as a blow directed at the heart of the nation and the foundation upon which it stood. He resolved to get Texas into the space race on the side of the United States.

What was worse, the Soviets had been challenged, but to no avail. The United States had tried to respond, only to suffer still more humiliation. The year before—in March 1958—ARPA, the Department of Defense's newly created Advanced Research Projects Agency, had also decided to go to the Moon. ARPA was supposed to stimulate innovative defense-oriented technology by providing seed money to promising projects. Making it to the Moon, it was felt, would add enormous credibility to the military presence in space, help to improve the reliability and performance of long-range missiles, and preempt a similar attempt by any civilian agency that was invented to muscle in on the space program. (It was only too aware that NASA was in its embryonic stage.)

ARPA had therefore funded five flight opportunities: three for the Air Force and two for the Army. Space Technology Laboratories had built diminutive probes under contract with the Air Force, while JPL had done the same for the Army. The Air Force version had been shaped like two flattened cones joined by a wide belt. The probe was made of fiberglass, weighed eighty-four pounds, and carried thirty-nine pounds of scientific instruments, a tiny television camera, a battery, a transmitter and antenna, and a small retrorocket to slow it down so it could slip into lunar orbit.

The JPL design, also made of fiberglass, had been quite a bit more modest. It was cone-shaped and had as its primary payload a miniature slow-scanning television camera and a special lightweight magnetic tape recorder and transmission system to get the imagery back to Earth without suffering radiation damage.* The entire spacecraft weighed only thirteen pounds, or about the weight of the briefcase of one of its designers. Both the Army and Air Force programs were called Pioneer, a name that was blackened (or, more accurately, charred) in 1958, but which would survive to see better days.

The Air Force had led off on August 17, 1958, when it sent up the first of its spacecraft in the nose of a Thor-Able launcher (a Thor Intermediate Range Ballistic Missile with a surplus Vanguard rocket used as an upper stage). The launch vehicle had erupted in a ball of fire only seventy-seven seconds after it left the pad at Cape Canaveral because a turbopump in its motor had seized. The attempt was referred to as Pioneer O.

The pump problem corrected, another Thor-Able, carrying Pioneer 1, had been launched on October 11. This time the problem was

*Data on the radiation field surrounding Earth that had been collected by the Explorers had already been carefully analyzed by Van Allen and his associates. They indicated that unshielded standard 35 mm film, which JPL had planned to use with an onboard wet processing system, would fog as it passed through the cosmic ray flux.

a premature shutdown of the second stage. This launch was particularly frustrating because the spacecraft had separated properly and was aimed in the right direction. The shutdown meant that the probe had simply lacked enough momentum to reach the Moon. Its velocity had dropped to zero a third of the way there, so it tumbled back down to Earth the next day and was duly incinerated after returning forty-three hours of data on radiation and micrometeoroids.

Pioneer 2, the Air Force's last hope, had gone up on November 8. It, too, had come to an ignominious end when the launch vehicle's third stage simply failed to turn on. The spacecraft had made it as high as 963 miles before plummeting back down without returning so much as a scrap of useful data.

The Army's JPL-built Pioneer 3 then blasted off on top of one of Huntsville's Junos on December 6, 1958, following a route that was supposed to take it past the Moon and into an orbit around the Sun. The date marked the first anniversary of the first Vanguard disaster. It turned out to be propitious. The first stage had shut down almost four seconds before it was supposed to, causing the tiny fiberglass cone to fall back toward Earth after reaching an altitude of 63,500 miles. During its thirty-eight-hour life, though, Pioneer 3 had managed to send back important data not only confirming the presence of Van Allen's high-intensity radiation belt circling Earth about three thousand miles out, but revealing the presence of a second belt some seven thousand miles beyond the first one.

Pioneer 4 had been launched without incident on March 3, 1959—two months after Luna 1—and had made it to within about thirty-five thousand miles of the Moon before continuing on to a solar orbit. It, too, had sent back radiation data. Perhaps the most important information it returned showed that radiation levels beyond the Van Allen belts were low enough so that properly protected astronauts could survive there.

On the whole, however, the first Pioneer program had been an almost unmitigated failure. If there was any consolation for those who had designed the probes at Space Technology Laboratories and at JPL, it no doubt came with the knowledge that their tiny spacecraft apparently functioned quite a bit better than did the as-yet-unperfected rockets upon which they had to ride.

Out of that maelstrom emerged three spacecraft that would actually make it to the Moon to perform the four basic missions developed by the Working Group on Lunar Exploration. Two of them would be developed by JPL and one by NASA's Langley Research Center in Virginia. They would be called Ranger, Surveyor, and Lunar Orbiter. And Ranger itself would initially be part of a flexible design that would produce yet a fourth class of spacecraft, though this one would be intended to go to the other inner planets—Mercury, Venus, and Mars—and not to the Moon. Those built for the exploration of the planets would be christened Mariners because of the long distances they would have to travel. The Rangers and the first of the Mariners, born as they were from a common concept, would at first have a clear family resemblance. As Mariner-series spacecraft evolved to suit particular mission requirements, though, they would come to take on more of their own identities.

While JPL was encouraged to develop Mariner and plan planetary missions, Headquarters went into 1960 increasingly convinced that the Moon had to be NASA's first stop. By that August, in fact, the first big mission to the Moon had been set to take place in only eighteen months. But there was a problem. And it went beyond designing the spacecraft itself.

Little Explorer 1 had been hastily shot into orbit with a make-do cluster of miniature Sergeant rocket motors on top of a large booster. And ARPA's little Pioneers had each weighed less than ninety pounds. No one, however, believed that it was possible to get payloads of any consequence into orbit, let alone to the Moon, with such anemic propulsion. The answer was the powerful upper stage: a high-thrust final boosting rocket that would blast away from the main launch vehicle when it shut off, hurling the satellite or space probe to a point where its own small engine could take it the last mile, or even stay attached to it throughout part or all of its flight.

Given the fact that the design of rocket engines was JPL's traditional area of expertise, the engineers of the Arroyo Seco naturally took it upon themselves to design their own upper stage, which they called Vega. Their lunar-planetary spacecraft and the Vega upper stage, they reasoned, would fit together perfectly and work smoothly because of the high degree of coordination that came with both pieces of equipment almost literally being designed under the same roof. It certainly made sense. Vega and its spacecraft would leave Earth on top of a General Electric second stage, which, in turn, would be attached to a General Dynamics Atlas launch vehicle. It would therefore be called Atlas-Vega. This seemed reasonable to Headquarters too, at least at first. It therefore programmed start-up funding for Vega development in 1959 with the understanding that it would be increased in 1960.

But there was a wrinkle. Three years earlier, in 1956, the Air Force Ballistic Missile Division had quietly contracted with Lockheed Missiles and Space Company at Sunnyvale, four hundred miles up the coast, for its own upper stage, named Agena. The Air Force had no interest in probing deep space, but it did have a galaxy of satellites it planned to put into many different kinds of orbits around Earth. The most important of these were supposed to collect photo and signals intelligence from around the world, provide early warning of a Soviet missile attack, and maintain command, control, and communication links for the armed forces as a whole. So even before NASA saw the light of day, much less gave JPL approval to create its own upper stage, Vega had a formidable and entrenched competitor.

To make matters even more complicated, General Dynamics was working on its own upper stage, called Centaur. This powerful rocket was the brainchild of Krafft Ehricke, von Braun's former colleague, and was being developed under his supervision. Konstantin Tsiolkovsky had postulated the theory that hydrogen and oxygen combined to make the most powerful rocket fuel because of their exceptionally high thrust-to-weight ratio. Ehricke had read this in Germany as a young man and taken it seriously. He therefore carried the idea with him when he parted ways with von Braun after the war and went to work for General Dynamics, builder of the Atlas. When the thirty-two-foot-long stainless-steel upper stage and the launch vehicle were mated, in fact, they could hardly be told apart. Centaur started as an Air Force program under ARPA's auspices, but was transferred to NASA over strenuous Air Force objections in July 1959.* Since its two main engines combined liquid hydrogen and liquid oxygen (the latter popularly known as LOX) to produce fifteen thousand pounds of thrust each, it was coveted by both the civilian and military space programs as a heavy-duty workhorse.

But Centaur had severe design and development problems that played havoc with the spacecraft engineers who depended upon it, even as they labored over the drawing boards trying to make the

---

*Control of Centaur illustrates the often intimate relationship between the civilian and military aspects of the space program. Following strong pressure by the Air Force and ARPA to keep Centaur even after the decision had been made to give it to NASA, a plan was worked out in which the Air Force established a Centaur project director at its Ballistic Missile Division in Los Angeles who would report to the Centaur program manager at NASA Headquarters. There was also a joint program management coordinating committee consisting of members from NASA, ARPA, and the Air Force.

powerful upper stage and their own creations compatible. The worst
of the trouble had to do with the volatility of the liquid hydrogen,
which tended to evaporate because of heat transfer between its tank
and the adjacent tank holding the liquid oxygen inside Centaur.
Both chemicals must be kept very cold if they are to remain in liquid
form and therefore be useful. Yet each has a substantially different
boiling point. Centaur's designers were therefore faced with a daunting challenge. With the liquid hydrogen and liquid oxygen tanks
close to each other inside Centaur's thin cylindrical shell, the LOX
had to be prevented from vaporizing the liquid hydrogen, which was
colder, while the hydrogen could not be allowed to overcool the LOX.
In other words, their proximity would cause each to alter the other's
temperature, in the process changing their states and reducing their
efficiency.

JPL was well aware of the temperature exchange problem, as well
as others that plagued Centaur. One of the reasons the lab wanted
to develop Vega, in fact, was to have it as an interim propulsion
system until the bugs were worked out of Centaur. Another was to
get its own upper stage in ahead of the Air Force's. Unless work on
Vega progressed quickly, Pickering believed, JPL and NASA would
be faced with either having to wait God knew how long for one Air
Force upper stage—Centaur—or having to adapt quickly to another—Agena. So he pushed Washington all the harder for the development of Vega. NASA responded by indicating that Vega was a
viable project. Yet no funds were forthcoming.

Pasadena itself might as well have been on the Moon where Headquarters was concerned, JPL's director mused angrily. How could
one go about the complicated business of mating a spacecraft to an
upper stage when Washington wouldn't even make it clear whether
there was going to be an upper stage? Here was a perfect example
of what could happen when a world-class institution like the Jet
Propulsion Laboratory became ensnared in the great bureaucracy's
elephantine, wheezing, inefficient duplicate and triplicate civil service gears. They couldn't get out of their own way back in Washington. It hadn't been like this with the Army. The Army would have
told him to go build Vega and be done with it. The Army would have
unleashed the cheetah of the space world so it could overtake the
opposition, not bind it in red tape. The Army had recognized JPL's
inherent excellence from the beginning. The good old Army. . . .

Pickering's patience began to crumble as exasperation took hold.
Finally, on March 24, 1959, his anger welled to the point where he

got off a sharp three-page letter to Glennan. The "private communication" began by emphasizing the upper stage's importance to
NASA on two counts. First, the Mars mission, set for the following
year in JPL's five-year plan, would be impossible without Vega. And
that, he hastened to remind the administrator, would mean "a con-
sequent loss of prestige to both the U.S. and NASA." Second, foot-
dragging on Vega could cause it to be abandoned in favor of Centaur,
which would result in the civilian space program being "subordi-
nate" to Air Force requirements for its own upper stage.

Then JPL's director laid bare frustrations that went quite a bit
deeper than Centaur. He stacked them under the heading of "Problem Areas." Pickering complained bitterly that "Headquarters is
not yet willing to treat JPL like one of its own laboratories," and
that, for its part, the lab did not understand Washington's "operating principles. JPL tries to cooperate when asked to do something by
Headquarters, but it is all too frequently frustrated when the expected results are not forthcoming." Pickering's nostalgia for the
Army days spilled onto the page. In case Keith Glennan missed the
point, he amplified his message: "Headquarters appears to be too
concerned with technical details of projects," William H. Pickering
snapped. "JPL is prone to compare the Headquarters negotiations
on the Vega program with the similar type of negotiations necessary
when the Sergeant program was set up with the Army. The result
is not flattering to Headquarters."

Less than two months later, Dryden informed Pickering that a
little more than $24 million was being allocated to Vega for research
and development, with a third of it set aside for the remainder of
1959 and the rest going toward 1960. Headquarters, it seemed, was
finally emerging from its long nap: it apparently wanted Vega.

And the president wanted it, too. But even more, Ike wanted no
costly duplication of upper stages. Pickering's view, from the other
side of the Rockies, was necessarily limited. Whatever he thought
about Headquarters' handling of Vega, Glennan did spend considerable time that autumn of 1959 defending it against determined attacks by the Department of Defense and grumbling of cost-cutting
in the Executive Office. On the morning of October 26, at a meeting
in the White House, in fact, Glennan clashed with representatives
of the Pentagon, who wanted Vega killed outright.

Later that day he and George Kistiakowsky briefed Eisenhower on
the conflict. The president angrily denounced those "subordinates"
who had defied orders he had issued prohibiting duplicate upper

stages. And he went on, no doubt to Glennan's relief, to point out that his "firm orders" on the subject precluded Agena.

But development of the Air Force's prized upper stage had already progressed to an improved model called Agena B. Agena, as they said in Washington, was already in the loop. Kistiakowsky was generally sympathetic to NASA in proportion to being as wary of the military as his boss was. But he also worried about what he saw as the space agency's penchant for spreading itself too thin and scattering large sums of money in all directions as it went. NASA's urge to build "vehicles," he noted in his diary on October 7, 1959, convinced him that it was trying to "cover the waterfront and is terribly eager to get hardware, where hardware is not called for at present. He therefore found himself sympathizing with NASA while at the same time wondering whether Vega was really necessary, given the availability of Agena. The whole effect," he reflected, "is that when they don't have good ideas, they build expensive equipment. I am sure that my dear friend Keith will be unhappy when I tell him that, but I will."

Glennan meanwhile saw that it was wiser to give in to the Air Force's superior firepower than continue an unseemly battle with it, so he decided to abandon Vega. The upper stage had already cost $17 million, but, as he saw it, adapting Agena B to NASA's needs would at least save further expenditures in the development of Vega. He

"Three ships is a lot of ships. Why can't you prove the world is round with one ship?"

called Pickering with the news during the first week of December, just as design work on the upper stage was nearly complete. Then a telegram went to Pasadena that sealed the matter: THIS CONFIRMS ORAL UNDERSTANDING BTWEEN [*sic*] YOUR WILLIAM PICKERING AND NASA ADMINISTRATOR T. KEITH GLENNAN TO TERMINATE WORK ON THE VEGA VEHICLE AS OF THE CLOSE OF BUSINESS DECEMBER 11, 1959. AS TO SUBCONTRACTS AND PURCHASE ORDERS, FOLLOW THE GUIDELINES SET FORTH IN CLAUSE 11 OF THE GENERAL PROVISIONS OF CONTRACT NASW-6. CONFIRMATORY LETTER WILL FOLLOW CONCERNING REDIRECTION OF JPLS EFFORTS.

On December 16, Richard E. Horner, the space agency's associate administrator, wrote Pickering a lengthy letter outlining agency-wide responsibility for the various programs. Huntsville would be responsible for launch vehicle development, he explained, while Goddard and JPL would concentrate on space science. JPL, specifically, would be responsible for the planning and execution of lunar and interplanetary space exploration. It was to plan the missions, develop the appropriate spacecraft, integrate the instruments that went into the spacecraft, acquire and analyze data during the mission, and record the results.

This was exactly what Pasadena wanted. But there was a caveat. Since it would not be possible for JPL to undertake all of that by itself, Horner added, it was expected that "a part of the developments will be contracted with industry and the Laboratory will assume the responsibility of monitoring such contracts."* The work, in other words, would be spread around the private sector in order to broaden the agency's power base and bring Pasadena still further into the still-coalescing fold.

The redirection stipulated by Headquarters would force JPL to concentrate on producing the spacecraft that were shortly to embark on the exploration of the solar system. It was now out of the rocket business forever.

• • •

*Emphasis on the allocation of projects to contractors is fundamental to the working of NASA, as has been noted. In a letter of January 8, 1968, to A. O. Beckman, chairman of the board of Beckman Instruments and an important Caltech trustee, Oran Nicks as much as said that contractors' participation was preferable to the government's. "There are several cases of record where the solution to a contractor problem at JPL has been to bring the task in-house. While many of these may have been appropriate, it is possible that emphasis by management at the proper time could have precluded the necessity for bringing the work in-house. *Management emphasis on relationships with industrial contractors is of extreme significance considering the fact that from 75 to 90 percent of the funds go for procurements.*" (italics added; Caltech Archives, File 20.7).

Late in December 1959, two months after the flight of *Luna 3* and barely ten days after Vega was officially killed, Headquarters directed JPL to set up an interplanetary flight calendar with missions programmed through the next three years. It was strongly suggested that five Atlas–Agena B missions to the Moon, all carrying Ranger spacecraft, be launched during 1961 and 1962. It was also stipulated that while the Rangers would carry an unprecedented battery of scientific instruments for experimentation, the most important part of their payload would be cameras to be used for lunar reconnaissance.

Pictures were particularly important for three reasons. First, they would provide geologists and other scientists with better views of the lunar surface than were obtainable from Earth. Second, they were indispensable for scouting landing sites for robot soft-landers and then for astronauts.* And, inevitably, there were the requirements of public relations.

"What was the thing that JPL could sell to the public as the plot for what they do?" Arthur L. "Lonne" Lane, the longtime member of JPL's Space Sciences Division, was to ask years later. "Pictures . . . the bottom line. To this day, the thing that drives the PIO [Public Information Office] is in fact: 'Can you give me a picture we can publish?' "

Pickering heartily agreed. "If you just had scientists running the program, there would have been a lot less attention paid to the photographic work," he has observed. "Scientists are perfectly happy measuring fields and particles, or temperature, or atmospheric phenomena. And you can do an awful lot of that—maybe all of it—without ever taking pictures. But from the political point of view, pictures are important." While some scientists would disagree

---

*NASA's plans to send astronauts to the Moon, despite bitter Air Force objections, predate John Kennedy's declaration to do so in May 1961. Eisenhower had assigned NASA responsibility for the nation's manned space flight program, however sketchy it was, in mid-1958, not because he favored such an endeavor, but because there was no rationale for allowing the Department of Defense to do it. But while Ike did not take the prospect of landing astronauts seriously, NASA did. By mid-1960, with Eisenhower's last term running out, NASA planning had gone beyond the Mercury program phase and was consciously directed at a manned landing in 1975. Photographs of suitable landing places were therefore imperative. When Eisenhower was briefed on the mission in December 1960, and was reminded that Queen Isabella had financed Columbus, he responded emphatically that he would not "hock the family jewels" to bankroll the counterpart of Columbus's voyage. "This won't satisfy everybody," someone in the room quipped. "When they finish this, they'll want to go to the planets." That brought a lot of laughter. (See Logsdon's *The Decision to Go to the Moon*, pp. 34–35.)

that much less attention would be paid to imagery if they ran things, none would dispute the extreme political importance of the exotic pictures that were soon to begin streaming to the press during each mission.

By the end of January 1960, the five lunar probes would be divided into two "blocks." The first two Rangers, comprising Block I, would be test vehicles that were supposed to fly near the Moon but miss it. They would be sent on elliptical trajectories, partly to perform some science experiments, but more important, so that they and the entire mission could be thoroughly tested. It was only prudent to know precisely how the entire launch system—the Atlas, the Agena, and the Ranger—would function as an integrated whole.

The three spacecraft in Block II, however, were to carry television cameras as well as a seismometer and other instruments to the Moon, with the intention of sending back pictures of the lunar surface in the course of a rough landing. And in addition to their scientific apparatus, they would carry their own preprogrammed, midcourse maneuvering engines, making them the first probes capable of changing trajectories during a mission.

On June 30, 1961, the month after Kennedy declared that he wanted Americans to go to the Moon and return, JPL would send a proposal to Washington for four Block III missions—Rangers 6 through 9—to carry only television cameras. These would be crash-landers whose sole objective would be to return detailed imagery preparatory to the landing of advanced robots and then astronauts. They were to begin flying in January 1963. NASA would approve the plan in August, since the Apollo program would by then already be under way.

The Jet Propulsion Laboratory now faced the challenge of designing and building relatively large and sophisticated ships to cross Kennedy's "new ocean." There were, and remain, many similarities between the space voyagers and those that have explored Earth's oceans since the time of Odysseus.

Both craft must be designed and fitted to go on long, arduous journeys, often through uncertain or dangerous areas. They must therefore be rugged, as self-sustaining as possible, and adequately propelled. While the *Santa María* may have been slow and clumsy, she was large and solid enough to venture across the Atlantic even through the terrible storms Columbus ran into on the return voyage to Europe. And *Niña,* stuffed with as much as sixty tons of cargo, was a provision ship that could keep the expedition going even in the face of unexpected privation. This has its space-age counterpart in shielding a spacecraft from solar heat and excessive radiation and of providing it with redundant hardware, such as a backup computer and a second antenna. And the fact that Columbus and many of those who came after him sailed with more than one ship for safety's sake (Magellan started with five) has as its counterpart the use of two or more virtually identical spacecraft to increase the odds of at least one completing the mission even if the others suffer debilitating failure.

Both kinds of craft need to be adequately powered and propelled. Power is what keeps the vessel or the spacecraft functioning. In the case of an ocean liner, there are generators to keep lights on, refrigerators working, navigation and communication systems functioning, and so forth. Spacecraft derive their power from solar panels or from nuclear engines or isotopes to keep their own guidance systems, communication links, science instruments, and other vital components working. Solar panels are used to convert the Sun's energy to electrical power within the inner solar system. But spacecraft that range too far from the Sun to be able to use its energy must carry their own supply in the form of a nuclear isotope that produces heat, which is converted to energy.

Propulsion is the force that gets the spacecraft from Earth to wherever it is supposed to go. It was well known by the time JPL got to work on Ranger and Mariner that first-stage–upper-stage combinations would be necessary to lift spacecraft off Earth and propel them to their intended destinations. Aside from politics, the rhubarb over Agenas, Centaurs, and Vegas had to do with finding an adequate means of propulsion for Moon and planetary missions. Nautical and astronautical engineers were faced with the same basic propulsion problem: finding a means of power that can push a given amount of weight over whatever distance has to be covered. All other things being equal, the more powerful the engine, the heavier (or bigger) the spacecraft or ship can be. And weight translates into the amount or complexity of cargo—in this case, science instruments—that can be taken along.

In addition, spacecraft are equipped with tiny steering jets, or thrusters, that either alter their orientation relative to the Sun, Earth, and the stars for accurate navigation, or else supply extra power to increase their velocity. Additional velocity changes a spacecraft's trajectory in order to keep it pointed in the right direction to rendezvous with its target.

Both craft also have to go where they are supposed to go. This means knowing precisely where the place to be explored is located and then being able to navigate there. Fourteenth- and fifteenth-century navigators were not without some pretty accurate charts. The Portuguese had already sailed along the west coast of Africa and had ventured as far as the Azores, Iceland, Greenland, and possibly even Newfoundland. There were also good Genoese, Venetian, and Catalan maritime charts covering much of the Mediterranean and the eastern Atlantic to help explorers like Columbus and those who came after him get their bearings. And there were two ways to navigate: dead reckoning by means of a compass (favored by Mediterraneans), and celestial, using the stars (preferred by northern Europeans).

The whereabouts of the planets and their moons are established by astronomers. In fact, astronomers were for several centuries the timekeepers for mariners, who needed accurate clocks for navigation. Astronomers at the Greenwich Observatory traditionally would drop a red ball from the top of a tower every afternoon at one o'clock so that sailors could set their chronometers. As mariners are dependent on nautical charts for navigation, those who would send spacecraft to explore the solar system are dependent on ephemerides. A heavenly body's location—where it is in time and space—is called its ephemeris.

Although it is deceptively simple-looking, knowing where a planet or a moon is going to be at any given time—that is, *precisely* where it will be—is a fantastically complicated business that astronomers have been fine-tuning for centuries. At first glance, predicting the positions of objects in space comes down to Newtonian mechanics: to knowing how things move based on how they interact.

"The concept is very simple," explained E. Myles Standish, Jr., a JPL astronomer who is widely respected for the accuracy of his ephemerides. "We know how the planets move. We know what pulls them and pushes them. We know the forces upon them. So if you set up a bunch of planets out in space somewhere, knowing their masses, and you give them all a specific position and push, you can figure out how they're going to move." The motion of the planets and their moons, he said, is determined by the gravitational forces—the pulling—they all exert on one another and on the Sun. Everything in the solar system therefore affects everything else. The effect is sometimes small. But it is always measurable. "That," Standish asserted, "is Sir Isaac Newton. Ninety-eight percent of my job is Sir Isaac Newton."

The problem, though, is that exact masses, positions, and velocities are not generally known. So while everything that is seen or
deduced can be measured, it comes down to a question of the accuracy of those measurements. Standish takes what is known—typically a data set from about one hundred thousand observations—and
runs it through a computer, forward and backward. Then he com-
pares the result with independent measurements of the planets and
moons, some of them almost a century old, made with radar or
telescopes. Next, he takes all of those data and keeps massaging
them with his computer until each ephemeris becomes more and
more refined. But in the last analysis, the lanky Connecticut native
added, "Your nose tells you after a lot of experience. It's really a
black art." But magic or not, fixing an object's position in the cosmos
with extreme accuracy, like everything else in astronomy, gratifies
Standish because it has a stability and permanence that he finds
lacking in the life sciences, which he has eschewed since college.
"Nobody pours it down the sink at the end of the day," he explained,
triumphantly.

Using the ephemerides supplied by Standish and others, a spacecraft, like an ocean vessel, is guided to its destination by making a
series of course corrections based on observations of where it is
relative to where it is supposed to go. Its position is followed from
Earth by radar, by keeping track of elapsed time, and by seeing what
it sees through images that are picked up by its own telescopes and
relayed to those who control it. And the spacecraft's own guidance
system, like the seaman who uses a sextant or radio navigation on
a ship, keeps track of its own whereabouts, too. It locks onto its
cosmic aim points and maintains its bearings relative to where they
are. If the spacecraft sees that it is wandering off course, its computers signal tiny thrusters to fire just enough to swing it back again,
the way sails on a ship are trimmed or the rudder is moved slightly.

"It's analogous to what you'd do on Earth," said Robert J. Ceser-
one, who designs spacecraft trajectories at JPL. "If you want to sail
to Hawaii from Los Angeles, you plan your route, you determine
your path, and you use whatever seagoing navigators use. You adjust your sails when you find you're off course. And you don't just do
it once and know that you've got it because after you've tracked your
spacecraft and corrected its errors, more errors creep in. So you do
it again, and again, and again," he added. "By doing that, you step
your way to the planet."

Finally, space probes, like ocean vessels, are carefully crafted to perform specific tasks in an environment that is always taken to be hostile. A spacecraft designed to go to the Moon, such as Ranger, would no more be sent to Jupiter than would a Mississippi paddle wheeler be sent to war in the North Atlantic. Each vessel is carefully designed to survive a battering by the elements through which it must pass. Each is built to protect its cargo. Each has a restricted amount of usable space on board, so "cargo" must be chosen with utmost care and according to the rigid requirements of the particular mission. And that cargo not only must be stored as compactly as possible but, in the case of a spacecraft, must be arranged so that one piece of equipment does not interfere with the working of another. In addition, a great deal of thought must be put into making certain that it has enough fuel to do whatever maneuvering is necessary to reach its destination and that its communication system is up to receiving instructions and sending back data over whatever expanse it will traverse. That much and a great deal more was known by the time Ranger and Mariner were committed first to the drawing board and then to JPL's assembly facility. But as JPL and Headquarters were about to learn, a great deal was not known, too.

Design work for the pair of Block I spacecraft—Rangers 1 and 2—was completed by May 1960. Each looked like an ocean buoy with large flippers and a moveable concave eye. The flippers were hinged solar panels that would be kept folded close against the spacecraft like the arms of someone standing at attention while it rose through the turbulent atmosphere inside the Agena B. Once the upper stage's shroud parted and Ranger sprang out, the panels were supposed to pop open like a pair of flower petals and begin collecting sunlight to power both the spacecraft and the Agena to which it was bolted. The "eye" was a high-gain dish antenna that had to be pointed toward Earth for two-way communication.

The panels and antenna were attached to a five-foot-wide hexagonal "bus," which, seen from above, looked like a thick six-sided bracelet. Each of the bracelet's "links" was a compartment, or bay, that held scientific experiments or equipment for the operation of the spacecraft itself. The bus also sprouted the tiny pitch, roll, and yaw thrusters that were supposed to keep the spacecraft stabilized on all three of its axes, and the sensors that were supposed to keep it properly oriented. The bus was therefore the heart of the Rangers, as it would be the heart of every space probe that followed. While the bus's size and shape, as well as the hardware it contained and the antennas and other gadgets that protruded out of it would vary according to mission, its function would always be the same.

Ranger's brain was a miniature computer, extraordinarily primitive by current standards, and a sequencer that was supposed to see to it that tasks were performed in order. The space historian R. Cargill Hall has described the mechanism as a "complex alarm clock; it was to time and trigger events after launch and enable Ranger to convert from its role as a rocket passenger to that of an independent spacecraft," opening its solar panels, aligning them with the Sun, pointing its communication dish back home so that its radio could transmit pictures and science data, and tell its controllers how it felt. The antenna also acted as a beacon for the ground radars that would keep constant track of where it was. There were to be eight scientific experiments on both of the first two Rangers, including instruments that would measure solar plasma and cosmic radiation, the Moon's magnetic field, and cosmic dust.

Fundamental problems boded ill for Ranger, however. One had to

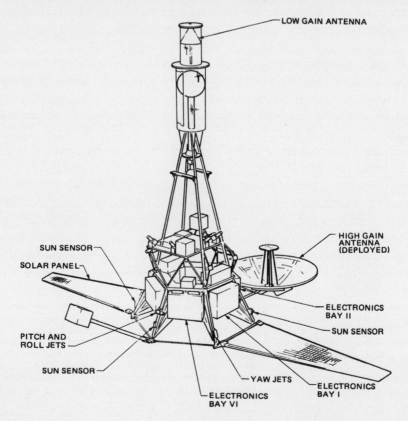

do with the different ways engineers and scientists saw the project. The engineers saw the Ranger mission as being reducible to equations that would, at least theoretically, make its mission predictable. But the scientists were interested in basic science: in what was not predictable. They were more interested in discovering new questions than in finding answers to existing ones.

For James D. Burke, the Caltech-trained mechanical engineer who managed Ranger for JPL, the important thing was to get his spacecraft to do what it was supposed to do. But for the scientists there was no point in having a mission in the first place unless it performed a useful service: primarily to carry experiments that would help gather data about the world out there. The two camps therefore argued incessantly over how much science the Rangers would carry. Burke reacted with fury, for example, when Headquarters agreed to an Atomic Energy Commission request to add an experiment that would help with space-based nuclear explosion detection just as he was about to freeze the Block I design.* He also noted sourly that NASA's approval of the AEC request only encouraged scientists at JPL to get Headquarters to wait until their experiments were ready, too. At that rate, Burke groused, when would the damned design ever be finalized?

To make matters worse, there were also disagreements as to whether Ranger's later experiments would concentrate entirely on lunar science and imagery in direct support of Apollo, as the Space Science Board suggested, or whether they would include atmospheric investigation, which Newell and some others in the Office of Space Science wanted.† But JPL, which had already prioritized its own experiments, contemptuously dismissed Newell's as mere "trinkets" and in effect told Headquarters as much.

Then there was sterilization. In January 1958, virtually at the outset of the space program, Joshua Lederberg, the eminent biologist and geneticist, had raised a telling point where the search for extraterrestrial life was concerned. If spacecraft that landed on the

*This was most likely to test infrared sensors in support of a program called Vela Hotel, in which sentinel spacecraft in very distant orbits were supposed to spot nuclear explosions as part of the proposed Limited Nuclear Test Ban Treaty.
†Until late 1961 space science came under Silverstein's Office of Space Flight Development. It became its own directorate in November of that year, however, as part of an agency reorganization. Homer Newell, who had led the space science group under Silverstein, was made associate administrator of the new Office of Space Science, where he remained until October 1967. There was also a separate Office of Applications, which in June 1963 was combined under Newell's Office to form the Office of Space Science and Applications (Ezell, NASA *Historical Data Book,* vol. II, p. 199).

Moon or elsewhere in the solar system carried organisms from
Earth, how could scientists who found signs of life in those places be
certain that they were not discovering the descendants of the hitch-
hikers? There were very few scientists who thought that life in any
form existed on the Moon. Yet ice or water trapped beneath the
lunar surface just might be insulating life in some form. However
unlikely that was, totally precluding such a possibility even before
exploration had begun was plain bad science. It was potentially a
mistake that could botch the search for life beyond Earth for all
time.

After a debate in the National Academy of Sciences and then in
the International Council of Scientific Unions, the decision was
therefore made to recommend that spacecraft bound for other
worlds be sterilized in some way, and both the United States and the
Soviet Union were urged to do so. But sterilizing a surgical scalpel
was one thing; sterilizing a 675-pound spacecraft that had to be
moved from Pasadena cross-country to Cape Canaveral was quite
another.

Nevertheless, on October 15, 1959, Silverstein sent an order to all
relevant centers requiring that "payloads which might impact a
celestial body" be sterilized and recommended the use of ethylene
oxide gas for the task. JPL decided that while the gas could decon-
taminate a spacecraft (or at least the areas it reached), it could not
by itself thoroughly sterilize them. Instead, it was decided that the
best practical way to do this was to heat all spacecraft components
to 257 degrees Fahrenheit for twenty-four hours, then use alcohol to
clean everything that had to be joined, ship the completed spacecraft
to Florida in a van with a controlled environment, and finally apply
the ethylene oxide to it when it was inside the shroud, on the pad,
and ready to go.

Sterilization, however, was not only expensive but potentially
dangerous. Any number of delicate components could be adversely
affected by exposure to intense heat for a full day. So the engineers
worried about sterilizing the Rangers. And their concerns, it would
turn out, were justified.

But that wasn't all. There was also the interface between the
experiments, the spacecraft, and its launch vehicle and upper stage.
Everyone connected with Ranger had to confront the iron law of
astronautical engineering, which does not bend: The size of the payload—what could be carried to space—depends on the amount of
thrust used to get it there. So as a consequence of the Rangers having

to carry the science experiments in addition to their own sterilized (and perhaps damaged) innards—nitrogen for the maneuvering thrusters, a battery, computer and sequencer, radio transmitter and receiver, and so forth—there was no room left for redundant systems; no room for backup apparatus in case of gross problems. This was dangerous and everyone knew it. But designing Ranger, like designing all other machines that ventured into space, was a matter of making trade-offs. It had to do with setting odds by making educated guesses and then committing what seemed to be one's soul and life's blood to the outcome.

In addition, the lab itself had more work in 1960–61 than even its growing capacity could keep up with. This affected all of its projects, but particularly Ranger. Pickering, no less than his opposite numbers at other NASA centers, knew that competition with the Soviet Union offered an unprecedented opportunity to grow, both in size and capability, and he made every effort to seize upon it for doing so.

The two JPL lunar programs, Ranger to impact the Moon and then Surveyor to land on it, were examples. But there was also Mariner, the crown jewel, which was more interesting because it was going to the planets. Yet as a consequence, Burke had to compete for engineering help with both of the other programs, as well as with assorted smaller ones, to keep his Rangers technically healthy and on schedule. He had to negotiate with section and division heads for guidance in specific areas, but because of the number of projects under way, they could not grasp the detailed requirements of any one of them, Ranger included.

Burke and his immediate subordinates therefore were often reduced to relying on junior engineers, some barely out of school, to solve Ranger's problems. In too many cases it was left up to them to decide whether a particular component was ready to go or not. System integration posed another problem. Not only did Ranger's thousands of components have to fit so they worked together perfectly, but outside contractors, such as RCA, which made the all-important television system that the Block IIs and Block IIIs were supposed to carry, also had to be consulted for close system coordination.

JPL's ledgers now looked robust enough. But they belied an insidious management problem. The budget for fiscal 1962 soared to $132 million from $35 million four years earlier. That same year the lab's employees numbered 3,500, up from 2,600 in 1960. The deep space probe incubator on the Arroyo Seco was growing quickly, to be sure.

As a result, however, some divisions were reporting that as many as 60 percent of their employees had been at the lab for less than two years. That was not a happy circumstance. Indeed, the combination of problems at JPL, both home-grown and inflicted by the home office, was about to start causing considerable trouble.

Ranger 1 roared away from Cape Canaveral at dawn on August 23, 1961. Its Agena B was supposed to get it to a so-called parking orbit around Earth, from where the best possible vector toward the Moon could be fixed, and then temporarily shut down. Once in perfect position, the Agena's motor was supposed to refire, sending the spacecraft the rest of the way toward its near miss with the Moon.

But a faulty valve in the motor closed prematurely during the second burn. Ranger 1 separated from the Agena as it was supposed to, but lacking enough velocity to escape Earth's gravitational pull, it merely settled into an orbit around the planet at an altitude that averaged only 187 miles. The spacecraft was therefore as much out of its element as a thoroughbred trying to race on sand.

Now a pathetic situation began to unfold. Since Ranger flew in darkness—at night—during half of every ninety-one-minute orbit around Earth, its two solar panels (which had deployed perfectly) abruptly stopped supplying power every forty-five and a half minutes. Its Sun sensor therefore did not collect energy half the time. Ranger 1 therefore became disoriented, then reoriented, then disoriented, and so on with each successive orbit. Every time the spacecraft flew back into sunlight the sensor kicked in, turning on the roll, pitch, and yaw thrusters, which obediently refired to stabilize it on all three axes. But as soon as it entered darkness, the sensor went blind, turning off the thrusters. Since the thrusters had to perform major maneuvering while they were on to compensate for the disorientation that developed during the passage through darkness, they guzzled the precious propellant in prodigious quantity. The nitrogen supply was therefore exhausted by the end of the next day, leaving Ranger 1 powerless to make the attitude corrections that were crucial in order to keep its solar panels aligned with the Sun.

But the corrections didn't matter, since the thoroughbred couldn't get out of the sand anyway. With its fuel and power gone, the crippled probe began tumbling steadily lower into the thickening atmosphere until it burned to oblivion over the Gulf of Mexico on August 30.

A little less than three months later—on November 19—Ranger

2 met the same fate after a flight of only twenty hours. Both spacecraft sent back a trickle of data on the environment through which
they passed before the end came, but it was of no real consolation
to those who wanted the Moon.

Ranger 3, the first of the Block II group that was supposed to
actually make a rough, not a crash, landing on the lunar surface,
arrived at Canaveral in a specially cushioned, air-conditioned van on
November 20, the day after its immediate predecessor was cremated
as it plunged through the atmosphere. The spacecraft's superstructure was topped by a thick balsa-wood sphere, called an impact
limiter. The engineers had put a seismometer (to measure possible
moonquakes and meteor impacts), a battery and related electronic
equipment, and a small transmitting antenna inside a fiberglass
sphere, which, in turn, was cushioned by flotation fluid inside the
balsa-wood.

The idea was for a small retrorocket to help brake the impact
limiter's fall by slowing its velocity from six thousand miles an hour
to a negligible speed at an altitude of eleven hundred feet above the
lunar surface. The delicate contents of the impact limiter would then
be cushioned against the full force of striking the Moon the way a
mammalian embryo is protected against shock. Besides the instruments inside the balsa-wood sphere, a gamma ray spectrometer for
analyzing the Moon's surface and the all-important video camera
were mounted below, on the bus itself.

At three-thirty on the afternoon of January 26, 1962, Ranger 3,
riding atop its Atlas-Agena B, rose into the clear, sunny sky above
Cocoa Beach to the cheers of Air Force and NASA personnel. The
first American spacecraft sent to take close-up pictures of the Moon
seemed off to a fine start. But it wasn't out of sight before the telemetry indicated that the Atlas's radio guidance system had failed. This
meant that its engine would not respond to the shut-down command.
Instead, the Atlas lifted the Agena and its Ranger payload beyond
the point at which the Agena itself was supposed to take over. And
as if that weren't bad enough, the Agena itself malfunctioned right
after separation because of an error in its own flight program.

The upshot of this was that Ranger 3 raced ahead of the Moon as
the two were converging, missed it by twenty thousand miles, and
kept going until it went into heliocentric orbit, round and round the
Sun. JPL and NASA had been done in for a third straight time by
an Air Force launch vehicle (though it turned out that Ranger 3's
main computer and sequencer also had failed).

Ranger 4 was dispatched on April 23. This time the Atlas-Agena B performed flawlessly. But now the spacecraft itself malfunctioned. The master clock in the central computer and sequencer simply stopped. All timed operations—everything that had to be activated in sequence, including the deployment of the solar panels—stopped. Since everything on a space mission has to be done in sequence, the mission itself effectively stopped. In the process the spacecraft also somehow became incapable of accepting commands from Earth. In the words of one dejected NASA official, Ranger 4 turned into an "idiot."

Sixty-four hours after launch, Ranger 4 skimmed low over the Moon's leading edge, or limb. Then, pulled down by gravity, it disappeared around the far side and crashed somewhere in the darkness. It plowed into the rough terrain over which Luna 3 had flown in triumph.

Ranger 5, now carrying the severely frayed hopes of Pickering, Burke, and the rest of JPL, not to mention an increasingly apprehensive but still supportive Headquarters, rose into a heavily overcast sky early on the afternoon of October 18, 1962. Three days later the spacecraft, stricken by a short circuit in its computer and sequencer that interrupted the flow of vital power from the solar panels to the battery, cartwheeled blindly and silently past the Moon's trailing limb at an altitude of only 450 miles. Then, like Ranger 3, it headed mutely toward the Sun.

The Cuban missile crisis, which was building during Ranger 5's flight and which technically started in earnest on the twenty-second, diverted public attention from this new space fiasco. It certainly diverted the White House's. But it did not divert the attention of Newell, Silverstein, or James E. Webb, who had succeeded Glennan when John Kennedy took office. Webb harbored an abiding dislike of JPL's independence and arrogance. And five successive failures in its Ranger program did nothing to soften his sentiments.

A stunned Pickering ordered an in-house board of inquiry on the twenty-second, the day after the hapless probe shot past its target without returning so much as a single picture. But where Headquarters was concerned, that would not quite do. A week later, on the twenty-ninth, Homer Newell, by then director of the Office of Space Science, formally ordered that a board of inquiry be set up to look into the causes of what had become an ongoing, increasingly embarrassing series of mishaps. The Ranger program was clearly in turmoil. In fact, it was now seen as threatening to disrupt the Apollo program itself. A deeply perturbed Headquarters wanted to know why JPL was screwing up and what could be done about it.

The NASA panel, chaired by Albert J. Kelley, head of the Electronics and Control Division of NASA's Office of Advanced Research and Technology, held an intensive series of inspections and conferences during the next three weeks, starting on October 30 with a site visit to JPL itself. Kelley and his colleagues, who were ordered by Newell to make recommendations that could include changes in management, systems, testing, quality control, operational procedures, component and reliability assurance, in effect looked over shoulders and asked pointed questions. The experience was embarrassing for engineers who had difficulty reconciling their elitist self-image with having to confront a board of inquiry sent out by the home office to investigate costly blunders. The Kelley committee submitted its report to the Office of Space Science on November 30, the day it was due.

From a technical standpoint the committee found that Ranger was too much like Mariner—that conceptually it was "not optimum for lunar missions" and was actually so complicated for its mission that it demanded an unnecessarily "high order of engineering skill and fabrication technology." In other words, while JPL had ostensibly designed Ranger to go to the Moon, its fixation with the Mariner interplanetary program had affected Ranger to the point of making it more complicated than it needed to be to fulfill its basic mission. Ranger had been overdesigned.

But even given that, the Kelley report went on, the level of sophistication and complexity that JPL was trying to attain required a degree of engineering excellence and craftsmanship that was lacking.

The report went on to cite "many potentially unreliable areas associated with design, choice of components, implementation and processes." It warned of weaknesses "so extensive that in combination they suggest that the present hardware comprising RA-6 [Ranger 6] through 9 . . . is unlikely to perform successfully." It singled out sterilization as a likely cause of trouble. And it called not for increased testing and replacement of parts for a "marginal design" but for a wholly redesigned spacecraft.

And the reason for the miasma at JPL, the panel concluded, was slipshod management. In a stinging indictment that clearly alluded to the old Army Ordnance days, the report charged JPL with having a "shoot and hope" attitude, "i.e., shoot enough and hope that sooner or later one of a series will indeed work." As an example, the panel found a damning passage from the Ranger 4 Information Plan and quoted it verbatim: "Since the likelihood of achieving complete mission success, i.e., that all mission objectives will be met, are relatively remote, the public information plan should be flexible enough to allow emphasis to be placed on a successful experiment." This was telling for two reasons. First, irrespective of the engineers' and managers' outward cockiness, there was an undercurrent at JPL that took initial failure for granted—a presumption that nothing would work satisfactorily the first time. Why, then, strive for it? Second, there was an unwillingness to assume public responsibility for serious problems, and instead a reliance on PR to put the best possible face on the situation. Emphasizing that one experiment succeeded even though the overall mission failed was like boasting that an airplane being tested had successfully recovered from a stall even though it had crashed for other reasons.

The report concluded with several recommendations, chief among them being that Ranger management be streamlined and simplified. It also suggested that mission objectives be clarified in support of Apollo; that either the Air Force or NASA be made responsible for the Atlas-Agena, but not both; that sterilization be abandoned immediately; that extensive modification, redesign, and testing be undertaken; and that an industrial contractor be used to make, integrate, and test all Rangers beginning with the tenth.

While JPL's own board of inquiry also found problems with the design and manufacture of the Rangers, it understandably viewed the overall situation from a different perspective. It found that the Rangers had been so limited by their weight, and so packed with experiments, that there was not sufficient room for the kind of redundant systems that could have taken over when primary systems malfunctioned. To its credit, the JPL report, too, pointed to management problems, though by implication more as a result of external factors than indigenous ones. It complained that design and integration errors were compounded by personnel turnover, by engineers who were often inexperienced, and by section chiefs who were unfamiliar with either the management of the project or with the exact nature of the subsystems they were supposed to furnish. That situation, the report asserted, left the functioning of the lab's spacecraft "heavily dependent on the inspiration, skill, and attention of individual cognizant engineers." Burke's constant push for adherence to tight schedules, the amount of time he had to spend negotiating science experiments, matters relating to the launch vehicles and their operation, and other aspects of the problem involving both Headquarters and the Air Force, were also aired.

The document ended by calling for a thorough review of the Ranger design, as well as for the introduction of new procedures for inspection, testing, and management. It also suggested that a revised schedule of operations be adopted and that the flight of Ranger 6 be abandoned. Instead of flying No. 6 to the Moon, the report said, it ought to be used as a test vehicle to evaluate the overall Ranger design.

Unless "specific and forceful action" was taken, the JPL report warned, Ranger 6 and those coming after it could be expected to meet the same fate as their predecessors. Here, JPL's finding and that of the Kelley panel were in absolute accord: unless radical measures were taken to avert it, more trouble was coming. More trouble was indeed coming.

5.

Beauty and the Beast: Mariner-Venus and the Great Galactic Ghoul

Mariner 1, America's first interplanetary spacecraft, was supposed to go to Venus. Instead, it went to the bottom of the Atlantic Ocean because of an error in punctuation.

NASA's abortive interplanetary debut took place at Cape Canaveral at a little after 4:00 A.M. on a steamy night, July 22, 1962. It happened in full view of Oran Nicks, an aide, and two congressmen who watched the launch and the ensuing explosion from the roof of the blockhouse of Mercury Launch Complex 14, a mile away. As NASA's director of Lunar and Planetary Programs, and therefore the senior space agency official present, Nicks had won the job of guiding the congressmen, James Fulton of Pennsylvania and Joseph E. Karth of Minnesota, through the launch's complicated and dramatic choreography.

Mariner 1 had the dubious distinction of extending NASA's calamitous record in the lunar program to the inauguration of the planetary program as well. JPL's first interplanetary probe thereby took its place beside its sisters in the space exploration program's hall of infamy. Indeed, except for continuing satellite programs, such as the Explorers, the Tiros weather observers, the Echo communication series, OSO-1, the Orbiting Solar Observatory that was developed at Goddard to collect data on solar flares, and a handful of other Earth-huggers, the only good news came from the manned program. That February, John Glenn had become the first American to orbit Earth, followed in May by Scott Carpenter. But all efforts to get a successful mission to the Moon, and now to Venus, had ended disastrously. And Mariner 1's loss was all the more galling because it happened not as the result of a seizure or some other catastrophic event that occurred deep within the Atlas-Agena's fiery bowels but for want of a simple punctuation mark—a hyphen.

The idea of striking out for the planets—of sending Mariners to Venus and then to Mars—had been the subject of a detailed briefing given to Glennan by JPL's Robert Parks in July 1960. Parks was JPL's lunar and planetary director. It was his job to carry the fire from Pasadena to Washington, to convince the administrator that flying beyond the Moon and going for both of Earth's neighboring planets was not only feasible but smart. This was not difficult, since the planetary missions had been high on NASA's agenda since the agency's inception. They had even been named Mariner two months earlier.

Parks had wasted no time in getting down to basics. He had begun by explaining to Glennan that it was too late to go for Mars later that year or for Venus early in 1961, since the space agency was not yet in a position to take advantage of the launch windows because of the continuing imbroglio over the upper stages.* But, he had added enthusiastically, there remained "exactly five opportunities to fire at Venus and four to fire at Mars" before the end of the decade. A sound ten-year plan would call for doing flybys—streaking past the planets at relatively close range with the sensors going—followed by orbital reconnaissance and then landings on both Venus and Mars. Ideally, Parks had added, Centaurs would be used through 1964 and von Braun's gigantic Saturn boosters thereafter. Since landers needed powerful retrorockets to slow them down during descent, they were necessarily heavier than orbiters, which merely circled, and they would therefore need the immensely powerful Saturns. In

---

*Lunar and planetary missions are the captives of so-called launch windows, the period during which the probe must be sent on its way if it is to reach its destination and complete its mission. The primary factor determining the window is the position of the Moon or the target planet relative to Earth. In the case of the Moon, the permissible launch period lasts for about six days a month, but only during certain periods, decreasing from about two and a half hours to about one and a half hours during those days. Lunar missions cannot be launched during either a new moon or a full moon, for example, because the Sun's position relative to the Earth does not permit a spacecraft's sensors to orient properly. The Sun is behind a new moon relative to Earth, while Earth comes between the Sun and the Moon during a full moon. Both situations mean that Earth, Moon, and Sun are essentially in a straight line, depriving the spacecraft's sensors of the angles they need to set navigational fixes. Communication is another factor, since the closer a planet is to the Sun as seen from Earth, the more radio interference there is. Pioneer 10's window for Jupiter had to be set so that it would not arrive there more than seven hundred days after launch, for example, to avoid proximity to the Sun. Other considerations include not straining the ground support system, because other missions are operating at the same time, and selecting the correct angles or the positions of particular areas of the target planet for the optimal operation of certain of the spacecraft's sensors. The upper stage's thrust is of extreme importance where windows are concerned because the more power it has, the more flexibility there is in planning the time of launch.

any case, Parks had warned, the preliminary planetary exploration missions would depend on the availability of the troublesome Centaur and, of course, on adequate funding.

Centaur would indeed prove to be as troublesome during actual tests as it had been in the design stage. During the first test of its two engines together that November of 1960, one fired when it wasn't supposed to, exploding liquid hydrogen in the other. This happened twice more before the ignition problem was solved. In the meantime, however, the upper stage's lifting capacity was downgraded. The engineers were disgruntled by this. While the Rangers were the packet boats of space, the Mariners were supposed to be the transoceanic liners, so they either had to go to space on Centaurs or be downgraded in weight and therefore in carrying capacity.

Mariner, like Ranger, was designed in blocks; that is, for serial production. The first block, which was supposed to ride on Centaur, consisted of two series: Mariner A and Mariner B. In addition, JPL also came up with a more modest Mariner probe, a relatively puny one that combined Ranger and Mariner A. Its chief and perhaps only asset was that it was light enough to get to Venus on an Atlas-Agena. The runt was shelved at the time Parks pitched Glennan about Venus and Mars, however, because NASA still believed that it was going to get Centaur on time.

The Mariner A series, which was funded for $11 million in 1961, consisted of three distinct spacecraft that were supposed to fly by Venus in 1962, 1964, and 1965 to measure the planet's surface temperatures and magnetosphere, and examine its atmosphere.

The B model was even more ambitious. It was to consist of a split capsule that would come apart at encounter, with the main part sailing by the planet and the smaller part, a passive probe, dropping down to make measurements before impacting on the target planets, Mars and Venus. And Mariner B, the more complex of the two, was itself to be the forerunner of the even more ambitious series, called Voyagers, that were supposed to begin exploring Venus or Mars in 1964. These highly advanced craft were to start by carrying soft-landers and then become progressively larger and more sophisticated until they hauled mechanized rovers to not only land on those planets but crawl over either or both of them.

Taken in conjunction with the Ranger, Lunar Orbiter, and Surveyor programs, the Mariner and then the Voyager flights represented a reasonably cohesive, carefully thought-out progression of missions in which the exploring craft would grow in size and complexity in order to collect increasingly sophisticated data from places that were ever more distant. That, at least, was the plan.

But by mid-August 1961 it was apparent that Centaur would not be ready for a 1962 launch to Venus or to anywhere else, for that matter. Plans to build the lightweight spacecraft were therefore hurriedly dusted off. Because most of the bastard spacecraft derived from the Moon probe itself, it was arbitrarily named Mariner R (for Ranger).

What made Headquarters particularly responsive to the notion of getting Mariner R into space whatever compromise it represented was the fact that a week before, on August 6–7, 1961, Gherman Titov had orbited Earth seventeen times in Vostok 2. Virgil I. Grissom, his American counterpart, had been able to fly only a suborbital mission on July 21. And even that had ended ingloriously when Grissom's Mercury capsule flooded after its hatch blew off during its ocean landing. The capsule, Liberty Bell 7, sank like a rock. Under those circumstances, NASA very badly wanted to beat the Soviets to the planets by firing at Venus, the closest of them, even with a stripped-down probe if that was what it took to get there. Accordingly, it was decided on August 30 to kill Mariner A, ready Mariner B for a Centaur launch at either Mars or Venus in 1964, and approve Mariner R for a quick shot at Venus in 1962.

So JPL began working furiously on Mariner R in the autumn of 1961 with Jack James, the veteran of the Corporal and Sergeant era, as project manager. James formalized the relationship between JPL's technical divisions—propulsion, guidance, and navigation, for example—and the project engineers who worked specifically on Mariner R. This had the effect of providing real support for the project people. Unlike what all too often happened in the Ranger program, they didn't have to grope for ad hoc solutions in isolation from those on lab who could help them. (The Mariner team was mindful that by November 18 both Rangers 1 and 2 had failed.)

Meanwhile, James worked with Lockheed to sweat one hundred pounds off the Agena B upper stage. At the same time he pushed his own engineers to cut the probe itself to the bone. Mariner-Venus would carry only six experiments weighing a total of forty-one pounds, and they would be relatively simple: a compromise, as one report put it, between what the scientists would have liked and what was technologically possible. There would be a microwave radiometer to take Venus's surface temperature and an infrared radiometer to measure thermal energy in its atmosphere, as well as instruments to measure the magnetosphere, charged-particle bombardment, the spectrum of the solar corona, and the density of the micrometeorites that hit the spacecraft itself.

The space agency, and certainly the always competitive Jet Propulsion Laboratory, were reduced to taking a leaf from the Soviets, book—The Russians produced essentially simple spacecraft on assembly lines and modified them for particular tasks. Mariner R didn't have to be a genius—it just had to fly close enough to Venus so the United States could claim to have gotten there first. That alone would be worth the probe's nearly $14 million price tag.

And so it was that the first Mariner R, now called Mariner 1, rose on top of an Atlas-Agena B in the predawn darkness at Cape Canaveral on July 22, 1962. Nicks, Karth, Fulton, and a NASA protocol officer named Bob Johnson watched from the top of the blockhouse less than a mile away as the launch vehicle and its upper stage cleared the tower with a thunderous roar and a light that almost seemed to turn night into day.

Elsewhere at the Cape, clusters of engineers and technicians sat secure inside their own blockhouses and within Hangar AE, monitoring the vital signs—voltages, temperatures, pressures, fuel flow rate, guidance systems—that came from the Atlas, the Agena, and the fragile spacecraft that was bolted inside the Agena's shroud. Those deep within the blockhouses better understood what was actually happening inside the Atlas-Agena-Mariner because their equipment was plugged into the system's various components the way a galvanometer's sensors pick up minute electrical changes in heart muscle to produce an electrocardiogram.

But, as Nicks explained, those who were hidden safely behind the reinforced concrete "could not glory in the smoke and flame of a launch" the way the four lone figures could on top of Complex 14's blockhouse. The engineers and technicians who sat deep inside the bunkers were safer than Nicks and the others, to be sure, but they were also deprived of the visceral thrill that came only when there was no barrier between their primal senses and the thundering monolith they shot at the sky. Night launches were especially dramatic. The lengthening stream of white fire, the expanding wall of back-lighted smoke, and a roar so deep that it made earth and water quake contrasted all the more starkly with the ethereal darkness and quiet that cloak the Banana River and the surrounding swamps before the giant comes to life and after it has gone.

Mariner 1 lasted a little less than five minutes. No sooner had it

begun to gather momentum after clearing the tower than its telemetry told the technicians in the bunkers that it was veering off course
and going out of control. Rather than endanger shipping and perhaps even the lives of people in communities around the space center, procedure called for the errant rocket to be blown to bits. A
range safety officer therefore pressed a destruct button on the console in front of him that sent a signal setting off explosive charges
secreted inside the Atlas.

The gleaming stainless-steel cylinder blew up on command, sending a shower of burning liquid oxygen and kerosene, encoders, actua-
tors, recorders, controls, gyros, gas manifolds and jets, the Earth,
Sun, and Canopus detectors, pumps, sensors, solar panels, combustion chambers, nozzles, igniters, injectors, pressure regulators, control valves, computers, vernier motors, antennas, transmitters,
transponders, the hexagonal bus, six separate instrument packages,
a labyrinth of tubes, pipes, wires and electrical tape, circuit breakers
and switches, and other brand-new junk, including more than two
hundred thousand pounds of torn and scorched sheet metal, some of
it no thicker than a beer can's, plummeting into the sea.

Nicks and the others watched incredulously as the explosion
turned the rocket and its fragile cargo into a pyrotechnic display of
burning shrapnel high in the blackness over the Atlantic. They kept
watching grimly as all of the debris rained down, some of it clearly
silhouetted in the glow from the blast, and then disappeared into the
murky darkness just to the east of the cape. Later, Orin Nicks was
moved to eulogize Mariner 1 in the opening lines of his memoir: "Our
friend died violently at 4:26 A.M. on a hot July night. Her finish was
spectacular; she was trapped amid the flaming wreckage of an explosion that lit the night sky. Four of us watched helplessly, standing
together at a site that gave us a perfect view. . . . We were soon to
learn that she had been blown up intentionally by a man with no
firsthand knowledge of her ability and promise. My emotion changed
from disappointment to bitterness when I learned that she was destroyed barely seconds before flying beyond his reach."

A postmortem showed that two separate malfunctions, neither of
which in itself would have been catastrophic, combined to end the
first shot at another planet almost as soon as it got off the ground.
The Atlas was steered by a signal from Canaveral that it picked up
with its guidance antenna. But the antenna on this particular Atlas
performed poorly, so the guidance signal came in imprecisely and
noisily, like an overwrought shout.

Yet that problem had been anticipated. In the event the external steering commands were degraded or lost, the Atlas's onboard guidance computer was supposed to take over and automatically control steering with its own stored program, much the way an autopilot controls the flight of an airplane. When the computer cut into the steering sequence, however, a second malfunction, otherwise pitifully trivial, developed to seal Mariner 1's fate. A hyphen had somehow been dropped from the guidance program that was loaded into the computer. Because of this, the program commanded the Atlas to veer left and nose down. This created a pronounced wobble that was taken by the range safety officer to be potentially life-threatening and which therefore ended with the huge explosion. Counting what by then were four successive Ranger failures, JPL's lunar and planetary exploration effort that summer of 1962 stood at 0 for 5.

But the opposition, also straining hard to reach the planets, was doing no better. The Soviet Union had taken its first shot at Venus on February 4, 1961, with Sputnik 7, which was sent into a relatively low parking orbit preparatory to being redirected toward the cloud-shrouded planet. But Earth orbit was as far as Sputnik 7 had gotten. A malfunction had sent both the probe and its booster back down into the atmosphere, where they burned up twenty-two days later.

Meanwhile, Venera 1, launched on February 12, had gone beyond its parking orbit to become the first spacecraft that was actually aimed at Venus. Typically, the probe had been heavy—1,416 pounds—which testified yet again to the lifting power of Soviet launch vehicles and upper stages. It had carried a magnetometer to study the Venutian magnetic field, a variometer to sample magnetic fields en route, and a charged-particle trap to measure ion density. The quality of the rocketry had been satisfactory and the scientific instruments, while rudimentary, had probably been capable enough.

But Venera 1 soon became a victim of a communication problem that not only sealed its fate but was to prove to be the most nettlesome aspect of the USSR's entire deep space program. The radio link to the probe had failed fifteen days after launch, at a distance of some fourteen million miles from Earth, and could not be reestablished. So desperate had the compulsively secretive Soviets been to reacquire communication with their muted spacecraft that they had even sought help from the Jodrell Bank observatory, outside Manchester, England, which operated the huge radio telescope. But it had been for naught. The probe had missed its target by about sixty

thousand miles in mid-May and had then continued on, incom-
municado, toward the Sun.

The next three Soviet attempts to reach Venus, all assiduously
cloaked in secrecy, had come in rapid succession on August 25, September 1, and September 12. Having been embarrassed by Venera,
the Soviets evidently had concluded that it was wiser to announce
risky missions only after success had been achieved, thereby limiting public relations damage. All three spacecraft had failed to make
it beyond Earth orbit.*

As it was to turn out, thirteen successive attempts to reach Venus
would go awry between February 4, 1961, and November 23, 1965,
because of launch failures, communication breakdowns, or inability
to get beyond Earth orbit. The furious launch rate reflected a determination to extend Soviet domination of lunar exploration to the
near planets as well. But the overwhelming influence the Soviets
sought would prove to be elusive.

The spate of Soviet failures at Venus (as well as Mars) during the
1960s and afterward, plus less severe problems experienced by some
U.S. spacecraft that passed in those environs, eventually led to the
conclusion that the mishaps were the work of an evil presence that
lived in deep space. The presence (or whatever it was) would first be
described by Donald Neff, who covered the space program for *Time*
magazine. He would proclaim that there was a force in deep space
that harbored nothing but ill-will for the emissaries from Earth and
kept trying to do them in, often with devastating results.

Neff saw that the Mariner 7 flight to Mars in July 1969, like many
of its ill-fated predecessors, was beset by a succession of unexplained
accidents. The probe would suddenly and mysteriously go dead en
route, for example, uttering not a bit of telemetry regarding its state
of health or its whereabouts. Seven hours later it would revive just
as mysteriously, though on a slightly different course and with its
telemetry reduced to a halting whisper. What better way to explain
the seemingly inexplicable than by applying some wit to conjure up
a mythical phenomenon that played havoc with even the most bril-

*The fact that a Venus window existed at that time and that the spacecraft were seen
to be in orbits precisely suited to a Venus mission made Soviet acknowledgment all
but superfluous. By the summer and fall of 1962 a wide variety of earth satellites doing
specific missions—reconnaissance, weather observation, navigation, communication,
and many scientific investigations—had been placed in highly specific orbits that
were chosen because they exactly suited the objectives of the particular mission. All
such orbits, in addition to optimal parking orbits for specific planetary probes, were
categorized by the Air Force, which tracked everything and still does.

liant of earthly designs? The malevolent presence, a remorselessly implacable bane of every astronautical engineer and deep space manager on Earth, was named the Great Galactic Ghoul by the imaginative reporter, and the name stuck.

The evil entity was readily embraced by the space exploration fraternity, and particularly by engineers at JPL (where its portrait hung in mute testimony to the fear it inspired), as a handy way of explaining otherwise unaccountable major glitches. The Ghoul was envisioned by some as being the equivalent of the Bermuda Triangle: an amorphous tract of space or a translucent amoebalike creature millions of miles wide into which probes disappeared forever. But others, including its portraitist, envisioned an androgynous creature of immense proportions (invisible on radar, of course, making it the first stealth monster) that clutched deep space probes the way King Kong held the biplane on top of the Empire State Building, whimsically bedeviled their navigation and communication equipment, or simply devoured them as though they were hors d'oeuvres. The Ghoul's nature may have been in the mind of the beholder, but one thing was virtually certain: it seemed to have it in for Communist spacecraft in particular.

Mariner 2 (or R-2), a near-carbon copy of Mariner 1, managed to make it past the Ghoul and into the history books. It blasted off from Cape Canaveral's Launch Complex 12 at 2:53 A.M. on August 27, 1962, on top of another Atlas-Agena B. But it didn't leave Earth without first rattling the inhabitants of the bunkers.

One of the Atlas's small vernier steering rockets stuck in an extreme position shortly after liftoff, causing the big booster to rotate one revolution a minute as it lifted the Agena and the probe high over Canaveral. For a long moment it looked as though Mariner 2 was going to join its sister under water. But the problem was overcome right after separation. The Agena's own guidance system suppressed the spin it inherited from the Atlas and stabilized itself. It then carried Mariner 2 to a parking orbit, where both remained for thirteen minutes before a final blast from the Agena's own rocket sent the probe on its way.

Mariner 2 dutifully unfolded and spread its solar panels, primed its dish-shaped high-gain antenna, found the Sun and Earth with its guidance sensors, stabilized on all three of its axes, and executed a perfect midcourse correction. It then continued its mission to Venus, sailing to within twenty-one thousand miles of the second planet— well within the limits of its instruments—on December 14, 1962.

Even as it sped toward Venus, Mariner 2 sent back a stream of data on the interplanetary magnetic field, solar plasma and radiation levels, and the amount of cosmic dust in the space between the two planets. Although the measurements provided few surprises, the unprecedented amount of information returned by the 446-pound spacecraft as it actually sailed through the interplanetary medium confirmed firsthand what had only been theorized before.

The nation's inaugural planetary probe bore out the fact that solar plasma flowing from the Sun formed a solar wind that radiated out toward the end of the solar system itself. The cosmic dust experiment, designed to register hits by dust particles, complemented similar experiments that had been done aboard Pioneer 1 and any number of satellites circling Earth. Whereas only two "definite hits" were registered on Mariner 2's detection plate during its four-month voyage, a hundred times as many hits had been recorded four years earlier as Pioneer 1 fell back to Earth after its abortive shot at the Moon. Even several of the Explorer satellites had registered hits in the many thousands. This lent credence to the theory that meteorites once impacted on the Moon with such force that debris in the form of dust was thrown up and caught in the gravitational fields of both bodies.

Total encounter time at Venus was a mere forty-two minutes. But the data return was out of all proportion to the duration of the flyby itself. The first scanning of another planet by an Earth robot showed Venus's temperature to be roughly the same on its light side, dark side, and terminator (the area dividing the two): some 800 degrees Fahrenheit, or about twice as hot as had been predicted. This indicated that the planet's temperature was evened out by its thick layer of clouds. For the most part, however, Mariner 2 confirmed observations made from Earth rather than finding unexpected phenomena. Perhaps most frustrating, there was no way for Mariner 2's camera to penetrate the thick clouds that perpetually shrouded the entire planet. Piercing the clouds would have to wait for probes that carried radar.

In common with any number of other astronomy books, one published in 1940 flirted with the possibility of life on other planets, including Venus. "One of the recent discoveries of astronomy," the authors quite properly noted, "has been that there are large quantities of carbon dioxide in the atmosphere of Venus." But then they undertook some tantalizing speculation. The carbon dioxide, they explained, "may have some bearing on the question whether or not there is life on this planet," adding that "both plants and animals give off carbon dioxide in the process of respiration." While the vast majority of astronomers lent no real credence to the possibility of life on Venus, no one would be able to say for certain that plants or animals of some species were not respiring in the blistering heat under all those thick clouds until spacecraft from Earth came to see for themselves.

Mariner 2's scientific return, while a respectable start, paled in comparison to its achievements in the areas of astronautics and politics. The mission established the fact that a spacecraft could be sent to a neighboring planet with accuracy. Furthermore, it proved that a probe could collect and transmit data and respond to commands over a distance of fifty-four million miles. Finally, Mariner 2's journey to Venus gave the United States a victory in deep space. It was a triumph that partly—but only partly—lessened the despair that was growing with each attempt to get Ranger to the Moon.

The Soviets' unbroken string of failures to get to Venus, starting in 1961, would come to an end only on the fourteenth try when Venera 4, launched on June 12, 1967, reached Venus four months later. It dropped a spherical descent capsule, about a yard in diameter, to test the planet's atmosphere. The probe's carrier bus contained its own instruments, including a magnetometer, cosmic ray counters, charged-particle traps, and ultraviolet radiation detectors to sample for hydrogen and oxygen. The bus released its descent capsule and then made its own measurements as it plunged to destruction on impact with the blisteringly hot planet.

Judged by the results of the mission, Venera 4 was a notable success; judged as a contestant in a race with the United States, it was nearly five years late making it to the finish line. And the fact that twenty months passed between either of the two previous missions—Venera 3, which suffered a communication failure in November 1965 and Cosmos 167, which turned into a cinder after reentering Earth's atmosphere in June 1967—suggests that the Soviet interplanetary program was undergoing the same exhaustive self-examination, born of repeated, frustrating failure that the American lunar program had gone through a few years earlier.

All the world marveled at the data returned by the first interplanetary spacecraft to leave Earth and complete a mission. Mariner 2's twenty-one and a half photographs provided the first close-up glimpse of another world. What was not generally known, however, was that the power used to send the pictures home, as well as all of the other data, was less than that required to light the little bulb in the average refrigerator. In the case of Mariner 2, it was three and a half watts; more typically, later missions would transmit at power levels of ten to twenty watts. Such a feat was only possible because of a highly integrated communication system on Earth that consisted of huge antennas strung around the planet not only to communicate with the probes but to fix their positions with extreme precision.

The fact that data could be relayed to Earth on such low power levels depended largely on the antennas being pointed exactly at the transmission source—the probe itself. And that, in turn, depended on the spacecraft's continuously sending a signal to the antennas to help them keep their lock on it. In this way, and like so many other aspects of the engineering of space missions, one role of a system—tracking—was essential for the performance of another—communication—and vice versa.

The system through which tracking and communication are accomplished is called the Deep Space Network, or DSN. Its roots go back to March 1958, when the Advanced Research Projects Agency determined to send the first, small Pioneers to the Moon and set a requirement for a tracking system to keep tabs on them. ARPA's need to develop a system to follow the whereabouts of things that flew in space soon evolved into two separate tracking and data acquisition networks. One of them would handle missile tests such as those in the Corporal, Sergeant, and long-range ballistic missile programs, plus Earth satellites such as the Explorers. The other network would be assigned to the Pioneers and other deep space probes that everyone in NASA and in the Pentagon knew were coming.

The network for missiles and satellites was called Microlock. The other was the first operational deep space tracking and communication facility. It was at first given one of those severely strained acronyms for which the federal government and its industrial contractors have become notorious: TRACE (Tracking and Communication, Extraterrestrial). TRACE was in turn part of a larger network called the Deep Space Instrumentation Facility, which itself was soon given its final name: the Deep Space Network. The system's antennas were hastily erected at Cape Canaveral, at Mayagüez, Puerto Rico, and at Goldstone, California, to support the Pioneer Moon shots and the Echo communication satellite program.

TRACE was a primitive network having a number of drawbacks, perhaps the worst of which was that it did not span the globe. This meant that spacecraft could not be kept under surveillance around the clock, but only when they were in sight of the Western Hemisphere. Obviously, that wouldn't do. Total, constant coverage of everything that went into deep space was a pressing requirement. Spacecraft, whether Earth-huggers or probes headed for distant planets, were inherently stupid (until relatively recently), whatever the quality of their onboard programs. Most therefore needed constant attention, or at least attention at regular, closely spaced intervals. This is called housekeeping. They also needed precise, unbroken tracking, and only a global system of antennas could do that. In addition, antennas that girdled Earth also provided a constant downlink capability. The stream of data coming back from space could flow more smoothly and efficiently, in other words, because it would not be obscured by blackouts.

It was therefore decided to build three large parabolic antennas, roughly equidistant at intervals of 120 degrees around Earth, so that every space probe would always be within straight-line range of one of them. By the time Mariner 2 was shot at Venus in 1962, eighty-five-foot-wide parabolic dish antennas and supporting equipment, including sensitive receivers and powerful radio transmitters, had been set up at Goldstone; Woomera, Australia; and Johannesburg, South Africa. Goldstone was to become the DSN's crown jewel. It was situated in a natural bowl, rimmed by hills, on a dry lake on the Army's Fort Irwin reservation in the Mojave Desert, just on the other side of the mountains from Pasadena.

There were then, as there are today, three fundamental tasks assigned to the Deep Space Network. It is supposed to keep precise track of spacecraft. It also must receive their telemetry, or the downlink signals that carry the data they collect and the reports they send describing their condition. Finally, it provides the uplink capability by which they are sent commands, or computer "loads," for maneuvering or reprogramming their data collection systems to suit changed circumstances.

The three field stations were in turn fitted into an elaborate network of other tracking facilities, military as well as civilian, which were scattered around the world, plus a real-time or near-real-time radio relay system that was interconnected and used for exchanging commands or information.

The nerve center for this far-flung and immensely complicated enterprise was the Space Flight Operations Center at JPL, where the members of a mission team followed their spacecraft's progress, communicated with it, and received its data. Since the SFOC was not completed until October 1963, Mariner 2's operation was handled at JPL's Central Computing Facility and its Communications Center. But two months after the SFOC opened for business, the Deep Space Network was officially established as a separate directorate at JPL.

The DSN's role in the Mariner 2 mission to Venus bears brief mention because of its historical significance and also because it shows the rudiments of what would soon become much more complex undertakings.

As the Atlas-Agena B carrying Mariner 2 lifted off from Canaveral in the dead of night on August 27, tracking antennas at the launch site itself followed it into the sky. By eight minutes eleven seconds into the flight, the Atlas had fallen away and the Agena B was arcing over the Caribbean and heading for the southern tip of Africa, its engine temporarily turned off to put it into a parking orbit. At that moment it was being tracked by antennas at San Salvador, Antigua, and Ascension. At twenty-four and a half minutes, the Agena's engine was reignited. Ninety seconds after that, it was put into the slingshot trajectory that began its true route to Venus.

Johannesburg's—"Joburg's"—eighty-five-foot antenna picked up Mariner 2 a little more than thirty minutes after launch. Nineteen minutes later, Woomera's big dish heard it, too. The Australians lost the spacecraft at six hours fifteen minutes forty-three seconds after launch. But seven hours later—at thirteen hours nineteen minutes and one second after its departure from the Florida coast (to be almost as precise as the equipment that did the tracking)—Goldstone acquired it.

As Mariner 2 streaked out into deep space, the DSN's eighty-five-foot antennas continued to track it and feed back to JPL a stream of precise data on its position. Calculations showed that the probe was going to miss Venus by 233,000 miles. That was too great a distance for the experiments planned for close encounter to work. A course change was therefore necessary.

Accordingly, nine days after launch, midcourse maneuvering commands punched on tape were fed into the encoder at Goldstone, transmitted to Mariner 2, picked up by its command antenna, and then relayed to its own decoder-receiver and computer-sequencer. While the spacecraft was still only a million and a half miles from Earth, its own primitive computer turned on the tiny maneuvering thrusters for three hours and forty-five minutes, swinging the probe ever so gradually into a new trajectory. Soon the antennas on Earth showed that Mariner 2 was indeed on its way to an acceptably close encounter. The same antennas also pulled in the data that the spacecraft sent back during its approach to Venus and throughout its brief flyby. After encounter it went into orbit around the Sun. On January 4, 1963, when it was fifty-four million miles from home, Mariner 2, its job done, fell silent forever.

Deep Space Network operations, like all others having to do with communication over the vast distances of space, are subject to the restrictions of something called the Inverse Square Law. Everybody in the space business knows about the law, which has it that the communication power required to maintain contact between Earth and the spacecraft varies inversely to the square of the distance between the transmitter and the receiver. All this means is that as distance is doubled, four times as much power is needed to keep up communication.

Peter T. Lyman, JPL's deputy director, likened communication signals between a spacecraft and Earth to the light bulb in a refrigerator. "As you double your distance from the light bulb, you only get one fourth the amount of light," Lyman explained. "If you double it again, you only get one fourth of that. So as you move away, you rapidly receive a weaker and weaker signal. You really have to have a lot of power and a big antenna on the spacecraft, or a big antenna—a very sensitive big antenna—on the ground."

The size of a probe's antenna is limited by the size of the upper stage's shroud. Most antennas, including those on Mariner spacecraft and the majority of those that came after them, were bowl-shaped, rigid, and extraordinarily small, given what was expected of them. Mariner 2's antenna, for example, measured a mere four feet across.* It was therefore imperative that they be aimed back home with extreme precision: on the order of a tenth to a twentieth of a degree over distances that could stretch into billions of miles. But however carefully they were pointed, their diminutive size severely constrained them. The difference therefore had to be made up on the ground.

*Galileo, the problem-plagued probe that went to Jupiter in October 1989, on the other hand, was crowned with a large mesh antenna that popped open like a beach umbrella once it was on its way. The fact that it could be unfurled allowed it to measure fifteen and a half feet across. Galileo's antenna or any other that is more than twelve feet across could transmit back to Earth from the edge of the solar system on a mere twenty watts of power provided it was precisely aimed, according to Lyman, in an interview with the author.

The signal that radiates from a probe is sent out in a narrow cone. By the time it reaches Earth it is spread over an almost unimaginably large area. What hits the planet and is picked up by the DSN's or other huge antennas is therefore a tiny fraction of the signal. Weak to begin with, that signal is further reduced to the barest whisper. "The idea is to build the antenna big enough, accurate enough, and have sensitive enough receivers so that the energy you receive is sufficient to recover the information," Lyman continued.

He likened the problem of communicating over the increasingly long distances in deep space to trying to do so in a similar situation at a cocktail party. "When you're the first two people at a cocktail party, in the room by yourselves, you talk very quietly. It's easy," Lyman explained. "But as more and more people come it gets noisier. And you get separated farther and farther apart. If you're still trying to communicate, you have to talk louder and louder. You've got to shout with a megaphone. You've got to cup your ears; that's the antenna listening. And pretty soon you've got to talk slower because if you talk fast the noise is going to interfere more. If you talk slowly you have a better chance to get through the noise. Pretty soon you say words twice, as they do in the military, because some of the words will get hit with some other noise burst. We say things twice, too. We code our data so we can lose some of it and still recover."

Perhaps the biggest technological leap in the history of the Deep Space Network, and certainly the most visually dramatic, was the sixty-four-meter dish antenna at Goldstone. Construction of the DSN's premier monster antenna, which was originally called the Advanced Antenna System, or the Mars Dish, began in October 1963. It became fully operational in May 1966 and was duplicated in 1973 outside Canberra and Madrid.* While by no means the largest radio telescope in the world,† the 210-foot steerable paraboloid dish at Goldstone and its two sisters remain the biggest in NASA's deep space system and also the most imposing. The antenna's alidade— the framework of steel girders supporting the dish itself—weighs

---

*The Johannesburg site was abandoned because of South Africa's potentially tumultuous situation and because of NASA's sensitivity to the adverse public relations impact of maintaining a major segment of its communication and tracking system in the land of apartheid.
†The world's largest radio telescope is the twenty-acre dish at Arecibo, Puerto Rico. Its platform and subreflector—the unit that collects signals from the huge dish and focuses them for analysis—itself weighs more than six hundred tons and hangs from cables that extend from three towers, each of which is higher than the Washington Monument.

more than two million pounds; the whole structure, including its massive concrete pedestal, weighs about fifteen million.

"The first time I ever saw the Goldstone DSS-14—the sixty-four-meter dish—we drove out and were waaaaay far away. You could see it from the road. I thought, It don't look that goddamned big," Bobby Brooks, the sequence integration engineer at JPL, recalled. Brooks is known around the lab as its aging hippie because of his motorcycle, ponytail, penchant for black T-shirts that often carry graphic messages, and his otherwise nonconformist life-style. But he is also known as an expert at integrating the sequence of experiments that spacecraft do during encounters, as well as for the time he spends visiting schools to tell children about the space program. But Bobby Brooks is probably best known among his own coterie for the often vivid, earthy descriptions of things he himself encounters. "But we were real far away and I didn't know it. Then we got closer and closer and closer, and finally we walked right up to it. And it was so big," he said, pausing, "that it just didn't even look three-dimensional. It looked like a big goddamned picture. It just blew me away, except

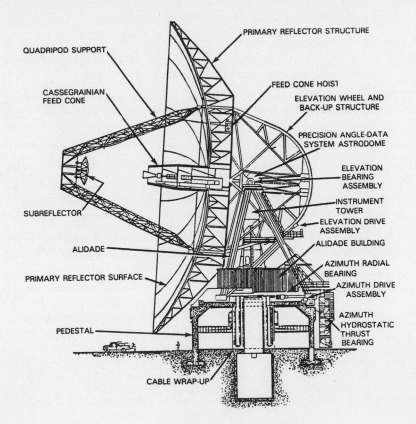

I knew it was real because we walked around on it," he added, still in wonder at the recollection.

The great gray ear upon which Brooks took his walk, a sluggish and obstinate contrivance from all appearances, can be pointed at a single tiny target across the solar system and beyond with an accuracy of 0.015 degree.

With Goldstone at its heart, the Deep Space Network steadily evolved throughout the 1960s, mostly in support of the accelerating Apollo Moon-landing program, but also for NASA's far-ranging space probes. Besides the 210-foot dishes, each of the three main stations was provided with two 111-foot dish antennas and one measuring eighty-five feet across. By the end of the decade, DSN Tracking Data and Acquisition Stations included dozens of lesser antennas measuring twenty-nine, forty-six, and eighty-five feet, plus a handful of relatively tiny ones. They literally spanned the globe.* In addition, eleven ships, a few of them belonging to the Department of Defense, also provided tracking and communication support for the space program.

The acquisition, tracking, and guidance of far-ranging spacecraft, together with the ability to receive and use the data they returned, depended squarely on an effective communication network on Earth—on how quickly and unambiguously data could be routed around the system. Nor was this a problem unique to the exploration of deep space. Tracking and communicating with Goddard's and other centers' fleet of navigation, weather, and communication satellites circling the planet, plus the spacecraft that were to take Americans to the Moon in incremental stages, also required the ability to stay in close touch all the time.

If scores of operations had to be integrated, which was always the

*The 210-foot dishes outside Madrid and Canberra became operational in 1973. Other dishes, a handful of which were dismantled before 1970, were built at Ahmedabad (India), Alaska, Antigua, Antofagasta (Chile), Ascension, Maryland, Brasilia, Canberra, Canton Island, Cape Canaveral and elsewhere in Florida, Carnavon (Australia), Cebreros (as well as other locations in Spain), Texas, Darwin (Australia) Minnesota, Puerto Rico, Georgia, Goldstone (which had four eighty-five-foot dishes and a few smaller ones, as well as the 210-foot giant) and other locations in California, Grand Bahama, Grand Canary, and Grand Turk islands, Guam, Guaymas (Mexico), Hawaii, Honeysuckle Creek (as well as other locations in Australia), Johannesburg and Pretoria, Kano (Nigeria), Kashima Machi (Japan), Hawaii, Kwajalein, Lima, Majunga (near Madagascar), Quito, North Carolina, Santiago, Singapore, Solant (South Atlantic), St. John's (Newfoundland), Tananarive (Malagasy Republic), Wake Island, Virginia, New Mexico, Winkfield (England), and Zanzibar. Some sites, such as Patrick Air Force Base in Florida, Point Arguello in California, and Pretoria, also supported Department of Defense operations. Finally, it might be mentioned that a station was opened in Havana in 1957 and moved two years later in anticipation of the revolution.

case, then communication links needed to be maintained not only with the spacecraft themselves but with other centers, stations, and outposts on Earth. A Space Tracking and Data Acquisition Network (STADAN) was therefore set up to handle the Earth satellites, while a Manned Space Flight Network was put in place for the Mercury missions and, it turned out, for Gemini as well. Together with JPL's Deep Space Network, they formed a comprehensive global acquisition and tracking system.

The idea from the outset was to keep the three networks elastic, not static, so that each could expand or contract as needs required while being mutually supportive. Twelve of the stations in the Manned Space Flight Network, for example, were co-located with either STADAN or DSN facilities or both.

Communication traffic between the various facilities in the three networks and whichever center they served was handled by state-of-the-art high-speed computers working in a data link system that used ordinary landline wires or cables, microwave facilities, under-ocean cables, or high-frequency radio circuits. The system stretched from Canaveral to Pretoria to Nairobi to Singapore to Adelaide to Honolulu to San Francisco to both Goddard, in Maryland, and JPL and back to Canaveral. While NASA did inherit bits and pieces of its far-flung tracking, acquisition, and communication empire from the various programs it was given in 1958, including the Army's and remnants of the Navy's Vanguard support system, it is fair to say that putting together and integrating such an extensive system by 1969 was a notable achievement.

But the DSN soon became a victim of its own success. As was true elsewhere in the space agency during the long prelude to the Apollo landings, the Deep Space Network was also pressed into service to support the manned program. This drew the ire of DSN managers and others at JPL who thought they had plenty of work to do without being held captive by Apollo. A Manned Space Flight Network had been set up specifically to support astronauts. By 1965, when the Apollo program was moving into its highest gear, the MSFN had nineteen land sites and assorted instrumented ships and planes to track Gemini and Apollo capsules. Yet the MSFN was only able to support relatively simple Earth orbit missions. There was no way it could effectively track two Apollo spacecraft—a command module and a lander—simultaneously.

It was therefore decided to get support from the Deep Space Network, even if doing so confounded JPL by overloading a system that was already straining to cope with a variety of planetary missions. Even NASA's own record of DSN involvement with the Apollo program calls the use of the system an intrusion (though a necessary one). The intrusion may have been irritating, but, all in all, it was a small price to pay for an expansion of activity that benefited science and exploration, even if it also benefited the manned program as well. The difference was a matter of degree.

The drive to send one astronaut at at time into Earth orbit in the Mercury capsules, followed by Kennedy's all-out push to land them in pairs on the Moon, placed the whole space program in sharp relief. Beginning with the first tentative answers to Sputnik, followed inexorably by the bold rhetoric about going to the Moon in full view of the world, and finally settling into stride against the quickening drumbeat of Apollo, space and everything associated with it had come to grip the nation's attention. The race to beat the Soviets to conquer the final frontier had become a national priority, if not a fixation. It was certainly ready fodder for a press that had a seemingly insatiable appetite for photo opportunities and patriotic tales of high adventure and the raw courage of those who, in the test pilots' jargon, pushed the outside of the envelope.

And while pushing the outside of the envelope involved nothing more dangerous than using the interoffice mail for most scientists and engineers in lunar and planetary exploration, they nonetheless benefited directly from the national obsession with the astronauts and their voyage to another world in search of the new grail. After all, if the pathetic state of mathematics and science in the United States was responsible for its trailing the Soviet Union, as was widely alleged, then it stood to reason that the mathematicians, engineers and scientists who *were* around had to be nurtured. The eggheads were therefore hurriedly enlisted to help salvage the national honor.

So however obscure they were in the parade to the Moon, the space scientists and engineers were swept up in its momentum and marched right along with everyone else, reaping monetary rewards as they went. The robot people, it was often said then and afterward, rode on the coattails of the manned program and would have all but starved without it. That is not quite true. Space science and exploration had been an integral part of NASA from the beginning. In fact, as a rule of thumb, all of space science, applications, and exploration accounted for a more or less steady 15 to 20 percent of the space agency's entire budget.* Yet even the sort of pupil who was suddenly being derided for arithmetical incompetence knew that 20 percent of $5 billion was twice as much as 20 percent of $2.5 billion. So while space science and exploration would in no sense have evaporated without Apollo, they did benefit from the fact that it was swelling the space agency's budget and therefore their own cut of the bigger pie.

Indeed, the scientists and engineers soon came to understand that it was in their best interest to support Apollo, not complain about it. And why not? If it was a circus, as most of them believed, they at least had the consolation of knowing that they numbered among its shareholders. Many of them were arrivistes who had been drawn into space science and exploration from remote and under-appreciated academic environments by the availability of funding. Now they had the opportunity to chart exciting new directions—to start a whole new discipline—and bask in the adulation of a grateful public to boot.

"Studying planets with Earth-based telescopes had basically dried up" by the time NASA started, said Joseph N. Tatarewicz, an assist-ant curator and specialist in the history of astronomy at the Na-tional Air and Space Museum in Washington. "The astronomers were just yawning at the prospect of working on the planets," he added, explaining that their interests had long since become more far-ranging.

"They [NASA] looked around for a community of people to do the science and found nobody." Scientific communities flourish when they have specific intellectual problems and are given the technolo-gies to solve those problems. "What NASA had to do," he continued, "was cajole people working in other areas to move into working on the planets, and also to provide enormous incentives for people to come in and work on planetary science."

NASA did this by spreading pollen—money—around the nation's institutions of high learning, by coaxing universities and institutes

*NASA's total appropriation for 1960 was $523.6 million, for example, while the space science and applications share was $95.7 million. By 1963 the total budget had risen to nearly $3.7 billion, with science and applications accounting for $615 million. The figures for 1966 were $5.1 billion and $759 million, respectively. Appropriations for the intermittent years are roughly the same.

Budget figures for NASA as a whole are from Jane Van Nimmen, Leonard C. Bruno, and Robert L. Rosholt, *NASA Historical Data Book,* Vol. I, NASA Resources 1958–1968, SP-4012 (Washington, D.C.: National Aeronautics and Space Administra-tion, 1988), p. 128. OSSA figures are from Ezell, *NASA Historical Data Book,* Vol. II, Resources and Projects 1958–1968, p. 204.

into establishing interdisciplinary departments. "NASA would give you a building," Tatarewicz said, "but you had to call it the space science building, or something like that. You had to move everybody into that building who was working on space-related research so that they would learn how to do interdisciplinary work by running into one another in the halls. NASA really conjured up a community of people to work on the planets.

"The social bonding of the encounters, where everybody gets together intensively and works together day and night for weeks and weeks and weeks; it's an incredible force for social cohesion," the historian continued. "You get a tight-knit community in which almost everybody knows everybody else, and who have participated together in exploring a part of the universe where nobody has ever been.* And these guys are in their twenties!" The result, Joseph Tatarewicz added, was that NASA got "a really feisty, interesting group of people who thought that the boundaries were limitless and that the exploration of the solar system was their birthright." Whether this would have happened without Apollo is problematical. But the fact of the matter is that it did happen under the aegis of a space program that was invigorated and dominated by Apollo.

This led to an understandable ambivalence within the space science and planetary exploration communities. Consciously or otherwise, their members were beholden to the manned program for much of the space agency's largess. At the same time, they stubbornly differentiated between politics in all of its manifestations and the majesty—the purity—of science and exploration. They believed implicitly that it was they and their instrument-laden spacecraft, not astronauts carrying the Stars and Stripes to the Moon, that could respond in the most profound way to humanity's highest and noblest aspiration: the accumulation of knowledge for its own sake. Next to that, they ruminated darkly, the manned program amounted to little more than a flying circus. And, at least where they were concerned, it was a mighty wasteful circus, whatever dividend it gave them.

The sentiment was echoed by an ad hoc Committee on Space,

*Oran Nicks echoed this in reflecting on the Surveyor missions to the Moon, calling them a once-in-a-lifetime experience. "In addition to the wonderful opportunity to land sophisticated spacecraft on the moon, the trials and tribulations during the effort promoted the maturing of such undertakings. . . . I know for certain that the Surveyor experience bonded a group of us Earthlings together in a way that nothing but struggling and succeeding as a team can do" (Nicks, *Far Travelers*, p. 140).

chaired by Jerome Wiesner of MIT, which on January 10, 1961, reported to President-elect Kennedy that there were not only grave
deficiencies where planning and direction within NASA were concerned, but that the space agency was grossly overemphasizing the
manned program at the expense of scientific satellites and lunar and
planetary probes. Wiesner, who was soon to become Kennedy's science advisor, argued that the Mercury program exaggerated "the
value of that aspect of space activity where we are less likely to
achieve success. . . . We should stop advertising Mercury as our
major objective in space activities," he urged, and instead place
greater emphasis on science and exploration. Kennedy, of course,
would do exactly the opposite.

6.

JPL: Damnation and Redemption

The worst day of William Pickering's career began with a disembodied voice running through a couple of wires that came to an end inside the throat of a speaker in a television monitor. The harbinger of doom was describing the final moments of Ranger 6 as it bore down on the Moon. And it was doing so in technospeak: in an impersonal cadence, almost devoid of inflection, that was supposed to settle the nerves and inspire confidence. Pickering's nerves were not settled, however, because it was "Put up or shut up" day for Ranger.

"The latest status report we have from the SFO indicates that the spacecraft is 'Go' and ready to receive commands. The SFO itself is 'Go.' The communication lines to Goldstone are 'Go,' and the DSIF installation at Goldstone is 'Go.' "

SFO, or Space Flight Operations, was responsible for virtually everything that happened to Ranger 6 after it separated from its upper stage. It was in a sense the infrastructural equivalent of the spacecraft itself: an amalgam of complex subsystems, including JPL's computer group, and assorted people who specialized in communication and data analysis and reduction, which combined to monitor and control every aspect of the mission.

SFO's real name was the Space Flight Operations System. It operated out of the Space Flight Operations Facility at JPL—Building 125 at that time—whose darkened main room held the computers, communication equipment, charts and pins, assorted clocks, and other accouterments that even by 1964 had become commonplace in all civilian and military space control centers. The DSIF, or Deep Space Instrumentation Facility, was, of course, soon to become the Deep Space Network.

"We have the current announcement to make concerning the spacecraft," the voice continued. "Earlier today it was determined that the trajectory of the spacecraft is such that the cameras are oriented to properly view the desired lunar surface area; therefore, a terminal maneuver will not be performed."

That was good news. It meant that Ranger 6 was approaching its target—Mare Tranquillitatis, the Sea of Tranquility—so accurately that final course adjustments were unnecessary. Indeed, with one seemingly minor exception, the mission was going so well that Pickering had ventured to tell the reporters who were present that he was "cautiously optimistic." Coming from Pickering, that amounted to an outpouring of enthusiasm.

It was now just after midnight on February 2, 1964, and lights burned all over JPL. Despite the inconvenience of the hour, the newsmen, convinced that a historic event was unfolding, were gathered in von Karman Auditorium to follow the spacecraft's progress on the television monitors that had been provided for that purpose. No one wanted to be beaten ("scooped," as the uninitiated called it) on Ranger 6's expected triumph. A little more than fifteen months had passed since the demise of the last of its predecessors: long enough, everyone supposed, for even the most pernicious of the bugs to have been worked out.

At Headquarters, on the other side of the continent, a "mission status room" had also been set up to dispense up-to-the-minute information on Ranger's performance and position. It, too, was supposed to show real-time pictures of the Moon to reporters, assorted dignitaries, and other interested individuals as Ranger 6 plunged toward the lunar surface with its electric eye wide open.

Success now would all but wash away the memory of five successive failures and the embarrassment and ridicule they had caused.* Ranger 6 was the first of the Block III series and, it was hoped, represented a new beginning. Radical changes had been made by Christmas, 1962, following the Kelley board's stinging indictment of the Block I and II spacecraft. Not only had the notion of sterilization been abandoned, but any components that had been sterilized before being installed on the Block IIIs were discarded.

*A few weeks before Ranger 6 was scheduled to fly, NASA decided to begin calling it Ranger A, with the next three in the block lettered B through D. If it was successful, it would publicly be referred to as Ranger 6; if it failed, however, it was hoped that the name Ranger A would disassociate it from its five numerical predecessors. Understanding this, the lettering system was mostly ignored by the press. There did seem to be some confusion on the matter, within NASA itself, however. A covering memorandum on actions taken by the Office of Space Systems and Applications in response to the Hilburn report referred to both "Ranger VI" and "Ranger B." For the sake of consistency, either VI should have been A, or B should have been VII (Memorandum of July 25, 1964, 2-2471a, from Newell to Seamans, on file in the NASA History Office).

More important, the development of planetary exploration technology (like Mariner) as an integral part of the Ranger program had come to be seen as a dangerous distraction and had therefore been eliminated. The space agency had resolved that where Ranger was concerned, science had to give way to the needs of Apollo. There would be no experiments on the Block III spacecraft. They would be stripped down to carry only the vidicon cameras that were necessary to help find a landing site for the astronauts. Whatever JPL's interest in space beyond the Moon, it had been ordered to give Ranger its highest priority attention. That had included a thorough design review, management changes, and the recommendations for an outside contractor to build all Rangers beginning with those in Block IV. It had also been decided that Ranger 6 would under no circumstances fly until both JPL and NASA were convinced that the mission would succeed and that they had signed off accordingly.

When it came right down to it, then, NASA saw its primary mission as supporting manned spaceflight: to get Americans into orbit and then on to the Moon by whatever means necessary. If that meant abandoning anything that was considered extraneous, science included, so be it. Burke, who was tainted by the string of failures, had also become extraneous. He had therefore been replaced as the Ranger project manager by Harris M. "Bud" Schurmeier, his friend and Caltech classmate.

The best launch window for a shot at the Moon early in 1964 started on January 30 and ended on February 6. Ranger 6 and its Atlas-Agena had been subjected to what the Air Force and JPL considered to be a meticulous checkup and both had come through fully certified to fly. It had therefore been decided to go through the window as soon as it opened. So at 10:49 on the morning of January 30, the sixth Ranger had thundered off its pad at Cape Canaveral and disappeared into an overcast sky in what appeared to be a perfect launch. Two minutes twenty-one seconds after liftoff, the Atlas's two booster engines had separated and fallen away, leaving the main section of the launch vehicle and its upper stage to arc far over the Atlantic and head east with the spin of Earth.

At that moment channel eight of Ranger's telemetry package had unexpectedly activated and remained on for sixty-seven seconds. Channel eight was supposed to monitor the television system during the cruise portion of the flight, which wasn't even to begin until after Ranger 6 had separated from its Agena upper stage, forty-seven minutes after launch. At any rate, having turned on for no apparent reason, channel eight had then abruptly switched off three minutes and twenty-eight seconds into the flight, also seemingly without reason.

Everything from that point had progressed according to plan. The Atlas itself had separated and fallen away five minutes ten seconds after launch, followed twenty-five minutes later by the Agena B. The upper stage's separation from Ranger 6 had automatically started the timer that turned telemetry channel eight back on, as it was supposed to do. An hour and a minute after launch, the solar panels had extended and turned toward the Sun. Sixteen hours and forty minutes after launch, Ranger 6 had executed its complicated mid-course maneuver perfectly. It was then unquestionably on its way to the Moon, which it was supposed to begin televising forty-nine hours later, shortly before impact.

The forty-nine hours had passed with irritating slowness. It was now 1:00 A.M. The monitors told the reporters in von Karman that Ranger 6 was carrying two "parallel and separate" TV cameras, one of which would begin warming up in exactly five minutes. It was supposed to begin taking pictures of the Sea of Tranquility five minutes later and continue doing so during its final moments as a coherent machine. The other TV system would be turned on from the ground at 1:08 and would start imaging at 1:13, eleven minutes before impact. The reason for Ranger 6's existence came down to a mere twenty-five minutes of television transmission.

"For those JPL personnel not in the auditorium, we are panning around through the auditorium to give JPL personnel in other conference rooms that are in this net some idea of the activity here," said the voice on the monitors, killing time. "Some of you will recognize familiar faces in the audience. As we swing farther forward you will see the various networks which have come in to cover the event here at the laboratory this evening, or early this morning, I should say."

JPL's own television camera began taking pictures of the television cameras that were there to take pictures of the pictures Ranger 6's television cameras took of the Moon. "As we swing farther forward there are some members of the press now coming into view with the stage, various displays, the lunar map, the impact point on it . . ." It was the space program's first tele-love-in, and like those that followed, it was unabashedly incestuous.

What the metallic voice failed to mention was that, where Apollo's mission planners at the Manned Spacecraft Center in Houston were concerned, Ranger 6's pictures had long since become irrelevant.

The Apollo engineers had waited in vain for images of possible landing sites for nearly two and a half years while five successive Ranger
reconnaissance missions ended without returning so much as a single usable frame. They had originally counted on using the pictures
for clues as to the composition and density of the terrain on which
their Lunar Module would have to set down. That was important
where its weight, power plant, and the design of its landing gear
were concerned. But they had finally tired of waiting and froze the
LM's design. Anything Ranger 6 or its successors sent back "could
only confirm or deny that design," one Ranger project scientist was
told. At that point, he added, Houston "frankly didn't care where we
put Ranger 6."

The spacecraft had been stripped of its scientific instruments,
then, with the single-minded purpose of having it send back pictures
to support a manned landing on the Moon. But with the bright
crater-pocked Sea of Tranquility looming larger by the second as
Ranger 6 streaked in for what was to be a near-perfect bull's-eye, this
salient fact haunted its creators, irrespective of what the voice in the
monitor said: It could not collect the data that was wanted by the
scientists and no one in the Apollo program wanted the data it *could*
collect.

With nineteen minutes to go before impact and its speed accelerating to nearly five thousand miles an hour because of the Moon's
increasing gravitational pull, Ranger 6 signaled that the first camera system had begun its five-minute warm-up. A few minutes later
the spacecraft reported to its increasingly jubilant masters that the
second camera system was also warming up. Both were supposed to
go on automatically at any moment. Video receiving equipment was
therefore switched on at Goldstone for instantaneous relay to
Pasadena. Pickering and Robert Parks, the lab's lunar and planetary programs director, had been joined by Newell and Parks's counterpart at Headquarters, Edgar Cortright, NASA's own head of
lunar and planetary programs. Newell and Cortright had flown out
from Washington for the event. Now, sitting in the Space Flight
Operations Facility, they watched the activity on the floor of the
control center and listened to the voice in the monitor nearest them.
They listened, and as the time at which the cameras were supposed
to switch on came and went without a picture, they looked at the
clock with growing apprehension.

"The signal level is steady but there is still no indication of full-
power video," the voice announced. "There is still no indication of

full-power video. We have just passed impact minus five and a half minutes. . . . We are approaching impact minus four and a half minutes. We still have no indication of full-power video."

The press, which had started murmuring at the first indication that something was wrong more than ten minutes earlier, had fallen absolutely silent over in von Karman. It was as if the sweep second hand on every clock at JPL was a wand that was turning a dream mission into a nightmare of epic proportions.

"Still no indication of full-power video as we approach impact minus three and a half minutes . . . Still no indication of full-power video . . . Still no indication of video . . . We still see no full-power video as we come up on impact minus one and a half minutes—just passed . . ." Pickering could do nothing but watch and listen, transfixed, as the catastrophe continued to unfold relentlessly. "We are coming up on impact minus one-half minute. We still have no indication of full-power video. . . . Still no video . . . Coming up on impact minus ten seconds. No indication of full-power video . . . Still no indication of full-power video. We have our first report of impact. . . ." Impact! "DSIF reports loss of signal. . . . We have no indication of switch-over to full-power video throughout the terminal event," the voice coming out of the blank monitor added. It was as if a gravely ill patient's vital signs had abruptly stopped without his having opened his eyes. "Goldstone had lost lock." Ranger 6 was no more. The patient was dead.

In Washington, where NASA's near-record $5.3 billion budget request for fiscal 1965 was due to go to Congress within a matter of days, the same narrative—with one exception—was piped into the NASA auditorium for reporters, space agency officials, and others. With "Goldstone has lost lock" still echoing in their heads and the reality of what had just happened slowly beginning to sink in, many in the stunned audience winced when they heard this finale reverberate through the room because an audio technician had accidentally crossed lines: "Spray on Avon Cologne Mist and walk in fragrant beauty, or splash on an Avon . . ."

Ranger 6's ignominious end was not as bad as it seemed. And it was worse. It had gone almost precisely where it was supposed to go, executing its midcourse maneuver so perfectly that further adjustments hadn't been necessary. All major systems except the television cameras had functioned without a hitch. It had hit the Moon only twenty miles from where it had been aimed: on a flat plain about seventy-five miles east of the crater Julius Caesar and halfway between two smaller craters, Ross and Arago. This proved that JPL could hit what it wanted to hit. Certainly that was requirement number one in lunar and interplanetary exploration.

"It was a beautiful shot until the last fifteen minutes," Pickering later reflected. "That really was, in a sense, the low point, and in a sense, the high point, at JPL. It was the low point in our realization that we had failed and that there was a very likely possibility that somebody was going to wipe us out of existence. But there was also a realization that 'we know how to fix this and we're going to pull ourselves together and do it.' "

Edgar Cortright sent a condolence letter to Pickering, Parks, and Schurmeier three days after the Ranger 6 calamity, echoing Pickering's feelings. "From the point of view of maintaining laboratory morale, I think you can take some pride in the fact that the bus appeared to work so beautifully." But then he noted ominously that the months ahead "are apt to be a great strain on all of us."

Three primary committees of inquiry were formed almost before the dust had settled at Ranger 6's final resting place and even as the press was carrying reports that Congress was mulling over the possibility of postponing a manned landing on the Moon because of the "trouble-plagued $252 million Ranger project." One committee was formed at JPL itself, one was formed by NASA, and one was created under the auspices of the House Subcommittee on NASA Oversight.

The JPL report, stamped DISCREET and completed on February 14—only twelve days after the event—concluded that the problem had come during the sixty-seven seconds right after liftoff, when the channel eight telemetry had been inadvertently turned on, causing electricity to arc. That had in turn knocked out the high-voltage power supply to the television system. But the reason for the error eluded JPL.

On March 17 the space agency's own board of inquiry submitted a politically charged report, pinning the blame not only on an unnecessarily complicated and not truly redundant television system but on inadequate test and inspection methods by JPL engineers and technicians. The five-member board, which was headed by Earl D. Hilburn, NASA's Deputy Associate Administrator for Industry Affairs, concluded that at least two failures had occurred within Ranger 6's television system and that such an occurrence indicated serious procedural shortcomings. Because of this, the confidential, seventy-page document asserted, "the Board broadened its investigation to include an evaluation of any general weaknesses in Ranger design, testing philosophy, and procedures which might have contributed to, or enhanced the possibilities of, in-flight failure." It went on to list several problems with the RCA-made television system (which JPL agreed with) and warned that Ranger 7 would probably fail unless a host of improved test and inspection procedures were adopted (which JPL vehemently disagreed with). It was like the Kelley report all over again.

Two weeks later Webb, evidently angered by JPL's and Caltech's stubborn resistance to direction from Headquarters, sent identical four-page letters to Clinton P. Anderson, chairman of the Senate Committee on Aeronautical and Space Sciences, and George P. Miller, chairman of the House Committee on Science and Astronautics. The letters detailed the Hilburn board's criticism of JPL's handling of the Ranger program but omitted the recommendations. Copies were telegraphed to Pickering and to Arnold O. Beckman, chairman of Caltech's Board of Trustees.

Webb's letter deeply disturbed both Newell and Oran Nicks, among others, because of the negative impact they felt it would have on Capitol Hill and at JPL. Nicks was so distressed by what he and others saw as inaccuracies and blatant politics in the Hilburn report that he wrote a rebuttal to his boss. Webb's letter, coming on the heels of the stinging report, and even citing it, only convinced Pickering and his senior aides that Headquarters was out to beat JPL into submission.*

The congressional hearings, which began on April 27 and lasted four days, were held in the Longworth Building under the auspices of the House Committee on Science and Astronautics' Subcommittee on NASA Oversight. Joseph E. Karth of Minnesota was chairman. Testimony was taken from Webb, NASA's Robert Seamans, Newell, Nicks, William Cunningham, NASA's Ranger program chief, and Cortright, representing the space agency, and Pickering, Parks, and Schurmeier, representing the laboratory.

Almost at the outset Karth noted that design work and engineer-

---

*The Hilburn report began with a brief acknowledgment of JPL for its help. Schurmeier's copy, on file in the NASA History Office, shows that someone amended ". . . the board wishes to give special thanks to Dr. Pickering and the staff. . . ." by inserting "A" and "KNIFE OF" to make it read ". . . the board wishes to give A special KNIFE OF thanks to Dr. Pickering and the staff. . . ." Further on, where the mission's mistakes were listed under Findings and General Observations, someone repeatedly and with apparent anger printed "RCA," usually underlined twice, beside several of the evidently contentious findings.

ing of the Apollo and lunar modules had so overtaken Ranger that its missions now seemed to be superfluous. Newell responded with a multifaceted defense of the program. Ranger pictures, he began, would still be valuable for providing a check on whether the "range of capabilities of the LEM design is adequate."* He went on to show what he termed to be one of the best photographs ever taken of the Moon from Earth and noted that objects smaller than one thousand feet were indistinguishable. Newell then compared the photograph with one taken of part of Boston in which objects no larger than five feet could be seen. That was the sort of resolution, he carefully explained, that the Ranger cameras would achieve during the final moments before impact. Earth-based telescopes, then, simply could not get close enough to provide the information that a robot could. Newell's message—there is no substitute for being there—was to run through the planetary science program for the next quarter century.

Newell also stressed that Ranger was an integral part of a three-spacecraft team that included Surveyor and Lunar Orbiter. He put to rest the argument that Mariner had infected Ranger with unnecessarily complicated technology, pointing out that work on Ranger had contributed directly to Mariner 2's singular success at Venus. JPL was still getting some mileage out of the triumph. The point that everything depended upon everything else—space systems were ultimately related, so the development of one benefited the others—was another theme that would continue for years to come. Finally, in answer to the inevitable question from Karth, Newell assured the committee that Ranger was indeed every bit as complex and sophisticated as its Soviet counterparts.

The Karth committee made four broad recommendations, all of them having to do with management. It advised NASA: supervise JPL more closely; alter the relationship of the two institutions to make JPL more responsive to Headquarters; consider one-year contracts with Caltech rather than longer ones; and bring in a deputy lab director who would be right under Pickering and who would be responsible for the day-to-day supervision of flight projects.

Headquarters, of course, could have liked nothing better. A strong deputy director who would control management decisions on a daily basis not only would tighten the design, testing, and production process, but might even help lessen the tension that persisted be-

*Lunar Excursion Module, or LEM, was eventually shortened to Lunar Module.

tween Headquarters and the laboratory. Certainly Karth was mindful not only of policy disagreements between Washington and
Pasadena, but also of conflicts on a personal level that affected policy, as evidenced by this exchange between him and Pickering:

> MR. KARTH.   Dr. Pickering, I am not sure that you would want to answer
> this, but if you feel that you are not inhibited in any way, I would appreci-
> ate it if you could.
>
> In your opinion, are there personality clashes that exist, let's say, be-
> tween top NASA management and top Caltech or JPL management that
> might cause some of the problems that we at the moment feel do exist?
>
> DR. PICKERING.   Mr. Chairman, I would prefer not to answer that ques-
> tion.

Under pressure from NASA, Pickering selected retired Air Force
Major General Alvin R. Luedecke, the general manager of the
Atomic Energy Commission, to be Washington's martinet at JPL.
Luedecke's presence as deputy director of the lab "mollified" NASA,
Pickering later recalled, but it proved nettlesome in a place that still
stubbornly clung to a semblance of independence, irrespective of the
damage caused by the successive Ranger disasters. The general
"wanted to be much more responsive to Washington" than Pickering
thought necessary. "When NASA proposed something, he wanted to
jump," William Pickering recalled with unbridled disdain. "Luedecke and I came to a parting of the ways a few years later."

Meanwhile, JPL and RCA's Astro-Electronics Division set to work
to correct the many problems in Ranger's imaging system through
the use of what the lab would come to call a "tiger team": a group
that concentrated on only one problem, brainstorming it intensely,
with an undefined but implicit time constraint. RCA, in Hightstown,
New Jersey, did its own brainstorming there, with specialists
brought in from its nearby Princeton Research Laboratory.

JPL and RCA developed a joint interlocking problem-failure reporting system, while NASA sent its own team to Pasadena to oversee the testing and inspection of Ranger 7. Nicks specifically ordered
that the Headquarters representatives write their own reports
rather than assign them to JPL people. It was understood, though
not articulated, that careers were now on the line: another failure
would end Ranger. Another failure, in fact, could likely end JPL as
well. The pressure to succeed, according to one participant, was
"unbelievable."

But it was that pressure which found the root cause of the short circuit in Ranger 6's television system. The cause of the failure turned out to be not in the system itself but rather in the launch environment. And that revelation would come only after some persistent detective work by a JPL electrical engineer named Maurice Piroumian.

Within less than a second after the Atlas's engines had separated, the television subsystem had turned on because of electrical arcing, Piroumian discovered. As was the case with other upper stages, the Agena's nose section contained a cluster of male pins that were connected by an "umbilical cord" to an external power source before launch so that the television system could be monitored. These pins were a quarter of an inch away from a single "hot pin" that was connected to the TV system's battery. At the moment of liftoff the umbilical cord fell away, a hatch covering the pin cluster snapped shut automatically, and the television system went on its internal battery power as the Atlas and Agena began to rise off the pad. The battery pin held twenty volts. The male connector pins, a quarter of an inch away, could be set off by only a three-volt charge. That tiny gap somehow seemed to have been bridged. But how?

More clues were supplied by General Dynamics, Atlas's manufacturer. At engine separation, Piroumian was told by GD engineers, 250 pounds of liquid oxygen and 150 pounds of kerosene were released into the atmosphere when their respective lines were severed. This highly combustible mixture was then ignited by the Atlas's separating engines, turning into a flash wave that moved up the length of the booster and over the Agena at six hundred feet a second, despite the fact that both the booster and the upper stage were at that instant climbing at three and a half times the speed of sound. Since the hatch that covered the pins in the Agena's nose was closed mechanically, rather than sealed hermetically, the burning fuel vapor got into the pin area and bridged the gap between both sets of pins, causing twenty volts from the battery to strike a cluster of pins that could be activated by only three volts.

The failure of Ranger 6 to collect even a single picture of the Moon, then, was caused by a design error of a quarter of an inch and by a little hatch that did not close tightly enough. It was not caused by at least two faults in the imaging system itself, as Earl Hilburn had asserted. The margin between the success and failure of these large and immensely complex machines, as Mariner 1's missing hyphen and Ranger 6's imperfect hatch design showed, was appallingly narrow.

Early on the afternoon of July 24, 1964—six months after its immediate predecessor's infamous end—Ranger 7 rose off Launch Complex 12 and into a clear blue sky with Mare Nubium, the Sea of Clouds, as its destination. It carried not only new television cameras but JPL's future as well.

The following morning Pasadena sent the order for Ranger 7 to execute its midcourse maneuver. The spacecraft did as it was told. Then Pickering, Parks, and Schurmeier went to von Karman to confront the cynical newsmen and women who had come from around the world to cover the seventh attempt to get a proven loser to do its job. Schurmeier reported that there had been "no anomalies whatever" to that point. Then he was asked whether he thought the cameras would work this time. "Very definitely," Ranger's project director shot back, unhesitatingly.

And they did. By 6:00 A.M., Pickering, Cortright and, once again, Homer Newell were perched in seats in the visitors' gallery in JPL's spanking new three-story Space Flight Operations Facility in Building 230, immediately behind the towering Administration Building. They looked down on the floor, called the net control area, where teletypewriters spewed Ranger's encoded telemetry as it came in from Goldstone. Closed-circuit television monitors showed other data and allowed face-to-face discussion between Ranger's guidance and flight analysis teams, who were off in their own rooms, and those who were responsible for the spacecraft's television system and the imagery it was supposed to produce. Rear-projection screens showed the probe's controllers, who were fanned out behind their consoles, what was happening to Ranger 7 at all times.

At 6:07 the monitors told reporters and some JPL people in von Karman (which was packed) that the command to warm up the first video system—two full-scan cameras—had been relayed to Ranger. The atmosphere in von Karman, in the net control area and in the gallery behind and above it, as well as in the NASA auditorium in Washington, approached catalepsy. The contingent in the capital included several NASA officials, a gaggle of congressmen and the ubiquitous reporters.

Ninety seconds later the monitors announced with ill-concealed glee that the cameras had full video power, "strong and clear." Von Karman erupted with applause. And ninety seconds after that orders went out for the second camera system—a brace of four partial-scan cameras with telephoto lenses—to begin warming. A minute and a half later Goldstone reported that the second system was also returning pictures. The applause in von Karman turned to cheers.

Now the telemetry was coming in without interruption. Ranger 7 was streaking toward destiny at a speed approaching six thousand miles an hour, its cameras showing the Sea of Clouds with ever-increasing clarity. "Seven minutes . . . all cameras continue to send excellent signals. . . . Five minutes from impact . . . video signals still continue excellent. . . . Everything is 'go,' as it has been since launch. . . . One minute to impact . . . Excellent . . . Excellent . . . Signals to the end . . . Impact!"

Ranger 7's telemetry ended abruptly at 6:25 and gave way to roars of jubilation in von Karman, in the Space Flight Operations Facility, and back at Headquarters. Some JPL employees in von Karman threw paper into the air and shouted. Others, unable to suppress tears, wept silently. Controllers on the floor of Building 230 abandoned their consoles for handshakes and backslapping under a blizzard of more paper. Several cases of champagne Bud Schurmeier had bought in anticipation of a successful Ranger 6 flight appeared and were quickly opened. Within an hour, President Johnson was on the phone to Pickering and Newell, congratulating them on a "magnificent achievement" that would provide "the scientific knowledge necessary for man's trip to the Moon."

On August 1, even as newspapers throughout the country extolled Ranger's triumph, Newell and Pickering briefed LBJ in the Cabinet Room of the White House, where the president again expressed his and the nation's gratitude. "We started behind in space," Lyndon B. Johnson said, portraying the nation as the come-from-behind underdog so beloved by Americans. But "we know this morning that the United States has achieved fully the leadership we have sought for free men."

While their contribution to the nation's space program was publicly acknowledged, apparently neither Newell nor Pickering was considered worthy of the kind of decoration Alan Shepard had been awarded after his fifteen-and-a-half-minute uncontrolled suborbital flight down the Atlantic test range in the Freedom 7 Mercury capsule a little more than three years earlier. But they and their associates—from Administrator Webb down to the lowliest janitor in "the remote test laboratory"—Johnson explained solemnly, had the "gratitude and the admiration of all Americans of all faiths, of all parties, of all regions." The election was ninety-six days away.

Ranger 7's feat brought redemption to the Jet Propulsion Laboratory and its beleaguered director. Not only were its pictures first rate, but the probe itself had impacted within ten miles of where it had been aimed, a telling accomplishment for its navigation and guidance teams. But the ramifications of the mission went far beyond that. Ranger 7's success may have prevented an embarrassing reassessement of the entire Apollo program. And it probably even helped the program by paving the way for the Surveyor-landers that were to follow in short order, as well as by showing that the design parameters of the Lunar Module's landing gear seemed to be sufficient. For the nation as a whole, Ranger 7 represented a badly needed riposte in the duel for the Moon. And a duel it was.

Luna 3's spectacular flight around the Moon and the amazing photographs of the far side it had returned nearly five years earlier were triumphs of the first magnitude for the Soviet Union. Indeed, the first three Luna missions were precedent-setting for their scientific achievements and were splendid supplements to the Earth-circling Sputniks.

But for all of Nikita Khrushchev's bombast about his nation's achievements and goals in space, there was also an unpublicized agenda that drove the Soviets to send their robots to reconnoiter the Moon, the same agenda for which the Rangers were being used. The reconnaissance robots were scouts for the cosmonauts who were supposed to follow. The Soviet Union was determined to beat the United States to a manned circumlunar flight around the Moon and then land on it in the late sixties or early seventies. The audacious plan was ultimately abandoned, however, because of the death of Sergei Korolev, the USSR's chief rocket designer, in 1966, and also because of a series of failures of the heavy boosters that were to have propelled the Soviet crews. The flight of Apollo 8's three astronauts around the Moon at Christmas, 1968, finally convinced Khrushchev that the United States was going to make good on Kennedy's pledge to land Americans on the Moon before the decade was out. For the Soviets, dropping out of the race without acknowledging ever having been in it was the most prudent course.*

*U.S. satellite reconnaissance imagery in June 1969 corroborated rumors of an enigmatic Soviet monster booster, named the G-1 by the intelligence collectors (later known to be called the N-1 by the Soviets), that stood 360 feet high and was estimated to have been able to develop 4.7 million pounds of thrust: enough to send sixty-three tons to the Moon. The booster was overpowered either to be used as a weapon or to place satellites in Earth orbit, leading analysts to conclude that it was intended for carrying cosmonauts to the Moon. Three of the launch vehicles were lost in accidents before the program was abandoned. Cosmonaut Vladimir Komarov told reporters

Because of the need for reliable data to support such a mission, as well as relentless pressure from Khrushchev to demonstrate his country's technical and scientific virtuosity by topping one "space first" after another, Soviet scientists and engineers were being pushed to their limit well before Rangers 1 through 6 foundered and after Ranger 7 and two successors accomplished their missions with distinction. The furious spate of early Mars and Venus missions, which began in October 1960 and February 1961, respectively, were clearly intended to keep the momentum of the Soviet program going. But they were unmitigated failures. If there was one thing that could sustain Pickering, Silverstein, Newell, Burke, Schurmeier, Nicks, and the others, in fact, it was the knowledge that in most respects the opposition was faring no better than they were, and probably quite a bit worse. That certainly applied to the Moon race.

The Soviets' inaugural attempt to send a probe to the Moon (as opposed to around it) that was capable of making the necessary midcourse adjustment maneuver ended on January 5, 1963, when the spacecraft incinerated in Earth's atmosphere. It had no official name. Neither did its apparent immediate successor, which plunged into the Pacific the following month without so much as making it to orbit. Luna 4 was launched at the Moon on April 2, 1963, but it went wide of its target by fifty-one hundred miles, slipped into a highly elliptical orbit around Earth, and finally headed off in the direction of the Sun. While some data from the cosmic ray and solar instruments it carried have been published, the precise nature of its

before his death in 1967 that "the Soviet Union will not be beaten by the United States in the race for a human being to go to the Moon." Other cosmonauts echoed Komarov, with one doing so in a private conversation with astronauts at an air show. In November 1989, evidently in the spirit of *glasnost,* six MIT and Caltech engineering professors visiting the Moscow Aviation Institute were told authoritatively that the Soviets had actually tried desperately to land a lone cosmonaut on the Moon by 1968, using relatively unsophisticated Soyuz orbital and descent modules. The plan called for an N-1 carrying the lunar landing craft to rendezvous with a reliable Proton booster carrying two cosmonauts in a spacecraft designed to fly in lunar orbit. Both were then supposed to fly to the Moon, with one of the cosmonauts descending in the landing craft while the other remained in orbit awaiting his return. Prof. Oleg Alifanov, who conducted the tour and made the revelations, confirmed that developmental problems with the N-1 caused the program to be put on hold in 1972 and scrubbed two years later. (Reconnaissance data on the G-1/N-1 is from Burrows, *Deep Black,* pp. 240–41. The confirmation by Alifanov is from "Now, Soviets Acknowledge a Moon Race," *New York Times,* December 18, 1989; Craig Covault, "Soviet Manned Lunar Mission Plan Used Modified Soyuz Spacecraft," *Aviation Week & Space Technology,* January 8, 1990, p. 44; and "Russian Moon Non-Landing," *Science,* January 12, 1990, p. 157. See also Steven Young, "Soviet Union Was Far Behind in 1960's Moon Race," *Spaceflight,* January 1990, pp. 2–3. The last article, as well as the January 1985 issue of the *Journal of the British Interplanetary Society,* has information on the N-1.)

mission has never been explained, leading some experts to speculate that it was supposed to make a soft landing on the lunar surface. A year later another unnamed spacecraft, reportedly also a lunar probe, failed right after launch. A year after that, on March 12, 1965, Cosmos 60 was parked in Earth orbit with the intention of rerouting it to the Moon. But there was yet another glitch and it decayed five days later.

The fusillade of red arrows shot at the Moon did not slacken. In May another unnamed spacecraft was put into Earth orbit and then vectored to a point at which it was supposed to collide with the Moon. Once its owners saw it was safely on its way, they announced that it was called Luna 5 and that it was going to land softly on the lunar surface. But it did no such thing. It made quite a hard landing, in fact. The probe's retrorockets apparently failed to brake its momentum, causing it to plow into the lunar surface with such force that a German observatory claimed to have seen a 135 by 49 mile dust cloud where it impacted. The cloud lasted for about ten minutes before settling.

And there were still others. Luna 6, the next attempt, missed by a little less than 97,000 miles because of a motor malfunction during midcourse adjustment; it continued on toward the Sun, around which it was soon circling. Zond 3, launched on July 18, 1965, passed within 5,600 miles of the far side of the Moon, photographed a substantial part of it, and then headed toward a heliocentric orbit while testing various systems that had previously failed on Mars and Venus probes. Luna 7 was higher than it was supposed to be when its retrorockets fired in preparation for another soft-landing attempt on October 8, 1965. They therefore cut off sooner than they were supposed to, causing the spacecraft to free-fall and smash into the surface. Its successor, Luna 8, had the opposite problem, but the result was the same. Its retrorocket fired too late to break its fall adequately. It, too, crashed on impact.

The Soviet Union would suffer five unsuccessful attempts to soft-land on the Moon in 1965 alone. While this indicated that its vaunted space program was in the throes of the same kind of pernicious engineering problems plaguing its American counterpart—and was indeed as far ahead in failures as it was in firsts—it also showed beyond doubt that Moscow was committing resources to space science and exploration in quantities which indicated a degree of competition that could be called furious.

Success would finally come with the launch of Luna 9 on January

31, 1966. It managed to make a successful soft landing on the Moon three days later, obediently opened its four "petal" doors, and promptly began beaming back pictures of its immediate environment. It is unlikely that paper flew around the control center outside Moscow when Luna 9 sent back word that it had landed safely, but there was probably a lot of backslapping and maybe some weeping, too.

Meanwhile, there continued to be general exultation over Ranger 7, which had staged a clear triumph. From NASA's point of view, the 4,308 pictures returned to Earth by Ranger 7 were extraordinary. The last one, taken from a height of only fifteen hundred feet a fraction of a second before impact, clearly showed craters as small as three feet. By comparison, the best resolution that could be attained by Earth-based telescopes was less than one thousand feet.

At nine o'clock on the morning of July 31, 1964—within three hours of Ranger 7's lunar impact—Pickering and his colleagues had starred at a nationally televised news conference in von Karman. Gerard P. Kuiper, director of the Lunar and Planetary Laboratory at the University of Arizona and a world-renowned astronomer, was the principal investigator—the PI—for Ranger's imagery. He was therefore in charge of its imaging team.

"We have made progress in resolution of lunar detail not by a factor of ten, as [was] hoped would be possible with this flight, nor by a factor of 100, which would have been already very remarkable, but by a factor of 1,000," Kuiper said, showing an assortment of Ranger's pictures. Preliminary evidence would help explain how the Moon's surface evolved, the astronomer added, but not when the Moon itself had originated. Almost parenthetically, Kuiper noted that the evidence also suggested that the lunar surface was dense enough to walk on. In other words, it was now held extremely unlikely that the Lunar Module and its two occupants would sink as if on quicksand. Though there was some disagreement among scientists on the exact density of the lunar surface, it was no longer a question that kept people in the Apollo program up at night. Harold Urey, however, was one scientist who did believe that the Moon's soil could prove to be treacherous for LMs. He postulated that the lunar maria could consist of lava, which would support a lander, or be composed of very fine material, which might not. Science instruments, rather than just television cameras, would probably have put the matter to rest, he insisted glumly.

A month later, on August 28, Kuiper, Eugene M. Shoemaker (a geologist with the U.S. Geological Survey) and Ray Heacock (the manager of the Lunar and Planetary Instruments Section at JPL) met at Headquarters for an interim scientific-results conference with the press. Both Shoemaker and Heacock were on the Ranger science team. The meeting was chaired by Nicks. All four were due to leave shortly for the International Astronomical Union meeting in Hamburg, where Ranger 7's findings were to be presented in a series of papers. As was to become traditional in lunar and planetary science, investigators lost no time in presenting and publishing the results of the findings.

Kuiper showed the reporters photographs of the Moon taken by Earth-based telescopes and by Ranger 7's full- and partial-scan cameras to illustrate the new breadth of detail that was afforded because of the spacecraft. He also ran a five-minute film made by splicing successive pictures taken as the spacecraft had bored in on the Sea of Clouds. The moving picture was effective, giving viewers the feeling of plunging toward the lunar surface with the spacecraft. Not only were hundreds of new primary craters clearly visible, but tiny secondary craters caused by rocks and other debris that flew out when meteorites struck with terrific velocity could be seen as well. Many of the images showed ridges and flow patterns associated with the movement of lava on Earth, Kuiper announced. This indicated volcanic activity at some distant, but as yet undetermined, time. Shoemaker, the geologist, agreed.

In recognition of Ranger 7's achievement, the International Astronomical Union decided at the Hamburg meeting to name the area where Ranger 7 impacted Mare Cognitum, the Sea That Is Known.

Rangers 8 and 9 were the last of the Block III spacecraft and the last in the Ranger series. Their intended successors had been half-heartedly planned during most of 1963, but by that Christmas they had fallen victim to budgetary problems, terrible publicity because of the disastrous first five missions (the imbroglio over Ranger 6 was barely two months away), and the fact that the more advanced lunar explorers, Surveyor and Lunar Orbiter, were by then firmly harnessed to the Apollo program and required increasing human and financial resources.

Ranger 8 left Earth on February 17, 1965, and flew another flawless mission, landing three days later within fifteen miles of its aim point in the Sea of Tranquility. It returned 7,137 more pictures.

Ranger 9 went out on March 21, its destination a seventy-mile-wide, 10,500-foot-deep crater named Alphonsus, located near the center of the Moon and immediately east of the Sea of Clouds.* Alphonsus was an intriguing target because it has a large central peak and small craters with dark halos around them on its floor. Similar craters on Earth, such as Crater Lake in Oregon, are thought to have been created by repeated explosions or by molten lava. This, in addition to the Soviet astronomer N. A. Kozyrev's having detected what he thought was glowing volcanic gas coming from the central peak in 1958, whetted Urey's appetite. He had therefore recommended it to Newell as a likely landing site at the outset of the Ranger program.

Just before dawn on the morning of March 24, 1965, Urey, hunched in a chair in the darkened Space Flight Operations Facility, watched as Ranger 9's 5,814 pictures unfolded live on national television as it completed its plunge into Alphonsus. The show lasted eighteen minutes. Shoemaker and Ewen Whitaker, another member of the Ranger team, sat at the venerable chemist's feet, legs outstretched as if they were screening a home movie.

"Everyone in North America with access to a television set had been able to watch the event and, as if holding a visual subscription to the *National Geographic,* experience firsthand the thrill of exploring the unknown," the historian R. Cargill Hall said.

What Rangers 7, 8, and 9 showed with their high-resolution close-up images of the Moon was that it was far more heavily pocked with meteorite hits than had been supposed, that there existed ample flat plains for manned and unmanned landings, and that its surface would most likely support Apollo spacecraft. In doing this the three vehicles served a strictly utilitarian—not scientific—purpose. They also helped to perfect the system integration, testing, navigation, and guidance procedures that would be necessary for the Lunar Orbiter, Surveyor, and Apollo spacecraft that were shortly to follow them to the Moon, as well as for the Mariners and other deep space probes that were soon to fan out across the solar system on long journeys of exploration and scientific investigation.

But Harold Urey, for one, was underwhelmed by the Rangers, which he dismissed as little more than technology demonstrators. On December 30, 1963, less than a year before the flight of Ranger 7, the iconoclastic chemist had complained bitterly about the severe

*The crater was named after Alphonso X, a thirteenth-century Spanish king who was nicknamed the Learned One by astronomers mainly because, unlike most other people, he took an interest in what they did.

limits of scientific investigation in the Apollo program and the narrow uses that were going to be made of the Ranger and Surveyor
missions. Urey was one of the investigators on the Ranger project,
but with the science instruments having been eliminated in favor of
only the television system, how could he investigate anything? Scientists had craved to examine the Moon, to pry into its delicious
secrets, for centuries. Now, at long last, they finally possessed the
wherewithal to do so: very possibly, to unlock the secrets of the
creation of Earth itself. Yet that glorious undertaking was being
impeded by the crass demands of show business. Speaking at a news
conference at the conclusion of the American Association for the
Advancement of Science's annual meeting in Cleveland on December 30, 1963, Urey had growled that it was false economy to curtail
scientific exploration of the Moon. "The first thing sacrificed is always science," he told the press.

Urey, however, was a fervent believer in the Apollo program. He
was convinced that landing men on the lunar surface had considerable scientific potential because of the first-hand observations they
could make and the rock and soil samples they could collect and
bring back. He steadfastly maintained that Apollo afforded an unparalleled opportunity for humans to conduct scientific investigations that were beyond the capability of robots. And he was therefore
adamant in insisting that the program ought to have been shaped
primarily by the requirements of scientific investigation—by its potential science returns—not by the simple need to land astronauts
on the lunar surface to go cavorting around for the sake of politics.
So Urey pelted Homer Newell and other NASA officials with often
acerbic complaints about incompetent science advisers, the whole
circuslike atmosphere surrounding the manned program, and about
the probes' instrumentation, which he considered pathetic.

". . . I understand the importance of TV photographs from the
engineering standpoint," Urey had written to Newell in 1962 to
complain about the paucity of experiments on the Rangers, "but I
do think they have small scientific value. We will find small, large,
and intermediate sized craters far apart or close together. So of what
significance are they? Terrestrial meteor craters have contributed
essentially nothing to the unraveling of the magnificent history of
the earth. We can reasonably assume that this will be true of the
small craters on the moon." The seismometer and gamma ray experiments, on the other hand, might have been extremely helpful in
understanding the structure and history of the Moon, Urey added,

deploring their removal. "I wish to assure you that I and many other people who are working on the problem of the structure and history of the moon, and who have worked on this program for many years, are immensely disappointed in the failure to secure any information on this subject up to the present time . . ."

He also took very strong exception to anyone who suggested that there was or had been volcanic activity inside the Moon, a theory that was particularly favored by geologists. This was known as the "hot moon–cold moon" battle. Urey fought it with abiding passion, not only because he didn't agree with hot-moon geologists, but because he didn't think much of what they did, either.

"You have turned heavily to geologists," he was to complain to George E. Mueller, the space agency's associate administrator for the Office of Manned Space Flight, about the scientific aspects of the Apollo program soon after Eagle landed in July 1969. "I know of some good, brilliant geologists, but mostly they are a second rate lot. This is known in university circles very well. I do not agree with Jim Conant who as president of Harvard abolished the Geology Department on these grounds, but we all know that geology attracts the less brilliant type of scientists. After all, it is descriptive, and very often they do not learn more than the most elementary things about chemistry and physics. The Geological Survey is filled with people of this kind," Urey noted sourly. He would nevertheless see the day when the geologists came to constitute the vanguard of those who conducted the most important analyses of the terrestrial planets and, perhaps even more important, of moons that were so amazing they were literally inconceivable during his lifetime.

Nor was Urey impressed by the professional qualities of the astronauts themselves. Of the astronaut selection process, he complained that more emphasis ought to have been placed on scientific expertise and less on sex appeal. But given the acknowledged purpose of the Apollo program—to simply get people there—"any man or woman with an attractive personality would do," Urey said contemptuously.

Now it was time to get comprehensive pictures of large tracts of the lunar surface and actually descend onto it to test possible landing areas in preparation for the Apollo missions. As was always true with exploration, or with reconnaissance of any kind, for that matter, the general would inevitably lead to the specific.

As early as May 1958, planners at the old NACA had suggested that the new space agency send orbiters to the Moon to collect data on its mass, radioactivity level, and magnetic field. Two years later NASA approved plans for a lunar exploration program in which a combination orbiter-lander spacecraft, called Surveyor, was supposed to go to the Moon and then separate. One part would circle and take pictures; the other was supposed to make a soft landing and return more imagery and scientific data from the surface.

As it was to turn out, such a dual-purpose spacecraft would not be used for lunar reconnaissance. Problems with Ranger, developmental difficulties with the Centaur, and Apollo's requirements for more detailed information than a single spacecraft could provide obviated such a complicated and heavy probe. But the orbiter-lander concept—a "mothership" circling overhead while an offspring collected data from the surface—was to prove itself on future missions, most notably the two Viking probes that reached Mars in 1976 and Soviet missions to Venus in 1965 and 1975 and to Mars in 1971. The Galileo mission to Jupiter, launched in 1989, would also be a highly complex variation on that theme. It would comprise an orbiter that was supposed to circle Jupiter for almost two years and a probe that would descend into the giant's radiation-soaked atmosphere under a parachute, sending back data until it expired in the lethal soup.

Using orbiters and landers in this way, on separate missions or in combination, made sense because it broadened the dimension of the investigation. Each type of spacecraft had its own, distinctive role. Orbiters circling a planet or a moon at a distance of hundreds or thousands of miles provide a perspective that is impossible to attain from up close. Getting up close, however, can yield important details that are unobtainable from far away. Scientists who study planetary atmospheres, for example, like to use pictures from orbiters to observe entire weather systems. But they also rely on measurements from landers or penetrators, which get right into the atmosphere itself, for precise data on the composition and characteristics of that atmosphere which are unobtainable from orbiters. Used in combination, orbiters and landers would provide scientists with a synergistic effect that was impossible if either type of probe alone was used. That was the rationale for the spacecraft that were to conduct the next stages of lunar reconnaissance: Surveyor and Lunar Orbiter.

A single spacecraft to accomplish both orbiting and landing, and called the Surveyor Lunar Orbiter, had been approved in May 1960. But the problems with Centaur, the only upper stage powerful enough to lift such a dual-purpose spacecraft, had forced NASA to divide the project into its component parts. In 1962 and 1963, even as the Rangers were failing, Headquarters and its Langley Research Center in Virginia studied the requirements of an orbiter mission. By March 1963 Langley's engineers had completed plans for a light-weight lunar orbiter and won approval for it not long afterward. The decision by Washington to go to Langley for a Moon orbiter was a curious one. Although the Tidewater engineers were renowned for their experience in aeronautics, and also had done some work with sounding rockets and Earth satellites, the orbiter was their first major spaceflight project. It is conceivable that the Office of Space Science and the Office of Manned Space Flight, which were jointly interested in the orbiter, went to Langley because the Ranger fail-ures indicated to them that JPL had more to do than it could handle. It is not inconceivable, however, that Langley was given the project to spite Pasadena for its arrogance and what was perceived as its belligerent attitude.

Having decided that Langley could manage the Lunar Orbiter project but not totally design the mission and build the orbiter itself, requests for proposals for a planned mission and spacecraft were released to industry. A Lunar Orbiter Project Office was duly set up at Langley under the direction of Clifford H. Nelson in late August 1963. Boeing Aerospace was eventually selected as the prime con-tractor for the orbiter and the shroud under which it would ride to space. Several months later Eastman Kodak was awarded a contract for the photographic subsystem. The Lunar Orbiter was also Boe-ing's first venture into the detailed planning of a space mission and the design and building of a spacecraft to perform it. Its contract called for the production of five orbiters at a total cost of $75.8 million.

Meanwhile, work was under way on the "soft-lander" itself, which came into sole possession of the name Surveyor. This spacecraft was going to push technology well beyond that of machines like Ranger, which struck the Moon like catapulted rocks, or orbiters, which circled it. Surveyor would have to land on the lunar surface so gently that its photographic apparatus and scientific instruments could gather the final, crucial data that were necessary before men fol-lowed. Surveyor, in fact, had a dual purpose. Not only was it sup-posed to collect data for a final determination of whether the Moon's surface would support Lunar Modules, but the very act of its land-ing—of its using retrorockets firing downward to brake its descent

against the pull of gravity—amounted to a test of its larger manned
cousin, the Lunar Module itself.*

JPL had been given responsibility for developing the lander in the
spring of 1960, when Surveyor was conceived as a two-part spacecraft
(and more than a year before the first Ranger mishap), and it kept
it. Barely minutes before he left office on January 19, 1961—the day
before John Kennedy became president and brought in Webb as the
new NASA administrator—the outgoing Keith Glennan approved
Hughes Aircraft as the contractor that would actually build seven
of the robot lunar landers under JPL's supervision.

The cost of the program—of designing and building the spacecraft
and getting them to the Moon—was claimed by NASA to be $58
million. But that figure, which was given to the press and to Congress, was a gross underestimation. Not untypically for either the
space agency or the Pentagon, the estimate neatly omitted the cost
of everything but the spacecraft themselves. The final figure, which
included all relevant operational expenses as well as overruns that
were caused for a variety of reasons—mainly a lack of understanding by either JPL or Hughes of the magnitude of the job, but also
including the confounding problems with the Centaur—would be
more than eight times that much: nearly $483 million.

The lander was to be squat, roughly triangular, and have two
equipment bays, a mast holding a solar panel and a slew of antennas,
and three legs, each of which sprouted a footpad. It would ride an
Atlas Centaur (the upper stage at last having come on line and been
successfully tested late in 1963). Surveyor would be slowed on descent by its single retrorocket, while three smaller vernier engines
would be fired to make minute adjustments to keep it level. At that
point—1963 and 1964—Surveyor, like Ranger, was heavily oriented
toward scientific experiments, according to W. E. Giberson, who first
managed the spacecraft for JPL. But as was the case with its cousin,
Ranger, that was to change.

Besides the absolute primacy of landing men on the Moon, which
had almost the same effect on Surveyor that it did on Ranger, Centaur's performance estimate kept fluctuating as its own engineers
labored to make it more dependable. Each time that happened, Sur-

---

*The Lunar Module comprised two main parts: a descent stage and an ascent stage.
The first, which operated like Surveyor, was to use its retrorockets to lower the Lunar
Module and its two occupants to the Moon's surface. The ascent stage would then be
detached from the descent stage and lift the astronauts back to where they could
reunite with the orbiting Command Module that would take them home.

veyor's designers had to recalculate its weight and the amount and size of the hardware it could carry. Like the crew of an airplane desperately tossing nonessential equipment out of the door to reduce its weight in one of those hackneyed movies, Surveyor's engineers had to reduce its scientific payload from 345 pounds to 20 pounds on the first four Surveyors and then back up to only 114 pounds on the last three.

Giberson nevertheless termed the spacecraft itself nothing short of "exotic," particularly for its time. It had an advanced array of communication antennas, radars that were used for making measurements of the distance to the surface as it drew closer to the Moon, its own throttleable engine, and, of course, the small science package.

There were, however, the usual development problems. When a full-size version of the lander was finally put together, for example, it was hoisted up to a tethered balloon some two thousand feet over Holloman Air Force Base in New Mexico and, with its radar on and its retrorocket going full blast, it was dropped to simulate landing on the Moon. This was perfectly sensible, since the engineers needed to know whether the braking system would work at the crucial instant. "The idea," Giberson explained, "was to actually soft-land on the ground. The first one crashed."

As counterpoint to the wearing out of pencils at Hughes and JPL and the smashing of steel at Holloman, there was the usual unrelenting clash of wills between Headquarters and Pasadena. "After all that had happened following the Ranger 6 failure . . . one would have thought that JPL had the message," Homer Newell was to note incredulously. Evidently not.

He and Cortright were "shocked" to learn in a conversation with Pickering in early July 1964 "that JPL considered Surveyor a low-key project which could be kept on the back burner, with the contractor [Hughes] left pretty much to his own devices." Letters to Pasadena followed in which Pickering was warned to tighten management and grasp the fact that Surveyor was "one of the highest priority projects in the space science program." Pickering, who maintained that he was merely following orders which stipulated reliance on outside contractors, still seemed to have his head beyond the Moon and his eyes on the planets.

JPL's vexing independent streak, plus a reputation for angering experimenters by being overbearing with them, at one point led NASA to consider insisting that Caltech fire Pickering. Another option mulled over by the exasperated space agency management was to convert JPL to civil service status, just as with the other centers. (How Webb relished that thought!) But there were sound reasons for abandoning both notions, however tempting they were. Pickering had too much to offer to make his removal "palatable," Newell wrote. And "the fierce pride that JPL people took in their heritage as part of the Caltech family left grave doubts as to whether the laboratory could be converted without seriously disrupting the ongoing program."

For its part, Pasadena tended to consider much of the tampering back East as superfluous and irksome, as usual. As late as January 1968, for example, Nicks was to write a six-page letter to Arnold Beckman outlining "key management functions" that he thought would improve the way the laboratory operated. B. P. Huber, Pickering's executive assistant, promptly got off a letter to DuBridge which dismissed Nick's recommendations as a broadbrush treatment that was applicable to any organization. "It rings of motherhood without providing any substantive issues," Huber sniped.

In the meantime, work progressed on both Lunar Orbiter and the Surveyor lander. Besides its photographic system, the 847-pound orbiter carried mapping equipment, as well as instruments to measure meteoroid activity and radiation intensity.

On August 10, 1966, Lunar Orbiter 1, riding atop an Atlas and inside one of the new Agena-Ds, was launched at the Moon. It was shortly to go into a perfect orbit, sending back 207 pictures covering 18,600 square miles of possible Apollo landing sites and more than ten times that much area on the Moon's far side. The orbiter thus became the first U.S. spacecraft to circle the Moon. The four missions that followed were as good as the first. The last in the series, which was launched on August 1, 1967, sent back 212 medium- and high-resolution pictures through August 28, and in the process completed coverage of the far side. When Lunar Orbiter 5's reconnaissance was completed, it was sent crashing into the surface of the Moon, as were its predecessors. No one wanted derelict probes circling the Moon to become navigation hazards for the Apollo spacecraft that were to follow in just under eleven months.

Langley's first deep space mission ended on a very positive note. Lunar Orbiter not only provided a wealth of data about the surface of the Moon, but its mission was executed within budget and in a cooperative spirit with Headquarters. NASA would remember Langley's performance a few years later when it came time to prepare for a landing on Mars.

Meanwhile, JPL's Surveyor 1 rose from Canaveral on its Atlas Centaur on May 30, 1966, and headed to its destination. The fact that Luna 9, launched four months earlier, had beaten it to a soft landing on the lunar surface did little to dampen spirits in Pasadena. Following a midcourse correction using the three verniers, the spacecraft closed to within fifty miles of the Moon on June 2. As it approached, the spacecraft fired its retrorocket and the verniers, slowing its descent to 230 feet a second.

With its verniers still on, Surveyor 1 slowed until it was practically hovering thirteen feet above Oceanus Procellarum, the Sea of Storms. The tiny steering jets were then turned off in order to minimize contamination of the landing area and not stir up dust. Then the spacecraft, cushioned by shock absorbers and crushable pads on its three outstretched legs, landed gently on the Moon.

Surveyor went right to work. It sent 11,237 high-quality television pictures back to Earth during the next six weeks, though it remained operational until the following January. The quicksand scenario, which still lingered as a dangerous possibility for some in NASA and elsewhere, evaporated. Surveyor 1's landing indicated that the lunar surface would support loads of about 350 grams per square centimeter: about the same as wet beach sand or plowed soil. That would be just fine.

Surveyor 2 got off all right on September 20, but its verniers failed it on descent, causing it to crash just southeast of the crater Copernicus. Surveyor 3 landed successfully on April 19, 1967. No. 4 was also afflicated with a malfunction immediately before it was due to land, so it, too, hit the Moon hard and was smashed into uselessness. But it was the last failure NASA was to have on the Moon.

All three of its successors performed perfectly. Surveyor 5 landed on Mare Tranquillitatis on September 11, 1967, and promptly began the first chemical analysis of the surface of another world. It shot a stream of alpha particles into the soil over which it squatted. Counting the number of alpha particles that richocheted back to the spacecraft's sensor allowed scientists to estimate the composition of the soil, which turned out to resemble terrestrial basalt. This not only further confirmed that the soil would support heavier landers, but also provided the first hard evidence of a chemical relationship—a kinship—between the Moon and its mother planet. The last of the series, Surveyor 7, alighted near the rim of the crater Tycho on the Southern Highlands on January 9, 1968. It returned 21,274 TV pictures and a chemical analysis of its surroundings, which differed from Mare Tranquilitatis.

In the end, and after an expenditure of nearly $905 million, the three main lunar reconnaissance programs—Ranger, Lunar Orbiter, and Surveyor—proved to be a mixed bag. Mostly relegated to the role of mere scouts for the men who were to follow, they returned precious little of scientific value and did nothing to resolve the debate on the origin and composition of the Moon itself.

Two of the programs, Ranger and Surveyor, were the objects of such bitter contention between JPL and Headquarters that they effectively became consciousness-raisers, the way errant children can cause arguments that reveal and even exacerbate otherwise unrelated marital problems. The Ranger failures also forced JPL to acknowledge that its smugness was compromising its genius. On the other hand, the program's eventual successes, as well as those of Surveyor's, forced Headquarters to come to terms with the fact that excellence was not the exclusive province of the civil service. Both sides came away from their contention over the Moon with a better understanding of how the other functioned and what it saw as its real needs and aspirations. That knowledge would prove to be increasingly important in the stressful but challenging years after Apollo.

In the realm of space, itself, some real achievements lay all but obscured beneath the debris of conflict. Whatever Houston thought about the value of lunar reconnaissance, the Surveyors did show that spacecraft could alight safely on the Moon. Six manned landings would follow without loss of life. In addition, the probes launched a revolution in lunar and planetary mapping, capturing details that were well beyond the capability of ground-based telescopes. And while easily unnoticed, the rockets themselves had improved in power and reliability to the point where they could be depended upon to keep the momentum of exploration going without undue setback.

Perhaps most important, the Ranger, Surveyor, and Lunar Orbiter missions provided NASA and its science community with a prodigious amount of solid experience in whole new areas of deep space operations, both technical and scientific. Their voyages to the Moon were an appropriate means of practicing what was necessary to go beyond it. And that experience would lead the way to the inner planets, then to the outer planets, and eventually beyond. Kepler would have been pleased.

7.

Mariner-Mars: The Road to Utopia

There was one place, and only one, where the whole disparate space program really came together during the time of Apollo, where the urge to send men and machines out to touch another world coalesced with the most profound longings for clues not only to the origin of the solar system but to the search for life beyond Earth itself. That place was not the Moon. It was Mars.

It was Mars, not the Moon, that von Braun envisioned as the destination for the armada of manned caravels he wanted to see strike out on the heavenly breezes. It was Mars, not the Moon, that most whetted the appetite of William Pickering and others at JPL who wanted their increasingly obedient robots to range ever farther out across the solar system, not only to gain scientific knowledge but to prove that they could be crafted to go on long and rigorous missions over almost unimaginable spans of time and space, and survive. And it was Mars, not the Moon, that most piqued the imagination of scientist and layman alike because it held the possibility of extraterrestrial life.

No one in the science community doubted the technological achievement that Apollo represented. Nor were the scientists oblivious to the knowledge that was gained through analysis of the rock and soil samples returned by the astronauts, the measurements made by the seismological instruments they planted, or the richly detailed close-up photographs that were taken of the lunar surface by them and by the robot spacecraft that supported them. Still, the origin of the Moon remained a matter of conjecture in the wake of Apollo. And whatever the program's scientific achievements, they were overshadowed by the fact that Apollo had turned the Moon into a blatant instrument of foreign policy. Mars, on the other hand, held its allure because it held its distance. That distance was a shroud that all scientists knew concealed the promise of treasures the Moon could never match. One of them was the remote but real possibility that it contained either traces of life itself or evidence that it had once existed there.

Although Venus, the morning star, is closer to Earth than Mars and certainly shines more brightly, it is the red planet that has most intrigued humanity through millennia. Mars was closely associated with both war and rebirth in ancient mythology and both facets of its character have remained remarkably durable until quite recently. The Babylonians, who were among the first to follow it methodically, named it Nergal after their god of war. It was the Roman name for their own war god, Mars, that stuck. Its two tiny moons, Phobos (Fear) and Deimos (Panic), take their own names from the attendants of Ares, the Greek god of war. More recently astronomers have noted interesting similarities between Mars and Earth. Mars makes one rotation every twenty-four hours and thirty-seven minutes, compared with Earth's twenty-three hours and fifty-six minutes; its rotation velocity at the equator is very close to Earth's; and it tilts an average of 25 degrees, compared with Earth's 23.45. The tilting means that Mars has seasons as Earth does, since its hemispheres take turns leaning closer to the Sun. It is the tilting that causes the Martian polar ice caps to advance and retreat according to the season, a phenomenon that, coupled with what appeared to be an elaborate network of canals and signs of vegetation on its surface, led some observers to conclude that life in some form could exist there.

Those who scrutinized Mars through telescopes in the mid- and late-nineteenth century saw a blurred planet divided into bright areas and dark ones beneath the ice caps. The bright places, which give off Mars's characteristic reddish hue, were thought to be deserts, while the darker ones, which variously appeared as gray, brown, blue, or green, were at first believed to be large bodies of water and were therefore called maria, or seas. But since the maria were seen to change from blue-green in the spring and summer to faded brown in the fall and winter, and then back again, the idea that they supported vegetation began to take hold as the century wore on. Some astronomers also thought they saw thin, straight lines spanning hundreds of miles in several directions and these, too, appeared to change color seasonally, as the maria did.

Giovanni Schiaparelli, the most renowned Mars mapper of the

time, called the lines *canali* (channels, not canals) and noted in 1877, without absolutely committing himself, that they could have been the work of intelligent beings. In 1893 Schiaparelli published a paper in which his views of the planet were explained in considerable detail. He concluded that the polar caps were an "immense mass of ice and snow" that advanced and retreated just as their earthly counterparts did. From that observation the astronomer forged a theory that was to shape the vision of Mars held by much of the world right up to the time when the first actual exploration of the planet began.

Schiaparelli reasoned that there could be no snow and ice without the precipitation of vapor, that the vapor was almost certainly water, and that it was carried by an appreciable atmosphere. Turning to the *canali,* he pointed out that those in the areas surrounding the ice and snow expanded, becoming "blacker and wider," as the polar caps melted, and then receded when the polar melting stopped. He therefore concluded that the channels seemed to form a "true hydrographic system," though he did not attribute them to artificial creation. "It is not necessary to suppose them the work of intelligent beings, and notwithstanding the almost geometrical appearance of all of their system, we are now inclined to believe them to be produced by the evolution of the planet, just as on Earth we have the English Channel and the Channel of Mozambique."

It was largely from this long paper that Percival Lowell, a Boston Brahmin and self-taught astronomer, concluded that a race of extremely intelligent and stalwart beings not only populated Mars but was desperately trying to save itself from extinction by irrigating a parched, dying planet.* Lowell's deliberations were scrupulously recorded. The resulting theory was meticulously constructed, carefully illustrated, and tenaciously defended. It was also absolutely wrong and stands to this day as a classic model of scientific sophistry. Yet Percival Lowell, utterly wrong but never in doubt, is owed a debt of sorts by the planetary exploration community. He was the one who brought Mars to the masses.

Lowell was a Harvard-educated Phi Beta Kappa whose blood

*Lowell was so awed by Schiaparelli that he dedicated a book, *Mars and Its Canals,* to him. "To Schiaparelli the republic of science owes a new and vast domain. His genius first detected those strange new markings on the Martian disk which have proved a portal to all that has since been seen. . . . He made there voyage after voyage, much as Columbus did on Earth, with even less of recognition from home," Lowell intoned poetically. If Schiaparelli was the Columbus of Mars, Lowell implied, then he was its Amerigo Vespucci (Sheehan's *Planets and Perception,* p. 164).

flowed directly from the same Lowells and Lawrences for whom two cities in Massachusetts remain named. It was not only Schiaparelli, but also Charles Darwin, who brought Lowell to amateur astronomy in 1894 and to his unshakable belief that there was life on Mars. Lowell had traveled extensively in the Orient and had published several articles and four books describing his experiences there with typical Victorian ethnocentrism. He was well acquainted with Darwin's theory of evolution and drew from it the notion that if intelligent life was an evolutionary process, it was at least theoretically possible that such life could evolve in places other than Earth. And just as Darwin had used the rigor of the scientific process to develop his theory of evolution on Earth, so, too, could Lowell use it to do the same for Mars.

"In our exposition of what we have gleaned about Mars, we have been careful to indulge in no speculation. The laws of physics and the present knowledge of geology and biology, affected by what astronomy has to say of the former subject, have conducted us, starting from the observations, to the recognition of other intelligent life," he proclaimed. "We have carefully considered the circumstantial evidence in the case, and we have found that it points to intelligence acting on that other globe, and it is incompatible with anything else."

Unsatisfied with observing conditions under an eastern sky that had been made relatively hazy by humidity and unbridled industrialization, Lowell moved to Flagstaff in the Arizona Territory early in 1894 and built an observatory under some of the clearest sky in the country, in a place, as the astronomers would say, that had exceeding good "seeing."* The town in those days was a rough ranching and lumbering community of about eight hundred people. Only eight years before Lowell set up his twelve-inch and eighteen-inch refractors, Geronimo and his band of marauding Apaches had finally been caught and shipped off to a detention camp in Florida.

Beginning in the late spring of 1894 and continuing for many years afterward, Lowell and successive assistants turned out thousands of drawings, many of them quite intricate, of Mars and what they took to be its features. However inaccurately Lowell interpreted what he saw, his observations were nonetheless rigorous and therefore quite valuable, producing quantities of detailed notes and journal entries.

---

*As Norman Horowitz has pointed out, Lowell did not neglect to point out that his observatory had a superior location when other astronomers said that they were unable to see what he saw (*To Utopia and Back,* p. 79).

Lowell's theory, painstakingly worked out with multiple analogies to the evolution of Earth, was based on the fact that Mars seemed to contain air, water, and a temperature range conducive to life. This, plus the fact that the planet tilted seasonally and had polar ice caps, as Earth did, led to the deduction that the green patches were oases of vegetation. Lowell maintained that the canals, as he called them, averaged about thirty miles wide, were "as fine as they are straight," and extended for hundreds and even thousands of miles in all directions. It was Lowell's insistence on their absolute straightness, uniform width, and systematic radiation from the oases that took him a giant step beyond Schiaparelli. Lowell could not bring himself to believe that such exquisite geometry had been created by nature at random.

And if nature hadn't made them, he reasoned, then intelligent beings had. The most likely reason for this, he became convinced, was that the inhabitants of Mars knew they were on a dying planet and were engaged in a brave (but ultimately futile) effort to survive for as long as possible by carefully managing what remained of their water. Lowell tirelessly preached his theory to audiences in public lectures and in articles in *Astronomy and Astro-Physics, Popular Astronomy, Atlantic Monthly,* and other publications.

Most scientists (Schiaparelli being an exception) dismissed Lowell's contention out of hand, some with unconcealed scorn. "It is a point to be noted that the conclusions reached by Mr. Lowell at the end of his work agree remarkably with the facts he set out to prove before his observatory was established at all," Edward S. Holden, director of the Lick Observatory in California, said icily. W. W. Campbell, Holden's successor, flatly labeled Lowell an opportunist.

Public reaction was another matter, however. It ranged from accepting wonder to skeptical but tolerant amusement. Newspapers carried vivid accounts of Lowell's revelations and his lectures were often oversubscribed, however much he was scorned and ridiculed by the scientific establishment.

Yet for all of the enormity of his error, Lowell was to bequeath a lasting legacy on the space program. He and his colleagues broke ground on many of the investigative techniques, such as spectroscopy, radiometry, polarimetry, and photography, that were to become indispensable research tools for later astronomers. And he did so, not insignificantly, with his own money. He also popularized Mars and the subject of space in general by igniting the imagination of successive generations. Finally, he provided a good deal of the motivation—the selling point—for sending robot spacecraft to the red planet to search for some form of life, however unintelligent it might be. The possibility of there being some form of life on Mars, or at least evidence that it once existed, is still used as a selling point to mount expeditions.

Although science scoffed at the possibility of intelligent life on Mars, it nevertheless remained an enduring myth among ordinary folk long after Lowell's death in 1916. On October 30, 1938—forty-four years after Lowell postulated his theory—thousands of people took the possibility of intelligent life on Mars so seriously that they fled their homes in terror when they heard Orson Welles deliver a dramatic "news account" of H. G. Wells's *The War of the Worlds*.

Unlike Lowell's Martians, which were physically undefined but benevolent, Wells's were huge, hideous, armed with heat rays, and definitely mean-spirited. "Those who have never seen a living Martian can scarcely imagine the strange horror of its appearance," Wells noted before describing creatures with no chins, quivering mouths, tentacles, and immense eyes. "There was something fungoid in the oily brown skin, something in the clumsy deliberation of the tedious movements unspeakably nasty. Even at this first encounter, this first glimpse, I was overcome with disgust and dread."

"I heard the broadcast and almost had a heart attack," one man in the Bronx told *The New York Times*. "I didn't tune it in until the program was half over, but when I heard the names and titles of Federal, State, and municipal officials, and when the Secretary of the Interior was introduced, I was convinced that it was the McCoy. I ran out into the street with scores of others, and found people running in all directions."

Well into the twentieth century, reputable scholars writing in popular college-level astronomy texts continued to hold out the possibility of life in some form, however primitive, on Mars. "It seems now to be the consensus of opinion among astronomers that very probably there is life on Mars, at least plant life," one textbook explained in 1940. "And since plant life and animal life developed together on the Earth," it added, following Lowell's faulty logic, "perhaps they are both present on Mars." That same year, no less an authority than H. Spencer Jones, the Astronomer Royal, concluded that "The presence of free oxygen almost certainly demands the existence of vegetation" on Mars. "The temperature and atmospheric conditions on Mars make vegetable life seem a possibility," another astronomy book noted nine years later, "and the color changes observed make it seem rather a probability." But, it hedged prudently, "conditions for animal life, unless of the lowest orders, must be very inhospitable from the climatic point of view."

The coming of the space age and the real possibility of being able to search for life on Mars, rather than merely hypothesize about it through lenses, seized the imagination of many scientists and lay-men alike. The public, or at least an alert segment of it, came to believe that the wherewithal for resolving the question was finally at hand. The following letter, which appeared in a Baltimore news-paper in 1984, probably spoke for many lay people in the United States and throughout the world when it asked: "Whatever hap-pened to the Martian canals? When I was little I distinctly recall seeing pictures of Mars that showed an elaborate network of lines that some thought were the remnants of an irrigation system built by a lost race of intelligent beings. But there was always some dis-claimer to the effect that we'd have to wait for further exploration before we could know for sure. Well, NASA has since sent any number of satellites [sic] flying by Mars equipped with cameras—and yet I don't remember hearing a peep about the canals. What's the story? Is there something they're not telling us, or was the whole thing a con intended to drum up support for the space program?"

Here's the story. There were many reasons for wanting to go to Mars, including the usual urge to inspect another world up close, to get to know it for its own sake, and also to see how it related to Earth and fit into the larger scheme of the solar system. But the question of the existence of life on Mars, whether stated explicitly or not, permeated nearly all discussion about the planet. It constituted an invariable undercurrent whenever planetary scientists got together. It haunted their literature and nagged at their souls. But whether or not they believed in the possibility of life in some form on the red planet, however primitive, there was one thing that was beyond debate. Everyone accepted the fact that the matter would not be settled until in situ experiments could be made—experiments that could be conducted not in some laboratory but on Mars itself. Explor-ing machines would have to go there and look.

But two fundamental questions had to be addressed before serious exobiological studies, or studies of life beyond Earth, could be planned at Mars, much less carried out. First, the scientific commu-nity had to decide what in fact it was looking for. It had to make an attempt to define life itself in an unambiguous way. And having done that, it had to decide which instruments would be most helpful for conducting the search.

Norman H. Horowitz, the Caltech biochemist who was to figure prominently in the search for life on Mars, put the matter simply but eloquently: "Our concept of 'life' must be broad enough to let us recognize it in any guise and precise enough to prevent our finding it where it does not exist."

Living things differ from inanimate ones in two fundamental respects, Horowitz said: they are far more complex and they have mechanisms that assure their survival (the most basic being self-replication and mutation, or the ability to reproduce and adapt). "Any system with the capacity to mutate freely and to reproduce its mutations must also inevitably evolve in directions that will ensure its preservation. Given sufficient time, the system will acquire the complexity, variety, and purposefulness that we recognize as 'alive.' " This is called the genetic model and it is widely (though not universally) accepted. Its premise is that life elsewhere must in some basic way mirror life here.

Life on Earth, as Horowitz has noted, is based on the chemistry of carbon. The system that constitutes the genetic model is built primarily of carbon compounds and such other light elements as hydrogen, oxygen, and nitrogen. Carbon atoms have properties that are particularly suitable for combination with other atoms to make highly complex, often very large yet stable arrangements of molecules. They are in turn the basis of proteins and nucleic acids, the foundations of Earth life. The organic compounds that are made of carbon and the other elements are in turn inherently unstable, yet they are inert. Instability means that these compounds change by reacting with other elements—with heat or water, for example. But, being inert, the change occurs slowly enough so that they have time to form highly elaborate and long-lived molecular structures.

This ability to change according to biological or chemical circumstances, but not so quickly that there would be perpetual chaos, explains why carbon is uniquely qualified for the construction of genetic systems. "Carbon is so superior for the building of complex molecules that the possibility of forming genetic systems with other elements has never seriously been considered," Horowitz explained. "While we cannot prove that no element but carbon can accomplish these functions," he added, "the possibility appears so remote that we shall assume carbon to be unique in this respect." Most scientists agree.

But Gerald Feinberg and Robert Shapiro, a Columbia University physicist and a New York University biochemist, respectively, aren't so sure about carbon's being the sine qua non of life. They therefore have taken a far more expansive approach to defining the quality of living. The two scientists have made an interesting case for the possibility of life existing elsewhere in the universe (and even inside Earth itself) in forms that depend on the laws of physics and chemistry but bear no relation whatever to the genetic model. Feinberg and Shapiro suggest the possibility of life throughout the cosmos, including within stars, that is not based on carbon at all. They do not say that Horowitz and other mainstream biologists and chemists are wrong. They do think, however, that looking in other directions—shaking off humanity's biocentrism—is at minimum good for the spirit and possibly even scientifically valid as well.

Whatever the definition of life, all agree that finding it elsewhere in the universe would have the most profound consequences for the human spirit. "Were we gifted with a vision of the whole Universe of Life," Feinberg and Shapiro concluded, "we would not see it as a desert, sparsely populated with identical plants which can survive only in rare specialized niches. Instead, we would envision something closer to a botanical garden, with countless species, each thriving in its own setting. If this latter vision is accurate, another argument for the distinction of Earth and its inhabitants will disappear," so that humankind will come to feel more like a local representative of life throughout the universe rather than existing alone in a vast and sterile void.

The physicist Philip Morrison has reflected that the discovery of life elsewhere in the cosmos would temper the human race's ethnocentric arrogance. It would transform life, he has said, from being a miracle to being a statistic.

The planetologists, and particularly those who were interested in geology, climate, and the overall way in which planets are affected by the universe in which they exist, had their own agenda for Mars.

"From the point of view of comparative planetology, the relations between Venus, Earth, and Mars were ideal," Homer Newell wrote. "Earth was clearly intermediate between the two others in many respects, and many scientists felt that a detailed study of all three should be of special benefit in understanding Earth." He specifically referred to the study of halogens* in the atmosphere of Venus as being helpful for understanding how chlorine and Freon might dan-

---

*Fluorine, chlorine, bromine, and iodine, which are closely related chemically, are halogens.

gerously deplete Earth's protective ozone layer and how an understanding of dust storms in the thin Martian atmosphere could lead
to new knowledge about how dust affects the climate of this planet.*

But the science, as usual, was also driven by politics. The Soviets
took the world's first shots at Mars on October 10 and 14, 1960. They
decided to use an improved version of the standard Vostok launch
vehicle, though they lengthened its third stage for use as an orbital
platform that would circle Earth and from which the Mars probes
could be fired. As it turned out, it didn't matter. Both attempts failed
because of booster malfunctions, so the spacecraft remained anony-
mous. Named or not, though, they would prove to be the harbingers
of a three-decade-long streak of profoundly bad luck where Soviet
Mars missions were concerned.

The next opportunity came a little more than two years later. As
was becoming customary, the Soviets relied on a multiprobe exploration strategy, and accordingly dispatched three more spacecraft toward Mars on October 24, November 1, and November 4, 1962. The
first apparently exploded while still in Earth orbit. The second actually made it into a trajectory aimed at Mars, a development that
prompted its optimistic controllers to christen it Mars 1. Three days
later what would have been Mars 2 failed to make it out of Earth
orbit and was incinerated during reentry. Then, on March 21, 1963,
all contact with Mars 1 was lost as it closed in on the red planet. The
probe apparently became disoriented, which would have simultaneously broken its communication lock with Earth and moved its
solar panels out of alignment with the Sun, cutting off its main
power supply. It looked like the work of the Ghoul. The five abortive
Mars shots, the failed attempts to get Sputnik 7 and Venera 1 to
Venus in February 1961, and then eleven successive failures to get
other probes to Venus through the autumn of 1965, were an unmistakable indication that the Soviet leadership was driving its space
establishment hard. It wanted to beat the West to deep space as well
as to Earth orbit. And their rivals felt the heat.

*Skeptics like Robert Shapiro are dubious about the quality of the scientific returns
as a function of the cost of such missions. In an interview with the author in 1987
Shapiro maintained that while such "big science" questions as whether life exists
elsewhere in the cosmos, or whether humans can colonize other parts of the solar
system, are worthwhile, there is no real need to scrutinize other planets to understand Earth. The best way to spend resources for understanding Earth, he maintained, is to examine the planet itself, not its neighbors. Proponents of such missions
argue that the varying dispositions of the planets compress a time scale that would
be impossible to duplicate on Earth.

"To JPL," the historian Clayton R. Koppes has written, "the Russian program was both a political setback and a professional affront." In April 1961 Pickering had gone so far as to establish a committee to come up with ways for Pasadena to salvage the national honor. He charged it with devising a plan that would "take into account the primary importance of the propaganda and geopolitical aspects of space achievements, as well as the value of missions having scientific merit."

The JPL report weighted the value of missions in three categories on a scale of 100. The results were telling: 45 percent thought that national prestige was the most compelling reason for staging deep space missions; 35 percent believed they were important as a means of improving technology; only 20 percent put down science as the principal driving factor. The primary goal of going to space, the report emphasized, was to be first, rather than to do "a better engineering job or obtain . . . more scientific data." Whatever inner philosophy the committee members brought to the report, they also took their cues from Pickering himself, who the year before had stated unequivocally that it was "the U.S. against Russia," and that the "most important campaign is being fought far out in the empty reaches of space." James Burke, then the Ranger project manager, tacked a picture of Venera 1 to the wall in front of his desk and pasted an old proverb beside it: "The better is the enemy of the good." It was like pumping up for the big game.

And so it was that a complex array of factors—scientific, technological, political, and perhaps even mystical—combined to set the course for Mars, even as it was being set for the Apollo landings on the Moon, in what the competitors saw as a matter of manifest destiny and national honor no less than the quest for knowledge.

In the spring of 1960 NASA established an Office of Life Sciences specifically to study the biological and physiological aspects of manned space flight and to search for extraterrestrial life. That year Headquarters also authorized JPL to study the possibility of getting a lander on Mars to search for life.

In 1962 an Exobiology Division was established at the Ames Research Center. The following year it was specifically charged with evaluating the many scientific instruments and experiments that were being suggested for the Mars life investigation by such luminaries as Wolf Vishniac of the Yale University School of Medicine, Melvin Calvin of the Department of Chemistry at Berkeley, and Joshua Lederberg, then of Columbia University. A summer study group sponsored by the Space Science Board in 1962 called for an investigation of life and other matters of scientific interest on Mars. A second summer group convened in 1964. That one, which included thirty-seven of the top life scientists in the country, issued specific proposals for the exploration of the planet.

While no one quibbled with the fact that soft landings by instrument-carrying spacecraft would eventually have to be made, it was also understood that, as was the case with the Moon, probes would first have to fly by to reconnoiter suitable landing places and collect data on surface conditions, atmospherics, and other phenomena that would help to prepare the way for the advanced mission. The order of attack, so to speak—flying by, orbiting, and then landing—had by then become established. First to go out, according to a plan tentatively approved by NASA in November 1962, were two identical JPL spacecraft—Mariners 3 and 4 (or C and D, or Mariner-Mars 1964, as they were also called)—that would fly past the planet and keep going. And as had been the case with Mariners 1 and 2, there was to be a setback before the mission succeeded.

Work on the two Mariner-Mars probes began late in 1962, the year after work started on Mariner-Venus, and two years before the next window was due to open for Mars itself. Throughout the autumn and winter of 1962 and into 1963, even as the Ranger debacle continued, Jack James's Mariner-Mars project office considered the special problems that would have to be overcome to get to Mars.

For one thing, the trip would take up to seven thousand hours— 290 days—which was almost three times as long as it was going to take to get to Venus. That meant almost three times the likelihood of equipment failure. Furthermore, Mariners 3 and 4 would be heading away from the Sun, not toward it like the Mariner-Venus probes. The reduced sunlight meant that the Mars spacecraft would have to carry seventy square feet of solar panels for their power as opposed to only twenty-seven square feet for Mariners 1 and 2. And the communication distance between Earth and Mars would be three times longer at near encounter than it would be at Venus. The inverse square law therefore dictated that the communication system on Mariners 3 and 4 would have to be nine times better than the one on Mariners 1 and 2. Navigation would be different, too. The lunar and Venus missions used Earth as a reference point. The Mars missions would have to use the Sun and Canopus to get and keep their bearings, however, because Earth would move across the face of the Sun for a long period during the flights and would therefore be all but useless as a navigation point. Failure to anticipate that kind of situation and hundreds like it—seemingly trivial matters next to thrust-to-weight ratios, the reliability of upper stages, or the accuracy of an ephemeris—could kill an otherwise flawless mission.

Finally, there was the problem of the engineering subsystems and the scientific instruments themselves, which would weigh substantially more than they did on Mariner-Venus. To the bare structure of the spacecraft itself—its skeleton—the engineers had to stuff in what amounted to a roomful of equipment. There was a radio (and its antenna), a data encoder, video storage equipment, a command system, attitude control equipment, a central computer and sequencer that were supposed to give commands in a prescribed order, a power system (including the four solar panels, an eighteen-cell battery, voltage regulators, and battery-charging, load-switching, and frequency-control devices), a pyrotechnics system to supply power specifically to fire the latches that would open the solar panels and the scan platform, and a cold gas jet propulsion system for midcourse trajectory correction. Temperature control equipment was particularly important. Unlike Mariner-Venus, which headed in the general direction of the Sun and therefore grew warmer, Mariner-Mars was to go the other way and would therefore get colder. If everything else was to work right, it was imperative that the spacecraft have stable internal working temperatures.

The science instruments included a narrow-angle telescopic television camera for taking pictures of part of the Martian surface; a helium magnetometer designed to measure the strength of the magnetic field on the interplanetary segment of the flight and as the Mariners closed in on Mars; a cosmic dust detector to measure the momentum and distribution of the dust the spacecraft would hit; an ionization chamber (which included a Geiger counter) to detect and measure radiation; a cosmic ray telescope to measure certain kinds of charged particles; a special radiation detector to measure the distribution, energy, and identity of magnetically trapped particles around Mars; and a solar plasma probe to measure the density, velocity, temperature and direction of the low-energy protons streaming out from the Sun.

In addition, the Mariner-Mars 1964 spacecraft were to be the first to carry out a new experiment, called occultation, which did not require special equipment beyond the requisite radio transmitter used to communicate with Pasadena. Radio signals beamed through the Martian atmosphere to Earth after the spacecraft had passed the planet and was on its far side would be measured to see how much they bent. This would be done by comparing the amount of time it took the bent signal to reach Earth with a signal that was beamed in a straight line. The bent signal would of course take longer. Exactly how much longer it took would indicate how much it bent. And that, in turn, would provide data on the composition, density, and height of the Martian atmosphere.* Occultation measurements would become integral to virtually every deep space mission after Mariner-Mars 1964. The atmosphere people loved them. And the beauty of it was that where weight was concerned, the experiment rode for free.

Although the Deep Space Network would be in almost constant communication with the spacecraft, the central computers and sequencers they carried were programmed to automatically carry out the various experiments in order and without further instruction from Pasadena. They would also do housekeeping, including deploying the four solar panels, activate the attitude control jets, and everything else that kept the spacecraft functioning.

Since the launch vehicle for Mariners 3 and 4 was to be the combination of an Atlas D first stage and the new Agena D upper stage, the overall weight of the spacecraft had to be held to a bare minimum. This was accomplished in part by making the spacecraft's electronic packages the buses themselves, rather than building buses and then filling them with equipment; it was the equivalent of using the chassis of an automobile as the entire vehicle without covering all of its innards with a body. In addition, the science packages were miniaturized to an extent that would have been unbelievable only a few years earlier (the cosmic ray telescope and the trapped radiation detector each measured less than seventy-two cubic inches, or less than a box of facial tissues, for example). Even the shrouds that were supposed to protect the spacecraft during their ascent were made of fiberglass in order to minimize weight while ensuring adequate strength. As was so often the case where sending complex machines to space was concerned, the use of fiberglass, an otherwise fine idea, would cause yet another major accident because of simple oversight.

*This is far trickier than it may seem, since all other factors producing the apparent motion of the spacecraft—its actual motion, the motion of the receiving stations on the rotating Earth, the lengthening of the time it takes the signal to reach Earth, and the refractivity of the Earth's atmosphere—must be accounted for with extreme accuracy. With those factors precisely known, remaining unexplained changes in the radio signal can be attributed to the refracting effects of the atmosphere of the target planet itself.

The Mariner-Mars spacecraft weighed precisely 574.74 pounds (or 128 pounds more than their sisters that were designed for the trip to Venus), were nearly nine and a half feet high and, with their solar panels extended, measured a little more than twenty-two feet across. Each was composed of 138,000 parts. Mariners 3 and 4 may have looked more as if they were designed to hang from a ceiling to keep air moving than to reconnoiter a distant planet, but they were in fact superb pieces of astronautical engineering for their time.

By early November 1964 both were poised to fly from the space center that just under a year before had been renamed to honor the president who had fixed the nation's sights on the Moon but who had been murdered before he could see that goal realized.

Mariner 3 was first to go. At 2:22 on the afternoon of November 5 it rose off Launch Complex 13 and headed east over the Atlantic. But it became apparent within sixty minutes of liftoff that there was a serious problem. Telemetry showed that while the science instruments were functioning as they should, no sunlight was shining on the solar panels. And it wasn't shining on them for good reason: they hadn't opened. There was a sudden, alarming drop in power.

The reason for the blackout soon became apparent. The fiberglass shroud that protected the spacecraft as its upper stage sliced through the atmosphere was supposed to be released by springs and pop off at high altitude, allowing the probe's solar panels to deploy and start collecting energy for the start of the mission. But as was apparent from the telemetry streaming into the Kennedy Space

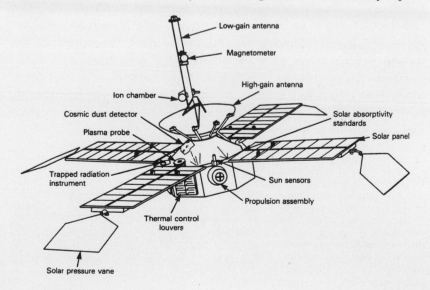

Center's launch control facility, the shroud hadn't popped off. It had stayed attached to the top of the Atlas, exactly where the technicians had secured it before launch. So Mariner 3, its solar panels pinned against its sides and its batteries drained, expired eight hours and forty-three minutes into the flight. Imprisoned within the darkness of its own shroud like a chrysalis entombed in its cocoon, it headed into a useless orbit around the Sun, taking its place as a tiny planetoid in the solar system.

Since Mariner 4 was scheduled to go on the twenty-fifth—at the end of a launch window that opened only every twenty-five months— engineers from JPL, NASA's Lewis Research Center in Cleveland, and Lockheed Missiles and Space scrambled to find out why the shroud had failed to separate and to correct the problem. Lewis was technically responsible for the shroud because it ran Mariner operations from launch to injection. But Lockheed had made the thing. The manufacturer therefore quickly conducted what it called a "comprehensive test program" to determine why its shroud had failed, but ended up reporting that no reasonable explanation could be established.

But JPL did better than that. Within four days, a series of tests of the shroud material in a heat chamber showed that the pockets of fiberglass honeycomb insulation exploded—"popped like popcorn," according to James—because of a heat buildup that was not vented. The explosions caused the honeycomb to separate from its own thin outer skin and stick to Mariner 3 like warm chewing gum. Lockheed's failure to adequately test its shroud, James noted years later, reflected the same sloppy management and engineering that his own laboratory had been guilty of during the outset of the Ranger program. Everybody was learning.

Mariner 4 rose into an overcast sky on the morning of November 28, dutifully shed its shroud, performed its other functions as commanded, and then headed for Mars almost without a hitch.*

---

*It did have some worrisome navigation trouble. Its Canopus sensor first locked onto a cluster of the wrong stars, then located the right one, only to lose it again during the midcourse maneuver on December 4. It reacquired the bright star, only to lose it again three days later, fixing on Gamma-Velorum instead. Mariner 4's controllers at JPL allowed it to stay on Gamma-Velorum until the seventeenth, when they broke its lock and got it to locate and stay on Canopus for the last time. The problem was eventually attributed to dust particles near the sensor's lens that reflected sunlight into it, creating a confusing situation for the little machine. The incident gives another indication, however, of how sensitive the Mariner-Mars instrumentation was.

Seven and a half months later, on the evening of July 14, 1965, the lone spacecraft sped past the red planet at an altitude of 6,188 miles with all sensors going. Its television camera took twenty-one and a half pictures of 1 percent of the Martian surface from distances of between 10,500 and 6,200 miles. Resolution was up to thirty times better than anything coming through earthbound telescopes. Meanwhile the other instruments collected data in considerable detail for transmission back to Pasadena. Mars had finally been reached.

Throughout the approach, JPL and NASA were careful to explain that Mariner 4's imagery would lack the resolution necessary to detect life, either animal or vegetal. In addition, they were careful to point out that the search for life was not running the mission, so photographic requirements had to give way to higher priorities in selecting Mariner 4's flight path. The probe could not be allowed to enter Mars's shadow, for example, or it would lose its fix on the Sun. It could not fly above the planet or it would lose Canopus. It could not get directly behind it or the occultation experiment wouldn't work properly. And, finally, California and Mars had to be facing each other at the time of encounter so that last-minute commands could be sent to the spacecraft if necessary. The camera's scan path therefore started at the planet's limb, at about 37 degrees north latitude, then swept down across the equator to about 52 degrees south latitude, and finally curved back up again to about 38 degrees south latitude. It was not an area that showed a great many canals on Lowell's charts.

Ever so slowly, the pictures began to come down to Goldstone and were immediately relayed to Pasadena for analysis. By current standards they might as well have been cave paintings, but by the standards of the time they were splendid.

The first pictures to come back to Earth from Mars were taken by the world's most sophisticated space probe. They were relayed through a network of antennas and computers that were on the cutting edge of the technology of their time. Yet each took ten and a half hours to materialize at an agonizingly slow rate of eight bits a minute. In addition, the pictures were composed of numbers that represented the hues of the Martian landscape. Each number was coded to correspond to a specific value, from white (0) to black (63). The numbers were printed in sequence on two hundred strips of paper tape (with two hundred pixels on a strip) as they came in. The strips were then cut into lines of numbers and stapled, side by side, onto a large piece of beaverboard. This made the entire picture look like a kind of uncolored number painting that had to be filled in. And that's exactly what the imaging team did. A color to match each number was selected arbitrarily. Then chalk of the appropriate color was painstakingly applied by hand to turn all forty thousand numbers into a yellow, brown, ocher, and red panorama. The first in the series hangs on permanent exhibition at JPL, a "priceless Rembrandt," according to Jurrie J. van der Woude of JPL's Office of Public Information.

On July 29 the Mars imaging team, led by principal investigator Robert B. Leighton, a Caltech physicist, told the world what it saw (and by clear inference what it didn't see) in the twenty-one and a half fuzzy pictures that had taken a little more than eight days to trickle in. Gone were the straight canals that Schiaparelli, Lowell, and some others had insisted crisscrossed the planet. Gone were the oases that were supposed to have held the precious water needed by the imperiled Martians. Gone were the creatures themselves (at least as could be determined from images whose best resolution was three kilometers, a little less than two miles). Certainly none bearing Wells's description showed up. More significantly, gone too was any semblance of terrain similar to Earth's, whatever the two planets may have had in common in terms of inclination, rate of rotation, temperature range, and so forth. The pictures, limited as they necessarily were, revealed no ocean basins—*maria*— or mountain ranges, no great valleys, and no continental plates.

What the imaging team did find was a lot of craters. Seventy of them, ranging from three miles to seventy-five miles across, were clearly visible in photos number five through fifteen in the camera's narrow scan path. Some appeared to rise three hundred feet high, while others had interiors several hundred feet deep. Mars seemed to bear no resemblance to Earth at all. What it looked like, in fact, was the Moon.

"Man's first close-up look at Mars has revealed the scientifically startling fact that at least part of its surface is covered with large craters," the imaging team's statement said. "Although the existence of Martian craters is clearly demonstrated beyond question, their meaning and significance is, of course, a matter of interpretation." Leighton and the others did go so far as to add, however, that the craters would lead to some "far-reaching fundamental inferences" about the evolution of Mars.

One inference was that Mars must be very ancient—perhaps as old as five billion years, or half a billion years older than Earth. Its remarkable state of preservation indicated that its thin atmosphere was never significantly denser than it is at the moment. The absence of severe erosion indicated that large quantities of water never existed on the planet. And the absence of a significant magnetic field or signs of topographic stress indicated a lack of internal activity such as exists in the Earth.

Finally, as predicted, the imaging team—or "television" team as they were called in those days—hedged on the big question. It said that its pictures neither demonstrated nor precluded the possibility of life. A search for fossils would hardly be promising in the absence of oceans, the scientists pointed out, though on the other hand the truly primitive surface of the planet might well hold preserved clues to some kind of early organic development. And, in a reference that was to be often repeated, they noted mellowly that what they found on Mars only enhanced the uniqueness of their own planet within the solar system.

The scientific return of the nonimaging instruments carried by Mariner 4 was significant. The absence of protective radiation belts did not bode well for the existence of life as it is known on Earth. The atmospheric pressure was measured at between four and seven millibars, or about what would be found at an altitude of twenty miles on Earth. That, too, did not speak well for the presence of life forms. Neither did the fact that the major constituent of the atmosphere was seen to be carbon dioxide by an overwhelming margin. Knowing this, and closely examining the planet's heat balance a year later, Leighton and Bruce C. Murray, another Caltech scientist and member of the television team, concluded in a celebrated paper that the polar caps themselves were made mostly of frozen carbon dioxide, not water, as had been widely supposed for several decades. This was yet another blow to the notion that a life form dependent on water could exist on Mars.

The Mariner 4 imagery provided a setback, but not a decisive one, to those who continued to hold out the possibility that either life in some form existed on Mars or it once had. In the face of growing skepticism within the scientific community itself, Lederberg and a few other self-described "diehards" met in late October 1965 to sift through Mariner 4's findings and come up with a course of action. They soon concluded that the search for life on Mars was a noble undertaking in its own right, irrespective of whether it was actually found, because the nature of the investigation itself would help to evaluate the uniqueness of life on Earth and allow a more valid inference about the abundance of life elsewhere in the universe. The fact that "new space technology" was available for such exploration for the first time, the group maintained, was reason enough to continue the quest.

Besides, there were two technical points that buttressed the case for pushing on. First, data on 1 percent of Mars—the swath under Mariner 4's route—was a very small sample. It was like trying to deduce the features of Earth based solely on information about Egypt. No one knew precisely what further reconnaissance would turn up elsewhere. Second, no amount of imagery and remote sensing could take the place of actually going down, landing, and analyzing samples on the spot.

However valuable flybys were, they were no substitute for going down for a look at the surface, so the notion of landing took an increasing hold on both the space science and planetary exploration communities and on the space agency itself. The urge to touch Mars intensified.

The instrument chosen to do this was originally named Voyager and then Viking. It stands to this day as an example of how a project can endure and even prevail despite being forced to run through a gauntlet of political rivalries; competing and highly charged scientific priorities; formidable design, navigation, and guidance challenges; managerial complexity without precedent for a probe; and a budgetary process so haphazard, labyrinthine, and parochial that it reduced all attempts at long-range planning to utter futility and grown men to near tears.

The idea was sound enough. As envisioned by the Office of Space Science and Applications, the Voyager program was to be the model of an orderly, progressive, logical method of exploring the planets in incremental stages. It was seen as "an evolving long-term program which will include flights during several opportunities," Homer Newell wrote to Caltech president Lee DuBridge. "Thus, later missions will be based on information from earlier missions. As the program evolves, significant changes in the scientific instruments are anticipated. These changes will result from scientific results from earlier missions, advances in scientific instrumentation, and increases in spacecraft and capsule capability," Newell explained, adding that while the basic bus would vary a bit to suit each mission, it would be of a "reasonably common design."

This made sense. The inherent commonality of the spacecraft would minimize their cost and allow those who used and operated them to gain increasing experience from one mission to the next. At the same time their built-in flexibility, which would permit them to be modified to suit the requirements of a given mission, could be expected to maximize the science they returned. It was a thoroughly impressive idea. But it ended as a debacle.

Voyager was first considered early in 1960 as a much heavier follow-on series after the Mariners. It was supposed to be a two-part spacecraft, with one part orbiting Venus or Mars the way the Lunar Orbiter would and the other making a soft landing, like Surveyor. And like Surveyor, Voyager was conceived at JPL.

But unlike Surveyor, which was created almost under duress for an Apollo program JPL viewed as both threatening and inadequately challenging, the lab relished Voyager because it was both highly advanced and planetary—a Rolls-Royce conceived for a noble purpose. Pasadena therefore took an early proprietary interest in both designing and assembling the big spacecraft in-house. This alarmed Headquarters. Laid on top of Ranger, Surveyor, and Mariner, it was felt, a fourth major project would tax JPL beyond its capability. And that, need it be said, could impinge on the most sacred of NASA's cows: Apollo itself. It was therefore determined that JPL would manage the project. That meant it would formulate the basic requirements for the spacecraft and for the missions as a whole. But an outside contractor would build the probes based on a design worked out jointly with the lab. In addition, other centers—Ames and Langley—would participate in areas that could benefit from their expertise.

But animus soon developed, as if by spontaneous generation, virtually everywhere. The science community became embroiled in a competition, refereed by Ames's new Exobiology Division, over which experiments would prove most fruitful. If the heart of the mission was the search for life, the competitors correctly reasoned, then the means used to look for it would obviously have to have the highest priority. And since the science team that discovered life beyond Earth would become immortal (no doubt picking up a Nobel Prize along the way), the contest to see whose experiment would go to Mars took on an especially keen edge. For his part, Lederberg was just as convinced that germs from Earth could ruin the search for life on Mars as they could on the Moon, and he therefore continued to press for sterilization.

Then there was the matter of the launch vehicle. Mariner 4 had found the Martian atmosphere to be thinner than anticipated. This meant the lander would need an enhanced way to slow its descent: a larger shell to brake its fall, larger parachutes, or more powerful retrorockets. That meant more weight. And more weight meant using a more powerful booster. The original plan called for the use of one of Huntsville's Saturn IB boosters—the large and extremely powerful forerunner of the Saturn V that would carry astronauts to the Moon—topped by a Centaur upper stage. JPL engineers, working on the assumption that they were designing Voyager for the Saturn IB-Centaur, did preliminary designs that called for a maximum weight of 1,865 pounds. Then, in mid-October 1965, Headquarters abruptly announced that the Saturn IB was to be terminated and as a consequence no Saturn IB-Centaur would be available for Voyager. The spacecraft would instead go to space on the even more powerful Saturn V.

That sounded fine. But Saturn V was a Trojan horse. For one thing, the massive booster (it was 6.6 times more powerful than Voyager needed) wasn't even supposed to fly until 1967, with the first of them earmarked for the Apollo program itself. This meant a delay of the Voyager test flight from 1969 to 1971 at the earliest, and therefore a postponement of the mission until 1973. Then, too, the change of boosters meant that the interface between the spacecraft and its new launch vehicle had to be reengineered. Electrical connections had to be redesigned, for example, and so did the insulation that would protect Voyager from the Saturn V's unique kind of vibration. The changes sent up the projected cost of the entire Voyager program to about $2 billion, according to one estimate. It therefore ran headlong into an Apollo budget that was entering its critical 1966–67 phase. There was no serious contest between the overwhelming imperative of landing men on the Moon versus sending robots to outer space to measure rare elements, photograph extinct volcanoes, and search for fossils. As it was, the Bureau of the Budget reduced NASA's fiscal 1967 budget from the $5.6 billion requested to $5 billion, since most of the Apollo hardware and support system had already been bought. And nearly three fifths of that amount went to Apollo anyway. Voyager's cut for 1967 was a paltry $10 million.

The total request of the Office of Space Science and Applications for the following year, fiscal 1968, was $695 million. Of that, it budgeted $71.5 million for Voyager's full-scale design and development. But the Senate authorization committee, concerned about the cost of going to the Moon, responded to OSSA's request by voting to give

Voyager nothing. Then, acceding to the House authorization committee's urging that exploration of the near planets was, after all,
one of the most important aspects of the space program, it grudgingly agreed to authorize $42 million for fiscal 1968.

Voyager's end came that summer. The House committee, fretting
over the bill for the war in Vietnam, the price of social services being
demanded at home, and the cost of Apollo (exacerbated by design
changes that had to be made following the fire the previous January
27, which killed astronauts Edward White, Virgil Grissom, and
Roger Chaffee), reversed itself, denying funds to Voyager. The senators were only too glad to follow suit: they voted it out of existence
on August 16, 1967. There were last-minute efforts to resuscitate
Voyager in both the Senate and the House that October, but they
came to nothing. The August vote stood: Voyager was officially dead.

There was a special irony to Voyager's demise. In July, the month
before the Senate wiped Voyager off the books, management at the
Manned Spacecraft Center in Houston, which ran Apollo, took it
upon itself to send twenty-eight prospective contractors a request for
proposals to bid on a study of manned missions to Venus and Mars
beginning in 1975. This was no trivial matter. Manned missions to
the planets would require decisions of the highest magnitude on the
national level and involve a financial commitment that would dwarf
even the costs for Apollo. And here was Houston, taking it upon
itself to solicit bids in an evident attempt to keep the manned program alive after Apollo by showing the nation that the structure and
inertia were in place to push on. Webb was duly informed that
Houston and its rocket supplier, the Marshall Space Flight Center,
were beginning a Mars-Venus initiative on their own. The news gave
him the vapors.

"People at Huntsville and other places . . . say they'd like to keep
the image before the country that somehow man is going to go to
Mars and Venus," the administrator snapped. "But I do think that
the image of NASA, when we're fighting for our lives here in the
major programs, ought to be one of controlling those things, or at
least not make them a major matter of publicity on the theory that
maybe they will elicit support. . . ."

That was an understatement. Congressman Karth, who had actually been trying hard to keep Voyager alive, exploded on hearing
that Houston was soliciting proposals to send people to the near
planets even as blood was being squeezed out of the existing budget.
He was "absolutely astounded," he growled at one reporter, adding

that new starts were absolutely forbidden. "Very bluntly, a manned mission to Mars or Venus is now and has always been out of the question—and anyone who persists in this kind of misallocation of resources at this time is going to be stopped." Clearly, Pasadena was not the only outpost in the empire where Headquarters had less control than it would have liked. From Washington's point of view, somebody out there always seemed to be doing something that threatened anarchy.

The Office of Space Science and Application's consolation prize for losing Voyager was three flybys to the near planets by Mariners before Apollo 11 landed on the Moon in July 1969 and one a little more than two years later.

The notion that Mars was like the Moon (dead, cratered, and therefore not all that interesting) put a crimp in plans to return there until 1969, when two more Mariners—Mariners 6 and 7—were dispatched on top of Atlas-Centaurs.* Neither flyby added appreciably to what was then known about Mars. Indeed, both missions underscored the bleak, pervasively uninteresting view depicted by Mariner 4 because, like their predecessor, their field of view was restricted to pockmarked areas that looked like surfaces of the Moon. Mariner 6 flew past Mars on July 30, skimming over its equator at an altitude of 2,131 miles. Mariner 7 followed it five days later, passing over the Southern Hemisphere at a distance of 2,130 miles, and in the process flying one of the most baffling and hair-raising missions in the history of the planetary exploration program. Its mysterious afflictions—going dead just before encounter, mysteriously straying off course and then returning to it, tumbling out of control and then righting itself, and having its telemetry interrupted for no apparent reason—were what inspired Donald Neff to theorize that it was the quintessential victim of that metaphor for calamity the Great Galactic Ghoul. Between them, the two spacecraft returned 201 pictures.

In 1971 NASA readied two more Mariners for missions to Mars. These were to undertake phase two exploration: not merely speeding past the planet but orbiting it in a more leisurely fashion while photo-mapping everything below. Their mission was not only to re-

*Mariner 5 had in the meantime gone on a successful flyby past Venus in October 1967. It passed within twenty-five hundred miles of the planet and returned important data on the structure of the atmosphere, radiation, and the magnetic field. In addition, the planet's mass was further defined, helping astronomers to narrow its ephemeris. Mariner-Venus 1967 was officially ended in December.

turn scientific data, but to search for possible landing sites for Voyager's successor, which had already been named Viking.

Mariner 8 didn't get very far. On May 8 it was dropped into a watery grave by its Centaur upper stage, which tumbled out of control soon after separation because of a faulty stabilizer control circuit.

Mariner 9 blasted off from the Kennedy Space Center twenty-two days later. It reached its destination on November 13 and became the first spacecraft to orbit another planet. But Mars would not give up its secrets easily. Even as the improved 2,200-pound spacecraft approached, its narrow and wide-angle cameras ready to go, the worst dust storm ever recorded on the red planet began building. Mariner 9 was therefore instructed to keep circling until the storm subsided, which would turn out to be in late February 1972. And as it circled it flew over a drama taking place on the Martian surface below. It was a drama concealed within the fierce storm itself.

The Soviets had also seized the 1971 opportunity to go to Mars, this time with a pair of soft-landers and orbiters named Mars 2 and Mars 3 that were the rough counterparts of what Voyager was to have been. Having never gotten pictures of the Martian surface from a spacecraft, the Soviets evidently decided to combine an imaging and landing operation in a single program. They tried to compress several missions in order to catch up to and surpass the United States. It was a bold move but yet another that was fated to fail. Both spacecraft arrived at the height of the storm.

On November 27, Mars 2's descent module separated from its orbiter and dropped into the Martian atmosphere for an attempted landing. But it disappeared into the cloud of ocher dust after suffering some sort of malfunction and slammed onto the planet's surface without sending back a single piece of useful data. Mars 3's descent module followed five days later. It entered the atmosphere at a blistering 13,320 miles an hour, was slowed by its braking parachute, and finally by its main chute. Then its retrorocket kicked in while it floated less than one hundred feet above the Martian surface. It landed seconds later. The sterilized capsule unfurled its petal covers, as it had been programmed to do before it left home, and began transmitting to Earth via its orbiter, which passed overhead. The first soft-landing on Mars belonged to the Soviet Union. Then disaster struck. Twenty seconds after the lander began transmitting, all signals abruptly stopped. They never resumed.

Two reputable Soviet scientists have suggested that the culprit was the orbiter, not the lander. They maintained that the lander transmitted data it collected, but the orbiter never passed it on to the USSR. Others have suggested that the lander was simply blown over by the wind and lay on its side, hidden and helpless, in the swirling clouds of dust while its orbiter passed overhead listening for a transmission that would never come.

Whatever the immediate cause of the problem, the Soviets' inability to keep their landers safely in orbit until the storm subsided—to wait it out as Mariner 9 did—said a great deal about their planetary program as a whole. It said that their missions were dangerously inflexible—that their spacecraft were more like zombies than robots.

"They can't modify what the spacecraft is really going to do," Nicholas L. Johnson, the specialist on the Soviet space program, noted. "They can't reprogram very well from the ground. They wanted a dead-shot trajectory for the planet; it was then or never, so they went down into some of the worst storms that we know about, and neither one of them survived. They just don't have the onboard [computer] processing," Johnson explained, adding that such capability not only speeds data transmission but adds a degree of artificial intelligence that could have helped the spacecraft to survive.

This shortcoming, which forced the Soviets to stick rigidly to a mission's sequence once it was under way, would profoundly affect the nature of the science they collected for decades to come. Preprogramming without the ability to adjust as circumstances change would mean that the Soviets had to know what they were after before the missions began. But if good science entails pursuit of the unknown—of being able to deviate from a set course when necessary in order to explore unforeseen opportunities—then Soviet space science would necessarily be hamstrung by its inherent inflexibility. It would be as if Columbus, having set out to find an ocean route to the Orient, never stopped at North America because it wasn't on his itinerary.

Mariner 9 kept circling and watching as the storm below devoured the two Soviet landers while continuing to play itself out. Then in late December the dust began to settle and the first imagery, initially fuzzy and then increasingly clear, began to come in as though through a parting veil. The imaging team at JPL, which until that moment had seen only crater-covered terrain in pictures from Mars, was almost literally stunned at what was materializing before it.

"Four huge, dark mountains poked through the dust-laden atmosphere," recalled Clark R. Chapman, a planetary scientist. "Each was crowned by interlocking craters that resembled not meteor-impact craters but rather the volcanic crater or caldera atop the Kilauea volcano in Hawaii. The largest of these volcanoes, Olympus Mons, is the size of the state of Colorado."

Then immense canyons came into view. One of them ran along the planet's equator like a gigantic wound that had been made by some cosmic weapon of formidable proportions. As the imaging team stared at the television screen in astonishment, the canyon's full size unfolded, line by line. "It is the length of the United States and so vast that one of its tributary canyons almost dwarfs the Grand Canyon," Chapman related in wonder. "Such extraordinary canyon-lands imply Martian geological forces like those in the Earth." The great canyon would be named Valles Marineris after the spacecraft that found it.

The walls of the Martian canyons showed layering, which might have come from lava flowing out of volcanoes that obviously had once been very active. It was also determined that the canyons them-selves most likely formed through a tectonic process in which large masses of the planet heaved and buckled under enormous internal pressure. The canyons seemed to have walls that looked as though they had been eroded by water. Water! Elsewhere some channels appeared, looking for all the world like dried riverbeds, while others were unmistakably the route of old lava flows.

Mariner 9 provided NASA with more than seventy-three hundred photographs covering 100 percent of the planet during its 349 days in orbit operation.* It also provided fresh data on the composition, density, pressure, and thermal properties of the Martian atmo-sphere and the first detailed photographs of Phobos and Deimos, the Martian moons. Mars was suddenly seen to be a far more dynamic planet than anyone had reason to believe based on the prior evi-dence.

Mariner 9 thereby left a dual legacy. It gave the scientists renewed reason to believe that life or its remnant might in fact exist on Earth's enigmatic neighbor and that it was worth returning for a closer look. And it gave the mission planners enough clear pictures so that they could find a place where, in a manner of speaking, the scientists could land to take that look.

*In all, the probe sent back more than thirty billion bits of data, or an amount equal to thirty-six times the text of the *Encyclopaedia Britannica*. This was far more information than the total from all previous planetary probes combined.

Viking: Utopia Visited

However else they may differ, NASA administrators and clerics share at least one fundamental belief: there is life after death. Certainly the space program has its own examples of formidable exploring machines that were killed—wiped off the books—only to be resurrected and ultimately sent on their way. The orbiter-lander that died as Voyager on Capitol Hill in 1967 and alighted on Mars to search for life as Viking nine years later was an example of this phenomenon. But it was a great deal more than that. Viking is prominently woven into the tapestry of the space age because it was one of the most technically and scientifically elegant yet abidingly enigmatic missions in the history of planetary exploration.

Congress virtually destroyed the Office of Space Science and Application's budget during the summer and early autumn of 1967, leaving no planetary mission intact except Mariners 6 and 7, which were supposed to go to Mars in 1969. Mariners 8 and 9, scheduled to reconnoiter Mars in 1971 preparatory to Voyager's landing there two years later, evaporated with Voyager itself.

But then NASA regrouped. Early in November, less than two weeks after Voyager officially expired, James Webb appeared at congressional hearings to explain his agency's proposed operating plan for fiscal 1968. While the Mariners and Voyager had been excised from the budget itself, the legislators nonetheless wanted to hear about NASA's plans, immediate and long-term. What they heard would impact on the fiscal 1969 budget.

Senator Margaret Chase Smith gave Webb his opening by asking what NASA planned to do in the way of planetary exploration. OSSA was proposing five new Mariner missions to fly to Venus and Mars between 1971 and 1975, Webb said, in addition to a lightweight Voyager-type mission to Mars in 1973 involving a pair of orbiters and

two small probes, plus a more ambitious soft-lander mission, also
called Voyager, to go there in 1975. The new 1971 Mariner-Mars
mission, he explained, would replace an earlier one that had been
slated to fly by the planet and release its own probe to sample the
Martian atmosphere. The new spacecraft would instead orbit the red
planet for a long time, conducting extensive observations in preparation for the Voyager soft-lander mission of 1975.

Webb went on to explain that costs would be kept to a minimum
in several ways. Since the new Mariner-Mars 1971 mission would not
carry a probe, he said, money would be saved by not developing it.
In addition, Mariner-Mars 1971 would use equipment left over from
its orbiting predecessor, Mariner-Mars 1969. Webb pointed out that
two of the five Mariners, which were supposed to go to Venus in 1972
and 1973, could use the Air Force's off-the-shelf Titan 3 launch vehicle to save still more.* So could the Voyager set for launch in 1973,
which had first been designed in a heftier version for the Saturn V,
and then scaled down. The big Voyager that NASA wanted to soft-
land on Mars in 1975, however, was still sized for the colossal booster.

Having finished describing NASA's plans for the exploration of
deep space, its administrator, following a well-established pattern
when testifying before Congress, next drew his listeners' attention
to matters having to do with terra firma. Webb pointedly noted that
Surveyor, Lunar Orbiter, and Mariner 5 were concluding simultaneously, even as Voyager was being eliminated. He then reminded
the Republican from Maine and her colleagues that the fiscal 1969
budget would therefore determine whether "these teams, representing an estimated 20,000 to 30,000 man-years of experience, are to be
disbanded. Together, they have launched sixteen spacecraft toward
the Moon and the planets. It cost over $700 million to do the work
represented by their competence." President Johnson's decision on
the 1969 space budget "and further consultations with this and other
committees of Congress," Webb added dryly, "will guide our reprogramming action."

Nor was Capitol Hill the space agency's only target. Throughout

---

*Titan was originally developed by Martin Marietta as an ICBM for the Air Force and
was deployed in the early 1960s. It became a standard launch vehicle for military and
civilian satellites and for deep space probes during the period when Minuteman
gradually replaced it as the nation's standard operational intercontinental ballistic
missile beginning in the mid-sixties (Thomas B. Cochran, William M. Arkin, and
Milton M. Hoenig, *U.S. Nuclear Forces and Capabilities*, Vol. I (Cambridge, Massachusetts: Ballinger, 1984, pp. 111–19). Titan evolved into a family of launch vehicles
designed to lift extremely heavy payloads—the KH-9 and KH-11 photo reconnaissance
satellites, each of which was the size and weight of an intercity bus, being but two
examples (Burrows, *Deep Black,* pp. 199–251).

the autumn and winter of 1967, Webb and his colleagues in Headquarters tried to generate support from the Lunar and Planetary
Missions Board, a respected internal advisory group of outside scientists that scrutinized agency planning, and from the Space Science
Board itself.

That November, John E. Naugle, who had replaced Homer Newell
as associate administrator for space science and applications, briefed
the Space Science Board on his office's dire situation even as his boss
did the same in Congress. Harry Hess, the board's chairman, responded on cue by writing to Webb to tell him of its "concern over
the weakness of the whole NASA science program and the planetary
program in particular." At a time when the space agency was cutting back on planetary exploration, Hess added, it was "fairly evident that the Soviets [would] have flights to Mars and Venus at every
opportunity as they have had for the last few years." Soviet missions
were "apt to be successes," Hess continued. Great discoveries "in
this area can only be made once. Shall succeeding generations look
back on the early 1970s as the great era of Soviet achievement while
we did not accept the challenge?" No, said the Space Science Board,
which went on to recommend that the planetary science program
take precedence over all other NASA activities.

Once again, the Soviets were used as ready kindling to keep probes
firing into space. The members of the Space Science Board, no less
than their counterparts in other areas of science, were loath to come
in second in the discovery derby. Discovery by definition meant
placing first: winning. If you didn't win, you lost. Who remembered
the name of the second mathematician to prove the law of universal
gravitation; the second chemist to conclude that vaccine could prevent disease; the second astronomer to see Uranus for the planet it
was? All the world remembered Newton, Pasteur, and Herschel.
Who could name the runners-up? Who cared? The race to the planets
certainly tested the mettle of the participants' science and technology. But it did more than that. It tested the very nature, the essence,
of the two opposing systems from which the competing science and
technology sprang. Space science and technology, unlike biology and
the health sciences, were overwhelmingly the domain of males, perhaps because of the brutish nature of the machines that carried the
instruments, perhaps because of the instruments themselves;
women did not tend to flock to physics. Losing was therefore taken
to imply weakness and perhaps even a diminution of masculinity, a
failure of the will. Losing smacked of culture rot. Or so it might have
seemed to a disinterested observer listening to the furor. That ob-

server might even have concluded that where the U.S. space program was concerned, had the Soviets not existed they would have had to be invented.

But Lyndon Baines Johnson, for one, was highly receptive to the culture-rot message. In an evident effort to keep the momentum of space exploration going in spite of (or perhaps because of) the coming end of a series of Apollo missions that had yet to even approach the Moon, he informed Congress in his budget message on January 29, 1968, that planetary exploration would not be abandoned. He specifically called for the development "of a new spacecraft for launch in 1973 to orbit and land on Mars," a reference to a lightweight version of the deceased Voyager. "Although the scientific results of this new mission will be less than that of the Voyager [in the previous budget] it will still provide extremely valuable data and serve as a building block for planetary exploration systems in the future." The corpse was stirring.

Within two weeks of Johnson's speech, Naugle asked the Langley Research Center and JPL for detailed studies of Titan 3-type missions to Mars to be flown by a spacecraft that would essentially be based on the Voyager orbiter-lander combination. Langley had already been tapped as the supervising center for the mission. It had earned that right for two reasons. First, its experience in aerodynamics—in vehicles flying through the atmosphere—had gotten it interested in spacecraft penetrating the Martian atmosphere as far back as 1964, when it was clear that the red planet was a prime target for on-the-spot exploration. It had therefore done its own studies of a combined orbiter-lander mission (as had Ames and JPL), which impressed Headquarters. In addition, not only had Langley successfully run the Lunar Orbiter flights (the first of which returned excellent imagery in August 1966), but it had done so with fewer cost increases and schedule slips than JPL had with Surveyor.

In fact, there had been some dueling over responsibility between Langley and JPL in 1965, during the program's initial incarnation as Voyager, and the memory of it lingered three years later. In July 1965, after JPL had been designated as the manager of Voyager's reentry capsule, a twelve-member delegation from Pasadena visited Tidewater, Virginia, to discuss Langley's role in support of the capsule. According to one participant in the meeting, it soon became apparent that the Pasadenans wanted to get Langley out of the systems area altogether and into the narrower area of specific technological tasks. For its part, Langley let it be known to Headquarters that it wanted Voyager to be the focus of its research programs and, more to the point, that it was more appropriate for a "real" NASA center to run the program than for the "contractor" facility in Pasadena to do so.

By December 6, 1968, planning for the new Mars mission had progressed to the point at which an interim project office was started at Langley and an organizational structure was adopted. Langley would supervise the development of the lander, which would be designed and built by Martin Marietta in Denver, and it would also integrate the entire program. JPL would be responsible for designing and building the orbiter. The Lewis Research Center would oversee development of the launch vehicle. The project manager would be James S. Martin, Jr., who had twenty-two years' experience at Republic Aviation Corporation, including work in space systems requirements, before coming to Langley as assistant manager of the Lunar Orbiter project in September 1964. Martin had established a reputation as a tough, no-nonsense administrator during the days when Langley's Moon probe was under development. That experience would serve him well.

Formalizing the program's structure also provided a good opportunity to give it a name. Although packaging could not get the project off the ground in a literal sense, its managers understood as well as their counterparts in the breakfast cereal and automobile industries that there were intangible but real benefits to having a good name and avoidable problems to having a bad one. When Ames was shortly to be faced with the prospect of naming the first spacecraft to venture to Jupiter and Saturn, for example, it would select Pioneer in order to make it seem as though another program—a quite successful one also named Pioneer—was in effect merely being continued. It would be a subtle, almost subliminal, way to get a new start going under the apparent aegis of an existing one. This, as they said, involved the time-honored use of smoke and mirrors. Nothing wrong with that. But the Office of Space Science and Applications and Langley had the opposite problem with the Mars orbiter-lander. They wanted everyone concerned, and certainly the Bureau of the Budget and Congress, to forget that it had until recently been called Voyager (Voyager, the Plucked Turkey; the Dead Duck). So they picked a name that was synonymous with intrepid, rugged seamen embarked on long expeditions in sturdy vessels. The program was rechristened Viking.*

*Voyager, however, would be reincarnated for an extended mission to the outer planets and would do nobly.

The advent of the Nixon administration in January 1969 brought good tidings to Viking, at least initially. As was the custom, the outgoing administration's space agency chief, Webb, was replaced by the new president's man, Thomas O. Paine. Paine had been Webb's deputy and had earned a solid reputation within the space agency as a balanced and able bureaucrat. As he prepared to take office following the election in November 1968, Paine could not help reflecting on the fact that the landing of astronauts on the Moon four months earlier had occurred during his predecessor's term of office and would therefore be linked to Webb. What, Thomas Paine wondered, would be his crowning achievement while at NASA's helm?

Of all the projects in the offing—Mariner Mars 1971 and the Apollo Applications Program (i.e., Skylab, the orbiting laboratory that was to use Saturn launch vehicles and other Apollo technology) being two of the foremost—none came close to the stature of Viking. Paine believed implicitly in planetary exploration and saw Viking, even in its preliminary planning stage, for what it was: a truly bold, extraordinarily complicated mission that had the potential of becoming one of the milestones in the history of exploration—*all* exploration. He therefore signed off on it enthusiastically, much to Naugle's delight, as well as that of Langley, JPL, Lewis, and the exobiology people at Ames.

Viking was an organizational nightmare. It was the first planetary program to involve several NASA centers and contractors, plus a huge number of subcontractors, in the development and operation of a single mission system. And that system had four basic elements, all of which had to be more closely coordinated—and certainly more dependable—than the working parts of the finest racing car. There would be two Vikings, each comprising two spacecraft—an orbiter and a lander—for a total of four individual spacecraft. The orbiters would be larger than the landers and would carry them to Mars in protective shells. There they would separate and carry out their respective assignments. In addition, there would be two main launch vehicles, two upper stages, and the entire command, control, communication, and tracking system. All of it—every single man, woman, and machine—had to be choreographed to perfection or the project would risk disaster.

In order to coordinate all of the disparate elements, the project manager invented the Viking Project Management Council in March 1969. Jim Martin's idea was to provide a forum in which representatives from the various organizations could review the status of their work, freely discuss engineering, science and management problems, and be kept abreast of the project's overall objectives and status. And not coincidentally, the council also allowed managers from Virginia to California to get to know each other on a face-to-face basis at meetings, rather than only over the telephone or through unending memorandums and status reports.

The first meeting was held at the Martin Marietta plant on August 18–19, with the various systems managers reporting to an audience of about fifty. The participants seemed impressed with the council and returned to their home facilities to report on what they had seen and heard before getting on with their respective jobs. Jim Martin's management style seemed to be working. From his and Naugle's perspective, and certainly from the perspective of everyone who reported to them, the exhausting effort to shape Viking and bring it to fruition appeared to be progressing. They had every reason to believe, based on what they saw and heard around them, that their world—the world of Viking—was in order. But they were wrong.

The effort to get men to the Moon, with its relentlessly accelerated tempo and intensity over the course of nine years, was like a kind of national love-in. Now, with the consummation at hand, many of the citizen-participants showed signs of delirium. But some also showed exhaustion. Of 1,517 persons polled by Gallop in July 1969, for example, 39 percent favored the Moon landing, while 53 percent opposed it. Most twenty-one- to twenty-nine-year-olds favored it (54 percent to 41 percent), but it was opposed by 60 percent of those over fifty. Citizen support for the space program seemed to be waning.

Then there was the budget. The chances are that the Bureau of the Budget and Congress would have found some way to buoy NASA's appropriation if there had been widespread public support, even with a costly and demoralizing war going on in Southeast Asia and a deep malaise running through much of society at home. In the absence of support, however, the space program—and particularly science and exploration—seemed to be relatively unimportant. That made it vulnerable to cutting.

Despite Naugle's admonitions to Langley and the other centers about keeping expenses down and avoiding cost overruns in a time of inevitable constraints, Viking went against the tide. The enormity of its requirements seemed to take hold irrespective of what he and Martin said. Viking was in fact already on its way to becoming the most sophisticated and expensive planetary explorer ever developed.

In March 1969, with the basic mission not yet totally defined, NASA guessed that it would cost $364.1 million. By August the figure had climbed to $606 million, not counting another $50 million for launch vehicles. And in October, Naugle admitted to the House Committee on Science and Astronautics that Viking's total bill was by then being projected at $750 million. Its considerable cost was a factor of its unprecedented complexity and many inevitable design changes. No matter how Viking's management tried to pare its cost—Naugle, Martin, and others fretted about it all the time—projections kept climbing relentlessly. It was like punching Robert Mayo, the director of the Bureau of the Budget, and everyone on the congressional appropriations committees in the nose, not once but repeatedly.

Finally, there was a development that did not affect Viking directly but would have extremely important long-term effects on planetary exploration in particular and on the entire space program in general.

Within six weeks of taking office, even as Viking's fiscal problems worsened, Richard Nixon had established a blue-ribbon Space Task Group to provide a "definitive recommendation on the direction which the U.S. space program should take in the post-Apollo period." Even before the astronauts whom Kennedy and Johnson had pointed at the Moon actually landed on it, Nixon was prudently casting about for a likely way to add his own mark to the space program.*

"Nixon went through a brief period asking, 'What should we do next?'" according to Bruce Murray, who was working on Mariner science experiments at the time and would replace Pickering as director of JPL shortly before the Viking landings. "He had to deal with it. He left Kennedy's people in there [at NASA] until the first successful landing [on the Moon] so that if anybody got killed, it would've been a Kennedy failure. When it was clearly a success, it became a Nixon success. They wanted to make sure nobody got killed on their watch," Murray added.†

The Space Task Group's members were Paine, Robert C. Seamans,

*He would in fact do just that in a literal sense, since the plaque carried by the Apollo 11 crew bore his name and signature, as well as theirs.
†John M. Logsdon, director of the Space Policy Institute at the George Washington University and a longtime observer of the space program, disputed Murray on the time it took Nixon to make the appointment. In a notation in his critique of this book, he has said that the position was offered to several potential candidates before it was offered to Paine, but that none took it.

the secretary of the Air Force, and Lee Dubridge, the former president of Caltech, who was then Nixon's science adviser. The group was chaired by Spiro T. Agnew, the vice president. Agnew had no expertise or even interest in space, as evidenced by the fact that he exercised no guidance whatever in the group's deliberations. His presence, however, had the effect of indicating that the White House meant to be involved in the space program. At a moment when Americans were about to embark on the most daring voyage of all time, the ghost of the popular martyred president who had ordered the mission in the first place loomed especially large. A Nixon presence in the Space Task Group's deliberations was therefore no doubt precisely what the new president wanted.

The chart for the nation's options in space, called "The Post-Apollo Space Program: Directions for the Future," was released in September, two months after the Moon landing. It listed four categories of potential activities in space: manned spaceflight (including a mission to Mars), a so-called Space Transportation System, scientific research, and such applications as remote sensing of Earth by satellites. The activities, arranged as a kind of Chinese menu of space projects, could be mixed and matched at different funding levels and various time periods.*

Agnew's panel forthrightly summed up the state of manned activity in space, noting that it permitted "vicarious participation by the man-in-the-street in exciting, challenging, and dangerous activity." But, it added, "Sustained high interest, judged in the light of current experience . . . is related to availability of new tasks and new mission activity." This was code. Translated, it meant that the man in the street had a low attention span that required progressively more daring and imaginative feats: he had to be entertained ever more grandly if his mind was to be kept from wandering.

The report went on to cite public unhappiness over the cost of the Apollo program and noted that scientists had been "particularly vocal" about the funds it was consuming and the problems they

---

*The grandest plan ("maximum pace"), for example, called for a space station in Earth orbit by 1975, a fifty-man space base by 1980, a 100-man base by 1985, an Earth-to-orbit Space Transportation System by 1975, a Mars expedition by 1981, multiple outer planet tours during 1977–79, a large orbiting observatory by 1979, and a great deal more. A less ambitious program would have pushed back the dates for some of these, while an even less ambitious one would have pushed back the dates for all of them, though by different degrees. The "maximum pace" suggested a manned lunar surface base by 1978 and a survey of the asteroids by 1975, for example, while the next less ambitious plan put the lunar base off until 1980, but kept the cheaper asteroid mission in 1975.

encountered in trying to do their experiments as part of that program. "Much of the negative reaction to manned space flight . . . will diminish if costs for placing and maintaining man in space are reduced and opportunities for challenging new missions with greater emphasis on science return are provided."

Then the Agnew report whittled its argument to a finer point. It suggested that costs could be kept down by fashioning a manned program that would emphasize "(1) commonality, (2) reusability, and (3) economy." In other words, it called for major manned space vehicles that could be used for a variety of missions over long periods, and with an absolute reduction in the number of "throw-away" components. What the drafters of the report had in mind, they went on to explain, was a manned space station, an eventual large space base consisting of several space stations joined together like the pieces of an Erector Set, and a Space Transportation System to shuttle all the necessary hardware to orbit.

Since nothing could be built in orbit without the means of getting materials up there, the Space Transportation System would be the obvious first choice for funding. The Space Task Group saw such a vehicle as being able to carry "passengers, supplies, rocket fuel, other spacecraft, equipment, or additional rocket stages to and from orbit *on a routine aircraft-like basis . . . in an airline-type mode*" (emphasis added). The reference to commercial airliners, with their scheduled departure and arrival times, fine safety record, and unquestioned dependability—their strictly routine operation—was reassuring. It brought to mind Dr. Heywood R. Floyd's commuter flight from Earth to the giant space station in *2001: A Space Odyssey,* which had premiered only the year before to critical acclaim and large audiences. Floyd's commute to the Moon was so tranquil that he dozed off to the strains of "The Blue Danube," the most serene of the Strauss waltzes, while even his pen floated gently nearby. This was the genesis of the space shuttle's actual development—a program that in NASA's estimation would mean its salvation.

At the same time, the Agnew committee rejected a manned mission to Mars, which had been mentioned as one possible post-Apollo program. Instead, it called for progressively more sophisticated unmanned missions to both Venus and Mars, as well as flybys to the outer planets in the late 1970s. These undertakings, which were not otherwise described, were lumped together with ground-based and satellite astronomy and Earth and life sciences; they accounted for only about one of the document's twenty-five pages.

Meanwhile, as 1969 drew to a close, Viking's future seemed as gloomy as the wind-driven slate clouds that scurried over Washington itself. The glow of July, when the Eagle had gently lowered Buzz Aldrin and Neil Armstrong onto the Sea of Tranquillity, had given way to the bitter cold of December, when malaise gripped the land. It was obvious that the war in Vietnam weighed heavily on the country because of what it was exacting in blood and treasure. Less obvious was the fact that it was also widely seen as the embodiment of technology gone haywire. And just as the technology spurred the armed struggle in the jungles of Southeast Asia, so, too, did it foment stubborn resistance and even backlash at home. The antipathy was focused mainly on the war, itself, of course. But it also extended to NASA. A nation beset by the scourges of poverty, pollution, urban decay, and racial turmoil, it was said, had no business squandering precious resources trying to get to other worlds. Better to concentrate on this one.*

It was against this background that the beleaguered Naugle faced the House Committee on Science and Astronautics in October. He tried to defend Viking's escalating costs by blaming erroneous early underestimates of its weight. That miscalculation, in turn, required a huge expenditure of man-hours to correct. And, the associate administrator for space science and applications added lamely, inflation was driving up the cost of man-hours. The congressmen were not persuaded by Naugle's explanation, nor by his assurance that NASA was doing all it could to hold down expenses. The space agency had "so far failed miserably in that regard," Joe Karth told John Naugle.

Paine, the old NASA hand, weighed what he saw in the congressional hearing rooms and on the evening news. Then he came to the conclusion that the space agency would have to rearrange its priorities or suffer the consequences. "We recognize the many important needs and urgent problems we face here on earth," he said in a public statement. "America's space achievements in the 1960s have rightly raised hopes that this country and all mankind can do more to overcome pressing problems of society. The space program should

*That argument was made to the author, in taped interviews in 1969, by the poet Mark Van Doren, the theologian Reinhold Niebuhr, and the historian Arnold Toynbee when the Apollo 11 mission was in the offing. Told of their position, Isaac Asimov, the writer, responded that carrying on the space program and addressing the nation's social and economic ills were in no way mutually exclusive. Speaking for others, including Carl Sagan, Asimov maintained that savings from the waste in the Department of Defense alone would have gone far in solving problems at home.

inspire bolder solutions and suggest new approaches. . . ." He went on to say that the 1971 budget would reflect a diminishing of NASA's total activities, but added that the "strong teams that sent men to explore the Moon and automated spacecraft to observe the planets" would not be dissipated. Among several other cost-reduction measures, Paine went on, Viking would be postponed from 1973 to the next Mars launch window, July 1975.

NASA as a whole was tumbling down the budget curve. The number of people working on projects for the agency dropped abruptly from 190,000 at the end of fiscal 1970 to about 140,000 a year later. Everyone, it seemed, had a story about a Ph.D. in astronautics who was driving a taxi. While the delay was disheartening, there was at least some consolation in the fact that most of the vast team that worked on Viking was being held together. (Only about 150 were pruned from the program, with most of them shifted to Mariner 10, which would be launched in November 1973 to reconnoiter both Venus and Mercury. Once the probe was on its way, many of them would be brought back to Viking to prepare for its launch.)

Gerald A. Soffen, Viking's chief scientist, tried to console the project's other scientists in late January by reminding them that "scientific research has never been an easy way of life. We expect to find favorable aspects of this Viking deferment in the form of improvements in the investigations and the better use of Mariner 71 [later known as Mariner 9] results," he added. Henry W. Norris, the orbiter manager at JPL, told his demoralized engineers that budgets were simply one of the many realities they (and their managers) had to live with and overcome in order to do their jobs.

As the new decade took hold, literally thousands of widely disparate parts and subparts of the Viking program began almost imperceptibly to come together. Yet the participants were continuously tested, cerebrally or emotionally or both, as they interacted to give shape to the project throughout that year and in the years that followed. They interacted against a background—*always* against a background—of money problems. There were contracts to be renegotiated, personnel turnovers, and altered requirements (Mars would be farther away in 1975 than in 1973, for instance, substantially changing Viking's trajectory and requiring hardware modification as well) that severely strained the budget.

By 1973, the year Viking was originally to have been launched, its cost had jumped to $830 million; a year later, to $930 million. It had become a glaring example of a pattern that was becoming so familiar at NASA because of chronic funding problems that it was virtually built into the scheme of things: put off today and get soaked tomorrow. Programs would consistently be delayed or diluted for lack of funding, only to end up costing more than had originally been estimated because of time slippage or some fundamental problem.

And there were the ubiquitous clashes, some subtle and some vituperative, between the scientists themselves. They debated vigorously over whether the lander or the orbiter should carry the bulk of the experiments, which experiments ought to be included, and whether theorists or actual experimenters ought to have more of a say in instrument design. There was also some discussion, but not a great deal of it, over whether the search for life should take precedence over other experiments. There was a clear consensus that the quest for life was the mission's top priority.

Bruce Murray was one who demurred, at least initially. Well before Viking even got off the ground, he reflected that the hell-bent search for life on Mars was premature, scientifically unjustified, and ill conceived. It would have been better for the first lander on Mars to start step-by-step exploration of the planet's surface, he believed, focusing on its chemical and environmental properties. Only later, with those things better understood, should the search for life begin. He was uncomfortable with what he perceived as the invocation of the search for life to whip up support for the program. And, in any case, he thought that such a quest was doomed.

"Ambiguous results seemed practically foreordained," he later recalled in his memoir. A test for life would have to detect and measure the growth or interaction of Martian microbes in a controlled experiment that involved feeding them especially mixed nutrients—a nutritious "broth," as some called it—and then observing whether or not the microbes multiplied or reacted in some other way. "Distinct interaction [between the microbes and the broth] could indicate the presence of life. But," Murray pondered, "what attitude should we adopt if there were no interaction—simply the neutral response of the nutrients to a passive, sterile soil?" How could the experimenters be certain they had used the right broth? What if Martian life reacted to the broth differently from the way anyone expected and therefore did not show up in a meaningful way? What if life happened not to exist under the pads of the landers, as it were, but did exist elsewhere? "A clear-cut determination of the presence of life—or of its absence—on Mars looked like an almost impossible task to me."

That made a certain amount of sense as far as it went. Yet with no follow-on mission in sight—or, given the financial situation, even realistically conceivable—the temptation to go for a "jackpot" shot was overwhelming. A positive result in one or more experiments would make a good case for life, while failure to turn up something would not in itself rule out the possibility that life in some form did exist, or had existed, out of the reach of the spacecraft. To ignore the opportunity, it was generally felt, would be scientifically unconscionable. That, at any rate, was how it looked to the seventeen scientists who submitted proposals to NASA for life-detection experiments. Of these, four were selected and three actually made the journey.*

All three were built into a so-called biology instrument that was to be fitted into the Viking landers. This machine in itself represented one of the space program's great feats of miniaturization. It was about the size of a one-gallon milk container and held about forty-thousand parts (half of them transistors), including tiny ovens to heat samples; ampules holding the broth that had to be broken on command; radioactive gases in tiny bottles; a xenon lamp to duplicate sunlight; Geiger counters and fifty separate valves. It amounted to a highly sophisticated miniature laboratory that would be fed soil samples by a kind of claw that came out of the lander, scooped up a bit of the terrain, and lifted it inside the biology instrument for analysis. TRW, which made the biology instrument, originally estimated that it would cost $13.7 million. The final cost was more than $59 million.

Living organisms on Earth give off gases as waste products: animals release carbon dioxide, plants release oxygen and carbon dioxide, and both exhale water. Two of the three life-search experiments inside the biology instrument would try to feed Martian organisms using the nutrients under Earthlike conditions and see how they

*Wolf Vishniac, a pioneer in the search for extraterrestrial life, designed an instrument he called the Wolf Trap. It consisted of a growth chamber with an acidity detector and a light sensor that were supposed to pick up the kind of changes in acidity that occur when microorganisms grow and measure the amount of light passing through the chamber itself. Since growing microorganisms turn clear culture mediums cloudy, Vishniac wanted to use the light-scattering aspect of the experiment as a check on the acidity detector. It was bumped from the flight, however, by a three-member panel of scientists (including Lederberg) who had no direct involvement with Viking experiments because it was considered less promising than the three experiments that actually flew. Vishniac, embittered, charged that he had been treated unfairly. He was killed in 1973, when he fell off a mountain in Antarctica while trying to prove that life forms could adapt to the region's extremely hostile environment.

The lander's two cameras were to participate in the search for life by scanning the terrain in its immediate area for tracks, fossil remains, artifacts, or anything that moved, though it was in no sense counted as an instrument for life detection.

reacted: specifically, whether they gave off a gas. The third would do the same thing, though by searching within the confines of the Martian environment itself. It would seek to measure not what microorganisms released but what they assimilated. All three experiments amounted to incubators that were supposed to warm and nourish any life form, active or dormant, and detect the chemicals they released.

The first was a gas exchange experiment designed by Vance T. Oyama, of Ames, which looked for evidence of microorganisms exchanging gases with the atmosphere that surrounded them. A soil sample was to be exposed first to water vapor alone and then to water containing a highly complex fifty-ingredient broth (called "chicken soup" by Oyama and his team). The chemical composition of the gas above the soil would then be continuously analyzed for changes that might indicate biological activity.

A second instrument, called the labeled release experiment, was devised by Gilbert Levin of Biospherics, Inc. It was also designed to cultivate Martian microorganisms in an Earth broth. It consisted of trying to feed the soil samples a simpler broth than Oyama's to see whether carbon dioxide was released, as it would be under similar circumstances on Earth. Levin's brand of chicken soup was "labeled" radioactively to help trace whatever gas might be expelled by microscopic Mars creatures.

The third experiment, which belonged to Norman Horowitz, was called the carbon assimilation, or pyrolytic release, experiment. It was designed to see whether microorganisms would create organic compounds out of radioactively labeled carbon dioxide and carbon monoxide. On Earth, organisms such as plants turn carbon dioxide in the surrounding air into the organic stuff that becomes their roots, branches, and leaves. Horowitz therefore wanted to add radioactive carbon dioxide to the atmosphere above the soil sample and then illuminate it with simulated Martian sunlight; if any microorganisms or other life forms converted the carbon dioxide into organic compounds, it could be detected by the radioactive gas, Horowitz felt. His was the only experiment that could succeed on Mars but not on Earth because it did not use a liquid nutrient solution. In other words, it was the only one that did not try to produce results under conditions that were more typical of Earth than of the world it was investigating.

In addition, a fourth experiment, called the gas chromatograph-mass spectrometer, or GCMS, was not intended as part of the life-search package, but it was to play an important role in the quest anyway. It was designed to detect and identify organic compounds containing carbon in the Martian soil.

However they were devised, and whatever their value, the life-detection experiments and the GCMS remained only one of a battery of instruments that would ride on either the Viking landers (in the case of the four instruments above) or the orbiters. The orbiters, which owed much of their design to their Mariner cousins, carried four instruments on independently movable scan platforms. There were two vidicon cameras on each orbiter to image the Martian surface, plus an infrared spectrometer for mapping water vapor, and an infrared radiometer for mapping the planet's heat profile.

Both Viking landers, which owed a great deal to Surveyor, carried their own cameras. They were also equipped with retarding potential analyzers that would sample the properties of the Martian ionosphere; mass spectrometers to measure the atmosphere's composition; pressure, temperature acceleration sensors to measure the atmosphere's structure; an X-ray fluorescence spectrometer for an analysis of inorganic compounds; sensors to measure pressure, temperature, and wind velocities; magnets to measure the surface's magnetic properties, and three-axis seismometers to measure the planet's subsurface vibration,* in addition to lesser engineering instruments.

Both the orbiters and the landers would carry radio and radar systems with which to carry out experiments in celestial mechanics, atmospheric properties, and tests involving general relativity. The landers' radar altimeters would measure their distance to the Martian surface as they descended.

The Vikings and their immensely complicated subsystems were so power-hungry that feeding them required 23,250 square inches of solar cells, plus a pair of SNAP-19 radioisotope thermoelectric generators, or RTGs, which would convert hot plutonium to still more energy. Each orbiter would weigh 5,125 pounds and measure nine and a half feet high by thirty-three feet wide (with its solar panels deployed). The landers would weigh 2,353 pounds and be a little over six feet high from the bottom of their footpads to the tips of their large disk-shaped high-gain antennas (they were squat and angular and about half that height without the antennas.) With their legs extended, they were a little less than ten feet across. The Vikings

*Lander 1's failed before it could be used.

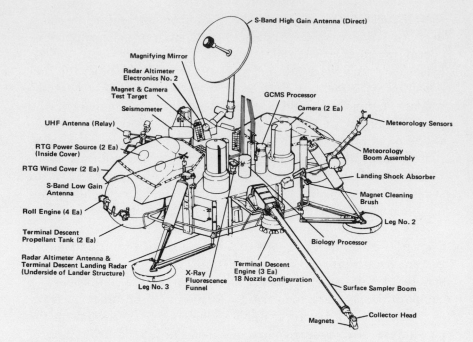

S-Band High Gain Antenna (Direct)

Magnifying Mirror

Radar Altimeter
Electronics No. 2

Magnet & Camera
Test Target

GCMS Processor

Seismometer

Camera (2 Ea)

UHF Antenna (Relay)

Meteorology Sensors

RTG Power Source (2 Ea)
(Inside Cover)

Meteorology
Boom Assembly

RTG Wind Cover (2 Ea)

Landing Shock Absorber

S-Band Low Gain
Antenna

Magnet Cleaning
Brush

Roll Engine (4 Ea)

Leg No. 2

Terminal Descent
Propellant Tank (2 Ea)

Biology Processor

Radar Altimeter Antenna &
Terminal Descent Landing Radar
(Underside of Lander Structure)

X-Ray
Fluorescence
Funnel

Terminal Descent
Engine (3 Ea)
18 Nozzle Configuration

Leg No. 3

Surface Sampler Boom

Collector Head

Magnets

were therefore the largest and heaviest interplanetary spacecraft
ever built by the United States, which is why they needed Titan
3-Centaurs to reach Mars.

As work progressed on Viking through the early seventies, the Space
Transportation System described by Wernher von Braun in *Collier's*
and on "Tomorrowland," and later stamped with the Agnew task
group's imprimatur, began to take on a life of its own.

And that was happening just in time. The key question faced by
NASA as the Apollo program wound down was this: What would it
take to keep the space agency and the aerospace industry that both
supported it and was suckled by it healthy in the decades ahead?
Certainly salvation would not come by developing aircraft technology, firing sounding rockets through the clouds, operating Earth
resources satellites, or even sending robot explorers to other planets.
All of that put together would amount to noise in the big-ticket
budget that was needed to replace Apollo. Which NASA administrator, to paraphrase Winston Churchill, would take office to preside
over the liquidation of the agency?

The shuttle was therefore seen as a vehicle that would at one and
the same time establish the basis for a permanent manned presence

in space—a key infrastructural building block upon which could be stacked a space station, a base on the Moon, an outpost on Mars, and God only knew what else—while not only keeping the space agency out of liquidation, but allowing it to thrive. And the beauty of the Space Transportation System, the effervescent technocrats in the Office of Manned Space Flight began assuring everyone, was that it would be cheap compared with expendables like Atlas and Titan. It would be cheap because it would be reusable. And so, amid deep and sometimes bitter controversy over exactly how cheap the shuttle would be, NASA lobbied Congress and the White House for it throughout 1970 and 1971, even as work on Viking progressed. It lobbied as if its life depended on it.

Nixon was mindful of the economic slump caused by the end of Apollo, of organized labor's taking an increasingly dim view of manpower reductions in the aerospace industry, and of NASA's having to start a major new program or face dismemberment or disintegration. He therefore made his selections for the space agency from the cheapest items on the Space Task Group's menu. He authorized the least expensive shuttle that could be produced and deferred the space station, probably hoping that it would become another president's headache. He approved the Space Transportation System on January 5, 1972.

James Fletcher, NASA's new administrator, flew out to San Clemente immediately afterward for the formal announcement. He carried a model of the space shuttle to present to the president, too. It was a model not of the shuttle Nixon had approved, however, but of a more expensive version that was deemed unaffordable by the White House. Nixon, ever the parsimonious Republican, took the occasion to predict that the shuttle would not only revolutionize space transportation but would take the "astronomical cost out of astronautics." Fletcher added that by the end of the decade "the nation will have the means of getting men and equipment to and from space routinely, on a moment's notice if necessary, and at a small fraction of today's cost."

Whatever was going to happen by the end of the decade, the president's endorsement of the shuttle had the effect of transfusing a bottle of whole blood into a patient who was hemorrhaging. Funding for the Space Transportation System nearly doubled from $100 million spent on research in fiscal 1972 to almost $199 million for actual development in fiscal 1973. Then the budget really started to climb and, with it, NASA's prospects for staying in business. Appropriations for STS reached $475 million in fiscal 1974; $797.5 million in 1975; and $1.2 billion in 1976, the year of the Bicentennial and the Viking twins' arrival at Mars.

Viking 1 rose into a cloudy sky late on the afternoon of August 20, 1975.* It was followed on the morning of September 9 by Viking 2. Both spacecraft headed for Mars.

Interplanetary cruise was mostly uneventful for the two probes, but in the meantime there was a great deal to do back home. Whereas the Mariner flights had been programmed to carry out their maneuvering and experiment sequence in an order that would not deviate except in an emergency, the Vikings had a more adaptable computer load. This meant that experiments could be altered as new information was received from the landers. The Viking team, including scientists, engineers, and technicians from NASA, Langley, JPL, the universities, Martin Marietta, and some of the subcontractors, therefore simulated operating the spacecraft in ways that deviated from what was expected even as the two robots closed in on their target. The simulations came to an end in June 1976, when the twins actually arrived at Mars. Allowing for the wide arc the Vikings had to make in order to rendezvous with Mars, their journey covered some four hundred million miles in 335 days.

The Viking 1 orbiter, carrying its lander in a protective clamlike aeroshell, began circling Mars in a highly elliptical orbit on June 21. Its first major assignment was to search the terrain below for a place on which the lander could settle. There were several criteria used for the selection of landing sites for Viking 1. It was important that the first landing be made around the equatorial zone, which was the best known; that there be no large rocks or boulders in the way; and that the site be a lowland. The site's low elevation was thought to have at least two advantages. First, the atmosphere would be denser than elsewhere, which would ease the lander's descent. Also, water would have collected in such a place, and where water had been, traces of life might remain.

*It was actually supposed to be Viking 2 (or Viking B as it was called before launch). Viking A, which was supposed to have been Viking 1, had trouble getting away. First, a valve in the Titan 3 had failed to work, causing a postponement. Then the nickel-cadmium batteries in the orbiter itself were discovered to have been nearly drained of their charge, apparently because a lightning flash had produced a signal in the control system that went from the command center to the spacecraft. Since it was possible that the dead batteries had damaged other components, Viking A had to be removed from its Centaur and replaced by Viking B. Their numbers were therefore switched (Burgess, *To the Red Planet,* p. 64).

But it was no good. The first pictures to come back showed hazards strewn all over sites that had looked promising in Mariner 9's imagery. They therefore had to be ruled out. Plans for Viking 1's lander to touch down on Mars on the Fourth of July—on the day of the Bicentennial itself—evaporated, along with a great public relations opportunity.

As it happened, those who wanted Viking 1 to commemorate an important event were not completely disappointed. Lander 1 came down on July 20, the seventh anniversary of the landing of the Eagle on the Moon. The site finally chosen, or "certified," as the Viking team called it, was based not only on imagery returned from Orbiter 1, but from radar signals bounced off the red planet from the dishes at Goldstone, the huge one-thousand-foot dish at Arecibo in Puerto Rico, and elsewhere. Although Goldstone's primary function was to communicate with spacecraft, and Arecibo's was to listen to the galaxy and beyond as a tool of radio astronomy, both could also be used to beam radar signals to the Moon and Mars with extraordinary accuracy.*

The site-selection process itself had taken months and was painstakingly conducted. Everyone understood that if one of the lander's legs struck a rock even a foot or so high it could be seriously damaged; a bigger one could turn it over, like a turtle flipped onto its back, making it absolutely useless. The site-selection team therefore compared in minute detail the radar imagery taken by Mariner 9 with that of the Viking orbiter itself. Finally, it was decided to go for a spot on a plain known as the Chryse Planitia, 22.27 degrees north of the equator.

At 1:15 A.M. Pacific daylight time on the twentieth, with the orbiter near the top of its apogee—the highest point in its highly elliptical swing around Mars—it released its lander. During the next couple of hours the squat robot, secure in its aeroshell, plunged toward the surface at a speed that reached ten thousand miles an hour. Throughout its descent, the radar altimeter constantly measured the distance separating it from the Martian surface and ordered the

*There were problems with radar, however. One had to do with the fact that, as a sphere, Mars's upper and lower latitudes could not be imaged because the signal would glance off rather than bounce back. In addition, some members of the landing-site working group feared that radar's low reflectivity in some seemingly excellent landing areas meant that its beam was being absorbed by a deep layer of dust. It was therefore possible that what the radar showed to be merely flat was a kind of quicksand, which, as Sagan and some of his colleagues put it, could cause the lander to sink "up to its eyebrows" (Ezell and Ezell, *On Mars,* p. 320).

landing sequence—the precise order of events—that was supposed to ensure a safe touchdown.

A little more than three hours after separation from the orbiter, the aeroshell slammed into the upper reaches of the Martian atmosphere like a meteorite, its forward surface burning off a layer at a time. It continued to decelerate until it passed the four-mile mark, by which time it had slowed to 995 miles an hour. Then the parachute popped open. Seven seconds later, the aeroshell was pulled off by the chute and, caught in the still-thickening atmosphere, drifted safely away. (The prospect of the lander's missing a number of potentially dangerous rocks only to come down on its own aeroshell was the sort of thing that kept the engineers up at night.) Twelve seconds after that, the lander's legs began extending. At just under a mile above the surface, its braking rockets started firing to slow it even more. Viking 1's lander hit Mars with about as much impact as if it had fallen off a low table. The instant the sensors in its footpads touched terrain, they turned off the descent engines, bringing quiet once again to the Chryse Planitia.

Immediately after it came to rest, Lander 1 shut off every system that had gotten it safely down except its computer. It also set its telemetry transmission rate to the highest level, deployed its high-gain antenna and meteorology boom, opened the cover to its biology instrument, and performed several other housekeeping chores. But housekeeping wasn't all the lander did during its first minutes on Mars. It also took a look around, with one camera staring at the rock- and pebble-strewn terrain at its own feet, and the other focusing its electronic eye upward toward the horizon. The scene might have been enough to frighten one of Percival Lowell's Martians nearly to death.

That first picture of the Martian surface, showing one of the lander's round pads in the lower right, took about twenty minutes to get to JPL's Mission Control and Computing Center, where it arrived at a little after five in the morning. As it unfolded line by line with startling clarity, the epic sense of the moment swept over the Viking team's hundreds of members, bringing a wave of shouting, backslapping, and self-congratulation. Fletcher and Naugle had flown to Pasadena for the occasion and now watched with Jim Martin as the envoy from Earth reported that it was alive and well and taking its first good look around.

"Look at the beautiful rocks," Martin shouted as that first image filled the monitor. "Fantastic!"

"We were looking at the surface of Mars as clearly as if we had been sitting on the lander," Eric Burgess, the lion-maned chronicler of much of planetary exploration, would later recall with undiminished wonder in a book describing the mission.

And steeped as he had been in the thousands upon thousands of dry details over the years, Martin himself was overcome with boyish wonder. "All of a sudden," he would say, "we were looking at the surface of Mars! And it was clear. It wasn't dusty.* It was sharp, and when we got to the end of that first picture, with the dust and pebbles in the footpad," he added, his square face beaming under a thick white brush cut that never varied, "it was just a . . . It was really a miracle."

However miraculous the pictures may have been, events the next day—the twenty-first—showed that vistas of Mars could also be subject to the parochial sensibilities of the earthlings who beheld them. Although the first two images that came in on the twentieth were black and white, the third, which came in the next day, was in color. It covered an area that began almost at the lander's footpad and extended for some distance to the horizon. As could plainly be seen, the ground was a shade of red reminiscent of the clay foothills on the north side of the Atlas Mountains in Morocco—a deep ocher. This was very interesting, especially since it could have indicated the presence of iron in the soil, but it was not especially surprising. What *was* surprising, though, was the fact that the sky was not blue, but pinkish orange.

Within eight hours of the arrival of that first color picture, James A. Pollack, a member of the imaging team, told a packed von Karman Auditorium that it showed the red planet to have a pink sky. This news was greeted with good-natured boos and hisses reflecting, as Carl Sagan put it the next day, "our wish for Mars to be just like Earth." The long-weary and now suddenly flustered imaging team, unwilling to commit itself publicly to this "provocative display" before making certain that the sky really was pink (as Tim Mutch, the lander imaging team leader put it) therefore quickly adjusted the color calibration apparatus so the sky turned a neutral gray. But to Mutch's and everyone else's chagrin, it then took on a bluish hue

---

*This may have been an allusion to Mariner 9's imagery. Although it returned excellent photographs by the standards of the time, enough dust remained in the Martian atmosphere after the great storm so that the pictures were not quite as clear as they might otherwise have been. This was a mild irritant to the site certification team.

while being reconstructed in final form. The reporters, now satisfied that the sky above Mars looked the way sky was supposed to look, sent the final version of the picture to their news organizations for reproduction.

Detailed analysis in the days that followed, however, confirmed that the Martian sky was indeed pink, or orange, because of a scattering of dust from its surface and a reflection of sediment suspended in the lower atmosphere. A second, accurate photograph was therefore released. This prompted a number of newspaper headlines to point out that the Martian sky had turned from "blue to red" almost overnight. Some of the reporters could not resist inquiring as to whether its next color would be green.

The first bit of soil scooped up by the lander's surface sampler, as its robot arm was called, was ingested on July 28. The sampler, which would have been appreciated by any model railroader who enjoyed working a crane car, was the ultimate in long-distance remote-control lifting and moving. It was the equivalent of the kind of manipulator arm used to handle radioactive materials in laboratories except that, of course, it reached across more than two hundred million miles of space.

The sampler was actually a retractable thirteen-foot-long boom made of two ribbons of stainless steel welded together along their edges. A flat electrical cable passed between them and carried power to the sampler's collector head. It moved vertically and horizontally across a 120-degree arc that was in full view of one or the other of the lander's cameras when it was working. The head itself was a combination scoop and backhoe that had a hinged lid with tiny holes in it and could move like a wrist. When ordered to scoop, the sampler boom was extended until its head, lid open, burrowed into the soil.

When the sample had been collected, the lid closed and the head was retracted and positioned over one of the experiment packages. It was then turned upside down and shaken so the holes in the lid acted like a sieve: they allowed samples two millimeters or less— roughly a sixteenth of an inch—to pass through. Coarser samples could be deposited in the X-ray fluorescence spectrometer for analysis, or be discarded. In addition, the head's toothy backhoe could be used to dig trenches and retrieve samples from them. Once, under the camera's watchful eye, the surface sampler even moved a rock to see whether the soil beneath it, protected from lethal ultraviolet light, might harbor microorganisms. An analysis of that sample produced the same result as other analyses done with unshielded soil. In both cases the results would prove to be ambiguous.

With the Viking 1 lander safely down on the Chryse plain and relaying data to Earth via its orbiter in one twenty-minute burst a day,* the site certification people could look for someplace else for Viking 2's lander to come down. After still more painful searching (this time using Viking 1 orbiter data, as well as those from the Viking 2 orbiter and everything else in JPL's quickly growing imagery collection), it was decided to order the Viking 2 lander down at the Utopia Planitia, or the Utopian Plain. This was some forty-six hundred miles from Viking 1 and, at a latitude of almost 48 degrees, considerably higher and therefore closer to the north pole. The more varied the locales, it was assumed, the more varied the data collected. Lander 2 duly settled on the stony Utopian plain on September 3 and, like its twin, promptly began returning information about what it encountered.

Although the Viking project did not divide all of the experiments and observations conducted by the orbiters and landers into two parts—the search for life and everything else—that was effectively where matters stood as the mission wound down in 1978.

Almost everything else amounted to a bonanza. In essence, the Viking twins provided a richly detailed catalog of the planet's orbital characteristics, geological composition, surface features, chemical components, atmosphere, and weather. (The last was studied in detail for several complete seasons and constituted the first real extraterrestrial weather reporting in history.)

While by no means complete, the quality of information returned by the four spacecraft would fill a small library.† The orbiters alone returned 51,539 images, while 4,500 came back from the landers. Ninety-nine percent of the Martian surface was photographed at high resolution (320 yards or better). Whatever else was learned from the surface imagery, it would surely provide a wealth of likely landing spots for a future mission. The orbiters also made more than one hundred million infrared observations, while the landers sent back more than three million weather reports.

Specifically, dried-up water courses, ranging from riverbeds to streams, showed that liquid water did exist in large quantities in

*The landers were also equipped to relay data directly to Earth. With Earth and Mars as far apart as they ever get, however, energy requirements were of paramount importance and the orbiter's relay system was more efficient. It could send twenty million bits of data a day, compared with only about one million that could be sent from the lander itself.
†Seismic data were totally lacking. Since Lander 1's seismometer failed to function, and Lander 2's was badly shaken by the wind, no results were returned.

Mars's distant past, though no one could be certain how it got there or where it went. Soil analyzed by both landers appeared to be about 45 percent silicon dioxide and 19 percent iron oxide, plus small quantities of magnesium, aluminum, calcium, sulfur, chlorine, and titanium. The landers also discovered that 2.7 percent of the atmosphere is nitrogen. Since that element is an essential ingredient of carbon-based life, it could be a clue to whether or not life ever in fact existed on the red planet. In that regard, the orbiters also confirmed the presence of water ice, not just frozen carbon dioxide, at the poles, while the landers found that soil samples contained traces of hydration, or water absorbed into its minerals. In addition, the evidence showed that there was very likely water ice in the planet's permafrost, indicating the presence of frozen subsurface oceans perhaps a hundred feet deep. Yet no liquid water was found.

The search for life itself, however, ended ambiguously and in an abiding controversy.

Oyama's experiment involving gas exchange showed that the soil did release four gases when water vapor was added to it: nitrogen, argon, carbon dioxide, and a relatively large quantity of oxygen. This was not expected. Neither life-bearing nor sterilized soils (including Moon rocks) that were tested in advance had produced oxygen under similar conditions. But the oxygen release was interpreted to show that the Martian surface was chemically, not biologically, active.

Levin's labeled release experiment actually produced positive results according to the protocols—the standards—set in advance. It found compounds that on Earth would have clearly established the presence of microbial activity in soil. Yet there were factors that made the conclusion questionable. First, the presence of intense ultraviolet light led some analysts to conclude that it produced compounds which themselves were mistaken for microbial activity. Also, organic matter itself was not found, which further clouded the issue.

The result of Horowitz's experiment was ambiguous, though perhaps more positive than negative. Some radioactivity was absorbed by the soil sample. Yet the degree to which the sample was heated would very likely have killed any organism that resembled life in its Earth form.

The GCMS experiment was negative. It did not seem to turn up any organic material. That might have been because none was there. But it was also possible that organic compounds were being produced and then destroyed by any number of elements, including a combination of ultraviolet light, oxygen, and some kind of catalyst from the soil. Then, too, it was conceivable that Martian microorganisms, unlike their counterparts on Earth, scavenge their own debris and therefore there was none. Finally, as Levin noted, as many as a million Earth-type bacteria could have gone undetected in the GCMS if they were not accompanied by a large mass of their own organic debris.

Norman Horowitz, creator of the pyrolytic release experiment, rebutted that argument. He concluded that not only did life not exist in the region around Landers 1 and 2, but that it could not exist anywhere else on the planet, either.

"Viking found no life on Mars, and, just as important, it found why there can be no life," the Caltech scientist explained. "Mars lacks that extraordinary feature that dominates the environment of our own planet, oceans of liquid water in full view of the sun; indeed, it is devoid of any liquid water whatever.* It is also suffused with short-wavelength ultraviolet radiation." Because of this, he continued, Mars lacks not only life but organic matter as well. And since Mars was the most promising habitat for other life in the solar system, he went on, it must be concluded that Earth alone harbors life, at least in this part of the galaxy.

Others, however, were not so sure. Harold P. Klein, who headed the Viking biology team, noted two years after the landings that Levin's results were "the most controversial." While pointing out that a number of "reasonably coherent" explanations based on purely chemical or physiochemical reactions could have accounted for Levin's findings, he nevertheless concluded that they remained enigmatic and that a great deal more analysis needed to be done for the Viking life-detection results to be "completely satisfying."

"We have awakened from a dream," Norman Horowitz wrote as a kind of eulogy to Viking. "We are alone, we and other species, actually our relatives, with whom we share the earth. If the explorations of the solar system in our time bring home the realization of the uniqueness of our small planet and thereby increase our resolve to avoid self-destruction, they will have contributed more than just science to the human future."

Horowitz's mellow sentiment notwithstanding, however, others were not at all sure that the question of life on Mars—or elsewhere

*There is disagreement on this. Bevan M. French, a NASA geologist with extensive experience analyzing data from both the Moon and Mars, has claimed that Viking data show as much as 1 percent water in both the soil and the atmosphere (French, *Mars; The Viking Discoveries*, p. 20).

in the solar system, for that matter—ought to be put to rest. Part of
the reason had to do with the fact that, taken collectively, the experiments were not conclusive. And another part had to do with the
restricted area under investigation.

"What might we find if we could roam the Martian surface and dig
around?" Oran Nicks wanted to know. "After all, its land surface
area of 55 million square miles is equal to about 40 percent of the
land area of Earth, and we have only been able to scratch 180 square
feet with our samplers."

"If we were able to do a thousand experiments, different experiments, on Mars, and do these in a wide variety of places on Mars—in
canyons, on the polar caps, in some deep areas of the surface—and
in all those experiments we got negative results, the answer to the
question 'Is there life on Mars?' would almost certainly be no," Klein
asserted. "But on the basis of just a few experiments done at only two
sites, very bland sites on the planet, I think it would be unscientific
of us to come to that conclusion. All we can really say for sure is that
we have run across some very interesting chemistry: the kind of
chemistry we do not see in surface samples from the Earth [or] from
the Moon."

Robert Jastrow, noting that an unambiguous resolution of the
question of life on Mars could well go on for decades, and also that
the Viking experiments yielded contradictory evidence, came out on
the positive side. They seemed to indicate that life, "or some process
closely imitating life, exists on Mars today," he has written.

Robert Shapiro, the iconoclastic chemist who is himself a widely
acknowledged expert on the origin of life, maintained that he was
"on the fence" where the possibility of life on Mars is concerned. But
he deplored the finality with which Horowitz tried to ring down the
curtain on the quest. "Congress, which only understands 'yes' or 'no'
answers, wanted to know whether life had been found on Mars after
the expenditure of $1 billion. Since it had not been found, they
(Horowitz and others) said no and tried to justify the thoroughness
of their work by insisting that life couldn't possibly be there because
they didn't find it," Shapiro maintained. "Follow-up experiments are
badly needed. The attempts to draw definite conclusions about life
were ill-conceived and have probably killed, or at least delayed for
twenty years or more, the follow-up mission. And," Shapiro added,
"who decided that Mars was the most promising habitat [for life]?
Europa, for example, is likely to have a huge ocean of water. How
can *anything* be concluded about this part of the galaxy?"

• • •

The Viking mission was technically concluded on April 1, 1978. But it went on anyway. Data continued to come in from the four spacecraft until, one by one, they succumbed to age. A worsening propellant leak that began in Orbiter 2 in the autumn of 1977 eventually caused it to drift out of alignment with the Sun and therefore to lose power. It went dead in late July 1978, during its 1,050th day in space.

There were problems other than those having to do with the condition of the spacecraft themselves, however. One was the very act of trying to stay in touch with them. The Deep Space Network had two other missions in the works in 1978—a Pioneer flight to Venus and the beginning of an extended flyby of Jupiter and Saturn by a pair of spacecraft carrying the resurrected name of Voyager—so it was heavily taxed. More important, funds were as scarce as ever, making it difficult to justify extending even further what had become an exhausted mission. (The Viking program, itself, would come in at a budget-busting $1 billion, however much Naugle, Martin, and the others struggled to keep costs down.)*

Lander 2 was therefore shut down on April 12, 1980—its 1,317th day on Mars—because transmission and other problems were seriously affecting its performance. JPL terminated Orbiter 1 a little less than four months later because it, like Orbiter 2, was almost out of fuel.

Lander 1 continued to transmit until 1982, even outlasting one of its most important scientists. In October 1980, Tim Mutch, the landers' first imaging team leader, was killed while leading a group of students on a climbing expedition in the Himalayas. He was by then on leave from the Geology Department at Brown University and was working at NASA Headquarters as the associate administrator for the Office of Space Science. Lander 1 was therefore subsequently named the Thomas A. Mutch Memorial Station. A stainless steel plaque commemorating his service to solar system exploration was dedicated in January 1981 with the understanding that eventually it would be attached to Lander 1.

*The situation became so grim by 1980 that a $60,000 Viking Fund was solicited from the public to finance two months of Deep Space Network data acquisition from Lander 1 the following summer. The collection was made under the auspices of the American Astronautical Society after NASA designated July and August 1981 as Viking Fund Months.

9.

Dreams of Frequent Flyers to Orbit Earth

The National Aeronautics and Space Administration, in common with virtually every other institution in the world, has two agendas: one is stated, the other is not.

The stated agenda, stipulated by the National Aeronautics and Space Act of 1958, is to operate the civilian space program of the United States. It does this to promote the "general welfare and security" of the nation in the realm of air and space. Specifically, NASA is charged with expanding knowledge, improving aircraft and spacecraft, sending instruments and "living organisms" to space, cooperating with other nations in space, and ensuring U.S. leadership there. These undertakings, as well as the space agency's relationship with the Department of Defense, were left open to broad interpretation and are therefore ambiguous. Its essential mandate, however—its stated agenda—is explicit: to keep the United States active in space.

NASA's unstated agenda concerns its survival. As with other institutions in Washington and elsewhere, the boxes that represent the space agency on organization charts are in reality thousands of people who have been harnessed to promote and achieve the stated agenda. They came together for a patriotic purpose in 1958 and have spent the ensuing years bonding as individuals and as an institution. And, also like other institutions, their collective enterprise has taken on a life of its own through shared beliefs and experiences. Where institutions are concerned, as with individuals, life resists death.

Yet theoretically at least, NASA the institutional entity leads a more precarious existence than most other government institutions because, as previously noted, the republic would not be in mortal danger without a civilian space program. If the United States

stopped exploring the Moon and the planets, stopped orbiting telescopes and other scientific instruments, and stopped sending astronauts and others to space, it would face no more peril than the
Grand Duchy of Luxembourg, which does none of those things.
Whatever NASA's enabling legislation says about promoting the
general welfare and security, those qualities as they relate to space
are in no sense applicable to the fundamental life, liberty, and pursuit of happiness of the people of the United States. So if NASA
evaporated tomorrow, life would go on without serious disruption,
much less widespread turmoil.

NASA knows this and has always known it. It therefore adopted
a strategy at birth that was designed to reduce its institutional
vulnerability as much as possible while maximizing its chances for
survival in an otherwise precarious world. That strategy is the core
of the unstated agenda. It has been embraced by every administrator
since T. Keith Glennan, by successive phalanxes of associate and
assistant administrators, and by every other manager who has been
able to influence or interpret policy (foremost among them being
those responsible for public relations). It has been adhered to by
them all. But it would be extraordinary if it has ever been articulated by even a single one of them. Instead, it is cloaked in
elaborate metaphor, and it always has been. The unstated agenda,
then, is unambiguous but it is not explicit.

The core of the agenda that is not discussed calls for feats of
massive engineering, which always involve sending humans to
space, to form the heart of the civilian space program. And those
feats—the individual programs—must in turn be grandiose, insepa-
rably linked to other programs so far as possible, and derive from a
broad socioeconomic and scientific base. It is no accident that
NASA's centers are positioned around the country, and not in any
one area, and that its contractors and scientists also represent a
diverse cross section of skills and locations. Besides having the obvious benefit of increasing the number of capable people and institutions plugged into NASA, this was meant to help garner maximum
political support from both politicians and academics: roots that run
wide and deep hold up big trees. Everyone in middle management
and above, not to mention outside contractors and those who study
the space agency professionally, understands and accepts the fact
that such programs are the agency's bread and butter because they
are expensive, long-term, and dramatic.

In addition, and just as important, huge undertakings are nearly impossible to stop once they have been started. The more money a large high-visibility program has consumed, the less likely are the Office of Management and Budget and congressional committees to kill it before it can accomplish enough to justify the funding they have already committed. And if this is true, it follows that one such program ought to lead logically and smoothly into the next, until there is an unbroken succession of them like links in a chain. As the use of individual links makes no sense, the wisdom had it, neither would any single phase in the sequence of massive man-carrying engineering projects. Each would lead to the next and all would be mutually dependent. Wernher von Braun, among others, grasped this instinctively.

Yet successive NASA administrators and their underlings have not approached the agency's existence in a particularly cynical way. On the contrary, their belief in a robust, many-faceted civilian space program seems only to have convinced them of the agency's abiding value. It's just that if NASA's continued existence is of paramount importance, then dramatic undertakings of immense proportions that can keep it functioning vigorously are easily justified. They are taken to be valuable not only in their own right, but because in helping the agency to stay healthy they automatically benefit all other programs, including space science and planetary exploration. In this way the institution itself and its huge engineering programs become a self-reinforcing closed circle. Politics and programs become indistinguishable.

It is understood that everybody and everything in the empire benefits one way or another from the engineering extravaganzas in the sky. The modest programs—space science and solar system exploration, for example—benefit from the big programs if only because the latter keep NASA alive in the first place. Few in science and exploration would argue that this is how the system evolved. Most of them, however, would argue quite strenuously that such a system seriously misplaces the space agency's priorities.

Apollo was the first of the gigantic agency-sustaining engineering programs—the prototype big-ticket item required by the unstated agenda. Both John Kennedy and Lyndon Johnson, his vice president, recognized the dynamic political possibilities inherent in landing men on the Moon (and necessarily risking their lives in the process). In sanctioning such a mission, the White House sent a clear message to NASA, to Congress, and to the nation: spending vast sums to undertake spectacular and dangerous feats in space for purely political ends was an acceptable instrument of national policy.

But sanctioning—not conceiving—the voyages to the Moon is what Kennedy and Johnson did. The idea was there all along. Sending people to the Moon was so technically audacious and politically adept that it fired the souls of many in the space community, including military strategists who dreamed of turning the lunar surface into the ultimate reconnaissance and guided missile platform practically from the moment they were actually able to get to space.

Serious planning for such an expedition originated with NASA itself, which started a Working Group on Lunar Exploration as early as February 1959, barely four months after it opened its doors. That June, it authorized the Army Ordnance Missile Command (which included von Braun's rocket team) to study possibilities for using the proposed Saturn launch vehicle for lunar missions.

The space agency fairly hummed with plans to go to the Moon well before JFK's speech of May 25, 1961. Two years earlier, in August 1959, a Space Task Group (a predecessor of the one chaired by Spiro Agnew a decade later) came up with plans for a three-man spacecraft capable of lunar flights. Abe Silverstein, meanwhile, had more on his mind during NASA's first year than jousting with JPL (William Pickering's and his colleagues' perception notwithstanding). On the last day of 1959 a team led by Silverstein recommended that NASA develop the huge Saturn booster, whose understood purpose was to transport people to the Moon.

Only seven months later, in July 1960, the name Apollo was given to the space agency's manned spaceflight program, which by then had expanded to include plans not only to land on the Moon, but also to build a space station. The first in a series of NASA-Industry Program Plans conferences to brief aerospace executives on the Moon program was even held at the end of the month. The space agency's agenda was therefore squarely in place well before Kennedy adopted it and took it for his own.

That agenda, featuring Apollo, was good to space science and planetary exploration. It carried with it a spate of programs— Viking being a prominent example—which might otherwise not have existed. Hardly anyone quibbled with that. Yet despite the relative windfall, which those who did science and exploration eagerly consumed, they despised Apollo anyway: they "detested" it, in the words of Norman H. Horowitz. "They criticized it for the same reasons the shuttle is criticized today," he wrote two decades later. "It consumed funds that should have been spent on space science, and its claims of being a scientific program were unjustified." The scientists were a malcontented bunch, apparently never satisfied with what came their way.

Homer Newell made the same point in his *Beyond the Atmosphere,* though from the different perspective of a NASA manager. At the agency's behest, he recalled, the Space Science Board held the first in a series of study sessions at the State University of Iowa in the summer of 1962 in the hope of trying to get the science community involved in the Moon program. The board favored Apollo for its potential for returning meaningful information about the origin of the Moon and other scientific data and wanted as broad participation as possible by scientists. It soon became apparent, however, that the discussions oozed with bile. Many of the participants objected to the manned program as a whole and steadfastly maintained that its funding, which would otherwise be wasted, ought to be redirected to space science.

Finally, in evident exasperation, Newell and his colleagues decided that they had to lay out the facts of life in explicit detail. "Study members were urged to recognize that the Apollo program would be carried out, that it concerned important national objectives other than science, a major one of which was the development of a strong national capability to operate with men in space," Newell recounted. "Since Apollo was going to be done, it behooved the scientists to take advantage of the opportunity before them and to help ensure that the science done in Apollo was the best possible."

Thus faced with the prospect of liking Apollo or lumping it, the scientists did both. Many participated in the program but badmouthed it anyway. Newell asked Harold Urey to list suggested landing places of particular scientific interest, for example. The chemist duly replied by sending Newell sites that extended over much of the Moon's surface. But Urey eventually learned that engineering constraints, not the needs of the scientists, dictated where the landings would have to be made: within a few degrees of the lunar equator, in the so-called Apollo zone. Years later, almost on the eve of the first mission to the Moon, he complained that he neither understood who was making the decisions on where to land or what the landing criteria were. When he was finally given the document he wanted, the irascible scientist grumbled that it was so full of unfamiliar acronyms as to be unintelligible.

Yet afterward, when scientists not only were included in the site-selection process but were assured that their views would be taken seriously, each repeatedly voted to give top priority to where he wanted his experiment conducted, according to one NASA planner. The meetings therefore often ended in stalemate, leaving frustrated NASA officials to make the decisions anyway.

Since the requirements of the unstated agenda were bigger even than Apollo or any other individual engineering program, plans to supersede it were well along even before the Eagle departed for the Moon. Serious thought about the two other massive undertakings that were within the realm of possibility—a space shuttle and a space station—had coincided with early thinking about the lunar mission itself. In 1959, for example, both a NASA Research Steering Committee on Manned Space Flight and the House Space Committee even concluded that a space station, not an expedition to the Moon, should follow the Mercury program that sent lone astronauts into Earth orbit. Von Braun believed in the primacy of a space station, too, and told NASA as much. As early as 1962 and 1963, NASA sponsored three corporate studies of a shuttle-type spacecraft, one of which involved a fully recoverable ten-passenger orbiter. Yet both the station and the shuttle had to be held in abeyance for financial reasons until Apollo wound down.

In the meantime the manned lunar program itself would set the stage for a series of far-ranging space exploration missions that would still be in progress more than a quarter of a century after the death of the president who first ordered the nation to go to the Moon. Mariner-Mars, Mariner-Venus, and Viking were three of them. But there would be several others, including two matched pairs—Pioneers 10 and 11 and Voyagers 1 and 2—that would go on spectacular long-distance flybys to the outer planets and then continue on, beyond the solar system itself. Because their impetus came as part of the immense explosion of energy that followed Kennedy's mandate, Bruce Murray of Caltech has gone so far as to call those voyages JFK's "last hurrah."

The choice of a major engineering program to follow Apollo was easy. Since a space station would have to be constructed in orbit, a fleet of flying trucks—a Space Transportation System—would first have to be built to carry the materials to where they were needed. It was therefore decided that reusable shuttles would replace Apollo as NASA's next big program. And unlike Apollo, which was single-goal-oriented—get men on the Moon—STS would form the first true link in the big chain. It would have two purposes that went beyond the requisites of its own existence: carrying people and hardware (including the next big element, a space station) to Earth orbit and launching probes on voyages across the solar system and beyond.

But irrespective of their relative places in the space agency's broad scheme, there was one fundamental difference between Apollo and the Space Transportation System. That difference would come to have a telling effect on space science, planetary exploration, and nearly the whole of the U.S. space program in general, military as well as civilian. Whereas Apollo was the signature program—the crown jewel—of the Kennedy administration and was nourished accordingly, the Space Transportation System, whatever its merits, was taken by an otherwise uninterested and cost-conscious Nixon administration to be little more than another flotation device that was required to keep NASA from sinking into oblivion. It, too, was nourished accordingly.

Those who ran the space agency knew, even as their astronauts gamboled on the Moon, that the shuttle was going to be a hard sell. Just about everyone in the executive branch and on the interested congressional committees understood about NASA's unspoken agenda and therefore why it needed the Space Transportation System.

Yet there was diminished public interest in space. In addition, Congress was determined to draw the nation's purse strings as tightly as it could. Senators Walter F. Mondale, William Proxmire, Clifford P. Case, and Jacob K. Javits, among others, spoke for sizable constituencies of scientists and others who were unhappy at the prospect of yet another manned program—perhaps of more stunts— that would divert precious funds from the space agency's already anemic budget. Finally, there was a president who was burdened by a frustrating and unpopular war, who was not especially enamored of space exploits, manned or otherwise, and who was as fiscally conservative as his old boss Dwight Eisenhower. It was therefore considered essential to convince Nixon, key members of the House and Senate, and the press (always the press) that the Space Transportation System was going to be so cheap to operate it would actually be profitable.

It certainly looked like an economical system on the face of it. Spacecraft that could be reused—emptied, refueled, reloaded, and sent out again like intercity buses or commuter planes—were bound to be cheaper than expendables, which hit the ocean like rocks and

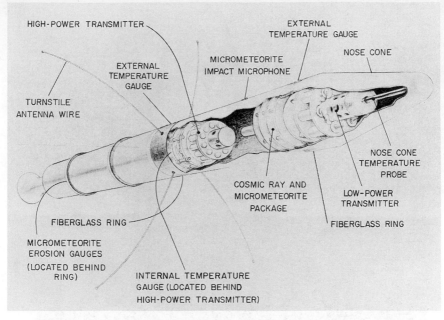

HIGH-POWER TRANSMITTER

EXTERNAL
TEMPERATURE GAUGE

NOSE CONE

MICROMETEORITE
IMPACT MICROPHONE

EXTERNAL
TEMPERATURE
GAUGE

TURNSTILE
ANTENNA WIRE

NOSE CONE
TEMPERATURE
PROBE

COSMIC RAY AND
MICROMETEORITE
PACKAGE

LOW-POWER
TRANSMITTER

FIBERGLASS RING

FIBERGLASS RING

MICROMETEORITE
EROSION GAUGES
(LOCATED BEHIND
RING)

INTERNAL TEMPERATURE
GAUGE (LOCATED BEHIND
HIGH-POWER TRANSMITTER)

William Pickering, James Van Allen, and Wernher von Braun share a
moment of triumph. They are holding a model of Explorer 1 (cutaway
above) which, hours before, had become the first U.S. satellite to
answer Sputnik 1 by going into Earth orbit. The cosmic ray and micrometeorite package, actually a sophisticated Geiger counter, was Van
Allen's experiment and discovered the radiation belt around Earth
that bears his name.

Mars explorer. Each Viking spacecraft consisted of an orbiter that circled the planet and a lander that alighted on it. The top photograph shows the orbiter with its solar panels deployed and the lander suspended beneath it in a protective bioshield. At bottom is a model of the lander in a Mars simulation laboratory. The boom and shovel that dug a trough and collected samples of the Martian surface is touching the sand, while meteorology instruments are at the end of the boom on the right. The canister at left protected the shovel and its claw during flight.

NASA administrator James C. Fletcher (left), Viking project manager James Martin, with crewcut, and John Naugle, the space agency's associate administrator for space science, watch as Viking 1's historic imagery comes in from Mars. The photo above is the first ever taken on the Martian surface. It was taken just minutes after the spacecraft settled on Chryse Planitia on July 20, 1976. The rock in the upper center is about four inches across.

Opposite page: Three historic JPL spacecraft. The artist's rendering notwithstanding, Ranger 1 (top) and five of its immediate successors failed to reach the Moon, embarrassing NASA and nearly ending JPL's activities in deep space. Mariner 4 (middle), the second U.S. spacecraft to reach Mars, flew by the red planet at very low altitude and sent back twenty-one pictures from a distance of up to 150 million miles. The probe's camera peers eerily out of its instrument-packed bus like a single eye. Voyager (bottom) conducted the first Grand Tour of the outer planets, with Voyager 2 completing its twelve-year odyssey at Neptune in August 1989. The sensor-loaded movable scan platform extends to the right.

THE GREAT GALACTIC GHOUL

The Great Galactic Ghoul, nemesis of planetary explorers, was conceived by *Time* reporter Donald Neff to explain the mysterious glitches that plagued Mariner 7 (shown in the Ghoul's grasp) and other deep space probes. The mythical monster has been especially prone to wreaking havoc on Soviet Mars-bound spacecraft. This rendition was done by a contractor's artist and hung for many years at JPL.

Laurence Soderblom, deputy leader of the Voyager imaging team, describes the qualities of the moons of Jupiter and Saturn to rapt science writers during the Saturn encounter in August 1981. From lower left are Thomas O'Toole of *The Washington Post*; George Alexander of the *Los Angeles Times*; Larry Eichel of *The Philadelphia Inquirer*; Julian Lowe of the *Pasadena Star News*; Robert Cooke of *The Boston Globe*; W. Mitchell Waldrop of *Science*; Robert Cowan of *The Christian Science Monitor*; Robert Locke of the Associated Press; Everly Driscoll of the United States Information Agency (kneeling); and John Noble Wilford of *The New York Times*. Ronald Clarke of Reuters and an assistant are behind Wilford, while William Hines of the Chicago *Sun-Times* is to Soderblom's left.

Opposite page: The Lord of the Rings yields some secrets to Voyager 1. The top photo, made on November 6, 1980, from a distance of 4.9 million miles, shows Saturn's extraordinarily complex ring structure —in this case, ninety-five individual concentric features. The spacecraft also discovered a fourteenth moon, barely seen at the upper right just outside the narrow F ring. A week later Voyager 1 captured the rings' elusive "spokes" from 581,600 miles. The shimmering spokes seen extending across the B ring, were more closely examined by Voyager 2 when it encountered Saturn in August 1981.

This hauntingly beautiful parting shot of Saturn was taken by Voyager 1 on November 16, 1980, four days after its closest approach. The giant planet's shadow falls on the rings, while its bright crescent can be seen through all but the densest part of the ring plane. The picture was taken from a distance of 3.3 million miles. Voyager 1 then climbed up and out of the solar system while its sister craft, Voyager 2, continued on to Uranus and then Neptune for the completion of the Grand Tour.

The four Galilean moons of Jupiter are, clockwise from the upper left: Ganymede, showing many bright impact craters, like the large one at right, which are relatively new; Io, variously called the "weirdest" object in the solar system and an "anchovy pizza" because of its reddish-orange appearance and tumultuous terrain, was found by Voyager 1 to be only the second body in this solar system (after Earth) to have active volcanoes; Europa, the smallest of the four, shows complex patterns on its surface that suggest ice was fractured at some point. The absence of many impact craters suggests that Europa's surface is still changing; Callisto, the darkest and most distant of the quartet, shows a large, bright impact basin measuring 360 miles across. Its concentric rings were probably caused by shock waves in the moon's icy crust when the impact occurred.

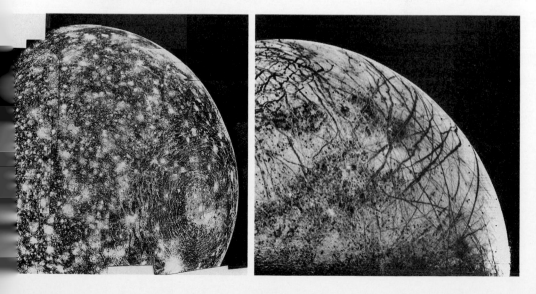

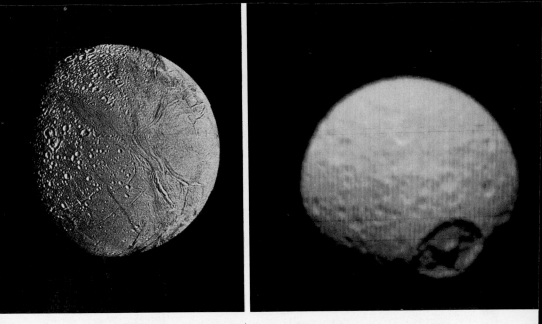

Four of Saturn's moons, clockwise from the upper left, are Enceladus, whose multiple terrains, including a fault system and ridged plains, indicate a complex history and an immense internal heat source sometime in the past; Mimas, nicknamed the Death Star from the movie *Star Wars* because of the sinister appearance caused by its dominating sixty-two-mile-wide impact crater; Tethys, whose heavily cratered region in the upper right and lightly cratered one in the lower right indicate a period of internal activity long ago; Dione, lower left, is also heavily cratered. The bright areas in the lower portion may be ice fields.

Laurence Soderblom, surrounded by other members of the Voyager imaging team (top) puzzles over evidence of active volcanism on Triton, Neptune's largest moon. Behind him, left to right, are three of the team's stalwarts: Eugene Shoemaker, Joseph Veverka, and David Morrison. Below, Torrence V. Johnson comes up with a possible answer to one of Soderblom's knotty questions. Besides being on the imaging team, "TV" Johnson was the Galileo project scientist. Tobias Owen, another longtime team member, sits on a desk at rear.

Voyager science teams met each morning at eight during encounters to sift the previous twenty-four hours' data before presenting their "instant science" to the news media. Carolyn C. Porco and other ring specialists (top) pore over fresh imagery in an effort to close one of Neptune's elusive rings. William I. McLaughlin (below left), manager of the Voyager Flight Engineering Office, ponders the state of the spacecraft's health while Rudolph A. Hanel, principal investigator of the Infrared Interferometry and Spectrometry team (at right with beard and holding pencil), makes notations on what his colleagues have discovered at Uranus.

With a dish that is 230 feet in diameter, the Deep Space Network's antenna at Goldstone in California's Mojave Desert looks so big up close that it appears to be two-dimensional, according to one of its users at JPL. Identical antennas are located near Madrid and near Canberra, providing worldwide two-way communication links with NASA's solar system explorers. Precise pointing is one reason why the antennas can pick up signals that are sent over billions of miles on less power than is used to light a refrigerator bulb.

The destruction of the space shuttle Challenger on the morning of January 28, 1986, came immediately before the final news conference of the Voyager-Uranus encounter. Several media and NASA representatives were in the Jet Propulsion Laboratory's von Karman Auditorium press area when the explosion occurred and saw it on the NASA Select channel. Clockwise from the upper left: Richard C. House and Jurrie van der Woude of JPL; George Alexander, then of National Public Radio and later head of public information at JPL; Curtis Hunt of the George C. Marshall Space Flight Center; and Mr. and Mrs. Lazlo Dosa of the Voice of America. The conference was postponed to the following day.

On October 18, 1989, Galileo finally got under way after one of the most tortuous development periods in the history of the space program. This artist's drawing shows the Jupiter-bound spacecraft being fired on its way by an Inertial Upper Stage while Atlantis orbits nearby. Ironically, it was the development of the shuttles themselves that caused most of Galileo's difficulties because of funding shortages.

Magellan used its radar to peer under Venusian clouds in August 1990 and returned an image of the crater Golubkina (lower right) with a resolution of 400 feet. The same crater was imaged by Soviet Venera 15 and 16 spacecraft in October 1983 with a resolution of up to 1.2 miles (upper left). The difference in picture quality is apparent. The bright ejecta surrounding the crater indicates that it is relatively young, while the dark interior suggests a possible lava pond.

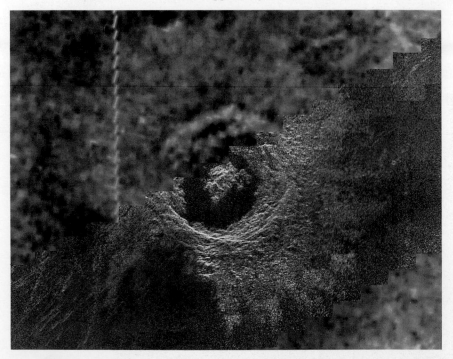

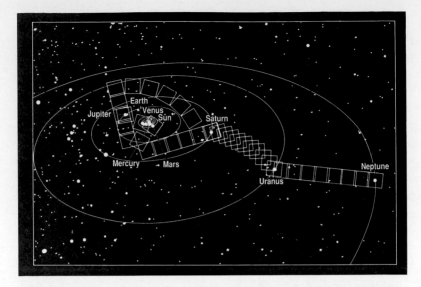

Voyager 1 took a historic first "family portrait" of the solar system from a distance of nearly four billion miles above the ecliptic on February 14, 1990. The drawing (top) shows the arrangement of the sixty-four frames that made the mosaic. Mercury and Mars do not appear because they were lost in sunlight, while Pluto was too small to be seen. Images of the remaining six known planets are shown below. Five months earlier Voyager 1's twin, Voyager 2, had completed the first Grand Tour of four of the outer planets.

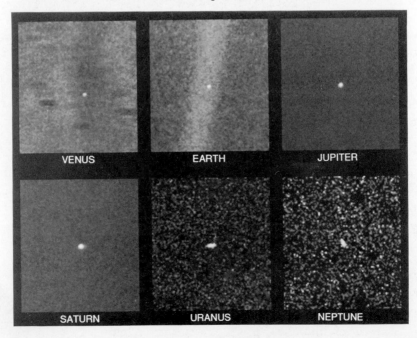

were never seen again. During the 1971–72 period, in the wake of the Agnew task group's report, and during the throes of the heaviest lobbying for the shuttle, the space agency projected some fifty-five flights a year when the system was fully operational—better than one roundtrip a week.

A month after the Space Task Group handed in its report, Wernher von Braun himself weighed in with an article for *Reader's Digest* that essentially reiterated the group's recommendations but provided new details about the shuttle. The vehicle's great value lay in the fact that it would "drastically slash" the cost of getting people and hardware to orbit, he wrote. "Present cost of orbiting one pound of payload is $500 or more. Completely reusable orbital space shuttle vehicles will slash this cost to about $50 or lower per pound." And because the manned orbiter would be so cheap compared with expendables, von Braun prophesied, "the reusable space shuttle will in due time replace most of the expendable launch vehicles presently used to launch unmanned spacecraft into orbit."

That same year, 1969, George Mueller, NASA's associate administrator for manned space flight, called for a shuttle that could carry as much as fifty thousand pounds to orbit for five dollars a pound or less.

NASA paid six hundred thousand dollars for a study by a Princeton think tank called Mathematica, Inc., which showed that a fully reusable shuttle would save a marginal $100 million during its write-off period (1978–90) at an investment of $12.8 billion. When OMB told James Fletcher, then the NASA administrator, that he would do well to get half that amount, he went back to Mathematica for a second study, this one based on an absolute maximum number of missions carrying the most weight possible divided by the cheapest conceivable design. At one point, Mathematica was instructed to use an almost mind-boggling 714 flights over the twelve-year period, which came to a little more than a flight a week. With each flight carrying a maximum 65,000-pound payload, this meant that almost four million pounds of cargo would have to be hauled to space every year in order to turn a profit. That would be the equivalent of four hundred 10,000-pound satellites. Six or seven such spacecraft would have to be carried on every trip, which was in itself impossible unless they were designed to be as heavy as possible while taking up minimal space in the payload bay. If any NASA official understood that there was no conceivable overall level of activity in Earth orbit, military or civilian, that could justify such a launch rate, there is no public record of it. (By comparison, forty-one satellites totaling 425,000 pounds were launched by the United States in 1971, a big year for such activity.)

Economics was at the heart of a debate that raged over the shuttle during most of the Nixon administration's first term—a debate that occurred even as NASA's budget continued to plummet. NASA's total appropriation for fiscal 1969 dropped to $4 billion (from $5.1 billion three years earlier). By fiscal 1973 it had been slashed even further, to $3.3 billion. No wonder the shuttle's advocates touted it as a money saver.

Yet others doggedly warned that the shuttle would be nowhere near as cheap to operate as its adherents predicted. Some pointed out that man-carrying spacecraft are by definition more expensive than unmanned ones because they have to be constructed to accommodate humans: their occupants must be able to function efficiently and in an environment that is both comfortable and safe. This requires more complicated and therefore more expensive engineering than do expendables.

People must have highly specialized life-support systems and other accommodations. Robots do not require pressurized space suits that cost many millions of dollars to develop. They do not need toilets. And they are not sensitive to odors—at least not to the point where extensive testing needs to be done to protect their sensibilities.

The odor evaluation experiment, an otherwise insignificant footnote in the history of the shuttle's development, would probably best be forgotten. But it reminded David Helfand, a Columbia University astrophysicist, of the kind of absurd undertakings that, collectively, added up to sums of money that might otherwise have benefited serious science and exploration.

Helfand recalled coming across a hundred-page NASA document describing odor evaluation experiments for the shuttle in considerable detail when he was a young graduate student. The guideline set up many procedures "to make sure that nothing smelled bad in the shuttle," Helfand explained. Every compound that was being considered for use on the shuttle therefore had to be tested by an Odor Evaluation Panel consisting of seven people who had themselves been tested for their ability to distinguish odors.

"They had to rate these odors: I think 'ethereal' was one of them, to 'earthy,' or 'scummy,' or something like that," Helfand remembered. There were adjectives for seven or eight different odors that had to be distinguished on a scale from one to five. "Picture this room with seven people sitting around with cards, like the Olympics, saying, 'That's a 3.2 ethereal.' They'd put little bags over their heads and breathe this stuff in," he said, laughing. "And this was described in a hundred pages in bureaucratese." The experiment amused Helfand, but he was less than amused by the funding it consumed in the name of life support.

Other experts, like Adelbert O. Tischler, who headed the chemical propulsion division of NASA's Office of Advanced Research and Technology, believed that it was not the exotic hardware itself that would drive up the cost of operating the shuttle, but the salaries paid to the thousands of white- and blue-collar workers who would have to support the Space Transportation System. The thirty thousand NASA employees at the Kennedy Space Center alone would draw almost $500 million in salaries a year, he predicted. When added to the salaries of thousands more at Houston who would have to control operations once the shuttles were in orbit, plus others around the world who would have to track them and run their communication system, plus still others at Headquarters who would have to process all the paperwork, the annual bill would be immense.

All but ignored in the fusillades of numbers that were exchanged during 1970 and 1971 was a six-page paper presented at the Third Annual Meeting of the American Institute of Aeronautics and Astronautics, held in Boston at the end of November 1966. Written by three RAND Corp. researchers working on their own with NASA data, the paper compared estimated costs based on maximum reasonable payloads on the standard Saturn expendable launch vehicles used for Apollo, and on horizontally and vertically launched two-stage reusable shuttles.

"In a major earth orbital program involving the placing into orbit of approximately 72 million pounds between 1970 and 1999," the study concluded, "it is more economical to use the current expendable Saturn IB and Saturn V launch vehicles than to develop and operate either a conventional or advanced reusable orbital transport. The reason for this is that even in an ambitious program there is insufficient payload to compensate for the high development cost of a reusable transport." What it came down to, in the authors' view, was the simple fact that there would not be enough business to warrant building reusable launch vehicles under even the most optimal conditions.

And there was more. "If the development of a reusable transport were to proceed it would seem apparent that either the total NASA budget must increase considerably or certain space programs may have to be seriously curtailed—programs that, if cancelled, would make the case for ROT [reusable orbital transport] even more tenuous. It is also interesting to note," the paper continued, "that when analyzing the space program involving a Mars landing as early as 1984 (implying a greatly reduced earth orbital program compared to the plan examined here), the reusable orbital transport is even less attractive because there are even fewer launch opportunities."

Unless NASA's budget was increased, the three RAND staff members were saying, the act of creating the space shuttle would automatically reduce or eliminate some of the very projects for which it was to be built. It would eat its own tail.

When the shuttles finally did fly operationally, beginning in November 1982, it would cost about three thousand in then-current dollars for them to get one pound to Earth orbit. And not counting food or space suits and other gear, it would cost more than a half million dollars to send up each astronaut.

Throughout 1970 and 1971, however, the debate over the shuttle raged on as one design after another took off and was shot down in a hail of highly charged verbiage and numbers that were used like grapeshot by Congress, NASA, the Office of Management and Budget, assorted consultants, the Air Force, and the White House.

A fully reusable system gave way to one that was only partially reusable. As originally conceived, the shuttle was supposed to consist of only two parts: a manned booster about the size of a Boeing 747 jetliner and an orbiter the size of a smaller but nonetheless hefty Boeing 707. After lifting the orbiter most of the way to its operational altitude, the booster was to have released it and then flown back down to the launch site for refurbishing.

But in May 1971 the Office of Management and Budget informed the space agency that it would receive no budget increases for the next five years. Since development of the fully reusable shuttle was calculated at about $10 billion, with a peak annual expenditure of some $2 billion, there was no way NASA could develop it and still keep at least some of its other programs going on its projected total annual budget of only $3.2 billion.

The engineers were therefore forced to radically rethink the original design. They ended up with an orbiter that was smaller and lighter than the original because it carried its liquid fuel and oxidizer outside in a single external tank and used two solid rocket

boosters that were "strapped on." What had been a single component—a reusable booster-spacecraft having its own engines and propellant—thus became three components, one of which (the external
tank) would be expended and two of which (the solid rocket boosters)
would parachute to Earth and be fished out of the ocean for use
again. And so, in order to save money, the Space Transportation
System's carrying capacity was decreased; it went from being fully
reusable to being only partly reusable; and the number of component parts doubled from two to four. It was now one flying craft, not
two, and it would require a pair of external boosters to get it to orbit,
plus an outsized propellant tank that would attach to its belly like
a big bomb.

A system that came in four parts was so much more complicated
than one that came in two that turn-around time—the time it would
take to collect the parts after a mission, refurbish them for a future
mission, and get everything put back together again—would increase markedly. With turn-around time lengthened, the number of
parts to be tightly integrated doubled, and with pressure to increase
the frequency of missions mounting for political purposes, it was
inevitable that taking otherwise unacceptable risks would become
ever more tempting.

The Air Force, which didn't particularly like the shuttle, to begin
with, but which was nonetheless enticed by NASA to support the
program because of its political clout on the Hill and at the Office
of Management and Budget, would have no skimpy space vehicle.
The Pentagonians would contribute not a cent to the cost of the thing
itself, but they extracted as their price for endorsement a very expensive system indeed.*

For one thing, the airmen insisted that the orbiter had to have a
sixty-foot-long payload bay and be able to carry up to 65,000 pounds.
The heavy-lift capability was important because the Air Force and

---

*The Air Force did make a considerable investment, however, in related hardware
and ground-support facilities. Through fiscal 1982, by which time it was operational,
the Department of Defense had spent $2.6 billion on the STS program, most of which
went to the construction of a special launch facility at Vandenberg Air Force Base,
the development of an inertial upper stage for it, and modifications to satellites that
would be launched from the shuttle instead of from expendables (Marcia S. Smith,
"Space Shuttle Issue Brief Number IB81175," Washington: Congressional Research
Service, December 2, 1981 (updated May 17, 1983), p. CRS-10). In August 1986, in the
wake of the Challenger accident and problems with the facility itself, it was announced that the Vandenberg shuttle launch site would be mothballed. (Colin Norman, "Air Force to Mothball Vandenberg, Reduce Reliance on Shuttle," *Science*,
August 15, 1986, p. 717.) It had by then reached a cost of $2.8 billion.

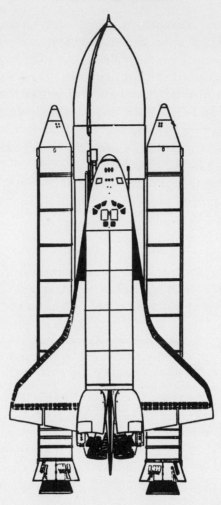

the CIA were planning a series of photo reconnaissance satellites, including one called the KH-9, that were the size and weight of a railroad boxcar (it would be nicknamed Big Bird). And the airmen also knew that even heftier spy satellites carrying more sensors, communication equipment, and maneuvering fuel were on the way.

Moreover, orbiters would also have to be able to carry an inertial upper stage—in essence, their own launch system—for sending signals intelligence, missile early warning, and other kinds of satellites all the way out to geosynchronous orbit (22,300 miles above the equator), where they would be parked over one spot on Earth to pull in missile telemetry and communication traffic like vacuum cleaners, watch for the missile plumes that signaled an attack, and more.

Finally, the Air Force wanted the orbiters to have a cross-range capability of eleven hundred to fifteen hundred miles. This meant they had to be able to turn and fly at least that distance to the left or right of their orbital path so they could get back to their takeoff point in case of emergency after one 90-minute orbit. This also would allow for a quick return during any orbit to one of the Department of Defense's secure air bases. The thought of an orbiter carrying a classified payload, such as a reconnaissance satellite, coming down on unfriendly or even neutral territory was frightening to most generals. But the requirement for additional glide range meant that NASA's simple straight wing had to become a delta, adding more complications and expense.*

The Air Force, then, wanted a top-of-the-line vehicle with immense lifting capacity and real maneuverability. NASA wanted a multipurpose carrier to secure a permanent foothold for manned spaceflight and in the process ensure its own survival. Congress wanted a guaranteed return on investment. The Office of Management and Budget wanted the lowest possible development cost. The result would be a spacecraft that satisfied no one because it had to satisfy everyone. It brought to mind the familiar quip, often heard on the general staffs of Western European nations, that the camel is a horse drawn to NATO specifications.

James Fletcher therefore faced a dilemma in 1971. He could either accept the camel and try to make the best of it or refuse it and take a chance on ending up with no beast of burden at all. Knowing as he did that the lack of a Space Transportation System would almost undoubtedly mark the beginning of the end of NASA, Fletcher decided to accept the compromise shuttle rather than fight to the bitter end for a superior version. ". . . if the shuttle was ever going to go," he later recalled, "it had to be that year."

It was a fateful decision in that it said something not only about Fletcher himself but about the precarious existence of the agency he headed. And the fact that he was forced to choose between an underfunded, second-rate system and no system at all amounted to a pathetic commentary on the entire process of acquiring and using spacecraft in the United States after Apollo. While the shuttle was the most visible victim of that sorry process, it was by no means the

*Ironically, NASA's Space Shuttle Task Force, which defined the shuttle design, initially called for a delta wing but was forced to drop the idea, also for budgetary reasons.

only one. Many other spacecraft, including any number of planetary explorers, would be afflicted in the same manner. In an odd sort of way, most civilian spacecraft tended to face the same kind of travel restrictions that the federal government placed on the humans who were responsible for them: Go economy; regulations strictly prohibit traveling first-class.

Nixon approved the camel over the New Year weekend of 1972 and made his decision public on January 5. He authorized the Space Transportation System despite sharply conflicting studies by OMB, RAND, and the president's Science Advisory Committee, all of which questioned its viability or scientific usefulness, and in the face of adverse reactions by the National Academy of Sciences and a slew of influential congressmen.

In certifying that the shuttle was going to be built, the president in effect signed the death warrant for expendables such as Thor, Atlas, and Titan, at least temporarily. It stood to reason that whatever the Space Transportation System's real carrying capacity was, it was not going to be enhanced by competing carriers. Those who planned NASA's agenda therefore resolved to put the competition out of business. The use of expendables would be terminated as shuttles were phased into service. That decision itself would drive up the cost of sending both military and civilian payloads to space. (It also drove the Air Force, which did not want to be dependent exclusively on the shuttle for pressing national security launches, into a prolonged frenzy.) This was due in part to the fact that Earth satellites and interplanetary probes had to be modified or designed from scratch to be carried and launched by the Space Transportation System.

But it was even more complicated than that. Space science and exploration, like the Department of Defense and the intelligence establishment, would also wait in a long queue for an available launch date. Unlike military and intelligence customers whose needs were held to involve national security, however, the science and exploration missions had relatively low priority on the STS manifest. The Hubble Space Telescope, which was scheduled for launch on the shuttle in late 1986, was only one example. Having been grounded by the Challenger accident, it was repeatedly bumped after shuttles began flying again in September 1988 because other missions were judged to be more important in an otherwise highly tenuous launch schedule. The delay not only added to the telescope's cost because of storage fees and the need to keep an unproductive infrastructure together until launch time, but it caused the spacecraft itself to become gradually outmoded without returning so much as a single picture.

Not satisfied with making extravagant claims about the shuttle's lifting capacity and launch rate or with eliminating its competition, the space agency also brought to bear its formidable public relations skills to line up allies, both as individuals and as huge groups, to help make it a pervasive element in the national space culture.

Senator Jake Garn (Republican from Utah), the influential chairman of the Senate Appropriations Subcommittee, which appropriates funds for NASA, would be a passenger on Discovery when it made the sixteenth shuttle flight in April 1985.* Representative Bill Nelson, a Democrat from Melbourne, a community just south of Canaveral, would go up on Columbia on January 12, 1986. Shuttles would also carry foreign nationals (a practice also favored by the Soviets): a Canadian, a Mexican, and a Saudi Arabian. In addition, Christa McAuliffe, the teacher, would be sent up to deliver a lesson to the millions of the nation's schoolchildren. There would also be plans to orbit a reporter or a writer who would be expected to describe for the country what he or she experienced. The Journalist in Space Project, as it was called, was canceled after the Challenger accident.

Another sales tool concerned the nature of some of the missions themselves. While heavy-duty work was planned to be the mainstay of the shuttle fleet—lofting Earth satellites, deep space probes, sections of the space station, and perhaps eventually parts of the rocket that would carry spacefarers to Mars and back—lesser stuff would in no case be ignored if it had some kind of public relations value, however indirect. There would be experiments to form crystals and other things in near-zero gravity, which it was hoped would attract some investment from the private sector. Science experiments by youngsters would also be carried to space, as would so-called Getaway Specials, which were small containers that held real experi-

---

*In May 1981, Garn, a former military pilot, asked space agency officials when he would be able to ride on a shuttle. He was told by a NASA official that his position was like that of an "800-pound gorilla: you can go whenever you want." At that point Senator William Proxmire, who had repeatedly ridiculed the space agency by giving it Golden Fleece awards for wasting taxpayer's money, quipped facetiously that if he ever went to space on a shuttle, he would not return. Garn's job as a so-called payload specialist was to conduct tests related to space sickness, earning Discovery the sobriquet "Vomit Comet" for that mission. ("When Can I Go on the Shuttle?—Garn," *Defense Daily*, May 13, 1981, p. 72).

ments by scientists who would be charged relatively little to get them taken along. NASA's managers understood that it was important for the Space Transportation System to seem to be accessible to all the people if all the people were going to support it.

No possibility for the shuttle's ingratiation with the people of the United States was too remote to ignore. It was therefore touted as being not only a cheap and efficient space ferry but the first truly humanitarian one as well. In February 1985, for example, NASA would announce that thirty pints of human blood, and possibly some bone marrow, was headed for orbit for experimentation in zero gravity. The experiments were to be done under the auspices of the Center for Blood Research at the Harvard Medical School; they were financed by NASA. Three months later the space agency would tell the press that the shuttle was to be enlisted in a Flight for Famine by using a special large-format camera to search for water in drought-stricken areas of Africa and elsewhere.*

Even AIDS research would be invoked. Discovery, which would be the first shuttle to return to work following the Challenger accident, carried an experiment designed to grow especially large crystals of an enzyme that played a role in spreading the disease. The crystals had been grown on Earth for years. But growth in the absence of gravity allegedly made them larger and therefore easier to see.

Whatever benefit there was in looking for water from the shuttle, or carrying minor biological experiments to orbit in its payload bay, such activity brought havoc to space science and exploration. While Viking survived as a robust mission, both the Pioneer and Voyager outer-planet missions would be racked by budget problems, at least initially.

Yet Pioneer and Voyager fared better than a rendezvous mission to Halley's Comet, planned for September 1985, which Murray fought hard to get for JPL. It fell victim to the shuttle and in the process caused renewed tension between Pasadena and Headquarters. Fred W. Bowen, who managed the Headquarters field office at JPL, recalled a few years later that the atmosphere was charged

*No mention was made, however, of the fact that Landsat earth resources satellites, which first went into service in 1972, were capable of doing such work and had been designed for that and similar purposes. The satellites were developed by NASA. Under pressure from the Reagan administration, their operation was turned over to a private firm, after which additional government funding for follow-ons was abolished (it was reinstated during the first months of the Bush administration).

when news came that Washington had decided to kill the Halley mission. "When I walked into the cafeteria," he said, smiling, "I could hear knives and forks scraping against plates."

A spacecraft called the Venus Orbiting Imaging Radar (later named Magellan), which was being designed to circle Venus and map its cloud-shrouded surface in unprecedented detail, was derailed for a time because of the funding crunch caused by the shuttle. So was another spacecraft, a large and ultrasophisticated one called the Jupiter Orbiter-Probe (eventually christened Galileo), which suffered a series of setbacks and suspensions because of the shuttle and its teething problems.

The shuttle's crippling effect on space science and planetary exploration would cause dismay and abiding anger among many scientists. Joseph Veverka, chairman of NASA's Comet Science Working Group and a Cornell University planetary scientist, fairly bristled when he was interviewed by *New York Times* science writer Malcolm W. Browne on the eve of the first shuttle launch in April 1981. "What's happened is that the space science program in this country has been almost destroyed," Veverka said. "The shuttle was built under very stringent financial conditions, and it was a very complex job done for less money than was really needed. Money to complete it was taken from science projects. The courageous thing would have been to go back to Congress or the White House and ask for more, instead of robbing those scientific programs. The single most important purpose of NASA, as defined by its charter, is exploration of the solar system," added the exasperated scientist. "But now, the institutions that control funds clearly regard science as not useful, and believe that applications, especially military applications, are sacred."

Veverka's point about the military had in a way been presaged by the RAND paper of November 1966, which explained that the Space Transportation System's cost would effectively eliminate much of its own civilian cargo throughout the 1980s and therefore a big part of the reason it existed in the first place. This would leave STS, in the words of *The New York Times'* John Noble Wilford, in the "unenchanting role of truckdriver for other people's freight."

The "other people" turned out to be largely the Air Force. So dependent would NASA become on Department of Defense payloads that cancellation of a Pentagon mission could automatically scrub a shuttle launch, even months ahead of time. When the Air Force announced in February 1984 that it was canceling a secret mission set for July, it effectively killed that launch. "If they remove the payload, we won't fly," said Glynn Lunney, the shuttle program manager, on hearing the news. They did and it didn't.

Whatever the Space Transportation System's real or imagined potential, even NASA's deft public relations skills could not obscure the fact that it was plagued from the outset by pernicious developmental problems. And it was those problems, no less than the base cost of the system itself, which crippled every part of NASA that was dependent upon it. Many of the problems would have plagued any new system as large and complicated as the shuttle. Both the United States and the Soviet Union had their share of problems in the development of several launch systems, including, respectively, Centaur and the giant N-1 booster that blew up three times while being tested to get cosmonauts to the Moon ahead of astronauts. Even Apollo had serious development problems, though they were drowned with money. But even throwing money at projects did not in and of itself insure against calamities, as Khrushchev's priority expenditures on the N-1 indicated.

From the outset, it was the orbiter's own main engines, not the solid rocket boosters, that caused the most trouble.* They amounted to a considerable improvement over those used on the Saturn series. Although each of the three engines was only seven and a half feet in diameter and fourteen feet long (measured to the end of its exhaust nozzle), it had to deliver 375,000 pounds of thrust when throttled to 100 percent of power and up to 417,300 pounds when set at the maximum 109 percent.† They had to be throttleable between 65 and 109 percent of power in 1 percent increments and have a service life of seven and a half hours, or fifty-five starts. These characteristics required highly complex engineering, including provision for all-important high-pressure turbopumps that had to push the liquid

*The fact that the SRBs ran on solid propellant, not liquid, lent them an aura of immunity from failure. Sensors that would have signaled trouble in the SRBs were left off them because it was taken for granted that they were "not susceptible to failure," William R. Graham, NASA's acting administrator, said five days after Challenger blew up. "They are considered primary structure, and not susceptible to failure. We designed them that way. They were designed with great care and great thought," Graham was quoted as saying by *The New York Times*.
†The engines' maximum normal power was rated by its manufacturer at 100 percent. They were able to achieve 9 percent more than that, however, in the astronautical equivalent of an automobile's overdrive. In the same way, jet engines used by military aircraft are given one maximum thrust rating when used without afterburners and another, higher one, when afterburners are ignited.

hydrogen–liquid oxygen mixture into the engines with so much force that all three engines developed the equivalent of five million horse-power.

Rockwell International's Rocketdyne Division, based in Canoga Park, California, won the $500 million engine contract in July 1971. That in itself raised eyebrows in the aerospace industry because it was awarded before Nixon approved the shuttle. "It's my feeling that the contract had to go to California for political reasons," said a disgruntled William R. Cotter, representative from Connecticut. Pratt & Whitney, an established jet engine manufacturer in East Hartford, had already tested most of the components for the high-pressure engine but lost out to Rocketdyne anyway. The Connecticut firm was so angered by this that it filed a protest with the General Accounting Office alleging that NASA had failed to observe relevant statutes governing procurement. It was the first time in forty-five years of doing business with the government that Pratt & Whitney had filed such a protest.

Meanwhile, Rocketdyne had its own problems right at the beginning, and they were far more technical in nature than political. Given the shortage of funds and the time pressure, NASA decided to adopt a "success-oriented" management approach for developing and testing the engines. This meant that instead of testing individual components before they were brought together to form a complete engine, the whole thing was tested only when it was finished. In other words, NASA and its main engine contractor were betting that when all of the pieces were finally put together and turned on, they would work. "This not only saves the time that would otherwise be spent on intermediary tests," Duke University historian Alex Roland observed with dry humor, but "it also creates an aura of confidence. No tests, no failures—and absence of failure is success."

But as the 1970s wore on, Rocketdyne waded ever deeper into a quagmire because incremental testing had not been adequately done. By 1978—the year Columbia, the first operational orbiter, was delivered to the Kennedy Space Center—Rocketdyne still could not get the engine to survive so much as a runup on the test stand. In five tests between 1978 and 1980 one turbopump and four separate engines were damaged because of pump, valve, or other malfunctions, resulting in further delays and $21 million in modifications.

Then there were the heat-resistant thermal protection tiles—some thirty-one thousand of them—that were designed to insulate the orbiter as it plunged into the atmosphere at twenty-five times the speed of sound. In order to maneuver the way the Air Force insisted it had to, the spaceship had to be made to withstand temperatures as high as 3,000 degrees Fahrenheit. The Ames Research Center, which had considerable experience in high-temperature aerodynamics, developed something called "reaction cured glass," made of molded silica, which could be baked into light tiles and glued onto a feltlike material that was in turn glued onto the orbiter's skin. The idea was that the tiles would absorb the heat so as to keep the craft's aluminum skin lower than 350 degrees at all times.

But there were two problems. First, each tile was unique. Each had to be precision-made to fit the contour of the particular spot on the orbiter where it was to go. Sticking on all thirty-one thousand of them was painfully slow work, the more so because spaces between tiles could be no more than 65/1,000ths of an inch wide, lest a gap cause a burn-through on the spacecraft's skin. The tiniest of scratches, or even fingerprints, on the tiles were not tolerated. Second, the tiles tended to come loose and fall off, as happened on Columbia's maiden voyage and on some subsequent flights.

Added to engine development and tile problems was a spate of others that were to plague the Space Transportation System well after it had become operational. There were several celebrated computer failures, a problem-plagued landing gear that once caught fire on landing, navigation instrument malfunction, and even a fire caused by a fuel leak in Columbia's rear compartment in December 1983.

At the time of the fire, Glynn Lunney told *The New York Times*'s John Noble Wilford of another accident—a "spooky" one—that had happened to one of the shuttles the previous August. The insulation lining one of the solid rocket booster's nozzles burned to within two-tenths of an inch of the metal, Lunney recalled. If the rocket had to fire a few seconds longer, the astronauts might have had to abort the flight and could even have lost control of the craft. "We were really fortunate," Lunney added. "There's no other way to put it." The orbiter was Challenger.

"If the high hopes of five years ago had been realized," Wilford pointed out on May 14, 1985, "today might have seen the 37th launching of a space shuttle. . . . Such was the optimism in December 1980 when the National Aeronautics and Space Administration issued its ambitious timetable listing for May 14, 1985, the flight of shuttle 37 with a secret military payload." With the first flight still four months off, the *Times* correspondent recalled, NASA had boldly predicted five hundred shuttle flights by 1991. "Reality has fallen far short of those early expectations," he added, noting that Challenger had returned from only the seventeenth mission the week before and that the space agency was then looking at only 165 missions through 1991. "Every now and then I go back and look at those early projections and have to close my eyes and shake my head," Wilford quoted L. Michael Weeks, a shuttle official in Washington as saying.

The schedule slippages led to cost overruns. The orbital test flights that started in 1981 were two years late. In 1971, when NASA was trying its best to sell the shuttle, its cost through the first four test flights in 1981 was estimated to be $5.15 billion. By 1983 that cost was figured at $9.91 billion real-year dollars, or $6.65 billion in fiscal 1971 dollars. That amounted to a 29 percent increase.

The situation had grown so dire by February and March of 1979 that the space agency was forced to do something it ordinarily loathes doing. It asked Congress for a supplemental appropriation of $185 million to keep the development program on schedule. But even that was soon lost in a well of red ink. Weeks later NASA submitted a $220 million budget amendment, which Congress approved. The additional money was needed because of pressing national defense missions, space agency officials explained. In January 1980 they again hit up Congress, this time for a $300 million supplemental ($285 million of which was granted). NASA's total budget request for the shuttle for fiscal 1981 was $1.87 billion, or some $800 million more than it had originally thought it would need. The runaway budget led many members of Congress to question whether NASA was competent to manage the shuttle program in the first place.

Whatever doubts Congress may have had about the way the space agency managed its finances, however, there seemed to be little or no doubt that given enough time and money, it could at least develop a shuttle that would operate safely.

Although catastrophic failure was a real possibility, its probability was always taken to be so remote as to be virtually nil. The near-fatal accident aboard Apollo 13, in which an explosion blew out one of the spacecraft's panels on the way to the Moon and caused the mission to be aborted, was an ominous portent of what could go wrong in the unforgiving environment of space. Yet the nine successful Apollo missions, including six landings and takeoffs on the Moon, obscured the danger and convinced NASA and its affiliates in industry that they could do no wrong, that engineering could purge error from a mission the way a turbopump could purge liquid hydrogen from a line or a tank. The shuttle's managers would come to believe, as their own publicists and they themselves had so often proclaimed to a gullible press and public, that propelling humans into space really was routine. They said it so many times they began to assume it was true. One day that hubris—the false pride that was the worst of the sins in the Greek myths—would literally explode in their faces.

Richard Feynman, the Nobel laureate from Caltech who served on the presidential commission investigating the Challenger accident, had revealing conversations with NASA employees about the odds of an accident happening. Louis J. Ullian, the range safety officer at the Kennedy Space Center who was responsible for putting explosive charges on launch vehicles so that the craft could be destroyed if they veered off course, told Feynman that NASA had told him that the probability of a calamitous failure was one in ten to the fifth power.

"I tried to make sense out of that number," the physicist later recalled. "Did you say 1 in 10^5?"

"That's right: 1 in 100,000."

"That means you could fly the shuttle *every day* for an average of *300 years* between accidents—every day, one flight, for 300 years—which is obviously crazy!"

"Yes, I know," Ullian answered. "I moved my number up to 1 in 1000 to answer all of NASA's claims—that they were much more careful with the manned flights, that the typical rocket isn't a valid comparison, et cetera—and put the destruct charges on anyway."

During the course of the Challenger investigation, Feynman would become convinced that a gap existed between how engineers and managers saw a given project, at least in terms of its viability. The engineers were the more objective. For the engineers, numbers, angles, and physical laws like the Bernoulli theorem were the truth, and the truth could not be bent. There was a naïve honesty in the way they clung to their numbers, in their stubborn belief that numbers honestly arrived at would never lie.

Managers, on the other hand (even those who had started as engineers but had "advanced" up the corporate or governmental ladder), were politicized and were therefore less objective than the engineers. For Feynman, a physicist who had been rigorously trained in the tenets of objective observation, that change perverted them. Once the managers had been told a project was in the works, it was their job to bring it to completion, even if that meant interpreting numbers in ways that were excessively optimistic. The "reality" of corporate or governmental life dictated that a manager put the best possible face on whatever his superiors wanted.

In order to get a clearer picture of what NASA insiders really took to be the odds of a shuttle having catastrophic failure, Feynman conducted an impromptu poll, in secret, of a manager and three of his engineers.

"I gave each person a piece of paper. I said, 'Now each of you please write down what you think the probability of failure for a flight is, due to a failure in the engines.'

"I got four answers—three from the engineers and one from Mr. [Judson A.] Lovingood, the manager. The answers from the engineers all said, in one form or another (the usual way engineers write—'reliability limit,' or 'confidence sub so-on—) almost exactly the same thing: one in about 200. Mr. Lovingood's answer said, 'Cannot quantify. Reliability is determined by studies of this, checks on that, experience here'—blah, blah, blah, blah, blah.'

" 'Well,' I said, 'I've got four answers. One of them weaseled.' I turned to Mr. Lovingood and said, 'I think you weaseled.'

"He says, 'I don't think I weaseled.'

" 'Well, look,' I said. 'You didn't tell me *what* your confidence was; you told me *how* you determined it. What I want to know is: after you determined it, what *was* it?'

"He says, '100 percent.' The engineers' jaws drop. My jaw drops. I look at him, everybody looks at him—and he says, 'Uh . . . uh, minus epsilon!'

"OK. Now the only problem left is, what is epsilon?"

"He says, 'One in 100,000.' "

The space agency would come to estimate that the odds of catastrophic failure in the shuttle's ascent—by far the most dangerous part of a flight—was one in seventy-eight. But it did that only after one actually exploded. The new reality that set in after the loss of Challenger fundamentally altered the way NASA saw its Space Transportation System. The accident was to have a sobering effect on the odds-makers and therefore on planners at the top levels of the space agency. Seymour C. Himmel, a member of NASA's Aerospace Safety Advisory Panel, would even predict that there was "clearly a finite probability that something will go awry over the next few years, that you'll clobber one."

Space "is in fact dangerous, and Challenger reminded us of that," Bruce Murray has observed. "NASA and the Congress, and journalists, are unindicted co-conspirators for selling us a fantasy which wasn't true: that space was easy, cheap, and that the shuttle was going to do it, and that there was great promise. None of those statements is true. It's not safe, it's not easy, and there's no great promise in a material sense. Challenger is a very important event in *this* sense: Not because somebody screwed up on an O-ring or because NASA made some bad decisions, but because it [the accident] helped to clarify this soup of feelings, analysis, special interests."

The former director of JPL added, "What the Rogers Commission never asked in the course of investigating the Challenger accident was why those people were up there; whether what they were doing was worth risking their lives."

10.

Pioneer: Pathfinders to the Outer Limit

Like an infant reaching out ever farther, first to find the extremities of its own body, then to define the boundaries of its crib, and finally to venture into the world beyond its immediate environment, the planetary scientists and the engineers who designed, built and guided the exploring machines had an instinctive urge to go to the outer planets, to see the two gas giants, Jupiter and Saturn, up close and take their measure.*

Telescopes had done very well in that regard. They had contributed a vast literature to the understanding of the solar system well before the first probe ventured beyond the vicinity of Earth. The sizes, shapes, probable compositions and orbits of the five outer planets, and particularly Jupiter and Saturn, had been calculated with some precision. So most astronomers looked far past them, even beyond this galaxy itself, for the challenge of discovery. Spectrometers plugged into giant telescopes like the two-hundred-inch monster at Palomar and the 157-inch one at Kitt Peak in Arizona had provided a great deal of hard information on the atmospheres of Jupiter and Saturn, the two nearest of the outer planets, while millions of observations of the way they interacted with their moons gave scientists a clear indication of their masses, densities, and gravitational pull. Their radio emissions, picked up by radio telescopes, helped to define their magnetospheres.

Jupiter, one planet removed from Mars, had been a likely target for telescopes since the time of Galileo because of its enormous size. Long before lenses were crafted and put into tubes, ancients looking up at the planet were so awed by its obviously huge proportions and

*Technically, both are composed mostly of hydrogen in liquid form, so "gas" is a misnomer. Yet they are commonly referred to as the gas giants. David Morrison, the astronomer, has wryly observed that "fluid" covers both bases.

by the shimmering white light it gave off that they named it after their greatest god. The Babylonians called it Marduk after the deity that ruled their city. The Greeks and Romans also invested the giant planet with the status of the king of their own gods: Zeus and Jupiter, respectively. It wasn't quite as bright as Venus, of course, but it more than made up for that by brazenly climbing high in the sky instead of merely skimming the horizon the way Venus, the demure "morning star," or "evening star," did at sunrise and sunset.

Jupiter is the dominating planet in the solar system and contains two thirds of all of its planetary matter. It has 1,317 times the volume of Earth. But it doesn't weigh 1,317 times as much, a fact that was deduced early in the history of modern astronomy. The motion of its moons told observers a great deal about its gravitational pull. And that pull, in turn, defined its mass: how heavy it is. It turns out that while Jupiter is 1,317 times the volume of Earth, it weighs only 318 times as much. This means it must be made of something considerably lighter than the rock, soil, and iron that constitute Earth.

The something is a liquid, and a pretty light one at that. An analysis of the spectrum of light given off by Jupiter—what the light was made of in chemical terms—showed that the planet is composed primarily of hydrogen and helium, the two most abundant gases in the universe. The combination made Jupiter slightly denser than water. And both elements are in roughly the same proportion on Jupiter as they are in the Sun. In fact, astronomers have calculated, if Jupiter had been perhaps one hundred times larger than it is, it might have become a sun instead of a giant gas ball. This tiny part of the galaxy would then have been a double star system. Earth would have been bathed in continuous daylight for much of the year, with night coming only when both stars were near each other. That, in turn, would have had profound effects on evolution (not to mention on Lotharios and other nocturnal creatures).

Telescopes were used not only by Galileo but also by Marius, a German astronomer, to spot the four largest of Jupiter's moons. Although Marius saw them first, in late December 1609, it was Galileo who published first and therefore reaped the glory (that much has not changed in three and a half centuries). But it was Marius who named the satellites after Jupiter's lovers: Io, Europa, Ganymede, and Callisto.*

*Callisto went on to become quite a celestial celebrity in her own right. Jupiter turned her into the Great Bear constellation.

Because Jupiter might have been a star, it and its moons—sixteen of them at last count—interact to the point of amounting to a miniature solar system. Where planetary scientists are concerned, in fact, they constitute a sort of small-scale model of the system as a whole and are therefore an important potential source of information about the dynamics of the larger system. The four lovers vary considerably and are fascinating in their own right, though there was no way of knowing just how fascinating until the exploring machines got there.

Seen through telescopes early on, Jupiter was a majestic sight: a spinning colossus of multicolored bands that paralleled its equator and were capped by gray hoods over both poles. In the 1660s Robert Hooke, the British scientist, reported seeing a gigantic spot with a diameter one tenth the size of the planet itself. Giovanni Cassini, an Italian-born astronomer who became the director of the Royal Observatory in Paris and who discovered four of Saturn's satellites and a great deal about its ring system, saw the spot at the same time. Similar sightings were made repeatedly during the following two centuries, though it was noted that the spot periodically seemed to fade or disappear, and then return. In the 1860s, for example, it was seen to be a faint oval, while a decade later it was the most conspicuous object on the planet, a thirty-thousand-mile-long brick-colored gash that came to be known as the Great Red Spot. Some mystified astronomers thought it was the top of an immense mountain; others speculated that it was an island floating in the Jovian clouds. Whatever it was, earthbound observations revealed that it and the clouds and bands around it were moving dramatically, which further intrigued those who peered at it. The astronomers also saw that Jupiter, by dint of its prodigious gravity, exerted a powerful influence on all of the neighboring planets.

To be sure, given its importance, Jupiter became a prime target for a visit as soon as long missions became feasible. But Saturn, Uranus, and Neptune were also highly tempting destinations. Tiny, frozen Pluto, usually the outermost of the known planets, but occasionally sliding inside Neptune's orbit, has been somewhat less subject to scientific curiosity.

Saturn, the second largest and certainly the most beautiful of the planets because of its exotic rings, was also taken to be a tempting target early in the space age. At a distance that ranges up to a billion miles from Earth, depending on where it is at any given time, Saturn looks bright yellow and somewhat indistinct through telescopes.

Saturn's rings were first seen to be what they were—bands (or at least one band) extending all the way around the planet—by Christian Huygens in 1655. (Galileo, who could not distinguish them against the brightness of the disk itself, drew them as ears.) Twenty years later Cassini, noting what appeared to be a separation in the ring, concluded that what had appeared to be one ring was in fact at least two. The dark line dividing them therefore came to be called Cassini's division. Later, the fact that Saturn's moons could be seen through the division and also through the Crepe, or the innermost of several rings, led astronomers to conclude that the rings themselves were not solid, but were made of many particles.

Like Jupiter, Saturn was accurately measured from Earth, its orbit calculated, and its surface analyzed for conspicuous features and chemical content. By timing how long it took some of the features to make one complete rotation it was revealed that Saturn, like Jupiter, is a fast spinner (Nine hours fifty-five minutes for Jupiter and ten hours thirty-nine minutes for Saturn). The planet's mass, also calculated by measuring the way it interacted with its inner moons, was seen to be about ninety-five times that of Earth's, though its density is only seven tenths that of Earth, leading the authors of one college-level astronomy text to note that it is "the only planet that would float in water." Uranus and Neptune, even farther out and therefore even fuzzier, were seen to be small bluish-green bodies that gave up little to the telescopes that scrutinized them.

What was most striking about the astronomy books of the postwar period, however, was their lack of hard data about all of the planets, including Earth. Although distant galaxies were described in impressive detail in any number of leading college texts, commensurate information about the planets in this solar system (which, by astronomical standards, crowd in on Earth like passengers on a rush-hour bus) was largely absent. A close reading of many of the texts years after they were published, in fact, shows a degree of equivocation and speculation that almost seem to reflect the frustration of those who wanted the robots to get in close and send back information that would finally turn question marks into exclamation points.

Jupiter's colored clouds "must in some way depend on circulation in the atmosphere," one of the textbooks guessed, adding that "certain molecules probably form more readily in some regions and decompose in others as a result of differences in temperature and pressure from one belt to another." On the other hand, it continued, "dust, clouds, or vapors may arise from the solid surface of the planet and float into the uppermost atmospheric levels." "Most of the volume of Jupiter seems to be atmosphere," said another. "The actual planet, thought to consist of a metallic-rocky core . . . [is] imagined to be overlaid by a thick layer of ice." "The apparent diameter of Jupiter varies. . . . The mass of Jupiter is best determined from . . . The rocky surface can hardly be more than . . . Callisto . . . is very likely a chunk of ice. . . . Perhaps Ganymede is partly rock, partly ice. . . . All four [moons] show a phase effect, so their surfaces are probably rough. . . . This remarkable group of moons possibly consists of asteroids that have been 'captured.' . . . On the long view, Jupiter may have a floating population of distant moons."

Planetary scientists in both NASA and academe wanted to get to Jupiter and Saturn at the earliest possible time, and so did the space agency's management. The slew of Mariners sent to Venus and Mars between 1962 and 1969 had been extremely successful, with the science return building from one mission to the next. Mariner 9's data return from Mars in 1971 was so good, in fact, that it even allowed mission planners to take seriously the possibility of sending the orbiter-lander there that would come to be known as Viking. With the first reconnaissance of Earth's closest neighbors complete, however, it was only natural for the planetary people to want to move farther out—out to the really big ones.

But first, some formidable problems had to be resolved. There was the severe budget crunch that began even before astronauts reached the Moon. There was also a president, Richard Nixon, who was not prone to lavish money on undertakings as relatively arcane as space science and planetary exploration (nor, for that matter, were the three chief executives who followed him).

"Space science was not high on Presidents Richard M. Nixon's and Jimmy Carter's list of space objectives," the historian Linda Neumann Ezell has written. "NASA was urged to build on the knowledge and experience of its first 10 years to develop a stronger program of practical applications satellites that would deliver a speedy return on the taxpayer's space dollars and improve the quality of life on Earth."* While Nixon's advisers did recommend a

*That message was to echo in 1989, another period of budgetary-belt-tightening, when the chairwoman of the Senate Appropriations Subcommittee admonished space scientists to keep their funding requests in "proper perspective." "I hope the science community understands that this investment is not a giveaway program of entitle-

strong program of lunar and planetary exploration, astronomy, physics, and studies of the Earth, she added, "this healthy program had to be accomplished on a bare-bones budget."

But the problems were by no means only political. There were physical difficulties inherent in getting to Jupiter and beyond it, the most obvious one being the sheer distance to be covered. When Jupiter is closest to Earth, it is roughly 367 million miles away as the crow flies (and 601 million when they are farthest apart). But planetary probes aren't crows: they are more like stones fired from slingshots that have to be aimed far ahead of a moving target in order to hit it, making a long, arcing trajectory. This substantially increases the total distance to be traveled. A probe sent to Jupiter would have to follow a 620-million-mile curved path. One sent to Saturn would travel two billion miles. Such distances would take so long to complete that it would require Rip Van Winkles to collect and analyze what the probes found once they finally reached their destinations. The propulsion system—the launch vehicle and upper stage—would therefore have to be up to the task of giving a Jupiter-bound spacecraft an adequate push.

Furthermore, while Earth is one astronomical unit from the Sun (roughly ninety-three million miles on average), the mean distance from the Sun to Jupiter is a little more than five AUs.* (Earth averages nine and a half AUs from Saturn; nineteen AUs from Uranus; almost thirty-one AUs from Neptune; and thirty-nine AUs from Pluto.) Since Jupiter and the other outer planets are five or more times farther from the Sun than is Earth, it was understood early on that solar panels would not be up to providing the electrical power needed to operate the spacecraft and their various scientific instruments. Power to do that would therefore have to be carried by the spacecraft itself in the form of nuclear power packs: a pair of radioisotope thermoelectric generators similar to those that would be put on the Viking landers.

The vast distances also pose serious communication problems. Even traveling at the speed of light, 186,000 miles a second, a radio

ment," Senator Barbara A. Mikulski warned. The Maryland Democrat's remark reflected a clear sentiment in Congress that space activities be more closely tied to specific benefits to the nation, such as improving its ability to compete internationally, rather than to the relatively abstract requirements of increasing knowledge for its own sake (*Aviation Week & Space Technology,* May 8, 1989, p. 15).

*The term "astronomical unit" refers to the distance between the Sun and Earth. It is used as a convenient way to express great distances without having to resort to either gaggles of o's or powers.

signal would take half a day to get from one side of the solar system to the other. This can cause a significant delay—forty-five minutes just to Jupiter and quite a bit longer to the planets beyond it— between the time when a signal is sent from Earth and when it is received by the spacecraft. One-way light time therefore figures importantly when operating spacecraft over long distances.

Controllers on Earth, for example, would have to send maneuvering or instrument operation instructions to a probe going to Jupiter at least an hour and a half before the actual event was to take place if they were going to allow the spacecraft time to acknowledge receipt of the signal. There would be no chance to change instructions within ninety minutes of a maneuver's having to take place or a sensor's being activated. Every contingency would therefore have to be anticipated by the probe's engineers.

In addition, the stream of signals carrying the collected data to Earth would be so faint as to amount to a whisper almost lost in all of the radio "noise"—the background static—coming from the planets themselves and from elsewhere around the galaxy and beyond. The Deep Space Network's big dishes would therefore have to be pointed at the outer planetary probes with consummate accuracy if the probes were to receive instructions sent to them and the information and other data they transmitted were to come back. (As it would turn out, the eight-watt signal transmitted to Goldstone and elsewhere in the Deep Space Network from either of the spacecraft that were to be the first to reach both Jupiter and Saturn would be so faint that if collected for nineteen million years, its energy would light a single Christmas-tree bulb for a thousandth of a second.)

Another problem relating to distance had to do with the reliability of the spacecraft themselves and their scientific instruments. The trip to Jupiter would take about two years. During that time the probes' guidance and maneuvering systems would have to perform flawlessly. At encounter, scan platforms holding cameras could not freeze or stick and none of the scientific instruments could degrade because of the severe cold or radiation bombardment.

As if that weren't challenge enough, engineers also had to consider the fact that any spacecraft going to Jupiter and beyond would have to pass through the asteroid belt and then perhaps through the huge planet's own murderous radiation field. The first asteroid was spotted in 1801. It was calculated by the end of the century that some thirty thousand of them circled the Sun between Mars and Jupiter. Yet they remained poorly understood at the start of the space age.

Some, like Ceres, Pallas, Juno, Hidalgo, and Vesta, were so big—
Ceres is nearly five hundred miles in diameter—that they were
given names. Others were known to be quite a bit smaller, but there
was no clear idea of how much smaller, how many there were, how
they were spaced, or how they got to be where they were in the first
place. All asteroids, no matter what their size, are called minor
planets. Whatever they were, though, they were taken to be a potential navigation hazard. A spacecraft slamming into a baseball-sized
asteroid at thirty thousand miles an hour would very likely come out
of the encounter looking like a tin can that had been subjected to an
exploding firecracker, while an asteroid no bigger than a grain of
sand could easily knock out one of the probe's subsystems. Emergency procedures would therefore have to be worked out for that
kind of contingency as well.

Finally, Jupiter itself was presumed to be a dangerous place for
probes. The planet was understood to have radiation belts a million
times more powerful than Earth's. High-energy protons and electrons could easily penetrate a spacecraft, it was feared, degrading or
completely zapping key transistors or circuitry, in effect electrocut-
ing them. One way to protect spacecraft from radiation was to
"harden" them: to use radiation-resistant materials as much as possible and provide shielding. Another was to keep them safely beyond
the point at which the radiation could be harmful. But what was that
point? No one knew for certain because Jupiter had never been
visited.

The door to the outer planets was opened by a physical law that
was dusted off in the mid-sixties. It has been known from the earliest
days of classical astronomy that the gravitational force of one planet
to some degree affects other bodies in the solar system: its own
moons, the other planets, and in the case of a body as massive as
Jupiter, even the Sun itself. This interaction of gravitational pulls,
which Newton articulated in 1666 as the law of universal gravitation, forms the basis of the theory of perturbations of planetary
orbits—that is, how each body's motion affects other bodies' motions.

It followed that if a planet's gravity attracts its own moons, comets, and other planets, it would also attract a spacecraft. The closer
the spacecraft came to the planet, the more the planet's gravity
would affect it, drawing it closer still. And the closer it came, the
more it would accelerate. If the spacecraft was aimed right at the
target planet, its velocity would reach its peak at the moment of
impact, which is what happened to the Rangers.

But if a spacecraft could be guided in such a way that it got close enough to a planet so that gravity increased its speed, it would swing partway around the planet, its acceleration increasing, and then zing off toward its next target at far greater speed than it had to begin with. The result was likened to the classic slingshot, used by David with stunning effect against a larger opponent, in which a cloth or leather sling was whipped around and then opened at one end to release a stone at high velocity. In the mid-sixties Michael Minovich, one of Pickering's young engineers at JPL, concluded that such a maneuver was entirely feasible. Homer Joe Stewart and another JPL engineer, Gary A. Flandro, then worked out the precise mechanics for such maneuvers.

Gravity assist, as the technique would come to be called, realized one of the astronautical engineer's oldest dreams: getting more velocity with no additional engine performance or fuel consumption. Higher velocity would mean arriving at the destination sooner. That might not be particularly important when driving to work, but where interplanetary distances are concerned, it can literally make the difference between seeing a mission to completion and perhaps not surviving it. But even the survivors could end up running a mission that seemed interminable.

"The management problems in organizing and carrying out a direct 30-year mission to Neptune (sheer boredom on the part of the participants) look great enough to deter even the most determined explorer," Homer Joe Stewart wrote in a pioneering paper in 1966. "In comparison, the eight-year trip by way of Jupiter seems quite tractable, particularly since we now have a number of spacecraft with useful life of over a year." Mission time to Saturn using Jupiter's gravity was reduced from six years to a little less than three, and to Uranus, from sixteen years to just under six.

Jupiter, indeed, is a blessing for rocketeers. It combines a mass that gives it more than twice as much gravitational pull as any other planet in the solar system (2.6 times that of Earth) with being first in the line of the outer planets. If a probe is aimed close enough to Jupiter for the planet's enormous gravity to increase its speed substantially, and it then whips partly around the gas giant like the stone in David's sling, it would be flying quite a bit faster on the way out than it had on the way in. Gravity assist is as close as trajectory engineers like JPL's Bob Cesarone ever get to a free lunch. It made Jupiter the gateway to the outer solar system.

But that wasn't all. In a report published the previous year, 1965,

Flandro presented calculations of the orbits of Jupiter, Saturn, Uranus, and Neptune, showing that all four would be strung out in a perfectly staggered formation beginning in the late seventies. This meant that a single mission could fly by each of them, in turn, using gravity assist from one to be slung to the next. The discovery was an amazing piece of luck, since such a formation occurs only once every one hundred seventy-five years.

The dream mission was soon given an appropriate name: the Grand Tour. It not only would offer the engineers and planetary scientists their first solid shot at all four of the big outer planets, but would do so at an attractive price, since a single spacecraft would theoretically be able to do the work of four. And if a second were sent along for the sake of redundancy, which was only prudent, it might even reach Pluto to boot.

Given the fact that hard times were clearly ahead as the Apollo budget peaked in 1965 and 1966, the cost of such a mission not only was significant but was very likely a decisive factor as to whether there would be any concerted exploration of the outer solar system at all. That much was obvious. It was far from obvious, however, that such a mission would be exclusively JPL's.

NASA's Ames Research Center at Moffett Field, California, had wanted to be included in space exploration from the outset of the space program. The facility, about an hour's drive south of San Francisco, was born in 1939 as the NACA's Ames Aeronautical Laboratory and still boasts several of the largest and finest wind tunnels in the world. It was renamed on October 1, 1958, when it became a NASA center. In the spring of 1960 Ames established a group to study the feasibility of managing space projects. Under the leadership of Charles F. Hall, the group came up with a small, relatively simple craft that could be used to explore space within Earth's orbit—that is, the two inner planets, Mercury and Venus, and the Sun itself.

In 1962 a small delegation from Moffett made a pilgrimage to Headquarters to present their case. Hall and his colleagues tried to persuade Edgar Cortright to let them have their own modest project: a series of solar probes.

Cortright approved the request, making it clear that he thought Ames's involvement in space exploration, along with JPL, Langley, and the Goddard Space Flight Center, would be good for the overall space science program because a degree of competition and diversity was healthy. That, at least, was Hall's recollection almost thirty years later. And it rings true. It was a time when the "spoiled brats" at JPL were showing undisguised hostility to Headquarters because of what they took to be excessive meddling even as the first of the Block I Rangers were failing.

The solar probes—five of them—were to be called Pioneers A through E. The name Pioneer had been borne by the five previous Air Force and Army spacecraft that had been fired at the Moon with decidedly poor results from 1958 to 1960.

The new Pioneers, managed by Ames and designed and built by TRW (formerly Space Technology Laboratories), did very well for the most part. Pioneers A, B, C, and D (which were numbered 6 through 9 after they were launched between 1965 and 1968), returned a mound of data on the Sun and on conditions in interplanetary space. Pioneer E would have become Pioneer 10 had its Thor-Delta first stage not suffered a catastrophic hydraulic failure within minutes of rising from Canaveral on August 29, 1969. The 148-pound, thirty-five-inch-high aluminum cylinder and its eight scientific instruments disintegrated when the range safety officer touched the booster's destruct button at liftoff plus eight minutes and three seconds. The number—10—was not to be retired, however. It would be saved, as it turned out, for the first man-made object to reach one of the outer planets and then sail beyond all of them.

Even as Ames's inner solar system probes were performing with distinction, momentum was building for a shot in the other direction: at Jupiter and beyond. In March 1967 several missions to explore the outer planets, and specifically Jupiter, were discussed at the Fifth Goddard Memorial Symposium in Washington. A spacecraft gaining gravity assist from Jupiter, it was said, could develop enough momentum to avoid being pulled into an orbit around the Sun and instead streak out of the solar system altogether. This, in turn, would provide the first clear picture of how far the Sun's influence—the solar wind—extended. That same year, the Goddard Center made its own move to establish a foothold in deep space exploration with a study calling for a Galactic Jupiter Probe—actually two spacecraft launched by Atlas-Centaurs in 1972 and 1973— that were to examine "solar, interplanetary, and galactic phenomena." The Goddard team certainly couldn't be faulted for setting its sights too low.

In 1968 the Space Science Board recommended that the exploration of Jupiter "be given high priority, and that two exploratory probes in the Pioneer class be launched in 1972 or 1973." The following year a Space Science Board–National Research Council committee chaired by James Van Allen published a report, *The Outer Solar System: A Program for Exploration,* which went even further. It called for missions that would begin at Jupiter and then strike out on two Grand Tours: to Saturn and Pluto in 1977, and to Uranus and Neptune in 1979. Jupiter was by then clearly earmarked as a kind of embarkation point from which the outer solar system was to be methodically explored.

Given the fact that the sort of deep space mission envisioned by the Space Science Board would require a spacecraft that was fundamentally different in almost every respect from the relatively small and simple solar Pioneers, it is not clear why the board recommended that the probes be called Pioneers. But Charles Hall, who would manage the program from its outset, very likely hit on the answer. "It generally seemed like it was always easier to get funding from Congress if you said this was an extension of an existing program" rather than a new one, he observed. "So you call it by the same name. Monday you buy a Volkswagen, and Tuesday you buy a Cadillac, but you call it a Volkswagen. See? That's how the name stuck."

In any case, Headquarters officially approved the Jupiter mission in February 1969, stipulating that two identical spacecraft be manufactured. The program was assigned to the Planetary Programs Office of the Office of Space Science and Applications in Washington.* It was to be managed by a Pioneer Projects Office at Ames, with design and fabrication of two identical spacecraft going to an outside contractor.

In giving Pioneer to Ames, Washington took it away from Goddard. "All of a sudden, Headquarters takes the Galactic Probe away from Goddard and hands it to Ames," said Hall. "Goddard lost out on this Galactic Probe; it was just taken away from them, no ifs, ands, or buts, and it was given to Ames. There's a little politics there, too," he noted.

The ostensible reason for choosing Ames was that it had more

*Planetary missions are called programs at Headquarters and projects at the centers that are responsible for them. Thus there was a Pioneer Program in Washington and a Pioneer Project Office at Ames. The director of the project reported to its program director. In the case of Pioneer, its program director at Headquarters reported to the associate administrator for advanced research and technology. JPL program directors reported to the associate administrator of Space Science (later changed to Space Science and Applications).

experience with the earlier Pioneers, which were spin-stabilized, just as the newer, larger ones were going to be. Spin-stabilization requires the whole spacecraft to spin around its vertical axis like a top. The other kind, three-axis stabilization, uses thrusters to keep the entire spacecraft steady. The Mariners were three-axis-stabilized, and so were the Viking orbiters and landers. Yet Goddard engineers had already demonstrated an excellent knowledge of what it took to stabilize spacecraft. They had already developed several types of Earth-huggers, including a long series of Explorers that came after the one that got the United States into space, plus an Orbiting Solar Observatory, an Orbiting Geophysical Observatory, the Tiros weather satellites, and such communication satellites as Telstar, Relay, Syncom, and Intelsat. Tiros, Telstar, Relay, and some of the others were in fact spin-stabilized. What is more likely is that Headquarters simply decided that three centers (including Langley) conducting deep space missions was quite enough, and that Goddard would be better off concentrating on a wide variety of platforms that circled the home planet.

Now the mission needed to be precisely defined; a prime contractor and subcontractors had to be selected; and proposals for science experiments had to be solicited. Given what had to be done, it looked as though the first window to Jupiter would come during late February through early March 1972. The first spacecraft, initially called Pioneer F (the next in line after the ill-fated E), was therefore scheduled for that launch opportunity. Pioneer G was scheduled to leave thirteen months later, when the next window opened. It was pretty well established by that point that having reached Jupiter, one or both of the spacecraft would be sent on to Saturn, too.

While the data sent back first from Jupiter and then from Saturn would be immensely important in their own right, the overall value of the mission went well beyond its scientific return. Although both of the Pioneers would not be going on the Grand Tour themselves, they would act as pathfinders for the spacecraft that were designated to undertake that long and potentially hazardous voyage. They would in effect travel through what was taken to be a likely minefield of asteroids and then an area of perhaps lethal radiation. The Pioneers' job would be to send back not only science data but information about how they themselves were faring in the new environment beyond Mars. If they emerged unscathed, other robots and missions would be designed to follow them within the then-accepted parameters. But if they came out of the flight and the encounter battered and poisoned, there would have to be some rethinking about the design of future missions and the spacecraft that would fly them.

The mission plan itself was identical for both probes. If Pioneer F ran into trouble, either with one or more of its experiment packages or because of a catastrophic systemwide failure, Pioneer G could duplicate its mission. But if the first flight went as hoped, the second could be modified to collect different data, as well as replicate experiments from the first mission.

Normal government procedure for selecting a contractor for a spacecraft requires that a Request for Proposal be circulated so that potential manufacturers will have a chance to submit their ideas based on the requirements of the mission. But Charlie Hall remembered ruefully that it had once taken 580 days from the time a Request for Proposal had been issued to when a contractor had finally been selected. If he was going to make it through both windows, he knew, waiting nineteen months was out of the question. Hall therefore decided to take an almost unheard-of measure within the stricture of federal government regulations. He took it upon himself to circumvent the usual procedure by writing a Justification for a Sole Source and named TRW as that source. The contract was signed in the autumn of 1969.

Meanwhile, an AO—an Announcement of Opportunity—drew more than 150 responses from scientists who wanted to send instruments to Jupiter and Saturn. Eleven of these were chosen for both Pioneer F and G. With one exception—the addition of a magnetometer designed to measure the intense radiation fields in the inner magnetospheres of both planets on Pioneer G—both would carry virtually identical science packages.

Some experiments would be conducted to determine the density and energy of the solar wind. Others would study the lives of cosmic rays, monitor solar and galactic cosmic ray particles and track high-energy particles from the Sun, and measure the energies of electrons and protons trapped by the magnetic fields of Jupiter and Saturn. Still others would gauge the scattering of solar ultraviolet light and the amount and distribution of heat energy coming from the two giant planets, and even the faint glow from deep space itself.

It was hoped that the Pioneers would confirm or disprove the data that had already been collected by peering at Jupiter and Saturn through telescopes. Yet so much remained a mystery. Although Jupiter gave off more heat than it absorbed, for example, no one knew for certain what went on beneath its surface—whether its core was solid or liquid. Nor were the depths of the Jovian atmosphere known with certainty in the first year of the seventh decade of this century, and nothing at all was known about the compositions and interactions of the gases making up that atmosphere. It was also suggested that the Great Red Spot was a column of gas, the center of an enormous vortex anchored to a prominent surface feature.

While estimates of the radiation around Jupiter had been calculated, its true potency was not known, and that worried Hall and others at both Ames and Headquarters. Gustav Holst's portrayal of Jupiter as the "Bringer of Jollity" notwithstanding, the gigantic gas ball gave off a level of radiation that could have proven lethal to the delicate instruments on any spacecraft that ventured too close. "We didn't know what we were getting into," Hall recalled. "The radiation in the vicinity of Jupiter could have damaged or killed the spacecraft." Although Pioneer F was to be bombarded in a test chamber with the amount of radiation it was expected to encounter at Jupiter, there was nonetheless concern about whether the probe would make it through the encounter "alive."

The fact that the planet was in effect a mass of deadly radiation, however, did nothing to preclude the project's publicists from holding out the possibility that it, too, contained the constituents of life. "Perhaps the most intriguing unknown is the possible presence of life in Jupiter's atmosphere," the lengthy Pioneer press kit suggested. "Jupiter's atmosphere contains ammonia, methane, and hydrogen. These constituents, along with water, are the chemical ingredients of the primordial 'soup' believed to have produced the first life on Earth by chemical evolution," the kit stated immediately after noting that scientists "appear to agree on the presence of liquid water droplets in the atmosphere. . . ."* Since Jupiter was known to have an internal heat source, the release continued, "many scientists believe that large regions below the frigid cloud layer are around room temperature." Such conditions, the press release went

---

*The primordial "soup" theory had its modern origin in 1952, when Stanley Miller, a young graduate student at the University of Chicago and a protégé of Harold Urey's, exposed reduced levels of methane, ammonia, and hydrogen to an electrical charge. The products produced by the reaction included two amino acids that are among the twenty used by living cells to make proteins. This was widely taken to mean that an infinite number of lightning bolts striking the right combination of chemicals in the ocean at some distant time could have produced the genesis of life. Miller's experiment, which was taken to be creditable by many scientists as well as journalists, was often replicated but it never yielded life in any accepted form.

on, "could allow the planet to produce living organisms despite the fact that it receives only $\frac{1}{27}$th of the solar energy received by the Earth." It concluded: "Jupiter could contain the building blocks of life." The reference to "room temperature" almost made Jupiter seem cozy. Once again the possibility of life on another world was used to help drive a mission.

And so was the possibility of actually proving what some had long suspected: that there is another planet out there, far beyond Pluto's outermost orbit. A subsequent press release held out the possibility that both Pioneers might detect "a tenth planet out beyond Neptune and Pluto—or alternatively a dark star companion to the Sun at perhaps 50 billion miles beyond Pluto." This would be the so-called Planet X. John Anderson, the JPL astronomer who was principal investigator for Pioneer's celestial mechanics experiments, concluded from studying old records that some massive object affected the orbits of the outer planets, causing them to behave erratically. The object, he theorized, might orbit the Sun at roughly a right angle to the other nine planets and travel such an elongated route that it returned only once in every seven hundred to one thousand years. It was hoped that when the time came for the two Pioneers to leave the solar system, they might register the kind of pulling—gravity effect—that would indicate the presence of the mystery planet.

Whether or not Planet X exists, however, the search for it provided a rare glimpse of how the respective methods of the scientist and the publicist can come into conflict. Anderson, a scientist, wanted to know whether Planet X was out there. Period.

But it was the job of Peter Waller, an Ames public information officer, to keep as many aspects of the mission as possible before the public. He was therefore supposed to dispense information— "news"—that would enhance the project, the center, and the agency as a whole. That is precisely what the public relations people at Ames, JPL, Goddard, Houston and elsewhere are supposed to do: generate stories in order to keep their centers in the public eye. Yet the differing views of what constitutes "news" between scientists, most of whom are intensely circumspect about their work, and the PR people, whose stock-in-trade is extroversion, can lead to occasional disagreement.

The Planet X episode was a case in point. Much later, in December 1985, as both Pioneers streaked toward the edge of the solar system, Waller would want to issue a press release saying that data from the two probes suggested that Planet X was out there somewhere. But

Anderson would balk. It wasn't that he didn't believe his data. It was just that he felt they were insufficient to warrant going to the press and, perhaps in the process, drawing ridicule from his peers as a headline grabber.

"I must admit that I have no great enthusiasm for this release, having been involved in a similar situation about three years ago," he would write to a colleague. "At that time I went out of my way to cooperate with Pete [Waller] and, despite a reticence on my part for press conferences, I did my best to make a coherent presentation before the TV cameras in support of his first release on Planet X. To do this a second time would be even more of a chore than the first, something I would only do as an institutional responsibility to NASA and the Pioneer Project. It certainly is not obvious to me that there is anything newsworthy here, though I have the highest regard for Pete's opinion on this, so I assume there is. Personally, I am more excited about the possibility of detecting gravitational radiation with the Pioneer 10/11 data than I am about Planet X, but Pete tells me that this would be pretty dry stuff in the absence of a detection. I accept his opinion."

Fortunately for Pete Waller and everyone else, nothing else having to do with the Pioneer mission to Jupiter and Saturn was quite so speculative as the existence or nonexistence of Planet X.

The spacecraft themselves—the first from Earth to venture to the outer planets—were remarkably simple, given the nature of their extended mission. Waller and his helpers provided copious details about them.

Each Pioneer weighed only 570 pounds, sixty-five of which were scientific instruments and sixty of which were propellant for attitude changes and course correction. The heart of each was a hexagonal bus that held the science packages, computers, guidance and communication systems, and propellant. Attached to the bus was a noncollapsible nine-and-a-half-foot-wide high-gain antenna, which fitted snugly inside a Centaur's ten-foot-wide shroud. The Centaur would, in turn, ride atop an Atlas. There were also three booms, one of which held the familiar magnetometer. Each of the two other booms supported a pair of radioisotope thermoelectric generators that would supply power. The four RTGs were loaded with plutonium-238 that would give off enough heat to provide 155 watts of power at launch and 140 watts at Jupiter.

Anticipating concern about how the highly toxic nuclear fuel

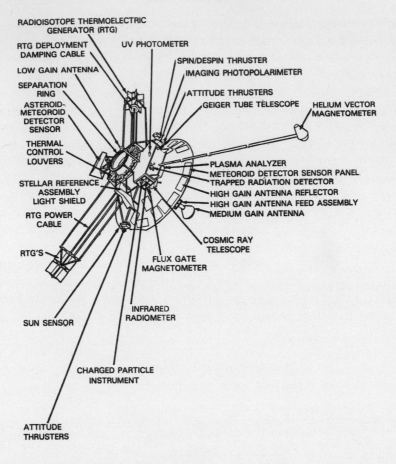

RADIOISOTOPE THERMOELECTRIC
GENERATOR (RTG)

RTG DEPLOYMENT   UV PHOTOMETER
DAMPING CABLE

LOW GAIN ANTENNA   SPIN/DESPIN THRUSTER

                                    IMAGING PHOTOPOLARIMETER
SEPARATION
RING   ATTITUDE THRUSTERS
ASTEROID-
METEOROID   GEIGER TUBE TELESCOPE   HELIUM VECTOR
DETECTOR   MAGNETOMETER
SENSOR

THERMAL
CONTROL
LOUVERS   PLASMA ANALYZER
                                                 METEOROID DETECTOR SENSOR PANEL
                                                 TRAPPED RADIATION DETECTOR
STELLAR REFERENCE   HIGH GAIN ANTENNA REFLECTOR
ASSEMBLY
LIGHT SHIELD   HIGH GAIN ANTENNA FEED ASSEMBLY
                                                 MEDIUM GAIN ANTENNA
RTG POWER
CABLE

                                         COSMIC RAY
RTG'S   TELESCOPE

                    FLUX GATE
                    MAGNETOMETER

                    INFRARED
                    RADIOMETER
SUN SENSOR

              CHARGED PARTICLE
              INSTRUMENT

ATTITUDE
THRUSTERS

would fare in an Earth or near-Earth accident, an Ames press release noted that the SNAP-19s, as the generators were called, had
been designed "for maximum safety in case of a launch pad explosion, abort, or reentry." Each was set out at the end of a ten-foot
boom to reduce the possibility that the radiation they gave off would
interfere with the spacecraft's science instruments and other equipment. All three booms would ride to space folded inside the Centaur's shroud and be extended after the probes were on their way.

After being stalled by an electrical power failure in the blockhouse,
then by the notoriously high winds that sweep over the area in
winter, Pioneer F (to be renamed Pioneer 10 once it was safely on its
way) lifted off the Kennedy Space Center's Launch Complex 36A on
top of its Atlas-Centaur at 8:49 P.M. on March 2, 1972. After it left the
ground, the Atlas, glistening in the reflection of its own flaming

engines, rolled eastward as it was programmed to do. Precisely 148 seconds after launch, as it arced out over the dark Atlantic, the Atlas's booster engines shut down and dropped off. Its sustainer engine—the main one mounted at the rear of its polished stainless-steel body—stayed on for another minute and thirty-two seconds, or until it was eighty-five miles high and going 7,926 miles an hour. Then, its propellant exhausted, the Atlas was separated from the Centaur by explosive bolts. Then it, too, fell away into the night.

The Centaur kicked in 245 miles from Florida and ninety miles into the sky. During the next seven and a half minutes the burning hydrogen and oxygen mixture pushed Pioneer 10 (and a third stage to which it was bolted) to a speed of 22,948 miles an hour. By that time the protective shroud had opened, separated, and been jettisoned.

Seventy seconds after the Centaur cut off, small thruster rockets mounted on a spin table holding the third stage and Pioneer 10 were fired, sending the spacecraft and its little booster into a sixty-rotation-a-minute spin (later reduced to 4.8 rpm). Next, the third stage fired for forty-four seconds and then was itself separated from Pioneer 10 by explosive bolts. At that point, Pioneer 10 was 280 miles over Africa and moving at 31,088 miles an hour. The launch had literally gone like clockwork. The Pioneer 11 launch a little more than a year later went precisely the same way.

Unlike the Voyager probes that would soon follow, the Pioneers' computers were not loaded with programmed instructions, but instead took their orders directly from their controllers. This was rationalized on the basis of increased mission flexibility, on the ability to react to new developments and to send appropriate commands in real time. Such a system was also cheaper than one in which instructions were loaded into an onboard computer.* It was therefore crucial for those who operated the Pioneers to stay in almost constant touch with them. Not doing so could have ended in catastrophe.

"We must communicate with these spacecraft daily," explained

---

*Ames took great pride during the 1970s in the fact that it flew less expensive missions than JPL. Richard O. Fimmel maintained that the cost of the Pioneer 10 and 11 missions through 1988 was a little more than $100 million, as opposed to JPL's Viking and Voyager projects, which were "billion-dollar missions." He added that on the basis of funding, the Pioneers were more productive than their JPL counterparts. Responding to a question in an interview with the author about the relative quality of imagery from Ames and JPL probes, Fimmel said, "their camera costs more than our spacecraft, so they *should* get better pictures!"

Richard O. Fimmel, who managed the Pioneer missions after Hall. "If we don't [contact them] within thirty-six hours, we're in trouble because the spacecraft has logic on board, and a timer which says 'My receiver has failed,' and starts switching to a backup receiver and a different antenna."

The Pioneers were designed so that, should their high-gain antenna communication links fail, there would be an automatic backup system. But the last thing Ames wanted was its probes' abandoning the established communication link for a fruitless search elsewhere. Should the switches "throw, and maybe hang up," he added, the result could be disastrous.

In addition, Washington had stipulated when it assigned Ames to the Pioneer-Jupiter project that JPL not only handle tracking and communication through its Deep Space Network, but deal with the navigation and trajectory planning as well. Hall objected to this for "competitive" reasons (as he put it) but was overruled. As a result, he and a colleague had to go to Pasadena to confer with Robert Parks, the guidance specialist and head of the Mariner program, and one of Parks's colleagues.

"God, I've never seen four guys who distrusted each other more in my life," Hall recalled, laughing, years later. "They didn't trust us, and we didn't trust them. It was like a couple of Arabs trying to sell a dead camel to each other." JPL didn't want to take responsibility for certain phases of the Pioneer mission, Hall added, and Ames didn't want to take responsibility for something else, though he didn't remember the details. But in the end, he said, the relationship with JPL proved to be a good and lasting one. "The group at JPL worked with us for twelve years, and we never had a single complaint the whole time: it was a beautiful working relationship."

Pioneer 10 crossed Mars's orbit on May 25, 1972, and entered the asteroid belt on July 15. While the larger asteroids may have been plotted for many years, there was a great deal of uncertainty about the location of most of the others, and they therefore caused concern.

Hits would be registered by a clever device designed by William H. Kinard and four colleagues at the Langley Research Center. The sensor, a meteoroid detector, was mounted on the back edge of the high-gain antenna; since the antenna pointed back toward Earth, the detector faced forward. It consisted of 234 cells filled with a mixture of argon and nitrogen. When a cell was punctured, the gas would leak at a rate proportional to the size of the hole and an electric current would jump between two electrodes. The instrument made it through the asteroids without registering any potentially deadly hits. Later, it would also provide clues that Jupiter had a ring because of particle strikes it picked up near the planet's equatorial plane.

On February 15, 1973—precisely seven months after it entered the asteroid belt—Pioneer 10 passed out of it, apparently without so much as a scratch, and continued to bear down on Jupiter. While it was true that there were a great many asteroids out there, scientists learned that there was also a great deal of space between them.

The mission's sequencing had been worked out with precision. All of Pioneer 10's science instruments had been turned on within ten days after launch, so a stream of data had started to come in long before it reached Jupiter. It sent back new information on the asteroids, on the nature of zodiacal light, a faint glow off dust particles along the zodiac, and, because of several unprecedented storms on the Sun in August 1972, important data on the solar wind and energetic solar particles.*

Nothing Pioneer 10 did was supposed to be more routine than mapping zodiacal light. Yet it was the mapping operation that provided a stark lesson on how one minute's routine can suddenly degenerate into the next minute's crisis. The map was being made by the imaging photopolarimeter. The instrument's heart was a phototube so sensitive to light that were it to look straight at the Sun, it would in effect be permanently blinded. Since this was the same instrument that was supposed to take the first close-up pictures of Jupiter, its being blinded would have amounted to a disaster. And that is exactly what almost happened.

While Pioneer 10 raced toward its destination, the imaging photopolarimeter mapped zodiacal light automatically in incremental steps. It was supposed to register the light and then be turned off before it pointed at the Sun. But just before that command was to have been sent, a trawler off the Azores snagged the transatlantic cable and broke the connection to the ground station in South Africa that was supposed to relay the order.

With about twenty minutes left, the controllers at Ames tried to

*There were three enormous storms on August 2 and another on the seventh, causing communication and power blackouts in Canada, Alaska, Sweden, and the northern United States. The one on the seventh was so severe that it generated enough energy in one hour to supply all the electrical power used by the United States for 100 million years at the rate of consumption that year. Since Pioneers 6, 7, 8, and 9 were at that time orbiting the Sun, data from all four were correlated with Pioneer 10's to provide a clear picture of how the solar wind and its magnetic field changed as it swept through space.

get word to South Africa to shut the photopolarimeter off by bouncing an emergency signal off a communications satellite. And that was when they learned that the relay satellite's ground station was in the Azores and used the same cable the trawler had ripped up. Now, suppressing panic, Pioneer 10's controllers declared a higher state of emergency. They in effect commandeered the most direct line possible through the Atlantic cable.

"I was told later that they pulled the plug on the White House connection—the phone line to overseas—and we went to England and all across the continent of Europe with teletype lines to get just one command to that ground station: to tell them to shut it off," Fimmel recalled. "We got it stopped just a couple of minutes before it would have been looking at the Sun. Sometimes," he added, his round face breaking into a grin, "you have a little bit of excitement."

Pioneer 10's encounter with Jupiter technically began on November 3, 1973, and lasted for two months, with near encounter coming on December 3. By that time the spacecraft had broken virtually every long-distance record. It had traveled farther and faster than any other man-made object—Jupiter's enormous gravitational pull increased its speed to a blistering eighty-two thousand miles an hour at closest approach—and had received instructions and returned data over unprecedented distances. Even more amazing, Pioneer 10's closest pass would come within a minute of when it was supposed to come after a flight of nearly two years. (It would arrive a minute early because of an underestimation of Jupiter's mass and therefore its gravitational pull, which would cause the probe to fly slightly faster than had been predicted.)

By encounter time, shifts of scientists and engineers, including experts on its subsystems, were watching Pioneer 10 around the clock. Everything was functioning perfectly. By November 29 the probe had crossed the orbits of all seven of the outermost of Jupiter's known moons and was speeding toward the planet's fearsome radiation belts. By then it had passed through the planet's bow shock, where the solar wind runs into its magnetic field and separates. The bow shock gets its name from the fact that it acts in roughly the same way as the bow of a ship plowing through the ocean, except that in this case, it is the solar wind that slams into and then around the planet's strong magnetic field at a million miles an hour while the planet itself moves relatively slowly. A 50 percent drop in solar wind speed as registered by Pioneer 10 told those who analyzed its data that the bow shock had been reached.

As this and other information poured into Ames, Hall went into a reverie with reporters in the center's main auditorium. As often happened at such moments, all of the tightly controlled engineering and management of the mission gave way to an outpouring of suppressed emotion. "We are really only twelve generations away from Galileo and his first crude look at the planet," he told the journalists, almost in disbelief. "Twelve generations later, we are actually there measuring many of the characteristics of the planet itself." Charlie Hall, totally amazed at the wonder of it all, had just found a place for himself in the annals of time.

Pioneer 10's imaging photopolarimeter was turned on November 4, twenty-nine days before near encounter. The instrument was scanning as the spacecraft on which it rode rotated. As each red and blue "slice" came down, it was displayed on television screens in the auditorium and joined to those that preceded it until recognizable images formed. The collation was done by a specially designed Pioneer Image Converter System, or PICS, developed at the University of Arizona. The red and blue imagery was in turn combined to make a synthetic green color, resulting in normal three-color pictures that came back in real time, or as they were taken. This had the double benefit not only of allowing mission scientists to monitor what was happening to their probe half a billion miles away, but of getting the press involved in the dramatic immediacy of the situation. The pictures that started to arrive a little less than a month before closest approach were still no better than those collected through telescopes. Yet the speed with which the Jupiter pictures were released throughout the encounter, together with the fact that they were the first taken of the planet by a spacecraft, would earn Ames an Emmy from the National Academy of Television Arts and Sciences.

By the twenty-sixth, seven days before the flyby, the pictures had improved somewhat. Twelve images of Jupiter and Io were taken, even as Pioneer was commanded to make its last, minuscule attitude change before it streaked past the giant planet. Twenty-three-hour-a-day imaging was begun at six that evening, with Jupiter now only four and a half million miles away. Twenty-six more pictures came back from the spinning spacecraft the following day, showing not only a growing planet but Io and Ganymede as well. By December 2, the quality of the imagery began to surpass anything that had been taken through telescopes. By that time—the day before closest approach—Pioneer 10 was working its mechanical heart out even as it slammed through radiation so intense that two of its cosmic ray detectors became saturated. (Others, specially designed to take the enormous hits, performed well, measuring the proton flux around Jupiter for the first time.) Ultraviolet measurements were being made of the planet itself, infrared data were being taken from Callisto to sample its heat characteristics as Pioneer crossed that moon's orbit, and twenty-three more images were taken of Jupiter, Io, Callisto, and Ganymede.

Periapsis, or closest approach, came at 6:26 P.M. Pacific standard time the next day. Pioneer 10 skimmed past Jupiter's cloud tops at an altitude of only eighty-one thousand miles, crossing its equatorial plane and plowing into a huge Jovian magnetic field that was canted at an angle to the plane. Its meteoroid detector was struck by particles that would help to provide the first solid clues that Jupiter had its own ring system, one that was invisible from Earth. The existence of the rings had long been postulated. But their existence was revealed, first by the Pioneers, and then by the Voyager spacecraft, one of which would actually make the Grand Tour. Pioneer 10's instruments measured the gigantic gas ball's atmospheric composition, temperature structure, and thermal balance in the infrared. It also took infrared readings of Ganymede, Io, and Europa as it made its closest approaches to those moons, too. At 3:45 that afternoon—less than three hours before periapsis—it began an hour's imaging of Jupiter's enigmatic Great Red Spot that would eventually indicate what seemed to be a massive Jovian hurricane. In addition, it sent back relatively clear images of Jupiter's terminator, the dramatic boundary between night and day.

The tensest time came at 7:42 P.M., when Pioneer 10 began a sixty-five-minute swing behind Jupiter, in the process losing communication with Earth. The question was whether the instruments would continue working after having been badly battered by radiation at close range. Reporters and scientists were transfixed as Pioneer 10 in effect dropped out of sight.

"We watched the PICS image displayed in real-time as the signals came back from the distant planet," Lyn R. Doose, an imaging experimenter from the University of Arizona, would report. Then "a single bright spot appeared, and then another, until a line gradually built up. We knew we were seeing sunrise on Jupiter as the PICS image showed a crescent-like shape. We survived passage through periapsis," the scientist exclaimed proudly in the first-person plural.

"We can say that we sent Pioneer 10 off to tweak a dragon's tail, and it did that and more," said Robert Kraemer, who represented Headquarters that day at Ames. "It gave a really good yank and . . . it managed to survive." Fimmel, Pioneer 10's irrepressibly jovial chief scientist, proclaimed, "This has been the most exciting day of my life."

Its encounter with Jupiter over, Pioneer 10 headed out of the solar system at about twenty-five thousand miles an hour. It would cross Pluto's orbital path early in 1990 and then head for interstellar space, all the while continuing to send back ever fainter signals describing the lessening effects of the Sun and other phenomena it encountered in the vast void. At last report, it was headed for the star Aldebaran in the constellation Taurus.

Pioneer 11 left on April 5, 1973. It could have duplicated its predecessor's mission. But since the flight of Pioneer 10 had gone so well, its controllers sent it off chasing new possibilities.

"We launched Pioneer 11 such that after Pioneer 10 went by, we could tweak up the trajectory a little to either have another equatorial or a polar pass. Since Pioneer 10 was successful, we went for the polar shot, and that allowed us to come back across the solar system and go by Saturn," Hall explained, adding that Pioneer 11's trajectory was changed by almost 180 degrees.

So Pioneer 11 was commanded to approach Jupiter from its left side, underneath its southern hemisphere, and then hurtle almost straight up, out of the plane of the ecliptic. It made its closest approach, at a height of only 26,725 miles, on December 2, 1974, sending back data that confirmed much of what Pioneer 10 had collected, and also provided new information on the Great Red Spot and, for the first time, on Jupiter's immense polar regions. Pioneer 11 returned some 460 images of Jupiter and its four Galilean satellites between November 18 and December 9, 1974, many of them taken at angles that were not possible from Earth. It then looped up and over Jupiter, racing high above its north pole, and swung back in the general direction from which it had come so it could rendezvous with Saturn, whose own orbit trailed far behind it at that time. Right after the Jupiter encounter, in fact, it was officially renamed Pioneer-Saturn in anticipation of its next flyby.

On September 1, 1979, after a journey that spanned more than two billion miles and took almost six and a half years, Pioneer 11 made its closest approach to the great ringed sphere. During the ten days of its encounter, it flew through the ring plane twice (coming and going), skimming just under it at a distance as close as 1,240 miles. Nearest approach to the planet itself was only thirteen thousand miles at a speed of 70,900 miles an hour.

Pioneer 11's most fundamental discovery at Saturn was that the planet has a strong magnetic field and magnetosphere, both of which had been considered likely to exist, but neither of which had been proven.* It was also learned that Saturn's radiation is made much less intense because of its rings, which absorb and wipe out high-energy electrons and protons. The probe found a new moon, dubbed 1979 S1, just beyond the outer edge of the rings. It also made photopolarimetry measurements of the known moons—Iapetus, Dione, Tethys, Rhea, and Titan—and ultraviolet observations of Hyperion, Rhea, Dione, Tethys, Enceladus, and Titan. With a diameter of thirty-six hundred miles, Titan, by far the largest of Saturn's moons, is also larger than the planet Mercury. That made it a tempting target for atmospheric experiments, an examination of its temperature and heat balance, magnetic wake, and other properties.

In their book, *The Grand Tour,* Ron Miller and William K. Hartman take strong exception to the "nine-planet gestalt," pointing out that there are many more valid worlds in the solar system than the officially designated planets. It is a point of view heartily endorsed by planetary scientists. And certainly everyone connected with the Pioneer-Saturn mission agreed that Titan, one of the most interesting objects in the solar system, warranted a close look by Pioneer 11. It would also come under close scrutiny by Voyager 1, which was to follow Pioneer 11 the following year.

Precise calculations of Pioneer 11's trajectory as it passed Saturn allowed project scientists to gauge the planet's shape and gravity more accurately than ever before. Analysis of its gravitational field, together with its temperature profile based on infrared measurements of the heat given off by its clouds in excess of what was absorbed from the Sun, provided new insight into the composition of its interior. Saturn's core, about the size of eighteen Earths, was suddenly understood to have two distinct regions: an inner core of iron-rich rocky material and an outer one composed of ammonia, methane, and water. It was concluded that the outer core was topped by liquid metallic hydrogen, a form of hydrogen whose high temperature and great pressure allow it to easily conduct electricity. (Liquid metallic hydrogen was also spotted on Jupiter.) Unlike Jupiter,

*A magnetic field is the region, or field of force, surrounding the magnetic pole that runs through a planet. It is roughly the equivalent of the force that would surround a long magnet buried deep inside the planet. The magnetosphere is much larger and is shaped by the interaction of the magnetic field and the solar wind. It is ordinarily doughnut-shaped and extends many thousands of miles beyond the radius of the planet itself.

whose atmosphere is fairly alive with swirling, moving belts, Saturn's showed surprisingly little contrast.

But whatever else Saturn was, its exotic ring system made it the most beautiful object in the solar system. Unfortunately, the photo opportunity was for the most part wasted on Pioneer 11, since its spin stabilization greatly reduced its capacity for taking high-quality imagery. Still, the pictures had their value. Saturn's rings—clouds of white hailstones more than 170,000 miles wide but less than a mile thick—were seen clearly enough to turn up a new one, called the F ring, and to show the structure and other properties of the rest in unprecedented detail.

By the time Pioneer 11 reached Saturn, Pioneer 10 was streaking toward the last of the outer planets at a rate of about 275 million miles a year. When Pioneer 11 left Saturn, it moved out on the opposite side of the solar system, also heading to a place far beyond the orbit of Pluto. As the two spacecraft moved into still deeper space at the end of the 1980s, they searched for the boundary between the solar system and the interstellar medium, where the solar wind runs into cosmic rays coming from distant parts of the galaxy. They also continued to look for the tenth planet.

Both Pioneers carried plaques made of gold-anodized aluminum showing a man and a woman, where and when their race lived, a schematic drawing of the hyperfine transition of neutral atomic hydrogen, the planets in this solar system, a silhouette of the spacecraft, a smaller diagram of the Pioneer with its antenna pointing right at the third planet from the Sun, and more. The plaque, which has been called an "intellectual cave painting," was designed by Carl Sagan and Frank Drake, also of Cornell, with the hope that some intelligent life form in a remote galaxy would one day find and decipher it.

The last spacecraft to carry the name Pioneer were numbers 12 and 13 or, as they were more commonly called, Pioneer Venus 1 and 2. Although quite a bit had been learned about the planet's atmospheric pressure and motion, as well as its temperature and mass from earlier missions, both American and Soviet, planetary scientists wanted to peer under the thick clouds and actually see surface features. They wanted to know whether there had ever been significant amounts of oxygen and water on Venus and, if so, where they had gone. The way to get under the clouds to find out was to use radar. This, among many other things, is what Pioneer Venus accomplished.

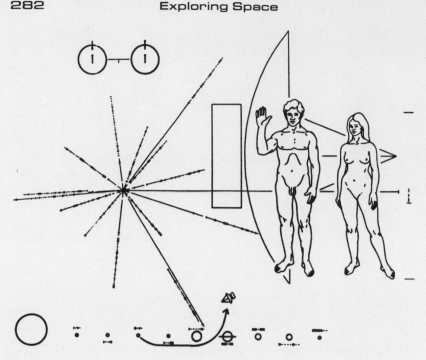

The mission was flown by two spacecraft. One of them, an orbiter, was launched on May 20, 1978. The other, a multiprobe, was sent on August 8. Both were essentially squat cylinders, sheathed with solar arrays, that measured a little more than eight feet in diameter. The orbiter circled the planet with a dozen science instruments, including a twenty-one-pound radar mapper that resolved features to about fifty miles across. The multiprobe was more interesting. It held four miniature probes that were released much the way the bus on an intercontinental ballistic missile releases individual warheads. One of them, the largest, floated to the Venusian surface under a parachute, while the others just rained down, sending back data as they went. The four were programmed to separate so that they landed on both the day and night side of Venus and above, below, and right on its equator.

The science return from Pioneer Venus was considerable. It was determined that the planet has no real magnetic field, that the temperature below its clouds was constant at a given altitude, and that the atmosphere was unexpectedly stable below the clouds. About 90 percent of Venus was mapped by the orbiter, which to this day circles the planet as an artificial moon. Perhaps the most interesting discovery was that large quantities of hydrogen escaped from Venus at one time, indicating that it may have had a great deal of water, perhaps as much as an ocean. If that is the case, scientists speculated, the water could have been lost because of a greenhouse effect similar to the one that is trapping solar heat on Earth and causing worldwide temperatures to rise. And as is the case with Mars, one of Venus's enduring fascinations for planetary scientists is the fact that it could well hold lessons about the evolution of Earth. Venus, in fact, would increasingly be viewed as a kind of model for what Earth was at a time very early in its history. Taken in that light, what happened to Venus might also be taken as a warning of the fate that could await Earth.

On June 13, 1983, Pioneer 10 crossed Neptune's orbit, which at that particular time was farther out than Pluto's, putting it at a greater distance from the Sun than any of the known planets.* By June 1988, sixteen years after it was launched, Pioneer 10 had traveled four billion miles from the Sun and was still riding the solar wind. It was far and away the farthest object mankind had ever flung into space. Earth was a mere pinpoint while the Sun itself was a pale disk so faint it was barely usable as a navigational reference point. But still its signals came, ever so faintly, from the black void beyond Neptune and Pluto as the venerable spacecraft continued to probe for the edge of the Sun's influence. Pioneer 10 was so far away that it took twelve hours and twenty-six minutes for signals to travel from Earth to it and back again; so far away, as Fimmel put it, that the radio waves it sent to the Deep Space Network would have to be collected and saved for eleven billion years to light a 7.5-watt night light for a millisecond.

So they held a celebration at Ames that June 1988 to mark the fifth anniversary of Pioneer 10's crossing Neptune's orbit. Someone in the crowd jokingly asked a representative of the company that built the tough little spacecraft whether it was under warranty. "TRW's position," he answered, "has been that if you bring it back, we'll fix it."

*The Office of Space Science's Public Affairs Office suggested to the Postal Service that the occasion be commemorated with a postage stamp and even sent two designs, one showing the spacecraft's location relative to the planets and the Sun, the other depicting the plaque it carried. No stamps were issued, however (a memorandum from OSSA Public Affairs to Robert Alnutt, Acting Associate Administrator for External Relations, dated March 9, 1983, provided by the Ames Department of Public Information).

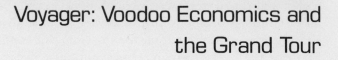

11.

Voyager: Voodoo Economics and the Grand Tour

KEY BISCAYNE, Fla., March 7 (UPI)—The chief of the U.S. space program said today that ordinary people without elaborate astronaut training will be able to travel in space by the late 1970s.

Dr. Thomas O. Paine, head of the National Aeronautics and Space Administration, said once space shuttles are developed to take passengers back and forth to orbiting space stations people "who are simply in good health" will be able to make the trip.

"In fact," Paine said at a news conference, "we will even be able to take healthy newsmen if we can find any."

There was a special irony about that story, which appeared in *The Washington Post* on Sunday, March 8, 1970. It came at the end of a much longer article, beginning on page one, in which President Nixon, reporting on the Agnew committee's recommendations, promised that U.S. spacecraft would embark on "two grand tours of the solar system" toward the end of the decade.

To this, Paine added some specifics. There would be a 1977 launch to Jupiter, Uranus, and Neptune, with a second Grand Tour launch to Jupiter, Saturn, and Pluto set for 1979. While Paine declined to estimate how much the missions to the outer planets would cost, the *Post* quoted another NASA official as guessing that sending a pair of probes on each mission would come to a maximum of $750 million.

The story went on to note, however, that the president had promised to ask for only $10 million in fiscal 1972 to plan the tour, even as gearing up for the shuttle began in earnest. NASA would, on the other hand, request ten times $10 million for the Space Transportation System for fiscal 1972, and it would get every penny of it.

It was ironic that the problem-plagued shuttle would rob the space science and planetary exploration programs of a great deal of funding for new programs while its developers tried desperately to make it a commuter vehicle that was supposed to carry the interplanetary spacecraft (and reporters) on a routine basis. And it was even more ironic that the shuttle would also come perilously close to killing the same Grand Tour that Nixon was talking about and even stopping exploration altogether. The president could have had no way of knowing that in 1970, of course, and neither could NASA Headquarters or centers like the Jet Propulsion Laboratory.

JPL, all but oblivious to what support of the Space Transportation System portended, meanwhile geared up for the Grand Tour: the once-every-175-year shot at the four big outer planets and, perhaps, even dumpy little Pluto as well. As early as June 1969 it had begun conceptualizing a long-distance spacecraft, ostensibly based on Mariner, which would weigh on the order of twelve hundred to fourteen hundred pounds and be capable of truly long-range missions.

Pasadena's high-endurance probe was called the Thermoelectric Outer Planet Spacecraft, or TOPS. As its name indicated, it would be powered by plutonium, so it would be able to get to the outer planets and beyond without solar power. It was also to have two highly advanced computer systems, the names for which also lent themselves to catchy acronyms. One, a self-testing and repairing unit (STAR), would incorporate artificial intelligence, so the spacecraft could take care of itself to an unprecedented degree as it penetrated the long and potentially dangerous regions beyond Mars. The other, a computer-aided telemetry system (CATS), would send data back to the Deep Space Network with far greater speed and efficiency than had ever before been possible.

TOPS was to be a deluxe spacecraft, complete with a fourteen-foot deployable high-gain antenna, a scan platform holding two television cameras as well as ultraviolet and infrared detectors, and a battery of other advanced science packages. By April 1971 a team of 108 scientists from the United States and six other countries had been chosen from five hundred applicants to work on thirteen experiments. They included many of the biggest names in planetary exploration: Merton E. Davies of RAND, Bruce Murray of Caltech, Carl Sagan of Cornell, John Anderson of JPL, Irwin Shapiro of MIT, Van Allen of the University of Iowa, John Wolfe of Ames, Thomas Donahue of the University of Pittsburgh, Tobias Owen of the State University of New York, and A.M.J. Gehrels of the University of Arizona.

There were to be four Thermoelectric Outer Planet Spacecraft.

They were supposed to follow the two pathfinders, Pioneers 10 and 11, across the solar system and then encounter Jupiter, Saturn, Uranus, Neptune, and possibly Pluto in the greatest planetary flyby program of them all. They were supposed to probe farther out and send back more data than all of the other flybys, U.S. and Soviet, combined. They were supposed to constitute a stunning finale to what was hoped would be a golden age of solar system exploration. They were supposed to do all of those things. But they never did. Instead, TOPS died on the draftsman's drawing board, bled to death by the shuttle.

Politics and exploration of the outer planets collided head-on during the winter of 1971–72, as NASA tried to sell the Space Transportation System to the White House, the Office of Management and Budget, and the Congress, literally for all it was worth. With an election looming in November, what Congress and the White House needed from space was not data on the thickness of the regolith in Ganymede's south polar region, but jobs. To be sure, the shuttle would carry the spirit of America to space. But it would also create fifty thousand jobs on Earth, half of them in California, and give a desperately needed lift to the aerospace industry. Accordingly, the Space Transportation System was duly approved by the president at the outset of 1972, with a projected cost through the end of the decade of $10 billion to $14 billion.

In those circumstances, a "grand tour" of anything, and certainly of the outer solar system, was taken to be a frivolous indulgence (particularly since the planetary scientists were already being placated with what would turn out to be the $1 billion Viking mission to Mars). To make matters even worse from the point of view of the planetary science community, Soviet activity in deep space was experiencing its own problems. While the Soviets were succeeding with their Venus missions, their record at Mars continued to be unaccountably wretched, and they seemed to be making no effort whatever to go to the outer planets.* Competition was a coin with two

*Timur M. Eneyev, a Soviet space scientist, claimed in May 1971 that he and his colleagues were studying a Grand Tour–like mission "from every angle," including the delivery of automatic science stations that would float under balloons in the atmospheres of the giant gas balls. "For all its exotic aspects and difficulties," he was quoted as saying in The New York Times of May 9, 1971, such a mission was probably the most promising "because it would yield far more data about the nature of the giant planets than could be obtained from fly-by trajectories." That may have been true, but there is no evidence that the idea ever advanced to the serious planning stage.

highly defined sides. If the obverse required racing when the Soviets wanted to race, then perhaps the reverse allowed for a rest when they showed no interest in racing.

But more important, there were more pressing calls on funds than bankrolling a mission as arcane and politically unrewarding as the Grand Tour. It was basically as simple as that, or so it appeared to the administration. TOPS was dead by the end of December 1971, the first major victim of the Space Transportation System.*

JPL's consolation prize was start-up funding for a mission to Jupiter and Saturn that was supposed to be a sophisticated follow-up to Pioneer. Expenses would be kept down by using a pair of spacecraft that amounted to souped-up versions of the tried-and-true Mariners. In fact, the probes themselves were at first even called Mariner 11 and 12 and the project was dubbed Mariner-Jupiter-Saturn 1977. It was officially begun on July 1, 1972, with a paltry $9 million and a projected total cost of $250 million.

In order to put the best possible face on Mariner-Jupiter-Saturn, it was said that excluding Uranus, Neptune, and Pluto from the mission would greatly shorten its time and lessen power and communications demands on the spacecraft. That, in turn, would mean the probes would not have to be as reliable as they would for a Grand Tour. This, according to some at Headquarters, was supposed to be good news.

But restricting the Pioneer follow-up mission to a Mariner flyby of Jupiter and Saturn was like forbidding Columbus to sail past the Azores or the Canaries and rationalizing it by telling him that they were easier to reach and would entail fewer provisions and less wear on his ships (and there would be fewer ships). Four spacecraft going to at least four planets had turned into two spacecraft going to two planets. Pasadena was not consoled. The last opportunity to take the Grand Tour had come in the administration of Thomas Jefferson and the next would be in about 2150. JPL's mission planners didn't need their big IBM computers to tell them that they weren't going to live

*Although press reports in late January told of its demise, the decision was in fact made in the Office of Management and Budget in mid-December. A letter out of James Fletcher's office to Caspar W. Weinberger, the OMB's deputy director, on December 22 mentioned an accompanying press release that announced "termination" of the mission. It also anticipated anger at JPL. ". . . as far as we know even the Jet Propulsion Laboratory people directly affected are not yet aware of the TOPS decision. We feel we can handle this situation better if JPL and the California Institute of Technology hear the decision directly from us; this is one reason we think it would be best to announce the decision as soon as we can." The document is in the NASA History Office.

long enough to see the next one. So limiting the mission to the two giant gas balls was not very good news at all (the more so because the JPL spacecraft would essentially only be following in the wake of two others developed by their rivals upstate). Uranus, Neptune, and Pluto eluded the disgruntled Pasadenans. Or so it seemed in the summer doldrums of 1972, even as Pioneer 10, the first of the Ames long-distance sprinters, was heading for Jupiter.

The JPL entries, eventually to be renamed Voyager 1 and Voyager 2 (notwithstanding still-bitter memories of the original Mars lander-orbiter that was killed and then resurrected as Viking), clearly showed the Mariner bloodline. Yet they were designed in-house to be bigger, tougher, and more sophisticated, and to go farther than either the Mariners or the Pioneers that preceded them.

Unlike Pioneers 10 and 11, Voyagers 1 and 2 were autonomous to the extent that their computers (each with a backup) could be "loaded" with mission instructions before launch. They would keep the spacecraft functioning semiautonomously for days, weeks, or months. But the computers were also flexible enough so that new loads for sequencing and guidance could be sent out as conditions dictated.* This built-in flexibility would prove decisive as the true dimension of Voyager 2's odyssey began to unfold four years into its mission.

The heart of each Voyager was a rugged ten-sided bus, to which was attached a twelve-foot high-gain antenna, three radioisotope thermoelectric generators stacked like drums, a pair of magnetometers set on a long boom, and a science package. There was also a second boom, the end of which held a movable scan platform containing the imaging sensors and spectrometers. The scan platform, mounted on a bearing, could swing from side to side and up and down like the bigger ones that held cameras on movie sets.

Each spacecraft weighed a hefty 1,808 pounds. And each was three-axis-stabilized so that it would remain perfectly steady while the scan platform "slewed" successive targets to collect pictures and other imagery. By the time of the Voyagers, JPL had so fine-tuned three-axis stabilization that the infinitesimal squirts of hydrazine

---

*The three computers were an attitude and articulation control system (AACS), which controlled the probe's position; a flight data system (FDS), which processed scientific and engineering data; and a computer command subsystem (CCS), which coordinated Voyager's various actions. Using loads transmitted from Earth and then updated, the three could command the science instruments to do their job or work the spacecraft's various systems and react automatically to problems or changed conditions. This made the Voyagers the smartest craft ever to go into deep space.

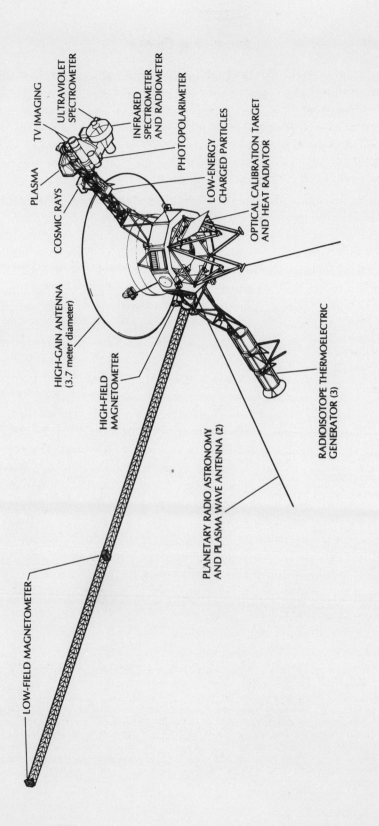

ULTRAVIOLET
SPECTROMETER

TV IMAGING

PLASMA

COSMIC RAYS

INFRARED
SPECTROMETER
AND RADIOMETER

PHOTOPOLARIMETER

LOW-ENERGY
CHARGED PARTICLES

OPTICAL CALIBRATION TARGET
AND HEAT RADIATOR

HIGH-GAIN ANTENNA
(3.7 meter diameter)

HIGH-FIELD
MAGNETOMETER

RADIOISOTOPE THERMOELECTRIC
GENERATOR (3)

PLANETARY RADIO ASTRONOMY
AND PLASMA WAVE ANTENNA (2)

LOW-FIELD MAGNETOMETER

would adjust a spacecraft's position at a rate ten to a hundred times slower than the movement of a clock's hour hand.

The small plaques identifying the time and place of origin of the two Pioneers were superseded by a more ambitious announcement fastened to the sides of the Voyagers: twelve-inch gold-plated copper discs—perhaps the most expensive long-playing records ever made—containing greetings from Earth. The salutation came in sixty of its languages. There were thirty-eight sounds, from rain to Morse code to auto gears to a kiss; 115 images, including a fertilized ovum, a snowflake, Bushman hunters, rush-hour traffic in India, DNA structure, and a supermarket; and ninety minutes of eclectic music, including selections from *The Magic Flute,* the Second Brandenberg Concerto, "Johnny B. Goode" by Chuck Berry, Senegalese percussion, a Navajo night chant, and a Peruvian woman's wedding song. The images and sounds were selected by a committee headed by Carl Sagan. Each record came with an aluminum jacket, cartridge, needle, and instructions.

It would be millions of years before either Voyager might encounter another planetary system, let alone one with intelligent life. But Sagan, looking inward as well as outward, was nonetheless optimistic. "The launching of this bottle into the cosmic ocean says something very hopeful about life on this planet," he mused. The records would provide extraterrestrials with no clue whatever, though, about the wars, famine, pestilence, pollution, repression, and cupidity that were just as endemic to the planet as dancing, grape and cotton harvesting, fishing, cooking, and other common activities portrayed on the records. Nor would they make note of the tortuous political process the Voyagers themselves would have to undergo in order to make it out of this solar system in the first place.

Voyager was officially born on July 1, 1972, following Nixon's speech and congressional approval. Seventy-seven proposals for instruments to go on the spacecraft were received in answer to an

Announcement of Opportunity, thirty-one of them from groups of scientists and forty-six from individuals who wanted to participate on the science teams. Twenty-eight proposals were eventually accepted. Nine of these would be for instruments and nineteen for individual participation in experiments using those instruments. Edward Stone of Caltech, an expert on magnetospheric physics, was named project scientist. Stone met with his newly appointed principal investigators and team leaders at JPL for the first time just before Christmas 1972.

All in all, there would be more than one thousand scientists, engineers, and technical managers, many from outside contractors responsible for major components, working on the new program. (Voyager would be built in-house, however, the way JPL preferred to do it). Many of them, like Bradford A. Smith of the University of Arizona, the imaging team leader, and James W. Warwick of the University of Colorado, who ran the planetary radio astronomy experiments, would stay with the project for its duration. Few if any of them could have realized in 1972, however, that they would be seventeen years older when that time came. Bud Schmurmeier, who had honed his managerial skills as Ranger's project manager, would be the first in a long series of JPL project managers for Voyager.

The Voyager team began bringing the project's various science and engineering elements together early in 1973 with two launches planned for the late summer of 1977. In addition to the planning of experiment sequences, trajectories, communication procedures, ground support, and a great deal more, there was the usual development and refinement of instruments; integration of the instruments with each other and with the spacecraft as a whole; and integration of the spacecraft with Centaur, its upper stage. While the particular aspects of Voyager were new, the essential method of bringing them together had been pretty well established by the mid-1970s and was basically done as usual.

There was something about Voyager, however, that was decidedly unusual. It was a notion that stirred, ever so faintly but relentlessly, deep within the program managers' souls: a thought so subtle though enticing that it was given no real credence in the normal scheme of day-to-day operations. Yet it would never go away. The managers were in effect instructed to limit Voyager's mission to Jupiter and Saturn. Yet the two spacecraft would leave Earth on a heading that could take them on the Grand Tour: a once-in-three-lifetimes chance to get all of the marbles with one spectacular shot.

The science and engineering were theoretically up to conducting a multiplanet sweep. What was lacking more than anything else was the will, and that was subject to the usual political vicissitudes, so it could change at any time. If the political winds did change after launch but the spacecraft were incapable of being modified to go for the whole tour, one of the greatest feats of exploration in history would die unrealized. Similarly, if the spacecraft were inherently capable of extending to Uranus, Neptune, and beyond, that fact in itself would provide impetus for pushing on. Accordingly, while Voyagers 1 and 2 were technically designed only to reach Saturn, they nonetheless were provided with the potential for going the extra distance if instructed to do so.

On the morning of August 20, 1977—two years to the day after Viking 1 left for Mars—Voyager 2 rose into the sky above Canaveral atop a Titan 3E-Centaur and headed for space. Voyager 1 left sixteen days later from the same pad. Although Voyager 1 followed Voyager 2, it would reach Jupiter four months ahead of its twin because it was fired on a shorter, faster trajectory.*

The Voyager twins' launch and first year in space was anything but auspicious. There was a double computer failure in Voyager 2 even before launch, followed by another while its Titan booster still burned within sight of Launch Complex 41. Less than an hour later, after the spacecraft had emerged from the Centaur's shroud, there were very worrisome indications that its scan platform boom hadn't fully extended. As it turned out, however, the warning amounted to only a heart-stopping false alarm.

Voyager 1's scan platform really did stop. It partly stuck early in the mission, before the completion of a routine operation. Since the platform held the instruments that were supposed to observe the Jovian and Saturnian systems, the probe's vision might have been seriously impaired as it passed those planets if the problem had gone uncorrected. The platform was eventually unjammed, but Voyager 1's controllers treated it warily for months to come.

Then there was the alarmingly high rate at which Voyager 2 was using hydrazine to maneuver. That problem was caused by a maneuvering thruster that was pointed in the wrong direction, firing hydrazine at the spacecraft itself. That was like hitting the aft side of

*Three weeks before the scheduled launch, the spacecraft that was originally to be Voyager 2 developed mechanical problems. As a result, a "spare" that actually carried the designation Voyager 3 became Voyager 2. Once repaired, the original Voyager 2 was made Voyager 1. The original Voyager 1 was shipped back to JPL.

a sailboat with a stream of high-pressure water. It required extra hydrazine to be used by the other thrusters to counteract the abnormality and keep the spacecraft on its correct course. In effect, Voyager 2 was pushing against itself, resulting in a considerable loss of fuel. This, too, was corrected.

Worse, a succession of minor calamities resulted in Voyager 2's losing its main radio receiver in April 1978, making it deaf in one ear. Not only that, but then the backup receiver malfunctioned, plaguing the spacecraft's controllers and the mission teams with the nagging fear of a seriously impaired or aborted mission. The culprit for the spate of problems may well have been the computers' very sophistication.

"Thrusters fired at inappropriate times, data modes shifted, instrument filter and analyzer wheels became stuck, and the various computer control systems occasionally overrode ground commands," observed astronomer David Morrison, a member of the imaging team, and Jane Samz, who co-authored a book on the Jupiter flyby. "Apparently, the spacecraft hardware was working properly, but the computers on board displayed certain traits that seemed almost humanly perverse—and perhaps a little psychotic. In general, these reactions were the result of programming too much sensitivity in the spacecraft systems, resulting in panic overreaction by the onboard computers to minor fluctuations in the environment. Ultimately," they added, "part of the programming had to be rewritten on Earth and then transmitted to the Voyagers, to calm them down. . . ."

Meanwhile, the Voyagers closed in on Jupiter. A planetary flyby is like a symphony in four movements. First, there is the initial observatory phase, done *andante* from far away. It sets the theme by viewing the object of the expedition in broad perspective and offering tantalizing hints of what is to come.

On December 10, 1978, just before the observatory phase actually started, Voyager 1 took photographs of Jupiter's spectacular horizontal belts and zones that were better than anything taken from Earth. The imagery, together with material collected by observatories, was in turn used by JPL scientists to pick final targets for study in the tumultuous Jovian atmosphere.

The observatory phase itself began early in January 1979 and ended about a month later, during which the probe sent back a stream of pictures—at one point, a picture every ninety-six seconds for one hundred hours—showing the planet, as well as Ganymede and Europa, in unprecedented detail. On February 13, when the probe was only 12.4 million miles from Jupiter, it sent back one of the most spectacular pictures to come out of the space exploration program: part of the giant's lower quadrant, clearly showing Io and Europa circling over the Great Red Spot and several of the swirling belts. At the same time the ultraviolet spectrometer was scanning the planet eight times a day; the infrared spectrometer analyzed heat emissions from the various latitudes of Jupiter's turbulent atmosphere, while the radio astronomy and plasma wave instruments searched for radio bursts from the planet and plasma disturbances.

Next came far encounter, *allegro vivace,* in which the drama started to build as Jupiter and its satellites loomed ever closer. Hour by hour the whirling globe seemed to expand until it finally overwhelmed the camera's field of view. Jupiter's turbulent atmosphere could be seen close up for the first time as immense, clearly delineated bands of violent weather surged past neighboring bands, sometimes curling into angry knots as they went.

As near encounter approached and the pace of data collection increased, sequencing—the precise order in which the various instruments were to operate—loomed ever more important. The Voyagers' eleven science teams contained ninety-five scientists, all of whom were determined to get their investigations done in acceptable fashion within a severely constrained period of time. Unlike an orbital mission, on which a planet or one of its moons can be reexamined repeatedly, there is no going back for a second look on a flyby. The finite nature of the opportunity made the Voyager scientists, already an accomplished lot by virtue of their competitive dispositions, all the more competitive.

"When you're far away, it's no big problem," said Arthur L. "Lonne" Lane, who acted as a kind of arbiter on the Voyager Science Integration Team at JPL until just before Voyager 1's near encounter. "However, when you get in close—in the case of the Voyager encounter, within, say, about five days—you end up with intense competition. That is, each instrument has an optimal time to make a certain kind of measurement because of the geometry, or because of the light level, or the flux of radiation coming out of the planet, or a certain satellite happens to be in a certain position as seen from the spacecraft."

This does not mean that squabbles erupt immediately before near encounter. Basic sequencing is set many months before encounter: in the case of Voyager's relatively short two-year trip to Jupiter, in fact, much of it was in place before launch. When the Voyagers were

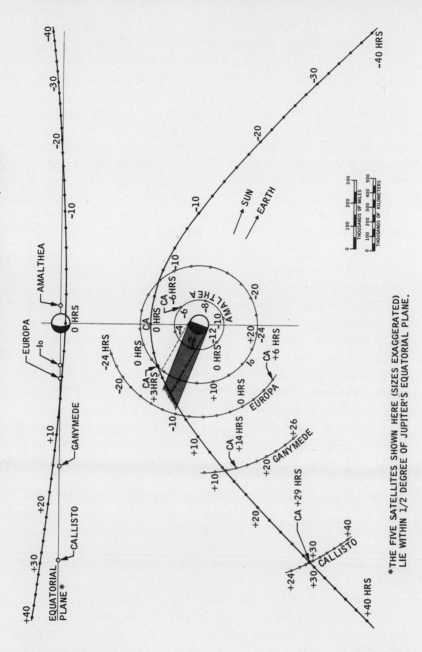

VOYAGER 1 FLYBY OF JUPITER March 3 - 6, 1979

*THE FIVE SATELLITES SHOWN HERE (SIZES EXAGGERATED) LIE WITHIN 1/2 DEGREE OF JUPITER'S EQUATORIAL PLANE.

130 days from Jupiter, and the planet barely filled 15 percent of the narrow-angle camera's field of view, experiments could be conducted at a leisurely pace. But as time shortens, and sequencing is modified to take advantage of unexpected opportunities, the science teams can become competitive to the point of contention.

Voyager 1's passage between Jupiter and Io was a case in point. One team wanted to investigate reports from Pioneers 10 and 11 that there were charged particles around Io, which would have been unusual for a planetary satellite. But another team was equally absorbed with the atmospheric dynamics of the planet itself, and wanted color pictures of it. The problem was that the instruments for collecting both sets of evidence—an ultraviolet spectrometer and one of the cameras—were mounted on a scan platform that could face only one direction at a time.

In order to get a good enough signal for a statistically meaningful measurement, Lane noted, the charged-particle investigators needed to work their spectrometer for half an hour or more at a time. But the imaging team wanted to take a sequence of pictures, one every forty-five minutes, so it could determine from the cloud pattern what the wind's velocity and direction were, whether the clouds were being sheared north and south, whether material was being convected up from below, and a great deal more. That was stuff the atmospheric people needed.

The respective priorities caused considerable debate, which, Lane recalled, was made even more complicated when the fields and particles investigators, a third group, weighed in by siding with the spectrometer operators against the imaging team. "And then," he added, smiling, "you get the infrared spectrometer [team] that says, 'no, we've got to integrate on the body itself for hours in order to be able to measure the heat flux coming out, so we really want to stay pointed at Jupiter, but not in the upper corner where you're watching the winds, but down in the center so we can get a global measurement.'"

In order to fit all of the requirements into a viable sequence, Lane had to try to weigh the merits of the competing experiments as they related to the successive blocks of time during the encounter and then adjudicate the conflicts. "This," he quipped, required "a Solomon and a half." When neither side would budge, the matter went to Ed Stone at Caltech, the project's chief scientist, for a binding decision. "It never came to fisticuffs," Lonne Lane explained with a hearty laugh, "but there were some pained and pointed discussions. . . ."

Its sequence set, Voyager 1 sailed on, crossing the orbit of Sinope, Jupiter's outermost satellite, on February 10, 1979. Excitement was building at JPL as the imagery started to come in. First, there were pictures of Callisto and then, on the twenty-fifth, of Ganymede. They were "clearly spectacular," said Lane, unable, as usual, to suppress his enthusiasm. "We're getting even better results than we anticipated. We have seen new phenomena in both optical and radio emissions. We have definitely seen things that are different—in at least one sense, unanticipated—and are begging for answers we haven't got."

The climax, *allegro con brio,* came when the far encounter gave way to the near encounter. By March 1, with periapsis only four days away, JPL was crawling with reporters and scientists from around the world. There were daily press briefings in von Karman, where project scientists were called on to provide "instant science"—play-by-play analyses of what was coming in. There were also hundreds of individual interviews in almost every corner of the place, as well as in the respective teams' offices.

Brad Smith couldn't contain himself. "It may sound unprofessional," he said at one point, "but a lot of people up in the imaging team area are just standing around with their mouths hanging open, watching the scenes come in." (On March 4, when the first color picture of Io, the most geologically active of the Jovian moons, came in, Smith was quoted in newspapers around the country as observing that it looked "better than a lot of pizzas I've seen." David Morrison, the astronomer, later added that the "piece of pepperoni" at the center of the stunning white, yellow, and orange tableau was the active volcano Prometheus. The image has been known as the "pizza picture" ever since). An active volcano on a moon!

The images of Jupiter itself were stunning and brought to mind van Gogh's thick, curved angry strokes or perhaps a psychedelic hallucination. There were massive orange and white cloud formations in a thousand hues, here shaped like a gigantic whirlpool, there snaking along like ribbons of pale cigarette smoke, mingling, passing, interacting.

There was the Great Red Spot itself, clearly seen to be a 25,000-mile-wide swirling mass, which computer simulation would eventually show to be not a volcano, not a column of gas, not a hurricane, not a floating island of ice, but a coherent structure of gas that more or less stays put in the middle of a stream of turbulent chaos, a structure that derives its own motion from the rotation of the planet itself.

Although Voyager 1's closest approach came on Monday, March 5, as it passed within 216,800 miles of Jupiter at a little more than 62,000 miles an hour, an almost giddy, carnival-like atmosphere pervaded JPL, starting the evening before, with everyone anticipating sharing an event of considerable historical significance. Scientists, engineers, managers, helpers of every stripe, reporters, writers, assorted politicians, a smattering of celebrities, and an occasional true believer of uncertain origin who made it past the front gate disguised as one of the herd were all caught spellbound by a cascade of imagery and other raw data that shaped new discoveries or confirmed old ones with astounding speed.

The solitary probe hurtling past the king of the planets, all of its instruments working to capture the physical essence of a moment never to be regained, was an extension of the beholders' own being. In a special way, the Voyager team and those who looked over its collective shoulder in awe were out there with their caravel on a voyage of the mind, riding it just as surely as Magellan rode the *Trinidad,* and Galileo his telescope. But the data came back in such prodigious quantity that it overwhelmed their capacity to absorb, let alone assimilate. In fact, only the computers could cope with the information that streamed in from the frozen reaches of deep space, giving shape and substance to a distant world at a rate of 115,200 bits a second.

Sunday night and Monday morning amounted to a "happening" for the reporters, the scientists and engineers, and the JPL support staff: an instant in the annals of the ages, a shared experience, a time for professional networking over coffee and stale crackers and champagne, played under von Karman's lights and in conference rooms and cubicles throughout the lab. "That's not Jupiter; it looks like a close-up of a salad," one science writer quipped. "They're not showing us Jupiter," said another, "that's some medical school anatomy slide." But the science writers knew perfectly well what they were looking at and relished it.

At one point that night, Jerry Brown, California's laid-back governor, appeared in the von Karman newsroom with his entourage, which included Rusty Schweikart, the baby-faced astronaut who had flown to the Moon on Apollo 9. Some gawkers clustered around Brown and his companions, creating a mini-event that angered the science and space reporters, some of whom snarled and warned them to "get the hell out of the way" of the TV monitors, which were full of Jupiter as it was coming back from the probe in real time. The governor tried to deflect the sarcasm with one of his well-known impromptu laid-back predictions, this one claiming that one day there would be a "JPL in orbit." Someone responded by wondering aloud whether the lab's relocating to space would finally mean adequate parking for the press.

Even before closest approach, Voyager 1 had begun making intensive observations of the enigmatic Io. What it sent back that night and into the morning astounded Larry Soderblom, an ordinarily taciturn geologist on the imaging team. Soderblom raved almost uncontrollably, calling Io one of the most spectacular bodies in the solar system. "This is incredible. The element of surprise is coming up in every one of these frames. I knew it would be wild from what we saw on approach, but to anticipate anything like this would have required some heavenly perspective. I think this is incredible," he said again. At 7:47 A.M., Voyager 1 made its closest approach to Io, passing at a distance of only 13,670 miles. Champagne corks could be heard popping in the particles and fields science offices as the spacecraft sliced through Io's inner magnetosphere, sending back data that showed electrical current in the moon's "flux tube" to be an astounding million amps.

Postencounter was a finale arranged *adagio*. It was a long good-bye, played as the planet and its companion worlds slowly receded against a starry backdrop that gradually widened to a breathtaking dimension. The symphony ended with the chorus trying to make real sense—science—out of what it saw and heard. That would take years.

Voyager 1's Jovian encounter was a bonanza, as was that of Voyager 2, which had its closest approach on July 9. The two spacecraft followed trajectories that complemented each other. Voyager 1 skimmed very close to Io, where it collected extraordinary imagery and very important data on the satellite's magnetic flux, which affects Jupiter itself and its fifteen other satellites. It also went moderately close to Callisto, Ganymede, and Amalthea, but stayed far from Europa. Voyager 2, on the other hand, made its closest pass at Ganymede and got closer to Europa than had its predecessor. Io was not positioned for a close look by Voyager 2, but the discovery by Voyager 1 that the vividly splotched moon had an active volcanic system—probably the biggest surprise of the entire encounter—persuaded JPL to reprogram Voyager 2 for a ten-hour "Io watch" from a little more than 702,000 miles away. In addition, Voyager 1's discovery of Jupiter's ring system, quickly confirmed by ground-based telescopes, was then reobserved with even better results by Voyager 2.

Voyager 1 sent back eighteen thousand images in ninety-eight days; Voyager 2 returned thirteen thousand. They inspected the planet and its five major moons in extreme detail, providing data that were being analyzed years after the conclusion of the encounter.

"For the first time, it was possible to see the Jovian satellites as individuals," David Morrison wrote in the introduction to a fat textbook devoted solely to Jupiter's satellites, a 972-page tome, packed with arcane scholarly papers (e.g., "Craters and Basins on Ganymede and Callisto: Morphological Indicators of Crustal Evolution"), that represented a colossal leap in knowledge about the solar system's largest and most imposing object. "We hope that some of the wonder and excitement of these discoveries have been preserved in the chapters of this book, in spite of the efforts of authors and editor to conform to the usual dry technical style," the astronomer noted wryly.

The Jovian moons certainly amounted to worlds unto themselves. The fact that they were seen to vary so much, from Callisto's heavily cratered surface of ice and rock to Io's explosive volcanoes, to Ganymede's "crazy quilt" pattern of craters and grooved terrain, stirred the imaginations of those who studied them in unprecedented detail on the Voyager imagery. Where had they come from? Why were they different?

And despite all of their obvious differences, the Jovian satellites interact with one another, with Jupiter and its ring, and with the entire magnetosphere. Taken together, they amount to a handy model with which to study the origin and workings of the solar system itself. Nor is the formation of the system the only model to come from Jupiter and its moons. The Great Red Spot is a weather pattern that has endured for at least three hundred years. As such, it also provides a model that scientists believe can yield clues to the weather on Earth, and specifically to hurricanes, tornadoes, and other fierce systems.

The Saturn encounters, in November 1980 and August 1981 for Voyager 1 and 2, respectively, were equally spectacular. "For sheer intellectual fun," the magazine *Science* observed in the wake of Voyager 2's flyby of Saturn, "there has never been anything quite like the Voyager encounters. Volcanoes on Io, ringlets around Saturn, *braided* rings—the observations are outrageous." That and more.

Saturn is almost twice as far from Earth as Jupiter and receives slightly more than 1 percent of the solar energy that hits our own planet. As a consequence, relatively little about Saturn was revealed through telescopes. Its disk was seen to consist of a series of dusky bands similar to the belts on Jupiter, but not nearly so colorful and distinctive. Fewer than a dozen spots had been seen on Saturn before the Pioneer flybys, and that was frustrating because spots or distinctive clouds—irregularities—are the markers that allow observers to measure a planet's rotation and the direction and force of its weather system. Before Pioneer, the huge gas ball was seen to have only three rings (Pioneer 11 found two more). In addition, only Titan could be seen as a disk from Earth; the other satellites were only discernible as points of light of varying brightness.

The Pioneers were first-rate precursors. They established the fact that the journey to Jupiter and Saturn could be made safely and they sent back an enormous amount of information. But their strongest suit was magnetospheric measurements, not imagery. While the pictures they returned were helpful in a general way—certainly to provide Voyager's mission planners with a better idea of where to point their own spacecraft's cameras—they were also disappointing. Since the Pioneers spun, the resolution of their pictures was necessarily poor, and that frustrated scientists who needed clear imagery above all else. Those who studied Saturn's atmosphere, for example, were disappointed because the pictures failed to reveal any identifiable discrete clouds. How could they delineate weather patterns in fuzz? Titan, the only moon to be meaningfully imaged by Pioneer, was similarly featureless where its atmosphere was concerned. Planetary scientists were therefore especially eager to see what the Voyagers would turn up. They would not be disappointed.

Once again the benefit of using two spacecraft became apparent. Sequencing was worked out so that Voyager 2, trailing Voyager 1 as the mission's ostensible "spare," could cover places that were missed by Voyager 1 or more closely examine those that seemed particularly interesting based on what Voyager 1 turned up. All of Saturn's known satellites were targeted for observation by Voyager 2, for instance, but special emphasis was placed on those not imaged by Voyager 1.

Voyager 1 had been looking at Saturn since midsummer of 1980.

The surprises therefore began well before its closest approach on November 12. Among the first was the discovery that dark "spokes" extended radially outward across Saturn's B Ring. Exhaustive investigation would show that the spokes are not permanent, that they can appear anywhere on the ring, and that they are caused either by tiny ring particles that are polarized by Saturn's electrical field, or simply by the way light strikes the particles at certain times.

Then three new satellites were found, two of them just inside and outside the narrow F Ring, and one orbiting just beyond the outer edge of the A Ring. It didn't take long to conclude that the tiny bodies (about sixty miles across in the case of those at the F Ring) were "shepherd" satellites that helped stabilize the rings against disruption and breakup, and helped keep order among them.

As first Voyager 1 and, nine months later,* Voyager 2 sliced through the Saturnian system on different trajectories, a nearly unbroken stream of data came down to the Deep Space Network and then to Pasadena.

First, and most obviously, the imagery was extraordinary.† Seen up close in brilliant color, the atmosphere of the planet itself could be defined by the dynamics of several cloud systems and small-scale spots. The colossal ring system was photographed, top and bottom, from far encounter, near encounter, and postencounter by both Voyagers. The imagery revealed the system's structure in fine detail, showing that there were not five rings, nor ten times five, but hundreds of delicate, gorgeous rings made mostly of water ice that shimmered in the light reflected off the butterscotch-colored planet and from the far-off Sun.

Yet the pictures also revealed new enigmas. Voyager 1, for example, sent back imagery clearly showing that the F Ring, in violation of the accepted principles of celestial mechanics, was kinky, clumpy, and seemed to be braided by three distinct strands of particles. During the months between the Voyager 1 and Voyager 2 encounters, scientists therefore went to great pains to come up with an explanation for the strange phenomenon.

---

*Encounter day for Voyager 2 was August 25, 1981.
†It came in relatively quickly, too. A memorandum sent by Stewart A. Collins of JPL to several members of the Voyager science and engineering teams on April 20, 1981, and whose title was "Amazing Trivia," noted that all twenty-one of the pictures Mariner 4 sent back from Mars in 1965 totaled just over five million bits, while each Voyager image alone contained 5.12 million bits, or more than the entire Mariner 4 return. Furthermore, the transmission rate had jumped from eight and a third bits a second to 44,800. At that rate, Collins concluded, "Mariner 4 would have returned 1 Voyager picture per year from Saturn!"

But when the Voyager 2 ring pictures came in, the imaging team pored over shots of the same ring and was even further confounded. Now there were five strands, not three, and the kinks, or braids, were gone. To confuse matters even more, there appeared a faint, very thin strand of water-ice particles wandering through the Encke division of the A Ring that had not shown up in the previous imagery. It was promptly named the "Encke doodle" because, in seeming contradiction to the accepted laws of physics, it, too, snaked around Saturn instead of being a nice, tidy, uniform circle.

The satellites themselves seemed eerie up close, especially against the pitch-blackness of the void behind them. Some of them, exposed to cameras for the first time, were vaguely reminiscent of the fantastically ugly prehistoric fish that suddenly appear out of the murk and into the strobe's glare as they swim up to the lens while being photographed during a science team's particularly deep dive in the ocean.

Titan, which is itself planet-sized and is the only other world in this solar system besides Earth to have a nitrogen-rich atmosphere, had shown practically nothing to those peering at it from Earth, since their telescopes could not penetrate its smog-shrouded blanket. But the Voyager instruments revealed a phenomenal world under a frozen orange atmosphere: a world loaded with methane as well as nitrogen, which most likely resembles conditions on the early Earth.

Enceladus, only 310 miles wide, revealed a surface that was heavily pockmarked with craters on one side but relatively smooth on the other, suggesting that it was "resurfaced" as recently as within the last 100 million years. This means that goeological activity, tectonic movement or volcanism, took place in the area and obliterated the impact craters, making the surface relatively smooth. Dione and Rhea showed evidence—bright, wispy streaks that could have been caused by material being thrown out from under their surfaces— that indicated internal activity at some distant time. Mimas, one of Saturn's inner satellites, was undoubtedly the spookiest of them all. It had an incredible impact crater named Arthur that is almost a third of its size. "As the image of Mimas and this absurd crater first appeared on our television monitors, there was a sense of déjà vu," Brad Smith recalled. "Of course! It was George Lukas's Death Star [in *Star Wars*]. The resemblance is uncanny."

In the end, long after the last of the TV and print people had left von Karman, and its legendary bottomless coffee urns had been put

away, scientists were still mining the lode that had come back from
Saturn. The Lord of the Rings, a mighty ball made almost entirely
of hydrogen and helium, had been reconnoitered in unprecedented
detail. Its magnetosphere had been charted with precision. Distinct
atmospheric features had provided a great deal of information about
the planet's weather and winds (which were clocked at eleven hundred miles an hour at the equator—four times faster than Jupiter's
and more than ten times faster than any measured on Earth).
Voyager 2's flight behind Saturn produced an occultation that allowed the atmosphere to be fixed in terms of both temperature and
density. Temperature measurements—they were as low as minus
312 degrees Fahrenheit in the upper atmosphere and minus 207
degrees Fahrenheit closer to the center—proved that Saturn, like its
bigger neighbor, gives off more heat than it absorbs. Perhaps Saturn,
too, is a failed star.

Voyager 1 and 2's historic accomplishments during the two years
that spanned the Jupiter and Saturn encounters—the summer of
1979 to the summer of 1981—were so impressive that Headquarters
decided to extend the mission to Uranus and Neptune, completing
the Grand Tour. The order, given in January 1981—seven months
before Voyager 2 even reached Saturn—called for Voyager 1 to climb
up and out of the plain of the ecliptic after Saturn. Its twin would
then continue on to Uranus and Neptune alone. The adaptability
engineered into the spacecraft therefore turned out to be fully justified.

The decision to go for the Grand Tour seemed auspicious—a hopeful
omen for the future. And it came even as data continued to pour in
from both spacecraft throughout the rest of that winter and well into
1981, climaxing with Voyager 2's encounter with Saturn in August.
But the order extending Voyager 2's mission had come the same
month that Ronald Reagan became president. It was a fateful juxtaposition of events. Reagan was shortly to embark on a cost-cutting
binge that would imperil both Voyagers and a great deal besides. In
a manner of speaking, budget problems would soon not only shake
the very ground from which the Voyagers had taken off, but would
even threaten to reach deep into space to terminate them as well.

James M. Beggs, Reagan's newly appointed NASA administrator,
went to Pasadena in August 1981 to help celebrate Voyager 2's rendezvous with Saturn. Standing behind the podium at the left side of
the stage in von Karman, he looked out at the national and interna-

tional press and offered the sort of hackneyed platitudes that speech-writers find irresistible for such occasions. It was feel-good talk: with a few nouns replaced, it could as easily have been used at a bridge dedication, the launching of a supertanker, or the start-up of a super-conducting super collider. "This nation, when it puts its mind to it, can do splendid things. . . . It staggers the imagination . . . one of the great scientific achievements of our age . . ."

Then Beggs took a seat behind the long table at which scientists normally sat during news conferences and waited for questions. If he had any illusions that the interchange would be gentle, they were quickly dispelled. The reporters, some of whom were unabashed space buffs, were upset because of the new administration's frontal assault on the space exploration program and of persistent threats to kill projects and even end planetary exploration altogether. They were in no mood to be drowned in warm honey. Beggs was therefore hit by hard questions that required specific answers about his agency's intentions, and especially about where it intended to go in planetary exploration. This was as close as the science writers and others had ever come to pelting a NASA official with ripe tomatoes, and although the administrator tried gamely to deflect the fusillade with still more platitudes ("I cannot conceive of NASA without a strong science program. . . ."), the reporters weren't buying it. They knew better.

As had happened before, and as would happen again, the space exploration program seemed fated to suffer a setback, perhaps a devastating one, just at a moment of triumph. It was as if the gods had decreed that the explorers would forever have to pay for some sin by having to accommodate a measure of defeat as the irreducible price for every victory—that the two somehow had to go together, like night and day or sickness and health.

Funding for planetary exploration was reduced by a factor of four between 1974 and 1977, and only one new planetary mission, the Jupiter Orbiter-Probe—or Galileo, as it would be named—was approved between 1974 and the end of the Carter presidency. Jimmy Carter had not been especially partial to space science and planetary exploration, notwithstanding the fact that he was the most scientifically and technically literate president since Jefferson. But those who faulted the Georgian for a lack of interest in space science and exploration would soon come to think of his presidency as halcyon compared with the one that followed.

Ronald Reagan came to office bearing an agenda that called for reducing the federal deficit to the point where the budget was actually balanced. (In fact, he ran on a platform that called for making a balanced budget a constitutional requirement, an idea that soon gave way to the largest federal deficit in history, due in great measure to unparalleled defense spending.)

David A. Stockman, Reagan's director of the Office of Management and Budget, believed in the classic tenets of a free market economy. Reaganomics, as it would come to be known, required that extraneous government spending be slashed by draconian means if necessary, that government involvement across the board be drastically reduced, that business be encouraged by tax incentives and other measures, and even that a return to the gold standard be sought. In his campaign for the Republican presidential nomination in 1980 George Bush, eventually to be Reagan's vice president, had contemptuously called the shell game "voodoo economics."

During the winter of 1980–81 Stockman wasted no time in targeting areas of federal spending he believed had to be drastically reduced in order to alter what he saw as a dangerously counterproductive economic system. Public welfare was the biggest of these, but no area except national defense would escape evisceration.

Stockman slashed Carter's proposed fiscal 1982 total NASA budget of $6.7 billion by $604 million. In the process, the Venus Orbiting Imaging Radar spacecraft was killed. So was the International Solar-Polar project, which understandably angered NASA's European partners in the program.

The situation worsened as the year progressed. Beggs learned that summer, even as the Voyager data from Saturn was pouring in, that his projected budget for fiscal 1983 was $6.5 billion. He nonetheless submitted a budget request for $7.2 billion in actual outlays, pointing out that it would be impossible to complete the shuttle, carry on space science and exploration, and do aeronautical research without that amount of money.

OMB's response was not long in coming. On September 24, Stockman sent the space agency its official budget target for fiscal 1983: $6 billion. That was half a billion less than what Beggs had already disregarded. Worse, the projected figure for fiscal 1984 showed yet another drop, to $5.6 billion.

David Stockman and James Beggs were now engaged in a test of wills. They were going through a bureaucratic exercise, endemic to Washington, in which a high premium is placed on bluffing. Stockman wanted to slash NASA's budget while trying to escape blame

for curtailing or ending its programs. He therefore submitted a budget to NASA, but left it to Beggs to accept or protest it and, in case
of the former, to decide which programs would live and which would
die. If the excisions generated heat from a particular constituency
within the space community, then the administrator would be the
one to take it, not the director of the Office of Management and
Budget.

Beggs understood this. He also understood, no less than those who
came before and after him, that the shuttle, whatever its problems,
was sacrosanct, since it constituted the underpinnings of his agency.
So he wrote a letter to Stockman on September 29 addressing the
OMB guidelines. He warned (in writing and therefore for the record)
that the reduced budget would mean "maintaining viable programs
in some areas" while closing down "other major programs that
NASA has operated since its inception." Planetary exploration was
at the top of the list of programs slated for termination. "In terms
of scientific priority it ranks below space astronomy and astrophysics," he explained to Stockman, adding that the next step in planetary exploration would involve sample returns. And those, James
Beggs explained, would require "full development" of the shuttle.
"Of course, elimination of the planetary exploration program will
make the Jet Propulsion Laboratory in California surplus to our
needs."

Beggs was in turn playing the Washington Monument Game, as
it is known inside the beltway. In this game, the Department of the
Interior threatens to close the monument to tourists if it doesn't get
its appropriation. Interior knows full well that closing the monument would result in a barrage of letters from outraged taxpayers,
all of which would be directed right back to the congressmen who cut
the budget in the first place. Knowing this, Congress is therefore
allegedly wary of cutting Interior's budget. Similarly, Beggs was
telling Stockman that the budget reductions would leave him no
choice but to end planetary exploration and, in the process, dissolve
NASA's relationship with JPL. Beggs also undoubtedly counted on
the fact that Stockman knew that JPL happened to be in the president's home state.

David Stockman, who called himself "as much of a space buff as
the next person," nevertheless held his ground. His priorities, in
fact, certainly did not reflect his professed affinity for space. When
Senator Harrison Schmitt, who held a doctorate in geology and who
had walked on the Moon, complained bitterly about cuts in applica-

tions programs, Stockman retaliated by saying that he had always found the technological spinoff argument "appalling." "NASA was in effect claiming that the way to build a better mousetrap was to go to Jupiter," he later wrote.

Beggs may have been bluffing, but Hans Mark, his deputy administrator, was not. Mark had been secretary of the Air Force in the Carter administration and had also headed the supersecret National Reconnaissance Office, which buys and runs the nation's spy satellites. An archconservative and kindred spirit of Edward Teller (the father of the H-bomb and the midwife to Star Wars), Mark was a fierce proponent of the space station and a staunch defender of the shuttle. Where he was concerned, the nation's defense requirements were of overriding importance, and he believed that NASA's proper role was in support of those requirements. When Mark came to NASA, Bruce Murray has observed, he "no longer had a blue Shuttle model on his desk, but his crew cut still symbolized his priorities." Mark maneuvered through the upper echelons of the aerospace fraternity, military and civilian, in successive administrations with considerable political acumen. One knowledgeable former space official who watched him over the years likened him to Richard III, whose deviousness and treachery gained him the throne while he pretended to be pious.

Hans Mark, himself the holder of a Ph.D. in physics, was no friend of planetary exploration or, apparently, the science that went with it. "In the last decade, the United States has spent an average of half a billion dollars on space science," he had complained in 1975. "This budget is roughly equal to that of the National Science Foundation and I, personally, find it difficult to believe that we have a cultural or intellectual justification for continuing our space science effort at the same level for the indefinite future. My concern," he added, "stems from the fact that unfortunately the results of space science to date have not been of major significance. While there have been a number of valuable findings, it is fair to say that no *fundamental* or *unexpected* discovery has been uncovered in the course of our exploration of the planets and the regions surrounding the earth. . . ."

While his boss, Beggs, may not have been serious about ending planetary exploration and bidding farewell to JPL, Mark was dead serious on both scores. He wanted to pull the plug on exploration and turn JPL over to the Department of Defense, not only because he thought its considerable resources could benefit the Pentagon, but because he believed that defense funding, the only segment of the budget that was beyond the reach of Stockman's ax, would be the lab's salvation.

And where the exploration of the planets was concerned, Hans Mark had an ally in George Keyworth, Reagan's late-appointed science adviser.* Early in December, Keyworth was quoted in *The Washington Post* as having recommended stopping all new planetary space missions for at least a decade—"an idea, he said, the White House seems to be buying." He told the OMB's Budget Review Board that he "totally" concurred with the decision to cancel Galileo (Jupiter Orbiter-Probe) and Magellan (the Venus radar mapper) because they would merely revisit Jupiter and Venus, while "the shuttle offers us a new capability to expand our horizons through . . . new astrophysical initiatives. Cutting planetary exploration," the nation's chief scientist assured OMB, "represents an example of good management."

Meanwhile, the engines that were supposed to power the vehicle by which the new astrophysical initiatives were to be undertaken were blowing up on their test stands or otherwise malfunctioning with appalling regularity. This and other setbacks during 1980 and 1981 not only were making delivery of the shuttle embarrassingly late, but were forcing NASA to raid every budget line it could for extra funding.

One scenario being given credence by Keyworth and the White House in the summer and autumn of 1981 had to do with Voyager 2's being turned off, along with the Deep Space Network. By then Headquarters had tentatively decided to go for Uranus and Neptune to complete the Grand Tour, and the spacecraft was being reprogrammed accordingly. But the budget cutters in the executive branch determined that the DSN was now prohibitively expensive to operate, especially since Voyager amounted to being its sole justification. Both of them—the DSN and the spacecraft—were suddenly seen as unnecessary indulgences. Voyager 2 might go on to Uranus, arriving in January 1986, and it might even sent back data without further instruction. But no one back on Earth would be listening. The planetary scientists' worst nightmare was coming true.

By the time the American Astronomical Society's Division of Planetary Sciences met in Pittsburgh for its 1981 annual meeting

*Keyworth was appointed on May 19, 1981, four months after the beginning of Reagan's first term. Beggs and Mark had been appointed on April 23.

during the week of October 12, it was clear to the thunderstruck astronomers and the planetary scientists that the administration was absolutely serious about ending deep space exploration. The astronomers, in particular, tended to be a politically naïve and inept bunch whose combative instincts generally didn't extend much beyond scraps over tenure, challenging refereed papers, and chairmanships of departments. "When trouble came," the Smithsonian historian Joseph N. Tatarewisz observed, "they'd form their wagons in a circle. Then they'd start shooting to the inside."

But it was different in Pittsburgh that October of 1981. The astronomers and planetary scientists reacted to the White House overtures with rage. They understood that suddenly they were in a fight, not merely for one program or another, but probably for the survival of solar system exploration.

With the probes gone, many of the atmosphere people would in effect have to go back to thinking about cold fronts over Canada and tropical depressions over the Gulf of Mexico; the geologists would have to return to the Geological Survey and to the petroleum companies; the fields and particles researchers would once again be looking at the aurora borealis. With neither the planetary probes nor the Hubble Space Telescope (which was also being menaced by OMB),* the astronomers and astrophysicists would for all intents and purposes be right back where they started—in balloons, rockoons, and sounding rockets. Those who looked to the sky would be revolving round and round forever under domes bolted to the tops of mountains or listening to what their dishes collected in valleys and deserts.

The exploration of the solar system and beyond—the majestic endeavor whose course had been set by the likes of Kepler, Galileo,

---

*In the winter of 1976, funding for the Large Space Telescope (later named for Edwin P. Hubble, a leading American astronomer) was dropped from the fiscal 1977 budget. Members of Congress and top NASA officials, including James Fletcher, were blitzed by letters from many of the nation's leading astronomers, including E. Margaret Burbidge, a professor at the University of California at San Diego and, at the time, president-elect of the American Astronomical Society. "The immediate angry reaction of many scientists," said another from the Institute for Advanced Study at Princeton, "is that NASA has disregarded the recommendations of its outside science advisory groups, as well as the overwhelming support of the scientific community. . . ." The latter actually hinted at a quid pro quo: "We fear that scientific support for the entire shuttle program might be affected by the backlash from the omission of LST from the FY'77 budget." (Burbidge's letter of February 10, 1976, was to Senator Charles McC. Mathias. The one from Princeton is dated January 21, 1976, and was signed by five well-known scientists, including Burbidge and Lyman Spitzer. The letters, as well as others from Steven Muller at Johns Hopkins and Richard W. Shorthill at the Utah Research Center, are in the NASA History Archive.)

Newton, and Tsiolkovsky, Columbus, Magellan, Drake, and Peary—was threatened with extinction by something called supply-side economics.

Everyone became galvanized in Pittsburgh. David Morrison, chairman of the Division of Planetary Sciences, sent out a "Dear Colleague" letter that got right to the point: "The time has come to politicize the planetary science community. . . . I realize this is distasteful to many, and I am sure all of us would much rather pursue our science. But we believe the danger is real and we are not crying 'wolf.' " The scientists learned how to lobby congressmen and work the press. They even grumbled darkly about forming a political action committee.

Eugene Levy, chairman of COMPLEX, the National Academy's Committee on Planetary and Lunar Exploration, delivered a stinging indictment of the decision-making process itself, which allowed space science and planetary exploration to be imperiled by the likes of economists and politicians. He deplored the lack of a dialogue on the merits of the case and attacked what he saw as a brazen fait accompli. Instead of open discussion, Levy charged, "highly placed government officials *assert* that most of the important things in planetary exploration have already been done! They *announce* that 'the era of planetary investigations is over'!

". . . Decisions are being made without serious study of the issues, without significant consultation with individuals and institutions that grasp the scientific questions, and with reliance instead on personal preconceptions," the enraged scientist said. "We may see important policy level decisions, affecting major scientific activities in the United States, formulated at the whim of a few randomly placed people in the administration—people who are neither informed on these issues, nor sensitive to the importance of science and technology for our society in the large."

The year before, at the meeting in Tucson, the astronomers had sniped at Carl Sagan, the author of *Cosmos* and the star of the somewhat melodramatic television series of the same name, for being a dreaded "popularizer." Popularizing equates with prostitution among the imperiously fastidious in academe, and if the culprit gets rich and famous in the process (which is what happened to Sagan), the denunciations become all the more venomous. But now, consciously or otherwise, they were trying to emulate the Cornell astronomer. They were going to have to reach out for help.

It suddenly began to sink in, as space observer Mark Washburn has written, that "In a year when Americans had spent 32 billion quarters shooting down video space invaders, most of them were unaware that their own space program was on the verge of being shot down for lack of a few hundred million dollars," or the cost each year of a single B-1 bomber. "In the absence of tangible support for space," Washburn added, "the legislators were likely to acquiesce to the Reagan Administration's attempt to gut NASA."

The counterattack was waged on several fronts. Morrison and Sagan wrote to Edwin Meese, the presidential counselor, asking his support and emphasizing that "a thousand years from now our age will be remembered because this is the moment we first set sail for the planets." Meese answered by acknowledging their position and assuring them that he had made their case to the president.

Arnold Beckman, the Caltech trustee, was more pragmatic in his own letter to Meese. The proposed budget cuts, he warned, threatened "to create total chaos and a rapid disintegration of a 5,000-person, $400 million Southern California enterprise. . . . There are obvious implications to the support of the President and to his Party should the Administration permit such a catastrophe to take place." John Rousselot, a conservative California representative, sent a letter to Meese that was drafted by JPL. Thomas Pownall, the president of Martin Marietta, told Meese that the company's work on solar system exploration had enhanced its ability to meet Department of Defense needs. Given the administration's drive to increase weaponry, Pownall's idea was an inspired one.

Mary Scranton, wife of the former governor of Pennsylvania and chair of an ad hoc Trustees Committee on JPL that had been started the previous January, contacted Charles Percy, Charles McC. Mathias, Mark Hatfield, Fred Bernthal (the top assistant to Senate Majority Leader Howard Baker), and Vice President Bush. Marvin Goldberger, the president of Caltech, went to Washington to lobby several senators, including Baker. The influential Tennessean in turn wrote to Reagan in support of Galileo, emphasizing that his interest in the matter was beyond parochialism. Baker's letter landed on Stockman's desk and, added to the chorus of other support, turned the tide.

OMB's Budget Review Committee met in December and agreed to a compromise, suggested by Keyworth, in which $80 million to $90 million would be added to the planetary exploration budget in order to save Galileo. However tenuously, the planetary exploration program was saved. By the following May, even Hans Mark was assuring a group of planetary scientists at the University of Arizona that he was "thoroughly committed" to planetary exploration. He had only maintained his previous position, he explained, because it was periodically necessary to look critically at the relative, as well as at the absolute, value of the science that was at issue.

Besides Galileo, the Deep Space Network emerged from the imbroglio intact, and so did Voyager. The latter's funding curve dropped precipitously after Saturn, leveled out during the interplanetary part of the mission, and then climbed just before the Uranus encounter: it was therefore derisively called the "bathtub" at JPL because of its shape. Galileo, while still alive, had its launch postponed until 1985, causing the mission to be redesigned so as to reach its destination in 1990. This understandably upset and frustrated the Galileo team and others at JPL who were itching to return to Jupiter to send a small penetrator toward its hot heart while an orbiter circled for the kind of long look that no flyby could provide. The Galileo people had no way of knowing, however, that the worst was yet to come. Nothing else, including the Halley's Comet rendezvous, survived that budget (though a downsized Venus radar orbiter would live to fly another day).

Bruce Murray, who was still pushing the Halley mission, was as thankful for the small favors bestowed by OMB as anyone else in planetary exploration. But given its many enemies in the new administration, he was far from sanguine about the program's prospects. He therefore penned an essay in *Science* titled "The End of the Beginning," in which he simultaneously rhapsodized about the recently concluded flybys and sounded an alarm over what he saw as a continuing menace to space science and planetary exploration.

"Voyager 2 journeyed 4 years from the warm sands of Florida to the icy environs of Saturn", Murray began. "Scientific specialists have been awed by the intricate and unexpected natural phenomena which characterize the Saturnian system, just as they were earlier bedazzled by Jupiter. Millions of others around the world have been carried along via instant global communications on this fantastic journey of the mind."

But, he continued, "While the Voyagers functioned relatively smoothly in space, circumstances in their terrestrial birthplace were not so harmonious." JPL's director supplied an endangered species list of threatened and disrupted missions, in addition to those that had been scuttled altogether, including the Jupiter Orbiter-Probe, two International Solar Polar Mission spacecraft, another to orbit

Venus with radar, and still another to meet Halley's Comet in 1986. Murray went on to cite high inflation, unprecedented interest rates, and continuing problems in the development of the shuttle as the main causes of the problem. Then he pleaded for the programs that were in jeopardy or already scrubbed, arguing that new missions would not require increased launch vehicle capability or strain the NASA budget.

In conclusion, Murray issued an oblique call for the science community—"the readership of *Science*"—to "help this uncertain nation once again look outward in space for the first time. Perhaps our national expectations will once again be rising 4 years hence when Voyager 2 reaches Uranus." (In fact national expectations would plummet during that encounter, but it would not be the spacecraft's fault.)

Meanwhile, Voyager 2, having run the gauntlet of asteroids, radiation, and Reaganomics, flew on. The decision to extend the mission to Uranus and then Neptune had been forced the previous January because a long lead time was necessary in order to make slight but crucial trajectory correction maneuvers. The route to both planets would not be a hole in one but, rather, a series of putts. More important, Voyager 2 was more than a billion miles—ten astronomical units—from Earth and about four years old when it flew by Saturn. When it arrived at Uranus in late January 1986, it would be twice as old and twice as far away, exceeding its original life expectancy by 100 percent.

This created two problems. First, while by no means incapacitated, the spacecraft was beginning to feel the effects of its long journey through time and space. Like any long-duration machine, key parts were becoming tired or failing altogether, and this had to be compensated for or corrected. Its primary receiver had died in April 1978, less than halfway to Jupiter, after its computer failed to get a routine check-in message from Pasadena and switched to an alternate receiver. Then the backup itself went tone-deaf and could hear only one narrow, shifting radio band. All instructions therefore had to be loaded on that single, fragile communications link. Then, right after Saturn, the gearbox that made the scan platform turn had seized and was freed only after a great deal of persistent effort. It had to be treated with extreme delicacy because everyone at JPL was afraid that there was no telling when it would stick again. Voyager 2 was therefore partly deaf and somewhat arthritic as it closed in on Uranus.

Second, the very distance to Uranus and Neptune—twenty and then thirty AUs—required radical changes in the way the spacecraft was programmed and how its data was collected on Earth. Voyager 2 had to be turned into a different exploring machine for it to reach Uranus and function there. If the pantheon of heroes in the U.S. space program includes individuals other than those who actually go to space, as it ought to, then the engineers at JPL who radically modified Voyager 2 to complete the Grand Tour earned the right to be there with the rest.

While distance between Earth and the spacecraft was steadily increasing, for example, the electricity produced by the radioisotope thermoelectric generators was decreasing from 470 watts to about 400. That power level was not enough to operate all of Voyager 2's subsystems at the same time. It also further decreased the probe's already feeble transmitting capability. This meant that some systems could be turned on only after others had been turned off. A "careful ballet" was therefore instituted to make certain that power on the spacecraft was distributed where needed while making certain that the system as a whole was not overtaxed. Hydrazine, used to operate the thrusters that kept the probe on course, was also diminishing and had to be carefully husbanded.

The amount of light available at Uranus would also be in very short supply. While the planet is twice as far from the Sun as Saturn, the inverse square law says there would be only a quarter as much light, which in turn meant that exposure time would have to be quadrupled if usable imagery was to be collected. This meant that some regular exposures would be fifteen seconds long, and others, taken through special filters, would require a full minute.

In addition, Voyager 2 was programmed to come so close to Uranus's five known satellites at high speed (nine miles a second) that "smear," similar to what happens when close-up objects are photographed from a moving automobile, was a certainty unless corrective action was taken. The engineers therefore worked out a complicated "anti-smear campaign." This entailed steadying the spacecraft by firing its thrusters for milliseconds to compensate for motion caused by the operation of its tape recorder and drifting.

Even more amazing, Voyager 2's operators reprogrammed its attitude control computer to reduce the thrusters' firing time and have them turn the entire spacecraft so that it panned the targets it photographed as it flew by them. The last operation was called image (or target) motion compensation. This maneuver bypassed the scan platform, whose faint vibration could have blurred the images, and instead turned the entire spacecraft into a scan platform. In order to get the attitude control subsystem to fire the thrusters as required, it had to be "fooled" into believing that Voyager 2 was drifting off course so it would compensate with the appropriate adjustment. This in turn meant tinkering with the spacecraft's attitude control logic, which had been forbidden since launch because a single slip could send it wandering out of control forever.

In addition, the great distance adversely affected the transmission of data, increasing the possibility that errors would come in. This was overcome by elaborate changes in the data processing software, which had the effect of cramming the same amount of data on fewer bits than were used in earlier encounters, and "compressing" the imagery so that a minimum number of picture elements—pixels— carried the same picture. The data rate was thereby reduced by almost 70 percent. Because of this, there would be less smear on the Uranus imagery than there had been on the pictures from Jupiter and Saturn.

Collection of the data on Earth was similarly enhanced by linking the main antennas in the Deep Space Network and adding Australia's 210-foot Parkes radio telescope so as to effectively make them one huge antenna that straddled the planet to form a big ear. Working in reverse, the global antenna system sent more accurate steering instructions to Voyager 2 and kept closer track of where it was. "Incredible" is not too strong an adjective for a system that placed Voyager 2's whereabouts to within fourteen miles from a distance of nearly two billion.

It turned out, too, that the probe had become partly demented. Six days before closest approach, on January 18, 1986, the imaging team was horrified to see pictures begin coming in that were seriously degraded by black and white streaks running through them horizontally, blotting out substantial sections. Satisfied that the problem was not on Earth, Richard Rice and Ed Blizzard, spacecraft data systems specialists, combed through volumes of computer printouts in a desperate effort to isolate the abnormality on Voyager 2 to prevent the most important part of the encounter's imagery from being ruined. An all-night search convinced Rice and Blizzard that a single bit of binary instruction inside the processor that compressed imagery data for transmission to Earth had switched irreversibly from "0" to "1," causing the system as a whole to slip into partial incoherence. Rice quickly wrote a program that acted as a patch to detour commands around the faulty memory part of the circuitry, tested it, and loaded it into Voyager 2 on January 20, only four days before nearest approach. It was that close.

The encounter with Uranus lasted 113 days—from November 4, 1985, to February 25, 1986. When it was over, scientists at JPL had a staggering amount of new information about Uranus and its satellites, much of it deliciously bewildering. It was no surprise that Uranus, alone among the planets, rotated perpendicularly to the Sun—"standing on its side"—with a pole pointed toward the center of the solar system like a gigantic bull's-eye. That and more—its mass, radius, temperature, and atmospheric composition, for example—had been calculated with reasonable accuracy through the use of telescopes.

But the planet's exotic moons, weird magnetic field, and bizarre weather system both intrigued and confounded the science teams that tried to analyze the flood of data that came as the encounter symphony played on. Because Uranus rotates on its side, and its rings and moons follow suit, Voyager 2 couldn't make a relatively leisurely flight through the ecliptic—the equatorial plane—but instead had to penetrate the bull's-eye head-on, like an arrow. Most of

VOYAGER 2's FLIGHT PAST URANUS
(VIEW IS VERTICAL TO PLANE OF FLIGHT PATH)

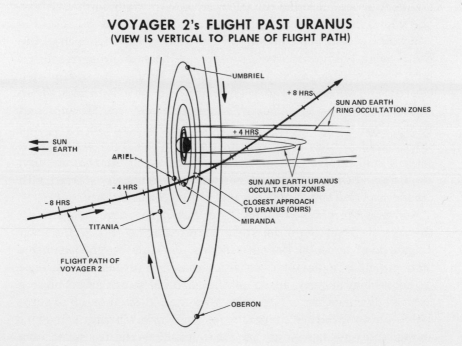

the close-in data were therefore collected in about six hectic hours on encounter day itself, January 24. Answers to many questions were so elusive that three days later one frustrated reporter demanded to know why explanations for the observed phenomena were not immediately forthcoming, why the science was not instant enough.

"We're happily bewildered," answered Ed Stone, who was weary but amused. "If you understand something the first time you see it, then you probably knew it already. So in a sense, the more bewildered we are, the more successful the mission was."

The planet's structure and composition were found to be as oddball as its tilt and askew magnetic field. While both Jupiter and Saturn are thought to have relatively small cores of rock and other heavy compounds that are immersed in thick blankets of helium and hydrogen, Uranus is distinctly different: it has far less gas around its heavy core. In that regard, it seemed like a near twin of what Neptune was thought to be. The chances are that Uranus's internal structure consists mostly of water, ammonia, and methane mixed into a dense, icy atmosphere that covers a rock core. Where core-to-gas ratios are concerned, Uranus and Neptune are structurally about midway between the terrestrial inner planets and the two gas giants: they are a kind of compromise. But why should that be? No one knows for sure.

Voyager 2 returned clear high-resolution pictures of each of the five previously known large Uranian satellites, and discovered ten new, much smaller, ones. The old moons—Titania, Ariel, Umbriel, Oberon, and Miranda—were seen to be worlds of ice and rock whose surfaces showed a wide array of geologic features. Titania and Ariel—at about one thousand miles in diameter, the largest of the satellites—had huge fault systems and canyons, but relatively few craters, indicating a geologically recent period of internal activity. Umbriel and Oberon, on the other hand, were heavily scarred with craters and therefore probably had little recent activity.

And then there was Miranda, innermost of the large moons. With the possible exception of Io, Miranda revealed itself to be the most enigmatic of the solar system's moons. The satellite, measuring a mere 310 miles in diameter, was immediately described by Laurence A. Soderblom, deputy leader of the imaging team, as a "bizarre hybrid" of the geology of Mercury and Mars, with a touch of some of Jupiter's and Saturn's large moons thrown in. Voyager 2 imagery showed canyons as deep as twelve miles, dramatic fractures, long ridges, and a bevy of craters, glacial flows, broad terraces, and strange-looking features, one of which looked like a racetrack and the other a chevron.

"It's all the strange places rolled into one. If you took all the bizarre features in the solar system and put them on one object, that would be Miranda," Soderblom said in astonishment two days after the pictures were taken at closest approach. One theory for Miranda's being so diverse is that it was blasted apart five or more times by large objects that struck it, each time coming back together again. Another explanation has it that when Miranda erupted for the last time it was a fairly uniform mixture of rock and ice, but the immense internal heat caused its various regions to form differently.

Voyager 2 photographed and measured Uranus's nine known charcoal-colored, spiderweb-thin rings, and found two new ones. Radio measurements showed that Epsilon, the outermost ring (and at a mere thirty-seven miles, the widest) was made mostly of boulder-sized particles measuring several feet across. Two tiny shepherd moons, which had been predicted but not seen, were also discovered on either side of the Epsilon ring. The dust and tiny particles common to the Jovian and Saturnian rings were for the most part absent from those circling Uranus, though there was a lot of dust around the planet generally. Instead, there were bands of black coallike material, measuring from the size of a softball to that of an automobile. The rings' dark color has yet to be fully explained. One possibility among several is that they contain unaltered material with the properties of primitive meteoroids, which contain large amounts of carbon. A number of factors, including incomplete rings and varying opacity in several of the main rings, led JPL scientists to consider the possibility that the entire ring system may be relatively new and formed after the birth of the planet itself.

As expected, hydrogen and helium were found to be the dominant gases in the Uranian atmosphere, though methane gives the planet its ethereal aqua color. Clouds could not be picked out of the atmosphere until colored filters were applied to the imagery. (Andrew P. Ingersoll of Caltech noted that "visually, the most striking thing about Uranus . . . is just how unstriking it seems: it is a nearly featureless blue-green ball.") But the filters and false color applied by computers on Earth revealed that cloud bands do indeed exist and run east to west, just as they do on Jupiter and Saturn. They are swept along by winds of up to 450 miles an hour. Because of a brownish haze that covered the pole facing Voyager 2 as it approached Uranus, the planet seen through a violet filter looked eerily like a giant eyeball floating in the blackness of space.

By the morning of January 28, four days after Voyager 2's closest approach to Uranus, the Jet Propulsion Laboratory was reveling not only in the deluge of data coming back from the planet that was knocked on its side, but also in the fact of the mission itself—that its spacecraft had gone where no other had been. A few of the Pasadenans were even beginning to savor the notion that Neptune was to be their spacecraft's next port of call. And then, some contemplated with relish, Voyager 2 would go on to become the first manmade object to leave the solar system altogether (a feat that Ames maintains belongs to its own Pioneer 10).*

At that particular moment, however, the dream of glory was abruptly interrupted by an awful explosion. It happened not on the far side of Uranus but over the Atlantic Ocean, right on the home planet itself.

*The distinction has been claimed by both centers. A news release (No. 83-10) issued by Ames on March 16, 1983, claimed the honor for Pioneer 10 by its very title: "Pioneer 10, First Spacecraft to Leave the Solar System, Passes Beyond All the Known Planets." Two years later, JPL issued a revised version of its *Flight Science Office Science and Mission Systems Handbook* for the Voyager Uranus Interstellar Mission, which noted that Voyager 1 was expected to be "the first man-made spacecraft to penetrate the heliopause and enter interstellar space." It even stated that Voyager 1 passed Pioneer 11 in April 1981 and Voyager 2 passed it in March 1988, while Voyager 1 was to overtake Pioneer 10 in January 1998 and Voyager 2 was to do the same thing in "about" 2014. And on February 24, 1990, TRW, which made the Pioneers, announced that Pioneer 11 had followed Pioneer 10 "beyond Neptune's orbit and out of the solar system." It was all in the way the solar system was defined, of course. Ames and TRW took it to be the outer limit of the planets, which Pioneer 10 reached first, while JPL saw it as the limit of the Sun's influence, which the faster Voyager 1 would reach first. At the time of the announcement about Pioneer 11, both TRW and NASA acknowledged that some scientists believe that JPL's definition is closer to the mark. Nevertheless, in a discussion with the author in March 1988 Peter Waller, Ames's longtime public information officer, expressed disgust at what he saw as the rival center's redefining the solar system to suit its own political ends after Ames had itself publicly taken credit for the achievement. (The JPL statement is on p. 1.5 of the handbook; the calculations are on p. 1.2. The Pioneer 11 information is from "Pioneer 11 Is Reported to Leave Solar System," *The New York Times,* February 25, 1990.)

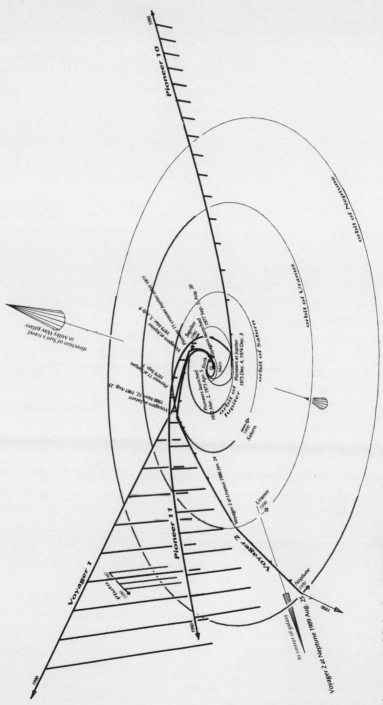

Astronomical Calendar 1990 by Guy Ottewell

Galileo: The Perils of Pauline

In 1977 Robert W. Carlson, a University of Southern California–trained physicist, was named principal investigator for a unique sensing instrument that was supposed to go to Jupiter. It had to do with looking at the planet's atmosphere and at the surfaces of some of its satellites by combining observations in the near-infrared with spectral analysis to determine cloud properties, mineral content, and other attributes.

The instrument was called a near-infrared mapping spectrometer, or NIMS, and it was enthusiastically approved to fly on the first spacecraft to revisit Jupiter after Voyager 2. The new exploring machine would be vastly different from Voyager, however. Rather than flying by the giant planet, it was designed to orbit for more than two years, and also to send a probe deep into the Jovian atmosphere. The spacecraft was therefore called Jupiter Orbiter-Probe, or JOP.

NIMS amounted to a new technique in planetary remote sensing. While devices to measure infrared wavelengths were hardly new, and neither were spectrometers, NIMS combined both in a way that allowed for a much more thorough investigation. It had first been suggested in the early seventies for a mission that would have sent a Mariner-type spacecraft to Jupiter and Uranus. That project was never approved, so the near-infrared mapping spectrometer remained grounded and in the experimental stage.

NIMS had been originally proposed by Torrence V. Johnson of JPL, who had worked on it with a team that included Carlson. When Johnson was appointed project scientist for JOP, however, Carlson was promoted to NIMS's principal investigator. The honor, which came in large part because of his expertise in spectroscopy, seemed to Carlson to portend a long and satisfying career. He was therefore understandably elated at the news. He would have been less than elated, however, if he had known in 1977, when he was thirty-six years old, that he would be fifty-four by the time the little device finally managed to make it to Jupiter and that, far from enhancing his career, participation in the project would nearly destroy it.

If the space age is about Neil Armstrong, Buzz Aldrin, and Yuri Gagarin, Wernher von Braun, Maxime Faget, and Sergei Korolev, James Van Allen, Carl Sagan, and Roald Sagdeev, and even about the martyrs—Grissom, Chafee, Komarov, Onizuka, Resnik, McAuliffe, and the others—it is no less about Robert Carlson and hundreds like him who have quietly offered their profound skills only to be just as quietly crushed, through no fault of their own, by the space gods.

No matter that Carlson was bright, energetic, hardworking, and extremely knowledgeable. He had the great misfortune to participate in an experiment on a planetary explorer that remained glued to Earth years after it should have been in space because of a degree of incompetence and mismanagement so great as to be almost unfathomable. The saga of this particular spacecraft amounts to a cautionary tale of what can happen to a project, however elegant, when its fate is left to the vagaries of partisan politics. Carlson and others who worked on Jupiter Orbiter-Probe were held hostage for more than a decade by people in Washington and elsewhere—the gods—whom they never even saw, let alone offended, but who nonetheless controlled their professional, and therefore personal, destinies: politicians, high-level space agency and defense planners, economists, OMB auditors, contractors, and others (including the designers of the shuttle's solid rocket boosters and those who decided that they were flight-ready on the morning of January 28, 1986).

Carlson's problem with JOP was not unlike taking a succession of steady losses at the gambling table or in the stock market; individually, each loss doesn't amount to enough to break the player or investor, so he stays in, hoping that his luck will change or his skill will improve to the point where he begins to win. So it was with Robert Carlson. There was no way of knowing when to get out. In the end, as he would come to admit, he had lost so much that he couldn't get out: there was no place to go.

Carlson had joined JPL in 1975. At the time, both Pioneers 10 and 11 had flown past Jupiter and the Voyagers were scheduled to follow. But a flyby, however close, was necessarily limited by its very nature. The spacecraft didn't hang around building data: it kept on going. As Lunar Orbiter had shown when it circled the Moon, and as Mariner 9 and the Viking orbiters had proven at Mars, however, hanging around—soaking up data during the course of repeated orbits—was the logical follow-up to a flyby.

Both Headquarters and JPL knew the value of orbiting and they wanted to do it at Jupiter, the planet that might have been a sun, the gateway to the solar system. They wanted to use the information sent back by the Pioneers and Voyagers to select the most promising scientific targets on Jupiter and then send out an advanced space-craft—with the exception of Viking, the most sophisticated space-craft ever made—to thoroughly scout the 89,000-mile-wide planet by orbiting it ten times in twenty-two months. But JOP would do even more than that. Rather than being "planet-specific," JOP would conduct a comprehensive survey of the entire Jovian system.

Not only that, but the orbiter would carry its own probe, the way landers were carried by the Pioneers and Veneras that went to Venus. Of course there was no possibility of landing on the great gas ball, as had been done on the terrestrial planets. But the Jupiter probe would nonetheless be released from the orbiter fifty days before encounter, plow into the Jovian atmosphere at 115,000 miles an hour, be slowed by parachute, and then relay data to the orbiter for about an hour before it succumbed to the thickening and increas-ingly deadly radioactive soup. The mother ship—the orbiter—would relay the information back to Earth just as was done by the Viking orbiters. Then the Jovian orbiter would continue on to do its own unparalleled orbital reconnaissance. Its highly elliptical orbit would allow repeated close encounters with Ganymede, Europa, Callisto, and Io, so they could be imaged in fine detail while intensive fields and particles experiments were conducted.

The idea for sending a follow-on mission to Jupiter gestated during the Apollo era and was articulated by James Van Allen's Science Working Group in 1976, even as the Vikings were heading for Mars and the Voyagers were being readied for what would turn out to be the beginning of the Grand Tour. By the spring of 1977 JOP was sufficiently shaped so it could be sent to Congress with a request for funding. But once inside the House Appropriations Subcommittee it ran into a rival for precious space science dollars: the Large Space Telescope.

The LST was the deep space astronomers' most cherished project because it promised to get them out once and for all from under the atmospheric distortions that shroud Earth. Its tenfold increase in resolution over the best ground-based instruments would open to

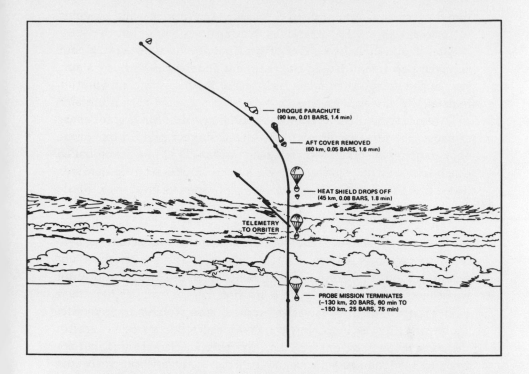

DROGUE PARACHUTE
(90 km, 0.01 BARS, 1.4 min)

AFT COVER REMOVED
(60 km, 0.05 BARS, 1.6 min)

HEAT SHIELD DROPS OFF
(45 km, 0.08 BARS, 1.8 min)

TELEMETRY
TO ORBITER

PROBE MISSION TERMINATES
(~130 km, 20 BARS, 60 min TO
~150 km, 25 BARS, 75 min)

view stars that are seven times farther away than those seen from Earth and objects that are fifty times fainter. The space telescope would allow astronomers to look far back in time, perhaps almost to the beginning of the universe. Having seen that the LST was not funded for fiscal 1977, the astronomers, as noted, bombarded Fletcher and key members of Congress with letters urging that the same mistake not be repeated in fiscal 1978 and threatening to withhold support for other programs if the telescope failed to make it on the Hill.

JOP had already been promised $21 million in start-up funding. But faced with recurring problems in the shuttle program, the Appropriations Subcommittee was loath to bankroll two new space science starts, so it bent to the astronomers' lobbying and appropriated $36 million for the LST while eliminating the Jupiter Orbiter-Probe. But the JOP group counterlobbied, both within NASA and in Congress, and finally got the original appropriation restored.

As matters stood in October 1977, the fifth trip to Jupiter (after the two Pioneers and two Voyagers) was to cost $410 million—$271 mil-

lion for development and $139 million for operations—and be ready
to go in January 1982 for arrival in 1984 and completion in 1986.

After more than two years of preliminary design work, NASA
received permission from Congress that October to start construction of the complicated spacecraft itself. But there were two problems at the outset.

The first, typically, had to do with funding. Total funding for space
science programs for fiscal 1978—the first year the orbiter-probe
showed up on the budget—was $404.7 million. That may have looked
like a lot, but when spread to cover several Earth-orbiting missions
(including the Explorer program, two orbiting observatories, Space
Lab, and the Space Telescope), plus sounding rockets, airborne research, balloons, data analysis, Pioneer, Viking, Voyager, support
research, and three separate bioscience programs, it became exceedingly thin. Space science, particularly as it related to planetary
exploration, was hemorrhaging. The new project's initial allocation
was therefore set at a paltry $21 million.

The Space Transportation System itself was problem number two.
To be sure, it was emptying the coffers of other space programs,
including planetary exploration. (Writing in *Scientific American*
early in 1986, James Van Allen, the most tenacious and respected
opponent of manned spaceflight, would decry the damage inflicted
on space science and exploration by the shuttle program, calling it
a "slaughter of the innocent.")

But in the case of the Jupiter Orbiter-Probe, there was a new
wrinkle. JOP, or Galileo, as it was renamed in 1978, was slated to be
the first planetary mission to ride the shuttle to space. Not only was
it financially strapped because of the Space Transportation System
but, unique among the planetary explorers (at that point), its actual
ability to get to space depended entirely upon the shuttle's getting
off the ground. It would suffer the consequences of any schedule
slippage because of the shuttle's development problems. Galileo
wasn't going anywhere without the shuttle. James Fletcher had seen
to it that nothing was going anywhere with the shuttle. It was as
simple as that.

The continuing sparseness of the science budget and the shuttle's
early birth pains were well known to Robert Carlson, to the scientists and engineers who worked with him, to everyone else at JPL,
and to the planetary exploration community as a whole. But neither
he nor they were oracles. They had no way of anticipating in 1977
and 1978 how bad things were going to get. Besides, as long as Galileo
remained a viable project—as in the old saw about life and hope—

they could continue to concentrate on their instruments in the splendid seclusion of their offices and labs and assume that the policymakers in Washington knew what they were doing (or, even if they didn't, that things would somehow work out anyway).

That was the way it was from 1977, when Carlson became principal investigator for his experiment, to 1982. He remembers the period as one of excitement, a "hectic" time in which he and the others raced to perfect the technology in time for that 1982 launch.

The near-infrared mapping spectrometer, combined in one experiment both spectroscopic and imaging capabilities and used a region of the infrared that, Carlson and his colleagues believed, would allow particularly good diagnostic analysis of Jupiter's surface and atmospheric features. Both of the instruments that combined to make up NIMS—a telescope and a spectrometer—had of course been around for a long time. But combining them in one system brought together the telescope's relatively high resolving power with the spectrometer's ability to analyze chemically important segments of satellite terrain and Jupiter's atmosphere.

The days were packed with intense, stimulating work, as the NIMS team tried to choose a path between being too careful and being "reckless," Carlson would recall nostalgically. "It was making sure that you weren't being too ambitious so that you couldn't deliver the product, and yet not being so conservative that you had an experiment that wouldn't be capable." He typically dropped his daughters off at school, got to JPL at about eight-thirty, worked there until five o'clock, went home with a briefcase full of papers relating to the next day's schedule, had dinner, and then worked some more: "sometimes until 9 o'clock, sometimes until midnight," he said. They were wonderfully busy days, with "lots and lots of meetings—meetings about everything—and lots and lots of paperwork and lots of talking on the telephone and responding to telephone calls." He spent many Saturdays on lab, too, "It was a rather consuming activity," Carlson said, "a busy time."

Busy, indeed. The challenge of exploring not just a planet but an entire planetary system was formidable. "We're really talking about exploring something that is the equivalent of a miniature solar system," Torrence V. Johnson, the Galileo project scientist, explained. "You've got a massive planet with, basically, starlike characteristics; you've got a set of planet-sized moons orbiting the thing, a very powerful magnetic field, and charged particles—things that make the Van Allen radiation belts look tame. So any exploration of the system really is an exploration of all aspects of the thing, plus their interconnections. I therefore tend to characterize Galileo as the first real exploration of an entire planetary system. And," he added, "that concept is what drives the complexity of the mission—the mission design—and spacecraft characteristics."

Galileo was originally conceived to ride a Titan-Centaur, as the Vikings and Voyagers had done. But that changed early on, when the shuttle-only rule was imposed. The engineers who got down to the business of actually committing Galileo to paper in October 1977 could take advantage of the shuttle's enormous power to design the heaviest and most complex planetary explorer ever produced by the United States. Furthermore, other design factors—how it was cushioned against vibration at launch, for example—were specifically suited to the shuttle, not to an expendable.

Galileo would weigh 5,620 pounds, be more than eighteen feet long (excluding its booms), and carry a record nineteen instruments, twelve of them on the orbiter and seven on the probe. The probe itself would be acorn-shaped, weigh 750 pounds, and be set inside a conical heat shield. The heat buildup would be so great that half of the probe's weight would consist of the ablative material necessary to insulate the instruments inside. It would be so severe, in fact, that new facilities had to be built at Ames to test several heat-shield materials. Ames would be responsible for managing development of the probe, with Hughes Aircraft designing and manufacturing it.

Except for the retropropulsion module (RPM), the orbiter would be built in-house at JPL. The RPM, which included ten small thrusters that would fire to adjust attitude control and make trajectory corrections, plus a more powerful thruster to insert the spacecraft into orbit around Jupiter, would be built by Messerschmitt-Bolkow-Blohm GMbH in West Germany (leading one wag at JPL to point out that NASA would therefore be first to send a Messerschmitt to space). In time, the attitude control and trajectory correction thrusters would develop their own problems, requiring extensive modification and ultimately contributing their share to the angst felt by Galileo's managers.

The spacecraft would also have a highly advanced telecommunications system, enough artificial intelligence so it could act autonomously for long periods, and a pair of powerful master computers. Galileo would also have the largest (sixteen feet) and most interesting high-gain antenna ever sent to another planet: it was made of gold-plated molybdenum mesh woven on a pantyhose machine (it would fly but not run).

The most challenging design problem had to do with stabilization. As usual, the fields and particles people wanted a full 360-degree single-axis sweep so that their instruments could collect unobstructed radiation from every direction. This would be particularly important for Jupiter, whose massive magnetosphere and intense field of radiation were largely responsible for the mission in the first place. But just as typically, the remote sensing investigators wanted a three-axis-stabilized platform so they could point their instruments at the planet and its moons to collect nice clear imagery from the camera, the photopolarimeter, and the two spectrometers (one of them being Carlson's).

The engineers at JPL solved the problem by coming up with something that was typically imaginative and audacious. Instead of choosing one type of stabilization or the other, as precedent would have had it, they gave it to both sides: they came up with a spacecraft that combined single-axis and three-axis stabilization, in effect creating a hybrid between Pioneer and Voyager.

Galileo was to be made of two parts, one of them "spun," the other "despun" (in the engineers' argot). The larger of the two, holding the big antenna, three long booms (two for radioisotope thermoelectric generators and one for the ubiquitous magnetometers), an eight-sided bus holding most of the orbiter's electronics, part of the command and data system, and the Germans' retropropulsion system, would be "spun." That is, it would spin. The other part, containing the scan platform, a radio relay antenna, five electronic equipment bays, another part of the command and data system, and the Ames/Hughes probe, would be "despun." That is, it would not spin.

In a way, then, Galileo would be like a man whose head remained stationary while his body kept rotating. Both parts would be connected by a single spin-bearing assembly containing the bearings upon which the spun part rotated. This was exceedingly clever. But it was also dangerous. If the spin-bearing assembly failed—if, for example, it seized up, or froze—Galileo's "head," the part with the camera and other remote sensors, would start spinning. The imaging equipment would therefore see everything as a blur, as if it were bolted to a merry-go-round. That, in turn, would force JPL to do some Voyager-like crisis engineering.*

*The contingency was anticipated. Engineers would then use the scan platform to point the imaging equipment in a direction parallel to the spin axis and then maneuver the spacecraft to point the spin axis to the target. In other words, the camera and other imaging sensors would be taking pictures in 360-degree swaths with every

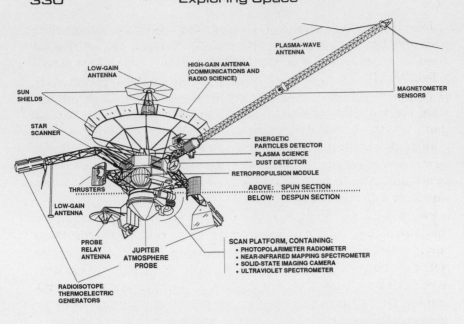

But the most problematic aspect of Galileo's voyage to Jupiter had to do with the fact of its going alone. Every explorer since Leif Ericson has believed implicitly in the safety of numbers, and those who planned the planetary missions were no exception. Not only did sending out two spacecraft increase the amount of information that was returned because it allowed for flexibility in selecting places to reconnoiter, but it provided insurance against a mission's collapse due to one spacecraft's becoming catastrophically disabled.

Not so with Galileo. There would be only one Galileo because there was no money for a second. And it would carry one camera, not the customary two, and but a single probe. A failure on any of these components could seriously impair the mission or end it altogether with no possibility for a second try.

But the fault tree had roots that went even deeper. Since the use of expendables was to be prohibited in favor of the shuttle, there was also only one way to get the spacecraft off Earth in the first place, and if that way failed, Galileo would be grounded. If the shuttle didn't work, and there was no other way of getting to space, a long line of spacecraft, military and civilian, would be stopped dead in their tracks like so many railroad cars behind a dead locomotive. This is called single-string failure, and it is the scourge of engineers everywhere.

rotation of the spacecraft's head. This would create substantial problems in several respects, but it could produce useful data.

John R. Casani, Galileo's project manager, was among those who from the beginning feared that total dependence on the shuttle greatly compounded the potential danger Galileo faced. Casani was a dedicated Dodgers fan as well as a politically astute engineer. Just as he understood the value of dependable relief pitching, he understood the value of dependable relief launch capability. He figured that if anything terrible ever did happen to the shuttle, Titan-Centaur would very likely go in as the relief launcher. During Galileo's formative design period, Casani therefore ordered his engineers to do nothing to the spacecraft that would keep it from fitting inside the shroud of a Titan-Centaur.

Indeed, JPL was so apprehensive about Galileo's dependence on the shuttle that on several occasions it tried to get Headquarters to buy it a Titan-Centaur exclusively for Galileo. But it got nowhere. Nobody told the Pasadenans in so many words that they couldn't have their own launch vehicle. Instead, Headquarters pointed out that the Titan-Centaur launch facility at the Kennedy Space Center had actually been dismantled. Since it required special equipment to handle the liquid oxygen and liquid hydrogen, getting the complex operating again would be unreasonably expensive, particularly since Galileo was at that time the only planetary exploration mission under active consideration.

Given the financial straits the space agency was in, Headquarters maintained, refurbishing the facility for a single mission would be prohibitive. If the Galileo project felt otherwise, however, it could pay for reconditioning the launch complex out of its own budget. And the same applied to buying one of the $80 million launch vehicles. If the Galileo program wanted a Titan-Centaur, Headquarters insisted, it would charge the giant rocket to the program. There was no other way such an expense could be justified for a single mission. Threatening to stick the project with such outlandish bills was also a not-so-subtle way of assuring that its team, like the shuttle's other customers, did not desert the Space Transportation System. "The shuttle was going to be the easy way to do it, the cheap way to do it, and the only way to do it," Torrence Johnson recalled with the barest trace of bitterness.

But the situation only worsened in the months and years that followed. Galileo and its embattled team were drawn into a deepening quagmire of contradictory orders, policy reversals, isolated decision making, and supposed fiscal restraints that simultaneously drove up the cost of the program and nearly brought it to ruin. The cumulative incompetence generated by the interaction of the White

House, Congress, the Department of Defense, and NASA was nothing short of stupefying.

There was the problem of how to get Galileo and other payloads on their way to their destinations after they had been disgorged by the shuttle, for example. The original plan for the Space Transportation System called for either the orbiter's remote manipulator system (its mechanical arm) or the astronauts themselves to remove Earth satellites or spacecraft bound for lunar and planetary missions and attach them to a "tug." The tug, like its nautical counterparts, was supposed to get them pointed in the right direction and then push them on their way. But the little workhorse fell early victim to the shuttle's lean budget.

NASA was therefore forced to improvise. The cheaper way to send Galileo and other spacecraft on their way from an orbiting shuttle was to attach an expendable minibooster to the bottom of each of them. It would fire them off in the proper direction and then detach. And the Air Force it turned out, had just such a device. It was first called an Interim Upper Stage, and then an Inertial Upper Stage, or IUS. The IUS was essentially a squat solid-fuel two-stage booster that would fit inside the shuttle.

The space agency was forced to try to adapt the IUS for its own shuttle operations. NASA soon found that the Air Force's minibooster was not powerful enough to give Galileo the push it needed to get to Jupiter, so the space agency tried adding a third stage onto it, but that did not work out very well either. Meanwhile, the airmen countered that Galileo weighed too much. At that point, JPL trajectory engineers began thinking that the only way they were going to be able to get their spacecraft on its way to Jupiter before the 1982 launch opportunity ended was to use the IUS to boost it to Mars, where it could pick up the necessary velocity through gravity assist to make it the rest of the way.

But there was no point in worrying about how to launch from the shuttle if there was no shuttle to launch from. Galileo was one of the spacecraft that were grounded because of the orbiter's recurring engine and tile problems. As they continued through 1978, it became increasingly clear that there could be no launch in 1982. Headquarters informed JPL accordingly, though no new launch date was set. John Casani's nagging concern about dependence on the Space Transportation System was turning out to be fully justified.

In January 1980 Headquarters decided to go for an early 1984 launch, but because the opportunity was less favorable than the one in 1982—Mars was not quite so well positioned—it also decided to split the mission. The orbiter would be sent on one IUS and use a Mars gravity assist for a twenty-eight-month flight. The lighter probe would then be launched thirteen months later on another IUS and use a direct trajectory to get to Jupiter, which it would reach about four months after the orbiter. Both launches, of course, were supposed to be from shuttles. And both the orbiter and the probe were scheduled to arrive in 1986.

"So what happens to the mission?" an incredulous John Casani asked rhetorically. "First of all, the cost of launching it doubles because we need two launch vehicles. The launch is delayed two years, and that increases the cost of the mission. And we have to develop a new vehicle to carry the probe: something called a probe-carrier." The carrier would have to be designed specifically to cradle the probe inside the shuttle's payload bay. The $410 million mission had suddenly become a $650 million mission "with no real increased value," he added. Nevertheless, JPL got to work on the changes, and specifically on planning both direct assent and Mars gravity assist trajectories for the probe and the orbiter.

In 1981 the planetary exploration program ran headlong into Reaganomics, and came out eviscerated. Reagan's would be the only administration since the space age began that did not send a single exploring machine to the Sun, the Moon, or the planets—not one in eight years. Supply-side economics, which tried to shrink government spending while bolstering the corporate sector, required space science's incredible shrinking purse to be drawn still tighter. With Stockman looking to chop millions from the space agency's budget, and Keyworth and Mark threatening to stop planetary exploration altogether, Galileo was once again perilously close to a death sentence.

Meanwhile, the IUS, which the Air Force had originally said it could develop at a cost of only $100 million, was now being projected at $900 million or more. But Congress would have none of that. It ordered NASA to abandon the expensive upper stage and instead adapt the by-then-proven Centaur to the shuttle for the Galileo mission.

The switch from the IUS to Centaur required reengineering the hardware and fundamentally changing the mission. Since the liquid-fuel Centaur was so much more powerful than the solid-fuel IUS, JPL could go back to where it had started from: a single payload on a direct trajectory. The plan for a dual launch, with the orbiter using

Mars gravity assist, and the probe going directly to Jupiter with a push by an IUS, had been painstakingly worked out in Pasadena. It was now sent to the lab's large wastepaper compactor. Then the time-consuming and expensive task of readapting Galileo to Centaur and Centaur to the shuttle was begun. Launch was now scheduled for 1985, with arrival in 1987. And the cost jumped again, to $695 million.

But late in 1981 the space agency decided that because of OMB and congressional cutbacks affecting other programs, there were really too few missions to justify adapting Centaur only for them and for Galileo. It therefore canceled its order for the powerful booster. Back to the IUS.

This time, Headquarters ordered a standard Air Force two-stage IUS and ordered Pasadena to develop an auxiliary upper stage, known as an injection module. The two-stage IUS was less powerful than either the three-stage IUS or Centaur. Galileo, it seemed, would have to use Earth instead of Mars for a gravity assist. This meant that Galileo would be fired in an elliptical orbit around the Sun, which would take two years to complete. It would then fly back to Earth, picking up additional velocity, and finally head right for Jupiter. Another trajectory therefore had to be worked out.

But it meant a great deal more than that. It also meant, as it did every time Galileo's course was altered, that the sequencing which was worked out with meticulous precision by the science teams also had to be changed. Not only did the time allotted to each experiment that was going to be done on the way to Jupiter require adjustment, but the fact that the spacecraft was to go around the Sun and then swing past Earth opened a whole range of other investigative possibilities.

The new trajectory, called Delta (meaning "change") VEGA (velocity Earth gravity assist) would require a fifty-two-month cruise. Galileo was now scheduled to leave Earth in 1985 and arrive at Jupiter in 1989. The mission's cost jumped to $834 million, $122 million of which would be consumed just by virtue of the additional time it would take to get to Jupiter.

But late in 1982 Congress, concerned about the amount of money that would be wasted by so long a flight to Jupiter, changed signals yet again. It ordered NASA to cancel the two-stage IUS and return to Centaur for a twenty-eight-month direct-trajectory cruise. Once again, the tricky job of adapting the volatile booster to the shuttle and to the spacecraft it was supposed to launch at Jupiter was begun.

This essentially put the mission back to where it had been before Headquarters and the OMB canceled Centaur a year earlier. This was as JPL wanted it. But the triumph was a small one because it came with still another time penalty. Centaur development had been interrupted for the better part of a year, so gearing up again meant that the launch would slip once more, this time to the spring of 1986. Galileo was now scheduled to arrive at Jupiter in December 1988, at a total mission cost projected to be $874 million.

And that was where matters seemed to stand by the spring of 1983. The shuttle manifest had Galileo scheduled for the thirty-eighth mission, due to leave from the Kennedy Space Center on May 21, 1986. It was supposed to be carried to a 130-mile-high orbit by Atlantis, according to the plan, and then be sent on its way by a Centaur.

Galileo's vexatious, wasteful five-year-long roller-coaster ride finally seemed to be over by that spring. Robert Carlson, like the rest of his colleagues, spent his days trying to perfect his experiment, bond with the others on his science team as well as with those outside it, and anticipate the data his mapping spectrometer was supposed to start returning in five years' time. Although he could have published research articles in areas other than the one that captivated him, he chose not to do so, concentrating instead on doing his best to ensure that NIMS would perform flawlessly at Jupiter. Then, he told himself, there would be any number of good solid papers to be published in the most reputable journals.

In mid-December 1985, as prospects for the launch continued to look good, the Galileo Project Office threw a "Movin' On" party at the Pasadena Civic Center, downtown. A large room was decorated with red, white, and green balloons and filled with 525 scientists, secretaries, engineers, administrators and others who were bound to each other not only by their pride in the project but by the Sisyphean nightmare that had been inflicted on them through no fault of their own for so long it had come to seem normal.

The Galileo people sat around large tables, danced to a disc jockey's "Mobile Music Service," and went through a buffet of chicken à la king, cheese-stuffed potatoes, peas with pimientos and mushrooms, and chocolate cake. They laughed and chatted animatedly around the tables or stood clustered in small groups, trying to shake off their long-endured demoralization. It was beginning to sink in that the end of Galileo's long period of house arrest in the Spacecraft Assembly Facility was practically at hand. Galileo was almost gone, soon to be spirited off to the Cape on a modified furniture truck, there to be readied for its rendezvous with destiny. The defeat of the gods seemed imminent.

John Casani, a veteran of Pioneers 3 and 4, Rangers 1 and 2, Mariner Mars 1964 and 1969, and the Voyager Project, had spent an appalling amount of time commuting back East to testify on the Hill, or plan strategy at Headquarters, or fend off attacks, all to keep the project alive. In the United States, in the 1980s, the project manager of a planetary explorer was a lawyer for a robot who had to keep pleading to stave off his client's execution. It had been a wearying, dispiriting business.

But now, decked out in a soft brown leather jacket and surrounded by his friends and colleagues, apparently closer to triumph than ever, Casani looked about as contented as he ever got. This was the moment, in the spirit of the holidays, to thank all for what they had done for the project and to ring in 1986 on an upbeat note. "We've got a great spacecraft," John Casani told the happy crowd that Friday the thirteenth, as it watched him silently from around the room. "We've got a great team. And from here on, we have only one way to go, and that's up, and we're on our way."

The week before Christmas, Galileo was taken from the clean room where it had been put together, a seventy-foot by seventy-foot cavern called High Bay 2 in JPL's Spacecraft Assembly Facility, and loaded onto a truck bound for Florida. Workmen wearing the technological equivalent of surgical garb labored under 19,200 watts of light coming from forty-eight mercury-xenon lamps to get the spacecraft into a specially built climatized aluminum container and then onto a truck that would be its life-support system during the journey to the Kennedy Space Center.

The trip began at 3:00 A.M. on December 19. The truck itself was a specially built tractor-trailer that had an air-ride suspension, temperature and humidity monitors with alarms, and air conditioners and heaters. It left Pasadena as part of a convoy whose constant escort included police and state troopers in patrol cars with flashing lights and government security officers armed with shotguns and automatic rifles.* Four days later its exhausted and edgy drivers—

*Federal law requires that shipments of radioactive material be moved under armed guard. The possibility that potential terrorists would try to hijack the plutonium was an obvious source of concern. But NASA also worried that thrill-seekers might take potshots at it simply because it was a moving target, or members of extremist political or environmental groups might try to stop it for ideological reasons.

engineers who spelled each other continuously day and night, stopping only for food and gasoline—pulled into the space center with
their fragile cargo. They were then let go for the holiday.

There was another party, this one at the Kennedy Space Center,
on January 24. It was thrown after four days had been spent filling
Galileo's tanks with the highly volatile hydrazine. But the party
wasn't given to celebrate the end of the dangerous operation. Its
purpose was to introduce the sixty-odd people from JPL to those of
their counterparts at Kennedy who would soon be preparing Galileo
for mating with the orbiter Atlantis and doing the countless other
things that were required before the May launch.

If both groups were going to work smoothly to send the spacecraft
on its way, it was thought, some socializing was a good way to begin.
A barbecue seemed perfect. And it was. The event was held at the
end of the workday, against a setting Sun that turned the horizon
vermillion, and talk was lively. The Californians and Floridians
exchanged stories, as workers in far-flung enterprises do when they
collect for a meeting. Mostly, they chatted about the mundane frustrations, minor victories, and perverse pleasures they got from what
they did.

With a single exception, and an apparently small one at that, the
barbecue went quite well. The exception had to do with the weather.
It was turning very cold. Out on Pad 39B, in the heavy darkness that
was creeping in from the Atlantic, Challenger stood waiting.

Between noon and 4 o'clock on the afternoon of the explosion—with
smoke still in the air and debris floating on the sparkling sea just out
of sight beyond the beach—Casani decided that under the circumstances, the most important thing he had to do right there and then
was hold the project together. With thoughts of the Challenger
crew's families and his own extended family at JPL racing in his
head, he called the JPL contingent together. The Pasadenans were
bewildered and numb, some still not believing what they had seen
happen practically above their heads. Others believed it to the point
of sobbing.

"I knew it was going to be a while before we got any direction. We
decided, in terms of what we were about, that probably the best thing
to do was continue doing what we were doing as if nothing happened," he would recall later. "How to keep four hundred people
working? How to keep them directed and focused, doing something
useful and rewarding, and not just something that they would think
would just be make-work?"

• • •

Thirteen months after Challenger blew up, Galileo, once again in its box, was returned to Pasadena. The world's most advanced planetary explorer had now made two voyages. But it had yet to fly an inch.

Nor was it clear during the weeks following the end of STS-51L when it would do so. Some believed that a relatively quick fix would get the shuttles back to space in a matter of months. As the Rogers Commission took testimony and collected evidence that spring, however, an early launch began to look more and more remote. James Van Allen, who had no experiment on Galileo, but who nevertheless was one of the mission's interdisciplinary investigators, mused that its plight reminded him of *The Perils of Pauline,* the silent film in which the heroine repeatedly escaped death by the narrowest of margins.

Meanwhile, Galileo was aging. Once back in High Bay 2, it was taken apart and minutely inspected. Some of the spacecraft's components were tested and seen to be nearing the end of their useful lives. Tapes that insulated electrical systems were losing their adhesive properties, some electrical cables were losing their flexibility, metal parts were corroding, and various sealing rings were fracturing. All of the defective or potentially defective parts had to be replaced. This was far from an easy feat given the fact, for example, that Galileo had almost twenty-five thousand feet of electrical cable and more than seven hundred connectors. In addition, the science instruments, including Carlson's mapping spectrometer, had to be removed and returned to their experimenters for modification and recalibration.

More worrisome, the radioisotope thermoelectric generators' forty-eight pounds of plutonium had been decaying, so they were producing less power. The engineers therefore had to figure out a way to get the same amount of work out of Galileo with less power. The RTGs were soon to develop political problems as well.

But that wasn't the worst of it. There was almost no doubt that one more disaster like Challenger would ground the surviving shuttles indefinitely, killing the space station in the process, and effectively driving the last nail in NASA's coffin. In that light, the gods began to see a shuttle-adapted Centaur not so much as a powerful space booster but as a flying bomb. It was not that there was a problem with Centaur per se. Rather, it was considered so poorly integrated with shuttle operations as to pose a serious potential danger.

The reason for this could be traced back, at least in part, to yet another managerial blunder by NASA. Instead of treating Centaur as an integral part of the shuttle itself, and therefore subject to the safety considerations inherent in the basic operation of the space-craft, it had been thought of as being merely another payload, a separate artifact. It was therefore modified for the shuttle under the direction of the cargo integration staff at the Johnson Space Center in Houston, rather than by the shuttle project management staff. Johnson, formerly the Manned Spacecraft Center, is responsible for the development of manned spacecraft. Casani has called this "arm's length" management. "The problem was understaffing at JSC [Johnson Space Center]," he said. "These problems could have, should have, and would have been caught earlier with Centaur if JSC had chosen to treat Centaur as an element of the shuttle instead of as a cargo element."

Two months after the accident, NASA's chief engineer, Milton A. Silveira, sent a six-page memorandum to Rear Admiral Richard H. Truly, who headed the shuttle program, making the same point. Silveira cited an alarming number of waivers involving critical Centaur flight safety items, inadequate hazard reports, several management changes in the preceding two years, and "less than desirable" reports on ground safety requirements, at places including the Kennedy Space Center itself. He recommended that if Centaur was to continue as part of the shuttle program, it had to be considered not a payload but a "shuttle program element."

In addition, the $1 billion program was experiencing cost overruns of $250 million because of the shuttle modifications, some of which were proving to be especially thorny. Unlike the Centaurs that had been flying to space on Atlases and Titans for twenty years, for example, those that would be carried on shuttles would have to have special "dump valves" so that their twenty-two tons of propellant could be jettisoned in case the spacecraft had to return to Earth for an emergency landing with a Centaur still on board. But General Dynamics was running into serious problems with the valve's reliability, driving up the cost of the modification program. The end finally came on June 19, 1986, five months after the accident, when NASA formally announced that it was abandoning plans to use Centaurs in the Space Transportation System.

Back to the two-stage IUS. Centaur would have delivered forty-five thousand pounds of thrust and gotten Galileo to Jupiter on a direct ascent in about two and a half years, just as it had done with the

Voyagers. Its considerable power would have made a direct approach to Jupiter feasible. The IUS, on the other hand, produced only about twenty-one thousand pounds of thrust and could therefore not get Galileo to Jupiter on a direct trajectory. After considering several possibilities, Roger Diehl, a trajectory specialist at JPL, dusted off the Delta velocity Earth gravity assist idea and substantially modified it.

VEEGA—Venus-Earth-Earth gravity assist—required Galileo to be launched not in the direction of Earth's motion around the Sun but against it. That would slow the spacecraft to the point where it would in effect fall toward the Sun. But it would never get there. Instead, it would meet Venus and whip around it at an altitude of 12,428 miles, increasing its velocity by about one and a half miles a second.

Assuming that Galileo was launched in October 1989, which came to be the plan, it would reach Venus in February 1990. The spacecraft would then head back toward Earth, swinging around it that December at an altitude of 2,237 miles. It would then pick up a little more than three extra miles a second before heading toward the asteroid belt. Out there, Galileo would be turned until it described a long ellipse and headed back toward the mother planet. In early December 1992, Diehl calculated, Galileo could make a final Earth flyby, skimming over the planet at a height of only 186 miles and picking up slightly more than two additional miles a second. The trip to Venus, then to Earth, then out to the asteroids, and then back to Earth once again would take thirty-seven months. And it would take almost exactly that long for Galileo to complete the final leg to Jupiter, with arrival (appropriately enough) scheduled for Pearl Harbor Day 1995. That would be thirty years after it was conceived and twenty after it was initially approved.

In order to put the best possible face on what had turned into a tragicomedy of Wagnerian proportions, the space agency found other things for Galileo to do on its way to Jupiter. It would collect some data at Venus and Earth, and from two of four large asteroids—Ausonia, Ortrud, Gaspra, and Ida—that would happen to be nearby during the fifteen months it was supposed to spend passing in and out of their belt.

From the point of view of the scientists, a swing by the Sun on the way to Jupiter seemed like a pretty good idea; it amounted to a two-for-one sale at which they could pick up free data. The engineers and project officials at JPL, however, were less enthusiastic. Besides the obvious problem of having to rework the trajectory yet again, they were faced with changing the spacecraft itself. Galileo had been designed to go from Earth to Jupiter—from a warm environment to a progressively colder one. But sending it to the Sun first meant that it would initially head from a warm climate to a very hot one, a situation that of course had not been considered by the spacecraft's original designers. Galileo would have to be fitted with an elaborate sunshade to keep it from baking. And even at that, no one could be absolutely certain it would come out of its rendezvous with Venus unharmed.

So the loss of Centaur, reappearance of the relatively puny IUS, and new route to Jupiter required still more modifications for the orbiter and its probe. Rather than going away from the Sun, as was originally planned, VEEGA would bring Galileo so close to it that the spacecraft would be exposed to three times the amount of solar radiation received on Earth. It therefore had to be protected from being roasted and from the barrage of deadly particles by thermal shielding and sunshades to cover the bus, the instruments, the magnetometer boom, and the antennas.

Normally, the antennas would point toward Earth, but during the launch to Venus and swing-back-toward-Earth phase of the mission they would have to be pointed toward the Sun for thermal control reasons. This meant the antennas would be unusable for several hundred days, so a third antenna had to be attached to one of the RTG booms in order to be certain that the communications link with the spacecraft did not break. Nor did the changes end there.

There was a good possibility that the science boom sunshade would block the Sun sensor used for navigation, so a second Sun sensor had to be considered. And since Galileo was now to fly close to Earth, its large high-gain antenna had to be made to close to prevent damage from solar heating; open, it would act like a large solar collector and therefore become damaged. It would be opened again, like a beach umbrella, once Galileo was safely past Earth. The mission planners didn't like that because opening and closing the antenna—working the mechanism—invited single point failure. If the antenna stuck in the closed position the mission was over.

And there were still more changes. The adapter ring had to be altered to bolt onto the IUS rather than the Centaur. Coolant lines to the RTGs had to be rearranged, and so did the umbilical wires that carried electrical commands between Galileo and the IUS. The materials used to fabricate several parts of the spacecraft had to be changed because of its new operating environment. And the sequencing had to be reshuffled as well because of Galileo's complicated new route. A new spin rate sensor had to be installed, since the original would not work when the spacecraft was pointed directly at the Sun. A new attitude control system, one that worked inside Earth orbit, also had to be added. The thermal control system had to undergo major changes, including the replacement of active electric heaters with small passive ones. This was necessary because the electric heaters ran off the RTGs, whose power kept diminishing as time passed.

Meanwhile the probe was sent back to its manufacturer, the Hughes Aircraft Company in El Segundo, for refurbishing. The parachute that would slow it as it entered Jupiter's atmosphere had to be rebuilt, as did its batteries, the cartridge that was supposed to deploy the chute, and other parts. This was estimated by Ames to cost a mere $1.5 million. Casani estimated that alterations to the orbiter, plus a three-and-a-half-year launch delay that required its continuous "care and feeding," totaled an additional $200 million. As of October 1987, according to a General Accounting Office estimate, the overall cost of the mission had increased by $952.4 million, to $1.36 billion.

To further complicate matters, there was also an ongoing controversy over Galileo's radioisotope thermoelectric generators. Although RTGs had been used on the Apollo, Viking, Pioneer, and Voyager missions without mishap, their use as power sources on Galileo had special significance for two reasons.

First, unlike its predecessors, Galileo was supposed to be launched from the shuttle, and studies in the wake of the Challenger accident indicated that the chances of another catastrophic mishap were only one in seventy-eight (down from one hundred thousand). It was feared that a similar explosion with an RTG-powered spacecraft in the payload bay would scatter deadly radioactive debris over a widely populated area around Canaveral. The half-life of the plutonium-238 used in the RTGs was eighty-eight years. Within two months after the Challenger explosion, in fact, the Energy Department released previously classified documents estimating that such an occurrence would contaminate up to 386 square miles of land and cause forty-three cancer deaths over a fifty-year period.* James J.

*David Morrison has taken exception to those numbers. They would be valid only if the plutonium was scattered over a wide area, which would not be the case, he has asserted in an annotation on the manuscript that became this book.

Lombardo, director of the DOE's Office of Special Applications, was quoted as saying that the risk to people in communities around Canaveral was "like the risk of being hit by lightning, or even less than that." He added, however, that the department's risk estimates would be reevaluated in the wake of the Challenger accident.

NASA also considered launching Galileo only when prevailing winds were blowing toward the sea if doing so could be shown to make a substantial difference in the risk level. A subsequent analysis showed that it would make no appreciable difference at all, according to Casani. (Still, there would have been a certain irony, harking back to Kepler, if the launch of an exploring machine bound for outer space had been held until a favorable breeze came along.)

Second, opponents of nuclear energy expressed fear that Galileo might plunge back into Earth's atmosphere as it streaked in low on the last leg of its gravity assist. As it disintegrated, the reasoning went, the RTGs would come apart, leaving a wake of radioactivity spread over much of the planet. The most vociferous of the antinuclear groups, the Florida Coalition for Peace and Justice, went so far as to publish a fund-raising brochure in the spring of 1989 that called Galileo a "bomb pointed at Earth." "While we might survive the Galileo or even the Ulysses,* we clearly understand that it only takes one Challenger-type explosion at launch or one Chernobyl accident in space to destroy life on our fragile planet," the brochure warned.

NASA wasted no time in counterattacking. One space agency official charged the coalition with preying on public fears and using scare tactics in order to raise funds. The space agency maintained that the RTGs' modular construction and triple encapsulation virtually guaranteed that they would survive a launch explosion intact and that their chances of reentering the atmosphere during closest approach were on the order of one in ten million. A fact sheet distributed to the news media asserted that the explosive pressure inside the shuttle's payload bay was well below the pressure of two thousand pounds per square inch to which the RTGs were tested and that, in any case, a rupture would cause only an estimated one-in-ten-million possibility of fewer than ten cancer fatalities in a population of seventy thousand in seventy years.

*Ulysses, originally known as the International Solar Polar mission, was the joint European Space Agency–NASA project to explore the Sun from above and below its poles. At the time the coalition was distributing its brochure, Ulysses, which carried one relatively large RTG, was scheduled for launch in the autumn of 1990.

Van Allen, showing some impatience with yet another obstacle to the Jupiter mission, asserted on television that were he in charge of Galileo, he would be more than happy to "sign off" on the safety of its nuclear power system.

But the coalition insisted that it was not convinced. It let it be known that it planned to picket and disrupt the spacecraft's launch. More noteworthy, though, was the absence of the larger, established environmental groups. Friends of the Earth, the Natural Resources Defense Council, the Sierra Club, and even the more aggressive Greenpeace would have nothing to do with protesting, let alone interfering with, Galileo's launch (though Greenpeace had a boat several miles offshore). Still, it seemed as though the gods would never let Galileo go.

Workers in the Galileo project office responded to the seemingly interminable delays with grim humor. They had organized an all-day Pre-Launch Picnic at a local park back in August of 1986, featuring softball and volleyball competition, as well as a wheelbarrow and other traditional contests (a "Guess the asteroids" game lent a distinctly JPL flavor to the festivities, however). There would be four such picnics, all marked by special T-shirts depicting the great astronomer, through the summer of 1989.

Back in 1983, Galileo had begun to take the edge off Robert Carlson's disposition. It didn't happen all at once. But slowly, imperceptibly, his attitude about the project became infected as it relentlessly wore him down. He no longer felt exhilarated. He felt trapped.

By his own reckoning, Carlson's enthusiasm for the mission to Jupiter had caused him to put too much time into the near-infrared mapping spectrometer and not enough into other areas. Except for some warmed-over research from his days at USC having to do with measurements of the Sun in the ultraviolet, and a little on data from Pioneer 11, there were no papers to speak of. And that, Carlson reflected in the winter of 1988—thirteen years after NIMS had been accepted by NASA—had been a serious mistake.

So the long hours gave way to regular workdays, and Saturdays were increasingly devoted to rock climbing and mountaineering. Both offered immediate gratification, he explained. Once every six months or so, his frustration would build to the point where he would do a lot of "swearing and cussing" at his wife, Kathie. "I allowed myself to get depressed," he added.

He and many others at JPL also allowed themselves to pick up desultory work with the Pentagon's Strategic Defense Initiative Office in the aftermath of Challenger. Carlson and several of his colleagues thought of Star Wars the way people who are impoverished think of consorting with rich but unsavory relatives: they weren't particularly proud of what they did, but the money was good, there was a little useful scientific spinoff, and it helped pass the time until something better came along.

He spent nine months working on a project called Pathfinder in which ballistic missile heat plumes were to be precisely tracked by infrared detectors that were to have been mounted on the shuttle and then on a satellite. Pathfinder was ultimately canceled, which Carlson thought altogether appropriate. Before that, however, he met with Air Force representatives on several occasions, all of them disquieting. "At one meeting they'd want to send up decoys and track them. Another time they'd want to put a radar experiment on. Another time they'd want an active laser experiment. Those guys were in technological heaven, dreaming up things you couldn't build in a year. It was more or less thought of as a joke. It was really an interim situation for most of us," Carlson explained. "We thought those guys were off the wall, unrealistic, and more or less crazy.

"I should have spent more time publishing, and not so much time getting involved—intensely involved—in this experiment," he said, getting back to NIMS. "If the Challenger accident didn't happen, we'd be launched and on our way now, and that'd be fine. But it's just dragging on and on and on. You can't just walk away from it," he added, because that wouldn't be responsible. "And my scientific credentials haven't been enhanced by this long period. It's publish or perish in a lot of places, and if you don't, then you can't just walk in somewhere and have someone offer you a job. You're basically stuck in science."

Lonne Lane's credentials, together with those of many others, weren't enhanced either by the Galileo fiasco and the loss of Challenger. "People such as myself, who are in their mid-40s, had planned an organized progression of a career. With missions that last twenty years, or ten years . . . All of a sudden, you find that there's a hiatus that represents, in the case of Galileo, close to ten years," Lane explained. "How do you keep the progression of knowledge and research interest alive?"

Moustafa Chahine, JPL's chief scientist, saw the broader panorama from his office on the ninth floor of the administration building. Chahine, slightly built and soft-spoken, brooded over what he saw. "This know-how, which was established through great struggle between JPL and NASA, which has helped us in the past twenty years or so, is about to disappear. We worry about this a lot. We are the only center in the U.S.A. with this capability. Now," he added in reference to the scientists and engineers who had been around since the Mariner days, "they are either retiring or doing something else. We are in a steady decline.

"Take Carlson. What can he do? The field of space science is very narrow. Can he go to work for a bank? A company? He has to go and teach, basically. But he can't go to a university because he doesn't have publications. He can go and teach in high school. So he goes, and he looks at himself, and he says: 'Do I teach in junior high, or high school, or do I continue this gamble?' He is chained."

Nor would Carlson's and the others' efforts as high school teachers be particularly appreciated, at least in Chahine's personal experience. The day before Chahine offered his observations on Carlson and on the demoralization of JPL, his son graduated from the local high school with high honors. La Cañada High, less than half a mile from the lab's main gate, has a student population at least half of which comes from JPL families. The frustrations those young men and women heard about at home spilled over at school: La Cañada students routinely compared horror stories.

Just before graduation, Mous Chahine said, an achievement awards banquet for 120 of the school's 320 graduating seniors was held at the local country club. Each student, in turn, took a moment to talk about his or her career plans. "There wasn't one single person who said space science—not one. And these are the people who got the achievement awards," he added wearily. Tony Chahine earned straight A's in physics, mathematics, English, and other subjects. "But when I asked him what he wants to do," Chahine sighed, his son answered, " 'I don't know, but not what you do.' "

As the October 1989 launch window approached, the trouble-plagued spacecraft's problems continued almost without interruption. On August 15, a compressor at the Kennedy Space Center that was supposed to pump dry temperature-controlled air to both the spacecraft and its inertial upper stage malfunctioned and, instead, sent them humid air, which could have adversely affected the IUS's performance. Electrical tests showed that no damage had been done.

Then, on September 28 the antinuclear groups that had warned they would go to court to prevent Galileo's launch made good on their threat. The suit requesting an injunction, filed in Federal District Court in Washington, gave Galileo the dubious distinction of being the first civilian spacecraft to have its launch challenged in court. "After the Challenger explosion, Chernobyl and the [Exxon] Valdez accident, we have learned that technology can go terribly wrong," said Bruce Gagnon of the Florida Coalition for Peace and Justice, one of the parties to the suit. Jeremy Rifkin, the activist whose Foundation on Economic Trends was another party, maintained that there was one chance in 430 that plutonium would be released in an accident. Once again, the major public interest groups were nowhere to be seen. To the contrary, a senior research analyst with the Federation of American Scientists, an independent, politically liberal organization, said he believed that "the risk is small and the scientific payoff is large."

Dudley G. McConnell, the NASA official in charge of Galileo's environmental impact statement, made it plain that he thought Rifkin's figure was nonsense; that it was "no number that we recognize." He countered that the space agency did two of its own analyses, neither of which found a significant risk.

On October 10, two days before the scheduled launch and with activist groups picketing at the Kennedy Space Center's main gate, Judge Oliver Gasch ruled that NASA had complied with environmental requirements and refused to grant a restraining order against the launch. In making his decision, Gasch noted that were he to rule for the plaintiffs, it would probably cause Galileo to miss its window, which closed on November 21. The next opportunity would not come until 1991. Answering the assertion that NASA did not have enough data about the risks of an accident, Gasch quipped, "I suppose Columbus didn't have that much data either."

But that night, with a court victory in hand, the space agency discovered that the computer regulating the amount of fuel and oxygen burned by one of Atlantis's three main engines was faulty and would have to be replaced. A new one was installed and tested. On Saturday, the fourteenth, Atlantis was once again pronounced fit to fly, with a new launch date set for Tuesday, the seventeenth.

Then it was the weather's turn. The seventeenth dawned with thick clouds and showers just north of Launch Complex 39B, upon which Atlantis stood. While the weather in the immediate launch area was marginally satisfactory, the clouds and showers were directly over the runway on which Atlantis would have to land if it got into trouble right after launch. Liftoff was delayed once again. The postponement was taken to be a mixed blessing by some at NASA when it was learned that a rogue computer program had attacked part of the space agency's worldwide computer network only two days before. The attacking program, which was designed to copy itself and send unwanted, sometimes vulgar messages, caused no damage but nevertheless forced NASA to disconnect several of its links because of potential trouble. Security experts speculated that the program might have been written by someone who opposed Atlantis's launch.

Even Earth itself seemed determined not to let go of Galileo. Late on that afternoon of the seventeenth, one of the worst earthquakes ever to hit California struck the San Francisco area—just hours before the spacecraft's scheduled liftoff—causing heavy damage in parts of the Bay area and in much of Silicon Valley, immediately to the south.

One of the buildings affected by the quake happened to be the Air Force's supersecret Consolidated Space Test Center, a six-story windowless structure hard beside Route 101 in Sunnyvale. The Big Blue Cube, as it is called, operates all U.S. reconnaissance satellites. In addition, it is responsible for providing final state vector updates for all Air Force rocket launches. These are computer calculations showing where the rocket is at all times and where it is supposed to go. Since the IUS to which Galileo was bolted belonged to the Air Force, it was included in the category of boosters whose vectors had to be updated by the Cube. The quake cracked walls and broke a water pipe at the center, the Air Force acknowledged, and also forced the evacuation for an hour of the section that was supposed to monitor Atlantis's launch. Technicians had to work all night checking the powerful computers before they reported to NASA at 2:00 A.M. Wednesday that Galileo would not have to be put on hold yet again.

After a four-minute delay caused by threatening clouds that eventually blew away, Atlantis finally roared into space at 12:54 P.M. the following day, Wednesday the eighteenth. The sky into which it headed was so clear that it could be followed with the unaided eye for at least five minutes—a rare event in shuttle launches—or until it reached a hundred miles out over the Atlantic.

Five hours and fifteen minutes later Atlantis, its payload bay doors open, was turned so that its belly faced the Sun and its nose pointed toward celestial north. An hour and six minutes later, with the shuttle cruising 160 miles above the Pacific, springs released

Galileo and its IUS so they rose gently out of the hold and pushed away from the orbiter. Sixty minutes after separation, with Atlantis maneuvered safely out of the way, the first-stage rocket motor behind Galileo automatically ignited and, its burn completed almost two and a half minutes later, separated. Then the IUS's second stage kicked in, slowing it down so it could begin falling into the inner solar system, toward Venus. Next, the spacecraft's seventeen-foot RTG and science instrument booms were deployed. Its thirty-six-foot-long magnetometer boom was also extended. Then Galileo started to follow Magellan, which had been launched five months earlier, on the first leg of its odyssey to Venus.

Those who gave the spacecraft its name did so with the hope that, in its own way, it would reflect the life and accomplishments of the great Italian astronomer. Yet they could scarcely have imagined that, like him, it would be severely tested and subjected to a long period of enforced confinement. The space gods exacted an inordinately heavy toll on that particular exploring machine and on those who developed it. But if Carlson, Casani, Chahine, and the other veterans of the "Movin' On" party were thinking about that, they weren't saying. Galileo was finally movin' on.

Astropolitics: No Parades for Robots

In the most honest of all possible worlds there would be two monuments, standing side by side, at the Kennedy Space Center. One would be dedicated to the Soviet space program; the other to the news media of the United States. A common tablet might read: "Without whose presence this establishment might not exist."

As NASA's programs have competed for years with their Soviet counterparts, they have also been sustained by them. It is fair to speculate, in fact, that had there been no Soviets, they probably would have had to have been invented. This is not to say that the United States would not have a civilian space program if not for the Soviet presence in space. But in a fundamental sense the Soviets boosted NASA's various programs almost as much as the space agency did itself.

Conversely, one of the great ironies of the "space race" is the fact that in both the military and civilian sectors, initial Soviet triumphs (or the appearance of them), accompanied by unbridled boasting, turned into the catalysts of defeat. Khrushchev's early warnings that his country was mass-producing thermonuclear warheads and ICBMs in great quantity—a lie he propagated in order to buy time to build the missiles he needed—touched off a frenzied arms buildup in the United States that only abated with the disintegration of the Warsaw Pact in 1989 and 1990 and the turning inward of the Kremlin itself. And three years of the Soviets' "cleaning up Earth orbit," as the historian Joseph Tatarewicz put it, and deriving immense propaganda benefit from each successive feat, only goaded Kennedy into going for the Moon.

The repeated attempts to send probes to Venus and Mars ahead of the United States galvanized the U.S. planetary exploration program, in the process leading to a string of achievements both on

Mars and at the outer planets that the Soviets were never able to match. The opponents were like two prizefighters. The Soviets, flashier and quicker on their feet, struck the first blows. But they lacked the stamina to go the distance: their physiognomy was in many fundamental respects more apparent than real. They therefore had to rely on equal measures of bravado and dogged persistence to at least stay in the ring.

Yet the history of U.S. planetary exploration and its Soviet counterpart are in fundamental respects inseparable. Kennedy's view— that the competition for space mirrored the battle of competing ideologies on Earth—had its clearly delineated place in the realm of space, including its exploration. In October 1968, even as Apollo 8 was being readied for its Christmas orbit around the Moon, Bruce Murray articulated what many felt to be the nature of that competition:

> The planetary exploration competition between the United States and the USSR should not be regarded as a muscle-flexing contest, but rather as a cultural confrontation. Style rather than scale, discoveries rather than exploitations, measure success in this contest. It comes down to our grasp of the noble motives of exploratory science. If the people of the world come to find knowledge of the solar system primarily in Soviet books, represented as the achievement of a revolutionary society, demonstrating, as they see it, the wave of the future, we will have forfeited an opportunity to shape the human mind and spirit in a crucial historical period. We will have done lip service to our ideals of ranging the frontiers of life and opening the world to every person.

That having been said, Murray and others grasped the importance of being able to use the Soviets to further their own ends, however idealistic they might be. When he was director of JPL, a term that overlapped the early years of the Reagan administration, Murray waged a losing battle for a mission to Halley's Comet that was so forceful it earned a place in the folklore of space science and exploration.*

*Murray always grasped the value of good public relations. Soon after he became director of JPL in April 1976, he divided all missions into one of two categories: Purple Pigeons or Gray Mice. While both would be scientifically valid, the former would also have considerable popular appeal. Sending wheeled robots around Mars, the establishment of an observatory on a Jovian moon, and launching a solar sail-powered spacecraft to meet Halley were examples of such "sexy" missions. Sending a polar-orbiting satellite around the Moon to measure geochemical and other properties, which he tried unsuccessfully to get funded after he arrived at JPL, was a Gray Mouse. (Murray, *Journey into Space,* p. 244.)

He has recounted how he met with a White House aide, Martin Anderson, in late March 1981 in an effort to sell the Halley Intercept Mission (HIM). Anderson worked for Edwin Meese, who determined what Reagan did or did not see, and whom the planetary science and exploration community was then lobbying because Keyworth, Mark, and others were threatening to kill Voyager and everything else in the exploration program. Murray's presentation included a special rendition of *The Russians Are Coming* (as he put it) with emphasis on the Soviet Halley mission and another that was supposed to map Venus with radar.

"This was fortunate because I rapidly discovered that competition with the Russians struck the single responsive chord. Otherwise, Anderson seemed interested only in 'privatizing' NASA," Murray has written. In the end, HIM was killed, another sacrifice to the shuttle. Although raising the specter of being beaten by the Soviets did not work every time, it is important to note that it was used incessantly and was usually enough to at least get the ear of whatever functionary had been targeted.

The news media and the trade press did not invent the race to space. But from the outset they combined generous doses of cheerleading with their reportage. This was certainly true during the period of panic that followed Sputnik, when the press turned into an all-too-willing conduit for government drummers and fist-shakers. But it has remained more or less constant through the years that followed. During the thirty-two months between the explosion of Challenger and Discovery's successful return to space, for example, the media and trade press ran a succession of warnings that the Soviets were forging ahead in the great race. If anyone in the American space community, in manned or unmanned programs, objected to the media's acting like Paul Revere riding Pegasus, there is no evidence of it.

Readers of the October 1986 issue of *National Geographic* could hardly have missed the point. On the cover, against the pitch-black of space, a cosmonaut peered at them over a headline that read (in red): "Soviets in Space: Are They Ahead?" While the long article inside dealt with the shortcomings of Soviet space technology, as well as its successes, it nevertheless portrayed the program as vigorous and threatening. The theme was repeated elsewhere; an *Aviation Week & Space Technology* cover story showed a cosmonaut's space suit, complete with backpack-type Manned Maneuvering Unit

Gary Brookins, The Richmond Times-Dispatch

for space walking, which said: "U.S./USSR in Space: the Quest for Leadership."

In October 1987, *Time* ran a cover story showing an Energiya, dwarfed by gigantic towers that reflected orange, blasting off from the Baikonur Cosmodrome in an eerie night launch. "Moscow Takes the Lead," the cover warned. "Moscow now has the world's most powerful rocket booster, unmatched expertise in manned spaceflight, a world-class planetary exploration program and an unwavering commitment to become the dominant presence in space," it said on the pages that followed. "Experts in the West think the Soviets are far ahead of the U.S.—and may stay there into the 21st century. Can America come back?"

And a year later, when the orbiter Discovery returned the shuttle program to operational status, *Time* ran a cover story that exclaimed: "Whew! America Returns to Space." David Morrison took strong exception to the magazine's proclamation, with its clear implication that being in space equated only with having people there. "We thought we were already there," the disgruntled astronomer said as he thought about the Pioneer, Voyager, and other missions then under way. "Just the fact that we hadn't had any manned flights for a few years did not mean that the U.S. did not have a successful space program."

If the managers of the space science and lunar and planetary communities in the United States were aware of fundamental Soviet shortcomings in those areas, they did not let on that they were. Instead, they became preoccupied not only with the Soviets' well-publicized achievements but with much of their rhetoric as well. The buzz word in the first decade of the space age was "race." This implied that both sides were engaged in a competition in which there would ultimately be a clear winner who captured some undefined grand prize, and a loser, relegated to becoming history's goat.

Speaking to the Electric Club of Los Angeles as early as November 1959, Eberhardt Rechtin, chief of JPL's Telecommunications Division, cited the claims of two Soviet scientists to prove that there was indeed a race on and that the opposition was dead set on winning it. Rechtin quoted the scientists as predicting that a spacecraft containing two men would orbit the Earth for two weeks by the end of the year. A month after that, he quoted the Soviets as saying, two other cosmonauts would circle the Moon with a TV camera. Two or three months later two men and two women would circle it for half a year. This would be followed in 1961 by launching probes to Mars and Venus, then to Mercury and Jupiter. Finally, he warned, manned spacecraft carrying from two to six cosmonauts would be dispatched to Mars and Venus.

"If this sounds fantastic to us, we should remember that from their advanced position, the view of the immediate future might well be clearer than what we can see from further back," Rechtin said. "Based on this kind of evidence," he added, "I think it is fair to conclude that we are in a race. What we may not have realized is that the Russians are in it whether we are in it or not. In a sense, we are so far behind that the Russian competition does not even look back to find out where we are."

A decade later, a more refined word, "leadership," became the buzz word. "The United States may not be in a position to assure itself of leadership in all aspects of solar system exploration, in view of the potential of a particularly vigorous Soviet planetary program," the Space Science and Technology Panel of the President's Science Advisory Committee warned in March 1970. "The full vigor of the USSR program in the planetary field has not been apparent because of a large number of mission failures," the report carefully noted. "Nevertheless, one can illustrate the scale of their program from their success in probing the atmosphere of Venus and the long series of launches toward both Venus and Mars at virtually every launch opportunity."

And in 1987 NASA's own Solar System Exploration Committee bemoaned the fact that there had not been a planetary launch since Pioneer Venus nine years earlier, and that the exploration budget for fiscal 1988 was to be slashed from an already meager $358 million to $307 million. The committee's report, which was sent to NASA Administrator Fletcher, warned that unless the situation was reversed, the United States might well remain a second-class power in planetary science through the end of the century. "The U.S. planetary exploration program is in worse shape now than when the SSEC was formed seven years ago," David Morrison, its chairman, complained. "NASA no longer leads the world in planetary exploration."

That same year, still in the throes of the Challenger disaster, a NASA Advisory Council Task Force on International Relations in Space cited a "widening recognition that the Soviet space program is surpassing it [the U.S. program] in manned flight, in planetary sciences and, with the recent launch of Energiya, in launch lift capability." The report went on to warn (correctly) that the Soviets were trying to join forces with European nations and were engaged in a vigorous effort to win a share of the commercial space market.

Taken in the context of the moment, the frustration and despair reflected by the media, Morrison, the advisory council, and others was understandable. There had been no planetary missions during the Reagan presidency; the Challenger accident had grounded Galileo, Magellan, and almost everything else, and the Soviets were at that moment preparing to send an extremely ambitious pair of spacecraft, called Phobos 1 and 2, back to Mars after an absence of thirteen years. Yet in the wider context of inherent U.S. science and engineering capability, let alone the approaching finale of Voyager 2's epic Grand Tour at Neptune, the Soviets were to remain only tenacious and plucky also-rans who had their own internal conflicts.

Energiya, itself, is interesting in the context of the use of competition as a driving factor for the U.S. program. It was designed to carry piggyback either their shuttle, named Buran (Snowstorm), or standard unmanned payloads. With a total thrust of 6.6 million pounds and a lifting capacity of 220,000 pounds, Energiya, first launched on May 15, 1987, was without doubt the world's most powerful booster. Ten days after it was launched, *Aviation Week & Space Technology* explained that the heavy-lift vehicle "extended the Soviets' lead in space" over the United States. "It is a tremendous achievement for the Russians," Dale D. Myers, NASA's deputy administrator, was quoted as warning. "I think it reinforces the need for this country to move ahead with the ALS [Advanced Launch System]. It gives the Soviets the opportunity to put up some very significant increases in space capability," Myers predicted grimly, "and if we do not chase them hard they are really going to establish a tremendous lead in space."

While that may have been true, it was not exactly the way one Soviet scientist at IKI, the Space Research Institute, saw it. Writing in *Pravda* two years later, Konstantin Gringauz not only questioned the need for the monster launch vehicle but for Buran, as well. Referring to the Ministry of General Machine Building, which was responsible for rocket production, Gringauz wrote: "It cannot be ruled out that the main reason for the creation of the Energiya-Buran system was the desire of the branch to assert itself and not the real needs of the country and science." Not content with bashing only the booster and shuttle makers, Gringauz then turned his pen on the agencies that design the kind of spacecraft that he himself needed to do his own work. Prognoz satellites were outdated twenty years ago, the frustrated scientist charged, and even the two advanced Phobos spacecraft had serious "shortcomings" because the engineers had not consulted with the scientists to determine what was required by way of instrumentation.

Given the amount of secrecy that Khrushchev and his successors continued during the three decades after Sputnik, a degree of ignorance about the exact nature of the Soviet activities, and certainly of plans, was understandable.* Yet von Braun and other expatriates from Peenemünde who found a haven in the United States, Medaris and some of his colleagues in the Army, a small group of senior Air Force officers, and countless NASA officials at Headquarters and throughout the empire had reason to know enough about the Soviet space program to understand that its successes were flawed by glaring weaknesses. Little if any mention was made of those weaknesses to the press and to the general public, however.

---

*At the same time, many sophisticated intelligence-collection methods, by far the best involving the use of reconnaissance satellites and listening posts that nearly ringed the USSR, plus first-rate space tracking facilities in the United States and elsewhere, kept the U.S. space community abreast of all developments of consequence in both the Soviet military and civilian programs. Most of the information was collected by the CIA and military intelligence, but a great deal of it was disseminated, officially and otherwise, throughout the space community as a whole. This was understandable, given the fact that most major contractors worked on military and civilian programs.

Eberhardt Rechtin, to take only one example, held a Ph.D. in electrical engineering from Caltech, knew his field thoroughly, and had a reputation for technical foresight of a high order. Yet with such attributes, his apparent eagerness to believe the blustery pronouncements that came out of the USSR vaunting its achievements and depicting its plans for space in blatantly unrealistic terms, suggests a suspension of analytical ability that borders on disingenuousness.

By fostering the notion that the opposition was ten feet tall, Rechtin and the others had much to gain—the technical challenge, funding, the adulation of a grateful public, and their place in history. Self-deception was therefore tempting. The military is notorious for doing the same thing, of course, and has largely been successful at it because generals and admirals really can win or lose wars. On the other hand, the space fraternity could lose the competition only if the race was actually declared over, with the Soviet Union the clear winner. But it has always known that would never happen.*

Out of all this and more—unenlightened self-interest, monumental engineering and elegant science, fortitude and duplicity, creative xenophobia, an establishment press, the profit motive, dreams of glory, battles over turf, rockets exploding over the Atlantic, knights in space armor saluting the Stars and Stripes and posing for photo opportunities on the Moon, opportunistic politicians at both ends of the Mall, rehabilitated weaponeers in league with Mouseketeers, unlikely heroes, relentless hubris and, with it all, the ubiquitous technocrats in government and industry carrying bagsful of rubber statistics and upbeat adjectives—came the space program. It was an undertaking that developed many facets, all of them resolutely institutionalized by the space gods themselves. It was astropolitics.

NASA's unstated agenda, requiring extravagant feats of engineering involving humans in space, carried several fundamental political as well as technical implications.

Foremost among these was the fact that the massive programs

*In their book, *A Shield in Space?: Technology, Politics, and the Strategic Defense Initiative,* Sanford, Lakoff and Herbert F. York discuss at length what they call the Fallacy of the Last Move. Their point is that a technological "man-against-nature" contest, such as going to the Moon, can be permanently resolved because nature does not know it is in the contest and therefore does not try to win. "Man-against-man" contests do not remain resolved, however, because once a particular problem has been solved by one side, the other finds a new one to take its place, thereby keeping the conflict alive indefinitely. Because of this, there can never be a last move. The authors apply this to Star Wars, but it has wider applications, including other forms of competition in space.

judged vital to the agency's survival were established in principle
before missions were found to justify them. As a consequence,
agency planners and those in the infrastructure that supports it and
feeds off it—contractors, lobbying groups like the American Institute for Aeronautics and Astronautics, grant-hungry applied science
departments in universities, and others—taxed their imaginations
trying to come up with missions that justified NASA's existence, and
specifically as it related to the three major space endeavors following
Apollo: the shuttle, the space station, and the mission to Mars. As
a consequence, many space scientists, both in and out of planetary
exploration, became disgruntled at what they saw as a blatantly
self-serving and misplaced desideratum that put great emphasis on
spending staggering sums of money on a kind of flying trapeze done
to Earth scale.

With NASA, said David J. Helfand, the Columbia University astrophysicist, "the next thing has to be much more spectacular than
the last thing or it isn't worth doing. They're not fundamentally
interested in doing the science. They're interested in the technological achievement—the engineering, the management. They go
searching for missions for themselves. And that goes from the
agency at the top . . . down to the individual, tiny directorates: the
astrophysics office, which has to keep finding bigger, more spectacular missions for itself." When a project is scaled down, either because
it isn't bearing fruit or because it has lost its competitive position
relative to other projects, it is "descoped," in NASA jargon. This has
proven to be extremely wasteful. But it is the inevitable result of
making work. "The agency, from top to bottom, as far as I can see,
is driven by creating reasons for itself to exist," the young scientist
complained.

Nowhere has the search for justifying missions been more ram-
pant than, first, in the shuttle program and then in the space station
project. The station described by von Braun in *Collier's* in the 1950s,
a voluminous wheel, which would have created its own gravity by
spinning and held scores of shirtsleeved occupants, has long since
given way to a bony version, made largely of exposed beams and
carrying outsized solar panels, which would house up to eight astronauts.

Proponents of that station insist it would be quite useful. But they
sharply disagree on what exactly it would be useful for. It has been
variously claimed that the station could serve as a departure point
for manned expeditions to the Moon and Mars; an orbiting science

laboratory and astronomical facility; a manufacturing center for materials best made in a near-gravity-free environment—particularly pharmaceuticals; a manned observation platform for Earth resources management and weather forecasting; a service and repair facility for satellites; a communication relay station for narrowband broadcasting because of its large antennas and power supply; and more. It is no coincidence that all of this is reminiscent of the arguments that were made to justify the Space Transportation System two decades earlier.

The technique of first selling a giant engineering program and only afterward getting down to the serious business of coming up with real missions for it has created long-standing frustration and angst in the space science and planetary exploration communities. This is because of a glaring anomaly. Whereas there is an inherent and overriding philosophical commitment to create manned programs before precise missions are found for them, the exact opposite is true in science and exploration, where there is an abundance of potentially valuable and clearly defined missions but not a commensurate philosophical commitment to support them. A maximum commitment has been lacking because science and exploration have not been taken to be vital to NASA's existence. Making the manned programs and the formidable infrastructure to support them the heart of the space program has necessarily resulted in relegating everything else, including science and exploration, to second-class status.

The space science and exploration community steadfastly believes that the space program's overwhelming emphasis on big-ticket engineering and the use of people to carry out tasks that would be more safely and cheaply done by automatons is unjust, wasteful, and counterproductive. And there is an irony about such a state of affairs that is particularly frustrating. Many of the attributes that NASA itself ascribes to a successful space program, both technically and politically, come not from manned missions but from planetary ones. Yet this is not widely perceived, not even within the space agency. The following are some examples.

NASA has made much of its crown jewel: the advanced technology necessary to send humans to Earth orbit, return them, or keep them there for long periods. It has therefore directed the greatest part of its funding to technology that relates to manned spaceflight. But it has been the planetary explorers more than the manned systems that have pushed space technology the hardest. Even the planetary community itself has given its engineering component shorter shrift than it deserves. While the community has emphasized the wonders of exploring new worlds and the benefits of the scientific knowledge derived from it, it has consistently understated the equally valid point that no instruments would get to those worlds in the first place unless they were carried across chasms of time and space so immense that they are all but ungraspable.

Burton I. Edelson, a scientifically literate engineer who headed the Office of Space Science and Applications from 1982 to 1987, was emphatic about the sheer impossibility of conducting scientific investigations in the solar system without an extremely high order of technology, a technology that not only goes untouted but is virtually ignored at encounter time, when science steals the show.

"One of the sad things about the space shuttle and the space station is that they really are not technology drivers," Edelson asserted. On the other hand, he cited both Galileo and the Hubble Space Telescope as being highly innovative works of engineering. He also reserved his highest accolades for Voyager 2's Grand Tour, which he described as nothing short of an engineering "miracle."

It arrived [at Uranus] within seconds of the time it was programmed to arrive years before, Edelson recalled. Then it "zips through the system, points a camera at Miranda going forty thousand miles an hour. . . . The precision of the tracking of a camera like that in order to get high resolution, and without blurriness of the camera . . . *a billion miles away* . . . *after eight and a half years* . . . *!*" Edelson paused to contemplate Voyager 2's streaking toward Uranus like a hypersonic arrow bearing down unerringly on an impossibly distant bull's-eye, or a hole in one from New York to Los Angeles. He took a moment to savor the sheer elegance of the engineering before abruptly snapping out of his reverie.

"Then the scientists look at it and say, 'Ah, well, I see *this* geological formation; I see *that* geological formation.' The big accomplishment there is an engineering accomplishment. It isn't a scientific accomplishment: it's a scientific *benefit* that they can get out there and look at that. The scientific benefit is a new understanding of how the solar system, and indeed the whole universe, were formed." And, Burton Edelson added, drawing the science and engineering together as he leaned slightly forward over his desk, "We did it for everybody on the face of the Earth."

The planetary explorers' singular accomplishments in the competition with the Soviet Union is another area that has not been adequately recognized. Solar system exploration has constituted NASA's main competitive advantage in the long run. While landing astronauts on the Moon was an unequivocal political triumph, there has been nothing since in the realm of manned spaceflight to equal it. Indeed, the Challenger accident and the thirty-two months of chaos that resulted from it amounted to a serious loss of both relative capability and prestige.

Nor are the shuttle and the proposed space station either unique or so inherently superior to their Soviet counterparts that they carry much, if any, competitive edge. Indeed, where the two space systems are concerned, both nations are locked in a cycle of technological copycat. The USSR launched its own shuttle, a near duplicate of its U.S. counterpart, for the first time on November 15, 1988, more than seven years after Columbia made its maiden voyage.* On the other hand, the Soviets launched Mir, a permanent (and expandable) space station in February 1986, while the United States was still in the throes of debating whether it would have its own.

The exploration of the planets and their moons, on the other hand, has been so dominated by the United States that the Soviet Union is not even a close second. While the improvement of technology in Earth orbit has come in small increments (e.g., increasing the capacity of spacecraft from three to seven; putting wings on them; keeping others in permanent orbit and adding sections to them, rather than bringing them back down), the immense distances and wide variety of destinations in solar system exploration have required a higher standard of engineering supported by a more robust technological base.

Not only has the United States had the outer planets all to itself because the Soviets were incapable of operating in those areas, but it has even excelled at the exploration of Mars, where the Soviets tried desperately to excel but failed. The close-up images of the Martian surface, the Great Red Spot of Jupiter, the rings of Saturn, and the astounding countenances of Io, Miranda, Triton, and other worlds that occupy this system were given to mankind, as Bobby Brooks, Burt Edelson, and others have said, not by Soviet explorers but by those that were made in America. If excelling at such competition really does enhance the stature of a nation throughout the world, and also flatters its self-image, then planetary exploration

---

*Buran made its maiden flight by remote control and without a crew. The Soviets used unmanned Progress rockets to carry supplies and fresh crews to their space station.

has accomplished those things for the United States far more than any endeavor except Apollo. Yet its reward for this has been to be cast in a supporting role while the manned program was kept in the limelight.

In that regard, the space program's insatiable requirement for heroes has been fundamentally misfocused (as has its counterpart in the USSR). The United States has deplored its own educational system because it has failed to produce scientists and engineers of the highest caliber in numbers that are adequate for maintaining a robust competitive society. At the same time, it has invested the quality of heroism exclusively in the crews that go to space, not in those who get them there or who explore distant worlds for the sake of pure knowledge.

Far from being out of tune with society, young people have grasped their elders' message all too clearly: heroism is the exclusive province of those who risk life and limb—who hang their hides on the outside of the envelope, as Tom Wolfe put it in *The Right Stuff*—be they high-wire performers in the circus, centers on hockey teams, astronauts who ride rockets to space, or others who engage in the most dangerous specialties of businesses with entertainment components.

NASA has understood from the beginning that only humans can be heroic. Franklin D. Martin, then NASA's associate administrator for the study of manned exploration to the Moon and Mars, put it succinctly at a meeting in Washington in the spring of 1989. "We don't give ticker tape parades for robots," he said.

There are no parades for robots because, by virtue of the fact that they are not alive, they cannot be heroic. That's fair enough. But those who conceive them, develop them, arm them with the means of comprehending Earth and the universe around it, and then send them on exemplary voyages of exploration are indeed heroic. If heroism is defined as overcoming great adversity to achieve success, rather than simply surviving physically dangerous situations, who could be more heroic than those who turned Voyager 2 into a new spacecraft in order to complete the Grand Tour, or who tenaciously protected Galileo and kept it mission-ready even as it suffered through a seemingly unending maelstrom of intrigue, bad luck, and sheer buffoonery?

Planetary scientists have studied much of the solar system close up and returned with knowledge so vast and profound that it has fundamentally and forever changed the way the inhabitants of this planet see themselves and their place in the greater universe. If those investigators are less noteworthy, let alone less praiseworthy, than quarterbacks who win Superbowls or the crews of Earth-orbiting vehicles that are run almost entirely by computers, such an assessment is a sure reflection of the values of the space agency, the executive and legislative branches of government, and society as a whole.

No one in planetary exploration is anticipating the day when Edward Stone, James Van Allen, John Casani, Bradford Smith, James Martin, Merton Davies, Torrence Johnson, and others engaged in this calling sell their life stories to television or appear on bubble-gum cards. But some serious recognition by the president, the Congress, and certainly by the agency for which they work would redress an oversight as old as astropolitics itself.

The budgetary process itself is also in need of reform. The constraints placed on the budget for exploration are bad enough, but the fact that there is no continuing base budget at all is probably worse. James Van Allen and David Morrison, among many others, have complained for years about the need to rejustify program funding every year.

"For some reason," Morrison observed, "NASA space science programs are not funded as if anyone thinks the agency will continue to exist beyond the next couple of years." The Department of Health and Human Services has no such problem, he said, and neither does the Department of Defense. The school lunch program in Rochester, he said, citing one example, is continuous and does not have to be renegotiated every year. And the same applies to aircraft carriers. "Once you have it," the astronomer added, "they let you run it."

But the "on-off" syndrome in space agency budgeting fosters often divisive and wasteful competition between individual scientists, between centers, and between the agency itself and other major organizations within the government. It also creates unnecessary and debilitating stress. NASA's primary way of trying to insulate itself from the vagaries of the budgetary process, of course, is through new-starts and the great man-carrying engineering projects. The Space Transportation System has a base budget of sorts, though, while a space station would have a real one. Who on the Senate or House appropriations committees would want to take responsibility for pulling the plug on the space station once it was in orbit and functioning? Space science and planetary exploration receive no such largess, however, with cost and time overruns on programs like Galileo the inevitable result.

If science and exploration have traditionally been forced to adhere to unpredictable budgets, and generally inadequate ones at that, the scientists, engineers, and managers themselves are in large measure responsible. This is because NASA has rigged its internal political system so that everyone has to support the giant engineering programs that help stabilize the overall budget, not just the direct beneficiaries of such programs. Those in science and exploration, in fact, are pressured by NASA to allow themselves to be co-opted if they know what's good for them. This, too, exasperates them.

"A large fraction of the [science] community feels that the manned space program is a waste of time," David Helfand maintained. Despite this, however, he and other scientists constantly receive letters from the leaders of their community, as well as from space agency officials on various levels with whom they work, strongly urging them to support the overall NASA budget. "You can't go in there [to Congress] and say, 'Cut out this manned crap and we could do some good science at a tenth of the cost.' That's a disaster on Capitol Hill. You're co-opted into playing the game, into not criticizing any aspect of the program."

Years ago, Helfand added, Headquarters agreed to devote roughly 20 percent of its budget to science and planetary exploration. This was a clever way of getting the astronomers and other scientists to help lobby for a bigger overall budget—to play the game—since the bigger the overall budget, the bigger would be their share.

The grievances harbored by the science and exploration people were long and varied. A few of them, such as Van Allen, thought that the manned program should be scratched altogether. Others, taking the opposite tack, convinced themselves that there would be no appreciable space science and solar system exploration without frequent flyers and crews in low orbit. They believed that for better or worse it was the people carriers, not the robots, that captured the public's imagination and therefore gave the space program its impetus.

Most of those in science and exploration believed, and rightly so, that there was room in the nation's space program for both manned and unmanned programs, for Earth-orbiting stargazers and planetary explorers, and for a generous mix of other endeavors as well. The problem was that NASA's priorities were woefully out of balance. Men and women belong in space. But they ought to go there to perform tasks that they are uniquely able to perform, such as building and inhabiting outposts on the Moon and perhaps on Mars, too. There is a place for humans in the exploration of Mars no less than there was on Earth itself, since only they can bring to bear the level of judgment that is necessary to extend a search when unanticipated developments occur. After all, as Merton Davies has said, the essence of exploration is turning up answers for which there are no questions. It would be important to have people on hand to raise the appropriate questions and then push the search for answers wherever it might lead.

What the majority in science and exploration wanted was recognition of their accomplishments and the potential of their work. Some of the engineers reflected, parenthetically, that getting a shuttle off the ground within a week of its scheduled liftoff was taken to be a major accomplishment. They, on the other hand, could send a spacecraft like Voyager on a trip across the solar system that took twelve years and get it there so close to the predicted time of arrival that the moment of nearest approach could be set at launch with total accuracy. Yet the system took that level of excellence for granted, grudgingly fed it just enough to keep it viable, and chose instead to lavish treasure on the frequent flyers. In a way, as David Helfand said, everyone in science and exploration had been co-opted.

Sergei P. Korolev, the rocket genius and designer of the first Sputnik, would have understood precisely what the Americans were talking about. He, like so many others, had been co-opted too. A "merciless" foe of unfounded "fantasizing," Korolev was nonetheless driven by Nikita Khrushchev's fantasies of landing men on the Moon before the United States did. While Khrushchev's braggadocio about his country's superiority in ballistic missiles and Earth-orbiting spacecraft echoed throughout the West, technocrats in the Communist party drove Korolev and other designers to come up with new extravaganzas by complaining incessantly that they were the underdogs and the oppressed, while their enemy was overcome by mad ambition.

Roald Z. Sagdeev, the director of the USSR's Space Research Institute, would have understood too. The period of increased openness that resulted from Mikhail Gorbachev's coming to power in the mid-1980s let loose an avalanche of revelations about widespread deeply impacted abuse, misdirection, and waste in essentially all sectors of government. It also prompted attacks by those who had been thwarted by the system for so long. And those in the intelligentsia, including Sagdeev, were in the forefront of the action.

What became clear as Sagdeev and a few of his colleagues openly railed against how the space program was run, and specifically the place science had in it, was the remarkable degree of similarity that existed between his nation's program and its competitor's. For three decades, Moscow's obsessive secrecy had obscured the fact that not only were both programs on parallel courses where technical objectives were concerned, but they functioned within very similar political frameworks. That is, science in general, including the variety that rode on lunar and planetary spacecraft, were relegated to supporting roles behind manned spaceflight. Meanwhile, work at IKI had to be done within an endless morass of turf protection, funding fights, and lobbying.

As events would show, the overall Soviet program, including spacecraft technology, looked better than its American opposite number during the time following the Challenger disaster only because NASA couldn't get its spacecraft off the ground. But that was a launch vehicle problem. The spacecraft themselves, as well as their capacity to carry out long missions, were all right. So was the scientific and technological base that produced and supported them. In fact, relatively speaking, they were quite a bit better than all right. It was politics, not technology, that was the problem. But the Soviets, as became clear during the new period of openness, had more than their own share of trouble, both politically and technically.

The Soviet lunar and planetary exploration program is remarkable, not only for what it has accomplished but for the fact that it has accomplished anything at all, given the horrendous obstacles it has had to overcome. Chronically poor computing capability has severely hampered tracking beyond Mars, all but eliminated the ability to take advantage of unexpected scientific opportunities once missions were under way, and virtually precluded the possibility of recovering from gross errors made in flight. Sagdeev would complain bitterly that his country's ineptitude at producing adequate computers had made research workers and engineers at IKI "resemble soldiers attempting to fight a modern war with crossbows."

In addition, reliability and maintainability problems have plagued Soviet space systems from day one. These are the principal reasons the Soviets have stayed relatively close to home, concentrating on the Mir space station and trying to explore Venus, Mars, and the Moon, while abandoning longer planetary missions to the United States. And even at that, the record on Mars has been abysmal. "They have never had a successful Mars mission," according to Merton E. Davies, the RAND Corp. pioneer in civilian and military space imaging. Davies has participated in a number of U.S. lunar and planetary missions and has been closely attuned to the general level of Soviet planetary capabilities.

He ticked off the list of failures, starting with the aborted missions of the early 1960s, and going through the notorious dust-storm landing of the Mars 2 and 3 spacecraft. "They didn't get any data from one, and ten seconds of data from the other, as I recall," he said. These were followed by still other failures. And the difficulties the United States had with launch vehicles during the formative years of its space program were mirrored in the Soviet Union, where there were an appalling number of failures of either first or second stages.

More insidiously, Soviet scientists and engineers in all sectors, including space, had to work in a dispiriting quagmire of competition and bureaucratic incompetence in which officials on almost every level drove them endlessly without understanding what they were doing. Khrushchev's demands on Korolev and his design bureau to produce ever more spectacular feats in space are legendary. But pressure came from the middle and lower levels as well.

Communist party functionaries, always mindful that their rears had to be covered, treated scientists the way they treated cabbage farmers and foundry operators. They took control of research institutes and set quotas. "In the 1960s, scientists even had to promise to achieve a specific amount of progress within a designated period," Sagdeev bitterly complained in a candid article in *Issues in Science and Technology* in the summer of 1988. "Physicists from Novosibirsk, recognizing the absurdity of the exercise, pledged to make one discovery of worldwide importance, two discoveries of all-Union importance, and three discoveries of Siberian importance to please political leaders at all levels.

"The shortcomings of Soviet science are apparent from the subatomic world of physics to the boundless world of astronomy," Sagdeev charged. "For too long, Soviet science has hidden its inadequacies behind official panegyrics to its success. In academic and political forums alike, exaggerated claims have been made for the achievements of Soviet science. Science has its own criteria for success, however, and Soviet achievements have not measured up to them."

Seen in the light of *glasnost,* even the vast sums spent on the Soviet space program have been deeply resented in many circles. The Soviet Union's colossal space budget, kept secret for years, burst into the open during elections in the spring of 1989 in a highly vocal

"butter versus rockets" debate. Newspapers, which acknowledged
that the subject of space has traditionally been a "sacred cow,"
began carrying stinging attacks on the cost of the program and urged
that it be directed more towards the needs of the economy in general.

"You cannot be satisfied with the vague replies heard at news
conferences about 'our spending being comparable with American
spending,' " an article in *Izvestia* charged. "If it really is comparable, why play at secrecy, why not name the sum directly? But when
it is not named, you inevitably imagine astronomic appropriations
which, when you look at empty store counters, you cannot help
wanting to cut."

The space scientists, thrown on the defensive, countered that the
$2.1 billion spent on space research in 1988 produced $3.2 billion
worth of technology that went directly to the national economy. It
was an argument that would make many in NASA smile knowingly.

Sagdeev, in fact, at one and the same time delivered a blow to
Buran and its sisters by using the American experience as an example. He could do this with some authority, not only by virtue of his
reading the popular press and professional commentaries published
in the United States, but by having discussed the situation with his
peers at meetings in the United States and elsewhere. Roald Sagdeev
surely got on far better with his opposite numbers from JPL, Caltech, and the Office of Space Science and Applications than he did
with the managers and engineers who masterminded the Soviet
shuttle program.

"We are witnessing a stormy, sometimes dramatic discussion in
the West about selecting the most sensible combination of manned
and automatic spacecraft, the optimum combination from the view-
point of scientific interests," Sagdeev wrote in an article published
in *Izvestiya* that ran on April 28, 1988. "The leaders of U.S. astronautics have recognized that the shuttle program was an historical
error," he asserted, adding that a number of "unique astronomical
instruments"* were waiting to be launched by the shuttle (at the
time, grounded because of Challenger).

Sagdeev went on to note that his counterparts in the United States
were expressing "serious anxiety" over the fact that scientific projects were going to be linked to the shuttle, and also to the space
station. "The aerospace business, which has received a substantial

*They would have included Galileo, Magellan, Ulysses (the International Solar-Polar
mission) and the Hubble Space Telescope.

order, has won this debate. But it is a pity, because life has shown that virtually all basic scientific results (except for space medicine) have been obtained by automated instruments. The establishment of the optimum balance on a sensible basis has not happened either in the United States or in our country," Sagdeev charged.

Sagdeev happened to be in the United States in late November 1988, a week after Buran made its first flight. Asked what he thought about the achievement, the bespectacled physicist told reporters: "It went up; it came down. But it had absolutely no scientific value."

Within a year, both the shuttle and space station programs had been hit by a kind of spasmodic paralysis due in large measure to economic pressure, but possibly also a trace of institutional weariness. Following the setting of a 366-day record in space by two cosmonauts on December 21, 1988, three others were brought down in mid-April without the typical replacement crew being sent up. Reports in the United States had it that electrical problems having to do with Mir's solar arrays required that repairs be made before a regular crew could be returned to it.

Soviet space officials denied that there was a malfunction, claiming that budgetary constraints were the real issue. But funding problems are rarely decisive when whatever it is that's being funded is considered worth the investment. It is quite conceivable that the issue arose because the managers of the Soviet space program grew increasingly restive about paying for cosmonauts to eat, sleep, exercise, and attend to small odds and ends in their cramped quarters while their bodies' vital signs, including the loss of calcium in their bones, were being measured for months at a time.

Four months later, in August 1989, it was announced that there would be no manned shuttle flight until 1992. While the delay was officially blamed on the need to install and test advanced flight safety systems required by the cosmonauts, "space policy" and scheduling issues were also cited.

The various problems experienced by the manned spacecraft would have been all too understandable to Konstantin Gringauz, Roald Sagdeev, and others in the Soviet space science and exploration program. They might even have found some small measure of satisfaction in knowing that their own "automated" spacecraft were performing far more satisfactorily than the cosmonaut-carriers. They might have, but they didn't, since two of their own planetary spacecraft were experiencing their own troubles at the same time.

If Gringauz's and Sagdeev's bitter accusations about infighting, lack of communication, empire building, and incompetence had a particularly sharp edge, it was because those pernicious traits had reached out to touch IKI's premier program as well.

Having run into the Great Galactic Ghoul on several Mars missions, the Soviets decided to abandon flights to Mars in 1974 after Mars 7, which carried a lander, missed it entirely because of a mysterious engine malfunction. Then they determined to return on a new and audaciously conceived mission that would use a pair of spacecraft that were in most respects highly sophisticated, even by American standards. But whatever their previous experiences at Mars, the Soviets' problems reached their nadir with the Phobos mission, which was flown by near-identical spacecraft named after the Martian moon that formed the focal point of their journey.

Phobos warrants a close look, technically as well as politically, because it shows what can happen when a bold and highly imaginative planetary exploration project is undermined by the very system from which it is spawned. Like Galileo, Phobos fell victim to partisan politics. Unlike Galileo, though, it was also sabotaged by systemic battles over turf that led to breakdowns in communication and therefore to seriously flawed coordination between the science and engineering teams. Phobos was conceived with hope and ended with heartbreak.

In a way, however, it may have contributed more in the realm of international relations than it did in science. Not only did Americans and other non-Soviets participate in the promising endeavor, working closely on it, but they shared the deep disappointment and sorrow of its premature demise. For them, it wasn't that a Soviet mission had run into disaster, but that a *mission* had. Where Americans who were closely involved with planning the Phobos flight, as well as others in planetary exploration who merely followed its progress were concerned, the loss was everyone's: it transcended nationality. That, too, is one of the facets of astropolitics.

The Phobos twins were designed to return the Soviet Union to Mars with a singular triumph. While previous Soviet planetary explorers had essentially been tried-and-true designs modified for Venusian and Martian missions, the Phobos spacecraft were new and relatively sophisticated. At almost seven tons, the probes were so heavy that they had to fire their own onboard engines to get out of Earth orbit. Unlike their American counterparts, whose instruments are mounted inside the bus, Phobos's instruments were set outside a central cylinder for what its designers believed would be a better field of view. The experiments themselves were truly international, representing scientists from East and West Germany, Bulgaria, Czechoslovakia, France, Finland, Sweden, Poland, and the European Space Agency. U.S. scientists, including Bruce Murray, consulted closely with IKI on the mission, and the Deep Space Network was supposed to help maintain radio contact and do some tracking. Both spacecraft were equipped with what was for IKI highly advanced computers with thirty megabit memories. As usual, however, the computers were loaded with instructions before launch. While the probes' trajectories could be altered, their sequencing was pretty much set before they left Earth.

After the two-hundred-day, four-hundred-million-mile flight, the spacecraft were supposed to orbit Mars and then its ugly little moon in a series of extremely complicated turn-and-burn maneuvers that would carry them to within five hundred miles of the red planet and to within 165 feet of its moon. A highly elliptical initial orbit around Mars that would have the spacecraft merely crossing Phobos's path would give way to a circular orbit around the planet that would position both spacecraft so that they were flying in formation with the moon. Given the fact that Phobos is only about fourteen miles in diameter, coming in as close as 165 feet would be a neat bit of navigation in itself.

But then the mission was supposed to get really interesting. While cruising slowly over Phobos at low altitude, each spacecraft was supposed to drop a lander equipped with cameras and instruments to measure the moon's soil composition, surface layer properties, and seismic disturbances. Because of Phobos's very low gravity, both landers would fire harpoonlike penetrators into the surface and then be winched down by electric motor until they were held snugly in place.

And because the gravity was so weak, IKI decided to put a "hopper" on Phobos 2 as well. This bizarre device was a 110-pound metal ball with spring-loaded legs that carried five additional instruments to make chemical, magnetic, and gravity experiments over a wide area. The idea was to collect data from the hopper's initial landing point and then use its springing legs to propel it about sixty-five feet away for another inspection. The hopper, a high-tech pogo stick, would bound over Phobos perhaps ten times, collecting fresh data at every leap. This, in addition to the information provided by the orbiters and landers, was expected to tell scientists where Phobos came from: whether it had broken off from Mars or was an asteroid that had become trapped there, or whether there was yet another explanation.

The Phobos mission was also important for the links it forged between the U.S. and the Soviet planetary exploration communities. Both nations were talking openly about the possibility of jointly exploring Mars, first with robots, then with astronauts and cosmonauts. Indeed, the Planetary Society had lobbied for years for such a mission because of an unshakeable belief that it would not only promote peace on Earth, but would be the only mission grand enough to inspire widespread public support in both countries.

Phobos was therefore a double blessing for the U.S. planetary exploration community. On the one hand, it represented renewed Soviet assertiveness, which could always be counted on to arouse some dormant support in Congress because of its competitive implications. It was an elegant, complicated, and dangerous mission that would be sure to rattle some politicians if it succeeded. On the other hand, it could be seen as the precursor to another golden age of spaceflight, in which both superpowers and perhaps other nations would join forces in the greatest, most daring feat of exploration in history: a multinational manned mission to Mars.

Phobos 1 was launched on a powerful Proton booster on the night of July 7, 1988; its sister followed five days later on another Proton. Two months later, the Great Galactic Ghoul struck again. Contact with Phobos 1 was lost when a single character was left out of a command sent by a ground controller (a development reminiscent of Mariner 1's missing hyphen back in the shoot-an'-learn days of 1962).

The error caused Phobos 1 to rotate, moving its solar panels out of alignment with the Sun and confusing its navigation system to the point where it became disoriented. The problem might have been corrected if caught immediately, but it wasn't caught because the controllers checked on the health of the spacecraft only every three days. Between times, it was left on its own. A new battery in the spacecraft apparently could not adequately compensate for the loss of power from the Sun for that long, but no one seems to have noticed until it was too late.

On September 9 a forlorn Roald Sagdeev, posing for photographers in shirt sleeves behind a model of the ill-fated spacecraft, announced at a reception at the U.S. ambassador's residence in Moscow that hope had been all but abandoned for Phobos 1. It was tumbling out of control ten million miles from Earth. By November it had officially been written off.

As had been the case when a nuclear reactor at Chernobyl blew up two years earlier, the authorities initially blamed human error, not system design. In this case, responsibility for the accident was laid at the feet of the hapless ground controller. But the real cause of the spacecraft's demise was indeed the system itself.

What happened to Phobos 1 could not have happened to any of its U.S. counterparts, including Voyager. When a spacecraft begins to wander, its radio communication link weakens and corrective steering directions are uplinked immediately. More important, the computers on Voyager, Magellan, Galileo, or any of the others would not have accepted an incongruous signal from Earth without challenging it. "The management system on one of our spacecraft would have said: 'Tell me that again. I didn't believe it the first time,' " Murray explained. "It's poor mission design."

Mert Davies echoed Murray, noting that such a problem is unimaginable in the U.S. program. On U.S. missions, Davies added, a tape is made of command sequences. "That's sent to the spacecraft and then the spacecraft is interrogated: 'What's in your command load?' Then it [the spacecraft] spits back the command listing, and then you put it in a computer and compare the two. If they're identical, you say, 'Implement.' You go through this check procedure; you don't just command a spacecraft and hope it will work out."

If there was any consolation to be had at IKI, it lay in the fact that the second spacecraft, which carried some instruments that were identical with those on Phobos 1, was still bearing down on Mars. On January 29, 1989, Phobos 2 entered an orbit around Mars, prompting Tass to announce that the planet "has acquired one more satellite" which "will bring mankind closer to unravelling mysteries of the planet."

But the mission was not going so smoothly as it appeared. As the previous autumn had turned to winter, disturbing reports of electrical problems on the Soviet spacecraft, of camera failure and serious transmission blackouts, came back to the West.

Then, on March 27, calamity struck again. Phobos 2, in orbit around Mars, was commanded to change its orientation for an imaging session. In order for its camera to point toward Phobos, its high-gain antenna had to be swung away from Earth. Once the imagery had been collected, the spacecraft was to have been turned so the antenna again pointed toward Earth. The pictures of Phobos were then to have been sent back. But there was no signal. As hours passed, dumbfounded controllers and stunned engineers and scientists, trying in vain to establish radio contact, began to realize that

Phobos 2 had met the same fate as its predecessor. Some imagery and other data were sent back before contact with the spacecraft was lost.* But the mission was nevertheless yet another resounding failure. Davies, contemplating the Soviets' plight in his office in Santa Monica, was philosophical and entirely sympathetic. "Phobos was their first new spacecraft in eighteen years," he reflected, "and all new spacecraft have teething problems."

But Sagdeev, less sanguine, aired an apparently long-festering dispute with the engineers. It was notable for getting beyond individual blame and concentrating, instead, on system failure. "On Project Phobos, we were at odds with General Designer Vyacheslav Kovunenko, who blames the breakdown on extraneous factors, whereas we are taking a different view." That view, which generally corresponded with Davies's interpretation and openly pitted the project scientists against the engineers, held that computer backup systems could have saved the mission but were not available on either spacecraft.

And it held a great deal more than that. Roald Sagdeev was denouncing the failure of the entire political-technological system to meet the needs of Soviet space science and exploration. He was castigating a technocracy in which his discipline was held captive to the vagaries of engineers who evidently were at odds with the scientists over basic mission design and who as a consequence held communication and cooperation to an absolute minimum. The engineers seem to have guarded their design prerogatives jealously, even to the detriment of the instruments their spacecraft were supposed to carry.

"I hope that, in the future, space technology producers will have their absolute freedom restricted so that the world scientific community, as the end user of this technology, can have a say in decision-making on spacecraft design," the Soviet scientist snapped.

But the engineers had their own case to make. "Space technology

*Yuri Zaitsev, of the Institute of Space Research, tried to put the best possible face on the mission by calling it a success. Writing in the November 1989 issue of *Spaceflight* (pp. 374–79), he noted that successful experiments were conducted during the interplanetary phase of the mission. In addition, he maintained that the spacecraft collected valuable data on the Martian magnetosphere and returned some imagery of both Phobos and Mars itself. Phobos 2's accomplishments were the subject of at least one other article (Stuart J. Goldman, "The Legacy of Phobos 2," *Sky & Telescope,* February 1990, pp. 156–59), which noted that it returned thirty-seven usable images of Phobos and provided new clues about Mars's magnetic field (or lack of it, since no certain detection was made). One expert, who requested anonymity, guessed that the combined mission accomplished about 15 percent of what it set out to do.

designers," retorted Roald Kremnev, a ranking Phobos engineer, "have to comply with a set of restrictions relating to funds and the weight and size of the spacecraft, etc." The scientists, then, could not always expect to have things their own way.

Closer cooperation between scientists and engineers might have overcome the restrictions imposed by the dimensions and weight of the spacecraft. But this was a position that Kremnev, who had his own colleagues to answer to, was unlikely to take in public. Instead, he promised that special attention would be paid to having adequate power, reducing human error, and enhancing computer-driven automation on future missions, and to making spacecraft more self-sufficient.

His reference to inadequate funding, however, reflected a more general malady, and one upon which both scientists and engineers would agree; there was not freedom, either economically or politically, to conduct space science and exploration as they ought to be conducted. The vehement interchanges between Sagdeev, Kremnev, and others really laid bare a situation so fundamental that it eclipsed the squabbling. There was little indication that those outside their own bailiwick, let alone in the space program as a whole, were able to do enough to help ensure the excellence of the Phobos project. It was simply confounded by the inherent weakness of the system within which it had to operate—a system that finally did it in. That's why there were no parades for Phobos 1 and 2, either.

Tomorrowland

If the decade of the 1960s was the one in which the United States first sent automated emissaries to the planets and men to the Moon, and the 1970s marked the zenith of the golden age of space exploration with the Viking mission to Mars, the flights of Mariner 10 to Venus and Mercury, the successes of the Pioneers at Jupiter, Saturn, and Venus and the beginning of Voyager's epic journey, then the 1980s were a time of self-assessment and searching for direction within a quagmire of political indifference, misshaped priorities, and finally the trauma of Challenger.

The Voyagers were being tended as they passed Saturn, one of them streaking upward, the other continuing on its Grand Tour. And the Pioneers continued to report back faintly as they headed in different directions toward the edge of the solar system. But there were no new starts; little or nothing for which to plan. Exploration seemed to be becalmed. Since the scientists, engineers, and managers in the planetary exploration business were prevented from starting missions, they tried to relieve their collective frustration in the traditional way of academics and bureaucrats everywhere. Some formed committees to produce reports that set goals. Others, alone in their melancholy, authored papers for journals that described the malady and prescribed cures.

At least six major studies addressing the future of the U.S. space program appeared between 1983 and 1988, in addition to a spate of articles, most of them written by disgruntled scientists, that were published in learned journals.

In 1980, even before the pall of the Reagan Revolution enveloped space science and planetary exploration, NASA understood that it was hemorrhaging. Shortly before he was killed in the Himalayas later that year, Tim Mutch, the agency's newly appointed associate administrator for space science, recommended that a blue ribbon panel be established to devise a rational sequence of goals for planetary exploration and define the missions to carry them out. This resulted in the creation of the Solar System Exploration Committee, composed of a galaxy of leading scientists and engineers, which worked under the auspices of the NASA Advisory Council. It delivered its detailed two-part report, *Planetary Exploration Through Year 2000,* in 1983 and 1986.

The SSEC study was followed by *Pioneering the Space Frontier,* a report prepared by the National Commission on Space, and released in May 1986. The commission was created in a venerable Washington tradition. That is, an administration assembles an eclectic group of notables to study a problem caused to a greater or lesser extent by its own vapidity. The group then makes recommendations, some of them quite sensible, which the chief culprits never even bother to read. The NCS included Thomas O. Paine (its chairman) and Neil Armstrong, Jeane J. Kirkpatrick, Generals Charles E. "Chuck" Yeager and Bernard A. Schriever, Luis W. Alvarez (the Nobel physicist) and Kathryn D. Sullivan (the first American woman to walk in space).

Next came *The Crisis in Space and Earth Science,* produced that November by the NASA Advisory Council's Space and Earth Science Advisory Committee. *Leadership and America's Future in Space,* the so-called Ride Report, appeared in August 1987 under the authorship of Sally K. Ride in the form of a report to the NASA administrator. That October the NASA Advisory Council's Task Force on International Relations in Space released *International Space Policy for the 1990s and Beyond.* Finally, the Space Science Board's National Research Council weighed in with its own seven-volume treatise, *Space Science in the Twenty-first Century: Imperatives for the Decades 1995 to 2015,* which was delivered to NASA Administrator Fletcher in 1988. No one could accuse the council of taking a once-over-lightly approach to the problem. The 763-page document represented a collaboration of a steering group and task groups specializing in earth sciences, planetary and lunar exploration, solar and space physics, astronomy and astrophysics, fundamental physics and chemistry, and life sciences.

While the substance of the studies varied according to their focus and breadth, they shared an unstated, but clearly implied belief that the U.S. space exploration program was seriously flawed. Implicit in each of the reports except the one on international policy was the underlying conclusion that the exploration of the solar system suffered from long-term institutional anarchy, that it lacked cohesion, direction, and adequately articulated goals. Overall, there was agreement that six basic curatives were required:

• The space science and exploration programs deserve to be taken with the utmost seriousness—certainly as seriously as other elements in the space program, including the manned presence in Earth orbit and beyond.

• Goals for planetary exploration should be clearly established, not be haphazard. Having conducted a quarter of a century of preliminary investigation of eight of the known planets, future missions should return to them and to their satellite systems for observations in ever-increasing detail.

• The exploration of the solar system should be conducted in a systematic and evolutionary way. Missions to the three main kinds of bodies—the inner planets, the outer planets, and the comets and asteroids—should progress in an orderly fashion that allows for the sustained accumulation of increasingly detailed knowledge, both scientific and technical. And those endeavors should also be pathfinders for a return of humans to the Moon and their journey to Mars.

• The national space program as a whole should be a careful balance between manned and unmanned activities. There was broad agreement that humans have a place in space, certainly where lunar and planetary exploration are concerned. Yet means ought to be matched to ends in a healthy mix, with men and machines complementing, not dominating, each other.

• Funding must be stable and judiciously apportioned. The executive and legislative branches should adopt a fresh philosophy regarding the commitment of resources for planetary exploration, the Solar System Exploration Committee suggested. "An emphasis on overall program cost should replace the arbitrary rationing of the rate of new mission activity: the control of mission costs depends upon increasing mission frequency . . . so that the economies of heritage of hardware and software can be realized," the SSEC added;

• International cooperation, particularly with the Soviet Union, should be encouraged. While the suggested degree of cooperation varied from merely coordinating data to flying coordinated parallel missions and to embarking on fully integrated joint ventures, there was a consensus that the time had come to undertake major feats of exploration in conjunction with other spacefaring nations.*

The idea of cooperating was not new. In fact, the U.S. planetary community and its Soviet counterpart had quietly flirted for years, even during times of political tension. In 1972 Nixon and Alexei Kosygin even held a summit from which a joint mission, the Apollo-Soyuz Test Project of 1975, was consummated. For nearly two days that July, an Apollo and a Soyuz spacecraft remained docked together, with their crews interacting. While the scientific and technical results of the mission were anything but extraordinary, it did mark history's first joint space exercise and it therefore set a notable political precedent.

The spirit continued throughout the 1980s, even as the U.S. space program began to founder. In May 1987 the Soviets unveiled grand plans for solar system exploration, largely having to do with Mars and its two moons, at the First International Conference on Solar System Exploration held in Pasadena. Valery L. Barsukov, director of the Vernadsky Institute of Geochemistry and Analytical Chemistry, and Roald Kremnev described in considerable detail spacecraft, launch vehicles, mission sequences, science experiments, and the expected results from several missions. These included the two Phobos probes, a rendezvous and landing on an asteroid, and several rover and sample-return missions to Mars before the end of the century.

Barsukov captivated his audience by describing the Mars rover

---

*Noting that space relations between the United States and the Soviet Union have traditionally reflected larger matters, NASA's Task Force on International Relations in Space added that such a relatively passive status—merely reflecting larger political matters—did not have to continue. To the contrary, the report suggested that joint ventures could act as a common bridge similar to those involving arms control, inhibiting nuclear proliferation, environmental protection, and large-scale food sales.

A number of individuals expanded on the theme. Bruce Murray held that cooperation would help reduce tensions, generate international support for a manned Mars mission, and spread out its huge cost. Murray's Caltech colleague Gerald Wasserberg also came out for U.S.-USSR cooperation, though he favored delaying a manned mission to Mars because its enormous cost would impair the science that he believed ought to come first by means of robots. John Logsdon came out for wider cooperation that would include Japan and the European Space Agency. Burton Edelson and Alan Townsend maintained that cooperation with the Soviets would have a "restorative" effect in the wake of the state of near limbo that was left by the Carter and Reagan administrations. (Murray's opinion is from his "Civilian Space: In Search of Presidential Goals," *Issues in Science and Technology*, Spring 1986, p. 34. Wasserberg's is from his "Exploring the Planets: A Strategic But Practical Proposal," *Issues in Science and Technology*, Fall 1986, p. 82. Logsdon's is from his "Leading Through Cooperation," *Issues in Science and Technology*, Summer 1988, pp. 44–47. Edelson's and Townsend's is in their "U.S.-Soviet Cooperation: Opportunities in Space," *SAIS*, Winter-Spring 1989, p. 187.)

and sample-return missions in considerable detail. The first expedition would come in 1992, the International Space Year, Barsukov maintained. It would consist of a small rover to scout the territory, penetrators to be fired into it, and a gondola suspended from a pair of balloons. The balloons would lose buoyancy at night, settling the instrument-laden gondola to the ground, then rise in the morning to carry it over new terrain.* Asked whether the Soviets would be willing to take along a large U.S. rover, Barsukov answered, "Why not?"†

Commenting on the tone of the meeting after it was over, one visibly disgruntled American participant said that "the Russians did all the talking." That was not quite the case, however. The United States also had plans for the exploration of space—beautiful, elaborate, carefully conceived plans. Elegant plans. It had plans to get itself out of the doldrums caused by a decade of neglect—some of it anything but benign—and the Challenger accident, to be back to a point at which it could once again catch Kepler's heavenly breezes. But those plans remained in a box that was kept locked by the space gods.

"We have fine plans," David Morrison had said in his keynote address at that same meeting. "We have a great inherent capability. But we have been very slow to turn those plans into actual programs. The budget history of the U.S. planetary program is somewhat depressing in that we have seen a steady decline in the amount of money spent for planets and planetary exploration as a fraction of the NASA budget for well more than a decade. We have been damaged by the loss of Challenger and the standdown in capability with the shuttle. But that is by no means the only source of our problem. The problem reflects a basic swing away from priorities for plane-

---

*The Soviets successfully used balloons on the Vega flights to Venus in 1985. Balloons have also been studied extensively in the United States and in France. Both nations have come up with designs that drag segments containing instruments on the ground snake-fashion. This would have the benefit of directly sensing the terrain and, of course, getting to places that would be inaccessible to a wheeled or even a tracked rover. As the helium supply became increasingly exhausted during the ten-day sojourn, segments of the snake would be released to keep its weight proportional to the balloon's lifting capacity. The French model would consist of a closed balloon and an open one (the latter called, appropriately, a montgolfier). (For data on one U.S. balloon design, see the box on p. 42 of *Aviation Week & Space Technology*, August 1, 1988. The French design, which was offered to the Soviets, is described in Jeffrey M. Lenorovitz, "French Offer Balloon Platform For Use on Soviet Mars Mission," *Aviation Week & Space Technology*, August 3, 1987, pp. 63 and 65.)

†Funding cutbacks and technical difficulties would force the Soviets to scale back their plans within two years (a tape recording of the proceedings and from John Newbauer, "Soviets: 'Join us to Mars?'" *Aerospace America*, July 1987, pp. 6–7).

tary exploration in favor of other kinds of science activities and non-science activities in the U.S. space program," the astronomer added in evident reference to the proposed manned space station.

Only four years before, Morrison reminded the crowd in Pasadena, the Solar System Exploration Committee of which he was chairman presented *Planetary Exploration Through Year 2000: A Core Program* to NASA. Three years later it had turned over part two, *An Augmented Program.* Both reports offered detailed, realistic ways to cover the Space Science Board's wish list of destinations and science objectives in planetary exploration.

The first, called a Core Program, was a sort of bare-bones plan that would cost $500 million a year, or 4 percent of NASA's projected budget (and 20 percent of the money in the Office of Space Science and Application's own coffers). The second, a grander "augmented" approach, could be had for $700 million a year if it was decided to have the exploration program go first-class instead of economy. The budget for planetary exploration at that moment, Morrison pointed out icily, was $300 million a year, or only 3 percent of the space agency's budget.

The two SSEC reports—the core and augmented programs—were impressively thought out and painstakingly detailed. Together, they amounted to a grand strategy for solar system exploration. The main idea was to carry out missions that were less expensive than the traditional kind while providing enough redundancy and system design inheritance from one mission to another—enough continuity—to protect the program from single point failures. Although the committee didn't necessarily envision multiple launches for particular missions, it did presume that there would be an ongoing series of new missions so that changes could be incorporated with relative ease in case of failures or if conditions were altered. Flexibility was the thing.

Within that context, the Solar System Exploration Committee devised two basic classes of spacecraft, each designed to accomplish a fundamentally different kind of mission. The first, called Planetary Observers, would be based on proven designs of Earth orbiters and would be built by contractors. They would lean heavily on off-the-shelf hardware and come in a standard size and shape. An orbiter, after all, was an orbiter: what could orbit Earth could orbit anyplace else. The Planetary Observers would be the workhorses of the inner solar system. The basic spacecraft would require only relatively minor modifications for adaptation to missions to study

the Moon, Mars, Venus, and Earth-approaching asteroids. They
would work the way the Landsat and French SPOT Earth observation satellites survey Earth itself: by making innumerable orbits and
scrutinizing what passed below in a variety of ways and in fine detail.
And like Landsat and SPOT, their power would come from arrays
of solar panels.

The first of this class, called the Mars Observer, was scheduled to
be launched in 1992 for arrival at the red planet in 1993. There it
would use cameras and other sensors to make detailed investigations
of the Martian climate and geology. (The Mars Observer, which
would be the first U.S. spacecraft to return to Mars since Viking,
would itself be a precursor to a highly advanced mission in which
either a rover would prowl the surface of the planet, collecting data
at first hand, or a sample-return mission would actually bring samples of the Martian surface back to Earth. That mission was spelled
out in the Augmented Program scenario.)

The second class of spacecraft would be far more sophisticated.
Explorers of this class would be built to operate semiautonomously
at great distances from the Sun, in the tradition of Voyager and
Galileo, and would be used to reconnoiter the outer planets, their
satellites and rings, and comets and asteroids in greater detail than
has ever been done before. And although their missions would vary,
emphasis would be on a maximum of inheritance from one spacecraft to another, on a basic commonality in design and operation. All
spacecraft in this class would essentially look alike. They would
share common antennas, electronic and data processing hardware,
and guidance and electric-power systems. Only some of their scientific instruments and portable probes would be individually tailored
to suit particular missions. Since their missions would focus on the
outer planets, they would carry nuclear-power packages. They
would be called Mariner Mark II and, like their namesakes, they
would be developed and built at JPL.

The first two Mariner Mark II spacecraft were called CRAF, for
comet rendezvous asteroid flyby, and Cassini. CRAF was designed to
collect data by passing close to an asteroid* and then continue on to
do the most detailed study ever of a comet—Kopff, as it turned out.
Comets and mainbelt asteroids are highly prized targets for scientists because their pristine primitive condition could yield a great

---

*The asteroid was planned to be Hamburga, named after the German city from which
it was first spotted.

deal of information about the early solar system. Unlike the International Cometary Explorer, which flew through Giacobini-Zinner's tail in 1985, or the fleet of spacecraft that met Halley the following year and simply crossed its path, CRAF's flight plan called for it to accompany Kopff—to fly in formation with it for 959 days—gradually closing in until it was circling its target at a distance of about forty miles. Part of the mission would entail firing a pointed penetrator—like shooting a harpoon—into the comet's core, where it would use a claw to scoop up a sample of ice or slush. The sample would be heated inside a chamber so its gases would boil off. They would then be analyzed. Data collected by the penetrator would be relayed back to CRAF for about nine days. The mother ship would in turn transmit the data back home.

Cassini, the other Mariner Mark II craft, would do at Saturn about what Galileo was supposed to do at Jupiter. Even before it reached the majestic gas ball, it would inspect the asteroid Maja and then use Jupiter for gravity assist to go the rest of the way. Cassini would make thirty-six orbits around Saturn in four years, taking the first comprehensive look at its rings, atmosphere, magnetosphere, and Titan, its largest moon. In fact, Cassini was designed to launch a disk-shaped probe into Titan's nitrogen atmosphere for detailed measurements.

The Solar System Exploration Committee's Core Program called for four initial missions, three of which involved the two new types of spacecraft: Mars Observer and the Mariner Mark IIs, CRAF, and Cassini. The fourth was Magellan (originally the Venus Radar Mapper), which was supposed to correct the imbalance in understanding in the Venus-Earth-Mars triad—that is, it was supposed to increase knowledge of Venus, the least understood of the three planets. Magellan left on May 4, 1989, and reached Venus on August 10, 1990.* It returned its first high-resolution imagery within two weeks.

The Augmented Program was spelled out in a richly detailed 239-page report. It outlined a wide variety of missions, some of them as exotic as searching for other planetary systems, and enumerated the

---

*Magellan was cut from NASA's fiscal 1982 and 1983 budgets and resurrected only after the space agency agreed to drop six atmospheric instruments, buy a cheaper radar mapper, and adopt hardware from other spacecraft. Like a bride's traditional wedding attire, it had something old (a spare Voyager bus and high-gain antenna), something new (a Hughes synthetic aperture radar with a 400-foot resolution), something borrowed (a propellant tank from the shuttle's auxiliary power unit), and something blue (its weary, long-demoralized team).

equally exotic technology that would be needed to accomplish them. For example, there would have to be software programs that mimic the human brain to the point of being able to diagnose, identify, explain, interpret, test, and monitor ongoing operations while keeping controllers on Earth advised the way a highly trained specialist would. Sensors would have qualities of perception also approaching that of humans.

But the heart of the Augmented Program had to do with yet a third class of spacecraft: the one that could rove over planetary terrain or collect samples from planets, moons, and comets. And where roving and sample collecting were concerned, there was but one planet that captured the imagination of the members of the Solar System Exploration Committee and their counterparts elsewhere: Mars. The SSEC wanted the United States to send a Mars Rover–Sample Return mission to the red planet as a precursor to a manned expedition.

The old infatuation would not go away. Both Sally Ride's report and that of the National Commission on Space—the so-called Paine commission—envisioned human settlements on Mars by the end of the twenty-first century. Ride wanted the Martian odyssey to unfold in three phases: robotic exploration and sample return in the 1990s; the establishment of a space station to test human response to long-duration missions;* and three "fast-piloted" round trips that would lead to a commitment to establish an outpost on the planet by 2010.

The Paine report was far more grandiose. It described "routine" exploratory missions involving complex transfers from Earth to a space station, then to a "Libration Point Spaceport," and then to a transfer vehicle that would carry people to still another vehicle that would deposit them on the surface of the planet or into a space station orbiting around it. It described the establishment of biospheres, in which inhabitants could live and work and where food could be grown.†

*The Soviet Union has much to contribute in this area because of its ongoing manned program. The 365-day record set by cosmonauts in the Mir space station in 1988 was roughly the amount of time it would take to reach Mars. Unlike many previous long-duration flights, the cosmonauts were able to shake off oppressive fatigue relatively quickly, according to the Soviets. (Nicholas N. Johnson, *The Soviet Year in Space: 1988*, Colorado Springs: Teledyne Brown Engineering, 1989, p. 87).
†The ultimate in adapting environments to a human presence is setting up not biospheres but "terraforming." This would entail making a planet inhabitable by altering its very nature. According to one study, for example, terraforming Venus would require removing most of its carbon dioxide, adding oxygen, importing enough hydrogen from Saturn to create oceans, and changing its angular momentum—speed-

But Ride, echoing the sentiment of just about everyone who had anything to do with planning for Mars, was emphatic in warning against a race to get there. "There is a very real danger that if the U.S. announces a human Mars initiative at this time, it could escalate into another space race," she wrote, adding that the consequence would be the kind of scheduling pressures that led to the Challenger accident. Such pressure, the former astronaut continued, would inhibit the design of a program with a sufficiently strong foundation to sustain itself beyond a few missions. "This could turn an initiative that envisions the eventual development of a habitable outpost into another one-shot spectacular." A theme expressed repeatedly during the National Commission on Space's public hearings, Sally Ride noted, was "a strong wish that our next goal for piloted space activity not be another *Apollo*—a one-shot foray or a political stunt."

For its part, JPL was not about to be left out of planning for manned Mars missions, either. On April 15, 1986, the lab released its own study, *The Case for Mars: Concept Development for a Mars Research Station.* The authors called for the establishment of a permanent fifteen-person base, which would expand every two years as a fresh crew arrived to relieve the established occupants. Automated lightweight plastic greenhouses, using both natural and artificial light and run by computers that would even regulate the spraying of roots, were described in some detail, as were the base's materials-processing facility, habitats, airshells, life-support system, power supply, rovers, tractors, and science vans, earth-moving equipment, and communications systems. Implicit in the study, as in several others, was the fact that propellants for both the rovers and the shuttle rockets could be extracted from Mars itself by reducing the carbon dioxide in the atmosphere to produce carbon monoxide and oxygen. This, as has often been pointed out, would mean that only enough fuel for a one-way trip would have to be carried from Earth to complete a round-trip mission.

Although the main reason for establishing a base on Mars would be for scientific research, the report also counted among the rationales the potential for a long-term economic "payoff," though specifics were not mentioned. Even psychological factors pertaining

ing it up to a twenty-four-hour day—by bouncing iron asteroids off it. Turning Venus into an Earthlike, even exotic, planet would take about 16,500 years, the study said. (M. J. Fogg, "The Terraforming of Venus," *Journal of the British Interplanetary Society,* 1987, pp. 551–64).

to long periods of confinement in both the spacecraft and on Mars were addressed. The study noted that emphasis on crew selection should go to people who can be "constructive and content" during long periods of interplanetary flight and that psychiatry should be one of the areas of competence among the crew. Even psychopharmacology and biological psychology—"management" of the biological aspects of behavior—would offer "effective ways of dealing with various manifestations of mental distress," the report explained.

The Solar System Exploration Committee's report and that of the National Research Council, *Space Science in the Twenty-first Century,* set a human presence on Mars as the ultimate goal of the robotic precursor missions. Noting that Mars is much more complex geologically than the Moon, the NRC study concluded that its exploration will eventually require "subtle judgments and interactions among observation, analysis, and interpretation" that can be done only by humans.

Yet, understandably, the space and planetary scientists and engineers who participated in the SSEC and NRC studies concentrated on the delicious intricacies of getting robots, not people, to Mars. Morrison's group made the telling point that fourteen months after Apollo 11 landed on the Moon, the USSR's Luna 16 dropped down on the Sea of Fertility, collected three and a half ounces of soil, blasted off, and returned home with its lunar sample. The feat was all but drowned out in the hullabaloo over Apollo, but it was important as a demonstration of the feasibility of sample-return missions. And the Soviets did it twice more, with Luna 20 in February 1972, and with Luna 24 in August 1976. The Solar System Exploration Committee even went on to list ten candidate landing sites for Mars sample-return missions, selected according to specific objectives (Arsia Mons West for young volcanic rocks, for example, and the Schiaparelli Basin Southwest for the oldest crustal rocks from ancient heavily cratered terrain).

As the 1980s gave way to the last decade of the twentieth century the space explorers were peering ahead to the new millennium and thinking about another great age of discovery. And as they thought, they spun their plans, some of which were literally fantastic. Ideas for new spacecraft, new ways to propel them, and new missions, as reflected in the spate of official and quasi-official reports, abounded.

Some conceived of ion engines. These would attain velocity by using positively charged atomic nuclei that chase electrons that have been stripped from them. Although a pair of ion engines weighing perhaps one hundred pounds each would only develop a couple of ounces of thrust at the outset of a long mission, they would work their way up to something like three hundred thousand miles an hour after ten years. Some say this would make truly immense journeys of exploration well beyond the solar system feasible.

The solar sail is the other extreme. Since solar energy radiates out from the Sun at speeds in the range of a million miles an hour with sufficient force to gradually push unguided spacecraft off course, it could also power them if they were equipped to catch it. That equipment, appropriately, would be a huge sail. Since the sail would be in continuous use throughout the voyage, rather than burn out in the initial stage and then just coast along as dead weight, it would be far more efficient than standard rockets.

In an article in *The New York Times Magazine* back in 1977, Carl Sagan had described such a sail and how it would be used to propel a space probe. He said it would be square, about half a mile long, and made of existing materials thinner than the thinnest Mylar. The sail, with probe attached, would be carried to Earth orbit by a shuttle. Then, the astronomer explained, it would be released, unfurled, and strutted. "It would be an extraordinary sight, easily visible to the naked eye as a bright point of light. With a pair of binoculars, detail on such a sail could be made out—perhaps even what on seventeenth-century sailing ships was called the 'device,' some appropriate graphic symbol, perhaps a representation of the planet Earth," Sagan wrote in his picturesque style.* The sight of a spaceship actually setting sail would certainly be stirring. It would also realize Kepler's dream of catching the heavenly breezes for long voyages of exploration.

Many engineers who contemplated spacecraft design saw planetary probes becoming not larger but smaller—in some cases, quite a bit smaller. Advances in the miniaturization of instruments, in fact, would allow microspacecraft weighing between two and twelve pounds to be sent out on lunar and planetary reconnaissance. Being able to, in effect, blanket the solar system with tiny spacecraft would have obvious advantages where expense is concerned, not to mention redundancy and increased scientific yield. According to one theory, the little probes would be launched from Earth orbit on the

*One possibility mentioned by Sagan was a mission to Halley's comet nine years later. He and his friend Bruce Murray, who had become the director of JPL the year before, lobbied hard for the Halley's program but, of course, to no avail.

same type of electromagnetic "railguns" that advocates of the falter-
ing Strategic Defense Initiative would like to use to fire small projectiles at incoming ballistic missile warheads. Ross M. Jones, a JPL
engineer, said that a microspacecraft shot at Saturn by a railgun
could get there in two years, or twice as fast as the Voyagers.

Not satisfied with flybys and orbiters, some engineers have even
designed "gnat robots" that would rove planetary surfaces. MIT's
Artificial Intelligence Laboratory's Mobile Robot Project has produced a small device that uses two legs to drag itself around on a
third point of contact—a kind of tail. With a single antenna, two legs
and a tail, and a pair of bulging telescopic "eyes," the MIT rover,
which is a little bigger than a beer can, looks like a metallic insect.
The diminutive spacecraft are thought to be particularly well suited
to imaging and radio science. The MIT group has also developed an
improved six-legged rover named Genghis that could handle more
difficult terrain.

One possible use for small spacecraft, as envisioned by JPL's
Bobby Brooks, would be to sprinkle the inner planets, several of the
outer planets' moons, and perhaps some asteroids with permanent
monitoring stations. These would send back a constant stream of
information on the body's position, velocity, atmospheric state, and
geological activity.

Meanwhile, the Japanese have moved from theory to practice.
They have begun an aggressive but far from grandiose space exploration program of their own, using diminutive robotic spacecraft. On
January 24, 1990, Japan became only the third nation to launch a
probe at the Moon, when a single booster launched two instrument-
laden spacecraft from the Kagoshima Space Center on Kyushu in
southern Japan. One of the probes, named Muses-A, was drum-
shaped and measured about four and a half feet across, while the
other, named Hagoromo (veil of an angel), was a mere fourteen
inches in diameter. The tiny spacecraft, a test vehicle, went into
lunar orbit on March 19, but its transmission system failed.

Representatives of the Institute for Space and Astronautical Science maintained at the time of the launching that it was only a
precursor to a lunar and interplanetary exploration program in the
1990s. "Our philosophy is that good space science does not need to
be expensive space science," said Jun Nishimura, director of the
institute. The leader of the launching team left no doubt about its
plans for the Moon. "Many countries are interested in the Moon
again," added Kuninori Uesugi, an associate professor at the institute, "and this time, we want to be part of it."

Whatever the potential of ion engines, solar sails, railguns, and other exotic propulsion devices, it seems certain that standard rocket engines are going to be used to get lunar and planetary explorers off Earth for many years to come. In addition, once missions are under way power will continue to come from the same sources that have been in use for years. Solar panels will be used for "close-in" work and radioisotope thermoelectric generators—the reliable RTGs—for exploration of the outer planets, their moons, and the asteroids. Nuclear power will also be used on the surface of Mars, as it was during the time of Viking, to supply dependable power there as well.

It also seems certain that these power sources will operate on increasingly smaller spacecraft and ones that share common designs, as does the Mariner Mark II series. "Ganging" very high speed computers will create a degree of artificial intelligence that should allow far-ranging spacecraft to self-diagnose their problems and either undo them or find ways to override them. The military is well on the way to devising such systems for its communication and reconnaissance satellites, and there is no reason to believe that the abundantly inventive minds in the space agency cannot do the same. Lasers will at some point undoubtedly handle two-way communication, substantially narrowing the beam coming from both Earth and the spacecraft, and in the process strengthening the respective signals and speeding their transmission rates.

The mechanics of designing, building, and sending on their way planetary explorers laden with scientific experiments, however, will by no means be the greatest of the challenges facing those who want humanity to extend its reach beyond Earth. Whatever improvements come in spacecraft design, whether they be in automation, sensing, power, or communications, they will be just that: improvements. The hardest task—learning how to get off Earth, go where it is interesting, and collect information—is already well developed. The robotic voyages that began with Mariner-Venus in 1962 and ended with Voyager 2's conclusion of the Grand Tour at Neptune in 1989 produced a golden age of space exploration. That epoch could stand by itself as a treatise on what the human race can accomplish when its instincts and imagination are harnessed in the drive to extend its world. Or it can constitute only the first chapter of a much longer (and grander) story. Which it is to be depends not so much on technology as on will.

If the will exists to extend mankind's presence in space, then one general rule would seem to apply where the people and the spacecraft themselves are concerned: Let the humans and the machines each do what they do best.

The Space Transportation System is an inherently valuable piece of technology whose fundamental worth was terribly—almost ruinously—diminished by those who wanted it to do everything. Its sponsors felt compelled to distort its true capabilities for the sake of its and their agency's survival. But they were not wholly to blame, since they were playing by long-established rules that forced them to wend their way through a political system in which subterfuge and deceit are rewarded, while honesty is often punished. They therefore calculated, probably correctly, that the consequence of not overselling the shuttle would be to have no shuttle at all.

What the shuttle can do best is carry people to orbit to do what they do best. This includes the service and repair of spacecraft already in orbit and the deployment of others that are particularly complicated or potentially troublesome. Repairing the defective mirror in the Hubble Space Telescope, which was launched by shuttle in April 1990, is a clear case in point. The tortured history of the device is appallingly similar to that of its distant cousin the Galileo spacecraft. After more than a decade of political setbacks, however, the huge telescope was finally orbited by Discovery. But the astronomical community's elation at finally being able to see to the edge of the universe and very far back in time quickly turned first to frustration when pointing difficulties arose, and then to abject despair when it was discovered that one of its two mirrors had been improperly ground, causing a persistent blur. Whatever else can be said about the shuttle (and about the failure to test the telescope adequately before it was launched), the $1.5 billion orbiting observatory would amount to a derelict glass eye—a severely impaired machine—without the possibility of being repaired by shuttle astronauts or returned to Earth for repair there. Such a mission is made to order for the Space Transportation System.

People riding to space on shuttles can also build a space station. Once the station (or stations) is in orbit, shuttles would have to be used to keep them supplied and to change their crews. That, after all, is precisely what the term "shuttle" means. This is a realistic job for manned spacecraft, at least for the foreseeable future. No automated shuttle could match the degree of human skill and ingenuity that would be necessary in the event of a life-threatening emergency (though unpiloted shuttles could easily carry the building materials themselves to orbit). Conversely, sending between four and seven people into the risky environment of space in order to launch a satellite or a deep space probe that could be sent on its way on top of an expendable rocket is as ethically flawed as it is economically wasteful.

Now, as if the saga of the overselling of the shuttle and its painful aftermath had never happened, the space agency and the greater space community seem bent on doing precisely the same thing with the space station. Just as the shuttle ought not to be the handmaiden of a severely fragmented and overambitious program, neither should the station be forced into the role of being an expedient contrivance with which to shepherd another generation of astronauts past Congress and into orbit.

There is ample work to be done on a manned space station, including carrying out studies that would supplement what the Soviets have done on how humans react to prolonged periods in space. There are no doubt many valuable biological and botanical experiments for which a manned station would be well suited. And perhaps the station's most important role would be to act as an assembly platform for the manned expedition to Mars. But there is broad agreement that space science has little or no place on a manned station, or at least on one that would be in an orbit optimized for dispatching the Mars mission.* Since vibration and contamination on the manned station would cause problems for scientific instruments (and perhaps for certain kinds of manufacturing as well), unmanned stations would be more suitable for those undertakings. It is even possible that a large committed unmanned science platform could accompany a manned station, flying in formation with it and being tended by its astronauts.

Mars itself is a perfect candidate for a manned mission. Yet clear distinctions need to be made, not only regarding the roles of men and machines relative to each other but regarding what it is people are supposed to do there in the first place.

If the well-established pattern of exploration that has developed during the space age shows anything, it is that robots should be optimized to do either what people cannot do, what is too dangerous

---

*Speaking at a space station symposium in 1983, Thomas M. Donahue, a leading planetary scientist and a member of the National Academy of Sciences, said that "on balance, the [manned] space station has no clear advantages except for very ambitious missions such as sample return from Mars, asteroids, or comets" (AIAA/NASA symposium, "Space Station: Policy, Planning and Utilization," held at Arlington, Virginia, on July 18–20, 1983).

for them to do, or what can most efficiently and cheaply be done without them. The Mars Observer and then the rover and sample-return missions would therefore be indispensable precursors for the arrival of humans. It would be the task of these machines to so thoroughly reconnoiter Mars—its surface features and atmospheric properties, for example, including radiation hazards—that the risk to the people who followed them would be reduced to an absolute minimum.

In addition, the reasons for the initial foray, perhaps followed by the creation of a modest base, need to be established honestly and explained with complete candor to those who are asked to pay for them. The three best reasons for sending people to Mars are to search for life or its remains; to see whether humans can exist there for long or indefinite periods; and to find things that cannot be anticipated. The three worst reasons for sending people to Mars are to manufacture ball bearings and antibiotics and find cures for cancer and AIDS; to mine minerals in order to supplement Earth's diminishing resources; and to set up a frontier outpost—an extraterrestrial Dodge City—from which an Oz-like metropolis would grow. The key to not overselling Mars is to reconcile the desirable with the possible.

What the late Richard P. Feynman said about the shuttle applies as well to the space station and to the expedition to Mars: "For a successful technology, reality must take precedence over public relations, for nature cannot be fooled."

Meanwhile the robots have more than enough of their own work to do. Every planet, moon, and planetoid of any significance in the solar system, plus any likely comet that wanders in, ought to be a candidate for detailed observation or reinspection. The essential criterion for such missions, however, must be that the resources put into them address science of the most profound sort. All data contribute something, however slight, to mankind's reservoir of knowledge. Yet the wherewithal to mount interplanetary missions is probably inverse to the vast amount of trivia in the universe. Priority should therefore continue to be given to missions that are most likely to contribute significant information to an understanding of the origin and formation of the solar system and to any modeling that could bear on the fate of the Earth itself.

All of the reports on the future of the space program that blossomed in the parched environment of the 1980s, like many that preceded them, had two basic components in common. They explained how to go to space. But they did not explain, in the most fundamental sense, why going there is important. Certainly those who drafted the reports, as well as many who wrote articles of their own, enumerated the usual litany of reasons for extending humanity's presence beyond Earth. These were given as scientific, technological, and occasionally even economic advancement, plus either gaining political leverage over other nations or working with them to foster a mutual understanding.

There was no allusion, however, to whatever it is that impels human beings to want to keep extending the boundaries of their physical world no less than those of their political and spiritual ones. Freedom to abandon the confines of the safe and familiar is a more subtle but no less universal goal than freedom to escape political oppression.

Nor is the accumulation of knowledge at the heart of the matter. Longing to learn is certainly the most valid rationale for undertaking voyages far from the protected precincts of home. Yet in the most basic sense, even the collecting of data—the stocking of libraries—is only a supremely honorable excuse to visit new worlds.

Rather, the core motivation for human beings to venture where they can, and to send robotic proxies where they cannot, is as sublimated but as real and ultimately unerring as the one that guides snow geese, salmon, and other migrators on their own immense journeys. It is a reason that transcends reason. We go because of a profound urge to leave our imprint on the universe. Doing so, physically as well as spiritually, is the only way we can fundamentally relate to it. That is why we explore.

The treasure invested in long voyages of high adventure could arguably be spent curing or preventing dread diseases, combating famine, or fighting other scourges. The compulsion to stave off illness and death is certainly understandable. But ultimately the imperative to merely survive, a trait we share with viruses, is not the most admirable of goals. Greatness is achieved not by putting out fires but by creating monuments to humanity's full capacity for enterprise, imagination, and courage. Certainly these include, as they always have, setting courses that lead straight into the heart of the unknown. The quality of a civilization, as Bruce Murray has observed, is measured not by what it has to do, but by what it wants to do. In that sense, even space itself is not the final frontier. The mind is.

EPILOGUE

Monday, August 21, 1989, dawned overcast and unseasonably chilly in Pasadena. A thick haze, dappled with puffs of smoke-gray and white, sailed over the San Gabriel Mountains behind JPL, alternately obscuring the rising Sun or filtering it to a perfect disk. Parked along Ranger Road, just outside the lab's main entrance, a line of tan trailers and mobile television studios, beaded with the night's condensation and connected to power outlets by thick black cables, began humming to life. Some pointed dish antennas to the south so that relay satellites could pick up Voyager 2's encounter with Neptune—the final encounter of the Grand Tour—as it progressed. The satellites would relay the first close-up pictures of Neptune to people around the world.

In front of von Karman, one or two of the lab's 160 full-time uniformed guards made sure that no one got into the building without a press badge or JPL identification. The Office of Public Information had been barraged for months by space enthusiasts from around the world, most of them hinged to rocket or space clubs or to schools and universities, who desperately wanted to be part of the encounter, if only at its outermost periphery. They wanted to be part of history as it was being made. And as usual there were some others, perhaps unhinged, who wanted to experience the event firsthand because they associated it with messianic or other supernatural events. Screening, both in terms of who got a press pass in the first place, and who was allowed into the auditorium and the adjoining newsroom every morning, was therefore scrupulously careful.

Calling it the prelude to "an extremely exciting week . . . a week of great drama," Lew Allen welcomed the reporters and cameramen at a quarter after ten that Monday morning. Allen was a tall, bespectacled, soft-spoken and politically adroit individual who was so competent, some wags at JPL snickered, that even a Ph.D. in physics had not prevented him from rising to the rank of Air Force chief of staff before he replaced Bruce Murray as Lab director. He believed implicitly in planetary science and exploration, and although he would not say so publicly for fear of raising hackles at Headquarters, it was said by those who knew him that he believed just as implicitly (as did many senior Air Force officers) that the manned program was wasteful, dangerous, and all but pointless.

"This is the last first encounter of a planet for quite a long time," said Allen, a taciturn individual who was not given to overstatement. Then he gave the news media their own benediction. "We have done all we can, I think, to try to make the environment in which you do your very important job productive for you. . . . I hope that we can keep the situation such that you can work effectively because we are very anxious to have you report what I'm sure is going to be an exciting series of events thoroughly and well." "Anxious" was the operative word. It was a fact of life in the closing years of the twentieth century, perhaps a sad one, that even a feat of exploration rivaling the voyages of Columbus was only as good as its press coverage.

The Fourth Estate—a small army of print and electronics media representatives—had come from around the world to report on Voyager 2's final performance. And some, particularly the younger ones, had come to cheer it on. They wore Voyager sweatshirts and buttons along with their press tags, a practice eschewed by John Wilford of *The New York Times,* David Perlman of the *San Francisco Chronicle,* Lee Dye of the *Los Angeles Times,* Robert Cowan of *The Christian Science Monitor,* and other older hands, including those from the wire services and the television networks, who made a clear distinction between reporting an event and advertising it.* Nonetheless, the reporters and writers would be as fastidious about the flyby and its myriad details as were their counterparts who savored a three-star meal, a particularly fine performance of *Die Meistersinger,* deft maneuvering on the floor of the Senate, or the exquisite nuances of the last game in a battle for the Pennant. A sizable

---

*This did not mean that they were humorless. Cowan arrived at von Karman one morning and grimly explained that based on calculations he had done, he was convinced that repeatedly using gravity assist around Earth to increase momentum, as Galileo was supposed to do, would over the course of several millennia force the planet out of its orbit and move it dangerously close to the Sun. In a parody of activist groups and their acronyms, Cowan then announced the formation of his own organization, called SAME, for Save the Angular Momentum of Earth.

number of them were veterans of previous encounters, including the last one: Uranus and the grisly finale that had been superimposed on it in the sky over Cape Canaveral only three and a half years earlier. For many of them, Voyager-Neptune would be a reunion as well as an assignment. They therefore relished being part of the last picture show, as they called it, not being merely its passive scribes.

Norman R. Haynes was next to speak after Allen. Like his predecessors, Voyager's seventh project manager knew Voyager as well as he knew the toaster in his kitchen, and could expostulate for hours, or even days, on its three computers and their complex coding systems, backup mission loads, the state of the RTGs, roll thruster maneuvers for velocity changes, and more.

Now, illuminated by a single overhead spotlight, Haynes told the reporters in the darkened auditorium about Voyager 2's final maneuvers before it reached Neptune and Triton, the largest of its known moons. At about eight-fifteen that morning, he said, the spacecraft's tiny roll thrusters had been fired to minutely change its velocity. The trajectory correction maneuver, as it was called, would move Voyager 2 ninety-one miles farther from the top of Neptune and 439 miles closer to Triton (which it would pass at a distance of about twenty-three thousand miles). As things stood before the adjustment, Haynes went on, the spacecraft was headed for the Earth occultation zone, the spot behind Triton where the moon came between Voyager 2 and Earth. But there was a spot on the other side of Triton, he added, where both Earth and Sun could be occulted—a "dual occultation zone"—and that was where the new course adjustment would put Voyager 2. This would improve its ability to measure the composition and density of the moon's atmosphere by radio transmission.

Ed Stone, the project scientist, opened on a philosophical note. "I suspect many of you are here for your sixth and final Voyager encounter. In a certain sense, this is the final movement of the Voyager symphony of the outer planets, which began with Jupiter ten years ago. And I think in true symphonic form, the tempo appears to be accelerated as we approach encounter, as we all hoped it would be. So, I think we're in for a good ride. . . ." The Caltech physicist then described the spacecraft and the story so far. For the benefit of those who were covering their first encounter, he not only described what was known at that moment about Neptune and Triton, its enigmatic companion, but touched briefly on the Grand Tour in general. The story, however, went much further back than that.

. . .

Neptune is so far away that it was the first planet to be discovered by mathematical calculation rather than by direct observation—it was surmised before it was seen. Its presence was given away by Uranus, which unaccountably seemed to accelerate a bit in its orbit before 1822 and then slow down after that. Two young mathematicians, John Couch Adams in England and Urbain Jean Joseph Leverrier in France, independently and unknown to each other calculated in the mid-1840s that if Newtonian physics was correct, only the gravitational influence of an eighth planet could cause Uranus's strange perturbations. But neither of them was able to convince his superiors that his theory was correct. So in September 1846 Leverrier, in frustration, sent his calculations to Johann Gottfried Galle at the Berlin Observatory. Using Leverrier's coordinates, Galle spotted the planet that tugged at Uranus on the night of September 23, hours after the Frenchman's letter arrived.

Galle originally wanted to name the new planet Janus after the Roman custodian of the universe. Leverrier rejected that, however, on the mistaken ground that Janus, who was also the two-faced deity of gates and doors, represented boundaries. Instead, he first suggested Neptune and then, thinking better of it, decided it was more appropriate that the new planet be named after himself. But the astronomical establishment, noting that such a precedent might cause Uranus to be renamed Herschel after its discoverer, and also finding Neptune and his symbolic trident appropriately mythological, rejected Leverrier's attempt at self-glorification. That was probably as it should have been since Adams was soon also credited with the discovery.*

*Recognizing that a period of intense exploration was at hand, the International Astronautical Union started a Working Group for Planetary System Nomenclature and five Task Groups in 1973. They are composed of scientists from several nations, including the United States and the Soviet Union. The Task Groups deal with the Moon, Mercury, Venus, Mars, and the Outer Solar System. The Working Group oversees the Task Groups to make certain that the names selected are not prejudiced. IAU rules have it that the names of patrons, politicians, or soldiers cannot be used and that no one's name can be used who hasn't been dead for at least three years. Moons are named after characters in Greek and Roman mythology or, in the case of Uranus, after characters in Shakespeare. That particular custom predates 1973: William Herschel's attempt to name Uranus after King George III was rebuffed. Attempts, including at least one from the White House, to name the newly discovered Uranian moons after those who died in the Challenger accident were similarly rejected. Instead, their names, together with other astronauts and cosmonauts, were given to craters on the far side of the Moon. But the process is not always free of dispute. In 1979 the Task Group for Venus Nomenclature drew fire from the National Organization for Women and other feminist groups who wanted newly discovered

Elusive Neptune, nearly three billion miles from the center of the solar system, whirling in light about one thousand times less than that falling on Earth, and invisible to the naked eye, has yet to make a single complete orbit around the Sun since it was discovered (the trip takes 165 years). The best telescopic observations from Earth showed a fuzzy globe a little smaller than Uranus with light regions toward both poles, which seemed to indicate ice crystals, and a darker section around the equator. Other images showed the planet as a kind of fuzzy cue ball covered with what appeared to be major cloud formations. A batch of these taken through filters by Heidi B. Hammel at the Mauna Kea Observatory in Hawaii in July 1988, even as Voyager 2—still more than a year away—was beginning to get its first clear imagery, suggested that Neptune's atmosphere was moving and that the planet, like Uranus, had a heart of rock and ice and a gaseous—actually a fluid—overlayer.

Spectrographic analysis of Neptune, which appeared to be pale green or perhaps blue, suggested a considerable amount of methane in the atmosphere. Neptune was also seen to have two moons: Triton (named after a sea god who was also the son of Poseidon), which was figured to be about the size of Earth's Moon, and the much smaller Nereid (a sea nymph). Triton was observed to move in a peculiar retrograde orbit—counter to the direction of its planet's spin—but no one knew why.

Finally, and most puzzling, astronomers had on occasion thought they saw partial rings around Neptune. What they actually saw was occultations of some stars behind the planet: interruptions, or strange flickering, that could only be accounted for by the presence of something that got between the star and the telescope. A ring would do that. But the rings, if that was what they were, appeared to be incomplete. They seemed to be shaped like horseshoes and were therefore called ring arcs. The existence of the ring arcs would be Voyager 2's first major discovery at Neptune.

The data were incontrovertible, but the whole notion of incomplete rings left many astronomers and others scratching their heads. Theory had it that dust, pebbles, ice chunks, or other stuff spinning around a planet as an incomplete ring would eventually close in on itself until its front and back joined to form a closed ring. If an eighth

features on Venus to be named after real women, not mythical ones. (The system governing nomenclature is from the interview with Merton E. Davies. The feminist problem with names on Venus is from "Scientists, Feminists Dispute Names of Features on Venus," *The Washington Post,* May 29, 1980.)

of a ring or less revolving lopsidedly around a body didn't defy the laws of physics, it was certainly unsettling. In fact the ring arcs, Triton's counterorbit, and many other things associated with Neptune were just plain weird. About all this the venerated university textbooks said nothing, usually in a couple of pages or less.

Late in May, Voyager sent back unambiguous pictures showing that Neptune had a spot—subsequently named the Great Dark Spot after Jupiter's Great Red Spot—that was as large or larger than the United States. Reexamination of imagery sent back in January showed that the spot had been there, too, but that it had been obscured by methane clouds that had since moved on or evaporated. Seen through five different filters, the huge spot was interpreted as probably being a swirling vortex, which, together with the rapidly moving clouds, suggested a lively weather system similiar to Jupiter's and, happily, quite a bit different from Uranus's.

In mid-June a JPL astronomer named Stephen P. Synnott thought he spotted a third moon. Four or five pictures coming back during the next few weeks left no doubt about the matter, since Synnott could compare the large object's movement relative to Neptune over an extended period. "It just came in right smack dead on the button," the elated scientist said. "I never really jumped and screamed," he later recalled, "but I clenched my fist, nodded my head to myself, and said, 'Yup, that one's real!' " The discovery of a new moon, made in the tradition of Galileo, would rank as one of the high points of Stephen Synnott's life. The new moon was promptly dubbed 1989 N1.

Three more moons, which first appeared as smudges on incoming imagery, were picked up during the first week in August, when Voyager was still twenty-two million miles from closest approach. They were christened 1989 N2, N3, and N4. Carolyn C. Porco, a ring specialist from the University of Arizona, guessed that the three might be shepherd moons and could therefore have a bearing on Neptune's peculiar rings because they were spotted in the ring area. People at JPL were by then telling each other that Neptune was going to be even "better" than Uranus.

But if the encounter was shaping up to be a triumph of science and engineering, it was no less one of political will. As Voyager 2, like an Olympic runner, drew closer to the Grand Tour's finish line, many of the journalists and all of the NASA and JPL scientists, engineers, administrators, and support personnel were mindful of the long string of triumphs and near tragedies that had happened along the way. The failed receivers, stuck scan platform, and weakening (but still adequate) memory were so deeply embedded in the mission's folklore that no one had to talk about them. Nor was there mention of the massive reprogramming and attendant course changes that had been necessary after it was finally decided (in retrospect, only God knew how) to go for Uranus and then for Neptune as well.

And certainly no one had to rekindle the memory of the shadow that had been cast by the shuttle on the project from its inception. Or how that shadow had lengthened, relentlessly stalking Voyager 2 even as it continued to bound from one world to another, obediently sending back a quantity of data that placed its flight among the great feats of exploration of all time.

And if anyone was thinking back to the dangerous political shoals through which the Voyager program had been maneuvered, he or she was repressing it in the exhilaration of the moment and in anticipation of what was about to unfold. But the ghosts were there: Carter's exasperating indifference, Reagan's appalling ignorance and theme-park mentality, Fletcher's obsession with keeping Americans in orbit at all costs, and Stockman's zealous "off with its head" budget cutting. And at bottom, of course, there was Keyworth's willingness and Mark's eagerness to pull the plug not only on the spacecraft itself but on the whole planetary exploration program in a vain effort to please a president who neither understood the consequences of such a decision nor cared. No wonder the little robot lent itself to heroic anthropomorphisms bandied about in von Karman and elsewhere at JPL and Caltech: hardy, intrepid, resilient, tough, indomitable . . . a survivor.

All through the ferment, however, the more orderly process of readying Voyager 2 for its meeting with Neptune had continued. One-way light-time would be four hours and six minutes at closest approach, meaning that maneuver commands had to be thought out well ahead of time. In addition, the twenty watts of transmission power that sent signals from the spacecraft to Earth arrived at an energy level about twenty billion times weaker than the battery power used to run a digital watch. The Deep Space Network's three large dishes were therefore stripped and rebuilt so that their bowls measured 230 feet across instead of only 210. This increased their capacity 58 percent. And other antennas, including all twenty-seven at the National Radio Astronomy Observatory's Very Large Array near Socorro, New Mexico, plus huge antennas in Australia and

Japan, were pointed right at Voyager 2. By encounter time, then, Earth had been turned into a giant ear.

Since available light at Neptune would be only 40 percent of what it was at Uranus (and a bare 3 percent of what it was at Jupiter), an elaborately planned "anti-smear campaign" had to be used to prevent blurring the imagery. This entailed pointing the whole spacecraft at the target while it was taking long-exposure pictures, and stabilizing it through ultradelicate use of its maneuvering thrusters. These techniques had been worked in time for use at Uranus, but they were further refined for Neptune. Yet again, they demonstrated Voyager's inherent flexibility and the sort of innovative solutions that the project engineers could bring to bear on potentially catastrophic problems.

Meanwhile the navigation team was doing late ephemeris updates—refining Neptune's and Triton's positions—almost around the clock. The probe's margin of error as it passed Neptune was at that moment being predicted by those who steered it from 2.8 billion miles away to be no more than twenty miles. And it would reach Neptune four minutes and forty-five seconds earlier than originally thought because its large blue-green target turned out to be slightly closer than had been anticipated. "That's not bad," E. Myles Standish, the astronomer who had calculated the planet's ephemeris years before, exclaimed with evident satisfaction. "Not bad at all!"

Now Voyager 2, its hearing and memory impaired, scan platform suffering from arthritis, voice reduced to the barest whisper, energy substantially expended, clock slowed by radiation damage inflicted at Jupiter, and high-gain antenna undoubtedly pitted by micrometeorite impacts, relentlessly continued to bear down on Neptune and its satellites. Streaking in at more than forty thousand miles an hour, the little spacecraft was going to cross the planet's ring plane, then skim over its north pole at an altitude of only slightly more than three thousand miles—by far the closest pass it had ever made to a planet—and finally take the first close look at Triton five hours later. If the Ghoul left Voyager 2 alone, the data return could be nothing short of colossal. After all, there was almost everything to learn. It was against this background that the long-awaited near encounter began.

As Neptune grew larger by the hour it became increasingly clear that the fourth largest planet was a wildly beautiful world, not a bland one like Uranus. It was a massive blue orb of violent, swirling storms set within a turbulent atmosphere of high white clouds, probably frozen methane, that looked like the cirrus type found on Earth. The clouds streaked rapidly along Neptune's girth. Unlike their earthly counterparts, though, most of Neptune's clouds moved from east to west.

The Great Dark Spot, an anticyclonic storm system floating below the equator, whose winds blew counterclockwise, was especially interesting. The imaging team had been following the spot for several weeks as it and the planet on which it swirled loomed ever larger. Now, as Neptune nearly filled the monitor screens in the Voyager office, it could plainly be seen to be "only about one Earth diameter across" and bearing an unmistakable resemblance to Jupiter's Great Red Spot. Neptune's version, color enhanced, was cobalt blue and barely tinged with red. Below the giant storm there was a patch of clouds moving so quickly that the imaging team called it the Scooter. And below the Scooter, welldown in the southern hemisphere, a second, smaller storm brewed.

Andy Ingersoll, the atmospherics specialist from Caltech—the "weatherman"—and his colleagues had done a computer simulation in which Jupiter's opposing bands of one-hundred-mile-an-hour equatorial winds had been made to "interface"—to speed past each other like express trains moving in opposite directions at a combined speed of two hundred miles an hour. Stone narrated the result to the reporters as a videotape of the experiment played on the large screen in front of von Karman. Turbulence could be seen to develop, grow, and evolve into a series of large circulating storm systems that looked just like the giant spots. The storm systems in the computer simulation, and possibly on Jupiter and Neptune as well, developed as part of chaotic processes, Stone added in an oblique reference to the still-emerging science of chaos. The Jupiter simulation was important for the Neptune encounter because eventually both weather systems would be compared to see how many traits they had in common.

As the minutes passed during that first detailed briefing, it became increasingly clear that an entire world that only weeks before had been beyond reach, veiled in cosmic ether since the dawn of time, was now materializing in a steady whisper that streamed to Earth from more than four hours away at the speed of light. An eighth planet, a new world, was being brought into the fold.

Neptune's core was probably melted ice and rock surrounded by a thick layer of water ice and gases. Its lower atmosphere looked as if it could be made of layers of hydrogen sulfide. The methane clouds that floated above it were 390 degrees below zero Fahrenheit, making Neptune the coldest planet yet visited by an Earth-launched probe. Back home, the same methane was used as a relatively clean source of energy to heat stoves and propel some cars. But excessive amounts of the gas were also thought to be partly responsible for the greenhouse effect that was very likely heating Earth's climate to potentially dangerous levels.

Disparate data were coming in from Goldstone and elsewhere in the Deep Space Net: a vast and complicated jigsaw puzzle that would slowly materialize into the basic profile of a distant world as the days passed. The Great Dark Spot now appeared to be twice as large as had been thought and was as proportional to Neptune's size as the Great Red Spot was to Jupiter's. While Earth-based observations had indicated that Triton was about the size of the Moon, Voyager 2's imagery was showing its diameter to be some four hundred miles smaller. "Triton has been shrinking as we approached. We feared that by the time we arrived it might be gone," Brad Smith quipped. He predicted that Neptune's largest satellite would turn out to be only about 1,740 miles in diameter. The first, fuzzy pictures of Triton showed it to be lighter than expected and have a pinkish hue, indicating that much of its surface was methane ice. The brightness, Smith said, indicated a high reflectivity which, in turn, probably meant that contrary to earlier speculation, it was too cold for lakes of liquid nitrogen to exist. A darkened area near its top was judged to be surface markings, but nobody at that point could know just how peculiar the markings were, or how different they were from the rest of Triton's surface.

Less than two weeks earlier—on August 11—Voyager 2 had returned the first photographs positively showing ring arcs: an inner arc revolving about seventeen thousand miles above the tops of the methane clouds, and an outer one, orbiting at an altitude of 23,300 miles. As the days passed, imagery coming back from the spacecraft continued to show the outer arc. It looked like an incomplete string of "pearls" or "sausages," though, because of the presence of relatively thick segments of particulate matter. That was peculiar enough. But to make matters even more confusing, the inner arc then simply dropped out of sight. Each day before near encounter began, fresh photographs, spread on a draftsman's easel and exposed under a large swivel-mounted magnifying glass in the Voyager Project Office, were scrutinized for any trace of the "lost" inner arc (as it was promptly called) and any meaningful extension, however skimpy, of the outer one.

Govert Schilling, an astronomer, correspondent, and amateur cartoonist from Utrecht, the Netherlands, who had a wry sense of humor, dashed off a series of cartoons throughout the encounter that captured several of its aspects. He commemorated the ring problem that first day with a drawing that showed Richard Terrile of JPL, a member of the imaging team, holding an incomplete ring like a broken Hula-Hoop and saying plaintively, "Hi, I'm rich . . . but still tryin' to make ends meet."

The ends met that Monday night, hours after the first briefing concluded. Following a lengthy backgrounder Tuesday morning on

Ring scientist Rich Terrile working hard to close the arc...

magnetospheres elsewhere in the solar system and on the bow shock that he said Voyager 2 was close to hitting as it neared Neptune—a kind of list of coming attractions—Stone, deadpan, turned the briefing over to Brad Smith.

"You've probably all seen the ring movie images that came down this morning," Smith said, drawing out each phrase. "And many of you, I know, have noticed that more than one ring could be seen in the divided images, the so-called ring arcs." Some of the reporters stirred with anticipation. "And it seemed reasonable that this was, indeed, the lost arc that our imaging team raiders were looking for.

"The answer to that is yes and no," Brad Smith continued. "It is, indeed, in exactly the right place. That's the yes. The no is that it's not an arc. It goes all the way around. It's Neptune's first complete ring."

Early that morning, Terrile and the others had painstakingly coaxed a thin line of dark matter out from among the background "noise" until it formed a complete ring just beyond the orbit of 1989 N_3, one of the new satellites. The outer ring, which still defied closing, was near N_4. Both of the new moons appeared to be associated with the rings, perhaps as shepherds, but it was too soon to come to that conclusion. It was also possible that other, smaller moons, yet to be discovered, might serve as the rings' shepherds. As usual, there were more questions than answers.

"When we get behind Neptune and can look back toward the Sun, we'll have the benefit of forward scattering of sunlight by the individual ring particles," Smith added. This would be like looking through an automobile's windshield while driving toward the Sun; dust and dirt that had been invisible becomes highlighted on the glass. "We can't tell how large or small the particles in the ring are, or how wide it is now because it's so faint," he said.

By Wednesday, the twenty-third, as usual, the laws of time and space were beginning to compress the encounter; everything seemed to be happening at once. Just after 10:00 A.M., with Voyager 2 less than 1.5 million miles from Neptune, Haynes announced that the trajectory correction maneuver on Monday had gone so well that the spacecraft was headed "almost smack, dab, in the middle of the Earth-Sun occultation region." It would be within twenty miles of the target area, he said, and would make its closest approach to Neptune within 2.4 seconds of its scheduled arrival time.

Haynes added that Voyager 2's final command load—its last instructions before the flyby—would be uplinked at 12:30, right after lunch. The instructions would be repeated six times, he said, with confirmation from Voyager 2 expected to come back between 8:30 and 9:00 that night. "The spacecraft is working fine, the instruments are all operating as we expected, and everything appears nominal," he said.

"Nominal" was engineering jargon for "as required." In fact, the instruments had been operating at capacity all through the night and were continuing to do so, even as the project manager spoke, and Voyager 2 sped past the 1.45-million-mile mark. Regardless of what the term meant, "nominal" somehow belittled what had happened.

Between midnight and the moment Norman Haynes stepped up to the lectern, another massive barrage of data had come in. There were eight fresh photographs of Neptune, plus eleven taken in the infrared. Two others, taken by the photopolarimeter, showed brightness levels on the planet's surface. Shuffled in with these were twenty-two new pictures of Triton taken by the vidicon camera, in addition to several taken by the photopolarimeter and the ultraviolet spectrometer. Nor did 1989 N1 escape having its portrait taken: four images of the newly discovered moon also came in.

The combined imagery and other data arrived at JPL in a steady stream, like a long line of boxcars coming into a rail yard on a single track. Then they were sorted out according to what they "carried" and routed onto other tracks that went all over the yard. Some of the cars were sent to the imaging team, where they were studied by the atmosphere people or by the geologists. Others went to Warwick's planetary radio astronomy group, while still others were sent over to the magnetic fields, radio science, ultraviolet spectroscopy, and other teams for detailed analysis. In the morning the contents of all the boxcars would be assembled and shown at one place: von Karman.

The quality of the freight had continued to improve. Brad Smith followed Haynes and could barely contain his excitement. "My colleagues in the imaging team are getting very excited. Voyager's images just keep getting better and better. The images we're getting now of the cloud features [of Neptune] and Triton are getting to the point where people are literally jumping up and down," Smith reported.

What else? Plenty. Images of the salmon-colored fuzzball that had been Triton were giving way to pictures that, while still blurred, clearly showed that the moon had a hard surface. Most of Triton was light and mottled, which could have been caused by water ice or by the presence of nitrogen, carbon monoxide, or methane ice. Its upper regions were dark.

But the curved area where the two regions met caused many in the darkened auditorium to stare in amazement at Smith's transparency, perhaps doubting their own senses. The old love song was right. There *was* a blue moon! Or at least there was a blue region separating much of the salmon and darkened regions, about halfway up in the northern hemisphere. There was some speculation—more instant science—that the color might have resulted from a freshly deposited frost of methane and nitrogen, which could scatter sunlight the way gas molecules do on Earth, causing the sky to appear blue. But no one knew for sure.

In addition, there were strong indications that Triton had an atmosphere (which the occultation following closest approach would show) and that some of the mottling was cratered (though no one could say at that point whether they were caused by volcanoes or meteor impacts).

Still the data kept coming in. The amazingly active dark spots on Neptune itself were now being seen from very close up. The outer ring, while not yet a complete circle, was beginning to look as though it would soon become one. Radio emissions from the planet were growing stronger and continued to have a periodicity of sixteen hours, or the length of the planet's day. And Voyager 2's plasma-wave detector had begun to pick up emissions from Neptune, telling the members of the plasma science team that their spacecraft was going to cross the boundary between the solar wind and the planet's magnetosphere—the bow shock—at about midnight.

The first people in von Karman Auditorium on Thursday, the twenty-fourth—Encounter Day—were not reporters. They were young Secret Service men who sized up the place and stuck silvery gray tape on a spot on the floor right in front of Voyager 3. That was where Daniel Quayle, the vice president of the United States, was supposed to stand the following morning when he answered reporters' questions following a speech he would make on the mall. Outside, the wrought-iron fence that separated the road leading to JPL's main gate from the area in front of von Karman was being covered by sheets of black plastic so that the vice president could not be seen from the street.

White and blue Voyager/Neptune banners had sprouted on the metal poles lining the wide stairs in front of Building 180, the administration building, on the north side of the mall, opposite von Karman. A long blue curtain had been strung out midway up the stairs, in front of which Quayle would address some five thousand JPL employees, guests, and reporters. Forty yards away, scaffolding was going up for the television cameramen and soundmen who would record the vice president's observations for posterity. Nearby, two stalls were also being set up: one to sell Voyager and Galileo sweatshirts, mugs, pins and other souvenirs; and the other, soft drinks and hot dogs.

Meanwhile, word was spreading that the vice president himself had committed a stunning gaffe on national television the previous Friday. On July 20 George Bush had unveiled his plan to build the manned space station that Ronald Reagan had approved and use it as a prelude to the program of returning astronauts to the Moon and eventually sending them on to Mars. The president had chosen the twentieth anniversary of the Apollo 11 landing to make the announcement. On August 11 the vice president was interviewed on the Cable News Network as a follow-up to Bush's new space initiative. One question had to do with whether Quayle believed that it was feasible to send people to Mars. "Mars is essentially in the same orbit [as Earth]," the vice president answered. "Mars is somewhat the same distance from the Sun, which is very important. We have seen pictures where there are canals, we believe, and water. If there is water, that means there is oxygen. If oxygen," Quayle added, straight-faced, "that means we can breathe." And where earthlings could breathe, he indicated, they could function quite nicely indeed. Thus did the chairman of the National Space Council not only endorse but elaborate on Percival Lowell's enduring conception of what Mars is really like.

Haynes opened the briefing on Thursday by ticking off where his spacecraft would be as the night progressed.* It would cross Neptune's ring plane (safely beyond any debris) at 11:59 that night. Closest approach would come at 1:01:39 Friday morning. Closest altitude would be 3,048 miles. Sun occultation would occur at 1:07:35, followed by Earth occultation at 1:08:03. "We'll then be behind the planet for nearly an hour," Haynes explained dryly. "We will exit Earth occultation—that is, come back into view of the Earth—at 1:56:49. . . . We then continue on. We cross the ring plane again on

---

*The times were given in so-called Earth Received Time, or local time, which was four hours and six minutes after the actual event had taken place.

our way to Triton at 2:20:56 tomorrow morning at a distance of 104,000 kilometers, which is safely away from any material. . . . Triton closest approach will be at 6:16:09 Friday morning. . . ."

"Well, this is the day," Ed Stone told a packed von Karman. "I hope you've all figured out when you're going to sleep; I haven't." Voyager 2 was due to hit Neptune's magnetosphere "any minute," he noted, adding that the spacecraft was now so close to the planet that its wide-angle camera had to be used to capture the immensity of the scene. "This is it: this is the twenty-four hours we've been waiting for."

Voyager's chief scientist then gave a detailed preview of what the night would hold, hour by hour, as data came in. Like a master magician, Stone concluded his presentation by showing the first animation of the blue planet, a fitting introduction to the night ahead. The short videotape had been made with the new Hypercube, the supercomputer. JPL's Visual Imagery Analysis Laboratory and its Hypercube group had taken individual images of Neptune, fed them into the computer for three-dimensional angle corrections, and gotten back a reconstructed picture of the whole planet actually moving. It was the first time the Hypercube had been used to make such an animation. There was Neptune, all but shapeless a month before, making six complete rotations right in front of the reporters, almost making them feel as though they were approaching it from just below the ring plane, along with Voyager 2.

Smith then presented his imagery. Now there were exquisite high-resolution pictures of both dark spots showing clouds that seemed to be moving upward on convection currents. And, for the first time on any planet Voyager had visited, cloud shadows could plainly be seen perhaps forty to sixty miles above the top of Neptune's gaseous atmosphere. The pictures were "magnificent . . . extraordinary," Smith said before going on to drop more nuggets.

The outer ring was closing, Brad Smith said, and he and his team were almost certain it was complete. Nereid had officially been replaced by 1989 N1 as the second largest of Neptune's moons. Blurred imagery showed that the satellite had a radius of about 120 miles and was irregularly shaped, indicating that it remained as rigid as it was when formed, rather than having been pulled into a round shape like most other heavenly bodies. And there were two new moons—pint-sized 1989 N5 and N6—bringing the total to eight.

Haynes, Stone, and Smith were finally asked to express their emotions now that closest approach to the last planet was finally at hand

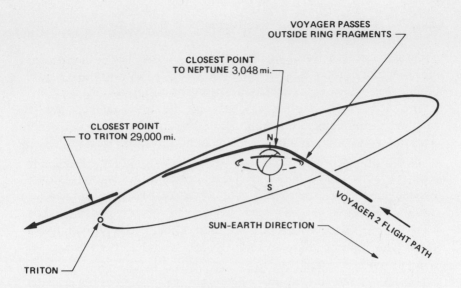

VOYAGER PASSES
OUTSIDE RING FRAGMENTS

CLOSEST POINT
TO NEPTUNE 3,048 mi.

CLOSEST POINT
TO TRITON 29,000 mi.

N

S

SUN-EARTH DIRECTION

VOYAGER 2 FLIGHT PATH

TRITON

VOYAGER 2 FLYBY OF NEPTUNE
AUGUST 25, 1989

after twelve long years. But Smith, speaking for the others, declined.
"We're all caught up in the encounter right now. It's all going to sink
in the next few days."

And caught up they were. Champagne corks popped in the
Voyager Project Office and in many other places throughout the lab
that night as the data continued to stream in. Meanwhile, the spacecraft cruised silently over the vast top of the frozen blue planet,
taking in the spectacular view and collecting all the other data it
could. Then, just as Haynes had predicted, Voyager 2 swung down
the far side of Neptune, toward Triton, at 9:00 P.M. local time, breaking contact with Earth as it entered the occultation region. This was
its last maneuver of the Grand Tour. The celebration had to do not
so much with where Voyager 2 was at that or any other moment but
with what it was sending back. And what it was sending back was
absolutely amazing. But the best was yet to come.

The chairs in the auditorium had been cleared earlier in the evening so that they could be rearranged to face Voyager 3, the full-
scale replica of Voyagers 1 and 2, for the vice president's appearance
in the morning. With the chairs gone, the place looked like a high
school gymnasium being prepared for a dance, particularly because
of the glare from television lights that were being used by several
film crews, including one from Japan that was broadcasting live on
the spot. The monitors in the background showed Torrence Johnson

and then Larry Soderblom doggedly continuing the play-by-play, which a knot of reporters, determined to stay awake throughout the night, were watching from the desks in the other room.

Into all that, making his way between the television commentators and technicians and stepping over their cables, walked George Alexander accompanying a distinguished visitor. Alexander, a pleasant, low-keyed former *Los Angeles Times* science writer, had been made head of the Office of Public Information the year before. The fact that he was personally conducting a tour of von Karman for a single individual suggested that the person was important. And he was. He was none other than the chancellor of the University of Texas and he was there to share NASA's and JPL's moment of triumph with everyone else.

Hans Mark had left the space agency in 1984 to accept his position in Austin. Now he wore a shiny silver Neptune encounter pin in the lapel of his conservative gray suit.

Mark studied Voyager 3 impassively while Alexander dutifully explained the meaning of the gold-plated record its sister was carrying on its way out of the galaxy. The fact that Voyager 2 had reached Neptune after such an arduous long-duration flight was a tribute to the quality of U.S. engineering, Mark told Alexander as he continued to appraise the spacecraft without visible emotion. He might have added that the feat was no less a tribute to its team's and the larger community's resilience, to their ability to withstand and ultimately prevail over duplicitous bureaucrats concerned only with what was politically expedient on the home planet as well. He might have. But he didn't. Instead, Hans Mark finally turned and purposefully retraced his steps to the rear of the auditorium, once more being careful to stay clear of the cables that were carrying the triumph at Neptune around the world. He did not smile.

The first of the twenty-three high-resolution pictures of the entire lighted surface of Triton started coming into the Voyager Project Office on schedule at 3:40 Friday morning. Cheese, crackers, pizza, and 1985 vintage champagne had been broken out as soon as the spacecraft made it safely past the ring plane. Now, with the bottles drained and stale munchies, crust, and Styrofoam coffee cups littering a large table, Stone, Soderblom, Smith, and the rest of the imaging team watched several monitors that showed the shrouds dropping away from Triton one after another. The resolution was sumptuous.

"Here we go!"

"Oh!"

"Look at that!"

"Holy cow!"

"Wow," Soderblom exclaimed, "what a way to leave the solar system!"

Stone, Soderblom, and Smith, peering intently at a small monitor, discussed interesting new lines on Triton, lines that made a large part of it look like a cantaloupe. In small offices nearby, others used their computers to zoom in on especially interesting surface features of the satellite, enhancing them in black-and-white so that they could extract more instant science, leaving the color for later. At that point someone rushed into the Voyager office waving yet another black-and-white Triton photograph, just in from Goldstone and practically still warm. "This is real evidence of volcanic features with multiple flooding incidents," he said excitedly. "We've got to go with this one!" The sky east of Pasadena was beginning to lighten.

"I really like to think of Voyager somewhat like a trained athlete," Stone told a packed von Karman auditorium on Friday morning. The vice president had just completed a congratulatory speech on the mall, followed by a short question-and-answer session as he dutifully stood on the silver tape in front of Voyager 3. He had then departed. "It's really working at the very limits of its capability," Stone added, "but not beyond. . . . We set ourselves an extremely challenging encounter and, essentially, everything has worked."

That day, and during the four that followed, an increasingly complex portrait of Neptune and its major moon, striking yet often baffling, began to come together. Neptune's magnetosphere, which Voyager entered about nine hours before closest approach, seemed to be roughly the same strength as Earth's. But, surprisingly, the field was found to be tilted 50 degrees off the planet's spinning axis. Uranus has a similar relationship between its magnetic and spin axes, but that was thought to be the result of its being tilted on its side. Since Neptune is not tilted, scientists were forced to begin rethinking their theories of planetary magnetic fields. In addition, the internal system that generates Neptune's magnetosphere does not pass through the center of the planet, but may in fact be relatively close to its surface. The magnetosphere itself undergoes dramatic and mysterious changes as the planet rotates.

Neptune's weather system was found to contain an enormously turbulent atmosphere, with winds whipping clouds at four hundred

miles an hour, and immense storm systems, the most striking of
which is the Great Dark Spot.* But project scientists were hard
pressed to explain how it could generate such violent weather when
it receives only about 5 percent as much solar energy as Jupiter.
They also found that its temperature range was similar to that of
Uranus, even though the latter is a billion miles closer to the Sun.
One likely explanation was that Neptune has a proportionately
stronger internal heat source than its neighbor. Yet, as usual,
Voyager 2's revelations produced more questions than answers. "It's
a mistake to think of the meteorology of the gas giants as the same
problem repeated four times," noted Ingersoll, the meteorologist. "It
teaches me a certain humility. All the great knowledge we have of
the Earth does not generalize very well. Uranus doesn't even generalize to Neptune."

But Voyager did nail down the moon and ring equation. It raised
the number of known satellites from two to eight, found that one of
them was larger than Nereid, and measured the others at between
seventy-five and three hundred miles in diameter. With their arcs
finally closed, four distinct rings were found around Neptune, plus
the faintest suggestion of two more. In addition, two "dust sheets"—
plateaus of small particles were also discovered, one of which seemed
to extend all the way down to the planet itself, in a way reminiscent
of a similar sheet that circles Saturn. But why the thick beads, or
arcs, on the outer ring? Why hadn't the arcs smoothed out until they
were uniform? No one knew. "Rings are not a geological monument
held together by old, strong forces," said Larry Esposito, a member
of the photopolarimeter team from the University of Colorado who
found the clumps similar to those on Saturn's F Ring. "They are
piles of debris." "None of the current hypotheses can explain the
persistence of the arcs," Smith would observe the following December. The implication was that previous theories of ring formation
would have to be drastically revised or scrapped altogether.

It was Neptune's foremost accompanying world, Triton, that stole
the show, however, just as Io had all but done at Jupiter. The blob
that was barely visible from Earth turned out to be not only the
coldest place yet visited by a spacecraft, but also one of the brightest
spots in the solar system, and certainly one of the most diverse.

*Subsequent close analysis showed that winds on Neptune's surface reach about 1,500
miles an hour, making them the fastest in the solar system, even beyond those on
Saturn, which have been measured at 1,100 miles an hour ("Neptune Winds Hit 1,500
M.P.H., *Los Angeles Times,* December 6, 1989).

Triton was fantastical pulp fiction come true. It seemed to have come from far away, only to be pulled into Neptune's orbit at an angle well off the equator and in a direction opposite to the rotation of the planet itself, clearing a path by obliterating everything in its way. The theory was supported by the fact that there were no other little worlds out at 205,000 miles, where Triton orbited.

It was also theorized that Triton's first billion or so years were spent in a gradually reduced elliptical orbit, drawing close to Neptune, then pulling away, then coming back again. The tremendous, repeated compression and expansion would have kneaded it like a celestial dough ball, causing its surface to be soft and its interior to convulse. This could explain its relatively new surface, as indicated by a general lack of impact craters, the presence of mysterious dark plumes next to some craters near the moon's south pole and huge flat basins that may from time to time have hardened into frozen lakes. It was at first theorized that the plumes—blackened swatches set across an otherwise pristine landscape—suggested volcanic activity on Triton. If true, it would have made the moon only the third body in the solar system after Earth and Io to have active volcanoes. It was later postulated, however, that the plumes are either geysers of nitrogen gas or so-called dust devils: wind-driven gusts of hydrocarbons that leave smudges on the surface. After a year of analysis the geologists would lean toward the nitrogen-release theory as the more plausible, calling it a kind of greenhouse effect.

No one at the time of encounter was sure of why so much of Triton's surface looked like the skin of a cantaloupe, either. Some said that the condition could have been caused by moonquakes, which ripped open its surface, causing the crisscrossing fissures. The rugged terrain elsewhere was most likely caused by the volcanoes, which were fueled by liquid hydrogen. But instant science had often been wrong during the twelve years of the Voyager mission, so the piles of imagery and other data would bear much closer scrutiny in the years to come. Leonard Tyler, the Stanford physicist who led the radio science team, explained at one point that his depiction of Triton's atmosphere was necessarily incomplete. "I'm waiting for 992 pounds of magnetic tape that's en route from the tracking stations," he explained.

The fifty-fourth and final news conference of the Voyager interplanetary mission took place on August 29, 1989. At nine o'clock that morning the "doughty little spacecraft that could" (as Haynes called

it) was 2,758,530,928 miles from Earth and heading out of the solar
system. Before it left the region of its fourth and final encounter,
though, it looked back and took a last portrait of Neptune and Triton
from only three million miles. The image showed the two ghostly
worlds backlighted by the Sun, the way Uranus as a blue crescent
had been forty-three long months earlier, when the exhilaration of
the first visit to the third giant suddenly evaporated in the anguish
of Challenger.

"As exciting as these and other discoveries we've made at Neptune
have been," Stone said in parting, "this encounter has really been
just the fourth and final planet that Voyager has revealed in an
unprecedented decade of discovery in its journey to the outer solar
system. The Voyager discoveries from this survey will serve as an
encyclopedia for the giant outer planets for decades to come. And
without any question, for those of us fortunate enough to have been
involved, this has been the journey of a lifetime."* He closed with
a line from T. S. Eliot: *Not fare well, but fare forward, voyagers.*

The longest and most bountiful mission in the history of the space
age was all but over. Data from the outer reaches of the solar system
would keep coming in for years, long after Voyager 2's cameras had
been turned off to save energy, just as it was still coming in from
Voyager 1 and the two Pioneers. But everyone at JPL that morning
understood that the first look at the great planets was finally at an
end. Not only had they gotten their spacecraft through a most extraordinary odyssey, reaping a quantity of knowledge that remained
incalculable, but they had managed to do so in what often seemed
to be a state of siege. The indifference and duplicity of the gods,
almost as much as the importance of the mission itself, had come to
define them both as individuals and as members of the larger team.

Now the exhilaration was suddenly giving way to emptiness as it
began to sink in that the Grand Tour was complete; there would be
no new planets. Jurrie van der Woude, his fists pushed into the
pockets of his fighter pilot's jacket, sat in the picture trailer beside
von Karman and barely managed to choke back a sob in midsentence
as he talked about the long mission, now suddenly concluded. He had
worked indefatigably throughout each encounter, not only getting
imagery to the news media every day but bringing to bear for them
a knowledge of JPL that was encyclopedic and widely venerated.

---

*It had its administrative as well as scientific rewards. In July 1990, Stone was named
to succeed Lew Allen as director of JPL. The appointment was in large measure
recognition of his decade-and-a-half contribution to the Voyager program.

Inside von Karman, a young man stood beside Voyager 3, a camera hanging from his neck and a blue timeline—the encounter's libretto—clutched in his hand. He seemed to speak for everyone when he said to no one in particular that it was "a sad day; a great day, but kind of a sad day, too." Then he asked Haynes to autograph the timeline.

Bobby Brooks, perched on a bench in the bright sunshine in front of the building that afternoon of August 29, watched among the last of the reporters heading for the parking lot on the other side of Ranger Road and down toward Oak Grove Drive, where the overflow traffic had been sent. The television cameras and portable antennas had been stuffed back into the large broadcast vans and for the most part been taken away the day before.

"We've given the people of this planet the solar system," Brooks said in a voice whose low intensity contrasted to the calm that was once again settling over the Jet Propulsion Laboratory. That seemed to say it all.

Except for one final photo opportunity, the last picture show was over. On February 14, 1990, Voyager 1, still climbing after having separated from Voyager 2 at Saturn, looked down on the solar system and shot an unprecedented family portrait. In effect, it had to step back about 3.7 billion miles to get almost all of the members of the family into the picture. Except for little Pluto, off to one side, they were strung out in a long, ragged line that started at the Sun. It was an appropriate souvenir of the Grand Tour.*

When Voyager 2's hydrazine is expended early in the twenty-first century, it will no longer be able to guide itself by the light of Canopus, the Sun, and Earth. Its antenna will gradually swing away from the direction of the Deep Space Network's antennas, breaking the communication lock with those who control it. Then, deaf, dumb, blind, and disoriented, the spacecraft will begin to tumble ever deeper into the frozen reaches of time and space without end. It will sail the heavenly breezes to eternity, long after the place from which it came is no more.

---

*Mercury and Mars were lost in the glare of the Sun and Pluto was too far away and too small to show up in the imagery. The picture was actually sixty-four frames that could be combined into one image.

SOLAR SYSTEM EXPLORATION MISSIONS

Spacecraft Nation	Launch Date	Objective Result
Unannounced USSR	May 1 58	Lunar flyby or impact Launch failure
Thor-Able 1 US	Aug. 17 58	Initial lunar probe Launch vehicle explosion
Unannounced USSR	Sep. 24 58	Lunar flyby or impact Launch failure
Pioneer 1 US	Oct. 11 58	Lunar orbiter Failed to achieve required velocity but returned 43 hours of data
Pioneer 2 US	Nov. 8 58	Lunar orbiter Failed to achieve required velocity
Unannounced USSR	Nov. 26 58	Lunar flyby or impact Launch failure
Pioneer 3 US	Dec. 6 58	Lunar flyby Failed to achieve required velocity but returned data on radiation bands around Earth
Luna 1 USSR	Jan. 2 59	Lunar flyby Passed within 3,500 miles and orbited the sun
Pioneer 4 US	Mar. 3 59	Lunar flyby Passed within 37,500 miles and returned radiation data
Luna 2 USSR	Sep. 12 59	Lunar Impact First man-made object to land on another celestial body
Luna 3 USSR	Oct. 4 59	Photograph far side of the Moon Hugely successful
Atlas-Able US	Nov. 26 59	Lunar orbiter Payload shroud broke away forty-five seconds after liftoff
Pioneer 5 US	Mar. 11 60	Solar orbit between Earth and Venus Returned data on interplanetary space and solar phenomena
Atlas-Able US	Sep. 25 60	Lunar orbiter Second-stage malfunction

Spacecraft Nation	Launch Date	Objective Result
Unannounced USSR	Oct. 10 60	Mars flyby Failed to achieve Earth orbit
Unannounced USSR	Oct. 14 60	Mars flyby Failed to achieve Earth orbit
Sputnik 7 USSR	Feb. 4 61	Venus flyby Failed to leave Earth orbit
Venera 1 USSR	Feb. 12 61	Venus flyby Communication failure 14 million miles from destination
Ranger 1 US	Aug. 23 61	Test spacecraft for lunar impact Entered wrong orbit because Agena failed to restart
Ranger 2 US	Nov. 18 61	Test spacecraft for lunar impact Entered wrong orbit because Agena altitude control system failed
Ranger 3 US	Jan. 26 62	Lunar rough landing and TV transmission Missed destination by 20,000 miles
Ranger 4 US	Apr. 23 62	Lunar rough landing and TV transmission Landed on the far side: no data
Mariner 1 US	Jul. 22 62	Venus flyby Blown up by range safety officer after booster went off course
Unannounced USSR	Aug. 25 62	Venus flyby Failed to leave Earth orbit
Mariner 2 US	Aug. 27 62	Venus flyby First spacecraft to visit another planet
Unannounced USSR	Sep. 1 62	Venus flyby Failed to leave Earth orbit
Unannounced USSR	Sep. 12 62	Venus flyby Failed to leave Earth orbit
Ranger 5 US	Oct. 18 62	Lunar rough landing and TV transmission Power failure: almost no data
Unannounced USSR	Oct. 24 62	Mars flyby Failed to leave Earth orbit
Mars 1 USSR	Nov. 1 62	Mars flyby Communication failure 69 million miles from destination

Spacecraft Nation	Launch Date	Objective Result
Unannounced USSR	Nov. 4 62	Mars flyby Failed to leave Earth orbit
Unannounced USSR	Jan. 4 63	Lunar soft landing Failed to leave Earth orbit
Unannounced USSR	Feb. 3 63	Lunar soft landing Launch failure
Luna 4 USSR	Apr. 2 63	Lunar soft landing Missed destination by 5,300 miles
Cosmos 21 USSR	Nov. 11 63	Venus test probe Failed to leave Earth orbit
Ranger 6 US	Jan. 30 64	Obtain TV imagery of the lunar surface before impact Camera failure: no data
Unannounced USSR	Feb. 27 64	Probable Venus flyby Apparent launch failure
Unannounced USSR	Mar. 4 64	Probable Venus flyby Apparent launch failure
Cosmos 27 USSR	Mar. 27 64	Probable Venus flyby Failed to leave Earth orbit
Zond 1 USSR	Apr. 2 64	Venus probe Communication failure: no data
Unannounced USSR	Apr. 9 64	Lunar soft landing Launch failure
Ranger 7 US	Jul. 28 64	Obtain TV imagery of the lunar surface before impact: returned 4,308 pictures
Mariner 3 US	Nov. 5 64	Mars flyby Shroud failure trapped spacecraft: no data
Mariner 4 US	Nov. 28 64	Mars flyby First successful Martian flyby: returned 22.5 pictures and other data
Zond 2 USSR	Nov. 30 64	Mars flyby Communication failure
Ranger 8 US	Feb. 17 65	Obtain TV imagery of lunar surface before impact: hit within 15 miles of aim point and returned 7,137 pictures
Cosmos 60 USSR	Mar. 12 65	Lunar soft landing Failed to leave Earth orbit

Spacecraft Nation	Launch Date	Objective Result
Ranger 9 US	Mar. 21 65	Obtain TV imagery of lunar surface before impact: returned 5,814 high-resolution pictures
Luna 5 USSR	May 9 65	First lunar soft-landing attempt Crashed on the lunar surface
Luna 6 USSR	Jun. 8 65	Lunar soft landing Missed destination by 100,000 miles
Zond 3 USSR	Jul. 18 65	Lunar test photographic mission: photographed far side
Luna 7 USSR	Oct. 4 65	Lunar soft landing Crashed on the lunar surface
Venera 2 USSR	Nov. 12 65	Venus flyby Communication failure just before arrival
Venera 3 USSR	Nov. 16 65	Venus atmospheric probe Communication failure just before atmospheric entry
Cosmos 96 USSR	Nov. 23 65	Venus atmospheric probe Failed to leave Earth orbit
Luna 8 USSR	Dec. 3 65	Lunar soft landing Crashed on the lunar surface
Pioneer 6 US	Dec. 16 65	Measure the Sun and its effects on interplanetary space: all experiments were successful
Luna 9 USSR	Jan. 31 66	Lunar soft landing First successful lunar soft landing: returned imagery
Cosmos 111 USSR	Mar. 1 66	Probable lunar orbiter Failed to leave Earth orbit
Luna 10 USSR	Mar. 31 66	Lunar orbit First satellite to orbit the Moon
Surveyor 1 US	May 30 66	Demonstrate lunar soft-landing capability and collect data Sent back more than 10,000 pictures.
Lunar Orbiter 1 US	Aug. 10 66	Lunar orbit in support of Apollo First US spacecraft to circle the Moon: heavy data return
Pioneer 7 US	Aug. 17 66	Solar investigation Detected tail of Earth's magnetosphere and made numerous solar measurements

Spacecraft Nation	Launch Date	Objective Result
Luna 11 USSR	Aug. 24 66	Probable lunar imaging orbiter failed to return imagery but sent back other data
Surveyor 2 US	Sep. 20 66	Demonstrate lunar soft-landing capability and collect data Crashed on the lunar surface
Luna 12 USSR	Oct. 22 66	Lunar orbiter Returned imagery and other data
Lunar Orbiter 2 US	Nov. 6 66	Obtain imagery and other data in support of Apollo Imaged 13 Apollo target sites
Luna 13 USSR	Dec. 21 66	Lunar soft landing Measured chemical properties of the surface and returned imagery
Lunar Orbiter 3 US	Feb. 4 67	Obtain imagery and other data in support of Apollo Transmitted data on landing sites
Unannounced USSR	Mar. 27 67	Probable Mars lander Rumored launch failure
Surveyor 3 US	Apr. 17 67	Lunar surface sample experiments and imagery Returned 6,315 images and other data
Lunar Orbiter 4 US	May 4 67	Do broad photo survey and gather data on gravity, radiation, and other areas First photos of the Moon's south pole
Venera 4 USSR	Jun. 12 67	Venus atmospheric probe First return of data from within the atmosphere
Mariner 5 US	Jun. 14 67	Venus flyby Returned data on atmosphere, mass, radiation, and magnetic field
Cosmos 167 USSR	Jun. 17 67	Venus atmospheric probe Failed to leave Earth orbit
Surveyor 4 US	Jul. 14 67	Lunar soft landing to get imagery and surface data for Apollo Crashed on the surface: no data
Lunar Orbiter 5 US	Aug. 1 67	Obtain detailed imagery and other data on both sides of the Moon Returned 212 excellent pictures

Spacecraft Nation	Launch Date	Objective Result
Surveyor 5 US	Sep. 8 67	Soft landing on the Sea of Tranquility for imagery, chemical analysis, and other data. Returned 18,006 pictures
Surveyor 6 US	Nov. 7 67	Collect data and perfect Moon landing techniques First lunar liftoff (hopped 10 feet)
Pioneer 8 US	Dec. 13 67	Make solar radiation and other measurements All experiments returned good data
Surveyor 7 US	Jan. 7 68	Soft landing near crater Tycho for imagery, material sampling, and alpha particle scattering: successful
Zond 4 USSR	Mar. 2 68	Probable precursor to a manned lunar spacecraft Probably destroyed a week after launch
Luna 14 USSR	Apr. 7 68	Lunar orbiter for probable TV coverage and study of the Earth-Moon relationship: no data released
Zond 5 USSR	Sep. 15 68	Precursor to a manned lunar spacecraft first flight to the Moon and back
Pioneer 9 US	Nov. 8 68	Measure how the Sun affects interplanetary space and explore area ahead of the Sun: successful
Zond 6 USSR	Nov. 10 68	Precursor to a manned lunar flight Circled the Moon and returned home after a "double-dip" reentry
Apollo 8 US	Dec. 21 68	First manned circumlunar flight The 147-hour mission included 10 orbits around the Moon
Venera 5 USSR	Jan. 5 69	Venus atmospheric probe Descent capsule returned data to an altitude of 16 miles from the surface
Venera 6 USSR	Jan. 10 69	Venus atmospheric probe Descent capsule returned data to an altitude of 7 miles from the surface
Mariner 6 US	Feb. 25 69	Mars flyby Passed within 2,070 miles and returned TV imagery and other data ·

Spacecraft Nation	Launch Date	Objective Result
Mariner 7 US	Mar. 18 69	Mars flyby Passed low over the southern hemisphere and returned 126 pictures
Apollo 10 US	May 18 69	Second manned mission to evaluate Lunar Module and collect data Came within 50,000 feet of the surface
Unannounced USSR	Jun. 14 69	Lunar rover or sample return Launch failure
Luna 15 USSR	Jul. 13 69	Lunar rover or sample retriever Orbited 52 times and then crashed
Apollo 11 US	Jul. 16 69	First manned landing on the Moon Conducted limited experiments and assessed the environment
Zond 7 USSR	Aug. 8 69	Third manned precursor to the Moon Took first Soviet deep space color pictures and returned to the USSR
Pioneer E US	Aug. 27 69	Solar mission similar to Pioneers 6–9 Blown up after launch vehicle malfunction
Cosmos 300 USSR	Sep. 23 69	Lunar rover or sample return Failed to leave Earth orbit
Cosmos 305 USSR	Oct. 22 69	Lunar rover or sample return Failed to leave Earth orbit
Apollo 12 US	Nov. 14 69	Second manned lunar landing mission Sampled more area, set up experiment package, and examined Surveyor 3
Unannounced USSR	Feb. 19 70	Lunar rover or sample return Launch failure
Apollo 13 US	Apr. 11 70	Manned lunar landing for seismological inspection, survey, sampling, imaging Accident aborted mission
Venera 7 USSR	Aug. 17 70	Venus lander First successful landing with 23 minutes of data from the surface
Cosmos 359 USSR	Aug. 22 70	Probably another Venus lander Failed to leave Earth orbit
Luna 16 USSR	Sep. 12 70	Moon sample return First automated return of material from another world

Spacecraft Nation	Launch Date	Objective Result
Zond 8 USSR	Oct. 20 70	Fourth and last manned precursor to the Moon Fiery splashdown in the Indian Ocean
Luna 17 USSR	Nov. 10 70	Land a Lunokhod (rover) on the Moon: it was steered five and a half miles and collected data
Apollo 14 US	Jan. 31 71	Third manned lunar landing for human activity and experiments Returned 95 pounds of samples to Earth
Mariner 8 US	May 8 71	Ninety-day Mars orbiter with infrared, ultraviolet, and other sensors Centaur malfunctioned shortly after liftoff
Cosmos 419 USSR	May 10 71	Mars orbiter-lander Failed to leave Earth orbit
Mars 2 USSR	May 19 71	Mars orbiter-lander Orbiter circled at low altitude: lander crashed
Mars 3 USSR	May 28 71	Orbiter circled at low altitude: lander sent first panoramic image of the surface before transmission ended
Mariner 9 US	May 30 71	Same mission as Mariner 8 Mapped 85 percent of Mars; sent first photos of Deimos and Phobos
Apollo 15 US	Jul. 26 71	Fourth manned lunar landing and the first to use a rover About 180 pounds of samples returned
Luna 18 USSR	Sep. 2 71	Lunar soil sample return Crashed on the Moon
Luna 19 USSR	Sep. 28 71	Imagery and a variety of sensor experiments from lunar orbit Successful
Luna 20 USSR	Feb. 14 72	Lunar soil sample return Drilled a hole, extracted samples, and returned them to Earth
Pioneer 10 US	Mar. 2 72	Jupiter flyby First spacecraft to investigate an outer planet and the interplanetary space leading to and beyond it
Venera 8 USSR	Mar. 27 72	Venus lander Returned data for 50 minutes

Spacecraft Nation	Launch Date	Objective Result
Cosmos 482 USSR	Mar. 31 72	Probable lander Failed to leave Earth orbit
Apollo 16 US	Apr. 16 72	Fifth manned lunar landing and the second to use a rover: 213 pounds of samples returned
Apollo 17 US	Dec. 7 72	Sixth and last manned landing in the series: 250 pounds of samples returned
Luna 21 USSR	Jan. 8 73	Land another Lunokhod on the Moon Returned data until June 3
Pioneer 11 US	Apr. 5 73	Jupiter and Saturn flybys Discovered Saturn's 11th moon, two new rings, magnetic field and much more
Mars 4 USSR	Jul. 21 73	Mars orbiter Engine malfunction prevented it from orbiting: flew by
Mars 5 USSR	Jul. 25 73	Mars orbiter to relay communication from Mars 6 and Mars 7 landers Entered orbit on Feb. 12, 1974 and apparently returned data
Mars 6 USSR	Aug. 5 73	Mars lander All signals from the capsule ended seconds before landing
Mars 7 USSR	Aug. 9 73	Mars lander Engine malfunction caused the spacecraft to miss Mars entirely
Mariner 10 US	Nov. 3 73	Venus-Mercury flyby Encountered Venus once and Mercury three times: excellent imagery and other data
Luna 22 USSR	May 29 74	Lunar orbiting imager Returned imagery and other data from different orbits for more than a year
Luna 23 USSR	Oct. 28 74	Drill for lunar soil samples Drilling device was damaged
Venera 9 USSR	Jun. 8 75	Venus orbiter-lander First successful orbiting of Venus: lander returned the first photo
Venera 10 USSR	Jun. 14 75	Venus orbiter-lander Returned a picture and data from the surface for 65 minutes

Spacecraft Nation	Launch Date	Objective Result
Viking 1 US	Aug. 20 75	Mars orbiter-lander First US landing on another planet: immense data return
Viking 2 US	Sep. 9 75	Virtual duplicate of Viking 1's highly successful mission: the search for life ended with ambiguous results
Luna 24 USSR	Aug. 9 76	Lunar sample return Returned to the USSR with a soil sample
Voyager 2 US	Aug. 20 77	Jupiter and Saturn system flyby extended to Uranus and Neptune for a Grand Tour: bonanza of data
Voyager 1 US	Sep. 5 77	Jupiter and Saturn system flyby In 1990 took first portrait of the solar system
Pioneer 12 US	May 20 78	Study Venus's atmosphere and the solar wind and make radar and gravity maps: worked in conjunction with Pioneer 13
Pioneer 13 US	Aug. 8 78	Multiprobe study of Venus's wind, circulation, atmospheric composition, temperature and pressure
ISEE 3 US	Aug. 12 78	International Sun-Earth Explorer 3 became the International Cometary Explorer to meet Giacobini-Zinner on September 11, 1985
Venera 11 USSR	Sep. 9 78	Venus soft landing Returned 95 minutes of data, including violent thunder activity: no imagery
Venera 12 USSR	Sep. 14 78	Venus soft landing Returned 110 minutes of data, including 460-degree C temperature
Venera 13 USSR	Oct. 30 81	Venus orbiter-lander Landed on March 3, 1982, and returned a color picture
Venera 14 USSR	Nov. 4 81	Venus orbiter-lander Landed on May 5, 1982, and returned a color picture
Venera 15 USSR	Jun. 2 83	Venus orbiting radar mapper Returned high resolution imagery, including over the northern pole
Venera 16 USSR	Jun. 7 83	Same mission and results as Venera 15 Surveyed regions not visible on Earth

Spacecraft Nation	Launch Date	Objective Result
Vega 1 USSR	Dec. 15 84	Mission to Venus in June 1985 and then to Halley's Comet in March 1986 Returned data from both encounters
Vega 2 USSR	Dec. 21 84	Same mission and results as Vega 1 Ejected a lander and an atmospheric ballon at Venus: bountiful data
Sakigake Japan	Jan. 7 85	Rendezvous with Halley's Comet Measured the effects of the solar wind on the comet's tail
Giotto ESA	Jul. 2 85	European Space Agency mission to Halley's Comet: made closest approach (336 miles from the nucleus)
Suisei Japan	Aug. 18 85	Rendezvous with Halley's Comet Returned ultraviolet imagery of the comet's 12-million-mile-long comma
Phobos 1 USSR	Jul. 7 88	Ambitious attempt to orbit Mars and set a lander on Phobos Faulty command ended mission en route
Phobos 2 USSR	Jul. 12 88	Mission similar to that of Phobos 1 On-board computer malfunction caused disorientation in late March 1989: some data received
Magellan US	May 4 89	Map Venus with radar in unprecedented detail: first shuttle-launched interplanetary spacecraft (Atlantis). Returned excellent imagery.
Galileo US	Oct. 18 89	Orbiter with probe to conduct intense examination of Jupiter and its system Also shuttle-launched (Atlantis)
Muses-A Japan	Jan. 24 90	A pair of small lunar orbiters made Japan the third nation to reach the Moon: transmitter failure before data could be returned

Sources:

TRW Space Log
Handbook of Soviet Lunar and Planetary Exploration
The Soviet Year in Space
Planetary Exploration Through Year 2000
The New York Times
The Washington Post
Aviation Week & Space Technology

NOTES

PROLOGUE

Faget, a National Aeronautics and Space Administration engineer, also figured prominently in design work for the Mercury and Apollo spacecraft and the space station.

Aborts, including those necessitating a return to the space center, are described in *Space Shuttle Transportation System,* a highly detailed press information guide that was published by Rockwell International, the shuttle's prime contractor, in January 1984. Hereafter it will be called *SSTS.* Abort procedures are on pp. 13–15.

Weather conditions before and at the time of launch are from the *Report of the Presidential Commission on the Space Shuttle Challenger Accident* (Washington: U.S. Government Printing Office, June 6, 1986), pp. 104–13. Hereafter it will be called the *Rogers Commission Report.* Icing on the Fixed Service Structure is from *Investigation of the Challenger Accident,* Committee on Science and Technology, House of Representatives, 99th Cong., 2nd Sess., October 29, 1986, pp. 233–40. Hereafter it will be called the *ICA.* Also see Appendix I, NASA Pre-Launch Activities Team Report, Rogers Commission Report Vol. II, I-9 and 10.

The Lamberth-Stevenson interchange is from *ICA,* p. 236. Also see "NASA Official Advised Against Liftoff," *The New York Times,* November 5, 1986.

Voyager 2's speed and distance from the earth on January 28, 1986, were calculated by Robert J. Cesarone of the Jet Propulsion Laboratory's Mission Design Section. Operational details for this time period are in the *Voyager 2 Uranus Encounter Timeline (Jan. 21 to Jan. 29, 1986),* published by the Jet Propulsion Laboratory in Pasadena, California.

The Voyagers are depicted in Richard P. Laeser, William I. McLaughlin and Donna M. Wolff, "Engineering Voyager 2's Encounter with Uranus," *Scientific American,* November 1986, p. 38. Also see Eric Burgess, *By Jupiter* (New York: Columbia University Press, 1982), Chapter 4.

Voyager 2's coordinates on the morning of January 28—1.78 billion miles from Earth and slightly more than three million from Uranus—are from Cesarone.

Voyager 2's navigational maneuver is the *Voyager 2 Uranus Encounter Timeline* for January 24, p. 2. The experiments and closest approaches are listed chronologically throughout that day's events, pp. 1–25.

Stone's remarks are from Joel Davis, *Flyby: The Interplanetary Odyssey of Voyager 2* (New York: Atheneum, 1987), pp. 190–91.

The first effort to get TDRS-B into space in March 1985 had failed. A space agency official was quoted at the time as saying that devices aboard the spacecraft "that encode secret signals" had caused the problem. "The TDRS spacecraft has encryption devices installed to protect the system from interfering signals," the official said. See "Satellite Problems Scrub Shuttle Flight," *The New York Times,* March 2, 1985. See also *Security Classification Guide: Tracking Data and Relay System (SCG 16),* a heavily censored 24-page document issued by NASA on April 4, 1983, that explains the satellite's basic classification procedure. Distribution of *SCG 16* included the National Security Agency, which is responsible for signals intelligence operations for the Department of Defense and the Air Force's Space Division in Southern California, which is in part a cover for the highly classified National Reconnaissance Office, responsible for operating U.S. reconnaissance and surveillance satellites.

TDRS-A's orbital mishap is in "Loss of TDRS-A Averted by Joint Action," *Aviation Week & Space Technology,* April 11, 1983, pp. 19–21. The communication problem is in *Aviation Week & Space Technology,* November 23, 1983, p. 29.

The TDRS-B material is from "Satellite Problems Scrub Shuttle Flight," *The New York Times,* March 2, 1985. The mission scheduled for March 3 was to have included Senator Jake Garn as a "test subject." Details of the flight are in "Shuttle Mission 51-E Will Carry Heaviest Payload Yet in Program," *Aviation Week & Space Technology,* February 18, 1985, pp. 121–27. For TDRS-B operational details, see "25th Shuttle Launch Will Inaugurate New Pad, Make Halley Observations," *Aviation Week & Space Technology,* January 20, 1986, pp. 88–92.

The plan for mission 51-L, as the operation that was to begin on January 28 was officially called, is tightly outlined in "25th Shuttle Launch Will Inaugurate New Pad, Make Halley Observations," *Aviation Week & Space Technology,* January 20, 1986. The acrimony at JPL over the failure of NASA to launch a Halley's probe was described by Fred W. Bowen, manager of the NASA Resident Office, in an interview on June 15, 1987.

Haeffele's remarks are from "Teacher Is Focus of Space Mission," *The New York Times,* January 25, 1986.

The Orlando conference is from "Teacher Is Focus of Space Mission."

Ambient air temperature at the time of launch is from the *Rogers Commission Report,* p. 70.

Engine start-up is from the *Rogers Commission Report,* p. 37.

The sensations of being in the shuttle's cabin during launch are described by a reporter who went through the process in a simulator. See Craig Covault, "Aerobatics at Mach 25," *Science 81,* May 1981, pp. 58–63.

The smoke puffs coming from the lower portion of the right SRB are pictured in sequence in the *Rogers Commission Report,* pp. 22–25.

The eight puffs of smoke are from the *Rogers Commission Report,* p. 37. The ensuing chronology is also from the report, pp. 37–39.

The description of the ascent from the pad is from Covault, "Aerobatics at Mach 25," p. 59.

Scobee's transmission to Houston and the roll maneuver are from "Challenger Lost While Leaving Region of Maximum Stress," *Aviation Week & Space Technology,* February 3, 1986, p. 20.

NASA news release 86–100 of July 28, 1986, which contained a transcript of comments made by the astronauts from the period just before the launch to the explosion of Challenger, quoted Resnik as having said, "[Expletive] hot." But the author has heard the term as given in the text repeatedly in high performance flying situations and believes that it was uttered in this instance.

Operation in the maximum dynamic pressure region and immediately after it is from the *Rogers Commission Report,* p. 37, and from NASA release 86–100, p. o6.

"Feel that mother go" is from NASA 86–100, p. o6.

The description of fire coming out of the SRB and the subsequent events leading to the destruction of Challenger are from the *Rogers Commission Report,* pp. 20–21 and 26–39 (including the color photographs and computer drawings).

Stone's comments are from an interview with the author at Caltech on June 16, 1987.

Lane's comments are from an interview with the author on June 22, 1987.

McLaughlin's recollection is from an interview with the author of June 25, 1987.

Stone's observation about Voyager disappearing is from the interview with the author.

Brooks's remarks are from the interview with the author.

CHAPTER 1

Galileo and his optics are detailed in Philip and Phylis Morrison, *The Ring of Truth* (New York: Random House, 1987), pp. 26–29.

Early Moon maps are mentioned in Bevan M. French, *The Moon Book,* (New York: Penguin Books, 1977), p. 39.

Gascoigne's micrometer is from Daniel J. Boorstin, *The Discoverers* (New York: Random House, 1983), pp. 400–401.

Galileo's description of the moon is from French, *The Moon Book,* pp. 38–39.

Berkner's and Odishaw's observation-experimentation point is from L. V. Berkner and Hugh Odishaw, eds., *Science in Space* (New York: McGraw-Hill, 1961), p. 4.

The excerpts from Kepler's *Dream* are from John Lear, *Kepler's Dream,* with the full text and notes of *Somnium, Sive Astronomia Lunaris* (Berkeley: University of California Press, 1965), pp. 106–7.

Kepler's letter to Galileo is from Lear, *Kepler's Dream,* p. 3.

Tsiolkovsky's theories are from David Baker, *The Rocket* (New York: Crown, 1978), pp. 17–21.

Material on Goddard's rocket is from Robert H. Goddard, "A Method of Reaching Extreme Altitudes" Smithsonian Miscellaneous Collections, Vol. 71, No. 2, 1919, pp. 1–4. Although this paper was dated 1919, it was released on January 11, 1920. It is on file in the NASA History Office.

Weather rockets are from the paper cited in the preceding note. pp. 53–54.

The moon shot is from the paper cited in the preceding note. pp. 55–57.

Times coverage of Goddard's paper is in "Believes Rocket Can Reach Moon," *The New York Times,* January 12, 1920.

The editorial attack was in Topics of the Times, *The New York Times,* January 13, 1920, p. 12. The Moon Man reference is from Baker's *The Rocket,* p. 24.

Goddard's rebuttal in "Goddard Rockets to Take Pictures," *The New York Times,* January 19, 1920.

The first rocket flight was described by Goddard in his "Liquid-Propellant Rocket Development," Smithsonian Miscellaneous Collections, Vol. 95, No. 3, March 16, 1936, pp. 2–3. A copy of this paper is in the NASA History Office.

The move to Roswell and related matters are from "Liquid-Propellant Rocket Development," pp. 3 and 5.

The formation of the VfR is reported in detail in Frederick I. Ordway III and Mitchell R. Sharpe, *The Rocket Team* (New York: Thomas Y. Crowell, 1979) pp. 12–16.

Dornberger's visit to VfR and his quote are from Ordway and Sharpe, *The Rocket Team,* p. 18.

Von Braun's "circus" quote is from the first segment of "Spaceflight," a documentary of the space age that was aired on public television in 1985.

The thrust of a rocket engine, called specific impulse, is described in Samuel Glasstone, *Sourcebook on the Space Sciences* (New York: D. Van Nostrand Co., 1965), pp. 86–87.

The guidance system is from Baker, *The Rocket,* pp. 45–46.

The working of the V-2's engine and related systems are from ibid., pp. 44 and 47.

Dornberger's remarks are from Ordway and Sharpe, *The Rocket Team,* pp. 41–42.

Production numbers are from Ordway and Sharpe, p. 406. Deaths, injuries, and destruction are from p. 252.

The antipodal bomber and monster missile are from James C. Sparks, *Winged Rocketry* (New York: Dodd, Mead & Co., 1968), pp. 66–87.

Von Karman's recollection is from Theodore von Karman and Lee Edson, *The Wind and Beyond* (Boston: Little, Brown & Co., 1967), p. 258.

Von Karman's remark about Goddard's being on a branch that died is from von Karman and Edson, *The Wind and Beyond,* p. 242.

The trip to New York is from Clayton R. Koppes, *JPL and the American Space Program* (New Haven: Yale University Press, 1982), pp. 7–8.

Details on research for JATO, including funding arrangements, is from Koppes's book on JPL, pp. 9–10.

Malina's and Tsien's report is from Koppes, pp. 18–19.

The contract is from Koppes, pp. 19–20.

JPL's size and staff is from Koppes, pp. 20–21.

The origin of WAC Corporal's name is from Koppes, p. 23. The rocket's measurements are from Baker, *The Rocket,* p. 269.

Von Braun's description of the space station is from Sparks, *Winged Rocketry,* p. 71.

The wayward V-2 is from Ordway and Sharpe, *The Rocket Team,* p. 355.

Ehricke's anecdote is from "Spaceflight," Part 1, a documentary produced by KCET-TV in Los Angeles that aired on public television in May 1985.

For the Army's study, see R. Cargill Hall, "Early U.S. Satellite Proposals," Eugene Emme, ed., *The History of Rocket Technology: Essays on Research, Development, and Utility* (Detroit: Wayne State University Press, 1964), pp. 412–15.

Van Allen's remarks are from an interview with the author.

Rockoons are described in Walter Sullivan, *Assault on the Unknown* (New York: McGraw Hill, 1961), pp. 118–21.

Green's fish story, originally told in *The New Yorker,* is from Ordway and Sharpe, *The Rocket Team,* p. 354.

The V-2 Panel's creation is from Homer E. Newell, *Beyond the Atmosphere: Early Years of Space Science* (Washington: National Aeronautics and Space Administration, 1980), pp. 34–35.

Military benefit from upper atmospheric research is from the interview with Van Allen.

The large NRL telemeters are in Newell, *Beyond the Atmosphere,* p. 35.

Tracking techniques are from Newell, *Beyond the Atmosphere,* p. 36. See also Samuel Glasstone, *Sourcebook on the Space Sciences* (Princeton: D. Van Nostrand Company, 1965), pp. 178–79.

Rocket problems, including reentry, are from Richard P. Hallion, "The Development of American Launch Vehicles Since 1945," in Paul A. Hanle and Von Del Chamberlain, eds., *Space Science Comes of Age* (Washington: National Air and Space Museum, 1981), pp. 117–18.

Newell's description of procedures is from his *Beyond the Atmosphere,* p. 36.

Bumper-WAC is from Hallion's "The Development of American Launch Vehicles Since 1945," p. 119, and from Baker, *The Rocket,* p. 234.

CHAPTER 2

Haviland's canceled paper is in "TV Rocket Kept Secret by Builders," *The New Haven Register,* October 14, 1951.

Corona is from William E. Burrows, *Deep Black: Space Espionage and National Security* (New York: Random House, 1987), pp. 107–11.

The substance of von Braun's and Rosen's remarks are in "Space Rockets with Floating Base Predicted," *The New York Herald Tribune,* October 14, 1952, and "2 Rocket Experts Argue 'Moon' Plan," *The New York Times,* October 14, 1952. Von Braun's honorarium was $75.

The introduction to the series "What Are We waiting For?" is from "Man Will Conquer Space *Soon,*" *Collier's,* March 22, 1952, p. 23.

Ride, Sally K., *Leadership and America's Future in Space* (Washington: National Aeronautics and Space Administration, 1987). See in particular pp. 23–31 for details of earth observation, solar system exploration by probes, and the landing of astronauts on the moon and Mars.

The orbiting observatory is described in Fred L. Whipple, *The Heavens Open,* which was included in the series' first installment, p. 32.

Use of the telescope for Earth observation is from Joseph Kaplan et al., *Across the Space Frontier* (New York: Viking Press, 1952), p. 43. Ryan was the editor.

The description of the station, shuttle, and related equipment is from von Braun's "Crossing the Last Frontier," *Collier's,* March 22, 1952, pp. 25–30.

The shuttle is described in von Braun's "Crossing the Last Frontier," p. 26, and in Kaplan et al., *Across the Space Frontier,* pp. 25–28.

Bonestell's depiction of reentry is shown in Kaplan et al., *Across the Space Frontier,* p. 61.

The moon material is from "Man on the Moon," *Collier's,* October 18, 1952, pp. 51–60.

Lunar exploration is in "The Exploration," *Collier's,* October 25, 1952, pp. 39–48.

The human dimension is in "Picking the Men," *Collier's,* February 28, 1953, pp. 41–48; "Testing the Men," *Collier's,* March 7, 1953, pp. 57–63; and "Emergency!" *Collier's,* March 14, 1953, pp. 38–44.

Eating is from Wernher von Braun, "The Journey," *Collier's,* October 18, 1952, p. 58.

Whipple's statement is from Fred L. Whipple, "Is There Life on Mars?" *Collier's,* April 30, 1954, p. 21. The possibility of different life forms in the universe is considered in a thoughtful and critically acclaimed book, *Life Beyond Earth,* by Gerald Feinberg, a Columbia University physicist, and Robert Shapiro, at biochemist at New York University. It was published by William Morrow in 1980. The Mars material from *Collier's* was also expanded into a book. See Willy Ley and Wernher von Braun, *The Exploration of Mars* (New York: Viking Press, 1956).

The author screened the "Tomorrowland" series at the Disney studios. The history of the project is recounted in David R. Smith, "They're Following Our Script: Walt Disney's Trip to Tomorrowland," *Future*, May 1978, pp. 54–63. Smith was the Disney archivist.

Killian's observation is from James R. Killian, Jr., *Sputnik, Scientists, and Eisenhower* (Cambridge: MIT Press, 1977), p. 3. Killian expressed a similar view in an interview with the author on February 11, 1985.

For Sputnik's effect, see Walter A. McDougall, . . . *The Heavens and the Earth* (New York: Basic Books), pp. 237–39.

Berkner's comment is from Baker, *The Rocket*, p. 133.

Introduction to Outer Space is reproduced in Appendix 4 of Killian's *Sputnik, Scientists, and Eisenhower*, pp. 289–99.

Killian's remarks about Medaris are from his *Sputnik, Scientists, and Eisenhower*, pp. 127–28.

The invention of "aerospace" is from McDougall, . . . *The Heavens and the Earth*, p. 166.

IGY experiments are in Herbert Friedman, "Rocket Astronomy—An Overview," in Paul A. Hanle and Von Del Chamberlain, eds., *Space Science Comes of Age* (Washington: Smithsonian Institution Press, 1981), pp. 37–40.

For Sputnik's role in the IGY, and the U.S. response, see Sullivan, *Assault on the Unknown*, pp. 49–107.

Nike capability, as well as those of the other sounding and surface-to-air rockets, are charted in Baker, *The Rocket*, pp. 269 and 271.

The National Space Establishment report and related matters are from Homer Newell, *Beyond the Atmosphere*, SP-4211 (Washington: National Aeronautics and Space Administration, 1980), pp. 46–47. Several of the members of the Rocket and Satellite Research Panel are listed in Appendix A, pp. 414–15.

The goal of the United States in space is from Section 102 (c) (5) of the National Space Act.

The presentations to Glennan are from Courtney G. Brooks, James M. Grimwood, and Loyd S. Swenson, Jr., *Chariots for Apollo: A History of Manned Lunar Spacecraft*, NASA SP-4205 (Washington: National Aeronautics and Space Administration, 1979), pp. 4–6.

Killian's speech is from his *Sputniks, Scientists, and Eisenhower*, pp. 142–43.

Webb's response to Vostok is from David Baker, *The History of Manned Space Flight* (New York: Crown Publishers, 1981), p. 66.

JFK's order to Johnson is from John M. Logsdon, *The Decision to Go to the Moon* (Chicago: The University of Chicago Press, 1976), p. 112.

MISS is described in Baker, *The History of Manned Space Flight*, pp. 32–33.

The Webb-McNamara quotation is from Logsdon, *The Decision to Go to the Moon,* pp. 125–26.

Kennedy's quote is from Logsdon, *The Decision to Go to the Moon,* p. 128.

For descriptions of the selection and training process, see "Picking the Men," *Collier's,* February 28, 1953, and "Testing the Men," *Collier's,* March 7, 1953.

CHAPTER 3

The conflicts among individuals is from Newell, *Beyond the Atmosphere,* p. 88.

Pickering's remarks about going to space are from the interview of June 15, 1987.

Von Braun's pleading with McElroy is from Koppes, *JPL and the American Space Program,* p. 83.

Vanguard's demise is from McDougall, . . . *the Heavens and the Earth,* p. 154. See also Baker, *The Rocket,* p. 134.

Pickering's quotation on competition is from an interview of June 15, 1987.

"Red Socks" is from Koppes, *JPL and the American Space Program* and from the June 15, 1987, interview with Pickering.

The atomic lunar explosion is mentioned in Koppes, *JPL and the American Space Program,* p. 85.

"Coffee table talk" is from the interview with Pickering of June 15, 1987.

Pickering's talk with Medaris is from Koppes, *JPL and the American Space Program,* pp. 85–86.

The Explorer prelaunch news blackout is in "Newsmen Agreed to Delay Reports," *The New York Times,* February 1, 1958.

Van Allen's description of waiting for Explorer 1 to orbit and the events that followed are from James A. Van Allen, *Origins of Magnetospheric Physics* (Washington: Smithsonian Institution Press, 1983), pp. 59–60.

Pickering's remark about Explorer relative to the Sputniks is from "Satellite Height Over 1,000 Miles," *The New York Times,* February 2, 1958.

Medaris's remark about Explorer 1's superiority is from "Eisenhower Announced Good News," *New York Herald Tribune,* February 1, 1958.

Explorer 1's specifications and arrangement are from *Space Explorers,* (Pasadena: Jet Propulsion Laboratory, undated), pp. 2–3.

Van Allen's remarks are from his "Observations of High Intensity Radiation by Satellites 1958 Alpha and 1958 Gamma," in Paul A. Hanle and Von Del Chamberlain, eds., *Space Science Comes of Age* (Washington: Smithsonian Institution Press, 1981), p. 59.

The analysis for symmetry is also from his seminal paper as quoted in Hanle and Chamberlain, eds., *Space Science Comes of Age,* p. 59.

The magnetic bar theory is from Bevan M. French and Stephen P. Maran, eds., *A Meeting with the Universe* (Washington: National Aeronautics and Space Administration, 1981), p. 80.

Ike's statement about Explorer 1 is from "Army Launches U.S. Satellite into Orbit; President Promises World Will Get Data; 30-Pound Device Is Hurtled Up 2,000 Miles," *The New York Times,* February 1, 1958.

Hagen's speech was in "Vanguard Chief Urges U.S. Elite," *The New York Times,* February 1, 1958.

Pickering's letter to Killian is from Edward Clinton Ezell and Linda Neuman Ezell, *On Mars* (Washington: National Aeronautics and Space Administration, 1984), pp. 17–18.

Newell's meeting with Pickering and his subsequent decision are from his oral history, taped on January 7, 1974, and on file in the NASA History Office in Washington.

Medaris's attitude about NASA is from Killian, *Sputnik, Scientists, and Eisenhower,* p. 127.

JPL's lobbying NASA is from the June 15, 1987, interview with Pickering.

The point about spreading out the empire to broaden the political and economic base was laid in particular to James Webb by G. J. Wasserburg of Caltech in an interview with the author. See the chapter on astropolitics for details.

Pickering's recollection of the early relationship with NASA is from the interview of June 15, 1987.

His description of relations with the Army are from the interview of June 15, 1987.

Giberson's remarks are from an interview on June 30, 1987.

James's recollections are from "The Early History of JPL and the Evolution of Its Matrix Organization," delivered on February 12, 1987, and videotaped by JPL.

Pickering's meeting with Dryden and Glennan is from the interview of June 15, 1987.

Glennan's pencil notations are on pp. 799 and 827 of Newell's comment draft of June 1978. His covering letter was written on January 2, 1979. Both are in the NASA History Office Archive.

Kistiakowsky's argument for unmanned probes is from page 34 of an oral history done in Cambridge, Massachusetts, on May 22, 1974, under the auspices of NASA. A copy of the transcript is in the NASA History Office.

Arguments for and against the Space Science Board are from Newell, *Beyond the Atmosphere,* pp. 203–4.

Glennan's complaint is annotated on p. 454 of the manuscript of Newell, *Beyond the Atmosphere,* Box 40, 25579-0649, NASA History Archive.

Newell's lament is from *Beyond the Atmosphere,* pp. 203–4.

The Committee on Interplanetary Probes and Space Stations' origin and recommendations are in Ezell and Ezell, *On Mars,* pp. 15–16.

Urey's role is mentioned in Ezell and Ezell, *On Mars,* p 17.

CHAPTER 4

Pickering's letter to Killian is from Ezell and Ezell, *On Mars,* p. 18.

Silverstein's memo to Pickering is from Ezell and Ezell, *On Mars,* p. 18.

JPL's space mission is from the interview with Homer Joe Stewart.

JPL's five-year plan is from Ezell and Ezell, *On Mars,* pp. 19–22.

The meeting between Pickering, Silverstein, and the others is from Newell, *Beyond the Atmosphere,* pp. 262–63.

Mercury details are from Baker, *The History of Manned Space Flight,* pp. 36–37.

Urey's criticism (cited in the footnote) about a lack of good scientists in NASA is from "Dr. Urey Assails NASA," *Huntsville Times,* April 25, 1963. His remarks about astronauts are from "Urey Criticizes Unscientific Astronauts," *San Francisco Chronicle,* January 1, 1964.

Jastrow's visit with Urey is from Robert Jastrow, *Red Giants and White Dwarfs* (New York: Harper & Row, 1971), pp. 3 and 5.

Newell's remark about the origin of Ranger and the Working Group on Lunar Exploration are from Cargill Hall, *Lunar Impact: A History of Project Ranger* (Washington: National Aeronautics and Space Administration, 1977), p. 15.

Sputnik 3 details are from George E. Wukelik, ed., *Handbook of Soviet Space Science Research* (New York: Gordon and Breach Science Publishers, 1968), pp. 28–30.

Details of the Automated Interplanetary Station are from Douglas Hart, *The Encyclopedia of Soviet Spacecraft* (New York: Exeter Books, 1987), pp. 57–58.

The three Luna missions are described in detail in Nicholas L. Johnson, *Handbook of Soviet Lunar and Planetary Exploration* (San Diego: American Astronautical Society, 1979), pp. 7–17.

Material on the first Pioneers is from R. Cargill Hall, *Lunar Impact: A History of Project Ranger* (Washington: National Aeronautics and Space Administration, 1977), pp. 6–10, from Baker, *The Rocket,* pp. 142–43, and from Madeline W. Sherman, ed., *TRW Space Log,* Vol. 19, 1983, pp. 27–28.

Vega chronology and budget are from Linda Neuman Ezell, *NASA Historical Data Book, Vol. II: Programs and Projects, 1958–1968* (Washington: National Aeronautics and Space Administration, 1988), pp. 311 and 22, respectively. Note: This and the other volumes in the series will hereafter be referred to only by title and volume number.

Tsiolkovsky's (and Oberth's) influence on Ehricke as they related to hydrogen and oxygen is from J. L. Sloop, *Liquid Hydrogen as a Propulsion Fuel, 1945–1959* (Washington: National Aeronautics and Space Administration, SP-4404, 1978), pp. 191–92.

Air Force-NASA-ARPA involvement with Centaur is from Sloop, *Liquid Hydrogen as a Propulsion Fuel,* p. 201.

Centaur's description is from *Jane's All the World's Aircraft, 1962–63,* pp. 191–92.

Centaur's problems are from Ezell, *NASA Historical Data Book,* Vol. II, p. 42.

For a discussion of the properties of liquid hydrogen and liquid oxygen as they relate to propulsion, see Glasstone's *Sourcebook on the Space Sciences,* p. 94.

Pickering's knowing about the existence of Agena is from the interview of February 18, 1988.

Pickering's remarks to Glennan about Vega and the relationship of the two organizations are from his letter of March 24, 1959, in the JPL Library archive.

The 1959 budget decision on Vega was contained in a letter from Dryden to Pickering, dated May 19, 1959, in the JPL Library archive. According to the *NASA Historical Data Book,* Vol. II, $14,291,000 was programmed for the remainder of 1959 and another $42.8 million—all of what NASA requested—was authorized for 1960 (p. 22).

Glennan's defense of Vega and Eisenhower's remarks are from George B. Kistiakowsky, *A Scientist at the White House* (Cambridge: Harvard University Press, 1976), pp. 128–29.

Kistiakowsky's notation about NASA's hardware is from his *A Scientist at the White House,* p. 110.

The telegram canceling Vega is from the Vega file in the JPL Library archive.

Horner's letter to Pickering, file 5-1164, is from the NASA History Office Archive.

NASA's orders regarding Ranger are from the *NASA Historical Data Book,* Vol. II, p. 311.

Lane's observation is from the interview with the author of February 19, 1988.

Pickering's remarks are from the interview of June 15, 1987, with the author.

Reasons for the testing of the Block 1 Rangers are from a typed history of the Ranger project that was taken to Washington for the *Ranger 6* hearings by Robert Parks and Harris M. "Bud" Schurmeier in April 1964 (p. 8). The document is on file in the JPL Library archive.

Plans for Block III are from the *NASA Historical Data Book,* Vol. II, p. 311.

Columbus's ships are described in Robert H. Fuson's translation of *The Log of Christopher Columbus* (Camden, Me.: International Marine Publishing, 1987), pp. 37–42.

Material on Old World charts and navigation is also from the Columbus log, pp. 25 and 42.

The explanation of ephemerides and Standish's work are from the author's interview with him.

Cesarone's comments are from the interview with the author.

For a fine detailed analogy between sea and space systems, see Oran W. Nicks, *Far Travelers: The Exploring Machines* (Washington: National Aeronautics and Space Administration, 1985), pp. 50–56.

Ranger's computer and sequencer description are from R. Cargill Hall, *Lunar Impact* (Washington: National Aeronautics and Space Administration, 1977), p. 60.

The Ranger 1 and 2 experiments are detailed in Albert R. Hibbs, M. Eimer, and M. Neugebauer, "Early Ranger experiments," [*sic*] *Astronautics,* September 1961, pp. 26–27. See also Parks's and Schurmeier's April 1964 monograph, pp. 9–10.

Burke and the Atomic Energy Commission experiment and the problem with Newell's "trinkets" are from Koppes, *JPL and the American Space Program,* pp. 121–22.

Sterilization is from Hall, *Lunar Impact,* pp 71–71.

Burkes's problems and the number of employees and budget are from Koppes, *JPL and the American Space Program,* p. 120.

Ranger 1's inclination was 32.9 degrees; its nodal period was 90.64 minutes; its perigee was 107 statute miles and its apogee was 268 miles. See D. G. King-Hele et al., *The R.A.E. Table of Earth Satellites: 1957–1980* (London: Macmillan Press, 1981, p. 14.

Ranger 1's and Ranger 2's flights are told in detail in Hall's *Lunar Impact,* pp. 101–8.

The Block II superstructure is clearly diagrammed in Hall's *Lunar Impact,* p. 62. Retro-rocket operation is described in John W. R. Taylor, ed., *Jane's All the World's Aircraft: 1962–63,* (London: Sampson Low, Marston & Co., 1962), p. 412.

Ranger 3's flight is from Hall, *Lunar Impact,* pp. 143–44.

Ranger 4's flight is from Hall, *Lunar Impact,* pp. 153–54.

Ranger 5's flight is from Hall, *Lunar Impact,* pp. 169–70.

Homer Newell has written that Webb wanted to use JPL, and therefore Caltech, as a "powerful drawing card" to get other academic institutions into NASA research and that he was therefore supportive of JPL while being critical of the way it operated (*Beyond the Atmosphere,* p. 262). But Joseph N. Tatarewicz, a historian at the National Air and Space Museum, has said that Webb was exasperated with the lab and used Ranger "as a club," threatening to take the project away from JPL (interview of January

28, 1988). Pickering generally supports the historian. Webb "felt that the JPL contract was the oddball in his setup," Pickering said. "Philosophically, he felt that this should be a civil service laboratory rather than a contractor-operated laboratory. He told me once that if the contract hadn't existed, he never would have signed it." Pickering also saw a somewhat more political side to Webb's interest in universities than can be inferred from Newell's book. The space agency administrator felt that since the universities "were taking all this [NASA] money from the government, they ought to be prepared to support the government when the government asks them to do something." Webb wanted to use the contract with JPL, and therefore with Caltech, as an "entree into the academic system" and thought that he and DuBridge ought to get together "to work out ways in which the universities could support NASA to a greater extent than they were doing," Pickering asserted. "He and DuBridge could never understand each other. He [Webb] never understood that a university, by its very nature, was going to be an independent body" (interview of February 18, 1988).

The Kelley panel's mandate is from Hall, *Lunar Impact,* p. 173.

The Kelley board's technical findings are from "Final Report of the Ranger Board of Inquiry," National Aeronautics and Space Administration, November 30, 1962, p. 4. (From the JPL Library archive.)

Management shortcomings and recommendations are from the Ranger final report, pp. 5–6 and 12–14.

The JPL Ranger report is from Hall, *Lunar Impact,* pp. 171–72.

CHAPTER 5

Park's briefing is from Ezell and Ezell, *On Mars,* p. 34.

Mariner A's budget is from Jane Van Nimmen and Leonard C. Bruno, *NASA Historical Data Book, Vol. I: NASA Resources, 1958–1968* (Washington: National Aeronautics and Space Administration, 1988), p. 155.

The Mariner-Voyager plan is related in detail in Ezell and Ezell's *On Mars,* pp. 31–36.

The decision to go with Mariner R is also from *On Mars,* pp. 38–40.

The compromise is mentioned in *Mariner-Venus 1962 Final Project Report,* SP-59 (Washington: National Aeronautics and Space Administration), p. 195. This report concerns the subsequent Mariner mission but the two spacecraft were identical.

Mariner R's (or Mariner 1's) instruments are from the *Mariner-Venus 1962* report, pp. 198–225.

The description of Mariner 1's end is from Oran W. Nicks, *Far Travelers* (Washington: National Aeronautics and Space Administration, 1985), p. 1.

The Atlas-Agena's trouble and end are from Nicks, *Far Travelers,* p. 3–4.

Sputnik 7 and Venera 1 are from Johnson, *Handbook of Soviet Lunar and Planetary Exploration,* pp. 137–38.

The thirteen Venus failures are listed in a Venus Probe Summary in *Handbook of Soviet Lunar and Planetary Exploration,* p. 136.

The Ghoul was the subject of an article by Harry L. Helms, Jr., "The Great Galactic Ghoul," *Saga,* July 1976, p. 52. John Casani of JPL, who was quoted extensively in the piece, smiles when The Ghoul is mentioned. See also James E. Oberg, "The Great Galactic Ghoul," Notes From Earth, *Final Frontier,* October 1987, pp. 10–11.

Mariner 2's launch and flight are from Hall, *Lunar Impact,* p. 160.

Mariner 2's cosmic dust experiment is detailed in "Mariner-Venus 1962 Final Report," NASA SP-59 (Washington: National Aeronautics and Space Administration, 1965), pp. 325–27.

Scientific data returned by Mariner 2 are from Arthur Smith, *Planetary Exploration* (Wellingborough, England: Patrick Stephens, 1988), pp. 69–70.

The carbon dioxide–life equation is from Clyde Fisher and Marian Lockwood, *Astronomy* (New York: John Wiley & Sons, 1940), p. 61.

Venera 4 is described in *Handbook of Soviet Lunar and Planetary Exploration,* pp. 146–50. The *Handbook of Soviet Space-Science Research,* edited by George E. Wukelic, and published in 1968, noted that the Soviets had "a remarkable lack of success" with their Mars and Venus probes to that point.

Microlock and TRACE are described in detail in William R. Corliss, "A History of the Deep Space Network" (NASA CR-151915) (Washington: National Aeronautics and Space Administration, May 1, 1976), pp. 10–19.

The three stations and their function are from Corliss, "A History of Deep Space," p. 63.

The completion of the SFOC and establishment of the Deep Space Network are from Ezell's *NASA Historical Data Book,* Vol. II, p. 573.

The acquisition-and-loss process is illustrated on a map in "A History of the Deep Space Network," p. 68.

The DSN–Mariner 2 mission sequence is from "A History of the Deep Space Network," pp. 67–70.

Lyman's remarks are from the interview with the author.

The antenna-design problem and the cocktail-party analogy are also from the interview with Lyman.

The Arecibo telescope and its capability are described in Dava Sobel, "Reaching across space," *Harvard Magazine,* December 1975, p. 19.

Brooks's description of the dish is from the interview of February 18, 1988.

The pointing accuracy of the 210-foot antenna is from N. A. Renzetti et al., *The Deep Space Network—An Instrument for Radio Navigation of Deep Space Probes,* JPL Publication 82–102 (Pasadena: Jet Propulsion Laboratory, December 15, 1982), p. 8.

Tracking data and acquisition stations are listed in Ezell's *NASA Historical Data Book, Vol II,* pp. 575–94. The tracking and communication ships are listed on pp. 594–96.

The three networks are detailed in Ezell, *NASA Historical Data Book,* Vol. II, pp. 521–95. Locations that served all three networks are on p. 548. Note, too, that a dozen Department of Defense facilities are also listed, though they are not necessarily the same as their NASA counterparts.

The communications lines were more extensive than indicated and included Vancouver, New York, London, and Tangier. See Corliss, "History of the Deep Space Network," pp. 136–37.

MSFN facilities are from Arnold S. Levine, *Managing NASA in the Apollo Era,* NASA SP-4102 (Washington: National Aeronautics and Space Administration, 1982), p. 220.

The intrusion is from Ezell's *NASA Historical Data Book,* Vol. II, p. 565.

Tatarewicz's remarks are from the interview with the author of January 28, 1988.

The Wiesner report recommendation is from Levine, *Managing NASA in the Apollo Era,* p. 17.

CHAPTER 6

Reference to Ranger 6's preliminary "Go" status is from "News Conference on Ranger VI Impact on Moon," NASA News Release 2-2509, February 2, 1964, p. 2. The release contains a verbatim account of the events of the culmination of the Ranger 6 mission and the subsequent press conference. It is on file in the JPL Library archive. Hereafter it is referred to as the "Ranger VI news release."

Pickering's remark about being optimistic is from Hall, *Lunar Impact,* p. 236.

The "mission status room" is from Hall, *Lunar Impact,* p. 234.

Changes in the Ranger program are from Hall, *Lunar Impact,* p. 237.

Ranger 6's flight from liftoff to midcourse maneuver is from "Final Report of the Ranger 6 Review Board," *Chronology of Events during Ranger 6 Flight (2-2472)* (Washington: National Aeronautics and Space Administration, March 17, 1964) pp. 32–34. (From the NASA History Office.)

The camera system description and the televising of the press corps are from the Ranger VI news release, pp. 2–3.

Houston's indifference to Ranger 6's landing site is from Hall, *Lunar Impact,* p. 232.

Narration to impact is from the Ranger 6 news release, pp. 8–9.

The Avon commercial is from the Ranger 6 news release, p. 9.

Pickering's reflections on Ranger 6 are from the interview of February 18, 1988.

Cortright's letter, dated February 5, 1964 (2-149), is from the JPL Library archive.

Possible congressional postponement of Apollo is from "Ranger's Failure Spurs Drive to Delay Lunar Trips," *The New York Times,* February 4, 1964.

JPL's findings are from "RA-6 Investigation Committee Final Report," EPD-205, Jet Propulsion Laboratory, February 14, 1964, p. v. This document is from the JPL Library archive.

The widened scope of the Hilburn board's investigation is from *Final Report of the Ranger 6 Review Board* (2–2472) (Washington: National Aeronautics and Space Administration, March 17, 1964), p. 6.

JPL estimated that the remaining flights in Block III had an estimated chance of success of 0.6 percent. The board said that JPL's estimate was valid only if it changed its procedures. Otherwise, the board put Ranger 7 reliability "at a value substantially less than that quoted by the Jet Propulsion Laboratory." See Appendix K, p. 65, of the report.

Webb's letter and Newell's and Nicks's response are from Hall, *Lunar Impact,* pp. 249–51.

Newell's testimony is from U.S. Congress, House, Committee on Science and Astronautics, *Investigation of Project Ranger,* Report of the Subcommittee on NASA Oversight, 88th Cong., 2nd Sess., 1964, pp. 11, 16, 21, and 23.

The Karth committee's four recommendations are from Hall, *Lunar Impact,* p. 254.

Karth's and Pickering's interchange on personality clashes is from *Investigation of Project Ranger,* p. 169.

Pickering's recollection of Luedecke is from the interview of February 18, 1988.

JPL and RCA Ranger 7 activities are from Hall, *Lunar Impact,* pp. 256–57. The "unbelievable" quotation is from a Hall interview.

The pin and hatch problem are from Hall, *Lunar Impact,* pp. 259–61.

The Ranger 6 launch and Schurmeier's remarks are from Hall, *Lunar Impact,* pp. 264 and 266.

Ranger 7's final minutes are from Hall, *Lunar Impact,* pp. 267–69.

Johnson's remarks are from Hall, *Lunar Impact,* p. 280.

Soviet soft-landing attempts are from Johnson, *Handbook of Soviet Lunar and Planetary Exploration,* pp. 21–25 and 187.

The number of pictures and the last one are from Raymond L. Heacock, "Ranger: Its Mission and Its Results," *TRW Space Log* (reprint), Summer 1965, pp. 10 and 12.

Kuiper's remarks are from Hall, *Lunar Impact,* pp. 273 and 278.

Urey's dissent is from Hall, *Lunar Impact,* pp. 284–85.

Kuiper's interim report is from Hall, *Lunar Impact,* pp. 284–85.

Urey's convincing NASA to land Ranger 9 on Alphonsus is from Stephen G. Brush, "Nickel for Your Thoughts: Urey and the Origin of the Moon," *Science,* September 3, 1982, p. 894.

Hall's *National Geographic* quotation is from his *Lunar Impact,* p. 302.

Urey's complaint to Newell is in his letter of October 24, 1962. (NASA History Archive)

The "hot moon–cold moon" battle is from Robert Jastrow, "Exploring the Moon," *Space Science Comes of Age* (Washington: National Air and Space Museum, 1981), pp. 46–47.

Urey's attitude about geologists is from his letter to Mueller of October 7, 1969. (NASA History Archive)

Urey's criticism is from "Urey Decries Cut in Lunar Project," *The New York Times,* December 31, 1963. Also see Hall, *Lunar Impact,* pp. 221–22. For earlier complaints about astronaut selection, see "Dr. Urey Assails NASA," *Huntsville Times,* April 25, 1963.

Early work on Lunar Orbiter is from Ezell, *NASA Historical Data Book,* Vol. II, p. 320.

The cost of the Surveyor program as predicted by NASA is from the interview with W. E. Giberson.

Surveyor's problems are from Koppes, *JPL and the American Space Program,* p. 173. Surveyor's final cost is from Ezell, *NASA Historical Data Book,* Vol. II, p. 205.

The reduction of science instrumentation on Surveyor is from Koppes, *JPL and the American Space Program,* p. 173.

Giberson's description of Surveyor is from the interview of June 30, 1987.

The Surveyor balloon-drop is from the Giberson interview.

Newell's difficulties with JPL's handling of Surveyor and its temptations are from his *Beyond the Atmosphere,* pp. 270–71.

The recommendations are in the letter from Oran Nicks to A. O. Beckman dated January 11, 1968 (File 20.7, California Institute of Technology Archives).

Huber's answer to Nicks is from his letter to DuBridge of January 18, 1968 (File 20.7 of the California Institute of Technology Archives).

Lunar Orbiter 1's mission is from Ezell, *NASA Historical Data Book,* Vol. II, p. 321.

Lunar Orbiter 5 material is from Ezell, *NASA Historical Data Book,* Vol. II, p. 325.

Surveyor 1's descent is from Kenneth Gatland, *The Illustrated Encyclopedia of Space Technology* (New York: Harmony Books, 1981), pp. 131–32.

The lunar surface's support capability is from French, *The Moon Book,* p. 80.

The soil analysis is from French, *The Moon Book,* pp. 81–82.

The cost of the three programs is from Ezell, *NASA Historical Data Book,* Vol. II, p. 205.

CHAPTER 7

Comparative rotation periods, velocities, and direction of axis is from Samuel Glasstone, *Sourcebook On the Space Sciences* (New York: D. Van Nostrand Co., 1965), p. 390.

The description of the planet and Schiaparelli's theory is from Horowitz, *To Utopia and Back,* pp. 77–78.

Excerpts from Schiaparelli's 1893 paper are from William Sheehan, *Planets and Perception: Telescopic Views and Interpretations, 1609–1909* (Tucson: University of Arizona Press, 1988), pp. 177–79. In regard to the apparent presence of a large quantity of water, Sheehan has noted that while spectroscopic observations of Sir William Huggins in England, Jules Janssen in France, and Hermann Vogel in Germany during the 1860s and 1870s indicated the probable presence of water, G. Johnstone Stoney of Ireland used the newly formulated molecular theory of gases to calculate that Mars was not massive enough to have hung on to a lot of water, and that what was frozen might be carbon dioxide. He was essentially right but was not given a great deal of credit for his deduction.

The influence of Darwin is from William Graves Hoyt, *Lowell and Mars* (Tucson: University of Arizona Press, 1976), pp. 55–56.

The invocation of earth science is from Lowell, *Mars as the Abode of Life,* p. 214.

Lowell's description of Mars is from Hoyt, *Lowell and Mars,* pp. 80–83.

Holden's remarks are from Hoyt, *Lowell and Mars,* pp. 90–91.

The possibility of fossils on Mars was raised by Louis Friedman, executive director of The Planetary Society, in a paper he gave at the American Association for the Advancement of Science's annual meeting in Boston on February 2, 1988.

Wells's description of the Martians is from his *The War of the Worlds* (New York: Pocket Books, 1988), p. 26.

Wells's broadcast was reported in "Radio Listeners in Panic, Taking War Drama as Fact," *The New York Times,* October 31, 1938. The Federal Communications Commission took the program so seriously that it asked the Columbia Broadcasting System for a transcript and a recording of the program. The chairman of the FCC called the program regrettable ("FCC to Scan Script of 'War' Broadcast," *The New York Times,* November 1, 1938).

The 1940 text is Clyde Fisher and Marian Lockwood, *Astronomy* (New York: John Wiley & Sons, 1940), p. 65.

Jones's conclusion is from H. Spencer Jones, *Life on Other Worlds* (New York: Macmillan Co., 1940), p. 241.

The 1949 text is William T. Skilling and Robert S. Richardson, *Astronomy* (New York: Henry Holt & Co., 1949), p. 413.

The letter is quoted in Joseph N. Tatarewicz, "The Persistence of Lowell's Legacy . . . : Life, Mars, and the U.S. Space Program, 1958–1967," prepared for the History of Science Society Annual Meeting, Bloomington, Indiana, November 1, 1985.

Norman H. Horowitz's definitions are from his *To Utopia and Back* (New York: W. H. Freeman, 1986), pp. 1, 2, and 13.

Horowitz's definition of life and explanation of carbon are from his *To Utopia and Back*, pp. 14–17.

For life in stars and on Cryobus, see Gerald Feinberg and Robert Shapiro, *Life Beyond Earth: The Intelligent Earthling's Guide to Life in the Universe* (New York: William Morrow & Co., 1980), pp. 380–93.

The spiritual argument is from Feinberg and Shapiro, *Life Beyond Earth*, pp. 435–36.

Morrison's quote is from Horowitz, *To Utopia and Back*, p. 18.

Newell's justification for planetary exploration is from his *Beyond the Atmosphere*, p. 337.

The Soviet Mars shots of 1960 and 1962 are from Johnson, *Handbook of Soviet Lunar and Planetary Exploration*, pp. 182–86.

The mood at JPL and the May 1961 report are from Koppes, *JPL and the American Space Program*, p. 116.

Pickering's warning is from Koppes, *JPL and the American Space Program*, p. 112.

Burke's Venera picture and proverb are from Hall, *Lunar Impact*, p. 65.

The birth of the Office of Life Sciences and Ames's involvement with evaluating experiments are in Ezell and Ezell, *On Mars*, pp. 57–66.

The Mariner 3 and 4 engineering problems are from Koppes, *JPL and the American Space Program*, p. 166.

Engineering subsystems on Mariner-Mars are from *Mariner-Mars 1964: Final Project Report*, NASA SP-139 (Washington: National Aeronautics and Space Administration, 1976), pp. 51–94.

The science experiments are described in detail on pp. 94–107.

The central computer and sequencer operation is detailed on p. 85.

The end of Mariner 3 is described in *Mariner-Mars 1964: Final Project Report*, p. 131.

Lockheed's investigation is described in *Mariner C Shroud Failure Evaluation Final Report (Vehicle 6931)*, LMSC-A734573, Lockheed Missiles & Space Company, March 1, 1965.

James's account of the Mariner 3 shroud failure is from the interview of February 22, 1988.

Mariner 4's resolution is from Bruce C. Murray and Merton E. Davies, "A Comparison of U.S. and Soviet Efforts to Explore Mars," January 1966, p. 12.

Coordinates for the pictures are from *Mariner-Mars 1964: Final Project Report*, p. 264.

The "priceless Rembrandt" is from the interview with Jurrie J. van der Woude of February 22, 1988.

The imaging team's statement is from Ezell and Ezell, *On Mars*, pp. 77–79. The theme of the uniqueness of the Earth was echoed, for example, by Norman H. Horowitz in the conclusion of his *To Utopia and Back*, which describes the search for life on the Viking missions (p. 146). In an interview in 1969 the late historian Arnold J. Toynbee told the author, for example, that he hoped landing on the Moon would give mankind "a better sense of proportion" regarding the political and physical fragility of the Earth itself.

The case for carbon dioxide polar caps was made in Robert B. Leighton, and Bruce C. Murray, "Behavior of Carbon Dioxide and Other Volatiles on Mars," *Science,* July 8, 1966, pp. 136–44.

Lederberg's and the others' points are from Ezell and Ezell, *On Mars*, p. 81.

The Saturn booster controversy and budget material are from Ezell and Ezell, *On Mars*, pp. 105–8.

The congressional seesawing over appropriations is from Ezell, *NASA Historical Data Book*, Vol. II, p. 217.

The MSC plan and Webb's remarks are from Levine's *Managing NASA in the Apollo Era*, p. 148.

Karth's remarks are from Ezell and Ezell, *On Mars*, p. 117.

The saga of Mars 2 and 3 is from Nicholas L. Johnson, *Handbook of Soviet Lunar and Planetary Exploration*, pp. 194–98.

Johnson's remarks are from the interview of October 11, 1988.

Chapman's description is in Clark R. Chapman, *Planets of Rock and Ice* (New York: Charles Scribner's Sons, 1977), p. 173.

The description of Valles Marineris is also from Chapman, *Planets of Rock and Ice*, p. 173.

The lava and tectonics theories are from Ronald Greeley, *Planetary Landscapes* (Boston: Allen & Unwin, 1985) p. 166.

Mariner 9 imagery, including a lava-bearing channel on the northwest flank of Olympus Mons, is in *Mars as Viewed by Mariner 9*, (SP-329) (Washington: National Aeronautics and Space Administration, 1976).

CHAPTER 8

Webb's testimony is from Ezell and Ezell, *On Mars*, pp. 134–35.

Naugle's briefing and Hess's response are from Ezell and Ezell, *On Mars*, pp. 142–43.

LBJ's remarks are from Ezell and Ezell, *On Mars*, p. 135.

The duel between Langley and Pasadena is from Ezell and Ezell, *On Mars,* p. 125. Langley's role in research on Mars and its record in space are from pp. 126–27.

The Viking Project Management Council is from Ezell and Ezell, *On Mars,* p. 173.

The poll is from Ezell and Ezell, *On Mars,* p. 186.

Viking's escalating cost in 1969 is from Ezell and Ezell, *On Mars,* p. 187.

The task group's mandate is from the NASA report "Goals and Objectives For America's Next Decades In Space," September 1969, p. i, which was appended to the task group's report.

Murray's remark about Nixon is from the interview with the author of July 2, 1987.

The task group's options were listed in "The Post-Apollo Space Program: Directions for the Future," Space Task Group Report to the President, September 1969, p. 20.

The need for ever-greater exploits in space is from the report cited in the preceding note, p. 5.

Cost reduction is from the report "The Post-Apollo Space Program."

The space station, base, and transportation system are from the report "The Post-Apollo Space Program," pp. 14–15.

Details concerning the Space transportation System are from the report "The Space-Apollo Space Program. p. 15.

Planetary and lunar exploration are from the report cited above. on pp. 13–14.

Naugle's testimony and Karth's response are from Ezell and Ezell, *On Mars,* p. 187.

Paine's decision is from Ezell and Ezell, *On Mars,* pp. 189–90.

The employment drop is from *On Mars,* p. 190.

The 150 who went to Mariner 10 are from Eric Burgess, *To The Red Planet* (New York; Columbia University Press, 1978), p. 51.

Soffen's remarks are from Ezell and Ezell, *On Mars,* p. 220. Norris's are from p. 192.

Murray's remarks are from Bruce Murray, *Journey into Space* (New York: W. W. Norton & Co., 1989), pp. 68–69.

The majority opinion for searching for life is from an untaped interview with Robert Shapiro on March 5, 1990, and from notes he made after reviewing this chapter.

The biology instrument is described in Ezell and Ezell, *On Mars,* pp. 229–30.

The three experiments are described in any number of places, including Ezell and Ezell. There is a simple description in Bevan M. French, *Mars: The*

Viking Discoveries, EP-146 (Washington: National Aeronautics and Space Administration), October 1977), p. 20.

Viking's science instruments are in the *Encyclopedia of US Spacecraft,* p. 160.

Spacecraft dimensions are from the *Encyclopedia of US Spacecraft,* p. 161, and Ezell and Ezell, *On Mars,* p. 243.

Nixon's and Fletcher's statements are from Alex Roland, "The Shuttle: Triumph or Turkey," *Discover,* November 1985, pp. 35–38.

Practice simulations are from Burgess, *To the Red Planet,* p. 66.

Burgess's recollection is from his *To the Red Planet,* p. 89. Martin's comments are from the video "Landing on Mars: Viking's Historic Mission," Cambridge: SSC, 1987.

The color photograph material is from Ezell and Ezell, *On Mars,* pp. 381–84, and from the interview with Jurrie van der Woude.

The surface sampler is described in fine detail in Ezell and Ezell, *On Mars,* pp. 396–97.

The quantity of imagery and other data returned is from Ezell and Ezell, *On Mars,* pp. 422–23.

Surface features and the quantity of nitrogen are from Arthur Smith, *Planetary Exploration: Thirty Years of Unmanned Space Probes* (Wellingborough, England: Patrick Stephens, 1988), pp. 110–11.

Levin's results are in Gilbert V. Levin and Patricia Ann Straat, "Life On Mars? The Viking Labeled Release Experiment," *BioSystems,* 9, 1977, p. 165.

The results of the GCMC are from the untaped Shapiro interview and from Levin and Straat, "Life on Mars?" p. 168.

Horowitz's pronouncement about the lack of life on Mars is his *To Utopia and Back,* pp. 141 and 145.

Klein's opinion is from Harold P. Klein, "The Viking Biological Investigations: Review and Status," *Origins of Life,* 9, 1978, p. 160.

Horowitz's conclusion about the fate of the earth is from his *To Utopia and Back,* p. 146.

Nick's observation is from his *Far Travelers,* p. 213.

Klein's point about a thousand experiments is from the video "Landing on Mars."

Jastrow's opinion is from Robert Jastrow, "Report From Mars," *Natural History,* March 1977, p. 53.

Shapiro's statement about the finality of Horowitz's conclusion is from the interview of March 6, 1990, and from Shapiro's commentary on the draft of this chapter.

CHAPTER 9

NASA's preliminary work on a lunar mission is from Linda Neuman Ezell, *NASA Historical Data Book*, Vol. II, p. 180.

NASA's lunar agenda before JFK's speech is from Ezell, NASA Historical Data Book, Vol. II, p. 180.

Horowitz's point is from Norman H. Horowitz, "Mission Impractical," *The Sciences*, March/April 1990, p. 48.

Newell's recollection of the study group is from his *Beyond the Atmosphere*, p. 208.

The Apollo zone is from Courtney G. Brooks, James M. Grimwood, and Loyd S. Swenson, Jr., *Chariots for Apollo: A History of Manned Lunar Spacecraft* (SP-4205) (Washington: National Aeronautics and Space Administration, 1979), pp. 363 and 365.

Lunar site selection is from Brooks et al., *Chariots for Apollo*, p. 365.

Early thoughts about the space station are from John M. Logsdon, "Space Stations: A Historical Perspective," a paper presented at the AIAA/NASA Symposium on the Space Station, July 18, 1983. It is reproduced in Mireille Gerard and Pamela W. Edwards, eds., *Space Station: Policy, Planning and Utilization* (New York: American Institute of Aeronautics and Astronautics, 1983), pp. 14–22.

The first shuttle study is from Ezell, *NASA Historical Data Book*, Vol III, p. 121.

Murray's observation is from the interview with the author of July 2, 1987.

The senators are mentioned in Wayne Biddle, "The Endless Countdown," *The New York Times Magazine*, June 22, 1980, p. 32.

The fifty-five flights a week is from Logsdon, "Space Stations."

Von Braun's manuscript, together with a covering letter to Cornelius Ryan dated October 6, 1969, is on file in the NASA History Office archive.

Mueller's numbers are from Roland, "The Shuttle: Triumph or Turkey?" p. 31.

The Mathematica material is from Biddle, "The Endless Countdown," p. 34.

Helfand's anecdote about the odor test is from the interview with the author.

Tischler's thesis is from Roland, "The Shuttle: Triumph or Turkey?" p. 31.

The AIAA paper is from A. Frank Watts, D. J. Dreyfuss, and H. G. Campbell, "The Economic Impact of Reusable Orbital Transports on the Cost of Planned Manned Space Programs, 1970–1999" (RAND report No. P-3465), November 15, 1966, p. 3. It also appeared as AIAA Paper No. 66-862.

The shuttle's impact on other programs is from Watts et al., "The Economic Impact . . . ," p. 3.

The $3,000 figure was quoted by Marcia S. Smith, a space specialist in the Congressional Research Service, who said in a telephone interview on March 1, 1990, that it was not precise and noted that estimates varied considerably. She also said that the cost per pound after the Challenger accident was generally taken to be about $5,000, although that, too, varied within wide parameters.

The figures for poundage and astronaut cost are from Ruth A. Lewis and John A. Lewis, "Getting Back on Track in Space," *Technology Review,* August/September 1986, pp. 35–36.

The shuttle's cross-range capability is from John M. Logsdon, "The Space Shuttle Program: A Policy Failure?" *Science,* May 30, 1986, p. 1101.

Fletcher's remark about "that year" is from Logsdon, "The Space Shuttle Program," p. 1100.

The blood/marrow experiment is from "Shuttle May Carry Bone Marrow into Space for Study on Radiation," *The New York Times,* February 11, 1985.

"Flight for Famine" is from "Shuttle May Be Used to Hunt for Water in Africa," *Los Angeles Times,* May 26, 1985.

The AIDS experiment is from "Experiment Tied to AIDS Battle," *Orlando Sentinel,* October 2, 1988.

Bowen's recollection is from the interview with the author. For a comprehensive account of the Halley debacle, including an interesting exposition on the relationship between the space science establishment and the overall political process, see John M. Logsdon, "Missing Halley's Comet: The Politics of Big Science," *ISIS,* 1989, pp. 254–80.

Veverka's observations are from "Worthy Projects Suffer Because of the Shuttle, Critics of NASA Charge," *The New York Times,* April 7, 1981.

Wilford's observation is from "Space Program Faces Hurdles Despite Cheers for Columbia," *The New York Times Week in Review,* April 19, 1981, p. 1.

Lunney's remark is from "July Shuttle Trip Placed in Doubt," *The New York Times,* February 15, 1984.

Space Shuttle main engine size, power levels, throttling characteristics and service life are from the *National Space Transportation System Reference,* Vol. I (Systems and Facilities) (National Aeronautics and Space Administration, June 1988), p. 199.

Pratt & Whitney's protest is from Biddle, "The Endless Countdown," p. 34.

Roland's comment is from "The Shuttle: Triumph or Turkey?" p. 38.

The tiles are mentioned in Biddle, "The Endless Countdown," p. 38.

The other malfunctions and Lunney's statement are from "Malfunctions Spur Extensive Space Shuttle Study," *The New York Times,* December 15, 1983.

Scheduled slights and Weeks's statement are from "In Harsh Light of Reality, the Shuttle Is Being Re-evaluated," *The New York Times,* May 14, 1985.

The shuttle's budget escalation is from Smith, "Space Shuttle Issue Brief IB81175," pp. CRS-11-12.

Feynman's conversation with Ullian is from Richard P. Feynman, *What Do You Care What Other People Think?* (New York: W. W. Norton & Co., 1988), pp. 179–80.

The interchange with Lovingood and the engineers is from Richard P. Feynman, "Mr. Feynman Goes to Washington," *Engineering & Science,* Fall 1987, p. 18.

Himmel's remark is from "High Risk of New Shuttle Disaster Leads NASA to Consider Options," *The New York Times,* April 9, 1989.

Murray's observation about the shuttle is from the interview with the author on July 2, 1987.

CHAPTER 10

Marius and the naming of the satellites is from Eric Burgess, *By Jupiter: Odysseys to a Giant* (New York: Columbia University Press, 1982), p. 3.

The Hooke and Cassini sightings are in Heather Couper with Nigel Henbest, *New Worlds: In Search of the Planets* (Reading, Mass.: Addison-Wesley Publishing Co., 1986), p. 70.

Speculation about the spot is from Burgess, *By Jupiter,* p. 7.

Saturn's ability to float in water is from Cecilia Payne-Gaposchkin and Katherine Haramundanis, *Introduction to Astronomy* (Englewood Cliffs, N.J.: Prentice-Hall), 1970, p. 250.

The description of Jupiter's cloud patterns is from Donald H. Menzel, Fred L. Whipple, and Gerard De Vaucouleurs, *Survey of the Universe* (Englewood Cliffs, N.J.: Prentice-Hall, 1970), p. 299.

The equivocations about Jupiter are from Payne-Gaposchkin and Haramundanis, *Introduction to Astronomy,* pp. 243–49.

Ezell's observations are from Ezell, *NASA Historical Data Book,* Vol. III, p. 127.

AUs are from Jay M. Pasachoff, *Contemporary Astronomy* (New York: Saunders College Publishing, 1981), p 251.

The Christmas-tree-energy analogy is from the first *Pioneer 10* news release issued by NASA and the Ames Research Center: "Pioneer F Mission to Jupiter," February 20, 1972, p. 3.

Asteroid material is from Glasstone, *Sourcebook On the Space Sciences,* pp. 396–97.

For gravity assist, see G. A. Flandro, "Utilization of Energy Derived from the Gravitational Field of Jupiter for Reducing Flight Time to the Outer

Solar System," Jet Propulsion Laboratory Space Programs summary, No. 37–37, October 31, 1965, and H. J. Stewart, "New Possibilities for Solar-System Exploration," *Astronautics & Aeronautics,* December 1966.

Stewart's treatise is in his "New Possibilities for Solar-System Exploration."

Flandro's calculations are in his paper cited above.

Hall's recollection is from an interview with the author.

Material on Pioneers 6 and 9 is from Ezell, *NASA Historical Data Book,* Vol. II *(Programs and Projects 1958–1968),* pp. 302–9.

The Goddard symposium is described in Richard O. Fimmel, James Van Allen, and Eric Burgess, *Pioneer: First to Jupiter, Saturn, and Beyond,* SP-446 (Washington: National Aeronautics and Space Administration, 1980), p. 26.

The SSB's recommendation is from Burgess, *By Jupiter,* p. 16.

The Space Science Board/NRC report is noted in Burgess, *By Jupiter,* p. 14.

Hall's remark about continuing programs is from the interview.

Hall's recollection of Pioneer's being taken from Goddard is from the interview.

The spin-stabilization argument is from Burgess, *By Jupiter,* p. 16.

Writing "The Justification for a Sole Source" is from the interview.

The flux-gate magnetometer is described in detail in Fimmel, Van Allen, and Burgess, *Pioneer: First to Jupiter, Saturn, and Beyond,* p. 55.

Hall's discussion of the radiation danger is from the interview.

The possibility of life on Jupiter is from the NASA press kit, "Pioneer F Mission to Jupiter," No. 72-25, p. 24.

The possibility of a tenth planet or a dark star is from "Pioneers May Find Tenth Planet," Ames Research Center press release No. 82-23, June 17, 1982.

The case for Planet X was made in John D. Anderson and E. Myles Standish, Jr., "Dynamical Evidence for Planet X," in Roman Smoluchowski, John N. Bahcall, and Mildred S. Matthews, eds., *The Galaxy and the Solar System* (Tucson: University of Arizona Press, 1986), pp. 286–96.

Anderson's balking at doing PR is in a memorandum of December 27, 1985, to W. L. Quaide: "Proposed NASA News Release No. 85–29, 'Data Suggest Tenth Planet in Far Out Orbit.'"

The RTGs are described in the "Pioneer F Mission to Jupiter" release (No. 72-25), p. 37.

The Pioneer launch sequence is from the "Pioneer F Mission to Jupiter" press release, pp. 64–66.

Fimmel's remarks are from an interview with the author.

Hall's remarks about JPL are from the interview with the author.

The meteoroid detector is described in James Elliot and Richard Kerr, *Rings* (Cambridge: The MIT Press, 1984), p. 93.

The zodiacal mapping story is from the interview with Fimmel.

The broken records are from Fimmel, Van Allen, and Burgess, *Pioneer*, p. 79.

Hall's remarks are from *Pioneer*, p. 80.

The PICS process and the Emmy are from Fimmel, Van Allen, and Burgess, *Pioneer*, pp. 83–84.

Pioneer 10's operation up to and through near encounter is described on the mission's time line, as given in the press release "Pioneer Will Reach Jupiter December 3" (73-243), National Aeronautics and Space Administration, November 19, 1973, pp. 38–44.

Doose's, Kraemer's and Fimmel's remarks are from Fimmel, Van Allen, and Burgess, *Pioneer*, pp. 84 and 90.

Hall's description of the Pioneer 11 trajectory is from the interview.

Miller and Hartman assert that there are some twenty-five bodies having diameters greater than 620 miles, making the distinction between those orbiting the Sun and those orbiting other bodies somewhat arbitrary. See Ron Miller and William K. Hartman, *The Grand Tour: A Traveler's Guide to the Solar System* (New York: Workman Publishing, 1981), p. 8.

Data on Saturn's magnetosphere, satellites, core, and atmosphere are from Fimmel, Van Allen, and Burgess, *Pioneer*, pp. 143–56.

The plaque is described and pictured in Fimmel, Van Allen, and Burgess, *Pioneer*, pp. 248–50.

The Pioneer Venus radar mapper is described in Richard O. Fimmel, Lawrence Colin, and Eric Burgess, *Pioneer Venus*, SP-461 (Washington: National Aeronautics and Space Administration, 1983), pp. 58–59.

Pioneer Venus's findings are from Earl J. Montoya and Richard O. Fimmel, *Space Pioneers*, EP-264 (Washington: National Aeronautics and Space Administration, 1987), pp. 7–8.

Fimmel's night-light remark is from "NASA Expects Pioneer 10's Useful Lifetime Will Be Extended by Decade," *Aviation Week & Space Technology*, June 27, 1988, p. 43.

The TRW statement is from *Aviation Week & Space Technology*, Washington Roundup, June 20, 1988, p. 15.

CHAPTER 11

Paine's shuttle and Grand Tour statements are from "U.S. Sets Tour of Planets," and "Space Travel by Public Seen," *The Washington Post*, March 8, 1970.

The shuttle appropriation is from Ezell, *NASA Historical Data Book,* Vol. III *(Programs and Projects, 1969–1978),* p. 69.

The Grand Tour spacecraft was the subject of a release, " 'Grand Tour' of the Planets," 69-84 (Washington: National Aeronautic and Space Administration, June 2, 1969.

TOPS computer systems are from "JPL Expresses Confidence in Grand Tour Spacecraft," *Space Daily,* June 30, 1971, p. 317.

TOPS was diagrammed in *Space Daily,* November 19, 1979, p. 79.

TOPS scientists and teams are in the press release "Grand Tour Scientists," Release No. 71-56 (Washington: National Aeronautics and Space Administration, April 4, 1971).

The fifty thousand jobs and $10–$14 billion shuttle budget is from "Doubling of Space Shuttle Funds Could Take Up the Slack in Jobs," *The New York Times,* January 25, 1972.

The Voyagers are described and illustrated in any number of places. There is a particularly good and clear rendition in *The Voyager Uranus Travel Guide,* PD 618-150 (Pasadena: Jet Propulsion Laboratory, August 15, 1985), pp. 57–73. Also see David Morrison and Jane Samz, *Voyage to Jupiter,* SP-439 (Washington: National Aeronautics and Space Administration, 1980), pp. 26–32.

The stabilization maneuver is from the interview with Torrence V. Johnson.

Voyager's records are described in Morrison and Samz, *Voyage to Jupiter,* pp. 28–29. They are also the subject of an entire book, Carl Sagan et al., *Murmurs of Earth* (New York: Random House, 1978).

The Voyager startup, including team assembly, is from Morrison and Samz, *Voyage to Jupiter,* p. 25.

The nature of the computer problems is from Morrison and Samz, *Voyage to Jupiter,* pp. 48–50.

Observatory and far-encounter material are from Morrison and Samz, *Voyage to Jupiter,* pp. 56–60.

Lane's description of sequencing deliberations are from the interview.

Lane's comment about the imagery is from Morrison and Samz, *Voyage to Jupiter,* p. 60.

Smith's open-mouth quote is from Mark Washburn, *Distant Encounters: The Exploration of Jupiter and Saturn* (New York: Harcourt Brace Jovanovich, 1983), p. 90.

The pizza quote is from Morrison and Samz, *Voyage to Jupiter,* p. 76.

The Great Red Spot theory is from "Jupiter's Baffling Red Spot Loses Some of Its Mystery," *The New York Times,* November 12, 1985.

The science writers' quips are from Morrison and Samz, *Voyage to Jupiter,* p. 75.

The Brown episode is from Washburn, *Distant Encounters,* p. 103.

Soderblom's quote is from Morrison and Samz, *Voyage to Jupiter,* p. 75.

Observation of the large Jovian satellites and the Voyager trajectories are from David Morrison, "Introduction to the Satellites of Jupiter," David Morrison, ed., *Satellites of Jupiter* (Tucson: University of Arizona Press, 1982), pp. 10–12.

Morrison's observation is from *Satellites of Jupiter,* pp. 10 and 12.

Use of Jupiter as a weather model is in Robert Pool, "Is Something Strange About the Weather?" *Science,* March 10, 1989, pp. 1290–93.

The "outrageous" remark is from M. Mitchell Waldrop, "The Puzzle That Is Saturn," *Science,* September 18, 1981, p. 1347.

Saturn sequencing is explained briefly in E. C. Stone and E. D. Miner, "Voyager 2 Encounter with the Saturnian System," *Science,* January 29, 1982, p. 500.

Spoke theory is in Jeffrey N. Cuzzi et al., "Saturn's Rings: Properties and Processes," in Richard Greenberg and Andre Brahic, eds., *Planetary Rings* (Tucson, University of Arizona Press, 1984), pp. 169–70.

The shepherd satellites are described in Bradford A. Smith, "The Voyager Encounters," in Beatty, O'Leary, and Chaikin, eds., *The New Solar System,* p. 114.

The braids, lack of them, and the Encke doodle are in Waldrop's "The Puzzle That Is Saturn," p. 1349.

Titan is vividly, if necessarily imprecisely, described in Ron Miller and William K. Hartmann, *The Grand Tour* (New York: Workman Publishing, 1981), p. 85.

Enceladus is described in David Morrison, *Voyages to Saturn,* SP-451 (Washington: National Aeronautics and Space Administration, 1982), p. 136.

Smith's Death Star analogy is from his "The Voyager Encounters," in *The New Solar System,* p. 115.

Beggs's press conference at JPL is from Washburn's *Distant Encounters,* pp. 220–21.

Funding for planetary exploration between 1974 and 1981 is from John M. Logsdon, *The Survival Crisis of the U.S. Solar System Exploration Program* (comment draft), Washington, June 1989, p. 6.

The fiscal 1983 and 1984 material is from Logsdon's study on the survival crisis of solar system exploration, pp. 13–14.

Begg's warning to Stockman is from the Logsdon study, p. 15.

Stockman's remarks about Schmitt and spinoff are from David A. Stockman, *The Triumph of Politics* (New York: Harper & Row, 1986), pp. 150–51.

The remark about the blue shuttle and crew cut is from Bruce Murray, *Journey Into Space* (New York: W. W. Norton & Co., 1989), p. 215.

Marks's observation regarding space science and exploration is from the *Bulletin of the American Academy of Arts and Science,* January 1975, as quoted in Logsdon's study of the crisis in solar system exploration, pp. 18–19.

Keyworth's statements are from Logsdon, pp. 25–26.

Keyworth's statement is from the first interview with Tatarewicz. Washburn alludes to the same thing in *Distant Encounters,* p. 222.

Wagons in a circle is from the interview of March 7, 1988.

Morrison's letter is excerpted in Washburn, *Distant Encounters,* p. 222,

Levy's remarks are from Logsdon's study, *The Survival Crisis of the U.S. Solar System Exploration Program,* p. 29.

Washburn's remarks about gutting NASA are from *Distant Encounters,* p. 223.

The campaign by Beckman, Rousselot, Pownall, Scranton, and Goldberger, as well as the Budget Review Committee meeting, are from Logsdon's study, *The Survival Crisis,* pp. 30–37. Mark's revision of his position is from p. 49.

"Bathtub" funding is in J. Kelly Beatty, "Voyager 2's Triumph," *Sky & Telescope,* October 1986, p. 338.

Murray's editorial was in *Science,* January 29, 1982, p. 459.

The reduced power supply is addressed in Richard P. Laeser, William I. McLaughlin and Donna M. Wolff, "Engineering Voyager 2's Encounter with Uranus," *Scientific American,* November 1986, pp. 37–38.

Fooling the attitude control subsystem is from "Engineering Voyager 2's Encounter with Uranus," p. 39.

The reduced data rate and low smear is from E. C. Stone and E. D. Miner, "The Voyager 2 Encounter with the Uranian System," *Science,* July 4, 1986, p. 39.

The 14-mile citation is from "Engineering Voyager 2's Encounter with Uranus," p. 42.

Rice and Blizzard's effort is recorded in "The Planet That Got Knocked on Its Side," a NOVA production for PBS that was aired on WNET in New York on October 29, 1986.

The nature of the problem was reported in "Voyager 2 Managers Resolve Imagery Problem Before Uranus Encounter," *Aviation Week & Space Technology,* January 27, 1986, p. 24.

Stone's defense of bewilderment was widely quoted with slight differences in wording. This one is from M. Mitchell Waldrop, "Voyage to a Blue Planet," *Science,* February 28, 1986, p. 916. See also Andrew P. Ingersoll, "Uranus," *Scientific American,* January 1987, p. 38.

Soderblom's description of Miranda is from "Scientists Report a Moon of Uranus Is 'Bizarre Hybrid,' " *The New York Times,* January 27, 1986.

Miranda is described and analyzed in Torrence V. Johnson, Hamilton Brown, and Laurence A. Soderblom, "The Moons of Uranus," *Scientific American,* April 1987, pp. 55–56.

The theory of why the rings are dark is from Jeffrey N. Cuzzi and Larry W. Esposito, "The Rings of Uranus," *Scientific American,* July 1987, p. 63.

Ingersoll's remark is from his "Uranus," *Scientific American,* p. 38.

The eyeball is pictured in Ingersoll's "Uranus," *Scientific American,* p. 39.

CHAPTER 12

"Planet specific" is from C. M. Yeates, et al., *Galileo: Exploration of Jupiter's System,* SP-479 (Washington: National Aeronautics and Space Administration, 1985), p. 2.

The Space Telescope and its capability are described in detail in John N. Bahcall and Lyman Spitzer, Jr., "The Space Telescope," *Scientific American,* July 1982, pp. 40–51. See also Riccardo Giacconi, "The Future of Space Astronomy," a paper presented at the Symposium on the Future of the Space Sciences in the United States, AAAS Annual Meeting in Chicago, February 15, 1987.

Letters in support of the LST are referenced in Chapter 11.

LST's and Galileo's start-up costs are in Ezell, *NASA Historical Data Book,* Vol. III, p. 133. Galileo's projected budget is in "Space Exploration: Cost, Schedule, and Performance of NASA's Galileo Mission to Jupiter," GAO/NSIAD-88-138FS (General Accounting Office, May 1988), p. 11, and hereafter referred to as the GAO Galileo report.

Budgetary material is from Ezell, *NASA Historical Data Book,* Vol. III, p. 132.

The initial budget allocation is from the data book, p. 143.

Van Allen's accusation is in his "Space Science, Space Technology and the Space Station," *Scientific American,* January 1986, p. 36.

NIMS is described in detail in C. M. Yeates et al., *Galileo: Exploration of Jupiter's System,* SP-479 (Washington: National Aeronautics and Space Administration, 1985), p. 49.

Carlson's recollections are from the interview with the author.

Johnson's remarks are from the interview with the author.

The MBB thruster problems are detailed in Michael A. Dornheim, "Repairs Completed, Galileo Thrusters Set to Undergo Reacceptance Tests," *Aviation Week & Space Technology,* January 23, 1989, p. 62.

The competitive computers are mentioned in *The Rocky Road to Jupiter,* produced for public television by NOVA. It aired on WNET on April 7, 1987.

The Galileo design, including explanations of "spun" and "despun," are in Yeates, *Galileo,* p. 102.

Material relating to Casani's order to his engineers, and expenses accruing from the Titan-Centaur complex and buying one of the launch vehicles, are from the Johnson interview.

James Fletcher mentioned Interim Upper Stage in the video *The Rocky Road to Jupiter*.

The shuttle's engine and tile problems are described in Biddle's article, "The Endless Countdown," pp. 34, 38, and 39.

The decision to run a split mission is from the GAO Galileo report, p. 7.

Casani's points about the added complications are from "The Rocky Road to Jupiter."

Events leading to the switch from the IUS to Centaur are from the video *The Rocky Road to Jupiter*.

The cost of VEGA is from the GAO Galileo report, p. 16.

The particulars of the projected Galileo launch are from "Space Transportation System/Space Shuttle Payload Flight Assignments," August 1983, p. 8.

The Christmas party and Casani's remarks are from the video *The Rocky Road to Jupiter*.

Details of High Bay 2 and the container and truck are from the interview with Richard F. Collins and Milton Goldfine.

Casani's recollection of the meeting after the explosion is from the interview.

Van Allen's allusion to *The Perils of Pauline* is from the interview with the author.

Aging problems are addressed in *Space Exploration: NASA's Deep Space Missions Are Experiencing Long Delays,* GAO/NSLAD-88-128BR (Washington: General Accounting Office, May 1988), pp. 18–19.

Casani's remarks about Centaur and the JSC are from notations he made on the manuscript.

Silveira's memorandum to Truly is from "Shuttle Centaur Flight Safety Issues Threaten Launch Planning," *Aviation Week & Space Technology,* May 12, 1986, pp. 18–19.

The end of the Centaur/shuttle program was reported in "NASA Drops Plans to Launch Rocket From the Shuttle," *The New York Times,* June 20, 1986.

VEEGA is detailed in John R. Casani, "Galileo's New Route to Jupiter," a paper presented at the American Astronautical Society's annual meeting at Boulder, Colorado, on October 28, 1986.

The Venus, Earth and asteroid investigations are in "Galileo VEEGA Mission to Jupiter," 1625-337 (Pasadena: Jet Propulsion Laboratory, April 1987). See also Bruce A. Smith, "Galileo Mission to Jupiter Will Involve More Travel Time, Additional Scientific Data," *Aviation Week & Space Technology,* December 14, 1987, pp. 115–16.

Shielding and antenna pointing are in Casani's paper "Galileo's New Route to Jupiter," p. 10.

Additional modifications to the orbiter are from Casani's annotations on the manuscript.

Modifications to the probe are from the news release "Galileo Probe Prepared for Longer Life," No. 88-02 (Moffett Field: Ames Research Center, December 21, 1987).

Casani's estimate is in the interview.

The GAO's estimate is from its Galileo report, p. 11.

The DOE documents and Lombardo's statement are in "Nuclear Reactor Hazard Is New Concern in Shuttle Flights," *The New York Times*, March 18, 1986.

The wind-risk result is from Casani's annotation in "Galileo's New Route to Jupiter."

The Florida coalition's brochure is quoted in Theresa M. Foley, "NASA Prepares for Protests over Nuclear System Launch on Shuttle in October," *Aviation Week & Space Technology*, June 26, 1989, pp. 83, 85, and 87.

NASA's response is from the same article, p. 87.

NASA's data on the RTGs is from an undated fact sheet, "NASA's Use of Radioisotope Thermoelectric Generators (RTGs) On the Galileo and Ulysses Missions."

Van Allen made the remark in the video *The Rocky Road to Jupiter*.

Carlson's recounting of his life after 1983 is from the interview.

Lane's remarks are from the interview with the author on June 22, 1987.

Chahine's remarks are from the interview with the author on June 19, 1987.

The humid air error is from Craig Covault, "Galileo Jupiter/Orbiter Probe Readied For Launch by Space Shuttle Atlantis," *Aviation Week & Space Technology*, September 4, 1989, p. 23.

Gagnon's remark is from "Suit Alleging Plutonium Danger Will Seek to Block Shuttle Launch," *Los Angeles Times*, September 28, 1989.

The FAS analyst is quoted in "Groups Protest Use of Plutonium on Galileo," *The New York Times*, October 10, 1989.

Rifkin's assertion and McConnell's rebuttal are in "Rifkin Tries to Stop Galileo Launch," *Science*, October 6, 1989, p. 30.

Gasch's decision is from "Judge Rejects Ban on NASA Launching," *The New York Times*, October 11, 1989, and "Court Rejects Activists' Bid To Halt Galileo/Shuttle Launch," *Aviation Week & Space Technology*, October 16, 1989, p. 21.

The engine computer malfunction and repair are in "Judge Rejects Ban on NASA Launching," and "Shuttle Problem Solved, NASA Says," *The New York Times*, October 15, 1989.

The weather delay is from "Rains Force 2d Delay in Launching of Shuttle," *The New York Times,* October 18, 1989. An accompanying story, "Computer Network At NASA Attacked By Rogue Program," described the attacking program.

Damage to the Consolidated Space Test Center is from "Quake rattles secret satellite control center," *Dayton Daily News,* October 19, 1989.

The launch is from "Shuttle Launched After Delay and Galileo Is Sent to Jupiter," *The New York Times,* October 19, 1989.

Galileo's launch sequence is from Craig Covault, "Galileo Launch to Jupiter by Atlantis Culminates Difficult Effort With Shuttle," *Aviation Week & Space Technology,* October 9, 1989, pp. 64–65.

CHAPTER 13

Tatarewicz's remark is from the interview of January 28, 1988.

Murray's statement is from Bruce C. Murray, "A New Strategy for Planetary Exploration," *Aeronautics & Astronautics,* October 1968, p. 43.

The presentation to Anderson is from Murray's *Journey into Space,* p. 269.

The National Geo article is Thomas Y. Canby, "Are the Soviets Ahead in Space?" *National Geographic,* October 1986, pp. 420–59.

The *AvWeek* cover story of December 12, 1988, represented two stories: "Soviet Manned Spaceflight: Blueprint for the Future," pp. 44–46, and a subseries of articles under the headline "U.S./USSR in Space: the Quest for Leadership," pp. 24–37."

The *Time* cover story, "Moscow Takes the Lead," was in the October 5, 1987, issue, pp. 64–70.

The return-to-space cover story appeared in the October 10, 1988, issue.

Morrison's remark about the *Time* cover is from the interview with the author.

Rechtin's address, dated November 16, 1959, is in the California Institute of Technology Archives (File 21.6).

The leadership question was posed in *The Next Decade in Space,* a Report of the Space Science and Technology Panel of the President's Science Advisory Committee, the White House, March 1970, p. 21. A copy of the report is in the NASA History Archive.

The SSEC report and Morrison's remarks are from Theresa M. Foley, "Scientists Urge Immediate Change in Planetary Exploration Policies," *Aviation Week & Space Technology,* June 15, 1987, p. 68.

The warning about the USSR is from "International Space Policy for the 1990s and Beyond," Washington: NASA Advisory Council Task Force on International Relations in Space, October 12, 1987, pp. 21–22.

Myers's remarks are from Craig Covault, "Soviets Test Massive New Booster For Station, Shuttle Missions," *Aviation Week & Space Technology*, May 25, 1987, p. 18.

Gringuaz's complaint is from "Space Rockets vs. Butter Is the Talk of Russia," *The New York Times*, April 17, 1989.

Rechtin's attributes are from Hall, *Lunar Impact*, p. 82. Rechtin would soon be promoted to director of the Deep Space Instrumentation facility.

Helfand's remarks are from the interview with the author.

Edelson's remarks are from the interview with the author.

The flight of Buran is in "Russian Shuttle Lifted into Orbit," *The New York Times*, November 15, 1988. See also "Moscow Scales Back Space Shuttle Program," *The New York Times*, August 15, 1989, and "Like Its American Cousin, Soviet Shuttle Is Criticized," *The New York Times*, November 22, 1988. The orbiter is described in some detail in Craig Covault, "Buran Inspection Shows Soviet Shuttle Details," *Aviation Week & Space Technology*, June 19, 1989, pp. 46–53.

Martin's remark was made at the Pathway to the Planets conference, sponsored by the Office of Exploration, in Washington on May 31 and June 1, 1989.

Van Allen's and Morrison's feelings about a steady-state budget are from the interviews with the author.

Helfand's remarks about the budget are from the interview with the author.

Davies's definition of exploration is from the interview with the author.

Korolev's work is from McDougall, . . . *the Heavens and the Earth*, p. 297.

The crossbow remark is from "Science and Perestroika: A Long Way to Go," p. 52.

Davies's remarks are from the interview with the author.

Sagdeev's discovery quota and charge of mediocrity is from Roald Z. Sagdeev, "Science and Perestroika: A Long Way to Go," *Issues in Science and Technology*, Summer 1988, pp. 48–50.

The butter-rockets debate is from "Space Rockets vs. Butter Is the Talk of Russia," *The New York Times*, April 17, 1989.

Sagdeev's remarks about the U.S. shuttle are from "Sagdeyev Assesses 'Crisis' of 'Big Science,' " *Izvestiya*, April 28, 1988. The translation is from the Foreign Broadcast Information Service (FBIS-SOV-88-085), May 3, 1988.

Sagdeev's remark about Buran's first flight is from "Like Its American Cousin, Soviet Shuttle Is Criticized," *The New York Times*, November 22, 1988.

The record is from "2 Soviet Astronauts Return With a 366-Day Record in Space," *The New York Times*, December 28, 1988. The problem on Mir is from "Soviet Station Electrical Problems Force Mir Repair Mission Plan,"

Aviation Week & Space Technology, April 17, 1989, p 22. The Soviet denial is from "Soviets Deny Flaw in Space Station," *The New York Times,* April 19, 1989.

The shuttle postponement is from "Moscow Scales Back Space Shuttle Program," *The New York Times,* August 15, 1989, and "Manned Soviet Shuttle Flight Delayed Until 1992 for Systems Installation," *Aviation Week & Space Technology,* May 8, 1989, pp. 20–21.

Phobos and the mission are described in Frank Miles and Nicholas Booth, eds., *The Race to Mars* (New York: Harper & Row, 1988), pp. 18–25. See also Jeffrey M. Lenorovitz, "Soviets to Study Phobos Surface From Fixed-Site, Mobile Landers," *Aviation Week & Space Technology,* August 29, 1988, pp. 48–49, and "Russia Readies 2 Craft For a Mission to Mars," *The New York Times,* July 5, 1988.

The Planetary Society's push for Mars is recounted in Kathryn Phillips, "Selling Mars," *Los Angeles Times Magazine,* June 25, 1989, pp. 21–27.

Phobos 1's affliction is from the interview with Bruce Murray of January 10, 1989.

Sagdeev's statement is from "Soviets See Little Hope of Controlling Spacecraft," *The New York Times,* September 10, 1988.

For a description of the Chernobyl accident and its causes, see "Report of the U.S. Department of Energy's Team Analyses of the Chernobyl-4 Atomic Energy Station Accident Sequence, DOE/NE-0076 (Washington: U.S. Department of Energy, November 1986).

Murray's remark about U.S. versus Soviet computers is from the second interview. Merton Davies agreed during the course of another interview.

The sequencing check procedure is from the interview with Davies.

The Tass statement is quoted in "Soviet Craft Orbits Mars on Way to Moon Phobos," *The New York Times,* January 30, 1989.

The last maneuver is from "Soviets Abandon Efforts to Regain Contact With Phobos 2," *Aviation Week & Space Technology,* April 10, 1989.

For the effect on U.S.-USSR exploration, see "Suddenly, Mars Seems a Little Farther Away," *The New York Times,* April 2, 1989.

Davies's remark about teething problems is from the interview with the author.

Sagdeev's and Kremnev's statements are from "Phobos Loss—Spacecraft Designers Blamed," *Spaceflight,* July 1989, p. 219.

CHAPTER 14

The reports were *Planetary Exploration Through Year 2000,* in two parts: a core program and an augmented one (Washington: National Aeronautics and Space Administration, 1983); *Pioneering the Space Frontier* (New York: Bantam Books, 1986); *The Crisis in Space and Earth Science* (Washington:

National Aeronautics and Space Administration, 1986); Sally K. Ride, *Leadership and America's Future in Space* (Washington: National Aeronautics and Space Administration, 1987); *International Space Policy for the 1990s and Beyond* (Washington: National Aeronautics and Space Administration, 1987); and *Space Science in the Twenty-first Century* (Washington: National Academy Press, 1988). The last consisted of seven relatively thin volumes.

The SSEC plea for stable funding is from *Planetary Exploration Through Year 2000* (A Core Program), p. 14.

Apollo-Soyuz is described in considerable detail in Edward Clinton Ezell and Linda Neuman Ezell, *The Partnership: A History of the Apollo-Soyuz Test Project,* SP-4209 (Washington: National Aeronautics and Space Administration, 1978).

Morrison's remarks are from the taped proceeding of the AIAA/JPL conference.

The Core Program is from *Planetary Exploration Through Year 2000: A Core Program* (Washington: National Aeronautics and Space Administration, 1983).

For detailed information on CRAF, see the slightly dated but comprehensive seventy-nine-page booklet, *The Comet Rendezvous Asteroid Flyby: A Search for Our Beginnings* (Pasadena: Jet Propulsion Laboratory, May 1987). See also the JPL fact sheet "CRAF: Comet Rendezvous Asteroid Flyby" (August 1988) and "CRAF Will Be First in Series of Missions Using Mariner Mk. 2," *Aviation Week & Space Technology,* October 9, 1989, pp. 99–109. For generic information on Mariner Mark II, see "NASA Turns from Custom Design to Standard Models," *The New York Times,* March 7, 1989.

For material on Cassini, see "Cassini to Provide Detailed, Extended Views of Saturn," *Aviation Week & Space Technology,* October 9, 1989, pp. 109–10, and the JPL fact sheet "Cassini Mission" (August 1988).

The so-called smart machines of the Augmented Program are mentioned in Part 2, pp. 226–27.

Ride's Mars option is from her report, p. 33.

The Paine Commission Mars scenario is in its report, pp. 65–71.

Ride's observation regarding one-shot stunts is from her report, p. 53.

The JPL Mars study is *The Case for Mars: Concept Development for a Mars Research Station,* JPL Pub. 86-28, (Pasadena: Jet Propulsion Laboratory, April 15, 1986). "Mental Health Maintenance" is on p. 91.

The NRC's treatment of humans on Mars is from the "Planetary and Lunar Exploration" part of the report, pp. 104–5.

The Luna sample return missions are described, together with a photograph of a replica of Luna 16, on pp. 52–53 of the Augmented Program report.

Sample return landing sites are from the Augmented Program report, p. 96.

Data on the ion engine is from the interview with John Brophy. One theoretical application would be to the so-called TAU, or Thousand Astronomical Unit, mission that would take fifty years to complete. This is under study by Aden and Marjorie Meinel at JPL.

The solar sail is from Carl Sagan, "The Next Great Leap into Space," *The New York Times Magazine,* July 10, 1977, p. 15.

The railgun idea and Jones's remark are from "Tiny craft touted to explore space," *The Washington Times,* January 11, 1988.

"Gnat Robots" and the MIT insect are from William McLaughlin, "Microspacecraft Conference," *Spaceflight,* November 1988, pp. 426–27.

Brook's idea about mass monitoring is from the interview with the author.

The launching of the Japanese lunar spacecraft and related matters are from "Joining Space Race, Japan Launches Rocket to Moon," *The New York Times,* January 25, 1990. For background, see Craig Covault, "Japan Readies First Moon Mission Launch as Companies Seek Lunar Base Role," *Aviation Week & Space Technology,* January 8, 1990, pp. 20–21.

Feynman's point about public relations is from the *Report of the Presidential Commission on the Space Shuttle Challenger Accident,* Vol. II, p. F-5.

Murray's observation about civilization is from the first interview with the author.

EPILOGUE

Allen's remarks are from the Voyager Neptune Encounter Tape of August 21.

Proceedings at the first news briefing and subsequent briefings were recorded by the author.

Hammel's images of Neptune are in H. B. Hammel, "Neptune Cloud Structure at Visible Wavelengths," *Science,* June 9, 1989, pp. 1165–67.

What was known about Neptune is nicely summarized in Beatty, O'Leary and Chaikin, *The New Solar System,* pp. 169–72.

Discovery of the Great Dark Spot is in two boxes: "There Is Weather on Neptune," *Science,* June 30, 1989, p. 1544, and "Voyager 2 Discovers Large, Dark Spot on Neptune," *Aviation Week & Space Technology,* June 26, 1989, p. 87.

The discovery of the third moon is from "Voyager Photographs Show Third Moon Orbiting the Planet Neptune," *Los Angeles Times,* July 8, 1989.

Smith's announcement of the discovery of the complete ring is from the Voyager Neptune Encounter Tape of August 22.

Smith's reference to forward scattering is from the JPL briefing summary for August 22.

Haynes's briefing on Voyager 2's location and condition are from the Voyager Neptune Encounter Tape of August 23.

Data that came in early on the morning of the twenty-third are from the *Voyager 2 Neptune Encounter Timeline (August 21 to August 29, 1989)*, D-6678, AUG 23 (DOY 235), pp. 1–5.

Smith's remarks are from the Voyager Neptune Encounter Tape of August 23.

The theory of the blue area is from "Uncannily Precise, Voyager Bears Down on Neptune," *The New York Times,* August 24, 1989.

The CNN interview with Quayle aired on August 18. The quotation is from "Scientists ponder Quayle's remark about water on Mars," *San Jose Mercury News* (from *The Washington Post*), September 1, 1989.

Encounter times are from the Voyager Neptune Encounter Tape of August 24.

Stone's and Smith's presentations are from the Voyager Neptune Encounter Tape of August 24.

Mark's statement about the quality of engineering is from a conversation the author had with George Alexander on April 26, 1990. The scene in von Karman was observed by the author.

The scene in the Voyager office is from "Triton Images Put Scientists in Party Mode," *Los Angeles Times,* August 26, 1989.

Stone's remarks are from the Voyager Neptune Encounter Tape of August 25.

Ingersoll's remark is from Richard A. Kerr, "Triton Steals Voyager's Last Show," *Science,* September 1, 1989, p. 929.

The dust sheet was announced by Carolyn Porco and is on the Voyager Neptune Encounter Tape of August 28.

Esposito's observation is from Kerr, "Triton Steals Voyager's Last Show," p. 930.

Smith's remark about the ring arcs is from "Scientists Puzzled by Unusual Neptune Rings," *The New York Times,* December 15, 1989.

The discovery of the active volcano is from Richard A. Kerr, "Neptune's Triton Spews a Plume," *Science,* October 13, 1989, p. 213. See also "Volcanoes Seen on Triton," *The New York Times,* October 3, 1989.

Material on Triton's geological history is from "Voyager Reveals Mysterious Moon," *Los Angeles Times,* August 26, 1989, "Triton May Be Coldest Spot in Solar System," *The New York Times,* August 29, 1989, and from the Voyager Neptune Encounter Tapes of August 26–29.

Stone's closing remarks are from the Voyager Neptune Encounter Tape of August 29.

The family portrait is described in "Voyager to Snap First Family Portrait of Planets Tonight," *The New York Times,* February 13, 1990.

SOURCES

BOOKS

Beatty, J. Kelly, Brian O'Leary, and Andrew Chaikin, eds. *The New Solar System.* Cambridge: Sky Publishing Corp. and Cambridge University Press, 1982.

Benjamin, Francis S., Jr., and G. J. Toomer, eds. *Campanus of Novara and Medieval Planetary Theory: Theorica planetarum.* Madison: University of Wisconsin Press, 1971.

Berkner, L. V., and Hugh Odishaw, eds. *Science in Space.* New York: McGraw-Hill, 1961.

Boorstin, Daniel J. *The Discoverers.* New York: Random House, 1983.

Brooks, Courtney G., James M. Grimwood, and Loyd S. Swenson, Jr. *Chariots for Apollo: A History of Manned Lunar Spacecraft* (SP-4205). Washington: National Aeronautics and Space Administration, 1979.

Buchheim, Robert W., et al., *Space Handbook: Astronautics and its Applications.* New York: Random House, 1958.

Burgess, Eric. *To the Red Planet.* New York: Columbia University Press, 1978.

————. *By Jupiter: Odyssey to a Giant.* New York: Columbia University Press, 1982.

Burrows, William E. *Deep Black: Space Espionage and National Security.* New York: Random House, 1987.

Chapman, Clark R. *Planets of Rock and Ice.* New York: Charles Scribner's Sons, 1977.

Cochran, Thomas B., William M. Arkin, and Milton M. Hoenig. *U.S. Nuclear Forces and Capabilities,* Vol. 1. Cambridge: Ballinger Publishing Co., 1984.

Columbus, Christopher. *The Log of Christopher Columbus* (Translated by Robert H. Fuson). Camden, Me.: International Marine Publishing Co., 1987.

Cooper, Henry S. F., Jr. *Imaging Saturn.* New York: Holt, Rinehart & Winston, 1981.

Couper, Heather, with Nigel Henbest. *New Worlds: In Search of the Planets.* Reading, Mass.: Addison-Wesley Publishing Co., 1986.

Davies, Merton E., and Bruce C. Murray. *The View from Space.* New York: Columbia University Press, 1971.

Davis, Joel. *Flyby: The Interplanetary Odyssey of Voyager 2.* New York: Atheneum, 1987.

Dyson, Freeman. *Infinite in All Directions.* New York: Harper & Row, 1988.

Elliot, James, and Richard Kerr. *Rings: Discoveries from Galileo to Voyager.* Cambridge: MIT Press, 1984.

Emme, Eugene, ed. *The History of Rocket Technology: Essays on Research, Development, and Utility.* Detroit: Wayne State University Press, 1964.

Ezell, Edward Clinton, and Linda Neuman Ezell. *On Mars: Exploration of the Red Planet, 1958–1978* (SP-4212). Washington: National Aeronautics and Space Administration, 1984.

————. *The Partnership: A History of the Apollo-Soyuz Test Program* (SP-4209). Washington: National Aeronautics and Space Administration, 1978.

Ezell, Linda Neuman. *NASA Historical Data Book, Vol. II: Programs and Projects, 1958–1968.* Washington: National Aeronautics and Space Administration, 1988.

————. *NASA Historical Data Book, Vol. III (Programs and Projects, 1969–1978).* Washington: National Aeronautics and Space Administration, 1988.

Feinberg, Gerald, and Robert Shapiro. *Life Beyond Earth: The Intelligent Earthling's Guide to Life in the Universe.* New York: William Morrow & Co., 1980.

Feynman, Richard P. *What Do You Care What Other People Think?* New York: W. W. Norton & Co., 1988.

Fimmel, Richard O., James Van Allen, and Eric Burgess. *Pioneer: First to Jupiter, Saturn, and Beyond* (SP-446). Washington: National Aeronautics and Space Administration, 1980.

Fimmel, Richard O., Lawrence Colin, and Eric Burgess. *Pioneer Venus.* Washington: National Aeronautics and Space Administration, 1983.

Fisher, Clyde, and Marian Lockwood. *Astronomy.* John Wiley & Sons, 1940.

Flight Science Office, Jet Propulsion Laboratory. *Voyager Uranus/Interstellar Mission Science and Mission Systems Handbook.* Pasadena: Jet Propulsion Laboratory, July 1, 1985.

French, Bevan M. *The Moon Book.* New York: Penguin Books, 1971.

French, Bevan M., and Stephen P. Maran, eds. *A Meeting With the Universe.* Washington: National Aeronautics and Space Administration, 1981.

Gatland, Kenneth. *The Illustrated Encyclopedia of Space Technology.* New York: Harmony Books, 1981.

Gerard, Mireille, and Pamela W. Edwards, eds. *Space Station: Policy, Planning and Utilization.* New York: American Institute of Aeronautics and Astronautics, 1983.

Glasstone, Samuel. *Sourcebook on the Space Sciences.* New York: D. Van Nostrand Co., 1965.

Greeley, Ronald. *Planetary Landscapes.* Boston: Allen & Unwin, 1985.

Grosser, Morton. *The Discovery of Neptune.* Cambridge: Harvard University Press, 1962.

Hall, R. Cargill. *Lunar Impact.* Washington: National Aeronautics and Space Administration, 1977.

Hanle, Paul A., and Von Del Chamberlain, eds. *Space Science Comes of Age.* Washington: Smithsonian Institution Press, 1981.

Hart, Douglas. *The Encyclopedia of Soviet Spacecraft.* New York: Exeter Books, 1987.

Horowitz, Norman H. *To Utopia and Back: The Search for Life in the Solar System.* New York: W. H. Freeman & Co., 1986.

Hoyt, William Graves. *Lowell and Mars.* Tucson: University of Arizona Press, 1976.

Johnson, Nicholas L. *Handbook of Soviet Lunar and Planetary Exploration.* San Diego: American Astronautical Society, 1979.

Jones, H. Spencer. *Life on Other Worlds.* New York: The Macmillan Co., 1940.

Kaplan, Joseph, et. al. *Across the Space Frontier.* New York: Viking Press, 1952.

Killian, James R., Jr. *Sputnik, Scientists, and Eisenhower.* Cambridge: MIT Press, 1977.

King-Hele, D. G., et al. *The R.A.E. Table of Earth Satellites: 1957–1980.* London: Macmillan Press, 1981.

Kistiakowsky, George B. *A Scientist at the White House.* Cambridge: Harvard University Press, 1976.

Koppes, Clayton. *JPL and the American Space Program.* New Haven: Yale University Press, 1982.

Kuiper, G. P., and B. M. Middlehurst, eds. *The Solar System,* Vol. III *(Planets and Satellites).* Chicago: University of Chicago Press, 1961.

Lakoff, Sanford, and Herbert F. York. *A Shield in Space?: Technology, Politics, and the Strategic Defense Initiative.* Berkeley: University of California Press, 1989.

Lewis, Richard S. *The Voyages of Apollo.* New York: Quadrangle, 1974.

Ley, Willy, and Wernher von Braun. *The Exploration of Mars.* New York: Viking Press, 1956.

Logsdon, John M. *The Decision to Go to the Moon.* Chicago: University of Chicago Press, 1970.

Lowell, Percival. *Mars as the Abode of Life.* New York: Macmillan Co., 1908.

McDougall, Walter A. *. . . the Heavens and the Earth.* New York: Basic Books, 1985.

Menzel, Donald H., Fred L. Whipple, and Gerard de Vaucouleurs. *Survey of Astronomy.* Englewood Cliffs, N.J.: Prentice-Hall, 1979.

Miles, Frank, and Nicholas Booth. *Race to Mars: The Harper & Row Mars Flight Atlas.* New York, Harper & Row, 1988.

Montoya, Earl J., and Richard O. Fimmel. *Space Pioneers* (EP-264). Washington: National Aeronautics and Space Administration, 1987.

Morrison, David. *Voyages to Saturn.* Washington: National Aeronautics and Space Administration, 1982.

Morrison, David, and Susan Samz. *Voyages to Jupiter.* Washington: National Aeronautics and Space Administration, 1980.

Morrison, David, ed. *Satellites of Jupiter.* Tucson: University of Arizona Press, 1982.

Morrison, Philip and Phylis. *The Ring of Truth.* New York: Random House, 1987.

Murray, Bruce. *Journey into Space.* New York: W. W. Norton & Co., 1989.

Murray, Bruce, and Eric Burgess. *Flight to Mercury.* New York: Columbia University Press, 1977.

National Aeronautics and Space Administration. *National Space Transportation System Reference* (Vol. 1: *Systems and Facilities*), June 1988.

Newell, Homer E. *Beyond the Atmosphere.* Washington: National Aeronautics and Space Administration, 1980.

Nicks, Oran W. *Far Travelers: The Exploring Machines.* Washington: National Aeronautics and Space Administration, 1985.

Oberg, James E. *Red Star in Orbit.* New York: Random House, 1981.

Ordway, Frederick I., III, and Mitchell R. Sharpe. *The Rocket Team.* New York: Thomas Y. Crowell, 1979.

Payne-Gaposchkin, Cecilia, and Katherine Haramundanis. *Introduction to Astronomy.* Englewood Cliffs, N.J.: Prentice-Hall, 1970.

Pasachoff, Jay M. *Contemporary Astronomy.* Newark: Sanders College Publishing, 1981.

———. *Scientific Results of the Viking Project.* Washington: American Geophysical Union, 1977.

Sagan, Carl, et al. *Murmurs of Earth.* New York: Random House, 1978.

Shapiro, Robert. *Origins: A Skeptic's Guide to the Creation of Life on Earth.* New York: Summit Books, 1986.

Sheehan, William. *Planets and Perception: Telescopic Views and Interpretations, 1609–1909.* Tucson: University of Arizona Press, 1988.

Sherman, Madeline W., ed. *TRW Space Log: 1957–1982,* Vol. 19. Redondo Beach, Cal., 1983.

Skilling, William T., and Robert S. Richardson. *Astronomy.* New York: Henry Holt & Co., 1949.

Sloop, J. L. *Liquid Hydrogen as a Propulsion Fuel, 1945–1959.* Washington: National Aeronautics and Space Administration, SP-4404, 1978.

Smoluchowski, Roman, John N. Bahcall, and Mildred S. Matthews, eds. *The Galaxy and the Solar System.* Tucson: University of Arizona Press, 1986.

Stockman, David A. *The Triumph of Politics.* New York: Harper & Row, 1986.

Sullivan, Walter, *Assault on the Unknown.* New York: McGraw-Hill, 1961.

Taylor, John W. R., ed. *Jane's All the World's Aircraft: 1962–63.* London: Sampson Low, Marston & Co., 1962.

Van Nimmen, Jane, and Leonard C. Bruno. *NASA Historical Data Book,* Vol I *(NASA Resources 1958–1968).* Washington: National Aeronautics and Space Administration, 1988.

Van Allen, James A. *Origins of Magnetospheric Physics.* Washington: Smithsonian Institution Press, 1983.

von Karman, Theodore, with Lee Edson. *The Wind and Beyond.* Boston: Little, Brown & Co., 1967.

Wells, H. G. *The War of the Worlds.* New York: Pocket Books, 1988.

Wolfe, Tom. *The Right Stuff.* New York: Farrar, Straus, Giroux, 1979.

Wukelic, George E., ed. *Handbook of Soviet Space Science Research.* New York: Gordon & Breach, 1968.

Yeates, C. M., et al. *Galileo: Exploration of Jupiter's System* (SP-479). Washington: National Aeronautics and Space Administration, 1985.

ARTICLES IN MAGAZINES

"Atlantis Extends the Shuttle's Reach," *Spaceflight,* August 1989.

Beatty, J. Kelly. "Voyager 2's Triumph," *Sky & Telescope,* October 1986.

———. "Welcome to Neptune," *Sky & Telescope,* October 1989.

———. "Getting To Know Neptune," *Sky & Telescope,* February, 1990.

Biddle, Wayne. "The Endless Countdown," *The New York Times Magazine,* June 22, 1980.

Bless, Robert. "Space Science: What's Wrong at NASA," *Issues in Science and Technology,* Winter 1988–89.

Brush, Stephen G. "Nickel for Your Thoughts: Urey and the Origin of the Moon," *Science,* September 3, 1982.

Campbell, Donald B., et al. "Styles of Volcanism on Venus: New Arecibo High Resolution Radar Data," *Science,* October 20, 1989.

Canby, Thomas Y. "Are the Soviets Ahead in Space?" *National Geographic,* October 1986.

"Cassini to Provide Detailed Extended Views of Saturn," *Aviation Week & Space Technology,* October 9, 1989.

"Court Rejects Activists' Bid To Halt Galileo/Shuttle Launch," *Aviation Week & Space Technology,* October 16, 1989.

Covault, Craig. "Aerobatics at Mach 25," *Science 81,* May 1981.

———. "Galileo Jupiter Orbiter/Probe Readied For Launch by Space Shuttle Atlantis," *Aviation Week & Space Technology,* September 4, 1989.

———. "Galileo Launch to Jupiter by Atlantis Culminates Difficult Effort With Shuttle," *Aviation Week & Space Technology,* October 9, 1989.

———. "U.S., Soviet Negotiators Agree to New Space Cooperation Pact," *Aviation Week & Space Technology,* November 10, 1986.

———. "Soviet Space Program Strife Threatens Mars Mission Plans," *Aviation Week & Space Technology,* May 22, 1989.

———. "NASA Accelerates Lunar Base Planning as Station Changes Draw European Fire," *Aviation Week & Space Technology,* September 18, 1989.

———. "Soviet Manned Lunar Mission Plan Used Modified Soyuz Spacecraft," *Aviation Week & Space Technology,* January 8, 1990.

"CRAF Will Be First in Series of Missions Using Mariner Mk. 2," *Aviation Week & Space Technology,* October 9, 1989.

Cuzzi, Jeffrey N., and Larry W. Esposito. "The Rings of Uranus," *Scientific American,* July 1987.

Dickson, David. "Europeans Decide on a Trip to Saturn," *Science,* December 9, 1988.

Dornheim, Michael A. "Repairs Completed, Galileo Thrusters Set to Undergo Reacceptance Tests," *Aviation Week & Space Technology,* January 23, 1989.

Dornheim, Michael A. "Latest Soviet Planetary Mission Plans Reflect Shift to Conservative Outlook," *Aviation Week & Space Technology,* August 28, 1989.

Edelson, Burton I., and Alan Townsend. "U.S.-Soviet Cooperation: Opportunities in Space," *SAIS Review,* Winter–Spring 1989.

Feynman, Richard P. "Mr. Feynman Goes to Washington," *Engineering & Science,* Fall 1987.

Foley, Theresa M. "NASA Prepares for Protests Over Nuclear System Launch on Shuttle in October," *Aviation Week & Space Technology,* June 26, 1989.

———. "NASA Apologizes for Illegal Lobbying To Preserve Budget, Space Station," *Aviation Week & Space Technology,* August 31, 1987.

———. "Scientists Urge Immediate Change in Planetary Exploration Policies," *Aviation Week & Space Technology,* June 15, 1987.

Gold, Michael. "Voyager to the Seventh Planet," *Science 86,* May 1986.

Goldman, Stuart J. "The Legacy of Phobos 2," *Sky & Telescope,* February 1990.

Goldreich, P., et al. "Neptune's Story," *Science,* August 4, 1989.

Graham, Loren R. "Toward a New Era in U.S.-Soviet Relations," *Issues in Science and Technology,* Fall 1989.

Hammel, H. B. "Neptune Cloud Structure at Visible Wavelengths," *Science,* June 9, 1989.

Heacock, Raymond L. "Ranger: Its Mission and Its Results," *TRW Space Log* (reprint), Summer 1965.

Helms, Harry L., Jr. "The Great Galactic Ghoul," *Saga,* July 1976.

Horowitz, Norman H. "Mission Impractical," *The Sciences,* March/April 1990.

"The Human-Voyager 2 Collaboration," *Science,* September 15, 1989.

Ingersoll, Andrew P. "Uranus," *Scientific American,* January 1987.

Jastrow, Robert. "Report from Mars," *Natural History,* March 1977.

Johnson, Torrence V., Robert Hamilton Brown, and Laurence A. Soderblom. "The Moons of Uranus," *Scientific American,* April 1987.

Kerr, Richard A. "Voyager Finds Uranian Shepherds and a Well-Behaved Flock of Rings," *Science,* February 21, 1986.

———. "Triton Steals Voyager's Last Show," *Science,* September 1, 1989.

———. "Neptune's Triton Spews a Plume," *Science,* October 13, 1989.

Kidger, Neville. "Glasnost and the Moon," *Spaceflight,* October 1989.

Kinoshita, June. "Neptune," *Scientific American,* November 1989.

Laeser, Richard P., William I. McLaughlin, and Donna M. Wolff. "Engineering Voyager 2's Encounter with Uranus," *Scientific American,* November 1986.

Lenorovitz, Jeffrey M. "Launch of Two Phobos Spacecraft Begins Ambitious Mission to Mars," *Aviation Week & Space Technology,* July 18, 1988.

———. "Soviets to Study Phobos Surface From Fixed-Site, Mobile Landers," *Aviation Week & Space Technology,* April 29, 1989.

———. "Surging Ahead," *Time,* October 5, 1987.

———. "Soviets, U.S. Make Progress On Space Cooperation Talks," *Aviation Week & Space Technology,* August 1, 1988.

Lewis, Ruth A., and John S. Lewis. "Getting Back on Track in Space," *Technology Review,* August/September 1986.

Logsdon, John M. "The Space Shuttle Program: A Policy Failure?" *Science,* May 30, 1986.

———. "Leading Through Cooperation," *Issues in Science and Technology,* Summer 1988.

McLaughlin, William. "Microspacecraft Conference," *Spaceflight,* November 1988.

———. "Voyager at Neptune," *Spaceflight,* October 1989.

McLucas, John L., and Burton I. Edelson. "Let's Go to Mars Together," *Issues in Science and Technology,* Fall 1988.

Miner, Ellis D. "Voyager's Last Encounter," *Sky & Telescope,* July 1989.

Morgan, M. Granger. "Space Policy: Getting There from Here," *Issues in Science and Technology,* Spring 1989.

Murray, Bruce. "Civilian Space: In Search of Presidential Goals," *Issues in Science and Technology,* Spring 1986.

Newbauer, John. "Soviets: 'Join Us to Mars?' " *Aerospace America,* July 1987.

Norman, Colin. "Air Force to Mothball Vandenberg, Reduce Reliance on Shuttle," *Science,* August 15, 1986.

Oberg, James E. "The Great Galactic Ghoul," *Final Frontier,* October 1987.

O'Lone, Richard G. "NASA Expects Pioneer 10's Useful Lifetime Will Be Extended by Decade," *Aviation Week & Space Technology,* June 27, 1988.

Phillips, Kathryn. "Selling Mars," *Los Angeles Times Magazine,* June 25, 1989.

Roland, Alex. "The Shuttle: Triumph or Turkey?" *Discover,* November 1985.

―――. "Shuttle Centaur Flight Safety Issues Threaten Launch Planning," *Aviation Week & Space Technology,* May 12, 1986.

―――. "Russian Moon Non-Landing," *Science,* January 12, 1990.

Sagan, Carl. "The Next Great Leap into Space," *The New York Times Magazine,* July 10, 1977.

Sagdeev, Roald Z. "Science and Perestroika: A Long Way to Go," *Issues in Science and Technology,* Summer 1988.

Scott, William B. "USAF Predicts Antimatter Propellants Could Be in Use by Early 21st Century," *Aviation Week & Space Technology,* March 21, 1988.

Smith, Bruce A. "Scientists Gain New Insights On Uranus From Voyager 2 Data," *Aviation Week & Space Technology,* February 10, 1986.

―――. "Voyager 2's Uranus Flyby Provides Detailed Images of Moon System," *Aviation Week & Space Technology,* February 3, 1986.

―――. "Voyager's Discoveries Mount on Final Rush to Neptune," *Aviation Week & Space Technology,* August 28, 1989.

―――. "Voyager Ends Neptune Flyby, Yielding Historic Triton Data," *Aviation Week & Space Technology,* September 4, 1989.

Smith, David R. "They're Following Our Script: Walt Disney's Trip to Tomorrowland," *Future,* May 1978.

Sobel, Dava, "Reaching Across Space," *Harvard Magazine,* December 1975.

―――. "Soviets Abandon Efforts to Regain Contact With Phobos 2," *Aviation Week & Space Technology,* April 10, 1989.

―――. "Soviet Moon Flight Admission," *Spaceflight,* September 1989.

Tatarewicz, Joseph N. "Federal Funding and Planetary Astronomy, 1950–75: A Case Study," *Social Studies of Science, Vol. 16,* London, Beverly Hills and New Delhi: SAGE, 1986.

"Ulysses Spacecraft Prepared for Long-Delayed Mission to Sun," *Aviation Week & Space Technology,* November 6, 1989.

Updike, John. "An Open Letter to Voyager 2," *Life* November 1989.

"U.S./USSR In Space: The Quest for Leadership," (several articles), *Aviation Week & Space Technology,* December 12, 1988.

Van Allen, James A. "Space Science, Space Technology and the Space Station," *Scientific American,* January, 1986.

"Voyager 2 Managers Resolve Imagery Problem Before Uranus Encounter," *Aviation Week & Space Technology,* January 27, 1986.

Waldrop, M. Mitchell. "The Puzzle That Is Saturn," *Science,* September 18, 1981.

―――. "Voyage to a Blue Planet," *Science,* February 28, 1986.

———. "Rifkin Tries to Stop Galileo Launch," *Science,* October 6, 1989.

———. "A Soviet Plan for Exploring the Planets," *Science,* May 10, 1985.

———. "Jet Propulsion Lab Looks to Life After Voyager," *Science,* September 8, 1989.

Wasserburg, Gerald Jos. "Exploring the Planets: A Strategic But Practical Proposal," *Issues in Science and Technology,* Fall 1986.

Young, Steven. "Soviet Union Was Far Behind in 1960's Moon Race," *Spaceflight,* January 1990.

Zaitsev, Yuri. "The Successes of Phobos-2," *Spaceflight,* November 1989.

ARTICLES IN ANTHOLOGIES AND SCHOLARLY PAPERS

Anderson, John D., and E. Myles Standish, Jr. "Dynamical Evidence for Planet X," *The Galaxy and the Solar System.* Tucson: University of Arizona Press, 1986, pp. 286–96.

Aston, Graeme. "Advanced Electric Propulsion for Interplanetary Missions," paper presented at the 33rd Annual Meeting of the American Astronautical Society (Aerospace: Century XXI), Boulder, Colorado, October 26–29, 1986.

Carr, M. H., et al. "Martian Impact Craters and Emplacement of Ejecta by Surface Flow," *Scientific Results of the Viking Mission,* published by the American Geophysical Union, 1977, (hereafter called SRVP), pp. 4055–65.

Casani, John R. "Galileo's New Route to Jupiter," presented at the American Astronautical Society, Boulder, Colorado, October 28, 1986.

Cuzzi, Jeffrey N., et al. "Saturn's Rings: Properties and Processes," Greenberg, Richard and Andre Brahic, *Planetary Rings.* Tucson: University of Arizona Press, 1984.

Donahue, T. M. "Use of Space Station for Science," AIAA/NASA Symposium on the Space Station, July 18, 1983.

Duxbury, T. C., and J. Veverka. "Viking Imaging of Phobos and Deimos: An Overview of the Primary Mission," SRVP, pp. 4203–11.

Horowitz, Norman H., G. L. Hobby, and Jerry S. Hubbard. "Viking on Mars: The Carbon Assimilation Experiments," SRVP, pp. 4659–62.

Klein, H. P. "The Viking Biological Investigation: General Aspects," SRVP, pp. 4677–80.

Levin, Gilbert V., and Patricia Ann Straat. "Recent Results From the Viking Labeled Release Experiment on Mars," SRVP, pp. 4663–67.

Levinthal, Elliott C, Kenneth Jones, Paul Fox, and Carl Sagan. "Lander Imaging as a Detector of Life on Mars," SRVP, pp. 4468–78.

Logsdon, John M. "Space Stations: A Historical Perspective," AIAA/NASA Symposium on the Space Station, July 18, 1983.

Martin, Franklin D. "Status of Human Exploration Studies," presented at the Pathway to the Planets conference, sponsored by NASA's Office of Exploration, Washington, D.C., May 31, 1989.

Morrison, David. "Introduction to the Satellites of Jupiter," in David Morrison, ed., *Satellites of Jupiter.* Tucson: University of Arizona Press, 1982.

Nock, K. T., "TAU—A Mission to a Thousand Astronomical Units," paper delivered at the 19th AIAA/DGLR/JSASS International Electronic Propulsion Conference, Colorado Springs, May 11–13, 1987.

Nock, K. T., et al. "Lunar Get Away Special (GAS) Spacecraft," paper presented at the 19th AIAA/DGLR/JSASS International Electric Propulsion Conference, Colorado Springs, May 11–13, 1987.

Oyama, Vance I. and Bonnie J. Berdahl, "The Viking Gas Exchange Experiment Results From Chryse and Utopia Surface Samples," SRVP, pp. 4669–76.

Rechtin, Eberhardt. "Who Says There's a Space Race" (speech presented at The Electric Club of Los Angeles, November 16, 1959). California Institute of Technology archive, File 21.6.

Soffen, Gerald A. "The Viking Project," SRVP, pp. 3959–70.

Snyder, Conway W. "The Missions of the Viking Orbiters," SRVP, pp. 3971–83.

Toulmin, Priestly, III, et al. "Geochemical and Mineralogical Interpretation of the Viking Inorganic Chemical Results," SRVP, pp. 4625–33.

Veverka, J., and T. C. Duxbury. "Viking Observations of Phobos and Deimos: Preliminary Results," SRVP, pp. 4213–23.

Watts, A. Frank, D. J. Dreyfuss, and H. G. Campbell. "The Economic Impact of Reusable Orbital Transports on the Cost of Planned Manned Space Programs, 1970–1999" (RAND No. P-3465), November 15, 1966.

ARTICLES IN JOURNALS

Blasius, Karl R., et al. "Geology of the Valles Marineris: First Analysis of the Imaging From the Viking I Orbiter Primary Mission," *Journal of Geophysical Research,* September 30, 1977.

Brooks, Robert N., Jr. "The Evolution of the Voyager Mission Sequence Software and Trends for Future Mission Sequence Software Systems," paper given at the 26th Aerospace Sciences Meeting, American Institute of Aeronautics and Astronautics, Reno, Nevada, January 11–14, 1988.

Ebersole, M. M. "The Space Flight Operations Center Development Project," *Journal of the British Interplanetary Society,* October 1985.

Flandro, G. A. "Utilization of Energy Derived from the Gravitational Field of Jupiter for Reducing Flight Time to the Outer Solar System," *Jet Propulsion Laboratory Space Programs Summary,* No. 37–35, October 31, 1965.

Fogg, M. J. "The Terraforming of Venus," *Journal of the British Interplanetary Society*, 1987.

Haynes, N. R. "Planetary Mission Operations: An Overview," *Journal of the British Interplanetary Society,* October 1985.

Hughes Aircraft Company, Space and Communications Group. "Pioneer Venus Case Study in Spacecraft Design," American Institute of Aeronautics and Astronautics Professional Study Series, undated.

Jones, C. P. "Engineering Challenges of In-Flight Spacecraft—Voyager: A Case History," *Journal of the British Interplanetary Society,* October 1985.

Jordan, J. F. "Navigation Systems," *Journal of the British Interplanetary Society,* October 1985.

Katz, B., and R. Brooks. "Understanding Natural Language for Spacecraft Sequencing," *Journal of the British Interplanetary Society,* October 1987.

Klein, Harold P. "The Viking Biological Investigations: Review and Status," *Origins of Life,* 9, 1978.

Leighton, Robert B., and Bruce C. Murray. "Behavior of Carbon Dioxide and Other Volatiles on Mars," *Science,* July 8, 1966.

Levin, Gilbert V., and Patricia Ann Straat. "Recent Results from the Viking Labeled Release Experiment," *BioSystems,* 9, 1977.

Linick, T. D. "Spacecraft Commanding for Unmanned Planetary Missions: The Uplink Process," *Journal of the British Interplanetary Society,* October 1985.

Logsdon, John M. "Missing Halley's Comet: The Politics of Big Science," *ISIS,* 1989.

Miner, E. D., C. H. Stembridge, and P. E. Doms. "Selecting and Implementing Scientific Objectives," *Journal of the British Interplanetary Society,* October 1985.

Murray, Bruce C. "A New Strategy for Planetary Exploration," *Aeronautics & Astronautics,* October 1968.

Murray, B. C., and M. E. Davies. "Space Photography and the Exploration of Mars," *Applied Optics,* June 1970.

Ostro, S. J., et al. "Radar Detection of Phobos," *Science,* March 24, 1989.

Smith, B. A., et al. "Voyager 2 in the Uranian System: Imaging Science Results," *Science,* July 4, 1986.

Smith, J. G. "Communicating Through Deep Space," *Journal of the British Interplanetary Society,* October 1985.

Smith, Robert W., and Joseph N. Tatarewicz, "Replacing a Technology: The Large Space Telescope and CCDs," *Proceedings of the IEEE,* July 1985.

Stewart, H. J., "New Possibilities for Solar-System Exploration," *Aeronautics and Astronautics,* December 1966.

Stone, E. C., and E. D. Miner. "The Voyager 2 Encounter with the Saturnian System," *Science,* January 29, 1982.

——. "The Voyager 2 Encounter with the Uranian System," *Science,* July 4, 1986.

REPORTS

The Case for Mars: Concept Development for a Mars Research Station (JPL 86-28). Pasadena: Jet Propulsion Laboratory, April 15, 1986.

Corliss, William R. "A History of the Deep Space Network" (NASA CR-151915). Washington: National Aeronautics and Space Administration, May 1, 1976.

Cost, Schedule, and Performance of NASA's Galileo Mission to Jupiter, GAO/NSIAD-88-138FS. Washington: General Accounting Office, May 1988.

Cost, Schedule, and Performance of NASA's Magellan Mission to Venus,

GAO/NSIAD-88-130FS. Washington: General Accounting Office, May 1988.

Cost, Schedule, and Performance of NASA's Ulysses Mission to the Sun, GAO/NSIAD-88-129FS. Washington: General Accounting Office, May 1988.

The Crisis in Space and Earth Science. Washington: National Aeronautics and Space Administration, November, 1986.

Final Report of the Ranger 6 Review Board, 2-2472. Washington: National Aeronautics and Space Administration, March 17, 1964.

Frye, Alton. "The Proposal for a Joint Lunar Expedition: Background and Prospects, (P-2808). Santa Monica: The RAND Corp., January 1964.

Goals and Objectives for America's Next Decade in Space. Washington: National Aeronautics and Space Administration, 1969.

Galileo VEEGA Mission to Jupiter, 1625-337. Pasadena: Jet Propulsion Laboratory, April 1987.

International Space Policy for the 1990s and Beyond. Washington: NASA Advisory Council Task Force on International Relations in Space, October 12, 1987.

Kloman, Erasmus H. *Unmanned Space Project Management: Surveyor and Lunar Orbiter,* SP-4901. Washington: National Aeronautics and Space Administration, 1971.

Logsdon, John M. *The Survival Crisis of the U.S. Solar System Exploration Program* (comment draft). Washington, June 1989.

Magellan Mission Plan, 630-50, Rev. A. Pasadena: Jet Propulsion Laboratory, May 1987.

Mariner C Shroud Failure Evaluation Final Report (Vehicle 6931). Sunnyvale: Lockheed Missiles & Space Company, March 1, 1965.

Mariner-Mars 1964 Final Project Report (NASA SP-139). Washington: National Aeronautics and Space Administration, 1967.

Mariner-Venus 1962 Final Project Report (NASA SP-59). Washington: National Aeronautics and Space Administration, July 1965.

Mars Studies with the Use of the Energiya Carrier-Rocket, Moscow: Space Research Institute, July 1988.

NASA's Deep Space Missions Are Experiencing Long Delays, GAO/NSIAD-88-128BR. Washington: General Accounting Office, May 1988.

The Next Decade in Space, A Report of the Space Science and Technology Panel of the President's Science Advisory Committee. The White House, March 1970.

Pioneering the Space Frontier, the Report of the National Commission on Space. New York: Bantam Books, 1986.

Planetary Exploration Through Year 2000: A Core Program. Washington: NASA Advisory Council, 1983.

Planetary Exploration Through Year 2000: An Augmented Program. Washington: NASA Advisory Council, 1986.

Planetary Exploration Through Year 2000: A Core Program: Mission Operations. Washington: NASA Advisory Council, 1986.

RA-6 Investigation Committee Final Report, EPD-205. Pasadena: Jet Propulsion Laboratory, February 14, 1964.

The Post-Apollo Space Program: Directions for the Future. Space Task Group Report to the President, September 1969 (NASA History Office)

Renzetti, N. A., et al. *The Deep Space Network—An Instrument for Radio Navigation of Deep Space Probes* (JPL Publication 82-102). Pasadena: Jet Propulsion Laboratory, December 15, 1982.

Report of the Presidential Commission on the Space Shuttle Challenger Accident, Vols. I and II. Washington: U.S. Government Printing Office, June 6, 1986.

Report of the U.S. Department of Energy's Team Analyses of the Chernobyl-4 Atomic Energy Station Accident Sequence, (DOE/NE-0076). Washington: U.S. Department of Energy, November 1986.

Ride, Sally K. *Leadership and America's Future in Space.* Washington: National Aeronautics and Space Administration, August 1987.

Smith, Marcia S. "Space Shuttle Issue Brief Number IB81175." Washington: Congressional Research Service, December 2, 1981 (updated on May 17, 1983).

The Soviet Programme of Space Exploration for the Period Ending in the Year 2000: Plans, Projects and International Cooperation. Moscow; Space Research Institute, October 1987.

Space Science in the Twenty-first Century: Planetary and Lunar Exploration, the National Research Council. Washington: National Academy Press, 1988.

United States Congress, House, Committee on Science and Technology. *Investigation of the Challenger Accident.* 99th Cong., 2nd Sess., 1986.

United States Congress, House, Committee on Science and Astronautics. *Investigation of Project Ranger,* Report of the Subcommittee on NASA Oversight. 88th Cong., 2nd Sess., 1964.

Voyager 2 Uranus Encounter Timeline (Jan. 21 to Jan. 29, 1986, Pasadena: NASA/Jet Propulsion Laboratory, undated.

LETTERS AND MEMORANDA

Homer E. Newell, to Robert C. Seamans, "Actions Taken by OSSA in Response to the 'Final Report of the Ranger VI Review Board,' " (2-2471a), July 25, 1964. (NASA History Office)

TAU Thinkshop, Interoffice Memorandum 315.2-SROP/MIR.86-162, September 11, 1986. (Aden and Marjorie Meinel)

JPL/Caltech Thinkshop on Science Unique to a Deep Space Mission, and subsequent report on the meeting of September 29, 1986. (Aden and Marjorie Meinel)

Letter from W. H. Pickering to T. Keith Glennan, March 24, 1959, extolling Vega and complaining about the relationship between JPL and Headquarters. (JPL Library)

Letter from Richard E. Horner to William H. Pickering, December 16, 1959, detailing JPL's responsibilities in the overall NASA framework. (NASA History Archive, 5-1164)

Letter from Oran W. Nicks to A. O. Beckman, January 8, 1968, presenting
a checklist of major elements important to "successful JPL management."
(Caltech Archive, File 20.7)

Telegram from Headquarters to JPL of December 14, 1959 officially terminating Vega. (JPL Archive)

Memorandum from OSSA Public Affairs Officer to Robert Alnutt, NASA,
suggesting commemorative stamps honoring *Pioneer 10*. (Ames)

Memorandum from J. D. Anderson to W. L. Quaide on the proposed News
Release, 85-29, "Data Suggest Tenth Planet in Far Out Orbit." (William E.
Burrows)

TAPED INTERVIEWS AND MEETINGS

Isaac Asimov		May 30, 1969
Joseph K. Alexander	NASA	Jan 29, 1988
Lew Allen	JPL	Jun 18, 1987
		Jan 6, 1989
Charles Beichman	Caltech	Jun 25, 1987
Roger D. Bourke	JPL	Jun 24, 1987
Fred W. Bowen	NASA	Jun 15, 1987
Bob Brooks	JPL	Feb 18, 1988
Jon Brophy	JPL	Jun 26, 1987
Robert Carlson	JPL	Feb 23, 1988
John R. Casani	JPL	Jun 24, 1987
Robert J. Cesarone	JPL	Jun 22, 1987
Moustafa T. Chahine	JPL	Jun 19, 1987
		Jan 6, 1989
Richard F. Collins	JPL	Jun 29, 1989
Stewart A. Collins	JPL	Jun 25, 1987
Merton E. Davies	RAND	Jan 4, 1989
Alphonso Diaz	NASA	Jan 27, 1988
Ronald F. Draper	JPL	Aug 28, 1989
James A. Dunne	JPL	Jun 18, 1987
Burton I. Edelson	SAIS*	Jan 29, 1988
Richard O. Fimmel	Ames	Mar 4, 1988
John P. Ford	JPL	Jun 23, 1988
Bevan M. French	NASA	Jan 28, 1988
Louis D. Friedman	Planetary Soc.	Feb 13, 1988
W. E. Giberson	JPL	Jun 30, 1987
Owen Gingerich	Harvard	May 29, 1969
Milton Goldfine	JPL	Jun 29, 1987
Charles F. Hall	Ames	Mar 1, 1988
Norman R. Haynes	JPL	Jun 23, 1987
David J. Helfand	Columbia	May 10, 1989

Allan S. Jacobson	JPL	Jun	26, 1987
Jack N. James	JPL	Feb	22, 1988
Nicholas L. Johnson	Teledyne Brown	Oct	11, 1988
Torrence V. Johnson	JPL	Jun	17, 1987
Carl A. Kukkonen	JPL	Jun	16, 1987
Arthur L. Lane	JPL	Jun	22, 1987
		Jun	29, 1987
		Feb	19, 1988
Bernard Lovell	JB**	Jun	13, 1969
Peter T. Lyman	JPL	Jun	29, 1987
William I. McLaughlin	JPL	Jun	25, 1987
		Feb	23, 1988
		Jan	4, 1989
Margaret Mead	AMNH***	May	28, 1969
Willis G. Meeks	JPL	Jun	17, 1987
Aden Meinel	JPL	Jul	2, 1987
Marjorie Meinel	JPL	Jul	2, 1987
David Morrison	Ames	Jan	18, 1989
Philip Morrison	MIT	May	29, 1969
Bruce Murray	Caltech	Jul	2, 1987
		Jan	10, 1989
William Pickering	Pickering Research	Jun	15, 1987
		Feb	18, 1988
		Jan	5, 1989
I. I. Rabi		May	15, 1987
Donald G. Rea	JPL	Jun	19, 1987
Ronald Schorn	Sky & Telescope	Feb	12, 1988
Robert Shapiro	NYU	Sep	16, 1987
E. Myles Standish, Jr.	JPL	Aug	18, 1987
Homer J. Stewart	JPL	Jul	2, 1987
		Jan	5, 1989
Edward C. Stone	Caltech	Jun	16, 1987
Joseph N. Tatarewicz	NASM****	Jan	28, 1988
		Mar	7, 1988
Arnold Toynbee		Jun	9, 1969
James Van Allen	Iowa	Feb	14, 1987
Jurrie J. van der Woude	JPL	Feb	22, 1988
Mark Van Doren		Jun	5, 1969
G. J. Wasserburg	Caltech	Feb	24, 1988

*School of Advanced International Studies, The Johns Hopkins University
**Jodrell Bank Observatory
***American Museum of Natural History
****National Air and Space Museum

AIAA/JPL First International Conference on Solar System Exploration, Pasadena, May 19–21, 1987.

Voyager-Neptune Encounter News Conferences, JPL, August 21–29, 1989.

Pathway to the Planets Conference, Washington, May 31–June 1, 1989.

Harrison H. Schmitt and Louis D. Friedman, "International Cooperation on Large Scale Space Ventures," AAAS Annual Meeting, Boston, February 12, 1988.

"Future of the Space Sciences in the United States," symposium conducted by James A. Van Allen at the AAAS Annual Meeting, Chicago, February 15, 1987.

"Reconstituting the U.S. Space Program," symposium conducted by John M. Logsdon at the AAAS Annual Meeting, Chicago, February 16, 1987.

"Images of the Future," symposium conducted by John M. Logsdon at the AAAS Annual Meeting, Chicago, February 16, 1987.

David J. Helfand, "Astropolitics: Science in the Backseat at NASA," talk given at the New York Academy of Sciences, April 27, 1989.

Galileo Briefing, JPL, August 20, 1989.

NEWS RELEASES AND BACKGROUNDERS

News Conference on Ranger VI Impact on Moon (2-2509), Washington: NASA, February 2, 1964.
"Pioneer F Mission to Jupiter" (72-25), Washington: NASA, February 20, 1972. This 73-page release summarizes all aspects of the mission.
"Pioneers May Find Tenth Planet" (82-23), Washington: NASA, June 17, 1982.
"Pioneer Will Reach Jupiter December 3" (73-243), Washington: NASA, November 19, 1973.
"Pioneer 10, First Spacecraft to Leave the Solar System, Passes Beyond All Known Planets" (83-10), Moffett Field: Ames Research Center, March 16, 1983.
"Grand Tour Scientists" (71-56), Washington: NASA, April 4, 1971.
"Jupiter Science Summary" (Voyager), Pasadena: Jet Propulsion Laboratory, April 27, 1983.
"Saturn Science Summary" (Voyager), Pasadena: Jet Propulsion Laboratory, August 6, 1987.
"Voyager to Saturn" (NF 100/10-80), Washington: National Aeronautics and Space Administration.
"Uranus Science Summary" (Voyager), Pasadena: Jet Propulsion Laboratory, August 6, 1987.
"Galileo Probe Prepared for Longer Life" (No. 88-02), Moffett Field: Ames Research Center, December 21, 1987.
"Magellan Venus Radar Mapper," JPL Fact Sheet, December 9, 1988.

"CRAF: Comet Rendezvous Asteroid Flyby," JPL Fact Sheet, August 10, 1988.

"Cassini Mission," JPL Fact Sheet, August 10, 1988.

"Voyager 2 Neptune Encounter Press Kit," NASA Office of Space Science and Applications, August 1989.

"Voyager at Neptune: 1989," Pasadena: Jet Propulsion Laboratory, March 1989.

"Radioisotope Thermoelectric Generators (RTGs) On the Galileo and Ulysses Missions," NASA Fact Sheet, undated.

"NASA Establishes Office of Exploration," No. 87-87, Washington: National Aeronautics and Space Administration, June 1, 1987.

AUDIO-VISUAL

Spaceflight (Part 1), Los Angeles: KCET-TV, May 1985.

Landing on Mars: Viking's Historic Mission, Cambridge: SSC, 1987.

The Planet That Got Knocked on Its Side (Voyager 2 at Uranus), NOVA, 1986.

The Rocky Road to Jupiter (Galileo), NOVA, 1987.

Jack N. James, *The Early History of JPL and the Evolution of Its Matrix Organization,* Jet Propulsion Laboratory, February 12, 1987.

Mars the Movie, Jet Propulsion Laboratory, 1989.

Miranda the Movie, Jet Propulsion Laboratory, 1989.

Houston, We've Got a Problem, National Aeronautics and Space Administration, (undated).

Magellan: Exploring Venus, Jet Propulsion Laboratory (undated).

ABOUT THE AUTHOR

WILLIAM E. BURROWS graduated from Columbia University in 1960 and earned an M.A. there in 1962. He has written about aviation and space for more than two decades. He has reported for *The New York Times, The Washington Post, The Wall Street Journal,* and the *Richmond Times-Dispatch.* His articles have appeared in *The New York Times Magazine, The Sciences, Foreign Affairs, Harvard Magazine* and *Harper's.* He is also the author of five books, including the best-selling *Deep Black,* a critically acclaimed investigative study of the U.S. space intelligence program.

Mr. Burrows is a professor of journalism at New York University and the founder and director of its graduate Science and Environmental Reporting Program.